Not For Tourists™ Guide to **LONDON**

Not For Tourists Inc

2009

Published and designed by:
Not For Tourists, Inc.
NFT.—Not For Tourists. Guide to LONDON 2009
www.notfortourists.com

NEW YORK STAFF

Publisher
Jane Pirone

Information Design
Jane Pirone
Rob Tallia
Scot Covey
Ben Bray
Jonathan Levy
Juan Molinari

Managing Editors
Rob Tallia
Craig Nelson

Database Manager
Michael Dale

Research
Melissa Burgos
Michael Dale
Bryce Evans

Cartography
Jonathan Levy
Nick Trotter

Graphic Design/Production
Scot Covey
Bethany Covey
Yumi Endo
Yanakarn Laksanaphrom
Jonathan Levy
Eleanor Renee Rogers
Aaron Schielke
Emily Steinfeld
Nick Trotter

Sales & Marketing
Lea Garrett
Sarah Hocevar
Annie Holt

LONDON EDITORS
City Editor: Jen Wight
Nightlife: Daniel Kramb
Restaurants: Julia Dennison
Shopping: Claire Storrow
Parks: Michael Lawrence
Sports: Rupert Raby
Landmarks: John Parton
Transport: Simon Cole
Proofreader: Anne Seymour

Neighborhood Writers
Kate Atwell
Trevor Baker
Judy-Meg Ní Chinnéide
Simon Cole
Julia Dennison
Mel Dias
Michael Kasparis
Frieda Klotz
Daniel Kramb
Michael Lawrence
Jimmy Lloyd
Esme McAvoy
John Myers
John Parton
Rupert Raby
Anne Seymour
Claire Storrow
Niklas Vestberg
Adam Welch
Jen Wight

Special Thanks
Stuart Farr

Maps derived from digital data © Collins Bartholomew Limited 2007.

Printed in China
ISBN# 978-0-9815591-0-0 $16.95 US / £9.99 UK
Copyright © 2008 by Not For Tourists, Inc.

Every effort has been made to ensure that the information in this book is as up-to-date as possible at press time. However, many details are liable to change—as we have learned. The publishers cannot accept responsibility for any consequences arising from the use of this book.

Not For Tourists does not solicit individuals, organizations, or businesses for listings inclusion in our guides, nor do we accept payment for inclusion into the editorial portion of our book; the advertising sections, however, are exempt from this policy. We always welcome communications from anyone regarding ANYTHING having to do with our books; please visit us on our website at www. notfortourists.com for appropriate contact information.

Dear NFT Reader,

You have here in your sweaty mits the first ever NFT guide for a city outside the US. And why did we choose London? Well we thought, due to the special relationship...

Nah, it is because London kicks arse (not ass mind) and us Londoner's need a guide like this. An urban manual that tells us, honestly, what each area of London is like, where to find the best shops, bars, pubs and cafes, and, even more importantly, where to find the nearest post office, hospital, library, or bank.

Even if you've lived here for years, or for ever, we GUARANTEE there is cool stuff in here you don't know about. Like the best Thai stall on Whitecross Market, the secret nature trail between Finsbury Park and Highbury, or that Hoxton has a few bars. Oh wait, hold on, you already knew that one. But there is so much more—we promise.

A thriving multicultural city, London is full of people from somewhere else, cheek-by-jowl with locals, some of whom have contributed to this guide. Thanks to them all. Imagine a group of Londoners including those originally from Battersea, Hackney, Scotland, the US, New Zealand and even Kent, arguing about where Tooting Broadway ends and Tooting Bec begins—and that was just one boundary between two of 152 'hoods in this guide.

We expect to get plenty of feedback, particularly from estate agents annoyed that we've let the cat out of the bag—Haringey isn't Upper Stoke Newington guys. So crack open the book and flick to your neighbourhood. Will you groan to see we've missed your favourite haunt? Or if we haven't, how you'll ever get a table there again? Either way, let us know what you think via www.notfortourists.com.

Here's hoping you find what you need.

Jane, Rob and Jen

Table of Contents

Underground Map and **Bus Map**
foldout, last page

Map 1 • **Marylebone (West)**

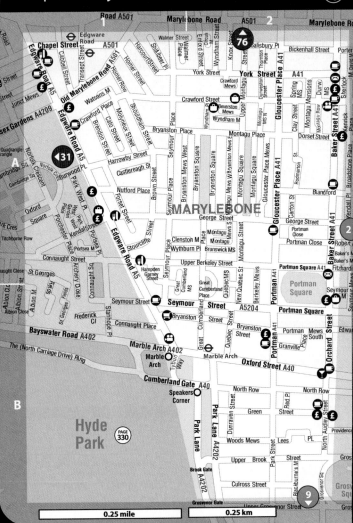

Marylebone (West)

Marylebone: old money meets the Middle East. Smell the mulah around Montague Square, sample hookahs and kebabs further towards Edgware Road. The Lebanese at Beirut Express can't be beat but shop at Maroush Deli if you want to cook at home. Wow friends at Nippon Tuk before mooching to Sequoia@RubyLo where you can bump, grind, get fuzzy on cocktails, and crash on the couches.

Map 1

£ Banks

- **Abbey** • 388 Edgware Rd
- **Barclays** • 9 Portman St
- **Barclays** • 93 Baker St
- **Barclays** • 127 Edgware Rd
- **Halifax** • 200 Edgware Rd
- **Halifax** • 20 N Audley St
- **Lloyds** • 195 Edgware Rd
- **NatWest** • 508 Edgware Rd
- **NatWest** • 81 Edgware Rd
- **NatWest** • 69 Baker St
- **NatWest** • 1 Portman Sq
- **NatWest** • 30 N Audley St

Cinemas

- **Odeon Marble Arch** • 10 Edgware Rd
- **Screen on Baker Street** • 96 Baker St

Coffee

- **Apostrophe** • 19 Baker St
- **Bagel Factory** • 39 Paddington St
- **Caffe Nero** • 184 Edgware Rd
- **Coffee Republic** • 1 George St
- **Eat.** • 400 Oxford St
- **Eat.** • 114 Baker St
- **Kings Café** • 177 Edgware Rd
- **Pret A Manger** • 556 Oxford St
- **Starbucks** • 29 N Audley St
- **Starbucks** • 207 Edgware Rd
- **Starbucks** • 34 Edgware Rd

O Landmarks

- **Marble Arch** • Oxford St
- **Speaker's Corner** • Cumberland Gate

Nightlife

- **Sequoia@RubyLo** • 23 Orchard St

Post Offices

- **Baker St** • 111 Baker St
- **Edgware Rd** • 354 Edgware Rd
- **Portman Square** • 2 Portman Sq

Restaurants

- **Beirut Express** • 112 Edgware Rd
- **Maroush IV** • 68 Edgware Rd
- **Nippon Tuk** • 225 Edgware Rd

Shopping

- **Maroush Deli** • 45 Edgware Rd
- **Phil Parker** • 106 Crawford St
- **Spymaster** • 3 Portman Sq
- **Totally Swedish** • 32 Crawford St

Supermarkets

- **Sainsbury's** • 55 Bryanston St

Map 2 • Marylebone (East)

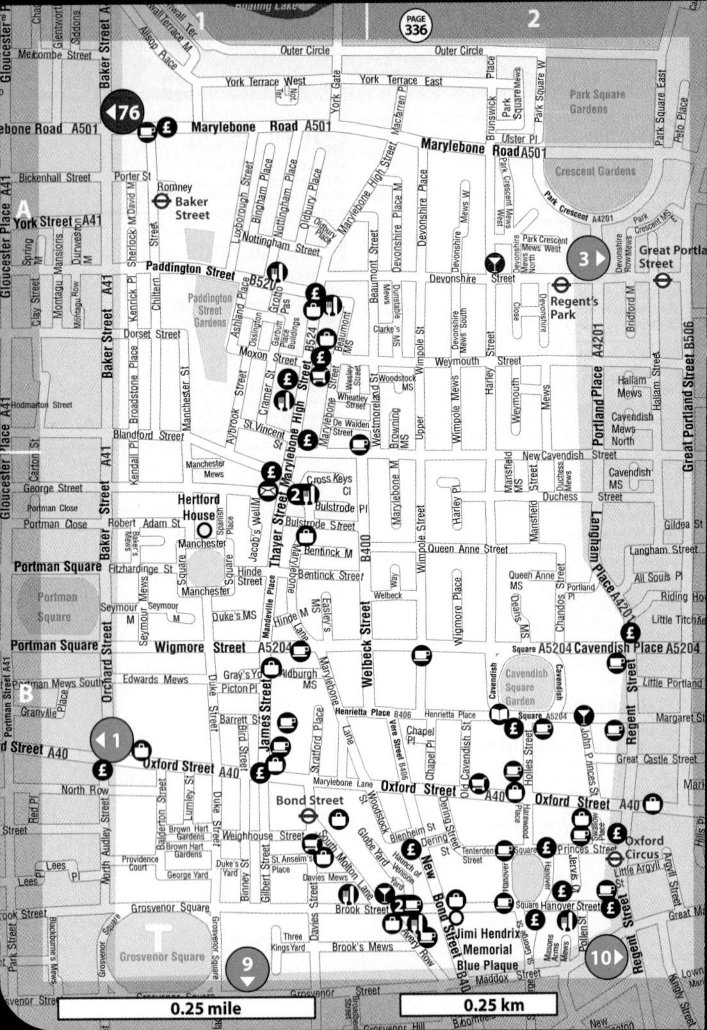

(N)

PAGE 336

Outer Circle

Boating Lake

York Terrace West — York Terrace East

Gloucester Place — Glentworth St

Melcombe Street — Siddons La

Allsop Place

Marylebone Road A501

◄76

Marylebone Road A501

Marylebone Road A501

Park Square East

Park Square Gardens

Park Square Mews

Brunswick Pl — Ulster Pl

Crescent Gardens

York Street A41

Bickenhall Street

Porter St — David M

Romney

Baker Street

Sherlock

Paddington Street

A — Park Crescent Mews West

Park Crescent Mews East

Crescent MG

Park Crescent A4201

3▶

Great Portland Street

Bingham Place

Luxborough Street

Nottingham Street

Paddington Street Gardens

Beaumont Street

Devonshire Place M

Devonshire Mews West

Devonshire Mews South

Devonshire Mews North

Devonshire Street

Regent's Park

Bridford M

Hallam Street

Great Portland Street B506

Chiltern St — Kenrick Pl

Dorset Street

Ashland Place — Cosway

Ossington

Moxon Street

Clarke's M

Weymouth St

Wimpole St

Harley Street

Weymouth Mews

New Cavendish Street

Cavendish Mews North

Cavendish MS

Portland Place

Langham Place A4201

Broadstone Place — Kendall Pl

Blandford Street

Cramer St

St Vincent St

Wheatley St — Wheatley MS

Woodstock St

Browning MS

De Walden St

Westmoreland St

Upper Wimpole St

Mansfield MS

Mansfield Street

Duchess Street

Cavendish MS South

Gildea St

Langham Street

Hanson St — Hodmarton St

Carlton St

George Street

Manchester Square

Hertford House

Manchester

Cross Keys Cl

2🅿

Bulstrode Pl

Bulstrode Street

Queen Anne Street

Portland MS

Chandos St

All Souls' PI

Riding House St

Little Titchfield

Portman Close

Portman Square

Fitzhardinge St

Robert Adam St

Jacob's Well

Spanish Pl

Hinde St

Bentinck M

Bentinck Street

B400

Welbeck St

Queen Anne St MS

Portman Square

Portman Mews

Seymour

Duke's MS

Manchester SW

Hinde S — SW

Way

Welbeck St

Wigmore St SW

Cavendish

Cavendish Square Garden

Little Portland

Wigmore Street A5204

B — Portman Mews South

Edwards Mews

Duke's

Gray's Yd

Picton PI

Aldburgh MS

Henrietta Place B406

Henrietta St

Cavendish Square A5204

Margaret Street

Granville

Barrett St

James Street

Stratford Place

Chapel PI

Old Cavendish St

Bolsover St

Great Castle Street

◄1

Oxford Street A40

Lumley St

Oxford Street A40

Marylebone Lane

Henrietta Place

Oxford Street A40

Oxford Street A40

Oxford Circus

Little Argyll

North Row

Balderton St

Brown Hart Gardens

Weighhouse Street

Duke's La

St Anselm's

Gilbert St

Binney St

Davies Mews

Blenheim St

Dering St

New Bond Street

Hanover St

Maddox

Princes St

Oxford Hanover St

Regent Street

Providence Court

George Yard

Three Kings Yard

Brook's Mews

Brook Street

Bond Street

Tenterden Street

Square Hanover St

Bullen St

Grosvenor Square

T

9▼

Jimi Hendrix Memorial Blue Plaque

Brook's Mews

Maddox

Grosvenor

10▶

Regent

0.25 mile   0.25 km

Head here to while away a sunny day and a month's pay. Marylebone High Street is a plush moocher's Mecca whilst St. Christopher's Place offers a last enclave of quiet eateries before the plebeian shopping madness of Oxford Street. Booze should be partaken at Inn 1888 or The Phoenix, kebabs at Diwan, and pastries at Patisserie Valerie. Luxurious eating, drinking, or sleeping? Claridges will do you right.

£ Banks

- **Abbey** • 14 Hanover Sq
- **Abbey** • 27 Marylebone High St
- **Barclays** • 8 Hanover St
- **Barclays** • 5 Marylebone High St
- **Halifax** • 5 Hanover St
- **Halifax** • 116 Marylebone High St
- **HSBC** • 90 Baker St
- **HSBC** • 19 St George St
- **HSBC** • 431 Oxford St
- **HSBC** • 19 Marylebone High St
- **Lloyds** • 399 Oxford St
- **Lloyds** • 10 Hanover Sq
- **Lloyds** • 324 Regent St
- **NatWest** • 10 Marylebone High St
- **Royal Bank of Scotland** • 97 New Bond St
- **Royal Bank of Scotland** • 28 Cavendish Sq

☕ Coffee

- **Apostrophe** • 23 Barrett St
- **Caffe Nero** • 273 Regent St
- **Caffe Nero** • Marylebone Rd
- **Coffee Republic** • 2 S Molton St
- **Costa** • 69 Wigmore St
- **Eat.** • 9 Avery Row
- **Eat.** • 319 Regent St
- **Eat.** • 25 Hanover Sq
- **Eat.** • 92 Wimpole St
- **Eat.** • 214 Oxford St
- **Pret A Manger** • 31 Cavendish
- **Pret A Manger** • 1 Tenterden St
- **Pret A Manger** • 18 Hanover St
- **Starbucks** • 22 Princes St
- **Starbucks** • 14 James St
- **Starbucks** • 63 S Molton St

O Landmarks

- **Hertford House** • Manchester Sq
- **Jimi Hendrix Memorial Blue Plaque** • 23 Brook St

📖 Libraries

- **Royal College of Nursing Library** • 20 Cavendish Sq

🍸 Nightlife

- **Claridge's Bar** • 55 Brook St
- **Inn 1888** • 21 Devonshire St
- **The Phoenix** • 37 Cavendish Sq

✉ Post Offices

- **Marylebone** • 24 Thayer St

🍴 Restaurants

- **Diwan** • 31 Thayer St
- **Eat and Two Veg** • 50 Marylebone High St
- **The Golden Hind** • 73 Marylebone Lane
- **Gordon Ramsay at Claridge's** • Brook St
- **Hush Brasserie** • 8 Lancashire Ct
- **La Galette** • 56 Paddington St
- **Patisserie Valerie** • 105 Marylebone High St
- **Sakura** • 9 Hanover St

🛍 Shopping

- **Browns South Molton Street** • 24 S Molton St
- **The Button Queen** • 19 Marylebone Ln
- **Daunt Books** • 83 Marylebone High St
- **Divertimenti** • 33 Marylebone High St
- **Fenwick** • 63 New Bond St
- **Gray's Antique Market** • 58 Davies St
- **John Lewis** • 278 Oxford St
- **Marimekko** • 16 St Christopher's Pl
- **Niketown** • 236 Oxford St
- **Noa Noa** • 14 Gees Ct
- **Paul Smith Sale Shop** • 23 Avery Row
- **Selfridges & Co** • 400 Oxford St
- **Zara** • 242 Oxford St

🛒 Supermarkets

- **Marks & Spencer** • Bond St Station
- **Tesco** • 311 Oxford St
- **Waitrose** • 98 Marylebone High St

Map 3 · **Fitzrovia**

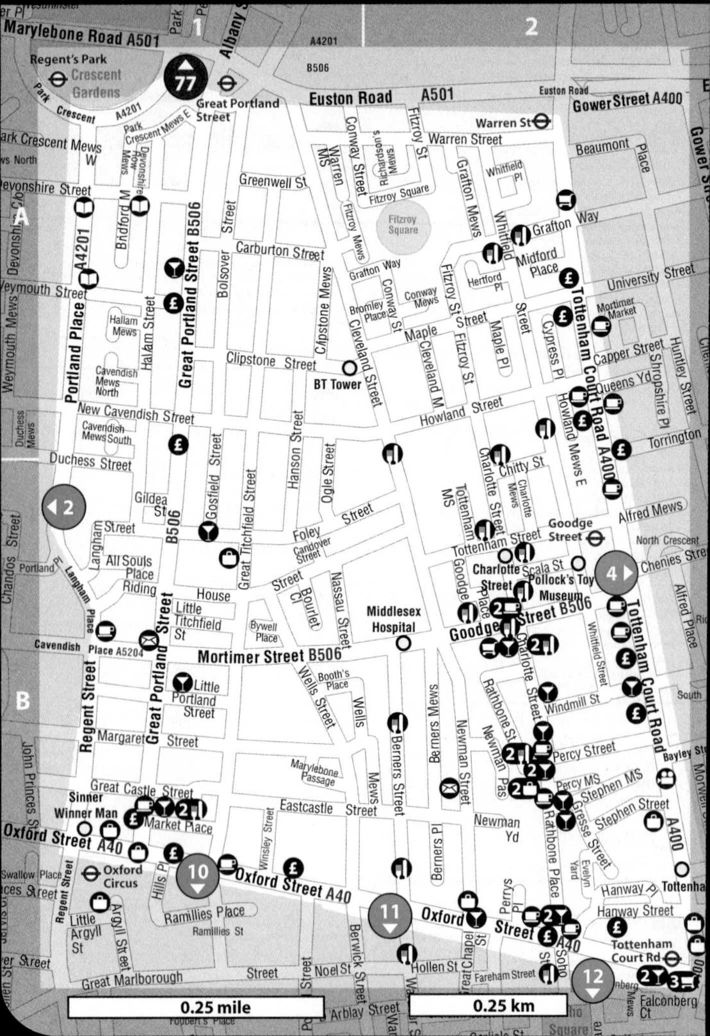

Marylebone Road A501

Regent's Park
Crescent
Gardens

77

Great Portland Street

Euston Road A501

Warren St

Gower Street A400

A4201

B506

Euston Road

Park Crescent Mews North

Devonshire Street

Park Crescent Mews West

Greenwell St

Warren Street

Fitzroy St

Conway Street

Grafton Mews

Whitfield Pl

Beaumont
Place

A

ark Crescent Mews
ews North

Devonshire Street

A4201

Portland Place

Bridford M

Hallam
Mews

Great Portland Street B506

Carburton Street

Bolsover Street

Clipstone Mews

Fitzroy
Square

Grafton Way

Whitfield St

Grafton Way

Midford
Place

University Street

Mortimer
Market

Tottenham Court Road A400

Weymouth Mews

Weymouth Street

Duchess
Mews

Hallam
Street

Cavendish
Mews North

Clipstone Street

Cleveland Mews

Bromley
Place

Conway
Mews

Maple
Street

Fitzroy St

Maple Pl

Hertford
Pl

Cypress St

Capper Street

Shropshire St

Queens St

Torrington

Duchess Street

New Cavendish Street

Cavendish
Mews South

Gildea
St

Gosfield Street

Great Titchfield Street

Hanson Street

Ogle Street

BT Tower

Cleveland Street

Howland Street

Charlotte St

Tottenham St

Charlotte
Mews

Chitty St

Goodge
Street

Alfred Mews

North Crescent

Chenies St

Duchess Street

Portland

Langham Street

B506

Gildea
Street

Foley
Gandover
Street

Nassau Street

Street

Tottenham
MS

Goodge
Street

Charlotte Street

Scala St

Pollock's Toy
Museum

Goodge
Street B506

Whitfield Street

Alfred
Place

2

2

Tottenham Court Road A400

All Souls
Place
Riding
House
Street

Little
Titchfield
Street

Bourlet

Bywell
Place

Middlesex
Hospital

Rathbone Street

Rathbone Pl

2

Windmill St

Percy Street

South

Bayley St

Morwell

Cavendish Place A5204

Langham Place

Great Portland Street

Mortimer Street B506

Wells Street

Booth's
Place

Wells Street

Berners Mews

Newman Street

Newman Pas

Percy St

Percy MS

Stephen MS

Stephen Street

A400

B

Regent Street

Margaret Street

Little
Portland
Street

Eastcastle Street

Marylebone
Passage

Berners St

Newman
Yd

Rathbone Place

Gresse
Street

Evelyn
Yard

Hanway St

Tottenha

John Prince's
Street

Great Castle Street

Sinner
Winner Man

Market Place

2

Winsley Street

Berners Pl

Newman

Hanway Street

Tottenham
Court Rd

2

3

Oxford Street A40

Oxford
Circus

10

Hills Pl

Oxford Street A40

11

Oxford
Street

12

Falconberg

Swallow Place

ces St

Little
Argyll
St

Argyll St

Ramillies Place

Ramillies St

Great Marlborough Street

Berwick Street

Noel St

Hollen St

Great Chapel

Greek

Fareham Street

A40

Soho

Arblay Street

Square

0.25 mile

0.25 km

2

4

Fitzrovia

In the heart of the advertising village, the Charlotte Street strip sees some super-slick schmoozing over lunch. From old-style (read "rude") French to the latest fad, the world is your (expense account) oyster. Get back on the 'corporate lash' later at a proper pub, like the Fitzroy Tavern. Beer boys grab a late curry while hipsters head to The Social for midweek madness.

Map 3

£ Banks

- **Abbey** • 165 Oxford St
- **Barclays** • 15 Great Portland St
- **Barclays** • 190 Tottenham Ct Rd
- **Halifax** • 60 Oxford St
- **Halifax** • 110 Tottenham Ct Rd
- **HSBC** • 39 Tottenham Ct Rd
- **HSBC** • 117 Great Portland St
- **HSBC** • 156 Tottenham Ct Rd
- **HSBC** • 196 Oxford St
- **Lloyds** • 190 Great Portland St
- **Lloyds** • 88 Tottenham Ct Rd
- **Lloyds** • 32 Oxford St
- **Royal Bank of Scotland** • 171 Tottenham Ct Rd

Cinemas

- **Odeon Tottenham Court** • 30 Tottenham Ct Rd

Coffee

- **Apostrophe** • 40 Great Castle St
- **Apostrophe** • 216 Tottenham Ct Rd
- **Caffe Nero** • 79 Tottenham Ct Rd
- **Caffe Nero** • 187 Tottenham Ct Rd
- **Caffe Nero** • 2 Charlotte St
- **Caffe Nero** • 48 Oxford St
- **Coffee Republic** • 23 Rathbone Pl
- **Coffee Republic** • 99 Tottenham Ct Rd
- **Costa** • 213 Tottenham Ct Rd
- **Eat.** • 44 Goodge St
- **Eat.** • 68 Oxford St
- **Eat.** • 94 Tottenham Ct Rd
- **Starbucks** • 1 Langham Pl
- **Starbucks** • 203 Oxford St
- **Starbucks** • 51 Goodge St

O Landmarks

- **BT Tower** • 60 Cleveland St
- **Charlotte Street** • Charlotte St
- **Middlesex Hospital** • Mortimer St
- **Pollock's Toy Museum** • 1 Scala St
- **Sinner Winner Man** • 216 Oxford St
- **Tottenham Court Road** • Tottenham Ct Rd

Libraries

- **British Architectural Library** • 66 Portland Pl
- **Institute of Contemporary History and Wiener Library** • 4 Devonshire St
- **Royal Institute of British Architects** • 66 Portland Pl

Nightlife

- **100 Club** • 100 Oxford St
- **The Albany** • 240 Great Portland St
- **Bourne & Hollingsworth** • 28 Rathbone Pl
- **Bradleys Spanish Bar** • 42 Hanway St
- **Bricklayers Arms** • 31 Gresse St
- **Charlotte Street Hotel** • 15 Charlotte St
- **The Fitzroy Tavern** • 16 Charlotte St
- **Ghetto** • Falconbery Ct
- **The Jerusalem Tavern** • 33 Rathbone Pl
- **Market Place** • 11 Market Pl
- **The Metro Club** • 19 Oxford St
- **Northumberland Arms** • 43 Goodge St
- **Punk** • 14 Soho St
- **The Rising Sun** • 46 Tottenham Ct Rd
- **The Roxy** • 3 Rathbone Pl
- **The Social** • 5 Little Portland St
- **The Yorkshire Grey** • 46 Langham St

✉ Post Offices

- **Great Portland St** • 55 Great Portland St
- **Newman St** • 19 Newman St

Restaurants

- **Archipelago** • 110 Whitfield St
- **Busaba Eathai** • 110 Wardour St
- **Carluccio's Caffe** • 8 Market Pl
- **Crazy Bear** • 26 Whitfield St
- **Eagle Bar Diner** • 3 Rathbone Pl
- **Elena's L'Etoile** • 30 Charlotte St
- **Govinda's** • 9 Soho St
- **Icco Pizza** • 46 Goodge St
- **Latium** • 21 Berners St
- **Market Place** • 11 Market Pl
- **Navarro's** • 67 Charlotte St
- **Neel Akash** • 93 Charlotte St
- **Ragam** • 57 Cleveland St
- **Rasa Express** • 5 Rathbone St
- **Roka** • 37 Charlotte St
- **Salt Yard** • 54 Goodge St
- **Sardo** • 45 Grafton Way
- **Squat & Gobble** • 69 Charlotte St
- **Stef's** • 3 Berners St
- **Thai Metro** • 36 Charlotte St

Shopping

- **Computer Exchange** • 32 Rathbone Pl
- **Harmony** • 103 Oxford St
- **Hobgoblin Shop** • 24 Rathbone Pl
- **Mango** • 225 Oxford St
- **Maplin** • 218 Tottenham Ct Rd
- **Paperchase** • 213 Tottenham Ct Rd
- **Scandinavian Kitchen** • 61 Great Titchfield St
- **Stargreen Box Office** • 20 Argyll St
- **Topshop** • 216 Oxford St

Supermarkets

- **Marks & Spencer** • 55 Tottenham Ct Rd
- **Sainsbury's** • 35 Mortimer St
- **Sainsbury's** • 17 Tottenham Ct Rd
- **Sainsbury's** • 145 Tottenham Ct Rd
- **Tesco** • 10 Goodge St

Map 4 · **Bloomsbury (West)**

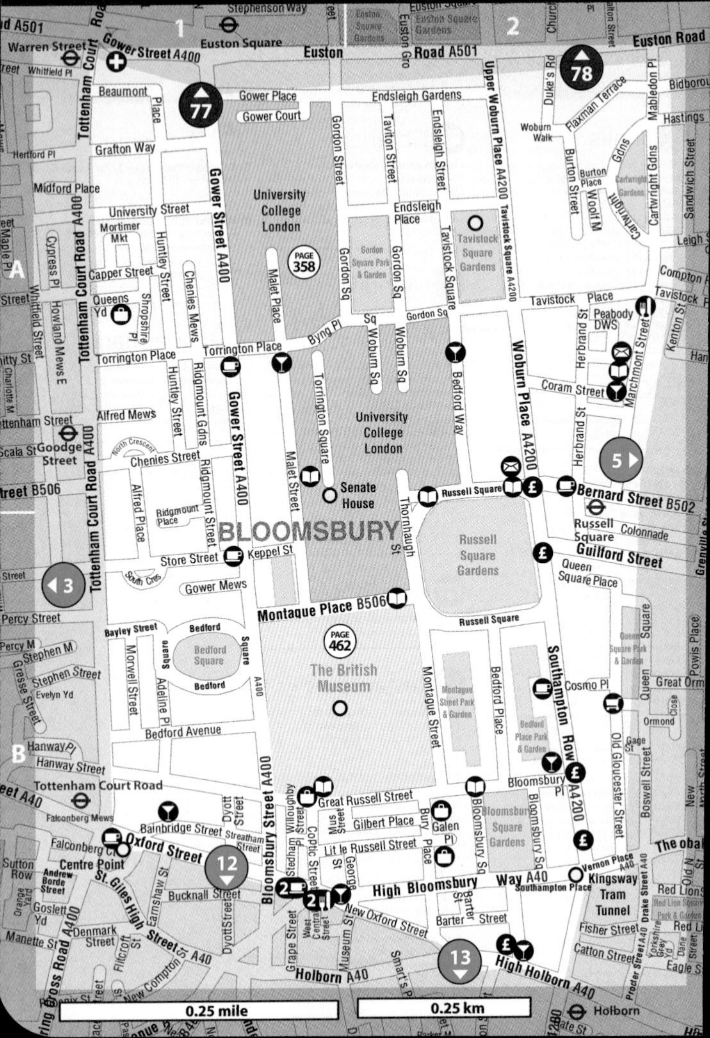

N

Warren Street
Gower Street A400
Euston Square
Euston
Euston Road A501
Euston Road

A501
Whitfield Pl
Stephenson Way
Euston Square Gardens
Church

1
2
78

77
Gower Place
Gower Court
Endsleigh Gardens
Upper Woburn Place A4200
Flaxman Terrace
Mabledon
Bidboroug

Beaumont
Place
Hertford Pl
Grafton Way
Tavistock Street
Endsleigh Gardens
Woburn Walk
Burton Street
Burton Place
Hastings
Cartwright Gdns

Midford Place
Mortimer
Mkt
University Street
Gordon Street
Endsleigh
Place
Tavistock Square Gardens
Woolf M
Sandwich Street

A
Capper Street
Chenies Mews
University
College
London
Gordon Square
PAGE
358
Gordon Sq
Gordon Square Park & Gardens
Tavistock Square A4200
Tavistock Place
Peabody
DWS
Leigh

Queens
Yd
Shropshire
Place
Torrington Place
Byng Pl
Woburn Sq
Herbrand St
Coram Street
Marchmont Street

Alfred Mews
Huntley Street
Ridgmount Gdns
Torrington Place
Torrington Square
Malet Street
University
College
London
Bedford Way
Woburn Place A4200
Herbrand St

Chenies Street
Ridgmount Street
Senate
House
Thornhaugh St
Russell Square
Bernard Street B502

5

Alfred Place
Store Street
Keppel St
Russell Square Gardens
Russell
Square
Colonnade
Guilford Street

3
Gower Mews
Montague Place B506
PAGE
462
Queen Square Place

Percy Street
Bayley Street
Bedford
Square
Bedford
The British
Museum
Montague Place
Montague Street
Russell Square

BLOOMSBURY

Bedford Avenue
Montague Street
Bedford Place
Bedford Place Park & Garden
Southampton Row A4200
Cosmo Pl

B
Hanway Pl
Hanway Street
Morwell Street
Adeline Pl
Bloomsbury Street A400
Bloomsbury Street
Great Russell Street
Bloomsbury Way A40
Bloomsbury Square
Bloomsbury Square Park & Gardens
Old Gloucester Street

Falconberg Mews
Dyott Street
Streatham Street
Willoughby St
Coptic Street
Gilbert Place
Bury Place
Galen Pl
Vernon Place A40
Kingsway Tram Tunnel

Oxford Street
Bainbridge Street
Falconberg Ct
Centre Point
12
Stedham Pl
West Central St
Lit le Russell Street
Southampton Place
Fisher Street
Red Lion

High Bloomsbury Way A40
13
High Holborn A40
Holborn

0.25 mile
0.25 km

Bloomsbury (West)

Map 4

Bloomsbury offers a chaotic throng of academics, belligerent tourists, and annoying Scientologists. The Virginia Woolf Effect is in its leafy squares, UCL, and the British Museum (blue plaques galore!). Traipse Tottenham Court Road for electronics, Gower Street for hotels, and the Brunswick centre for boutiques. Go posh bowling (All Star Lanes): booze at a Victorian gin palace (the Princess Louise), and do some collage (Paperchase).

£ Banks

- **Barclays** • 58 Southampton Row
- **Barclays** • 73 Russell Sq
- **Co-Operative** • 64 Southampton Row
- **HSBC** • 210 High Holborn
- **HSBC** • 1 Woburn Pl
- **Royal Bank of Scotland** • High Holborn

Cinemas

- **Horse Hospital** • 30 Colonnade
- **Odeon Tottenham Court** • 30 Tottenham Ct Rd

Coffee

- **Café Deco** • 43 Store St
- **Costa** • 44 New Oxford St
- **Costa** • 82 Gower St
- **Pret A Manger** • 40 Bernard St
- **Pret A Manger** • 23 Southampton Row
- **Pret A Manger** • 44 New Oxford St
- **Starbucks** • 124 Southampton Row
- **Starbucks** • 112 New Oxford
- **Starbucks** • 425 Oxford St

Emergency Rooms

- **University College Hospital** • 235 Euston Rd

O Landmarks

- **The British Museum** • Great Russell St
- **Centre Point** • 101 New Oxford St
- **Kingsway Tram Tunnel** •
- **Senate House** • University of London, Malet St
- **Tavistock Square** • Tavistock Sq

Libraries

- **Anthropology Library** • Great Russell St
- **Birkbeck College Library** • Malet St
- **German Historical Institute Library London** • 17 Bloomsbury Sq
- **Institute of Advanced Legal Studies Library** • 17 Russell Square
- **University of London, Senate House Library** • Malet St

Nightlife

- **All Star Lanes** • Victoria House, Bloomsbury Pl
- **Bloomsbury Bowling Lanes** • Bedford Way
- **The Fly** • 36 New Oxford
- **Marquis of Cornwallis** • 31 Marchmont St
- **Old Crown** • 33 New Oxford St
- **Point 101** • 101 New Oxford St
- **The Princess Louise** • 208 High Holborn
- **ULU** • 1 Malet St

Post Offices

- **Marchmont St** • 33 Marchmont St
- **Russell Square** • 9 Russell Sq

Restaurants

- **Alara** • 58 Marchmont St
- **Bi Won** • 24 Coptic St
- **Savoir Faire** • 42 New Oxford St

Shopping

- **Blade Rubber** • 12 Bury Pl
- **British Museum shop** • Great Russell St
- **Gosh! Comics** • 39 Great Russell St
- **London Review Bookshop** • 14 Bury Pl
- **Maplin** • 218 Tottenham Ct Rd
- **Paperchase** • 213 Tottenham Ct Rd

Supermarkets

- **Waitrose** • Old Gloucester St & Gage St

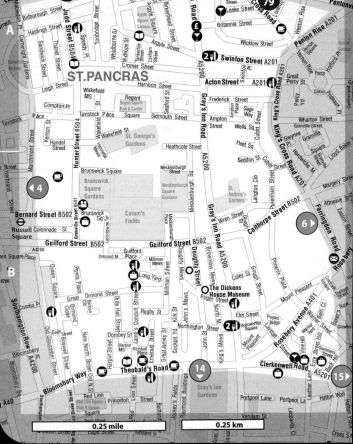

Map 5 · **Bloomsbury (East)**

Bloomsbury (East)

Map 5

Close to University College London, this area is a student's delight, where you can hang out in caffs and watch art-house films to your heart's desire. Convenient chains proliferate but shun them for the friendly Mary Ward Centre. Lamb's Conduit Street provides a range of cheap eateries such as the Thai Candle. The Brunswick Centre is an upmarket shopping alternative and is home to the excellent Renoir cinema.

£ Banks

• **Lloyds** • 344 Gray's Inn Rd

Cinemas

• **Renoir Cinema** • 1 Brunswick Sq

Coffee

• **Apostrophe** • Hunter St & Handel St
• **Caffe Nero** • 54 Theobald's Rd
• **Costa** • 118 King's Cross Rd
• **Pret A Manger** • 15 Theobald's Rd
• **Starbucks** • 57 Theobald's Rd

O Landmarks

• **The Dickens House Museum** • 48 Doughty St
• **Doughty Street** • Doughty St

Libraries

• **Holborn Library** • 32 Theobald's Rd
• **Royal National Institute of the Blind Research Library** • 105 Judd St
• **St Pancras Library** • Argyle St

Nightlife

• **06 St Chad's Place** • 6 St Chad's Pl
• **The Duke of York** • 156 Clerkenwell Rd
• **Monto Water Rats** • 328 Gray's Inn Rd
• **Smithy's** • 15 Leeke St

Post Offices

• **Mount Pleasant** • Farringdon Rd & Rosebery Ave

Restaurants

• **Acorn House** • 69 Swinton St
• **Aki Bistro** • 182 Gray's Inn Rd
• **Bread and Butter Sandwich Bar** • 100 Judd St
• **Ciao Bella** • 86 Lamb's Conduit St
• **Cigala** • 54 Lamb's Conduit St
• **The Food Bazaar** • 59 Gray's Inn Rd
• **Fryer's Delight** • 19 Theobald's Rd
• **Konstam** • 2 Acton St
• **La Provence** • 63 Gray's Inn Rd
• **Mary Ward Centre** • 42 Queen Sq
• **Swintons** • 61 Swinton St
• **Thai Candle** • 38 Lamb's Conduit St

Shopping

• **Bobbin Bicycles** • 31 Eyre St Hill
• **International Magic** • 89 Clerkenwell Rd
• **Joy** • The Brunswick
• **Magma Concept Store** • 117 Clerkenwell Rd
• **Romanian Charity Shop** • Lamb's Conduit St

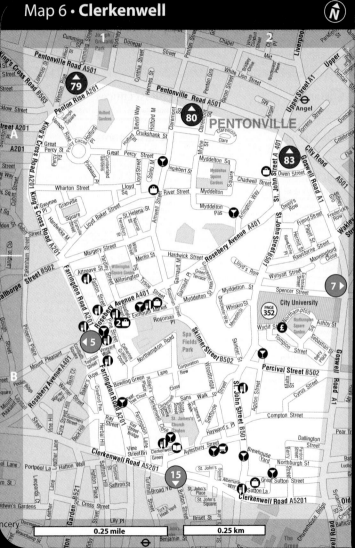

Map 6 · **Clerkenwell**

Clerkenwell

Clerkenwell is London's own little village, only without the cricket team and middle-class wife swapping. At its heart is Clerkenwell Green, an old-time square that pops up in Dickens (only the nice bits of his books, mind; the grim workhouse stuff he must have got from elsewhere). The Three Kings is part pub, part music museum, while Sandwichman does 65p lunches.

Map 6

Banks

• **Barclays** • 10 Northampton Sq

Libraries

• **Marx Memorial Library** • 37 Clerkenwell Green

Nightlife

• **Betsey Trotwood** • 56 Farringdon Rd
• **Café Kick** • 43 Exmouth Market
• **Cicada** • 132 St John St
• **Dollar Grills and Martinis** • 2 Exmouth Market
• **The Dovetail** • 9 Jerusalem Passage
• **Filthy McNasty's** • 68 Amwell St
• **The Harlequin** • 27 Arlington Way
• **Queen Boadicea** • 292 St John St
• **The Slaughtered Lamb** • 34-35 Great Sutton St
• **The Three Kings** • 7 Clerkenwell Close

Restaurants

• **Bada Bing!** • 120 St John St
• **Clarks Pie and Mash** • 46 Exmouth Market
• **Dans Le Noir** • 30 Clerkenwell Green
• **The Eagle** • 159 Farringdon Rd
• **Little Bay** • 171 Farringdon Rd
• **Moro** • 34 Exmouth Market
• **The Quality Chop House** • 94 Farringdon Rd
• **Sandwichman** • 23 Easton St
• **Sofra** • 21 Exmouth Market
• **Vic Naylor's** • 38 St John St

Shopping

• **The Black Tulip** • 28 Exmouth Market
• **Brindisa Retail** • 32 Exmouth Market
• **The Family Business Tattoo Shop** • 58 Exmouth Market
• **M and R Meats** • 399 St John St
• **Timorous Beasties** • 46 Amwell St
• **Wyvern Bindery** • 56 Clerkenwell Rd

Supermarkets

• **Waitrose** • Aylesbury St & St John St

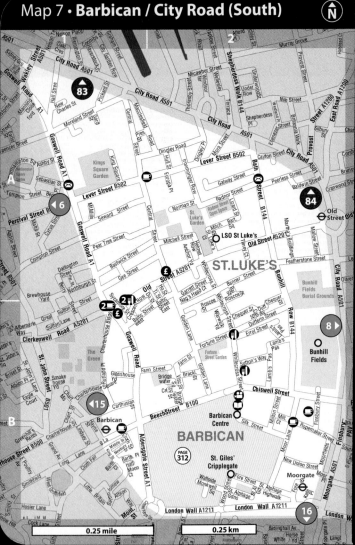

Barbican / City Road (South)

A no-man's-land that's neither Shoreditch, Angel, nor Clerkenwell, this area has been co-opted by the nu mee-djah crowd (spot Jefferson Hack cycling from the Dazed & Confused office). There's culture to be had at the Barbican and LSO St Luke's, and Turkish baths at Ironmonger Row. Food is fast and exceptional (Nusa and Warrin Thai), magnificent Whitecross Market has top-notch food stalls and there's plenty a coffee shop to keep resident caffeine-dependent office monkeys from rioting.

£ Banks

- **Barclays** • 128 Moorgate
- **HSBC** • 74 Goswell Rd
- **Lloyds** • 69 Old St

Cinemas

- **Barbican Centre Cinema** • Silk St & Whitecross St

Coffee

- **Caffe Nero** • 40 City Rd
- **Coffee Republic** • City Rd
- **Costa** • 68 Goswell Rd
- **Costa** • Ropemaker St
- **Eat.** • 143 Moorgate
- **Popular Cafe** • 85 Lever St
- **Pret A Manger** • 9 Goswell Rd
- **Pret A Manger** • 1 Long Ln
- **Pret A Manger** • Ropemaker St

O Landmarks

- **Barbican Centre** • Silk St
- **Bunhill Fields** • City Rd
- **LSO St Luke's** • 161 Old St
- **St. Giles' Cripplegate** • Fore St

Libraries

- **Barbican Library** • Silk St

Post Offices

- **Goswell Rd** • 151 Goswell Rd
- **Old Street** • 205 Old St

Restaurants

- **Carnevale** • 135 Whitecross St
- **De Santis** • Old St
- **NUSA Kitchen** • 9 Old St
- **Warrin Thai Kitchen Stall** • 77 Whitecross St

Map 7

19

Map 8 · **Liverpool Street / Broadgate**

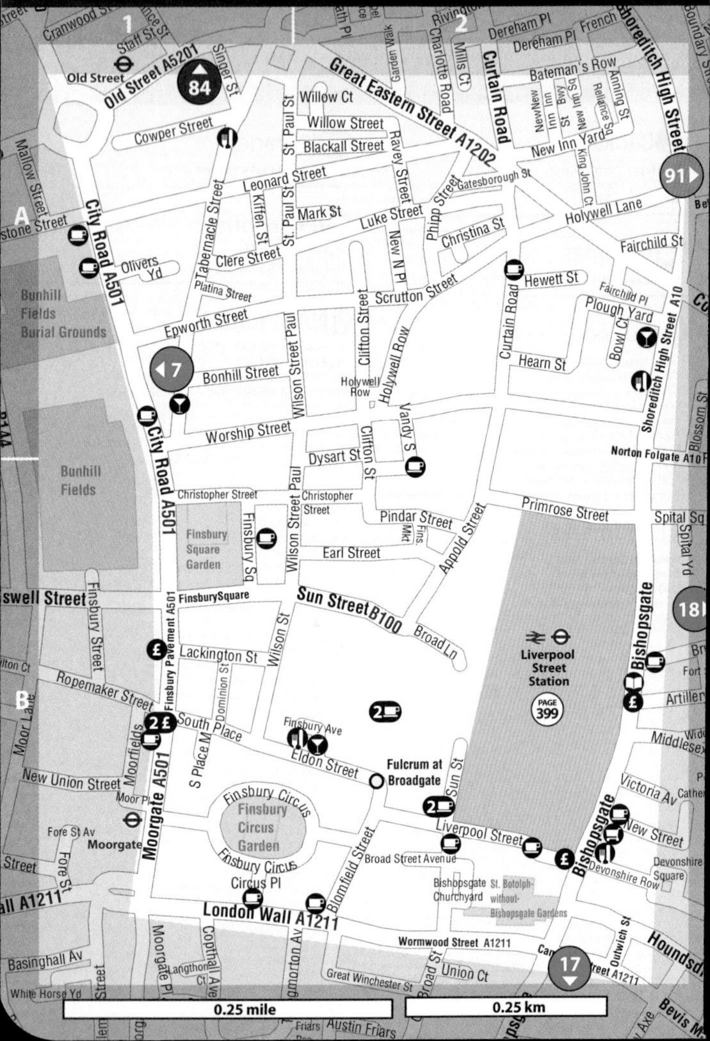

N

Cranwood St

Staff Rd

1

Old Street

Old Street A5201

84

Singer St

Cowper Street

Leonard Street

Mark St

St Paul St

Kffren St

Tabernacle Street

Clere Street

Platina Street

Epworth Street

7

Bonhill Street

Worship Street

Christopher Street

Finsbury Square Garden

City Road A501

Wilson Street St Paul

Christopher Street

Dysart St

Pindar Street

Earl Street

FinsburySquare

Finsbury Pavement

Lackington St

Ropemaker Street

Moorfields

S Place King St

South Place

Eldon Street

2

Moorgate

Finsbury Circus Garden

Finsbury Circus

Circus Pl

London Wall A1211

Fore St Ave

Fore St

Moorgate

New Union Street

Moor Pl

Basinghall Av

Coptall Ave

Moorgate

Langthorn Ave

all A1211

White Horse Yd

Circus Pl

Blomfield Street

Broad Street Avenue

Willow Ct

Willow Street

Blackall Street

Ravey Street

Great Eastern Street A1202

Garden Walk

Charlotte Rd

Mills Ct

Gatesborough St

Luke Street

New P St

Christina St

Scrutton Street

Clifton Street

Holywell Row

Holywell Row

Clifton St

Vardy S

Sun Street B100

Wilson St

Finsbury Ave

2

Broad Ln

Sun St

Fulcrum at Broadgate

2

Liverpool Street

Bishopsgate Churchyard

St. Botolph-without-Bishopsgate Gardens

Wormwood Street A1211

Gt Union Ct

Great Winchester St

Friars

Austin Friars

Rivington St

Charlotte Rd

Curtain Road

Dereham Pl

Dereham Pl

French

Bateman's Row

New

New Inn Yard

New Inn King John Ct

Holywell Lane

Fairchild St

Hewett St

Fairchild Pl

Plough Yard

Curtain Road

Bowl Ct

Hearn St

Norton Folgate A10

Primrose Street

Appold Street

Spital Sq

Spital Yd

Liverpool Street Station

PAGE 399

Victoria Av

New Street

Devonshire Row

Bishopsgate

18

Artillery

Fort

Middlesex

Devonshire Sq

Shoreditch High Street

Arming St

Reliance Sq

91

Co

Norton Folgate A10

Shoreditch High Street

St Union Ct

Houndsd

Bevis

Dulwich St

reet A1211

17

0.25 mile   **0.25 km**

The southern end of this hood is a pure suited-and-booted City zone, the northern end a slightly confusing mix of Shoreditch trendonites and looser suits—very little, if any, fraternisation between the tribes occurs. Plenty of bars, try Sosho for cocktails and The Light for a jolt of electric history and plenty of space. Hungry? Try the Gaucho Grill or the Eyre Brother's place.

Banks

• **Abbey** • 224 Bishopsgate
• **Barclays** • 128 Moorgate
• **Halifax** • 136 Bishopsgate
• **HSBC** • 1 South Pl
• **Lloyds** • 109 Finsbury Pavement

Coffee

• **AMT** • Liverpool St & Broadgate Circle
• **Caffe Nero** • 2 Bishopsgate
• **Caffe Nero** • 40 City Rd
• **Caffe Nero** • 75 London Wall
• **Coffee Republic** • City Rd
• **Coffee Republic** • 25 Exchange Sq
• **Costa** • 18 Liverpool St
• **Eat.** • 1 City Rd
• **Eat.** • 143 Moorgate
• **Eat.** • 176 Bishopsgate
• **Eat.** • 34 Broadgate Circle
• **Eat.** • 62 London Wall
• **Eat.** • 80 Old Broad St
• **Fab Food Patisserie** • 26 Curtain Rd
• **Starbucks** • Liverpool St Station
• **Starbucks** • 28 Broadgate Circus
• **Starbucks** • 50 Finsbury Sq

O Landmarks

• **Fulcrum at Broadgate** • Broadgate

Libraries

• **Bishopsgate Library** • 230 Bishopsgate

Nightlife

• **The Light** • 233 Shoreditch High St
• **The Red Lion** • 1 Eldon St
• **Sosho** • 2 Tabernacle Street

Restaurants

• **Damascu Bite Kebab** • 21 Shoreditch High St
• **Eyre Brothers** • 70 Leonard St
• **Gaucho Grill** • 5 Finsbury Ave
• **Ponti's Caffe** • 176 Bishopsgate

Supermarkets

• **Tesco** • 160 Bishopsgate

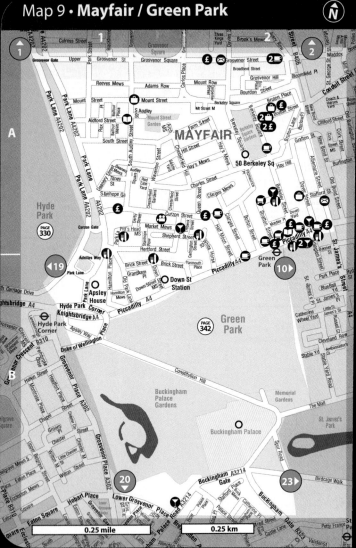

Map 9 · **Mayfair / Green Park**

In Monopoly, you can buy both Mayfair and Park Lane, build hotels, and end up really screwing everyone else. In real life you may struggle to afford a t-shirt here, though avant-boutique Dover Street Market is definitely worth a timid visit, and afternoon tea at the Ritz is a rite of passage for most aspirational yuppies. Check out Mahiki for young royals and paralytic celebrities.

£ Banks

- **Barclays** • 11 Bruton St
- **Halifax** • 51 Berkeley St
- **HSBC** • 18 Curzon St
- **HSBC** • 79 Piccadilly
- **Lloyds** • 14 Berkeley Sq
- **Lloyds** • 50 Grosvenor St
- **NatWest** • 63 Piccadilly
- **NatWest** • 4 Berkeley Sq
- **Royal Bank of Scotland** • 43 Curzon St
- **Royal Bank of Scotland** • 24 Grosvenor Pl

Cinemas

- **Curzon Mayfair** • 38 Curzon St

Coffee

- **Apostrophe** • 10 Grosvenor St
- **Caffe Nero** • 50 Curzon St
- **Caffe Nero** • 70 Piccadilly
- **Costa** • 4 Grosvenor St
- **Eat.** • 8 Berkeley Sq
- **Eat.** • 55 Stratton St
- **Starbucks** • 52 Berkeley St
- **Starbucks** • 84 Piccadilly

O Landmarks

- **50 Berkeley Square** • 50 Berkeley Sq
- **Apsley House** • Hyde Park Corner
- **Buckingham Palace** • The Mall
- **Down Street Station** • Down St

Libraries

- **Mayfair Library** • 25 South Audley St
- **Royal Society of Chemistry Library and Information Centre** • Piccadilly

Nightlife

- **1707** • 181 Piccadilly
- **5th View** • 203 Piccadilly
- **bbar** • 43 Buckingham Palace Rd
- **Funky Buddah** • 15 Berkeley St
- **Mahiki** • 1 Dover St
- **Shepherd's Tavern** • 50 Hertford St

Post Offices

- **Albemarle St** • 44 Albemarle St
- **Mayfair** • 32 Grosvenor St

Restaurants

- **El Pirata of Mayfair** • 5 Down St
- **Galvin at Windows** • 28th Floor, Hilton Park Lane
- **L'Autre** • 5 Shepherd St
- **Nobu** • 15 Berkeley St
- **The Ritz** • 150 Piccadilly
- **Theo Randall at the InterContinental** • 1 Hamilton Pl
- **The Wolseley** • 161 Piccadilly

Shopping

- **Diane Von Furstenberg** • 25 Bruton St
- **Dover Street Market** • 17 Dover St
- **Marc Jacobs** • 24 Mount St
- **Matthew Williamson** • 28 Bruton St
- **Stella McCartney** • 30 Bruton St

Supermarkets

- **Marks & Spencer** • 78 Piccadilly
- **Sainsbury's** • 50 Stratton St

Map 10 · **Piccadilly / Soho (West)**

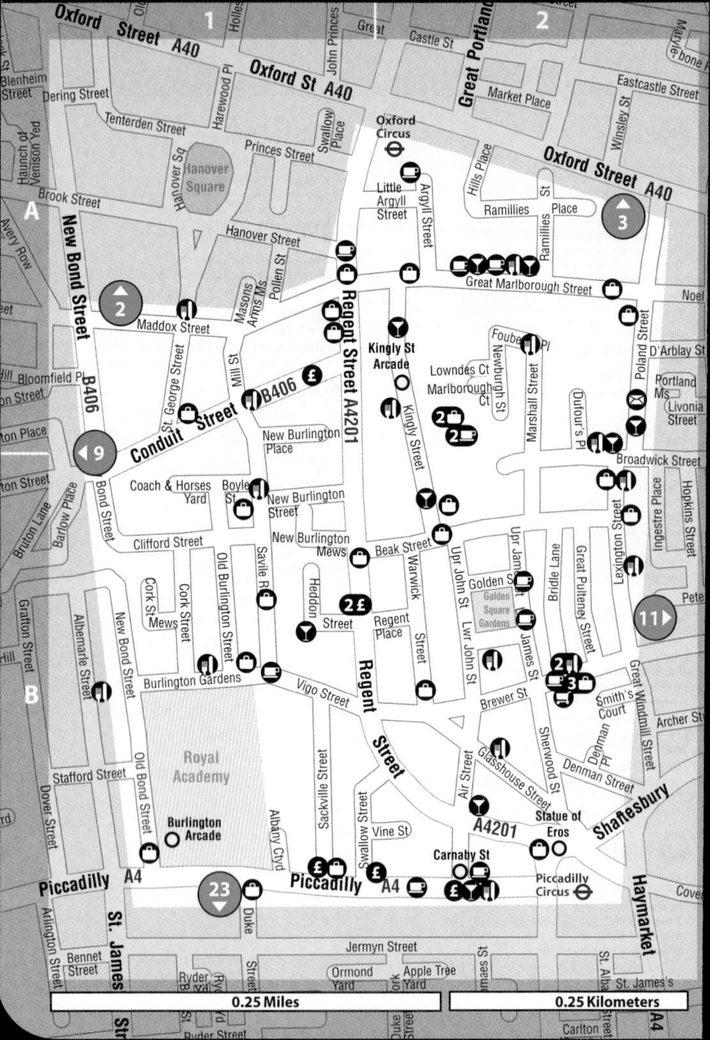

1

2

Oxford Street A40

Oxford St A40

Great Portland

Castle St

Eastcastle Street

Blenheim Street

Dering Street

Tenterden Street

Princes Street

Market Place

Winsley St

Oxford Circus

Oxford Street A40

Noel

Haunch of Venison Yard

Brook Street

Hanover Sq

Hanover Street

Swallow Place

Little Argyll Street

Argyll Street

Hills Place

Ramillies Place

Ramillies

3

Poland Street

D'Arblay Street

A

New Bond Street

Maddox Street

Masons Arms Ms

Pollen St

Regent Street A4201

Kingly St Arcade

Great Marlborough Street

Foubert

Newburgh St

St

Marshall Street

Portland Ms

Livonia Street

2

Conduit Street

St. George Street

Mill St

B406

£

New Burlington Place

Kingly Street

Lowndes Ct Marlborough Ct

Dufour's Pl

Broadwick Street

9

Boyle St

Coach & Horses Yard

New Burlington Street

New Burlington Mews

Beak Street

2£

2£

Upr John St

Golden Square Gardens

Lexington Street

Great Pulteney Street

Hopkins Street

Ingestre Place

Pete

Clifford Street

Savile Row

Warwick

Upr James St

Lwr John St

Bruton Place

Barlow Place

Bond Lane

New Bond Street

Cork Street

Cork St Mews

Old Burlington Street

Hedon St

2£

Regent Place

Regent Street

Lwr James St

Bridle Lane

2£

3

B

Grafton Street

Hill

Albemarle Street

New Bond Street

Old Bond Street

Burlington Gardens

Vigo Street

Brewer Street

Sherwood St

Denman Street

Smith's Court

Archer St

Great Windmill Street

11

Royal Academy

Stafford Street

Dover Street

(rd)

Burlington Arcade

Albany Cvd

Sackville Street

Swallow Street

Vine St

Air St

Glasshouse Street

A4201

Statue of Eros

Shaftesbury

Piccadilly A4

£

Piccadilly A4

Carnaby St

£

Piccadilly Circus

Haymarket

Cove

Arlington Street

Bennet Street

St. James

Duke

23

Jermyn Street

Ormond Yard

Apple Tree Yard

St James St

St. Alba

Dove

Ryder St

Carlton

| 0.25 Miles | 0.25 Kilometers |

This is where an outsiders' idea of London and 'real' London meet, but it's not a place for budgets or morals. Georgina Goodman will heel you and Carnaby Street will clothe you. You can gastronomically ruin yourself at Mrs. Kibbles and maybe have £20 left over for a seedy encounter with a 'model'. This is London and it's still swinging.

£ Banks

- **Abbey** • 34 Piccadilly
- **Barclays** • 27 Regent St
- **HSBC** • 133 Regent St
- **Lloyds** • 39 Picadilly
- **NatWest** • 208 Piccadilly Circus
- **Royal Bank of Scotland** • 60 Conduit St

Coffee

- **Caffe Nero** • 62 Brewer St
- **Caffe Nero** • 26 Piccadilly
- **Caffe Nero** • 225 Regent St
- **Coffee Republic** • 39 Great Marlborough St
- **Costa** • 11 Argyll St
- **Eat.** • 19 Golden Sq
- **Eat.** • 8 Vigo St
- **Pret A Manger** • 298 Regent St
- **Pret A Manger** • 27 Great Marlborough
- **Sacred Cafe** • 13 Ganton St
- **Starbucks** • 37 Golden Sq
- **Starbucks** • 16 Picadilly

O Landmarks

- **Burlington Arcade** • Burlington Arcade
- **Carnaby Street** • Carnaby St
- **Kingly Street Arcade** • Kingly St
- **Statue of Eros** • Piccadilly Circus

Nightlife

- **22 Below** • 22 Great Marlborough St
- **Ain't Nothing But The Blues Bar** • 20 Kingly St
- **Bar Red** • 5 Kingly St
- **Cheers Bar** • 72 Regent St
- **Courthouse Bar** • 19 Great Marlborough St
- **John Snow** • 39 Broadwick St
- **Milk & Honey** • 61 Poland St
- **Pigalle Club** • 215 Piccadilly
- **Strawberry Moons** • 15 Heddon St

Post Offices

- **Poland Street** • 1 Poland St

Restaurants

- **Atlantic Bar & Grill** • 20 Glasshouse St
- **Cecconi's** • 5 Burlington Gardens
- **Dehesa** • 25 Ganton St
- **Mildred's** • 45 Lexington St
- **Mosaico** • 13 Albermale St
- **Nordic Bakery** • 14 Golden Sq
- **Ping Pong** • 45 Great Marlborough St
- **Sartoria** • 20 Saville Row
- **Sketch** • 9 Conduit St
- **Taro** • 61 Brewer St
- **Ten Ten Tei** • 56 Brewer St
- **Thanks for Franks** • 26 Fouberts Pl
- **Toku @ The Japan Centre** • 212 Piccadilly
- **Wagamama** • 10 Lexington St
- **Wild Honey** • 12 St George St
- **Yauatcha** • 15 Broadwick St

Shopping

- **Abercrombie & Fitch** • 7 Burlington Gardens
- **Arigato** • 48 Brewer St
- **b store** • 24 Savile Row
- **Banana Republic** • 224 Regent St
- **Behave** • 48 Lexington Sreet
- **The Black Pearl** • 10 Kingly Ct
- **Burlington Arcade** • Burlington Arcade
- **Cos** • 222 Regent St
- **Deal Real** • 3 Great Marlborough St
- **The European Bookshop** • 5 Warwick St
- **Fortnum And Mason** • 181 Piccadilly
- **Georgina Goodman** • 44 Old Bond St
- **Hamley's** • 188 Regent St
- **Hatchard's** • 187 Piccadilly
- **Hoss Intropia** • 211 Regent St
- **Liberty** • 214 Regent St
- **Lillywhites** • 24-36 Lower Regent St
- **Mrs Kibble's Olde Sweet Shoppe** • 57 Brewer St
- **Muji** • 41 Carnaby St
- **Phonica** • 51 Poland St
- **Playlounge** • 19 Beak St
- **Richard James** • 29 Savile Row
- **Rigby & Peller** • 22 Conduit St
- **SKK (Lighting)** • 34 Lexington St
- **Twinkled** • 1 Kingly Ct
- **The Vintage Magazine Shop** • 39 Brewer St

Supermarkets

- **Fresh & Wild** • 73 Brewer St

Map 11 · **Soho (Central)**

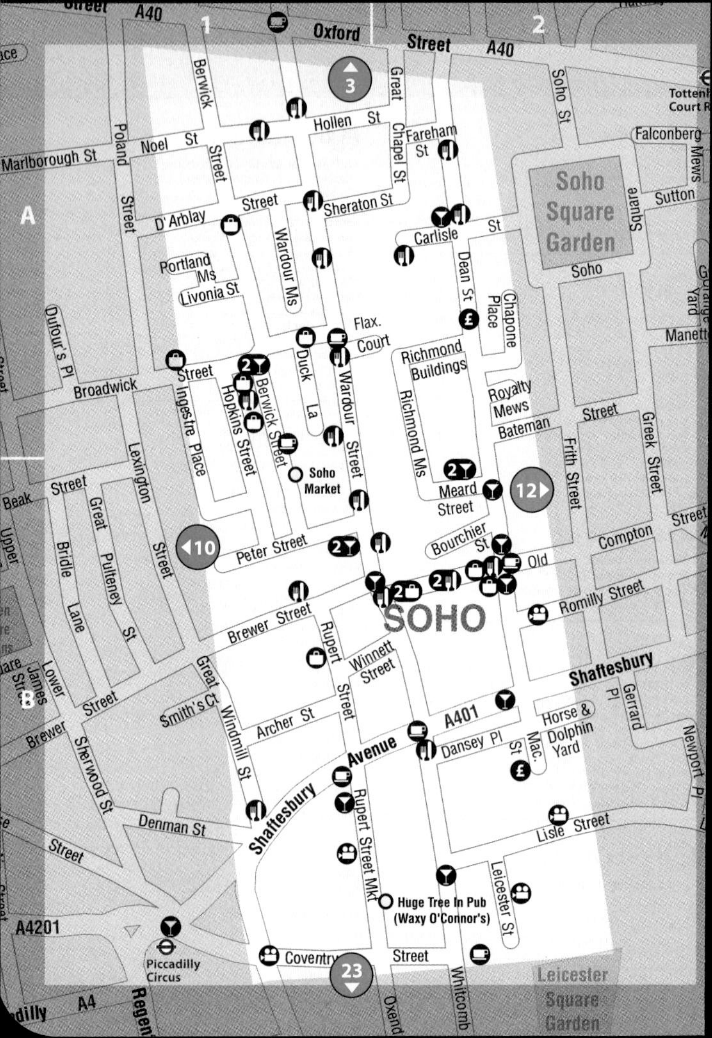

N

Street   A40   **1**   Oxford   Street   A40   **2**

3

Berwick   Hollen   St   Great   Fareham   St   Chapel St   Soho St   Tottenham Court Rd

Poland   Noel   St   Street   Sheraton St   Carlisle   St   Dean St   Falconberg Mews

Marlborough St   D'Arblay   Street   Chapone   Place   Sutton   Square   Goslett Yard

A   Street   Portland   Ms   Wardour Ms   Flax.   Court   £   Soho   Manett

Dufour's Pl   Livonia St   Duck   La   Richmond   Buildings   Royalty   Mews   Greek   Street

Broadwick   Street   Berwick   Street   Hopkins Street   Wardour   Street   Richmond Ms   Bateman   Street   Frith Street

Ingestre Place   Soho   Market   Meard   Street   **2**   Bourchier   St   **12▶**

Beak   Street   Lexington   Street   **◀10**   Peter Street   **2**   Old   Compton   Romilly Street   Street

Great   Pulteney   St   Bridle   Lane   SOHO   **2**   **2**

Upper   James St   Lower   James St   Brewer   Street   Rupert   Street   Winnett   Street   Shaftesbury   Gerrard   Pl

Smith's Ct   Windmill St   Archer   Street   A401   Horse &   Dolphin   Yard   Newport Pl

Square   James   Brewer   Sherwood   Street   Great   Windmill St   Shaftesbury   Dansey Pl   Mac.   St   £   Lisle   Street

Denman St   Rupert Street Mkt   Leicester St

Street   Huge Tree In Pub   (Waxy O'Connor's)

A4201   Piccadilly   Circus   Coventry   Street   Whitcomb   Leicester   Square   Garden

dilly   A4   Regen   **23**   Oxenden

Soho (Central)

Map 11

No longer the scuzzy, slightly dangerous Bohemia it used to be, Soho's red-light district, gay-friendly, café society buzziness keeps the punters coming (no, not like that). You can sup on the pavement like a true Soho drunkard at the French House, catch some cabaret at Madame Jojo's, or laugh it up at The Comedy Store before breaking your fast in the wee hours at Balans.

💷 Banks

• **HSBC** • 17 Gerrard St
• **NatWest** • 20 Dean St

😀 Cinemas

• **Cineworld Shaftesbury Avenue** • 13 Coventry St
• **Curzon Soho** • 99 Shaftesbury Ave
• **Empire Cinemas** • 5 Leicester Square
• **Prince Charles Cinema** • 7 Leicester Pl
• **Rex Cinema and Bar** • 21 Rupert St

☕ Coffee

• **BB's Coffee and Muffins** • Oxford St & Berners St
• **Coffee Republic** • 7 Coventry St
• **Coffee Republic** • 8 Berwick St
• **Costa** • 39 Old Compton St
• **Costa** • 62 Shaftesbury Ave
• **Starbucks** • 7 Leicester Sq
• **Starbucks** • 60 Wardour St

O Landmarks

• **Huge Tree In Pub (Waxy O'Connor's)** • 14 Rupert St
• **Soho Market** • Berwick St

🍸 Nightlife

• **Blue Posts** • 22 Berwick St
• **The Blue Posts** • 28 Rupert St
• **Candy Bar** • 4 Carlisle St
• **The Colony Room** • 41 Dean St
• **The Comedy Store** • 1 Oxendon St
• **De Hems** • 11 Macclesfield St
• **The Endurance** • 90 Berwick St
• **Freedom** • 66 Wardour St
• **The French House** • 49 Dean St
• **LUPO** • 50 Dean St
• **Madame Jojo's** • Brewer St
• **Rex Cinema and Bar** • 21 Rupert St
• **Shadow Lounge** • 5 Brewer St
• **Soho Revue Bar** • 11 Walkers Ct, Brewer St
• **Trash Palace** • 11 Wardour St
• **The Village** • 81 Wardour St

🍴 Restaurants

• **Balans** • 60 Old Compton St
• **Bar Bruno** • 101 Wardour St
• **Beetroot** • 92 Berwick St
• **Cafe Espana** • 63 Old Compton St
• **Hummus Bros** • 88 Wardour St
• **Imli** • 167 Wardour St
• **Italian Graffiti** • 163 Wardour St
• **Jerk City** • 189 Wardour St
• **Malletti** • 26 Noel St
• **Maoz** • 43 Old Compton St
• **Paul** • 49 Old Compton St
• **Pizza Express Jazz Club** • 10 Dean St
• **Randall & Aubin** • 16 Brewer St
• **Red Veg** • 95 Dean St
• **Soho Thai** • 27 St. Annes Ct
• **St Moritz** • 161 Wardour St
• **Sugar Reef** • 42 Great Windmill St
• **VitaOrganic** • 74 Wardour St
• **Won Kei** • 41 Wardour St

🛍 Shopping

• **Algerian Coffee Stores** • 52 Old Compton St
• **Bang Bang** • 9 Berwick St
• **Chappel of Bond Street** • 152 Wardour St
• **Cheapo Cheapo Records** • 53 Rupert St
• **Cowling & Wilcox** • 26 Broadwick St
• **Gerry's** • 74 Old Compton St
• **I Camisa & Son** • 61 Old Compton St
• **Paradiso** • 41 Old Compton St
• **Sister Ray** • 34 Berwick St
• **Sounds of the Universe** • 7 Broadwick St
• **Vinyl Junkies** • 94 Berwick St

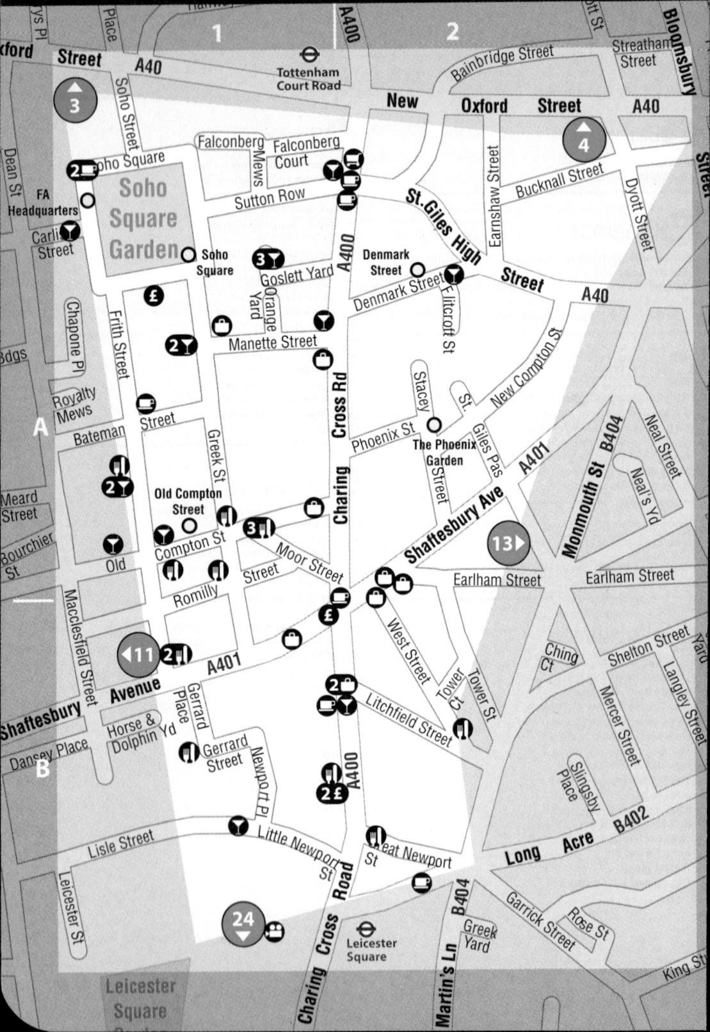

Map 12 · **Soho (East)**

1   2

Harwell

 Place

ky's Pl
xford   **Street**   A40   A40

Soho Street   Tottenham
Court Road

Bainbridge Street   Streatham
Street   Bloomsbury

3   **New   Oxford   Street**   A40

Falconberg   Falconberg   4
Mews   Court

Dean St

FA
Headquarters

Carli
Street   **Soho
Square
Garden**

Falconberg Mews   Sutton Row

Soho
Square   **St Giles High**

Earnshaw Street   Bucknall Street

Dyott Street

Street

Chapone Pl

Bdgs

£   Goslett Yard

3   Denmark
Street

Orange
Yard   Denmark Street   **Street**   A40

Manette Street   Ellcroft St

New Compton St

Frith Street

2

A

Bateman   **Street**

Royalty
Mews

Greek St

Charing   Cross Rd

Phoenix St

Stacey

St

The Phoenix
Garden   New Compton St

St. Giles Pas

Meard
Street

2

Old Compton
Street

St Giles

Street

Shaftesbury Ave   A401

Neal Street

Neal's
Yd

Monmouth St   B404

Bourchier
St

Compton St   3

Moor Street   Earlham Street   Earlham Street

Old

Romilly
Street

West Street

Tower St

Litchfield Street

13

Ching
Ct   Shelton Street

Shelton Street

Langley Street   Yard

Mercer Street

Macclesfield Street

11   2

Avenue   A401

Horse &
Dolphin Yd

Gerrard
Place

2

Tower Ct

2

Slingsby
Place   B02

Shaftesbury

Dansey Place

Gerrard
Street   Newport Pl

2   £

A400

Long   Acre   B02

Lisle Street

Little Newport
St   Great Newport
St

Leicester St

24

Charing   Cross   Road

Leicester
Square

St Martin's Ln

Greek
Yard

Garrick Street

Rose St

King St

Leicester
Square

Soho (East)

Whether bored, jaded, gay, drunk, high or low, this crowded corner of Soho will provide just what you need. Old Compton Street is your high street, although Greek Street and Soho Square offer equal excitement. Opportunities for liquid-fuelled misdemeanour abound, so line your stomach at the Gay Hussar or blot-up at the Friendly Inn, Chinatown (Gerrard Street). When you want it all to stop, beeline for the relative calm east of Charing Cross Road.

£ Banks

- **Barclays** • 27 Soho Sq
- **Barclays** • 25 Charing Cross Rd
- **HSBC** • 138 Shaftesbury Ave
- **Royal Bank of Scotland** • 49 Charing Cross Rd

Cinemas

- **Vue West End Cinema** • 3 Cranbourn St

Coffee

- **Caffe Nero** • 32 Cranbourn St
- **Caffe Nero** • 43 Frith St
- **Caffe Nero** • 155 Charing Cross Rd
- **Coffee Republic** • 19 Soho Sq
- **Costa** • 140 Shaftesbury Ave
- **Eat.** • 16 Soho Sq
- **Eat.** • 155 Charing Cross Rd
- **Foyles** • 113 Charing Cross Rd

O Landmarks

- **Denmark Street** • Denmark St
- **FA Headquarters** • 25 Soho Sq
- **Old Compton Street** • Old Compton St
- **The Phoenix Garden** • 21 Stacey St
- **Soho Square** • Soho Sq

Nightlife

- **12 Bar Club** • 22 Denmark St
- **The Astoria** • 157 Charing Cross Rd
- **The Borderline** • Orange Yard, Manette St
- **Comptons** • 53 Old Compton St
- **Crobar** • 17 Manette St
- **G-A-Y Bar** • 30 Old Compton St
- **G-A-Y Late** • 5 Goslett Yard
- **Garlic & Shots** • 14 Frith St
- **Green Carnation** • 5 Greek St
- **Jazz After Dark** • 9 Greek St
- **Ku Bar** • 30 Lisle St
- **Montagu Pyke** • 105 Charing Cross Rd
- **Ronnie Scott's Jazz Club** • 47 Frith St
- **Royal George** • 133 Charing Cross Rd, Goslett Yard
- **The Toucan** • 19 Carlisle St

Restaurants

- **Abeno Too** • 17 Great Newport St
- **Arbutus** • 63 Frith St
- **Bar Italia** • 22 Frith St
- **Barrafina** • 54 Frith St
- **Boheme Kitchen and Bar** • 19 Old Compton St
- **Café Emm** • 17 Frith St
- **Chinese Experience** • 118 Shaftesbury Ave
- **Corean Chilli** • 51 Charing Cross Rd
- **Ed's Easy Diner** • 12 Moor St
- **Friendly Inn** • 47 Gerrard St
- **Garlic & Shots** • 14 Frith St
- **Gay Hussar** • 2 Greek St
- **Haozhan** • 8 Gerrard St
- **Kettners** • 29 Romilly St
- **La Porchetta Pollo Bar** • 20 Old Compton St
- **Le Beaujolais** • 25 Litchfield St
- **New World** • 1 Gerrard Pl
- **Stockpot** • 18 Old Compton St
- **Taro** • 10 Old Compton St

Shopping

- **Angels** • 119 Shaftesbury Ave
- **Fopp** • 1 Earlham St
- **Forbidden Planet** • 179 Shaftesbury Ave
- **Kokon to Zai** • 57 Greek St
- **Macaris** • 92 Charing Cross Rd
- **Porselli** • 9 West St
- **Ray's Jazz** • 113 Charing Cross Rd
- **Turnkey** • 114 Charing Cross Rd
- **Wunjo Guitars** • 20 Denmark St

Supermarkets

- **Sainsbury's** • 137 Charing Cross Rd

Map 12

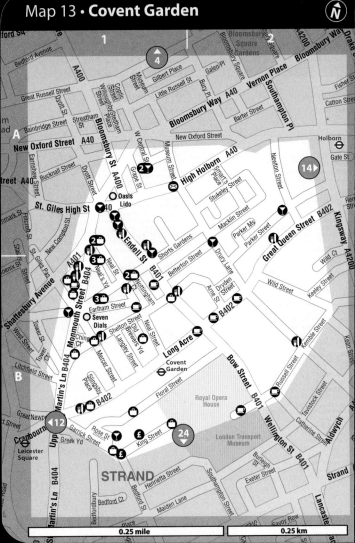

Map 13 · **Covent Garden**

Covent Garden

Map 13

Famed ex-barrow land. The old market square is a little too full of teen tour groups, head north for the finer environs of Neal Street and Seven Dials. Neal's Yard Dairy will cause cheese climax, relax afterwards at Rock and Sole Plaice (fish and chips). Thirsty? Stumble down to Freud or Bunker for basement boozing or the Lamb & Flag for a twee pint.

£ Banks

- **Abbey** • 36 King St
- **HSBC** • 16 King St

Coffee

- **AMT** • 14 Neal St
- **Bagel Factory** • 18 Endell St
- **Café Metro** • 33 Catherine St
- **Caffe Nero** • 30 Monmouth St
- **Caffe Nero** • 83 Long Acre
- **Pret A Manger** • 65 Long Acre
- **Starbucks** • 10 Russell St
- **Starbucks** • 55 Long Acre

O Landmarks

- **Oasis Lido** • 32 Endell St
- **Seven Dials** •
  Junction of Monmouth St, Mercer St and five others

Nightlife

- **AKA Bar** • 18 W Central St
- **Bunker** • 41 Earlham St
- **Coffee, Cake & Kink** • 61 Endell St
- **The Cross Keys** • 31 Endell St
- **The End** • 18 W Central St
- **Freud** • 198 Shaftesbury Ave
- **Guanabara** • Parker St
- **The Lamb and Flag** • 33 Rose St
- **Octave** • 27 Endell St
- **Poetry Cafe** • 22 Betterton St

Post Offices

- **High Holborn** • 181 High Holborn

Restaurants

- **Belgo Centraal** • 29 Shelton St
- **Café Mode** • 57 Endell St
- **Candy Cakes** • 36 Monmouth St
- **Food for Thought** • 31 Neal St
- **Great Queen Street** • 32 Great Queen St
- **Kulu kulu** • 51 Shelton St
- **Mon Plaisir** • 21 Monmouth St
- **The Photographers' Gallery** • Great Newport St
- **The Punjab** • 80 Neal St
- **Rock & Sole Plaice** • 47 Endell St
- **Sarastro** • 126 Drury Ln

Shopping

- **Cath Kidston** • 28 Shelton St
- **Cybercandy** • 3 Garrick St
- **David and Goliath** • 4 The Market Pl
- **Duffer of St George** • 34 Shorts Gardens
- **Koh Samui** • 65 Monmouth St
- **Libidex** • 49 Shelton St
- **The Loft** • 35 Monmouth St
- **London Graphic Centre** • 16 Shelton St
- **Neal's Yard Dairy** • 17 Shorts Gardens
- **Nigel Hall** • 18 Floral St
- **Octopus** • 54 Neal St
- **Orla Kiely** • 31 Monmouth St
- **Pop Boutique** • 6 Monmouth St
- **Scoop** • 40 Shorts Gardens
- **Screenface** • 48 Monmouth St
- **Slam City Skates** • 16 Neal's Yard
- **Stanford's** • Long Acre
- **Superdry** • 35 Earlham St (Thomas Neal Centre)
- **Twosee** • 17 Monmouth St
- **Urban Outfitters** • 42 Earlham St

Supermarkets

- **Sainsbury's** • 129 Kingsway

Map 14 • **Holborn / Temple**

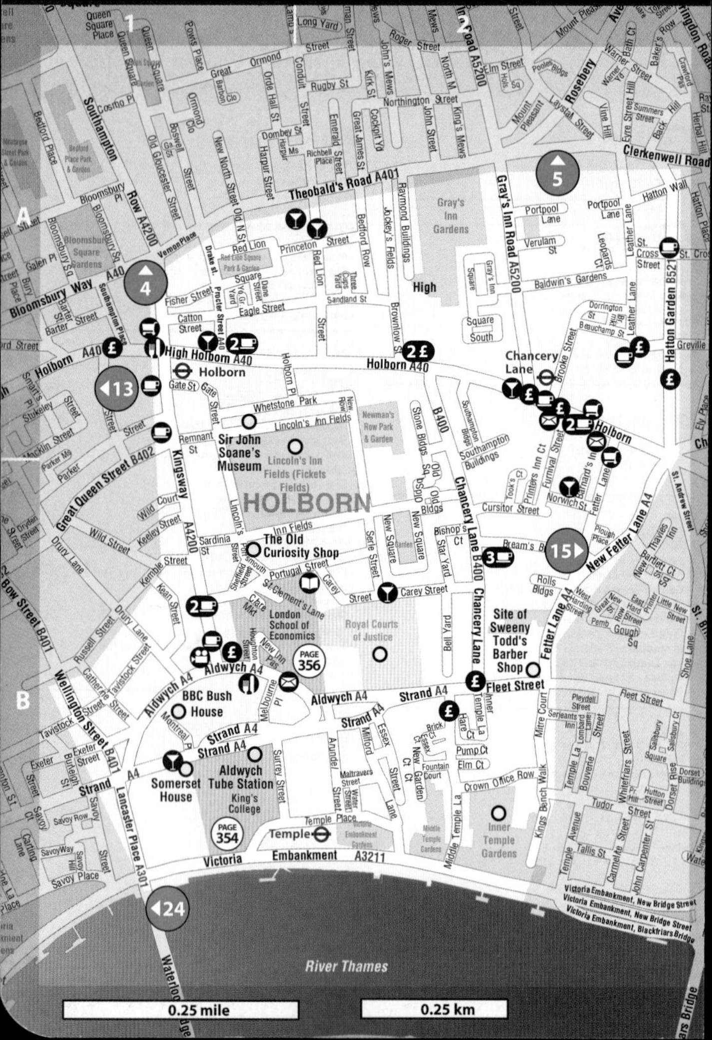

1

5

4

13

Theobald's Road A401

Gray's Inn Gardens

High

Chancery Lane

2£

High Holborn A40

£

Holborn

Holborn A40

£

Holborn

Whetstone Park

Sir John Soane's Museum

Lincoln's Inn Fields (Fickets Fields)

2£

HOLBORN

The Old Curiosity Shop

3£

Bream's B

15

New Fetter Lane A4

Rolls Bldgs

2£

£

Aldwych A4

PAGE 356

BBC Bush House

Strand A4

Strand A4

Aldwych A4

Strand A4

Site of Sweeny Todd's Barber Shop

£

Fleet Street

Somerset House

Aldwych Tube Station

King's College

PAGE 354

Temple

Inner Temple Gardens

Victoria Embankment A3211

24

Victoria Embankment, New Bridge Street
Victoria Embankment, New Bridge Street
Victoria Embankment, Blackfriars Bridge

River Thames

0.25 mile   0.25 km

Holborn / Temple

Step away from Covent Garden, as Holborn/Temple has everything, for less money, more class, and no human living-statues. For charming boozers explore the side streets off High Holborn; seek sanctuary in Inner Temple Garden; find historical thrills at the Old Curiosity Shop and Soane's Museum; and test your Polish pronunciation with a skinful of vodka in Na Zdrowie. Just, please, not Kingsway, OK?

Map 14

£ Banks

- **Abbey** • 10 Leather Ln
- **Abbey** • 306 High Holborn
- **Barclays** • 99 Hatton Garden
- **Barclays** • 147 Holborn
- **Barclays** • 19 Fleet St
- **HSBC** • 31 High Holborn
- **Lloyds** • 296 High Holborn
- **NatWest** • 65 Aldwych
- **NatWest** • 214 High Holborn
- **Royal Bank of Scotland** • 1 Fleet St

Cinemas

- **One Aldwych Cinema** • 1 Aldwych

Coffee

- **Caffe Nero** • 333 High Holborn
- **Costa** • 15 Chichester Rents
- **Eat.** • 105 Kingsway
- **Eat.** • 239 High Holborn
- **Eat.** • 34 High Holborn
- **Eat.** • 7 Kingsway
- **Eat.** • 77 Chancery Lane
- **Eat.** • 78 Hatton Garden
- **Pret A Manger** • 10 Leather Ln
- **Pret A Manger** • 240 High Holborn
- **Pret A Manger** • 29 Kingsway
- **Starbucks** • 10 Kingsway
- **Starbucks** • 28 Chancery Ln
- **Starbucks** • 90 High Holborn
- **Starbucks** • 99 Kingsway

O Landmarks

- **Aldwych Tube Station** • The Strand
- **BBC Bush House** •
- **Inner Temple Garden** • Inner Temple
- **Lincoln's Inn Fields** • Lincoln's Inn Fields
- **The Old Curiosity Shop** • 13 Portsmouth St
- **Royal Courts of Justice** • Strand
- **Sir John Soane's Museum** • 13 Lincoln's Inn Fields
- **Site of Sweeny Todd's Barber Shop** • 186 Fleet St
- **Somerset House** • Somerset House Trust, Strand

Libraries

- **British Library of Political and Economic Science** • 10 Portugal Street

Nightlife

- **Cittie of Yorke** • 22 High Holborn
- **Enterprise** • 38 Red Lion St
- **The Lamb** • 92 Lamb's Conduit St
- **Na Zdrowie The Polish Bar** • 11 Little Turnstile
- **The Seven Stars** • 53 Carey St
- **Tutu's** • Surrey St
- **Volupte** • 9 Norwich St

Post Offices

- **Aldwych** • 95 Aldwych
- **Grays Inn** • 19 High Holborn
- **Holborn Circus** • 124 High Holborn

Restaurants

- **Asadal** • 227 High Holborn
- **Indigo @ OneAldwych** • 1 Aldwych

Supermarkets

- **Sainsbury's** • 129 Kingsway
- **Sainsbury's** • 60 Fetter Ln
- **Sainsbury's** • 69 High Holborn

Map 15 • Blackfriars / Farringdon

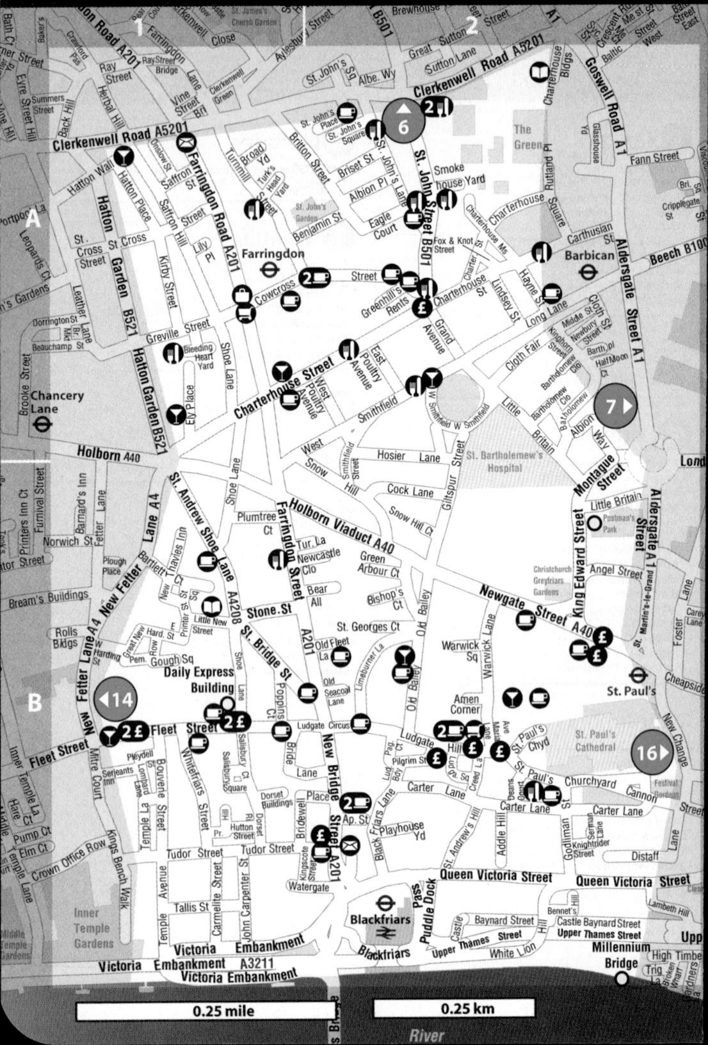

N

1

2

Clerkenwell Road A5201

6

2

St John's

Farringdon

2

Charterhouse Street

Smithfield

7

Barbican

St. Bartholemew's Hospital

Holborn A40

Holborn Viaduct A40

Newgate Street A40

St. Paul's

Daily Express Building

14

Fleet Street

2

16

Ludgate Hill

2

St. Paul's Cathedral

New Bridge Street A201

2

Blackfriars

Queen Victoria Street

Queen Victoria Street

Upper Thames Street

Millennium Bridge

Victoria Embankment

Victoria Embankment A3211

Inner Temple Gardens

0.25 mile	0.25 km

River

Blackfriars / Farringdon

Blackfriars Bridge is one of the gateways to The City but the area around Farringdon Road is a bit cooler and weirder. To the west there's Fleet Street where Charles Dickens used to go for a piss-up. To the east there's mega-club Fabric which has retained its haughty cool, despite having the frantic atmosphere and grim-faced security of Heathrow Airport in August. And in the middle, Smithfields for eats and drinks (Pho, Kurz + Lang).

Banks

- **Abbey** • 11 Ludgate Hill
- **Barclays** • 89 Charterhouse St
- **Barclays** • 81 Fleet St
- **Barclays** • 81 Newgate St
- **Halifax** • 71 Fleet St
- **HSBC** • 165 Fleet St
- **HSBC** • 1 St Paul's Churchyard
- **Lloyds** • 33 Ludgate Hill
- **NatWest** • 156 Fleet St
- **Royal Bank of Scotland** • 9 Paternoster Row
- **Royal Bank of Scotland** • 36 New Bridge St

Coffee

- **Apostrophe** • 3 St Bride St
- **Apostrophe** • 10 St Pauls Churchyard
- **Bagel Factory** • 54 Cowcross St
- **Café Deco** • Charterhouse St & E Poultry Ave
- **Caffe Nero** • Shoe Lane
- **Caffe Nero** • 118 Newgate St
- **Caffe Nero** • Paternoster Sq
- **Costa** • 13 New Bridge St
- **Costa** • 65 Ludgate Hill
- **Costa** • 46 Cowcross St
- **Eat.** • 88 Cowcross St
- **Fab Food Patisserie** • 15 Long Lane
- **Fab Foods Patisserie** • 97 Fleet St
- **Fab Foods Patisserie** • 37 St John's Ln
- **Oi Bagel** • 58 Ludgate Hill
- **Oi Bagel** • 74 Fleet St
- **Pret A Manger** • 101 Turnmill St
- **Pret A Manger** • 5 St John's Sq
- **Pret A Manger** • 19 Ludgate Hill
- **Pret A Manger** • 10 Pasternoster Sq
- **Pret A Manger** • 101 New Bridge St
- **Pret A Manger** • 143 Fleet St
- **Starbucks** • 1 Cowcross St
- **Starbucks** • 32 Fleet St
- **Starbucks** • 3 Fleet Pl
- **Starbucks** • 30 New Bridge St
- **Starbucks** • 30 Ludgate Hill
- **Starbucks** • 1 Paternoster Sq

Landmarks

- **Daily Express Building** • 121 Fleet St
- **Millennium Bridge** • Millennium Bridge
- **Postman's Park** • King Edward St

Libraries

- **Shoe Lane Library** • Little New St
- **Society of Genealogists Library** • 14 Charterhouse Buildings [Goswell Road]

Nightlife

- **Corney & Barrow** • 10 Paternoster Sq
- **The Deux Beers** • 3 Hatton Wall
- **Fabric** • 77 Charterhouse St
- **Smithfield Bar & Grill** • West Smithfield
- **Ye Old Mitre** • 1 Ely Ct
- **Ye Olde Cheshire Cheese** • 154 Fleet St
- **Ye Olde London** • 1

Post Offices

- **Farringdon Road** • 89 Farringdon Rd
- **Ludgate Circus** • 16 New Bridge St

Restaurants

- **Beppe's** • 23 West Smithfield
- **The Bleeding Heart** • Bleeding Heart Yard, off Greville St
- **Cafe du Marche** • 22 Charterhouse Sq
- **Kurz + Lang** • 1 St John St
- **The Larder** • 91 St John St
- **Pho** • 86 St John St
- **Portal** • 88 St John St
- **Smiths of Smithfield** • 67 Charterhouse St
- **St Germain** • 89 Turnmill St
- **St John's Smithfield** • 26 St John St
- **Tinseltown** • 44 St. John St
- **Vivat Bacchus** • 47 Farringdon St
- **Yo! Sushi** • 14 St Paul's

Shopping

- **Flaneur** • 41 Farringdon Rd

Supermarkets

- **Marks & Spencer** • Ave Maria Lane
- **Sainsbury's** • 23 Farringdon Rd

Map 16 · **Square Mile (West)**

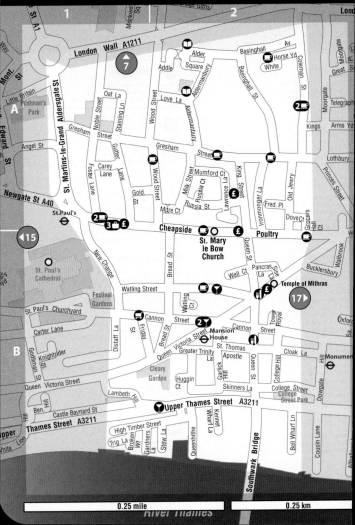

Square Mile (West)

You should have a fucking good reason to come here if you're not working in the City. Lunch at Sweetings, for example, where you feel like it's 1889, or the Roman leftovers at the Temple of Mithras. Drinking options are limited, but The Samuel Pepys comes with great Thames views, Bar Bourse with a healthy dose of elegance. Warning: On the weekend, this is ghost town.

£ Banks

- **Barclays** • 1 King St
- **Halifax** • 134 Cheapside
- **HSBC** • 60 Queen Victoria St
- **Lloyds** • 70 Cheapside

Coffee

- **Coffee Republic** • 32 Coleman St
- **Costa** • 99 Gresham St
- **Costa** • 65 Ludgate Hill
- **Costa** • 9 Bow Ln
- **Eat.** • 143 Cheapside
- **Eat.** • 15 Basinghall St
- **Eat.** • 88 Wood St
- **Fab Food Patisserie** • 19 Watling St
- **Fresco Café Bar** • 21 Masons Ave
- **Pret A Manger** • 30 Gresham St
- **Starbucks** • 1 Poultry
- **Starbucks** • 143 Cheapside

O Landmarks

- **St Mary le Bow Church** • Cheapside
- **St. Paul's Cathedral** • St. Paul's Churchyard
- **Temple of Mithras** • Queen Victoria St

Libraries

- **City Business Library** •
  1 Brewers Hall Garden [off Aldermanbury Square]
- **Guildhall Library** • Aldermanbury

Nightlife

- **Hatchet** • 28 Garlick Hill
- **The Mansion House** • 44 Cannon Street
- **The Samuel Pepys** • 48 Upper Thames Street
- **Ye Olde Watling** • 29 Watling Street

Restaurants

- **Bar Bourse** • 67 Queen Street
- **Sweetings** • 39 Queen Victoria St

Shopping

- **Church's Shoes** • 90 Cheapside
- **Manucci** • 5 Cheapside
- **Space NK Apothecary** • 145 Cheapside

Supermarkets

- **Marks & Spencer** • Cannon St Station

Map 16

37

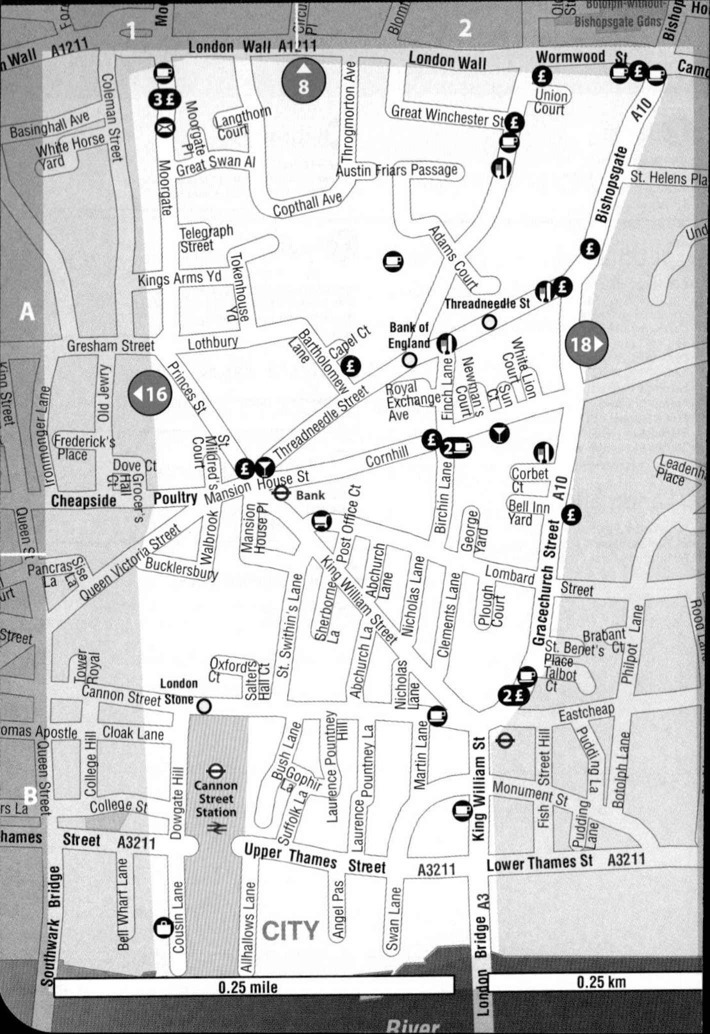

Map 17 · **Square Mile (East)**

N

1   **2**

London Wall A1211   London Wall A1211   Wormwood St

Botolph-without
Bishopsgate Gdns

Old
St

Bishopsgate Ho

Camo

London Wall

8

3£

Union
Court

Langthorn
Court

Moorgate Pl

Throgmorton Ave

Great Winchester St

Basinghall Ave

Coleman Street

White Horse
Yard

Moorgate

Great Swan Al

Austin Friars Passage

St. Helens Pla

Bishopsgate A10

Telegraph
Street

Copthall Ave

Adams Court

Und

Kings Arms Yd

Tokenhouse Yd

A

Gresham Street

Lothbury

Barthlomew Lane

Capel Ct

Threadneedle St

Bank of
England

White Lion
Court

◄16

Princes St

St. Mildred's
Court

Threadneedle Street

Royal
Exchange
Ave

Finch Lane

Nen__ Ct
Sun
Ct

18►

Frederick's
Place

Ironmonger Lane

Old Jewry

Dove Ct

Grocer's Hall Ct

Cheapside

Poultry

Mansion House St

Cornhill

Birchin Lane

Leaden__
Place

Bank

Walbrook

Bucklersbury

Mansion
House Pl

Post Office Ct

George
Yard

Corbet
Ct

Bell Inn
Yard

Gracechurch Street

A10

King Street

Queen St

Pancras
La

Queen Victoria Street

Lombard

Street

Plough
Court

Clements Lane

Brabant
Court

Philpot Lane

Rood La

Thomas Apostle

Tower
Royal

Cannon Street

London
Stone

Oxford's
Ct

Salters' Hall Ct

St. Swithin's Lane

Sherborne
La

King William Street

Abchurch
Lane

Nicholas Lane

St. Benet's
Place

Talbot
Ct

Eastcheap

2£

Cloak Lane

College Hill

Bush Lane

Gophir
La

Laurence Pountney Hill

Abchurch Lane

Nicholas
Lane

Martin Lane

King William St

Monument
St

Street Hill

Fish Street Hill

Pudding Lane

Botolph Lane

B

College St

Cannon
Street
Station

Suffolk La

Laurence Pountney La

Monument

Dowgate Hill

Laurence Pountney La

rs La

thames

Street A3211

Upper Thames Street A3211

Lower Thames St A3211

Southwark
Bridge

Bell Wharf Lane

Cousin Lane

Allhallows Lane

Angel Pas

Swan Lane

CITY

London
Bridge A3

0.25 mile   0.25 km

River

Square Mile (East)

London's most Jekyll and Hyde-like hood. By day, the Bank district hums with suits making their fortune. They like good sushi, steak and kidney pie, and a pint (Mercer) and Michelin stars (Rhodes 24). But by night the area's a no-man's land. Deserted and shut down, few people have business being around Bank after dark. If you do end up here at night, go elsewhere—or find yourself a new job.

💷 Banks

- **Abbey** • 51 Gracechurch St
- **Abbey** • 48 Moorgate
- **Barclays** • 29 Wormwood St
- **Co-Operative** • 80 Cornhill
- **Halifax** • 58 Moorgate
- **Halifax** • 33 Old Broad St
- **HSBC** • 100 Old Broad St
- **HSBC** • 95 Gracechurch St
- **Lloyds** • 34 Moorgate
- **Lloyds** • 39 Threadneedle St
- **NatWest** • 15 Bishopsgate
- **NatWest** • 1 Prince's St
- **Royal Bank of Scotland** • 62 Threadneedle St
- **Starbucks** • 48 Gracechurch St

☕ Coffee

- **Bagel Factory** • 59 Moorgate
- **Caffe Nero** • 22 Wormwood Stree
- **Costa** • 51 Gracechurch St
- **Eat.** • 54 Cornhill
- **Eat.** • 123 Cannon St
- **Oi Bagel** • 27 Throgmorton St
- **Pret A Manger** • 43 King William St
- **Starbucks** • 90 Old Broad St
- **Starbucks** • 74 Cornhill
- **Starbucks** • 5 Camomile St

⭘ Landmarks

- **Bank of England** • Threadneedle St
- **London Stone** • 105 Cannon St
- **Threadneedle Street** • Threadneedle St

🍸 Nightlife

- **The Counting House** • 50 Cornhill
- **Grand Cafe & Bar** • The Ctyard, Royal Exchange

✉ Post Offices

- **Moorgate** • 53 Moorgate

🍴 Restaurants

- **Gaucho City** • 1 Bell Inn Yard
- **The Mercer** • 34 Threadneedle St
- **Rhodes 24** • 25 Old Broad St
- **Wasabi** • 52 Old Broad St

🛍 Shopping

- **Sweatshop (City branch - at Cannon's Gym)** • Cousin Lane

🛒 Supermarkets

- **Marks & Spencer** • Cannon St Station
- **Sainsbury's** • 14 Lombard St

Map 17

Map 18 • Tower Hill / Aldgate

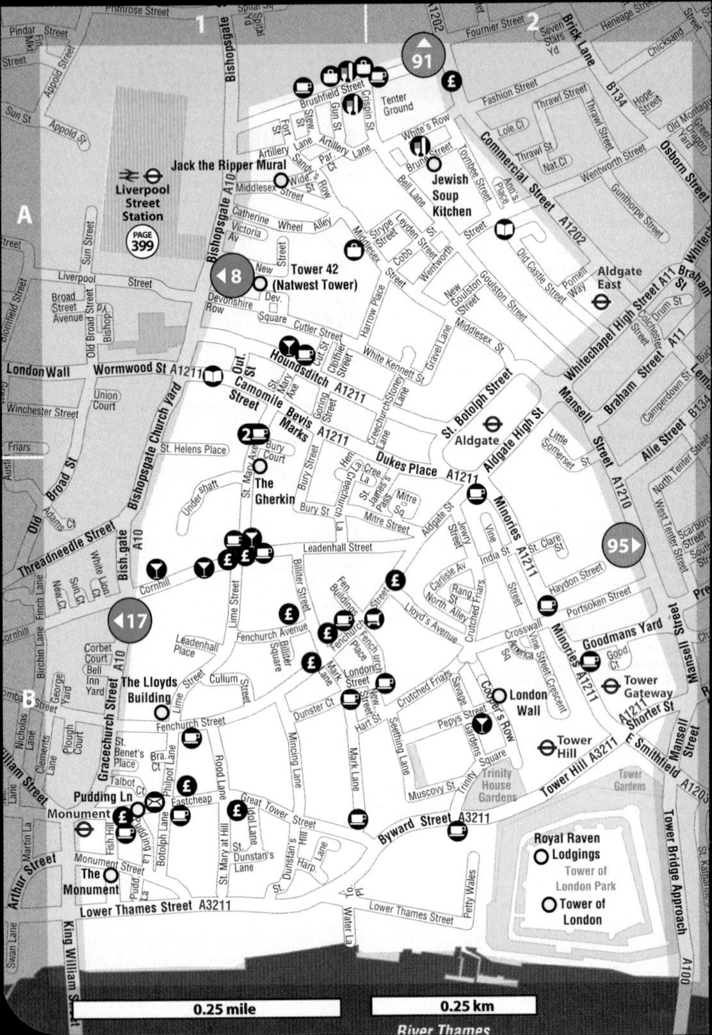

Primrose Street
Pindar St
Appold St
Bishopsgate
Sun St
Appold St

Brushfield St
Crispin St
Sun St
Tenter Ground
Fournier Street
Brick Lane
Heneage Street
Chicksand
St

91
£

Fashion Street
Thrawl Street
Hopetown St
Old Montague

Jack the Ripper Mural
Liverpool Street Station

PAGE 399

Artillery Lane
Middlesex St
Wide St
Par
Artillery Row

White's Row
Bell Lane

Commercial Street
Lole Ct
Thrawl St
Nat Cl
Wentworth Street

Jewish Soup Kitchen

B134
Old Montague Street
Osborn Street

A

Catherine Wheel Alley
Victoria Av
New St
Dev.

8
Tower 42 (Natwest Tower)

Strype
Leyden St
Cobb
Wentworth
New
Goulston Street
Old Castle Street
Pomell Way

Aldgate East
Whitechapel High Street A11

Braham

Liverpool St
Broad St Avenue
Bishop's
Devonshire Row
Square
Cutler Street

Narrow Place
White Kennett St
Middlesex St

London Wall
Wormwood St A1211
Union Court

Houndsditch
Camomile Bevis Street Marks
A1211

St. Helen's Place
Bury Court
2
Cree La
St. Mary Axe
Goring St
Harrow Pl

St. Botolph Street
Aldgate High St A1211

Whitechapel High Street A11
Mansell Street A1210
Braham
Alie Street A1210
North Tenter St
Scarborough St

Aldgate East
Camperdown St

Winchester Street
Friars
Austin

The Gherkin
Undershaft
St. Mary Axe
Bury St
Mitre Street

Aldgate
Little Somerset

95

Threadneedle Street
Old
Broad St
St Adams Ct
Finch La

Bishopsgate Church yard
Bishgate A10

Leadenhall Street
£

Minories A1211
Jewry St
India St
St Clare St
Haydon St
Portsoken Street

Cornhill
Lime Street
£

17
Cornhill
Birchin Lane
Finch La

Leadenhall Place
Fenchurch Avenue
£
£

Billiter St
Fenchurch Street
£

Lloyd's Avenue
Carlisle Av
Rang.Friars
North Alley
Crutched Friars
Crosswall

Goodmans Yard
Godol
£

Tower Gateway

B

Corbet Court
Bell
Inn Yard
George Yard
Nicholas
Lane

The Lloyds Building
Fenchurch Street
Leadenhall
Market

Lime Street
Mark Lane
London St
£

Dunster Ct

Crutched Friars
Cooper's Row
London Wall

Tower Gateway
Tower Hill A3211

Plough
Court
Talbot
Ct
St Benet's Place
Bra.
Fish St

Cullum St
Mincing Lane
Mark Lane
Hart St
Seething Lane
Pepys St

Cooper's Row
Tower Hill A3211

Tower Hill
Tower Gardens
Tower Bridge Approach A100

William St
Arthur St
Martin La

Pudding Ln
Monument
Monument Street
The Monument

Fish Hill
Botolph Lane
Eastcheap
St Dunstan's Lane
£
St Mary at Hill
St Dunstan's Hill
Harp La

Great Tower Street
£

Muscovy St
Trinity Square
Byward Street A3211
Cooper's Row

Trinity House Gardens

Tower Hill A3211
Tower Gardens
E Smithfield
Mansell Street A1210
Shorter St

King William St
Swan Lane

Monument Street
Pudd
Hill
Lower Thames Street A3211
St Mary at Hill
Lower Thames Street
Water La
Petty Wales

Royal Raven Lodgings
Tower of London Park

Tower of London

0.25 mile
0.25 km

River Thames

The eastern edge of finance-land, ruled by suits during the day, deserted over the weekend. Insurance brokers drink at Dion City, you'd be better off with lowbrow lunch at Jeff's, a jaunt atop the Monument, (expensive) dinner at Prism, and then heading eastward for more fun. If all else fails, go gawp at the Tower of London.

£ Banks

• **Barclays** • 114 Fenchurch St
• **Barclays** • 99 Commercial St
• **HSBC** • 20 Eastcheap
• **HSBC** • 60 Fenchurch St
• **Lloyds** • 72 Fenchurch St
• **Lloyds** • 113 Leadenhall St
• **NatWest** • 116 Fenchurch St
• **NatWest** • 2 Eastcheap
• **Royal Bank of Scotland** • 5 Great Tower St
• **Royal Bank of Scotland** • 54 Lime St

Coffee

• **Caffe Nero** • 1 Fenchurch Pl [Coopers Row]
• **Caffe Nero** • 23 Eastcheap
• **Caffe Nero** • 88 Leadenhall St
• **Costa** • 74 Mark Ln
• **Eat.** • 28 Brushfield St
• **Eat.** • 84 Aldgate High St
• **Eat.** • 2 Eastcheap
• **Eat.** • 155 Fenchurch St
• **Eat.** • 26 Leadenhall St
• **Eat.** • 122 Minories
• **Eat.** • 48 Mark Ln
• **Eat.** • 2 Tower Hill
• **Eat.** • 33 St Mary Axe
• **Pret A Manger** • 3 Cutler St
• **Starbucks** • 8 Brushfield St
• **Starbucks** • 20 Eastcheap
• **Starbucks** • 65 Fenchurch St
• **Starbucks** • 48 Minories
• **Starbucks** • 66 St Mary Axe

O Landmarks

• **The Gherkin** • 30 St Mary Axe
• **Jack the Ripper Mural** • Widegate St
• **Jewish Soup Kitchen** • Brune St
• **The Lloyds Building** • 1 Lime St
• **London Wall** • Cooper's Row
• **The Monument** • Monument St
• **Pudding Lane** • Pudding Lane
• **Royal Raven Lodgings** •
  Wakefield Tower (Tower of London)
• **Tower 42 (Natwest Tower)** • 25 Old Broad St
• **Tower of London** • The Tower of London

Libraries

• **Camomile Street** • 15 Camomile St
• **The Women's Library** • 25 Old Castle St

Y Nightlife

• **Dion City** • 52 Leadenhall St
• **Kenza** • 10 Devonshire Sq
• **Pepys Bar at the Novotel Hotel** • 10 Pepys St
• **Prism** • 147 Leadenhall St
• **Revolution in the City** • 140 Leadenhall St

Post Offices

• **The City of London BO** • 12 Eastcheap

Restaurants

• **Jeff's Cafe** • 14 Brune St
• **Leon** • 3 Crispin St
• **S & M Cafe** • 48 Brushfield St

Shopping

• **A. Gold** • 42 Brushfield St
• **Montezuma's** • 51 Brushfield St
• **Petticoat Lane** • Middlesex St

Supermarkets

• **Sainsbury's** • 45 Fenchurch St

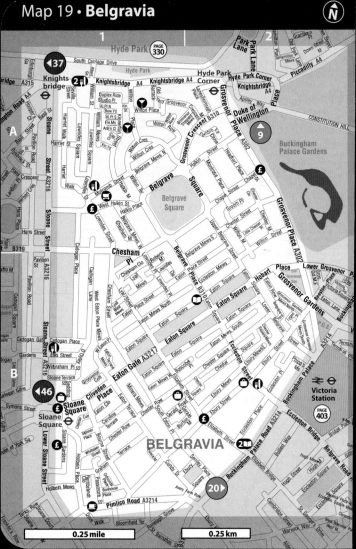

Green-welly brigade? We know where you live. Belgravia conjures images of tweed, Eliza Doolittle (post-makeover), and everything slightly soulless about upper-crust London. Embassies on Belgrave Square and the occasional Elizabeth Street boutique are about all it has to offer to outsiders. See where the other half buy their pug outfits at Mungo & Maud, flower arrangements at Moyses Flowers, and curries at Amaya.

£ Banks

- **Barclays** • 8 W Halkin St
- **HSBC** • 19 Grosvenor Pl
- **HSBC** • 13 Sloane Sq
- **NatWest** • 141 Ebury St
- **NatWest** • 2 Sloane Gardens

Coffee

- **Starbucks** • 53 Pimlico Rd

Libraries

- **Instituto Cervantes** • 102 Eaton Square
- **Victoria Library** • 160 Buckingham Palace Rd
- **Westminster Music Library** • 160 Buckingham Palace Rd

Nightlife

- **The Blue Bar** • Wilton Pl
- **Nag's Head** • 53 Kinnerton St

Restaurants

- **Amaya** • Halkin Arcade, Motcomb St
- **Boisdale, Victoria** • 15 Eccleston St
- **La Noisette** • 164 Sloane St
- **One-O-One** • 101 Knightsbridge
- **Yo! Sushi** • 102 Knightsbridge

Shopping

- **British Red Cross Victoria** • 85 Ebury St
- **Moyses Flowers** • Sloane Sq
- **Mungo & Maud** • 79 Elizabeth St

Supermarkets

- **Waitrose** • 27 Motcomb St

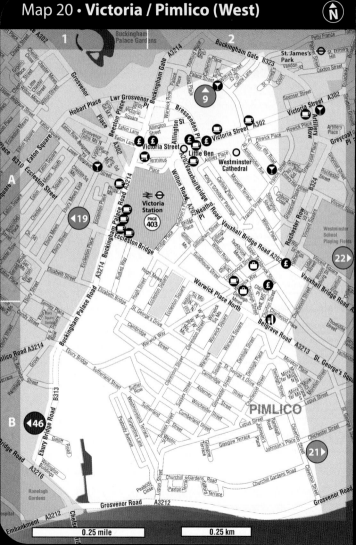

Map 20 · **Victoria / Pimlico (West)**

Map 20

Hectic Victoria station with its belching buses, coaches and tourist trains is grubby big sis to posh Pimlico—a dignified 'hood Churchill and Mozart called home. Stroll the magnificent rows of all-white houses north of Lupus Street, hit Warwick Way for high-street essentials, local caffs and delis, the village-y Cask & Glass for real ale, and gentle giant, Westminster Cathedral, for a moment's calm.

Banks

- **Barclays** • 1 Churton St
- **Halifax** • 62 Victoria St
- **HSBC** • 89 Buckingham Palace Rd
- **HSBC** • 166 Vauxhall Bridge Rd
- **Lloyds** • 98 Victoria St
- **NatWest** • 169 Victoria St

Coffee

- **Bagel Factory** • 115 Buckingham Palace Rd
- **Caffe Nero** • 31 Warwick Way
- **Costa** • 115 Buckingham Palace Rd
- **Costa** • 324 Vauxhall Bridge Rd
- **Eat.** • Cardinal Pl
- **Pret A Manger** • 12 Victoria St
- **Pret A Manger** • 173 Victoria St
- **Pret A Manger** • Victoria Station
- **Pret A Manger** • 92 Buckingham Palace Rd
- **Starbucks** • 137 Victoria St
- **Starbucks** • Buckingham Palace Rd & Lower Belgrave St

O Landmarks

- **Little Ben** • Victoria St/Vauxhall Bridge Rd intersection
- **Westminster Cathedral** • 42 Francis St

Nightlife

- **The Albert** • 52 Victoria St
- **The Cardinal** • 23 Francis St
- **Cask & Glass** • 39 Palace St
- **The Plumber's Arms** • 14 Lower Belgrave St

Restaurants

- **Grumbles** • 35 Churton St

Shopping

- **La Bella Sicilia** • 33 Warwick Way
- **Rippon Cheese Stores** • 26 Upper Tachbrook St

Supermarkets

- **Marks & Spencer** • Victoria Mainline Station

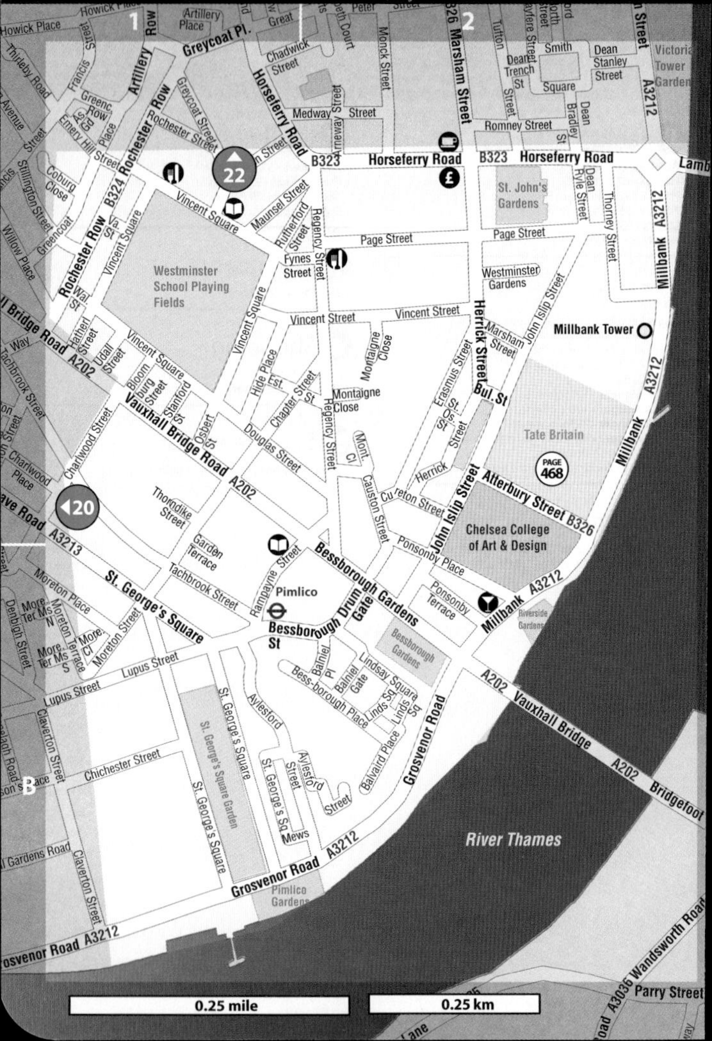

Map 21 · **Pimlico (East)**

N

Howick Place
Artillery Place
Artillery Row
Great
North Court
Monck Street
Tufton Street
Smith Square
Dean Stanley Street
Victoria Tower Gardens
A3212

1

Greencoat Place

Chadwick Street

Great Peter Street

Marsham Street

Dean Trench Street

Bradley

2

Thirleby Road
Francis Street
Greencoat Row
Greycoat Street
Rochester Row
Greycoat Place
Horseferry Road

Medway Street
Gayfere Street
Romney Street

Emery Hill Street
Emery Street

B323 **Horseferry Road**
B323 **Horseferry Road**
Lamb

Cobure Close
Greencoat
Rochester Row B324
Rochester Street
Vincent Square
Maunsel Street
Regency Street
Rutherford Street

St. John's Gardens

Dean Ryle Street
Thorney Street
Millbank

A3212

Willow Place
Shillington Street

22

Vincent Square
Page Street
Page Street

Westminster Gardens

Vincent Square

Fynes Street

Westminster School Playing Fields

Vincent Street
Vincent Street

Marsham Street
Herrick Street
Bul St

Millbank Tower

Vincent Street
Montaigne Close

Erasmus Street

Hide Place
Regency Street
Montaigne Close

Chapter Street

Tate Britain

Way
Tachbrook Street
Cureton Street

PAGE 468

Bridge Road A202
Cardwood Street

Douglas Street

Mont. Cl.

Causton Street

Herrick
Atterbury Street B326

Bloomburg Street

Vauxhall Bridge Road A202

John Islip Street

Millbank

Charwood Place
Charwood Street

20

Thorndike Street

Garden Terrace

Bessborough Gardens

Ponsonby Place

Chelsea College of Art & Design

ave Road A3213
Road A3213

St. George's Drive
Tachbrook Street
Hannington Street

Pimlico

Ponsonby Terrace

Millbank A3212

Moreton Place
Moreton Street

St. George's Square

Bessborough St
Bessborough Gate

Riverside Gardens

Denbigh Street
Moreton Terrace M
Moreton Terrace S
More. Ter. M
More. Ter. S

Lupus Street
Lupus Street

Bessborough Place
Balmial Gate
Lindsay Square
Lindsay Square
Lindsay

Bessborough Gardens

Chichester Street

St. George's Square Garden

Aylesford Street

Aylesford Street

Belgrave Place

Grosvenor Road

Gardens Road
Claverton Street

B

St. George's Square

St. George's Square Mews

Grosvenor Road A3212

A202 **Vauxhall Bridge**

A202 **Bridgefoot**

Pimlico Gardens

River Thames

svenor Road A3212

Road A3036 Wandsworth Road

Parry Street

Lane

| 0.25 mile | | 0.25 km |

Pimlico (East)

Map 21

Hugging the curve of the Thames, this princely patch of Pimlico combines the stately Tate with imposing embankment architecture and houses centuries old. Check out the town-house splendour of Vincent Square and bag some posh nosh sans posh prices at the Vincent Rooms. Enjoy one too many in the prisoner's pub of choice, the Morpeth, before breakfasting like Kings with runny egg fry-ups at the Regency.

 £Banks

• **NatWest** • 27 Horseferry Rd

 Coffee

• **Starbucks** • 35 Horseferry Rd

O Landmarks

• **Millbank Tower** • Millbank

Libraries

• **Pimlico Library** • Rampayne St
• **Royal Horticultural Society Library** • 80 Vincent Sq

Nightlife

• **Morpeth Arms** • 58 Millibank

Restaurants

• **The Regency Cafe** • 17 Regency St
• **Vincent Rooms** • 1 The Victoria Centre, Vincent Sq

Map 22 · **Westminster**

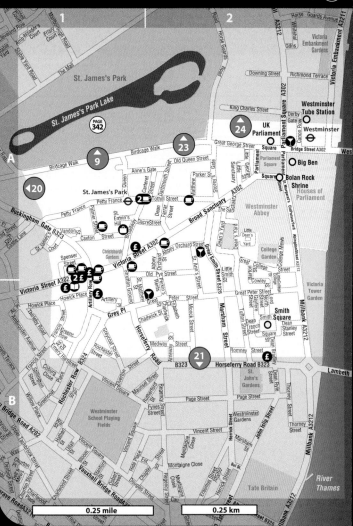

Westminster

Map 22

Historic 'hood featuring the seat of parliament, the rather gorgeous Westminster Abbey, and the demure delight of Smith Square. The preponderance of government offices limits late-night fun but Cinnamon Club is worth a special visit and (crowded) St Stephen's Tavern or The Speaker are both good booze anchors. Victoria Street is the main shopping drag with a mix of standard chains.

£ Banks

- **Abbey** • 115 Victoria St
- **Barclays** • 13 Artillery Row
- **Barclays** • 2 Victoria St
- **HSBC** • 8 Victoria St
- **Lloyds** • 4 Dean Stanley St
- **NatWest** • 57 Victoria St
- **Royal Bank of Scotland** • 119 Victoria St

Coffee

- **Caffe Nero** • 1 Bridge St
- **Caffe Nero** • 105 Victoria St
- **Eat.** • 37 Tothill St
- **Eat.** • 3 Strutton Ground
- **Fresco Cafe Bar** • 11 Tothill St
- **Pret A Manger** • 75 Victoria St
- **Pret A Manger** • 49 Tothill St
- **Puccino's** • 6 Victoria St
- **Starbucks** • 17 Palmer St
- **Starbucks** • 27 Victoria St

O Landmarks

- **Big Ben** • House of Commons
- **Bolan Rock Shrine** • Queen's Ride, Putney
- **Smith Square** • Smith Sq
- **UK Parliament** • House of Commons
- **Westminster Tube Station** • Bridge St

Libraries

- **St James's Library** • 62 Victoria St

Nightlife

- **The Cinnamon Club** • Great Smith St
- **The Speaker** • 46 Great Peter Street
- **St. Stephen's Tavern** • 10 Bridge Street

Shopping

- **Haelen Centre** • 41 Broadway

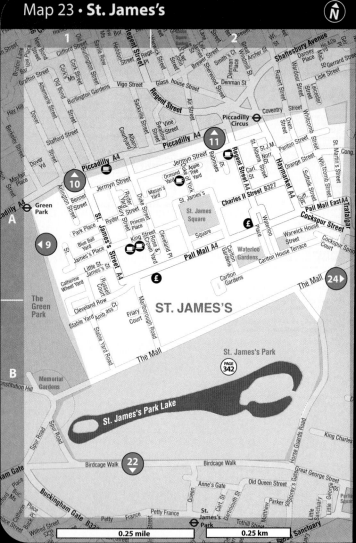

Map 23 · **St. James's**

Dignified, decadent, exclusive, Pall Mall and St.James's Street are where the aristobrats come out to play, with old-style gentlemen's clubs, bespoke tailors, and 'purveyors' of fine cigars dotted south of Jermyn Street. Count your pennies for a Laduree macaroon, then hit St. James's Park for a sarnie amid the commoners. Culture vultures congregate in the ICA bar, the peasants head for big portions at Stockpot.

£ Banks

- **Barclays** • 31 St James's St
- **HSBC** • 69 Pall Mall
- **Lloyds** • 8 Waterloo Pl
- **Royal Bank of Scotland** • 48 Haymarket

Cinemas

- **Apollo West End** • 19 Regent St
- **Cineworld Haymarket** • 63 Haymarket
- **ICA Cinema** • The Mall & Horse Guards Rd
- **Odeon Leicester Square Cinema** • 24 Leicester Sq
- **Odeon Panton Street** • 11 Panton St
- **Odeon West End Cinema** • 40 Leicester Sq

Coffee

- **Apostrophe** • 16 Regent St
- **Caffe Nero** • 35 Jermyn St
- **Coffee Republic** • 63 Haymarket
- **Eat.** • 18 Regent St
- **Eat.** • 3 Duke of York St
- **Eat.** • 9 Crown Passage
- **Pret A Manger** • 8 King St
- **Starbucks** • 171 Picadilly

O Landmarks

- **Economist Plaza** • 25 St James's St
- **Giro the Nazi Dog** • 9 Carlton House Terrace
- **Leicester Square** • Leicester Sq

Libraries

- **London Library** • 14 St James's Sq
- **Westminster Reference Library** • 35 St Martin's St

Nightlife

- **Aura** • 48 St James's St
- **ICA** • The Mall
- **The Sports Cafe** • 80 Haymarket

Restaurants

- **Inn The Park** • St James' Park
- **Laduree** • 71 Burlington Arcade
- **Stockpot** • 38 Panton St

Map 24 · **Trafalgar Square / The Strand**

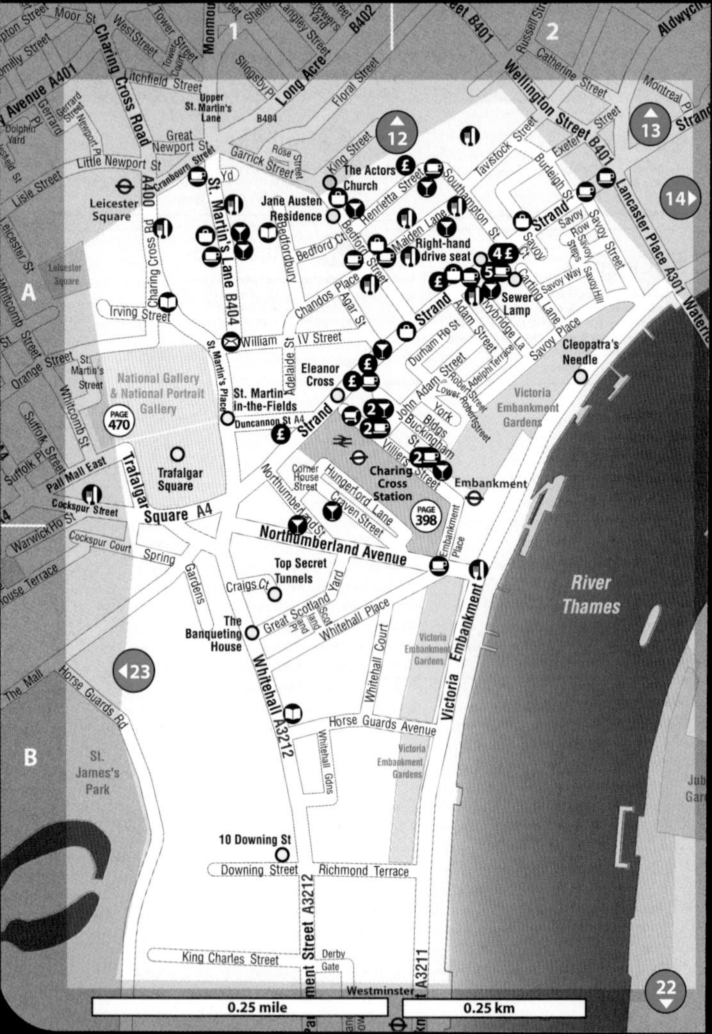

(N)

1

2

Aldwych

Piccadilly Avenue A401

Moor St

West Street

Tower Street

Monmouth St

Long Acre

B402

Floral Street

Wellington Street B401

Russell Street

Catherine Street

Montreal Pl

Strand

13

Gerrard

Newport Court

Litchfield Street

Slingsby Pl

Langley St

Dolphin Yard

Great Newport St

Slingsby Pl

B484

Floral Street

Exeter St

14▶

Little Newport St

A400

Charing Cross Road

Upper St. Martin's Lane

Rose Street

Garrick Street

Tavistock Street

Burleigh St

Lancaster Place A301

Gerrard

Cranbourn Street

St

Garrick Yd

King Street

The Actors Church

£

Southampton Street

Strand

Savoy St

Savoy Row

Savoy Steps

Leicester Square

St. Martin's Lane B404

Jane Austen Residence

Henrietta Street

Maiden Lane

Right-hand drive seat

£

Savoy Buildings

Waterloo

Lisle Street

Leicester Square

Charing Cross Rd

Cranbourn St

Bedford Court

Chandos Place

Adam St

4 £

5 £

Savoy Way

A

Irving Street

Whitcomb St

Orange Street

St. Martin's Place

William IV Street

Chandos Place

Strand

Adam St

Sewer Gas Lamp

Cleopatra's Needle

Eleanor Cross

£

Durham Hse St

John Adam Street

Robert Street

Lower Adelphi Terrace

Adelphi Terrace

Suffolk St

Pall Mall East

National Gallery & National Portrait Gallery

PAGE 470

£

St Martin's Place

St. Martin-in-the-Fields

Adelaide St

Duncannon St

£

Strand

2 £

2 £

York Buildings

George Ct

Victoria Embankment Gardens

Cockspur Street

Trafalgar Square

Trafalgar Square A4

2 £

Villiers Street

Embankment

Warwick Ho St

Cockspur Court

Spring

Northumberland Ave

Craven Passage

Charing Cross Station

PAGE 398

Embankment Place

River Thames

House Terrace

Gardens

Northumberland Avenue

Corner House Street

Hungerford Lane

Craven Street

23

Top Secret Tunnels

Craigs Ct

Great Scotland Yd

Scotland Pl

Whitehall Place

Victoria Embankment

The Mall

The Banqueting House

Whitehall A3212

Whitehall Court

Victoria Embankment Gardens

B

St. James's Park

Horse Guards Rd

Horse Guards Avenue

Victoria Embankment Gardens

Jubilee Gardens

Whitehall Gdns

10 Downing St

Downing Street

Richmond Terrace

Parliament Street A3212

King Charles Street

Derby Gate

Westminster

A3211

22

| 0.25 mile | 0.25 km |

Trafalgar Square / The Strand

Map 24

The word 'Strand' means beach. If you'd been strolling along here 150 years ago the Thames would have been lapping around your ankles. Then they built the Embankment so that Gordon's on Villiers Street could stop being a damp, riverside warehouse and transform into a famously louche winebar so the tourists stumbling towards Nelson's Column and the National Gallery could keep their feet dry.

£ Banks

- **Abbey** • 406 Strand
- **Barclays** • 366 Strand
- **HSBC** • 455 Strand
- **HSBC** • 194 Strand
- **Lloyds** • 48 Strand
- **Lloyds** • 222 Strand
- **NatWest** • 38 Strand
- **NatWest** • 34 Henrietta St
- **NatWest** • 217 Strand

Coffee

- **Apostrophe** • 215 Strand
- **Bagel Factory** • 45 Villiers St
- **Café Express** • 372 Strand
- **Caffe Nero** • 10 Bedford St
- **Caffe Nero** • 181 Strand
- **Caffe Nero** • 125 Strand
- **Caffe Nero** • 36 St Martin's Ln
- **Caffe Nero** • 20 Southampton St
- **Coffee Republic** • 79 Strand
- **Costa** • 17 Embankment Pl
- **Eat.** • 41 Bedford St
- **Eat.** • 39 Villiers St
- **Pret A Manger** • 135 Strand
- **Pret A Manger** • 421 Strand
- **Pret A Manger** • 78 St Martin's Ln
- **Starbucks** • 355 Strand
- **Starbucks** • 442 Strand
- **Starbucks** • 14 Villiers St
- **Starbucks** • 1 Villiers St

O Landmarks

- **10 Downing Street** • 10 Downing St
- **The Actors' Church** • St. Paul's Church, Bedford St
- **The Banqueting House** • Whitehall
- **Cleopatra's Needle** • Embankment
- **Eleanor Cross** • Charing Cross Station, The Strand
- **Jane Austen Residence** • 10 Henrietta St
- **Right-hand Drive Street** • Savoy Ct
- **Sewer Lamp** • Carting Lane
- **St Martin-in-the-Fields** • Trafalgar Sq
- **Top Secret Tunnels** • 6 Craig's Ct (entrance)
- **Trafalgar Square** • Trafalgar Sqaure

Libraries

- **Charing Cross Library** • 4 Charing Cross Rd
- **CILT Resources Library** • 20 Bedfordbury
- **Royal United Services Institute Library** • Whitehall

Nightlife

- **Asia de Cuba** • 45 St. Martin's Lane
- **The Chandos** • 29 St Martins Lane
- **The Coal Hole** • 91 Strand
- **Covent Garden Comedy Club** • The Arches, Off Villiers St
- **Gordon's Wine Bar** • 47 Villiers St
- **Heaven** • Under the Arches, off Villiers St
- **Maple Leaf** • 41 Maiden Ln
- **Punch & Judy** • The Piazza
- **Retro Bar** • 2 George Ct
- **Roadhouse** • The Piazza
- **The Sherlock Homes** • 10 Northumberland St
- **The Ship and Shovel** • Craven Passage

✉ Post Offices

- **Trafalgar Square** • 24 William IV St

Restaurants

- **Bistro 1** • 33 Southampton St
- **Cafe in the Crypt** • Trafalgar Sq
- **Covent Garden Market Cafe** • Covent Garden
- **Farmer Brown** • 4 New Row
- **Gourmet Burger Kitchen** • 13 Maiden Ln
- **India Club** •
  143 Strand (Second floor, Strand Continental Hotel)
- **J Sheekey** • 28 St Martins Ct
- **RS Hispaniola** • Victoria Embankment
- **Rules** • 35 Maiden Ln
- **Wahaca** • 66 Chandos Pl

Shopping

- **Austin Kaye** • 425 The Strand
- **Australia Shop** • 27 Maiden Ln
- **The Italian Bookshop** • 5 Cecil Ct
- **London Camera Exchange** • 98 Strand
- **Rohan** • 10 Henrietta St
- **Stanley Gibbons** • 399 Strand

Supermarkets

- **Marks & Spencer** • Charing Cross Station

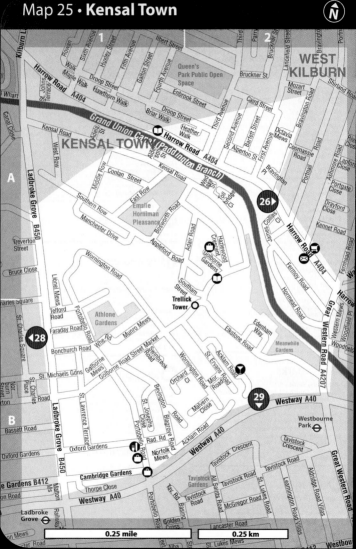

The "new Notting Hill" label weighs heavily on the Kensals. They look east for inspiration, ignoring the Harlesden yardies at their backs. Thai Rice serves eastern food, while Book Slam try to ship a little Shoreditch sauce to the manor Westbourne. Prepare for Carnival by visiting What Katie Did for exhibitionist outfits, while Trellick Tower is perfect for real—"I mean it, I'll jump"—attention-seekers.

O Landmarks

• **Trellick Tower** • 5 Golborne Rd

Libraries

• **Kensal Library** • 20 Golborne Rd
• **Queen's Park Library** • 666 Harrow Rd

Nightlife

• **Book Slam** • 12 Acklam Rd

Post Offices

• **Maida Hill** • 377 Harrow Rd

Restaurants

• **Thai Rice** • 303 Portobello Rd

Shopping

• **Honest Jon's** • 278 Portobello Rd
• **Rellik** • 8 Golborne Rd
• **What Katie Did** • 281 Portobello Rd

Supermarkets

• **Iceland** • 512 Harrow Rd

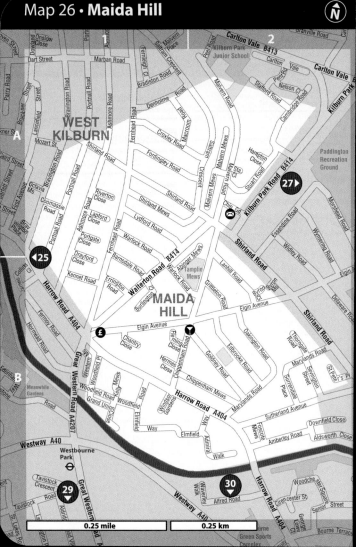

Map 26 · **Maida Hill**

N

Carlton Vale B413

Kilburn Park Junior School

Carlton Vale

2

Granville Road

Granville Road

Dowding Onslow Close

Dart Street

Marban Road

Fernleigh Ct

Saltram Crescent

Malvern Place

Peel

Kilburn Park

Carlton

Vale

Perch St

Stafford Road

Nelson Ct

Cambridge Road

Kilburn Park

Parry Road

Bruckner Street

Lancefield Street

Portnall Road

Bravington Road

Ashmore Road

1

Portnall Road

Marban Road

Bradiston Road

Denholme Road

Croxley Road

Fordingley Road

Shirland Road

Peel

Saltram Crescent

Malvern Road

Malvern Mews

Malvern Road

Hampton Close

Stuart Road

Sta. Ct

Kilburn Park Road B414

Paddington Recreation Ground

A

WEST KILBURN

Mozart St

Brackner Street

Faircourt

Caird Street

East Avenue

Octavia Ms

Coomassie Road

Brav Wington Place

Bravington Road

Portnall Road

Ashmore Road

Riverton Close

Lapford Close

Portgate Close

Drayford Close

Farmhead Road

Shirland Road

Shirland Mews

Lydford Road

Warlock Road

Barnsdale Road

Ernington Road

Shirland Road

Saltram Crescent

Malvern Road

Malvern Road

Chip Ct

Essendine Road

Widley Road

Wymering Road

Elgin

27

Moselband Road

Delaware Road

25

Kennet Road

Walterton Road B414

Abinger Mews

Warlock Road

Tamplin Mews

Lanhill Road

Shirland Road

Byron Mews

Shirland Road

Harrow Road A404

Fermoy Road

Hormead Road

Collins Ct

Fernhead Road

Burlington

MAIDA HILL

Elgin Avenue

Grittleton Road

Elgin Avenue

£

Chantry Close

Hermes Close

Fleming Close

Chippenham Road

Goldney Road

Oakington Road

Edbrooke Road

Byron Mews

Delaware Road

Thorngate Road

Marylands Road

Sevington Street

St Peter's St

Surrendale Place

B

Meanwhile Gardens

Edenham Way

Glastone

Great Western Road A4207

Woodfield Pl

Woodfield Mews

Woodfield Road

Woodfield Road

Kelfield

Grand Union

Elmfield

Way

Windsor Gardens

Chippenham Mews

Harrow Road A404

Marylands Road

Sutherland Avenue

Coscote Mews

Amberley Road

Downfield Close

Aldsworth Close

Westway A40

Westbourne Park

Tavistock Crescent

Tavistock Road

29

Great Western Rd

Elmfield Way

Admiral Walk

Westway A40

Waverley Walk

Alfred Road

30

Harrow Road A404

Cirencester St

Senior Street

George Cowp Ct

Bourne Terrace

Woodchester Square

Woodche ster Square

St Lukes St

Porteus

Bourne Green Sports Complex

0.25 mile

0.25 km

Not as posh as Maida Vale or as cool as Ladbroke Grove, Maida Hill is slightly grubby to the south, not helped by the distinctly unlovely Harrow Road. Things get more upmarket heading north where those who can't afford Notting Hill have settled. Hang out at The Skiddaw, popular with a lively crowd of booze hounds.

£Banks

• **Royal Bank of Scotland** • 2 Elgin ave

Nightlife

• **The Skiddaw** • 46 Chippenham Rd

Post Offices

• **Kilburn Park** • 5 Chippenham Gardens

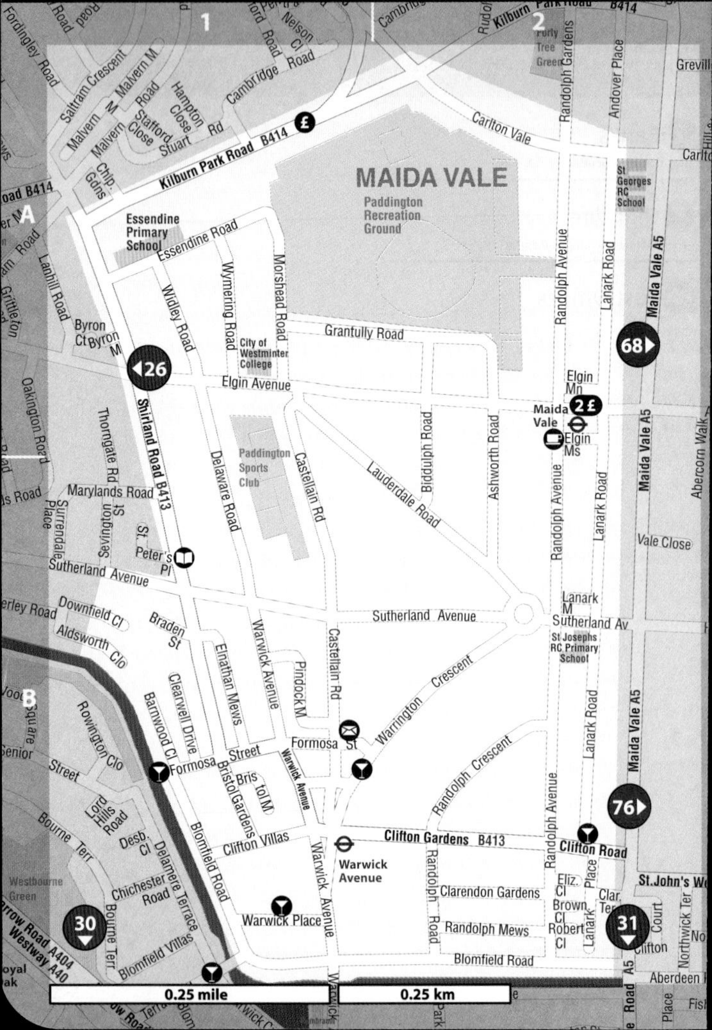

Map 27 • Maida Vale

N

1 **2**

Fordingley Road

Kilburn Park Road

Saltram Crescent

Malvern M

Malvern Road

Stafford Close

Stuart

Hampton Close

Cambridge Road

Nelson Road

St Peter's

Cambridge

Rudolph

Kilburn Park Road B414

Carlton Vale

Carlton Vale

Forty Tree Green Gardens

Andover Place

Randolph Gardens

Greville

Carlto

Road B414

Lanhill Road

Griffin

Chip Gdns

Essendine Primary School

Essendine Road

MAIDA VALE

Paddington Recreation Ground

St Georges RC School

A

Byron Ct

Byron M

Widley Road

Wymering Road

Morshead Road

City of Westminster College

Grantully Road

Randolph Avenue

Lanark Road

Maida Vale A5

Oakington Road

◄26

Shirland Road B413

Delaware Road

Elgin Avenue

Castellain Rd

Lauderdale Road

Biddulph Road

Ashworth Road

Randolph Avenue

Elgin Mn

2£

Maida Vale

Elgin Ms

Lanark Road

68►

Maida Vale A5

Abercorn Walk

Maryland Road

Thorngate Rd

St Peter's Pl

Paddington Sports Club

Vale Close

Sutherland Avenue

Downfield Cl

Braden St

Warwick Avenue

Castellain Rd

Sutherland Avenue

Lanark M

Sutherland Av

Lanark Road

Maida Vale A5

Aldsworth Clo

Elnathan Mews

Pindock M

Warrington Crescent

St Josephs RC Primary School

B

Rowington Clo

Clearwell Dr

Barnwood Cl

Bristol Gardens

Formosa Street

♦

Warwick Mews

Formosa St

♦

Randolph Crescent

Lanark Road

Maida Vale A5

Lord Hills Road

Desb. Cl

Delaware Terrace

Blomfield Road

Clifton Villas

Warwick Avenue

♦

Randolph Road

Clifton Gardens B413

♦

Clifton Road

76►

Chichester Road

Warwick Avenue

Warwick Place

Clarendon Gardens

Eliz. Cl

Brown Cl

Robert Cl

Clar. Ter

St John's W

Westbourne Green

30▼

Bourne Terr

Blomfield Villas

Warwick Place

♦

Randolph Mews

Randolph Road

Blomfield Road

Lanark Pl

Clifton

Court

31▼

Northwick Ter

Aberdeen

arrow Road A404

Westway A40

oyal ak

Senior

Bourne Terr

Place

Fish

| 0.25 mile | 0.25 km |

Maida Vale is a posh residential area and that's pretty much all there is to it. Immaculately trimmed trees line street after street of nearly identical Edwardian mansion houses. It's clean, peaceful, and nice (translation: quite dull).Locals frequent the cafés and eateries around the Maida Vale tube station and on Clifton Road. The Robert Browning does cheap beer and good Thai upstairs and the E Bar does basement.

£ Banks

- **Abbey** • 131 Kilburn Park Rd
- **Barclays** • 320 Elgin ave
- **NatWest** • 298 Elgin ave

Coffee

- **Starbucks** • 160 Randolph Ave

Libraries

- **Maida Vale Library** • Sutherland Ave

Nightlife

- **Bridge House** • 13 Westbourne Terrace Rd
- **E Bar** • 2 Warrington Crescent
- **Robert Browning** • 15 Clifton Rd
- **The Warwick Castle** • 6 Warwick Pl
- **Waterway** • 54 Formosa St

Post Offices

- **Formosa Street** • 12 Formosa St

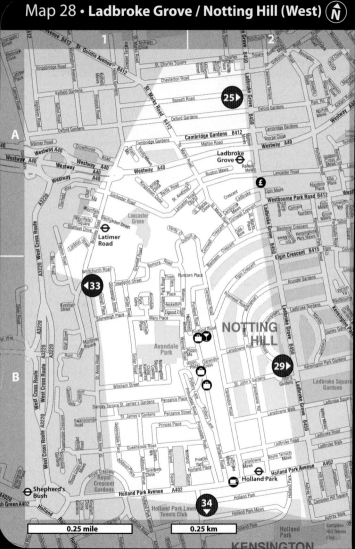

Ladbroke Grove / Notting Hill (West)

Look at that Westway and tell us you can't hear the opening chords of "London Calling." Maybe Rudie didn't fail but he moved up and moved out. This is leafy Notting Hill away from the Hugh Grant-hungry tourists scouring Portobello and there's not much doing. Around Portland Road try The Cross for expensive knick-knacks and Julie's for a bite. For other shopping and eating options head to Clarendon Cross.

£ Banks

• **Barclays** • 137 Ladbroke Grove

☕ Coffee

• **Starbucks** • 76 Holland Park Ave

🍸 Nightlife

• **Julie's Wine Bar** • 135 Portland Rd

🛍 Shopping

• **Cowshed** • 119 Portland Rd
• **The Cross** • 141 Portland Rd
• **Virginia** • 98 Portland Road

Map 28

Map 29 · **Notting Hill Gate**

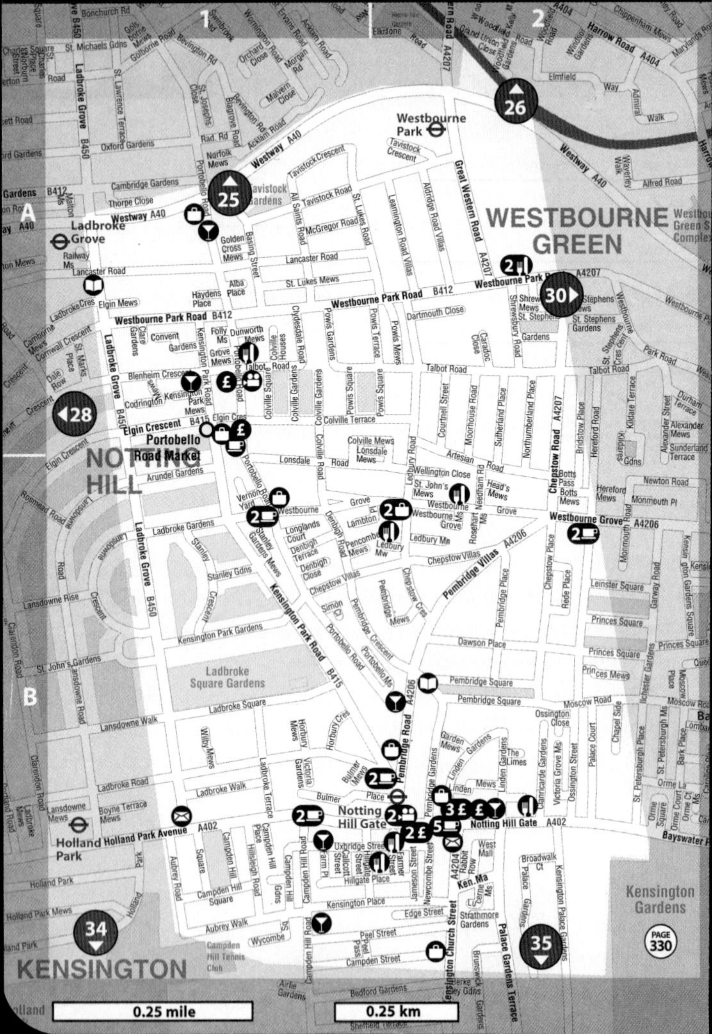

N

1
2

26

Westbourne
Park

WESTBOURNE
GREEN

25

A

Ladbroke
Grove
Railway

30

28

Portobello
Road Market

NO
HILL

35

B

Ladbroke
Square Gardens

34
KENSINGTON

Notting
Hill Gate

Holland
Park

Kensington
Gardens

PAGE
330

35

0.25 mile   0.25 km

Notting Hill Gate

Unbelievably, it's only recently that the mega-rich, minor gentry have conquered the Gate like posh rats (mink?). Traces of the area's counter- and multi-cultural past are in the wrinkles of the old eccentrics in the Uxbridge Arms or at the lively Portobello Road Market. Pig out at Costas or to feel old and bitter, go scowl at teenagers in the Notting Hill Arts Club.

£ Banks

- **Abbey** • 174 Portobello Rd
- **Abbey** • 88 Notting Hill Gate
- **Barclays** • 35 Notting Hill Gate
- **HSBC** • 152 Portobello Rd
- **HSBC** • 25 Notting Hill Gate
- **Lloyds** • 50 Notting Hill Gate
- **NatWest** • 46 Notting Hill Gate
- **Royal Bank of Scotland** • 78 Notting Hill Gate

Cinemas

- **The Electric Cinema** • 191 Portobello Rd
- **Gate Notting Hill** • 87 Notting Hill Gate
- **Notting Hill Coronet** • 103 Notting Hill Gate

Coffee

- **Apostrophe** • 138 Notting Hill Gate
- **Bagel Factory** • 61 Notting Hill Gate
- **Caffe Nero** • 113 Westbourne Grove
- **Caffe Nero** • 53 Notting Hill Gate
- **Caffe Nero** • 168 Portobello Rd
- **Coffee Republic** • 8 Pembridge Rd
- **Coffee Republic** • 214 Portobello Rd
- **Eat.** • 68 Notting Hill Gate
- **Pret A Manger** • 65 Notting Hill Gate
- **Starbucks** • 96 Westbourne Grove
- **Starbucks** • 227 Portobello Rd
- **Starbucks** • 26 Pembridge Rd
- **Starbucks** • 140 Notting Hill Gate
- **Starbucks** • 64 Notting Hill Gate

O Landmarks

- **Portobello Road Market** • Portobello Rd

Libraries

- **North Kensington Library** • 108 Ladbroke Grove
- **Notting Hill Library** • 1 Pembridge Sq

Nightlife

- **Mau Mau** • 265 Portobello Rd
- **Montgomery Place** • 31 Kensington Park Rd
- **Notting Hill Arts Club** • 21 Notting Hill Gate
- **The Sun in Splendour** • 7 Portobello Rd
- **Uxbridge Arms** • 13 Uxbridge St
- **Windsor Castle** • 114 Campden Hill Rd

Post Offices

- **Kensington Church St** • 190 Kensington Church St
- **Ladbroke Grove** • 2 Ladbroke Grove

Restaurants

- **Beach Blanket Babylon** • 45 Ledbury Rd
- **Cafe Diana** • 5 Wellington Terrace
- **Costas Fish Restaurant** • 18 Hillgate St
- **Crazy Homies** • 125 Westbourne Park Rd
- **The Electric Brasserie** • 191 Portobello Rd
- **Geales** • 2 Farmer St
- **Lucky 7** • 127 Westbourne Park Rd
- **Taqueria** • 139 Westbourne Grove

Shopping

- **& Clarke's Bread** • 124 Kensington Church St
- **Bodas** • 38 Ledbury Rd
- **The Grocer on Elgin** • 6 Elgin Crescent
- **The Hummingbird Bakery** • 133 Portobello Rd
- **Melt** • 59 Ledbury Rd
- **Music & Video Exchange** • 38 Notting Hill Gate
- **Negozio Classica** • 283 Westbourne Grove
- **Portobello Road Market** • Portobello Rd
- **R Garcia and Sons** • 248 Portobello Rd
- **Retro Man** • 34 Pembridge Rd
- **Retro Woman** • 32 Pembridge Rd
- **Rough Trade Talbot Road** • 130 Talbot Rd

Map 29

(63)

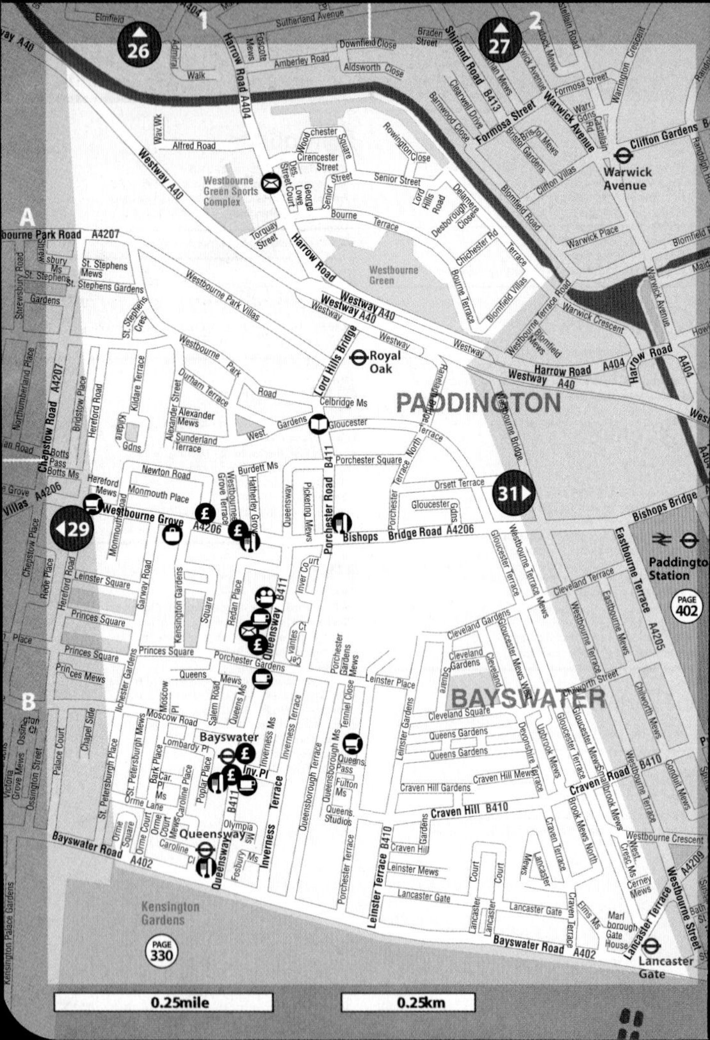

Map 30 · Bayswater

N

1   2

26   27

Elmfield
Sutherland Avenue
Harrow Road A404
Braden Street
Shirland Road B413
Downfield Close
Way A40
Amberley Road
Aldsworth Close
Formosa Street
Walk
Warwick Avenue
Cirencester Street
Clifton Villas
Clifton Gardens
Alfred Road
Chester
Senior Street
Blomfield Road
Warwick Avenue
George
Westbourne
Street Court
Bourne
Lane
Terrace
Chichester Rd
Green Sports
Complex
Torquay
Street
A
Bourne Park Road A4207
Harrow Road
Westbourne
Green
Warwick Place
St. Stephens
Mews
Westway A40
Blomfield Villas
St. Stephens
Gardens
Westbourne Park Villas
Westway A40
Warwick Crescent
Westway
Chepstow
Road
Westway A40
Harrow Road A404
Way
Westbourne
Park
Hereford Road
Durham Terrace
Royal
Oak
Road
Lord Hills Bridge
Westway
Blomfield Road
Alexander
Celbridge Ms
Gloucester
PADDINGTON
Bishops Bridge
Sunderland
Terrace
West
Gardens
Porchester Square North
Paddington
Station
Chepotts
Pass
Newton Road
Burdett Ms
Porchester Road B411
Orsett Terrace
PAGE
402
29
Hereford
Road
Monmouth Place
Westbourne Grove
Gloucester Terrace
Bishops Bridge Road A4206
31
Eastbourne Terrace A4205
Westbourne Grove
Bishops
Cleveland Terrace
Redan Place
Chepstow
Inver Court
Cleveland Gardens
Leinster Square
Garway Road
Porchester Gardens
Porchester Mews
Westbourne Terrace Mews
Kensington Gardens
Cleveland Gardens
Princes Square
Queensway B411
Leinster Place
Cleveland Square
B
Princes Square
Queens
Queens Gardens
Princes Mews
Queensborough Ms
Leinster Place
BAYSWATER
Moscow Road
Salem Road
Inverness Ms
Craven Hill Mews
Queens Gardens
Bayswater
Lombard Pt
Princess Ms
Queens
Pass
Craven Hill Gardens
Craven Road B410
Bark Place
Fulton Ms
St. Petersburgh Place
Inverness Terrace
Queensborough Terrace
Poplar Place
Palace Court
B411
Queensway
Orme Lane
Queens
Studios
Olympia
Queensway
Craven Hill B410
Queensway
Caroline
Leinster Mews
Westbourne Crescent
Bayswater Road A402
Inverness Terrace
Porchester Terrace
Leinster Terrace B410
Leinster Gardens
Lancaster Gate
Craven Road B410
West
borough
Gate
Kensington
Gardens
PAGE
330
Lancaster Gate
Bayswater Road A402
Lancaster
Gate

0.25mile   0.25km

Bayswater

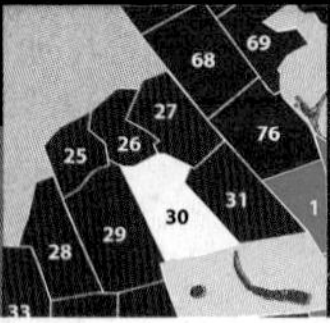

Map 30

Bayswater is notable for being next to other places that are far more interesting: Hyde Park, Marble Arch, Portobello Road. It's also a xenophobes' nightmare, with billions of hotels and tourists everywhere, not to mention the rich ethnic diversity. The rest of us can go smoke shisha at Berdees or eat tacky Austrian at Tiroler Hut or Indo/Malay at Kiasu.

Banks

- **Barclays** • 93 Queensway
- **Halifax** • 23 Whiteleys Of Bayswater
- **HSBC** • 43 Queensway
- **Lloyds** • 30 Westbourne Grove
- **NatWest** • 16 Westbourne Grove

Cinemas

- **Odeon Whiteleys** • Queensway & Porchester Gardens

Coffee

- **Coffee Republic** • 126 Queensway
- **Pret A Manger** • 127 Queensway
- **Starbucks** • 49 Queensway

Libraries

- **Paddington Library** • Porchester Rd

Post Offices

- **Harrow Rd** • 272 Harrow Rd
- **Queensway** • 118 Queensway

Restaurants

- **Berdees Coffee Shop** • 84 Bishop's Bridge Rd
- **Kiasu** • 48 Queensway
- **Royal China** • 13 Queensway
- **Tiroler Hut** • 27 Westbourne Grove

Shopping

- **Planet Organic** • 42 Westbourne Grove

Supermarkets

- **Sainsbury's** • 88 Westbourne Grove
- **Waitrose** • 38 Porchester Sq

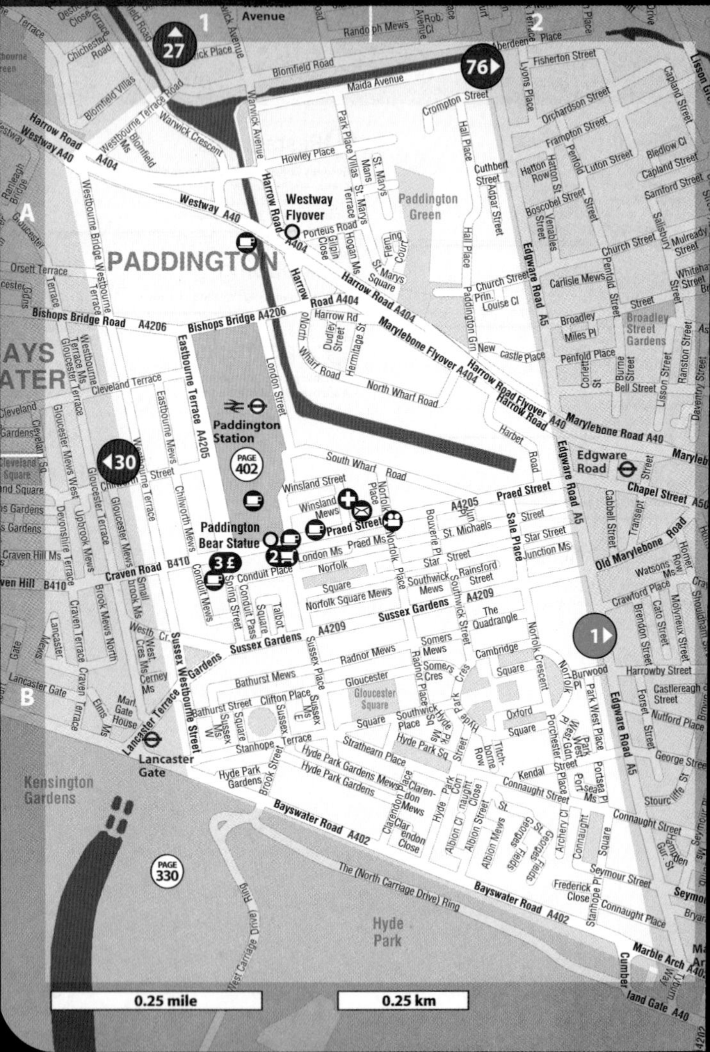

Map 31 · **Paddington**

N

1 27

2

Avenue

76▶

Randolph Mews

Chichester Road

Desborough

Warwick Place

Blomfield Road

Maida Avenue

Aberdeen

Fisherton Street

Capland Street

Clifton Villas

Warwick Avenue

Blomfield Road

Crompton Street

Orchardson Street

Harrow Road

Westbourne Terrace Road

Westway Bridge

A404

Howley Place

Park Place Villas

Westway A40

Hall Place

Frampton Street

Bledlow Cl

Samford Street

Westway A40

Porteus Road

St Marys Terrace

St Marys Mews

Cuthbert

Hatton

Penfold

Luton Street

A

PADDINGTON

Westway Flyover

Paddington Green

Hermitage St

St Marys Sq

Boscobel Street

Venables

Church Street

Carlisle Mews

Harrow Road A404

Harrow Rd

Dudley St

St Marys

Church Street A5

Prin.
Louise Cl

Bishops Bridge Road A4206

Eastbourne Terrace

Bishops Bridge A4206

Harrow Road A404

Marylebone Flyover A404

Harrow Road Flyover A404

Penfold Place

Broadley Miles Pl

Broadley Street Gardens

Cleveland Terrace

North Wharf Road

Harbet

Harrow Road A40

Bell Street

AYS ATER

Gloucester Terrace

Eastbourne Mews A4205

London Street

Wharf Road

Marylebone Road A40

Marylebone

Edgware Road A5

Chepel Street

Old Marylebone Road

🚆

Paddington Station

PAGE 402

South Wharf Road

Praed Street

A4205

St. Michaels

Sale Place

Star Street

Junction Ms

◀30

Chilworth Mews

Winsland Street

Winsland Mews

Norfolk

✚

Praed Street

Bouverie Pl

Star Street

Rainsford Street

Old Marylebone Rd

Crawford Place

Paddington Bear Statue

Praed Ms

Southwick Street

A4209

Watsons Ms

3£

2

Norfolk Square

London Ms

Southwick Mews

The Quadrangle

Brendon Street

Craven Road B410

Conduit Place

Conduit Street

Talbot

Sussex Gardens

A4209

Somers Cres

Cambridge Square

Norfolk Crescent

Burwood

1▶

Harrowby Street

Lancaster Ms

Sussex Westbourne Terrace

Radnor Mews

Gloucester

Somers Cres

Oxford Square

Porchester Place

Castlereagh St

Mulford St

B

Lancaster Gate

Bathurst Mews

Clifton Place

Gloucester Square

Southwick Pl

Hyde Park Sq

Row

Kendal

Connaught Street

George St

Bathurst Street

Stanhope Terrace

Strathearn Place

Hyde Park Gardens Mews

Connaught Place

Stourcliffe

Kensington Gardens

Lancaster Gate

Hyde Park Gardens

Bayswater Road A402

Albion Mews

Frederick Close

Seymour

PAGE 330

The (North Carriage Drive) Ring

Bayswater Road A402

Connaught Place

Marble Arch A40

Hyde Park

Cumberland Gate A40

0.25 mile   0.25 km

Mainly peopled by Little Venetians, B&B owners, and harassed commuters ("Go west young man, but avoid Reading") Paddington has that Oxford Street cosmopolitan-yet-bland vibe. Grab an anonymous meal with other transients in a café as you fill time before the Heathrow flight. If gazing at a statue of a bear in Wellington's doesn't appeal, banish evening boredom by listening to famous war correspondents' sordid stories over a meal at the Frontline Club.

£ Banks

- **Barclays** • 17 Spring St
- **HSBC** • 2 Craven Rd
- **NatWest** • 26 Spring St

Cinemas

- **Frontline Club** • 13 Norfolk Pl

Coffee

- **Bagel Factory** • 141 Praed St
- **Caffe Nero** • 14 Spring St
- **Caffe Nero** • Paddington Station
- **Eat.** • Paddington Station
- **Pret A Manger** • 9 Sheldon Sq

Emergency Rooms

- **St Mary's Hospital** • Praed St

O Landmarks

- **Paddington Bear Statue** • Paddington Station
- **Westway Flyover** •

Post Offices

- **Paddington** • 128 Praed St

Supermarkets

- **Sainsbury's** • Paddington Station
- **Sainsbury's** • 12 Sheldon Sq

Map 32 · Shepherd's Bush (West)

Map 32 · Shepherd's Bush (West)

1 **2**

Gravesend Road
Erica Street
Bryony Road
Bloemfontein Road
Commonwealth
India
Commonwealth Av
Canada Way
Avenue
Commonwealth
Avenue
Wormholt Park
Common
wealth Av
Australia Road
South Africa Road
White City Road
Sawley Road
Ormiston Grove
Oaklands Grove
South Africa Road
Ring Road
White

A

Dunraven
Road
Galloway Road
Willow Vale
Adelaide Grove
Oaklands Grove
Bloemfontein Road
Halsbury Road
Close
Close
Hammersmith
Park
Close Batman
Batman Close
SHEPHERD'S
BUSH

33

Loftus Road
Stadium - Queens
Park Rangers F.C.
PAGE 370

Adelaide Hal. Rd
Ellerslie Road
Ethelden Road
Loftus Road
Stanlake Road
Tunis Road
Stanlake Road
Wood Lane A219
Ring Road

Thorpebank
Road
Boscombe Road
Coningham Road
Bloemfontein Road
Ingersoll Road
Arminger Road
Close
Lime
Abdale Road
Tunis Road
Swindon Street
Stanlake Villas
Stanlake MS
Frithville Gardens
Macfarlane Road

Cingham Mews
Uxbridge Road A4020
Bloem
fontein Way
Helfey Road
Godolphin Road
St Stephen's Avenue
Thornfield Road
Warbeck Road
Coverdale Road
Uxbridge Road A4020
Stanlake Villas
Shepherd's
Bush
Uxbridge Road
High
Wood Lane A219

on Road
Boscombe Road
Findon Road
Shepherds
Bush Mkt
Shepherds Bush
A4020
Bulwer St

B

nville Road
Goodwin Road
Stowe
Stowe Road
Godolphin Road
Thornfield Road
Lime Grove
Shepherds
Bush Market
Market Lane
Pennard Road
Shepherds
Bush Comm
Cathnor
Park
Melina Road
Cathnor Road
Stowe Road
Godolphin Road
St Stephen's Avenue
Sthw
Scotts Road
Gainsborough Court
Woodger
Shepherds Bush Green A219
Millers Rd
Pd
Road
Coningham Road
Scotts Road
Stw Ct
Devonport Road
Minforc

40

Elgin Cl
Parbell
Close
Gold
hawk Ms
Titmuss St
Goldhawk Road A402
Goldhawk
Road
Bamborough
Gardens
Poplar
Terrace
West
Carthew Villas
Brackenbury
Gardens
Benbow Rd
Hamm Grove
Richford Street
Astrop Ter
Cromwell Grove
Sulgrave Road
Beauclerc Road

0.25 mile   0.25 km

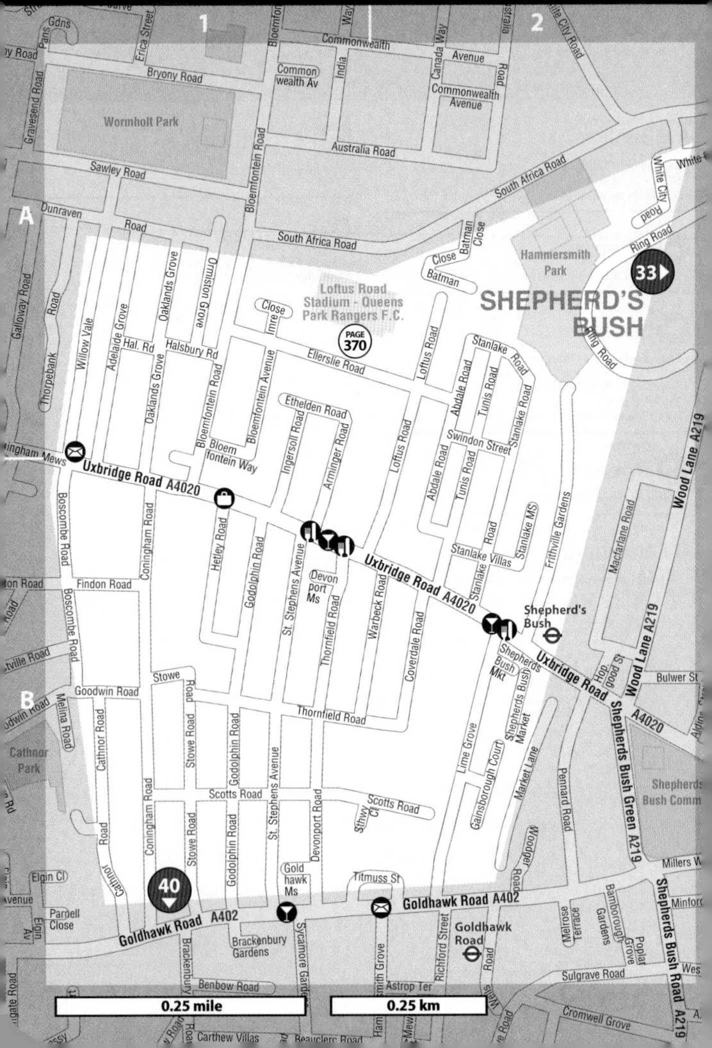

Infamous for shoot outs in Nando's and grim, locals-only boozers. Depending on your viewpoint, this bit of London is either pleasingly unpretentious or a bit of a dump. Pubs here are best avoided but foodies on a budget will be in heaven. For cheap, tasty, and totally authentic grub try Abu Zaad (Syrian), Esarn Kheaw (Thai), or Vine Leaves Taverna (Greek).

Nightlife

• **Bush Hall** • 310 Uxbridge Rd
• **The Goldhawk** • 122 Goldhawk Rd
• **The White Horse** • 31 Uxbridge Rd

Post Offices

• **Goldhawk Road** • 88 Goldhawk Rd
• **Uxbridge Road** • 420 Uxbridge Rd

Restaurants

• **Abu Zaad** • 29 Uxbridge Rd
• **Esarn Kheaw** • 314 Uxbridge Road
• **Vine Leaves Taverna** • 71 Uxbridge Rd

Shopping

• **Nut Case** • 352 Uxbridge Rd

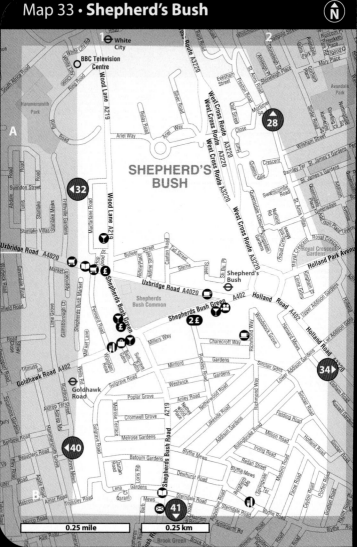

Map 33 · Shepherd's Bush

Shepherd's Bush

Map 33

This is the grimy, vibrant, international hub of West London. The market may be almost decrepit but we hope that it can survive against the titanic Westfield London Centre. Off the Green Shepherd's Bush Empire provides west London with up and coming bands, Jasmine serves awesome Thai, while those in the know drink at Albertine. Keep an eye out for the BBC's finest straying off the streets from nearby Television Centre.

£ Banks

- **Abbey** • 23 Shepherd's Bush Green
- **Barclays** • 74 Shepherd's Bush Green
- **HSBC** • 16 Shepherd's Bush Green
- **NatWest** • 25 Shepherd's Bush Green

Cinemas

- **Vue Shepherds Bush** • Shepherds Bush Green & Rockley Rd

Coffee

- **BB's Coffee and Muffins** • Richmond Way & Charecroft Way
- **Starbucks** • 62 Uxbridge Rd

O Landmarks

- **BBC Television Centre** • Wood Lane

Libraries

- **Hammersmith Library** • Shepherds Bush Rd
- **Shepherds Bush Library** • 7 Uxbridge Rd

Nightlife

- **Albertine** • 1 Wood Lane
- **Bush Bar & Grill** • 45 Goldhawk Rd
- **Ginglik** • 1 Shepherd's Bush Green
- **Shepherd's Bush Empire** • Shepherd's Bush Green

Post Offices

- **Shepherds Bush Road** • 146 Shepherd's Bush Rd

Restaurants

- **Jasmine** • 16 Goldhawk Rd
- **Popeseye** • 108 Blythe Rd

Shopping

- **Whole Foods Market** • 63 Kensington High St

Supermarkets

- **Co-Op** • 187 Uxbridge Rd
- **Sainsbury's** • 164 Uxbridge Rd

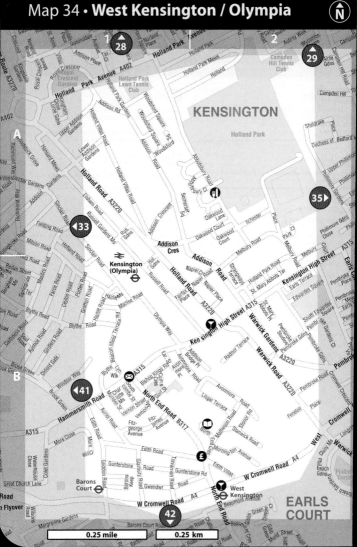

Map 34 • West Kensington / Olympia

Map 34

The stretch between Holland Park and the A4 is home to well-shod extras from a Richard Curtis film (oh sorry, they don't really exist) as well as Kensington Olympia which houses exhibitions such as Erotica ("look we're so chilled about sex we've got a whole hangar of this naughty shit!"). Try the Belvedere for top nosh or Famous 3 Kings for big-screen sports 'n beer.

£Banks

• **Barclays** • 137 N End Rd

Libraries

• **Barons Court** • North End Crescent

Nightlife

• **Famous 3 Kings** • 171 North End Road
• **Plum Bar** • 380 Kensington High St

Post Offices

• **Olympia** • 87 Hammersmith Rd

Restaurants

• **The Belvedere Restaurant** • Abbotsbury Road

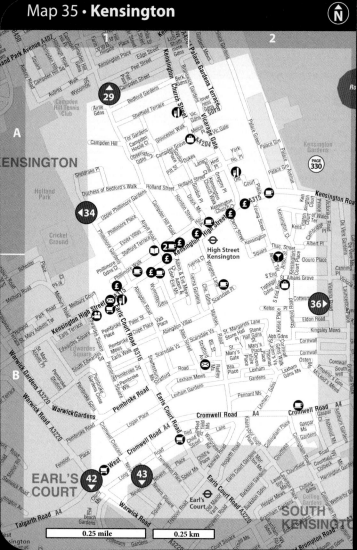

Map 35 · **Kensington**

2

PAGE
330

A

KENSINGTON

Holland
Park

Cricket
Ground

29

34

Campden Hill Tennis
Club

Airlie
Gdns

Bedford Gardens

Sheffield Terrace

Tor Gardens
Camden
House Cl

Campden Hill

Observatory
Gdns

Sheldrake Pl

Duchess of Bedford's Walk

Upper Phillimore Gardens

Holland Street

Phillimore Place

Essex Villas

Stafford Terrace

Phillimore Walk

Phillimore Gdns Cl.

Phillimore
Gdns

Melbury Court

Melbury Road

Phillimore

Abingdon Road

Wynnstay

Adam & Eve Mews

Adam & Eve Mews

Iverna
Gdns

Iverna Court

Chr. Gdns. Markets

Scarsdale Pl.

Scarsdale Vs.

Scarsdale Vs.

Bill St.

St. Margarets Lane

Stone Hall

Stone Hall Gdns

Strathmore

Allen Street

Stratford Road

Stratford

Pembroke Sq.

Pembroke Walk

Lexham Mews

Lexham Gardens

St.
Mary's
Gate

St.
Mary's
Place

St.
Thomas

Radley Mews

Bea. Place

Abb Gdns

Lexham Gardens

Lexham Ms

Pennant Ms

Kensington Place

Edge Street

Peel Street

Campden Street

Kensington Place

Bedford Gardens

Berkeley Gdns

Brunswick Gardens

Gloucester Walk

Campden Grove

Dukes
Lane

Pitt St.

Gordon Pl.

Holland Street

Horton Street

Drks.

Gregory Pl.

Kensington
Church Walk

Kensington Church Street

Vicarage Gate

Inver
nest
Gdns

Vic.
Gdns

Vic. Gate

York
Ho. Pl

Palace Green

Palace Grn

Palace Grn

Kensington
Gardens

Young Street

Kensington Square

Thac. Street

S End

St. Albans Grove

Douro Place

Stanford Rd

Cottesmore

36

Eldon Road

Kingsley Mews

Cornwall

Cornwall

Cornwall

Osten

Emperor's Gate

Southwell
Gdns

Ashburn Gdns

Stanwick Road

Harrington Gdns

Courtfield Gdns

Courtfield Gdns

Collingham Place

Gaspar Ms

Gaspar Road

Cromwell Road A4

Cromwell Road

Pembroke Road

Earls Court Road B316

Warwick Gardens

Warwick Road A3220

Warwick Gardens A3220

Pembroke Gardens

Edwardes Square

South Edwardes Sq

Pembroke Gdns Close

Logan Place

West Cromwell Road A4

Earls Court Road

Cromwell Road A4

Nevern Road

Child's Place

Child's Street

Trebovir Road

Spear Ms

Nevern Place

Kenway Road

Hogarth Road

Knaresborough Place

Barkston Gdns

Collingham Road

Collingham Place

42

43

EARL'S
COURT

Earl's
Court

Warwick Road

Talgarth Road A4

Holland Park Avenue A402

Camden Hill Rd

A4204

A4315

Kensington High Street

Kensington High Street

Holland Street

Kensington Road

High Street
Kensington

Kensington High Street

Cope Place

Pater St.

Abingdon Villas

Earls Court Road A3220

SOUTH
KENSINGTON

Brompton Road

0.25 mile   0.25 km

Witness the endangered Sloane ranger species in their natural habitat. Kensington reeks of money but shows that that doesn't necessarily translate into style. It's not a cool place to hang out but draws hordes of shoppers by day. After dark, try The Builders Arms for a good pint or chow down on arguably London's best burger at Byron, washed down with a thick shake before you waddle away.

Banks

- **Abbey** • 144 Kensington High St
- **Barclays** • 208 Kensington High St
- **Halifax** • 180 Kensington High St
- **HSBC** • 92 Kensington High St
- **Lloyds** • 112 Kensington High St
- **NatWest** • 55 Kensington High St
- **Royal Bank of Scotland** • 175 Kensington High St

Cinemas

- **Odeon Kensington** • Kensington High St & Edwards Sq

Coffee

- **Caffe Nero** • 160 Kensington High St
- **Caffe Nero** • 1 Wrights Lane
- **Costa** • 144 Kensington High St
- **Costa** • 149 Cromwell Rd
- **Pret A Manger** • 149 Kensington High St
- **Pret A Manger** • 123 Kensington High St
- **Starbucks** • 25 Kensington High St
- **Starbucks** • 197 Kensington High St

Libraries

- **Kensington Central Library** • Phillimore Walk

Nightlife

- **Builders Arms** • 1 Kensington Ct Pl

Post Offices

- **Kensington High St** • 257 Kensington High St
- **Startford Road** • 11 Stratford Rd

Restaurants

- **Byron** • 222 Kensington High St
- **Clarke's** • 124 Kensington Church St
- **Maggie Jones's** • 6 Old Court Pl

Shopping

- **Buttercup** • 16 St Albans Grove
- **Notting Hill Housing Trust** • 57 Kensington Church St

Supermarkets

- **Sainsbury's** • 160 Earl's Ct Rd
- **Tesco** • 100 W Cromwell Rd
- **Waitrose** • 243 Kensington High St

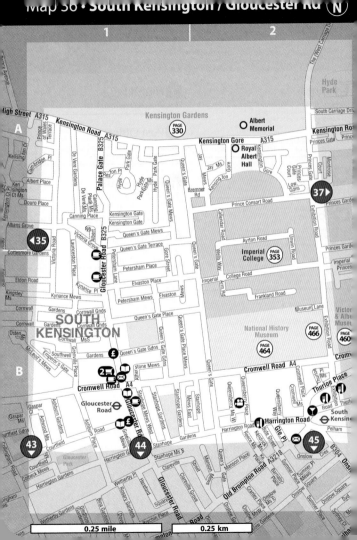

Map 36 • South Kensington / Gloucester Rd

South Kensington / Gloucester Rd

Befriend a millionaire and you can hang out here all the time, perhaps house-sitting his London 'base' while he unwinds in the countreh. You'll have great afternoons at the museums, the shops on Fulham Road, and at the Royal Albert Hall (which is a must for musos). Nightlife, however, is terrible---if you have to go out, make sure the millionaire comes with you.

Banks

• **Barclays** • 114 Gloucester Rd
• **HSBC** • 95 Gloucester Rd

Cinemas

• **Cine Lumiere** • 17 Queensberry Pl

Coffee

• **Café Deco** • 62 Gloucester Rd
• **Coffee Republic** • 121 Gloucester Rd
• **Starbucks** • 17 Gloucester Rd
• **Starbucks** • 83 Gloucester Rd

Landmarks

• **Albert Memorial** • Kensington Gardens
• **Royal Albert Hall** • Kensington Gore

Libraries

• **French Institute Library** • 17 Queensberry Pl
• **National Art Library** • Cromwell Rd
• **Natural History Museum** • Cromwell Rd

Nightlife

• **Boujis** • 43 Thurloe St

Post Offices

• **Gloucester Road** • 118 Gloucester Rd
• **South Kensington Station** • 41 Old Brompton St

Restaurants

• **The Kensington Creperie** • 2 Exhibition Rd
• **Little Japan** • 32 Thurloe St
• **Odonno's** • 14 Bute St

Supermarkets

• **Sainsbury's** • 158 Cromwell Rd
• **Waitrose** • 128 Gloucester Rd

Map 36

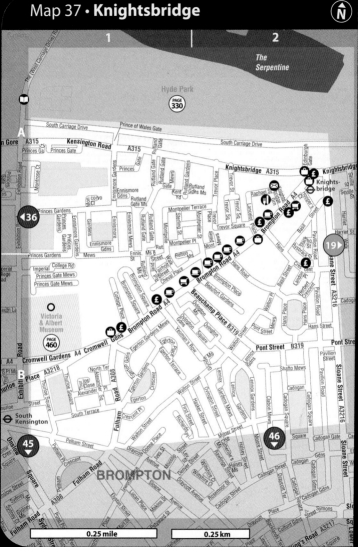

Map 37 · **Knightsbridge**

N

1

2

The
Serpentine

Hyde Park
PAGE
330

The (West Carriage Drive) Road

Prince of Wales Gate

A
South Carriage Drive

Kensington Road A315

South Carriage Drive

Knightsbridge A315

Gore

A315

Princes Ga

Princes Gate

Exhibition Road

Knightsbridge

Knights-
bridge

Montrose Ct

£

Princes Gate

Princes Gate

Seville St

Raphael St

£

Harriet St

Ennismore
Gdns

Princes Gardens

corvo

Princes
Gardens

Rutland
Gate Ms

Rutland
Gdns Ms

Trevor St

Brompton Road A4

£

Harriet St

36

Princes Gardens

Gardens

Ennismore
Gdns

Montpelier Terrace

Trevor Sq

£

£

Pavilion Road

19

Ennismore Gardens

Kent
Yd

Montpelier St

Trevor Sq

Hans Road

Basil St

Sloane Street A3216

Imperial
College Rd

Ennismore
Mews

Rutland
Gate

Montpelier Pl

£

Cadog

Princes Gate Mews

Cottage Place

Sterling St

Relton

Rut

Hans Pl

Herbert
Crescent

Pavilion Road

Princes Gate Mews

Ms

Brompton Road A4

£

Brompton Place

£

Hans Street

eum La

£

O

Cheval Place

£

Beaufort Gardens

Hans Place

Victoria
& Albert
Museum
PAGE
460

Brompton Square

Beauchamp Place B319

Ovington
Gardens

Walton Place

Walton Street

Hans Street

perial
lege R

£

Cromwell Gardens A4 Cromwell Gdns

Egerton Gardens Mews

Ovington
Square

Yeoman's Row

Pont Street B319

Pont
Street

B
Exhibition

Place A3218

Ter

Alexander
Sq

Egerton Gardens

Egerton
Terrace

Cromwell
Road

Joe
JJ

Close

Crescent

Lennox Gardens Mews

Shafto Mews

Cadogan Square

Pavilion
Street

Onslow

Egerton

Lennox Gardens

Cadogan Gate

Sloane Street A3216

Alexander Sq

hurloe

Thurloe Square

Walton Street

Lennox
Gdns

Cadogan
Square

Cadogan Square

Fulham Road

South Terrace

Haster Street

Crington Mews

First Street

Milner Street

Clabon Mews

Cadogan Gdns

hurloe

South
Kensington

Pelham Street

Crescent Pl

Draycott Avenue

Donne Place

Ixworth Place

Walton Street

Sydney Ms

Denyer Street

Moseley Street

Hasker Street

Halsey Street

Richards Place

Sloane Avenue

Draycott Ave

Whitehead's Gr

Whittard's Ct

Blacklands Terr

Rosemoor St

Draycott Ter

Culford Gdns

Cadogan Gdns

Cadogan Lane

Sloane Street

45

46

Onslow
Cres

Onslow
Square

Sydney
Street

Fulham Road

Sydney St

A308

BROMPTON

Elystan Place

Lucan Place

Makins St

Ixworth Place

Sloane Avenue

Symons

King's Road A3217

Fulham Road A308

0.25 mile

0.25 km

The perfect place to go to get that must-have item at a much higher price than anywhere else. Rammed Brompton Road features Harrods, Harvey Nichols, the flagship Burberry store, and a host of other credit crunchers, populated by hordes of aggressive tourists. Behind that: behold! Luxury apartments worth way more than the lives of your entire family.

£ Banks

- **Barclays** • 38 Hans Crescent
- **Barclays** • 137 Brompton Rd
- **Halifax** • 110 Brompton Rd
- **HSBC** • 237 Brompton Rd
- **HSBC** • 202 Sloane St
- **Lloyds** • 9 Brompton Rd
- **NatWest** • 186 Brompton Rd

💻 Coffee

- **Bagel Factory** • 88 Brompton Rd
- **Bagel Factory** • 102 Brompton Rd
- **Caffe Nero** • 124 Brompton Rd
- **Costa** • 197 Brompton Rd
- **Eat.** • 106 Brompton Rd
- **Pret A Manger** • 132 Brompton Rd
- **Starbucks** • 58 Brompton Rd

O Landmarks

- **Victoria & Albert Museum** • Cromwell Rd

📖 Libraries

- **Goethe-Institut Library** • Exhibition Rd

🍸 Nightlife

- **Knightsbridge BO** • 6 Raphael St

🍴 Restaurants

- **Zuma** • 5 Raphael St

🛍 Shopping

- **Burberry** • 12 Brompton Road
- **Harrods** • 87 Brompton Rd
- **Harvey Nichols** • 109 Knightsbridge
- **Skandium** • 247 Brompton Rd

🛒 Supermarkets

- **Marks & Spencer** • 179 Brompton Rd
- **Sainsbury's** • 112 Brompton Rd

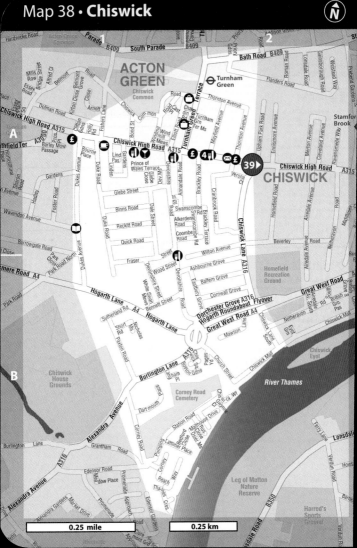

Map 38 · Chiswick

Lean, green, and thankfully not so mean, Chiswick's leafy, cosmopolitan pavement dining is the epitome of what makes west London, well, west London. Hit the High Road for café culture and Turnham Green Terrace for intimate boutiques. On Devonshire Road The Devonshire is a more affordable Gordon Ramsey venture, spice it up on the High Road at Boys Authentic Thai, Kalamari for authentic Greek, and Theobroma Cacao on Turnham Green Terrace for chocolate to die for.

 ## Banks

• **Halifax** • 91 King St
• **Lloyds** • 308 Chiswick High Rd

 ## Coffee

• **Starbucks** • 280 Chiswick High Rd

 ## Libraries

• **Chiswick Library** • Duke's Ave

 ## Nightlife

• **Carvossos** • 210 Chiswick High Rd

Post Offices

• **Chiswick High Road** • 110 Chiswick High Rd

Restaurants

• **Boys Authentic Thai** • 95 Chiswick High Rd
• **Chez Gerard** • 163 Chiswck High Rd
• **Chris' Fish and Chips** • 19 Turnham Green Terrace
• **The Devonshire** • 126 Devonshire Rd
• **High Road Brasserie** • 162 Chiswick High Rd
• **Kalamari** • 4 Chiswick High Rd
• **Zizzi** • 231 Chiswick High Rd

Shopping

• **Oxfam Books** • 90 Turnham Green Terrace
• **Theobroma Cacao** • 43 Turnham Green Terrace

Map 39 · **Stamford Brook**

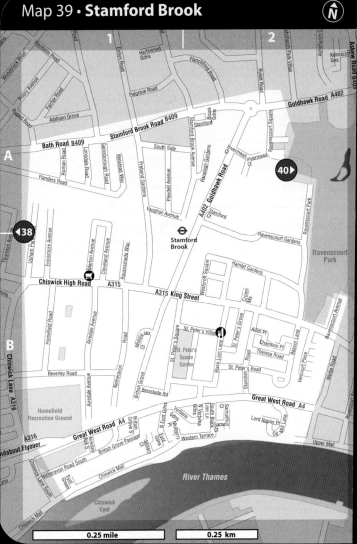

Wedged between Chiswick and Hammersmith, with the actual brook now a sewer, there's more to Stamford Brook than a tube station and some very expensive houses. Visitors should head either up King Street for international cuisine or Chiswick High Road with its outdoor dining for their shits and giggles.

Restaurants
• **Carpenter's Arms** • 91 Black Lion Ln

Supermarkets
• **Sainsbury's** • 120 Chiswick High Rd

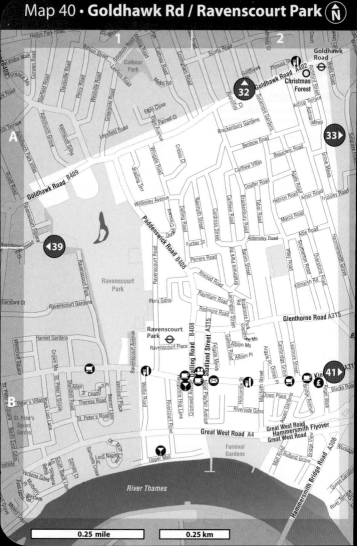

Map 40 · **Goldhawk Rd / Ravenscourt Park**

0.25 mile   0.25 km

Far enough on the tube to scare the tourists, this area is a haven for locals who want it all on their doorstep. International flavours? Please, it's like a Benetton ad here: try Lowiczanka, Sagar, or Blah Blah Blah. Pretty Thames walk? Check!—along with The Dove, one of the city's most picturesque pubs. There's even a Christmas Tree forest. Life's good in these parts.

£ Banks

• **Barclays** • 75 King St

Cinemas

• **Cineworld Hammersmith** • 207 King St

Coffee

• **Caffe Nero** • 1 King St
• **Coffee Republic** • 207 King St
• **Starbucks** • 38 King St

O Landmarks

• **Christmas Forest** • 83 Goldhawk Road

Nightlife

• **The Dove** • 19 Upper Mall
• **Ruby Grand** • 225 King St

Post Offices

• **King St** • 168 King St

Restaurants

• **Blah Blah Blah** • 78 Goldhawk Rd
• **Lowiczanka Polish Cultural Centre** • 238 King Street
• **Sagar** • 157 King St

Supermarkets

• **Iceland Foods** • 111 King St
• **Tesco** • 327 King St

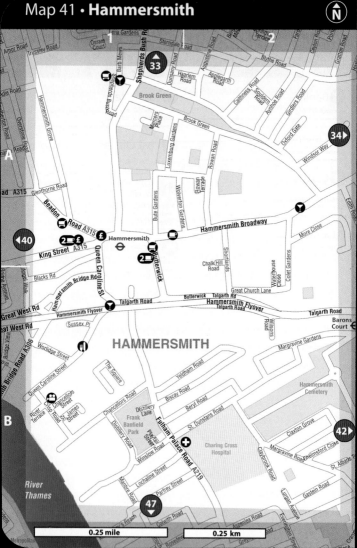

So the shops and pubs on offer are all pretty drab, but Hammersmith has three great venues for the more culturally inclined. Check out The Apollo for mainstream bands and big-name comedians, The Lyric for the latest in modern theatre, and The Riverside for an awesome selection of foreign/art house films. London's vegetarians flock to The Gate, with its seriously original and inventive menu.

Banks

• **HSBC** • 1 Beadon Rd
• **Lloyds** • 21 King St

Cinemas

• **Riverside Studios** • Crisp Rd & Queen Caroline St

Coffee

• **Café Brera** • King St & Angel Walk
• **Costa** • Butterwick
• **Costa** • King St
• **Pret A Manger** • Butterwick
• **Starbucks** • 200 Hammersmith Rd

Emergency Rooms

• **Charing Cross Hospital** • Fulham Palace Rd

Nightlife

• **Brook Green Hotel** • 170 Shepherd's Bush Rd
• **Hammersmith Apollo** • 45 Queen Caroline St
• **Lyric Hammersmith** • King St

Restaurants

• **The Gate** • 51 Queen Caroline St

Supermarkets

• **Sainsbury's** • Beadon Rd
• **Tesco** • 180 Shepherd's Bush Rd
• **Tesco** • Butterwick

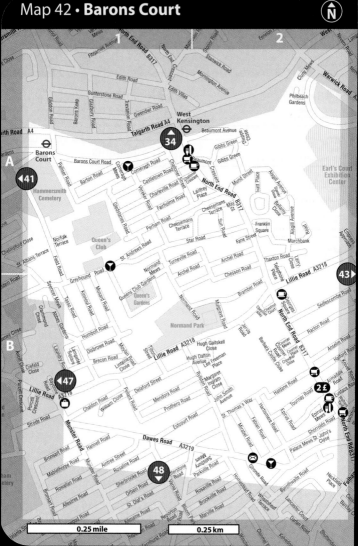

Map 42 · **Barons Court**

Barons Court

Barons Court doesn't have a scene as such, unless you're a yummy mummy or a Chihuahua. But it is elegantly lovely. Except North End Road—a fried-chicken blot among Edwardian mansions. Check out Lillie Road's antique stores, particularly Curious Science for the weirdest stock in London. If you need a change from polished chic, seek the Colton Arms for a jug-pint in its cottage-style garden.

Map 42

Banks

- **Abbey** • 421 N End Rd
- **Lloyds** • 417 N End Rd

Coffee

- **Café La Cigale** • 353 N End Rd
- **Coffee Republic** • 92 N End Rd
- **Costa** • 431 North End Rd

Nightlife

- **Colton Arms** • 187 Greyhound Road
- **Curtains Up** • 28 Comeragh Rd
- **The Fulham Mitre** • 81 Dawes Rd

Post Offices

- **Dawes Road** • 108 Dawes Rd

Restaurants

- **Bombay Bicycle Club** • 352 North End Rd
- **Ta Khai** • 100 North End Rd

Shopping

- **Curious Science** • 319 Lillie Road

 Supermarkets

- **Co-Op** • 88 N End Rd
- **Iceland** • 290 North End Rd
- **Sainsbury's** • 342 North End Rd

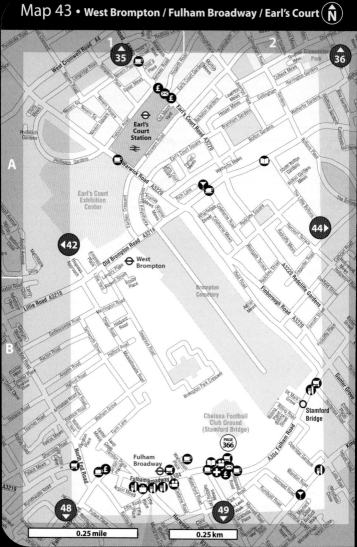

A lively mix of Aussie's, Saffa's, rich kids, and sweaty Chelsea fans occupy these neighbourhoods. Fulham Broadway is the focus of the action offering heaving bars and clubs. Earl's Court is slightly more sedate while West Brompton is positively sleepy in comparison. Try Chutney Mary for an upscale Indian while Vingt Quatre is a 24-hour institution serving fry ups to clubbers in the early hours.

£ Banks

- **Barclays** • 191 Earl's Ct Rd
- **Barclays** • 20 Fulham Broadway
- **HSBC** • 315 Fulham Rd
- **Lloyds** • 179 Earl's Ct Rd

Cinemas

- **Cineworld Fulham Road** • 142 Fulham Rd
- **Vue Fulham** • Fulham Rd & Cedarne Rd

Coffee

- **Caffe Nero** • 480 Fulham Rd
- **Caffe Nero** • 174 Fulham Rd
- **Coffee Republic** • 198 Earl's Ct Rd
- **Coffee Republic** • 142 Fulham Rd
- **Costa** • Warwick Rd
- **Costa** • 153 Earl's Ct Rd
- **Pret A Manger** • Fulham Broadway Retail Centre
- **Starbucks** • 259 Old Brompton Rd
- **Starbucks** • 186 Earl's Ct Rd

Emergency Rooms

- **Chelsea and Westminster Hospital** • 369 Fulham Rd

O Landmarks

- **Stamford Bridge** • Fulham Road

Libraries

- **Brompton Library** • 210 Old Brompton Rd
- **Institute of Cancer Research Library** • 237 Fulham Rd

Nightlife

- **The Coleherne** • 261 Old Brompton Rd
- **Nectar** • 562 King's Rd

Post Offices

- **Earls Court** • 185 Earl's Ct Rd
- **Fulham Road** • 369 Fulham Rd

Restaurants

- **The Blue Elephant** • 3 Fulham Broadway
- **Bodean's** • 4 Broadway Chambers
- **Chutney Mary** • 535 King's Rd
- **Vingt Quatre** • 325 Fulham Rd
- **Yo! Sushi** • Fulham Road

Shopping

- **Fulham Broadway Centre** • Fulham Road

Supermarkets

- **Sainsbury's** • 295 Fulham Rd
- **Sainsbury's** • Fulham Rd
- **Tesco** • 459 Fulham Rd
- **Waitrose** • 380 North End Rd

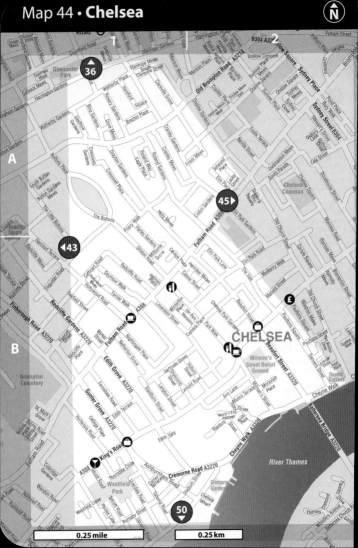

Map 44 · Chelsea

This area drips old money, 4x4s, and people who own rather large things, like, say, Devon. The only way to do Chelsea is to be seen doing it---and if you're paying all that money at least make it worthwhile. Drink one of Eight Over Eight's innovative cocktails, taste Michelin-starred food at Aubergine, and blow a week's wage on a designer sock from The Shop At Bluebird.

£ Banks

• **Barclays** • 348 King's Rd

🖵 Coffee

• **Starbucks** • 388 King's Rd
• **Starbucks** • 369 Fulham Rd

🍸 Nightlife

• **Rumi** • 531 King's Rd

🍴 Restaurants

• **Aubergine** • 11 Park Walk
• **Eight Over Eight** • 392 King's Rd

🛍 Shopping

• **Furniture Cave** • 533 Kings Rd
• **The Shop At Bluebird** • 350 King's Rd

Map 45 • Chelsea (East)

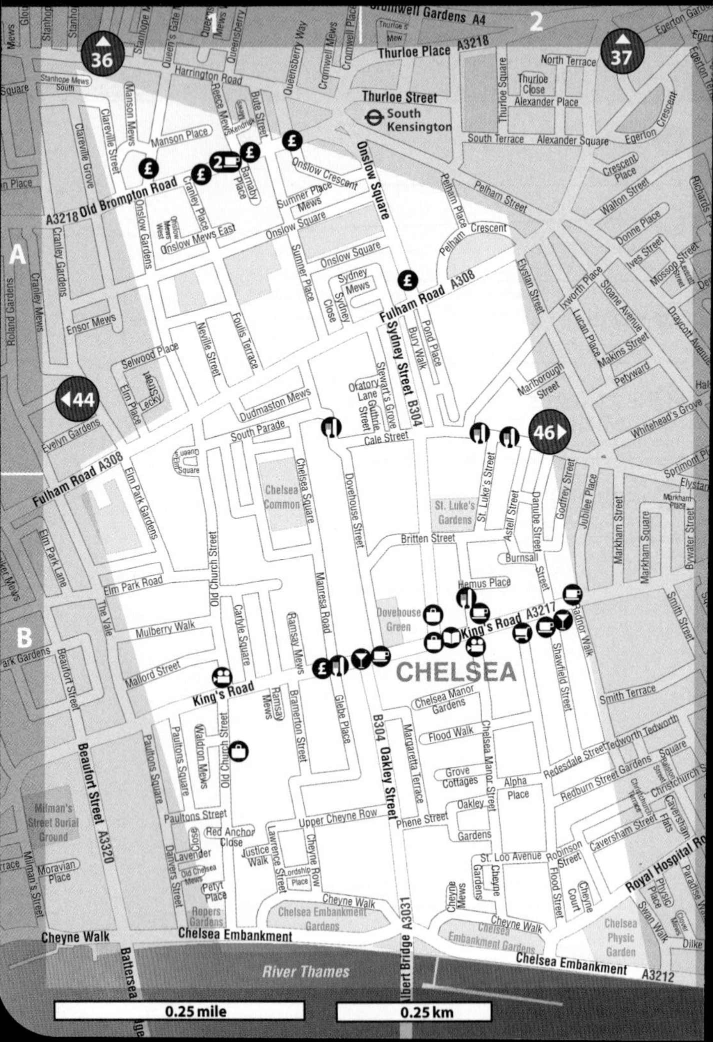
N
1
2
A
B
36
37
44
46
Cromwell Gardens A4
Thurloe Place A3218
Thurloe Street
South Kensington
Harrington Road
Stanhope Mews South
Queensberry Way
Cromwell Mews
Cromwell Place
North Terrace
Thurloe Close
Alexander Place
Thurloe Square
South Terrace
Alexander Square
Egerton Crescent
Egerton Gardens
Crescent Place
Walton Street
Pelham Street
Pelham Place
Pelham Crescent
Manson Mews
Manson Place
Reece Mews
Kendrick
Bute Street
Clareville Street
Clareville Grove
Old Brompton Road
A3218
Cranley Place
Barnaby Place
Onslow Crescent
Onslow Square
Sumner Place Mews
Sumner Place
Onslow Gardens
Onslow Mews West
Onslow Mews East
Cranley Gardens
Cranley Mews
Roland Gardens
Ensor Mews
Selwood Place
Elm Place
Lecky Street
Neville Street
Foulis Terrace
Sydney Mews
Sydney Close
Fulham Road A308
Sydney Street B304
Bury Walk
Pond Place
Elystan Street
Donne Place
Ives Street
Mossop Street
Sloane Avenue
Lucan Place
Makins Street
Petyward
Draycott Avenue
Marlborough Street
Whitehead's Grove
Dudmaston Mews
Oratory Lane
Guthrie Street
Stewart's Grove
South Parade
Cale Street
Evelyn Gardens
Queen's Elm Square
Fulham Road A308
Elm Park Gardens
Chelsea Common
Chelsea Square
Dovehouse Street
St. Luke's Gardens
St. Luke's Street
Astell Street
Danube Street
Godfrey Street
Jubilee Place
Markham Street
Markham Square
Bywater Street
Sprimont Place
Elystan Place
Markham Place
Britten Street
Burnsall Street
Elm Park Lane
Elm Park Road
Old Church Street
Hemus Place
Dovehouse Green
King's Road A3217
Radnor Walk
Smith Street
The Vale
Mulberry Walk
Carlyle Square
Ramsay Mews
Manresa Road
Mallord Street
King's Road
CHELSEA
Shawfield Street
Smith Terrace
Beaufort Street
Glebe Place
Bramerton Street
Chelsea Manor Gardens
Flood Walk
Chelsea Manor Street
Tedworth Square
Redesdale Street
Tedworth Gardens
Paultons Square
Waldron Mews
Margaretta Terrace
B304 Oakley Street
Grove Cottages
Alpha Place
Redburn Street
Christchurch Street
Christchurch Terrace
Ralston Street
Beaufort Street A3320
Milman's Street Burial Ground
Paultons Street
Upper Cheyne Row
Phene Street
Oakley Gardens
Caversham Flats
Caversham Street
Red Anchor Close
Lavender Close
Old Chelsea Mews
Justice Walk
Lawrence Street
Cheyne Row
Lordship Place
Petyt Place
Moravian Place
Milman's Street
Danvers Street
St. Loo Avenue
Robinson Street
Cheyne Gardens
Cheyne Mews
Flood Street
Cheyne Court
Royal Hospital Road
Physic Place
Swan Walk
Paradise Walk
Clover Mews
Dilke
Ropers Gardens
Cheyne Walk
Chelsea Embankment Gardens
Cheyne Walk
Chelsea Embankment
Albert Bridge A3031
Chelsea Physic Garden
Chelsea Embankment
A3212
River Thames
Battersea Bridge
0.25 mile
0.25 km

Chelsea (East)

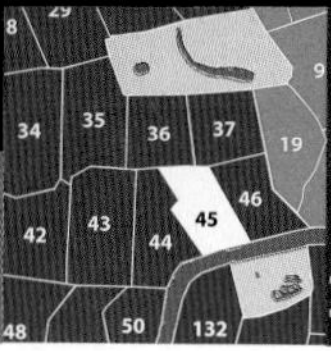

Chelsea East is what Hollywood thinks all of London is like, full of dapper English chaps and potential princesses (who, incidentally, donate their clothes to the Red Cross shop: rummage here for London's best bargains). King's Road buzzes as it did when it spawned the Swinging '60s, and foodies are spoiled around Cale Street. Tom's Kitchen is your place for Sloaney eating without the Sloaney allowance.

Banks

- **Abbey** • 90 Old Brompton Rd
- **Barclays** • 108 Queen's Gate
- **HSBC** • 1 Sydney Pl
- **Lloyds** • 67 Old Brompton Rd
- **NatWest** • 224 King's Rd
- **Royal Bank of Scotland** • 29 Old Brompton Rd

Cinemas

- **Chealsea Cinema** • 206 King's Rd
- **Cineworld Chelsea** • 279 King's Rd

Coffee

- **Caffe Nero** • 115 King's Rd
- **Caffe Nero** • 201 King's Rd
- **Caffe Nero** • 66 Old Brompton Rd
- **Coffee Republic** • 157 King's Rd
- **Starbucks** • 123 King's Rd
- **Starbucks** • 72 Old Brompton Rd

Libraries

- **Chelsea Library** • King's Rd

Nightlife

- **Apartment 195** • 195 Kings Rd
- **Chelsea Potter** • 119 Kings Rd

Restaurants

- **Four o nine** • 409 Clapham Rd
- **Le Columbier** • 145 Dovehouse St
- **My Old Dutch Pancake House** • 221 King's Rd,
- **Tom's Kitchen** • 27 Cale St
- **Tom's Place** • 1 Cale St

Shopping

- **British Red Cross Chelsea** • 67 Old Church St
- **Frock Me! Vintage Fashion Fair** •
  Chelsea Town Hall, Kings Rd
- **Kate Kuba** • 24 Duke of York Sq

Supermarkets

- **Waitrose** • 196 Kings Rd

Map 45

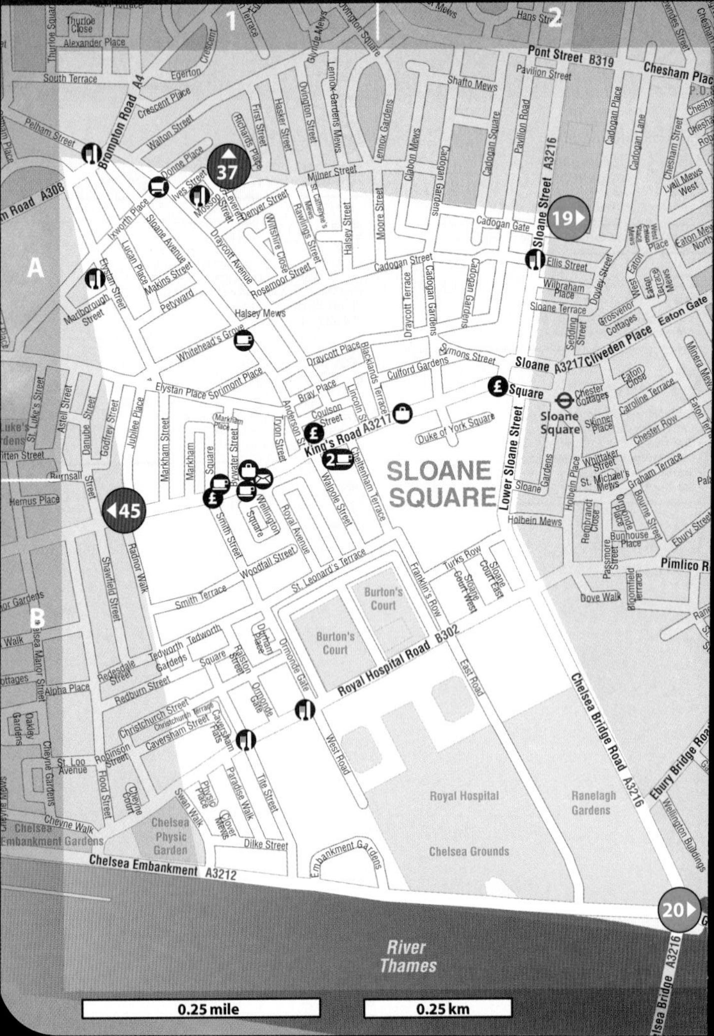

Map 46 · **Sloane Square**

N

1

2

Thurloe Square
Thurloe Place
Alexander Place
South Terrace
Pelham Street

Brompton Road A4
Egerton Terrace
Crescent Place
Walton Street

Pont Street B319
Chesham Place
Pavilion Street
Shafto Mews
Chesham Street

Hans Street

37

19▶

£ Square

SLOANE
SQUARE

45◀

Sloane Street

Lower Sloane Street

Sloane Street A3216

Sloane A3217 Cliveden Place
Eaton Gate

Sloane
Square

Pimlico Road

King's Road A3217

2

SLOANE
SQUARE

A

B

Burton's
Court

Burton's
Court

Royal Hospital Road B302

Chelsea Bridge Road A3216

Ebury Bridge Road

Chelsea Physic Garden

Royal Hospital

Ranelagh Gardens

Chelsea Embankment A3212

Chelsea Grounds

20▶

Chelsea Bridge

River
Thames

| 0.25 mile | 0.25 km |

Sloane Square

Map 46

You've got to love a place that spawns an adjective. If you've never met any 'Sloaney' types and are curious as to why the whole of London gets so riled about them, take a walk along the King's Road and observe. Other attractions in this rather beautiful nabe include a clutch of bank-breakingly expensive eateries and many lovely (but pricey) boutiques.

Banks

- **Abbey** • 138 King's Rd
- **Barclays** • 30 Sloane Sq
- **Lloyds** • 33 King's Rd

Coffee

- **Costa** • 138 King's Rd
- **Eat.** • 82 King's Rd
- **Pret A Manger** • 80 King's Rd
- **Starbucks** • 35 Sloane Ave
- **Starbucks** • 128 King's Rd

Post Offices

- **Kings Walk** • 122 King's Rd

Restaurants

- **The Admiral Codrington** • 17 Mossop St
- **Bibendum Restaurant & Oyster Bar** • 81 Fulham Rd
- **Foxtrot Oscar** • 79 Royal Hospital Rd
- **Gordon Ramsay** • 68 Royal Hospital Rd
- **Le Cercle** • 1 Wilbraham Pl
- **Tom Aikens** • 43 Elystan St

Shopping

- **Fresh Line** • 55 King's Rd
- **Space NK Apothecary** • 307 King's Rd

Supermarkets

- **Sainsbury's** • 75 Sloane Ave

Map 47 • **Fulham (West)**

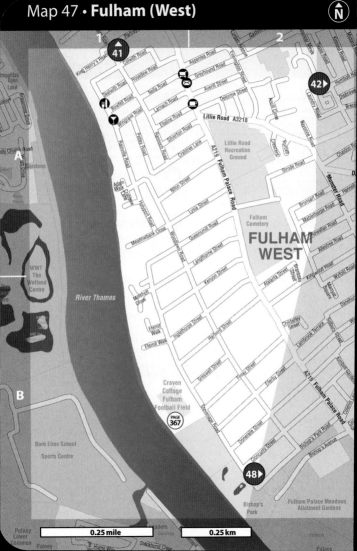

This area is an estate agent's wet dream. Leafy, well-heeled, on the river, the thing is, you can't afford to move here so dream on. Instead, live the lie—make the most of the riverside and grab a pint at The Crabtree Tavern. Now you're tipsy, head to The River Café where you'll feel less pained shelling out for top-notch, dead-posh grub.

Coffee

• **Starbucks** • 220 Fulham Palace Rd

Nightlife

• **The Crabtree Tavern** • Rainville Rd

Post Offices

• **Fulham Palace Road** • 185 Fulham Palace Rd

Restaurants

• **The River Café** • Thames Wharf, Rainville Rd

Supermarkets

• **Sainsbury's** • 179 Fulham Palace Rd

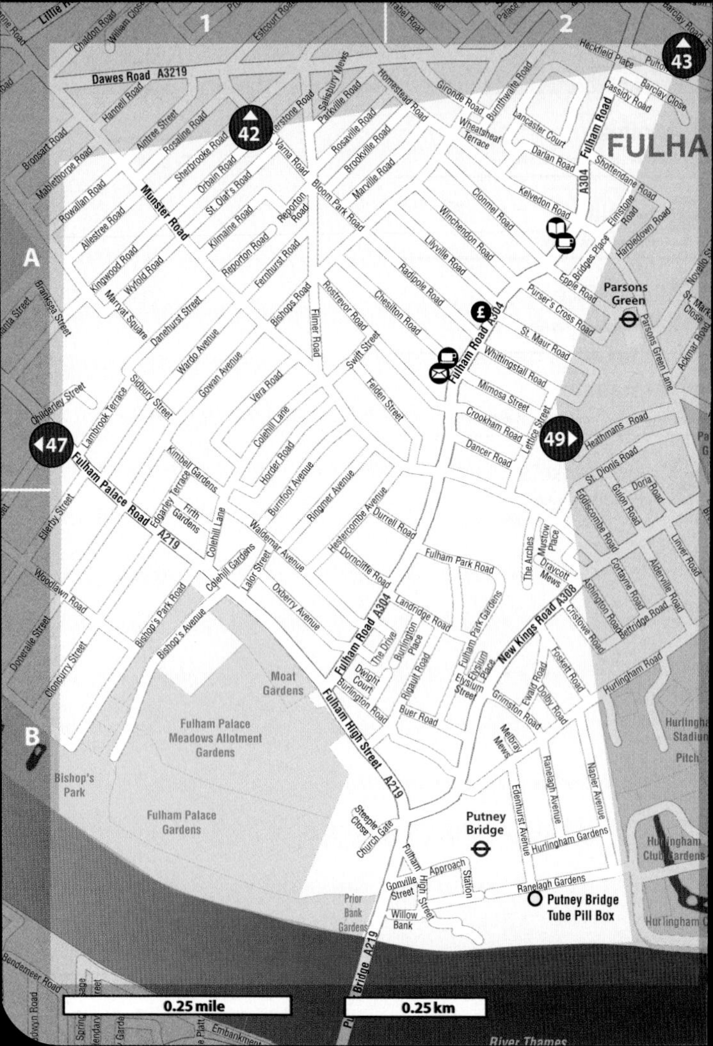

Map 48 · **Fulham**

N

1   2

43

FULHA

Little R...
Cheston Road
William Cob...
Falcon Road
Barclay Rd...
Barclay Close
Hickfield Place

Dawes Road   A3219
Hamel Road
Gironde Road
Southerville Road
Cassidy Road
Lancaster Court

Alfred Street
Rosaline Road
Fernhurst Road
Parfrew Road
Homestead Road
Wheatsheaf Terrace
Darian Road
Shorttenden Road
Einstein Road

42

Rosaville Road
Brossard Road
Mahlmoroc Road
Rowallan Road
Sherbrooke Road
Orbain Road
Varna Road
Brookville Road
Marville Road
Clonmel Road
Kelvedon Road

Munster Road
Allestree Road
St. Olaf's Road
Kilmaine Road
Bloom Park Road
Linville Road
Winchendon Road

A304   Fulham Road
Harbledown Road

Kingwood Road
Wyfold Road
Riporton Road
Redpole Road
Epee Place
Bodies Place

Merrial Square
Danehurst Street
Bishops Road
Fernhurst Road
Chesilton Road
Fulham Road A304
Purser's Cross Road
Parsons Green

Wardo Avenue
Gowan Avenue
Vera Road
Rostrevor Road
Filmer Road
Swift Street
St. Maur Road
Whittingstall Road
St. Dionis Road

Challoner Street
Lambrook Terrace
Sedlescombe Road
Colehill Lane
Telden Street
Mimosa Street
Crookham Road
Heathmans Road

47   Fulham Palace Road   A3219
Kimbell Gardens
Firth Gardens
Horder Road
Bunthorn Road
Rugmere Avenue
Dancer Road
Lettice Street

49

Doneraile Street
Waldemar Avenue
Heckfield Place
Durrell Road
Fulham Park Road
The Arches
Dorncliffe Road
Fulham Park Gardens
Greswell Street
Dora Road
Linver Road
Cloncurry Street
Woodlawn Road
Epirus Road

Coniger Road
Bishop's Park Road
Lakin Street
Oxberry Avenue
Fulham Road A304
Landridge Road
The Drive
Burlington Place
Fulham Park Gardens
Grimston Road
Bettridge Road
Burntfold Road

Moal Gardens
Dights Court
Elysium Street
Buer Road
Medora Mews
Napier Avenue
Hurlingham Road

A
B

Bishop's Park

Fulham Palace Meadows Allotment Gardens

Fulham Palace Gardens

Fulham High Street   A219
Burlington Road
Binfield Road
Rigault Road
Raynham Avenue
Edenhurst Avenue

Hurlingham Stadiu
Pitch

Hurlingham Club Gardens

Putney Bridge Station
Ranelagh Gardens
Hurlingham Gardens

Prior Bank Gardens
Willow Bank
Sharpe Close
Church Gate
Gonville Street
Fulham High Street
Approach

Putney Bridge Tube Pill Box

Putney Bridge   A219

0.25 mile   0.25 km

Embankment
River Thames

Fulham

Expensive home to rivals Fulham and Chelsea FC with a strong possibility of encountering some Chanel-clad WAGS. Fulham Road is where the good stuff is, but mostly on Map 43. See the Putney Bridge Pill Box for a little bit of WWII history at Putney Tube Station of all places.

Banks

• **HSBC** • 593 Fulham

Coffee

• **Caffe Nero** • 717 Fulham Rd
• **Starbucks** • 809 Fulham Rd

O Landmarks

• **Putney Bridge Tube Pill Box** • Putney Bridge Station

Libraries

• **Fulham Library** • 598 Fulham Rd

Post Offices

• **Fulham** • 815 Fulham Rd

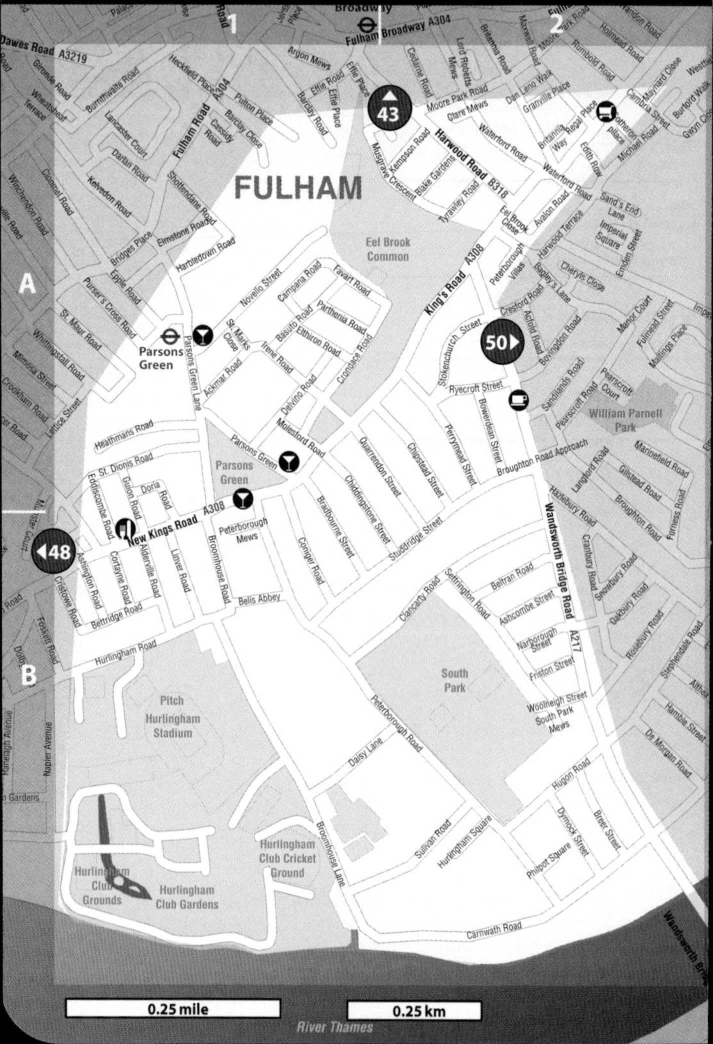

Map 49 · **Parson's Green**

Broadway

Fulham Broadway A304

1

2

Dawes Road A3219

Grenvale Road

Bramonfield Terrace

Westborough Road

Bridges Place

Elsmore Road

Harbledown Road

43

Harwood Road B316

FULHAM

Eel Brook Common

King's Road A308

Parsons Green

50

Parsons Green

New Kings Road A308

48

William Parnell Park

Heathmans Road

St. Dionis Road

Parsons Green

Peterborough Mews

Bells Abbey

Wandsworth Bridge Road A217

Hurlingham Road

Pitch Hurlingham Stadium

South Park

Peterborough Road

Daisy Lane

Hurlingham Club Cricket Ground

Broomhouse Lane

Sulivan Road

Hurlingham Square

Hurlingham Club Grounds

Hurlingham Club Gardens

Carnwath Road

Wandsworth

| 0.25 mile | 0.25 km |

River Thames

Parson's Green

You know you're in a classy neighbourhood when the kebab house (Kebab Kid) gets people travelling across London. Things here aren't cheap and you may be unnerved by all the people saying "terrific!" with their collars up. But they don't bite (despite their formidable buck teeth) so relax and enjoy a beer in the White Horse, known as the Sloaney Pony, or heavenly Sunday brunch at Duke on the Green.

Coffee

• **Starbucks** • 95 Wandsworth Bridge Rd

Nightlife

• **Amuse Bouche** • 51 Parson's Green Lane
• **Duke on the Green** • 235 New Kings Road
• **The White Horse** • Parson's Green

Restaurants

• **Kebab Kid** • 90 New Kings Road

Supermarkets

• **Tesco** • 601 King's Rd

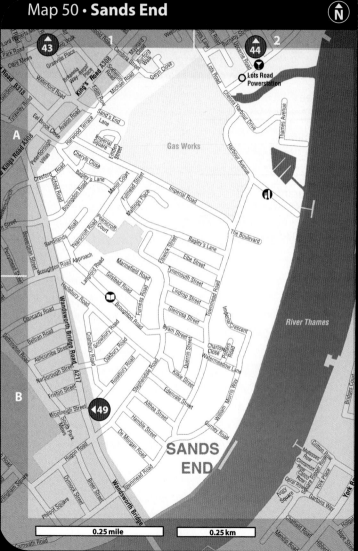
Map 50 · **Sands End**

Sands End

Ask any Londoner where Sand's End resides and you will get blank looks or possibly a bemused 'you wot?' Go on, try it now, stop the nearest person and ask for Sand's End. The reason they don't know is because there's sod all there. Perhaps it's a cartographer's idea of a joke. Hilarious. One for fans of Industrial estates and Gas works only.

O Landmarks
• **Lots Road Power Station** • Lots Rd

Libraries
• **Sands End Library** • 59 Broughton Rd

Nightlife
• **606 Club** • 90 Lots Rd

Restaurants
• **Deep** • The Boulevard, Imperial Wharf

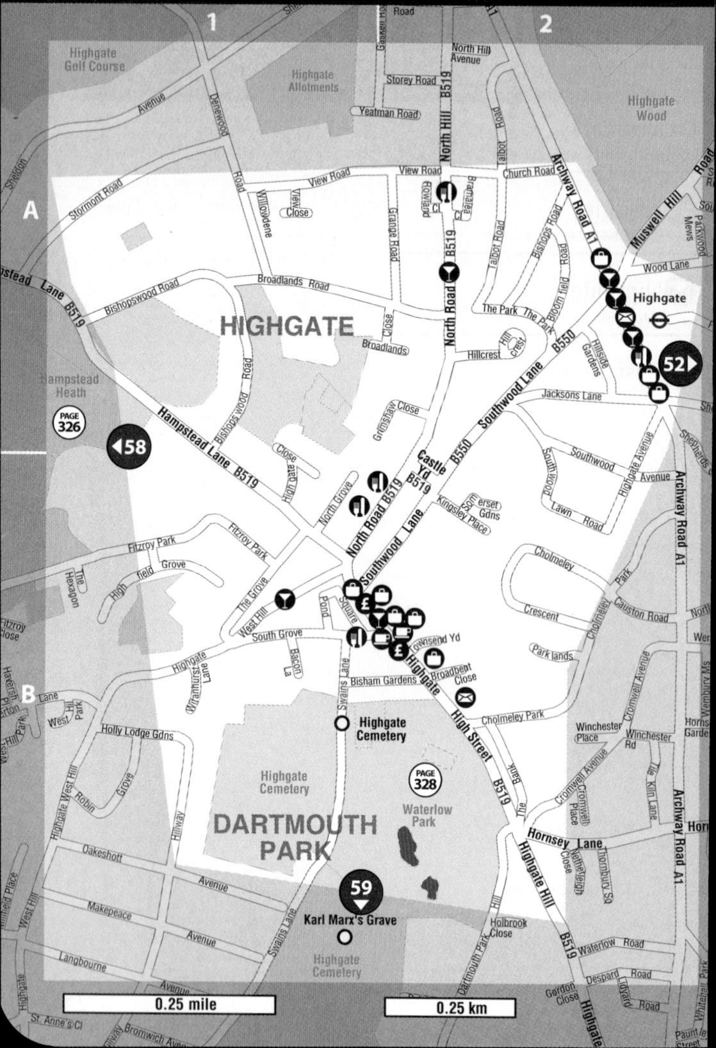

Map 51 · **Highgate**

N

1

2

Highgate
Golf Course

Greswell Road

North Hill Avenue

Storey Road

Denewood Road

Avenue

Highgate
Allotments

Yeatman Road

North Hill B519

Talbot Road

Church Road

Highgate
Wood

Muswell Hill Road

Park House Mews

A

Stormont Road

View Road

View Road

Rowland Cl

Grange Road

Willowdene

Bloomfield Rd

Bishops Rd

The Park

Wood Lane

Highgate

Road

Bishopswood Road

Broadlands Road

Close

North Road B519

Hillcrest

Hillside Gardens

52

HIGHGATE

Broadlands

Close

Southwood Lane

Jacksons Lane

mpstead Lane B519

Hampstead Lane B519

PAGE
326

58

High Gate

North Grove

Grovelands Close

Castle Yd
B519

Southwood Lane B550

Merton
Lane

Southwood Avenue

Southwood Avenue

Shepherd's Hill

Archway Road A1

Hampstead
Heath

Fitzroy Park

Fitzroy Park

The Grove

Field Grove

North Road B519

Kingsley Place

Somerset Gdns

Lawn Road

Cholmeley Park

Gaston Road

Archway Road A1

Fitzroy
Close

The Hexagon

West Hill

South Grove

The Grove

Swains Lane

Southwood Lane

Gainsend Yd

Broadbent Close

Cholmeley
Crescent

Park lands

North

West Hill

Holly Lodge Gdns

Bisham Gardens

High Street

Cholmeley Park

Winchester
Place

Winchester
Rd

Horns
Garde

B

Lane

West Hill

Highgate West Hill

Robin Grove

Hillway

Highgate
Cemetery

Highgate
Cemetery

PAGE
328

Waterlow
Park

King

Cromwell Avenue

Cromwell Place

Hornsey Lane

Southwood Lane

Highgate Hill

Makepeace Oakeshott

Avenue

Avenue

Langbourne

DARTMOUTH
PARK

59

Karl Marx's Grave

Highgate
Cemetery

Holbrook
Close

Waterloo Road

Gordon
Close

Despard Road

St. Anne's Cl

0.25 mile

0.25 km

Bromwich Avenue

Get your fix of village life here. Sample quaint local shops (The Corner Shop) on the High Street or a selection of book, music, and charity shops on the grittier Archway Road side. There's plenty of food options, but for the true Highgate experience head to The Flask for great modern pub grub and drinks. For nightlife The Boogaloo is the local hipster venue of choice.

 ## £Banks

• **Barclays** • 56 Highgate High St
• **Lloyds** • 51 Highgate High St

 ## Coffee

• **Caffe Nero** • 62 Highgate High St
• **Costa** • 66 Highgate High St

O Landmarks

• **Highgate Cemetery** • 1 Swain's Lane
• **Karl Marx's grave** • Highgate Cemetry

Nightlife

• **The Boogaloo** • 312 Archway Rd
• **The Flask** • 77 Highgate West Hill
• **Highgate Inn** • 385 Archway Rd
• **Prince Of Wales** • 53 Highgate High St
• **The Woodman** • 414 Archway Rd
• **The Wrestlers** • 98 North Rd

Post Offices

• **Highgate High St** • 7 Highgate High St
• **Highgate Near Station** • 361 Archway Rd

Restaurants

• **The Bull** • 13 North Hill Ave
• **Cafe Rouge** • 6 South Grove
• **Kiplings** • 100 North Rd
• **Papa Del's** • 347 Archway Rd
• **Red Lion And Sun** • 25 N Rd

Shopping

• **The Corner Shop** • 88 Highgate High St
• **Dragonfly Wholefoods** • 24 Highgate High Street
• **Highgate Butchers** • 76 Highgate High St
• **Le Chocolatier** • 78 Highgate High St
• **Oxfam Bookshop, Highgate** • 47 Highgate High St
• **Second Layer Records** • 323 Archway Rd
• **Sound 323** • 323 Archway Rd
• **Wild Guitar** • 393 Archway Road

Map 52 · **Archway (North)**

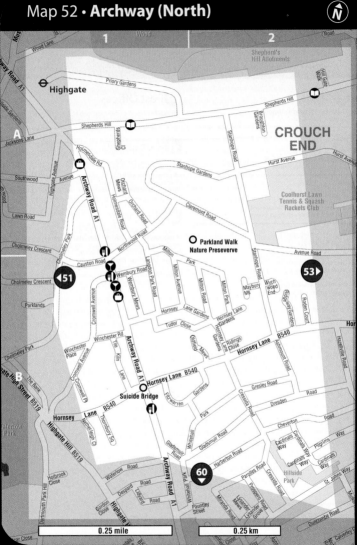

Archway (North)

Map 52

Estate agents will hate the fact that we've dubbed the area between posh Highgate and Crouch End 'Archway North' and Archway Road is a grimy, gritty thoroughfare for an area with so much cash sloshing on either side. Nevertheless it's dotted with jewels like no-nonsense pub The Winchester and the distinctly odd Caipirinha Jazz Bar.

O Landmarks

- **Parkland Walk Nature Reserve** • Parkland Walk
- **Suicide Bridge** • Hornsey Lane

Libraries

- **London Mennonite Centre Library** • 14 Shepherds Hill Heights

Nightlife

- **Caipirinha Jazz Bar** • 177 Archway Rd
- **The Winchester Pub Hotel** • 206 Archway Rd

Restaurants

- **Bengal Berties** • 172 Archway Rd
- **Fahrenheit** • 230 Archway Rd
- **The Lighthouse** • 179 Archway Rd

Shopping

- **Archway Video** • 220 Archway Rd
- **Magic Carpet** • 248 Archway Rd

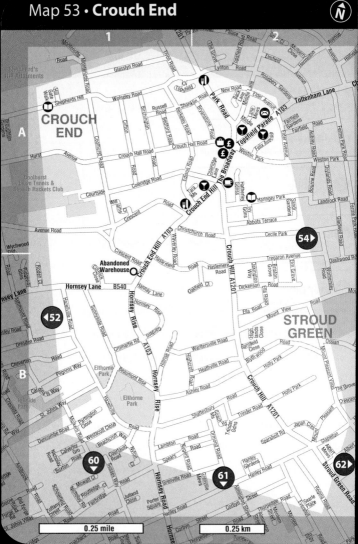

Map 53 · **Crouch End**

Crouch End

Crouch End was nominated in the famous "Crap Towns" book a few years ago under the heading "The Tyranny Of Pesto." Which is a neat way of saying that it's a nice, middle class place with baby-buggies jack-knifing along the crowded streets in front of numerous mid-priced restaurants. Check out Banners cafe if you don't mind people being cheerful at breakfast or Thaitanic if you don't mind terrible puns.

Banks

• **Barclays** • 8 The Broadway
• **Lloyds** • 34 The Broadway

Coffee

• **Starbucks** • 7 The Broadway

O Landmarks

• **Abandoned Warehouse** • Parkland Walk

Libraries

• **Highgate Library** • Shepherds Hill
• **Hornsey Library** • Haringey Park

Nightlife

• **Harringay Arms** • 153 Crouch Hill
• **Queens Pub & Dining Rooms** • 26 Broadway Parade
• **The Wishing Well** • 22 Topsfield Parade, Tottenham Lane

Post Offices

• **Crouch End** • 28 Topsfield Parade

Restaurants

• **Banners** • 21 Park Rd
• **Hot Pepper Jelly** • 11 Broadway Parade
• **Thaitanic** • 66 Crouch End Hill

Shopping

• **Haelen Centre** • 41 Broadway
• **Walter Purkis And Sons** • 17 The Broadway

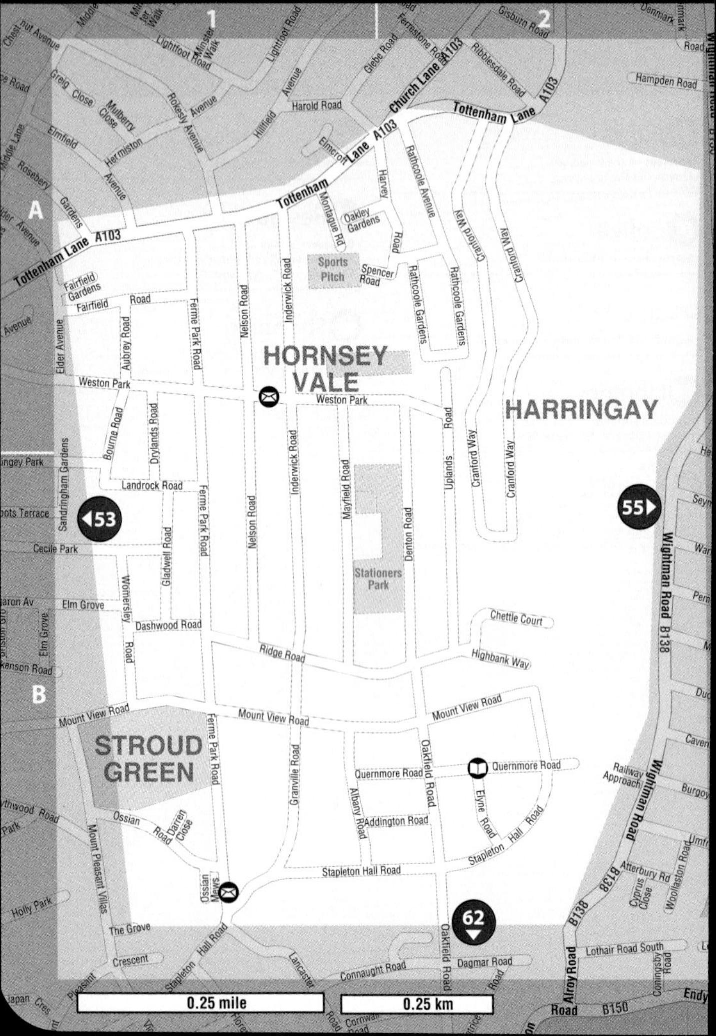

Map 54 · **Hornsey**

N

1
2

Chestnut Avenue
Modus Walk
Lightfoot Road
Lightfoot Road
Glebe Road
Ferrestone Road
Gisburn Road
Denmark
Road

Greig Close
Mulberry Close
Rosslyn Avenue
Hinfield
Harold Road
Church Lane
Tottenham Lane A103
Ribblesdale Road
A103
Hampden Road

Wightman Road B138

Elmfield
Hermiston
Avenue
Tottenham Lane A103
Elmore Lane
Montague Rd
Harvey
Rathcoole Avenue
Cranford Way

Roseberry
Avenue

A
Tottenham Lane A103
Fairfield
Gardens
Fairfield
Road
Oakley
Gardens
Road
Spencer
Road
Rathcoole Gardens

Elder Avenue
Weston Park
Ferme Park Road
Nelson Road
Aubrey Road
Inderwick Road
Sports
Pitch
Rathcoole Gardens
Cranford Gardens

**HORNSEY
VALE**
HARRINGAY

Bourne Road
Drylands Road
✉
Weston Park
Road
Cranford Way
Cranford Way

Landrock Road
Ferme Park Road
Gladwell Road
Inderwick Road
Mayfield Road
Uplands Road

Sandringham Gardens
◄**53**
Cecile Park
Nelson Road
Denton Road
55►

Elm Grove
Womersley Road
Dashwood Road
Ridge Road
**Stationers
Park**
Chettle Court

Highbank Way

B
Mount View Road
Mount View Road
Mount View Road

**STROUD
GREEN**
Ferme Park Road
Granville Road
Oakfield Road
Quernmore Road
🚇 Quernmore Road

Ossian Road
Darren Close
Albany Road
Eyne Road
Railway Approach

Mount Pleasant Villas
Addington Road
Stapleton Hall Road
Stapleton Hall

Holly Park
✉
The Grove
Crescent
Connaught Road
Oakfield Road
62▼
Dagmar Road
Alroy Road
Lothair Road South

0.25 mile
0.25 km

B150

People who live here will probably say they live in Crouch End or Stroud Green. Partly because it sounds better and partly because most people have no idea where Hornsey is. It's an area bullied on all sides by bigger, brasher neighbourhoods like middle class Crouch End and gritty Green Lanes with the locals taking refuge in ferociously unpretentious pubs like The Wishing Well (Map 53).

Libraries
• **Stroud Green Library** • Quernmore Rd

Post Offices
• **Ferme Park Rd** • 4 Ferme Park Rd
• **Weston Park** • 89 Weston Park

Map 55 • Harringay Ladder

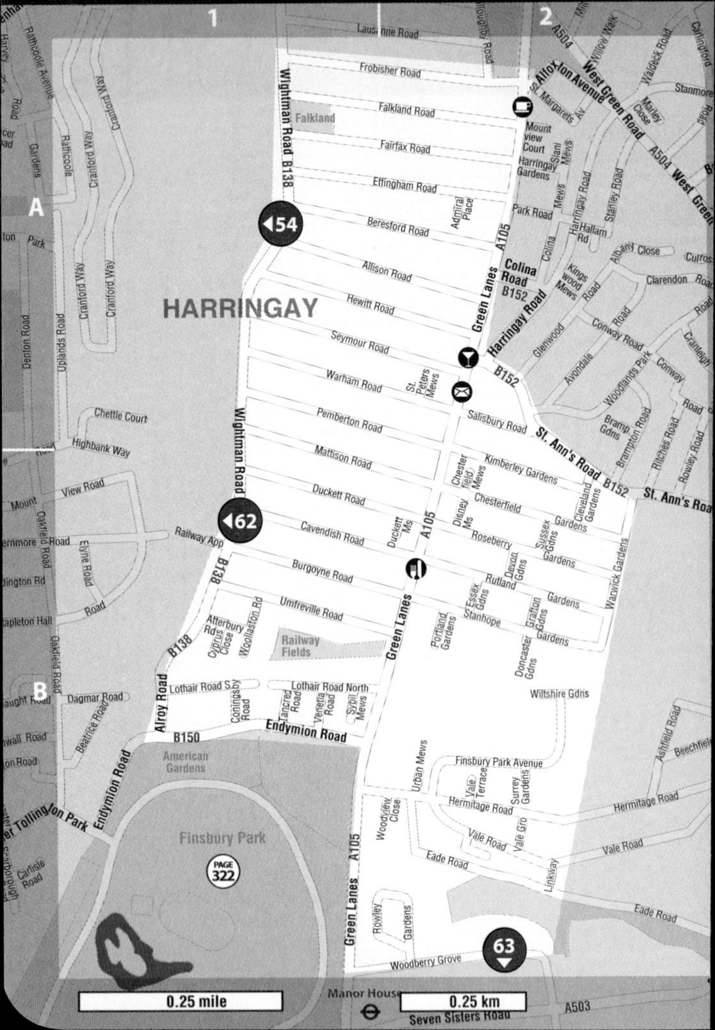

1
2
A
B
HARRINGAY
Lausanne Road
Frobisher Road
Falkland Road
Falkland
Fairfax Road
Effingham Road
Beresford Road
Allison Road
Hewitt Road
Seymour Road
Warham Road
Pemberton Road
Mattison Road
Duckett Road
Cavendish Road
Burgoyne Road
Umfreville Road
Wightman Road B138
Wightman Road
B138
54
62
63
Green Lanes
A105
Colina Road
B152
Harringay Road
Mount view Court
Harringay Gardens
Slani Mews
Park Road
Admiral Place
St. Peters Mews
Salisbury Road
St. Ann's Road
Kimberley Gardens
Chesterfield Mews
Chesterfield Gardens
Disney Ms
Duckett Ms
Roseberry Gardens
Sussex Gdns
Cleveland Gardens
Devon Gdns
Rutland Gardens
Essex Gdns
Stanhope Gardens
Grafton Gdns
Portland Gardens
Doncaster Gdns
Warwick Gardens
Wiltshire Gdns
Railway Fields
Atterbury Rd
Cyprus Close
Woollaston Rd
Alroy Road
Lothair Road South
Lothair Road North
Coningsby Road
Tancred Road
Venetia Road
Sybil Mews
Endymion Road
B150
American Gardens
Finsbury Park
PAGE 322
Urban Mews
Finsbury Park Avenue
Vale Terrace
Surrey Gardens
Hermitage Road
Vale Road
Vale Grove
Eade Road
Linkway
Woodview Close
Rowley Gardens
Woodberry Grove
Manor House
Seven Sisters Road
A503
A504
Alroy Avenue
St. Margarets Av
West Green Road
Willow Walk
Waldeck Road
Marley Close
Stanmore Road
Carlingford
Harringay Road
Stanley Road
Hallam Rd
Colina Mews
Albany Close
Kings wood Mews
Kingswood Road
Clarendon Road
Glenwood Road
Avondale Road
Conway Road
Woodlands Park Road
Cranleigh
Bramp Gdns
Brampton Road
Ritches Road
Rowley Road
Ashfield Road
Beechfield
Rathcoole Avenue
Rathcoole Gardens
Cranford Way
Uplands Road
Denton Road
Chettle Court
Highbank Way
View Road
Railway App
Oakfield Road
Etyne Road
Dagmar Road
Beatrice Road
Endymion Road
Tollington Park
Carlisle Road
0.25 mile
0.25 km

One of the only places in the world where Turks, Turkish Cypriots and Greek Cypriots live together happily, a stroll up Green Lanes means two things: eating and drinking. Any of the little Cypriot or Turkish restaurants will fill you handsomely but check out Sofra for real family fayre or just try doing a 'meze crawl' up the ladder! Alcoholic respite can be found in the grand Salisbury.

 Coffee
- **Cafe Delight** - 351 Green Lanes

 Nightlife
- **The Salisbury** - 1 Grand Parade, Green Lanes

 Post Offices
- **Harringay** - 509 Green Lanes

 Restaurants
- **Sofra** - 421 Green Lanes

Map 56 · **Hampstead Village**

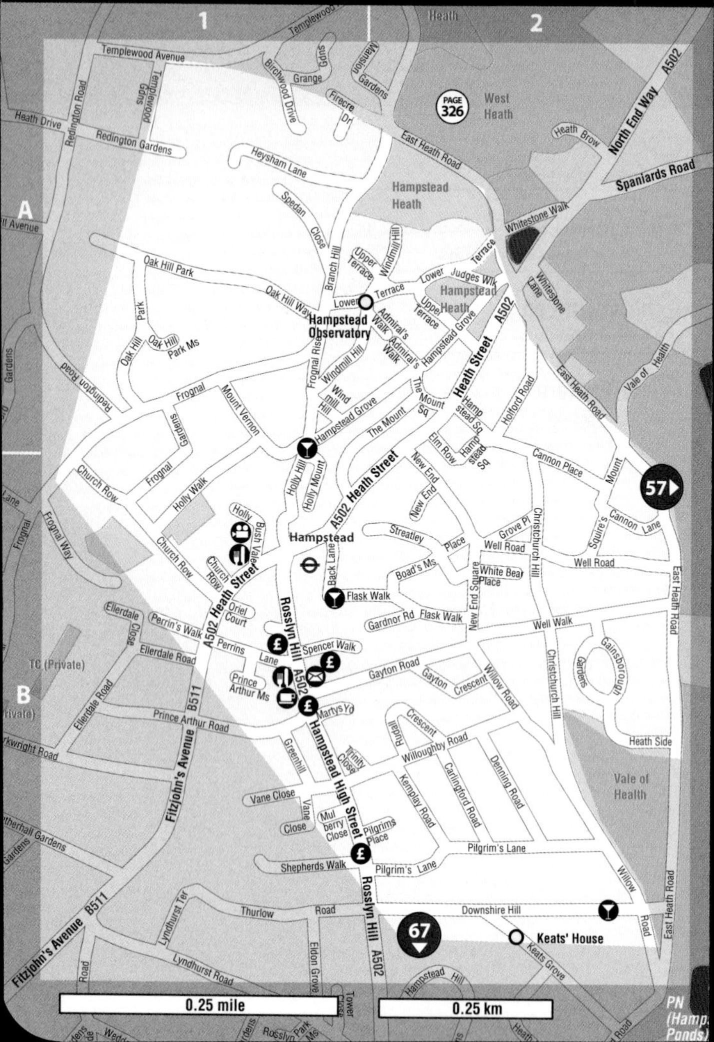

N

1 2

Templewood Gdns

Heath

Templewood Avenue

Brickwood Drive

Grange

Firecrest Dr

Redington Road

Heath Drive

Heath Gates

Pilgrims Pl

PAGE
326

West
Heath

North End Way A502

Heath Brow

Redington Gardens

Spaniards Road

East Heath Road

Heysham Lane

Hampstead
Heath

Heath Drive

A Avenue

Spedin Close

Oak Hill Park

Oak Hill Way

Branch Hill

Upper
Terrace

Lower Terrace

Terrace

Judges Wlk

Whitestone Walk

Hampstead
Heath

Whitestone
Lane

Oak Hill Park

Frognal Gardens

Oak Hill

Oak Hill Park Ms

Redington Road

Lower
Terrace

Hampstead
Observatory

Admiral's
Walk

Admiral's Wlk

Upper
Terrace

Hampstead Grove

Heath Street A502

East Heath Road

Vale of Health

Gardens

Lane

Frognal Way

Church Row

Frognal

Mount Vernon

Holly Bush Hill

Windmill Hill

Hampstead Grove

The Mount

The Mount

Hamp
stead
Sq

Hollybush
Sq

Holford Rd

New End

Cannon Place

Mount

57

Holly Walk

Holly
Mount

Back Lane

Streatley
Place

Boad's Ms

New End
Square

Grove Pl

Well Road

Christchurch Hill

Squire's
Mount

Cannon
Lane

Cannon Place

Well Road

East Heath Road

Church Row

Holly
Berry
Lane

Prospect
Pl

Oriel
Court

Hampstead

Flask Walk

White Bear
Place

Well Walk

Gainsborough
Gardens

Ellerdale Road

Perrin's Walk

Perrins
Lane

Spencer Walk

Gaynor Rd

Flask Walk

Gardens

Church
Row

Heath Street A502

Rosslyn Hill A502

Prince
Arthur Ms

Prince Arthur Road B511

Gayton Road

Gayton
Crescent

Willow Road

Heath Side

Vale of
Health

Ellerdale Close

Ellerdale Road

Perrin's Walk

TC (Private)

Martyrs Yd

St Mary's

Greenhill

Fitzjohn's Avenue B511

Hampstead High Street

Rosslyn Hill A502

Crescent

Willoughby Road

Kemplay Road

Carlingford Road

Denning Road

Christchurch Hill

Vane Close

Willow Road

Kingswell Vane Close

Mul
berry
Close

Pilgrims
Place

Pilgrim's
Lane

Pilgrim's Lane

Aberdare Gardens

Fitzjohn's Avenue

Arkwright Road

(Private)

Lyndhurst Ter

Shepherds Walk

Shepherds Walk

Thurlow
Road

Eldon
Grove

67

Downshire Hill

Keats' House

Willow Road

East Heath Road

Fitzjohn's Avenue B511

Lyndhurst Road

Hampstead Hill Gdns

Rosslyn Hill A502

Wedderburn Rd

Rosslyn Park Ms

Tower
Close

PN
(Hamp.
Ponds)

0.25 mile 0.25 km

Hampstead Village

Map 56

Leafy Hampstead Village is as genteel and calm as you're going to get. It's a literary, suburban place where Ye Olde England has been commodified and sold back to the yuppies, but there's still quiet pleasures to be had. Louis Patisserie is great for cakes and the Holly Bush is a quaint 17th Century oaky heaven. Keats wrote Ode To a Nightingale about some bird around here.

£ Banks

• **Barclays** • 28 Hampstead High St
• **HSBC** • 12 Hampstead High St
• **Lloyds** • 40 Rosslyn Hill
• **NatWest** • 25 Hampstead High St

Cinemas

• **Everyman Cinema Club** • 5 Hollybush Vale

Coffee

• **Caffe Nero** • 1 Hampstead High St

O Landmarks

• **Hampstead Observatory** • Lower Terrace
• **Keats' House** • Keats Grove

Nightlife

• **The Flask** • 14 Flask Walk
• **The Freemasons Arms** • 32 Downshire Hill
• **Holly Bush** • 22 Holly Mount

Post Offices

• **Hampstead** • 79 Hampstead High St

Restaurants

• **La Creperie De Hampstead** • 77 Hampstead High St
• **The Louis Patisserie** • 32 Heath St

117

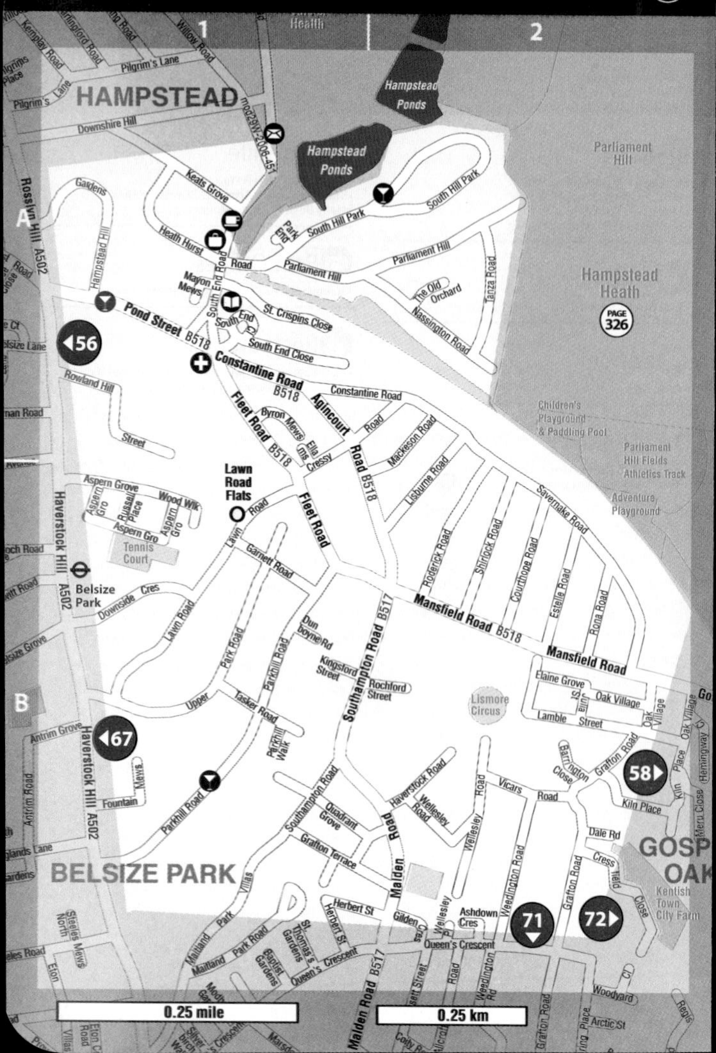

Map 57 · **Hampstead Heath**

HAMPSTEAD

Hampstead Heath

Hampstead Ponds

Hampstead Ponds

Parliament Hill

Hampstead Heath

PAGE 326

Pilgrim's Lane

Willow Road

Pilgrim's Place

Downshire Hill

Keats Grove

Thurlow Road B511

South Hill Park

Rosslyn Hill A502

Gardens

Heath Hurst

Road

Keats Grove

Downshire Hill

Rd

Heathurst

Maryon

Mews

Parliament Hill

Parliament Hill

The Old Orchard

Nassington Road

Tanza Road

Pond Street B518

South End

St. Crispins Close

South End

South End Close

Children's Playground & Paddling Pool

◀**56**

Rowland Hill

Street

Constantine Road

B518

Byron Mews

Ella

Cressy

Fleet Road

B518

Constantine Road

Agincourt

Road

Mackeson Road

Lisburne Road

Cahill Road

Parliament Hill Fields Athletics Track

Adventure Playground

Haverstock Hill A502

Aspern Grove

Aspern Gro

Wood Wk

Lawn Road Flats

Fleet Road

Rudall Road

Tennis Court

Belsize Park

Downside Cres

Garnett Road

Roderick Road

Shirlock Road

Courthope Road

Estelle Road

Savernake Road

Rona Road

Lamble Mews

Lawn Road

Dun Bonnet Rd

Kingsford Street

Rochford Street

Southampton Road B517

Mansfield Road B518

Mansfield Road

Elaine Grove

Oak Village

Lamble Street

Lismore Circus

Dalby Village

◀**67**

Upper Park

Tasker Road

Parkhill Road

Parkhill Walk

Haverstock Hill A502

Antrim Grove

Antrim Road

Mews

Fountain

Parkhill Road

Southampton Road

Quadrant Grove

Wellesley Road

Weedington Road

Vicars

Road

Barrington Road

Grafton Road

Grafton Close

Kiln Place

Dale Rd

Cressy

Grafton

Road

Cressy Close

Kentish Town City Farm

GOSP OAK

58▶

BELSIZE PARK

Grafton Terrace

Malden Road

Herbert St

Garden

Weedington Rd

Ashdown Cres

Queen's Crescent

Malden Road B517

71▼

72▶

Maitland Park Villas

Maitland Park Road

Herbert St

Bassett Street

Queen's Crescent

Malden Street

Weedington Road

Grafton Road

Woodyard

| 0.25 mile | 0.25 km |

It might not be quite as posh as Hampstead Village but the streets to the south of the wonderful heath still have all the advantages of the area—the chance to nip into the woods and have sex with George Michael if one wishes (always ask first), browse in Daunt Books or hang out in nice pubs like The Magdala or Monkey Chews.

Coffee
• **Starbucks** • 5 S End Rd

 Emergency Rooms
• **Royal Free Hospital** • Pond St

O Landmarks
• **Lawn Road Flats** • Lawn Rd

Libraries
• **Heath Library** • Keats Grove

Nightlife
• **The Magdala** • 2 South Hill Park
• **Monkey Chews** • 2 Queen's Crescent
• **Roebuck** • 15 Pond St

Post Offices
• **Hampstead Heath** • 65 S End Rd

Shopping
• **Daunt Books** • 51 S End Rd

Map 58 • **Parliament Hill / Dartmouth Park**

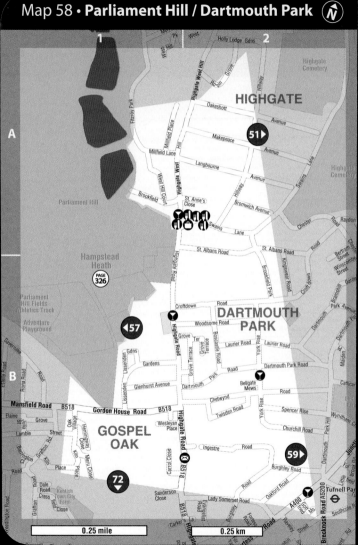

Map 58

Mainly a leafy residential area, but there's a bunch of good eateries around Swain's Lane/Highgate West Hill. Try Kalendar for a variety of all-day brekkies or Al Parco for their excellent pizzas. Locals get provisions from Corks and picnic on the Heath. If it wasn't for the rough (but gradually improving) Duke of St Albans pub you could almost forget you're in London.

Nightlife

- **Bar Lorca** • 156 Fortress Rd
- **The Bull and Last** • 168 Highgate Rd
- **The Dartmouth Arms** • 35 York Rise
- **Duke of St. Albans** • Highgate Road

Post Offices

• **Highgate Rd** • 111 Highgate Rd

Restaurants

- **Al Parco** • 2 Highgate West Hill
- **Cafe Mozart** • 17 Swain's Ln
- **Kalendar** • 15 Swains Lane

Shopping

• **Corks** • 9 Swain's Ln

Map 59 · **Tufnell Park**

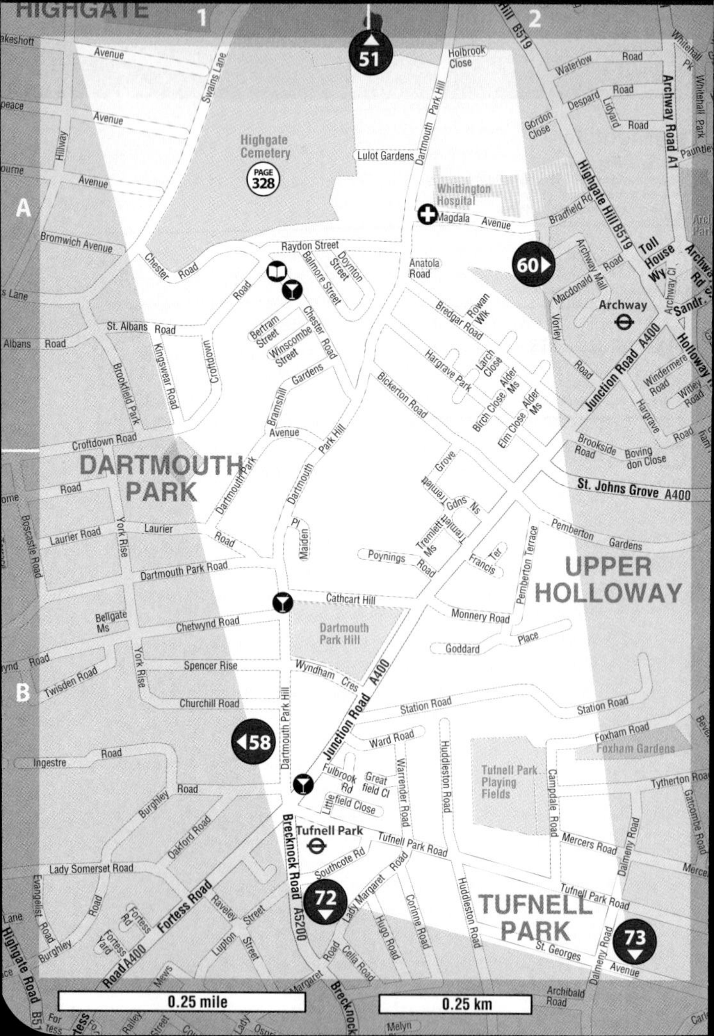

HIGHGATE

1   2

N

Avenue

Swains Lane

Holbrook Close

Waterlow   Road

51

Despard   Road   Gordon   Road

skeshott

peace

Avenue

Avenue

Hilway

ourne

Avenue

A

Bromwich Avenue

Highgate
Cemetery
PAGE
328

Lulot Gardens

Whittington
Hospital

Magdala

Avenue

Anatola
Road

60▶

Archway Road A1

Toll
House
Wy

Archway

Sandr.

Chester   Road

St. Albans   Road

Raydon Street

Bredgar Road

Rowan Wlk

Kingswear Road

Croftdown

Bertram
Street

Winscombe
Street

Chester Road Gardens

Hargrave Park

Larch
Cl

Alder
Ms

Birch Close

Elm Close Ms

Alder
Ms

Archway Mall

MacDonald's

Vorley

Junction Road A400

Windermere
Road

Witley
Road

Hargrave   Road

Albans   Road

Brookfield Park

Bramshill

Avenue

Bickerton Road

Grove

Brookside

Boving
don Close

St. Johns Grove A400

Croftdown Road

Road

DARTMOUTH
PARK

Dartmouth Park

Dartmouth   Park Hill

Laurier Road

Laurier

Dartmouth   Park   Road

Maiden   Pl

Tremlett
Ms

Gdns Ns

Grove

Tremlett
Gdns

Francis   Ter

Pemberton   Terrace

Pemberton   Gardens

UPPER
HOLLOWAY

Poynings

Francis
Place

orie

Bossante Road

York Rise

Belligate
Ms

Chetwynd Road

Cathcart Hill

Dartmouth
Park Hill

Monnery Road

Goddard

ynd   Road

B

Twisden Road

Spencer Rise

Churchill Road

Wyndham   Cres

Junction Road A400

Station Road

Station Road

Ward Road

Foxham Road

Foxham Gardens

58◀

Ingestre   Road

Burghley   Road

Oakford Road

Dartmouth Park Hill

Breaknock Road A5200

Fulbrook
Rd

Great
field Cl

Warrender Road

Linfield Close

Tufnell Park

Tufnell Park Road

Huddleston Road

Tufnell Park
Playing
Fields

Campdale   Road

Mercers   Road

Tytherton Road

Dalmeny   Road

Merc

Lady Somerset Road

Fortess Road A400

Raveley   Street

Lupton   Street

72

Southcote Rd

Lady   Margaret   Road

Hugo Road

Cardine   Rd

Celia Road

Huddleston Road

TUFNELL
PARK

Tufnell Park Road

Dalmeny   Avenue

St. Georges

73

Highgate Road B5

Fortess Road A400

Breaknock Road A5200

Archibald   Road

Melyn

| 0.25 mile | | 0.25 km |

Map 59

Surrounded by the rougher Archway, Kentish Town, and Holloway—and immortalised by Simon Pegg in cult comedies Spaced and Shaun of the Dead—unassuming Tufnell Park has been quietly fashionable for years. Keep it low key here—vaguely recognising 'that bloke off the telly' supping an ale in the Star, or taking in an unknown band at upstairs at The Boston.

Emergency Rooms
• **Whittington Hospital** • Magdala Ave

Libraries
• **Highgate Library** • Chester Rd

Nightlife
• **Boston Arms** • 178 Junction Rd
• **The Lord Palmerston** • 33 Dartmouth Park Hill
• **The Star** • 47 Chester Rd

Map 60 · Archway

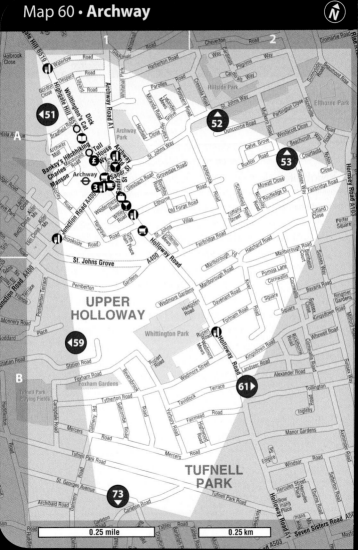

Dirty and more than a little rough around the edges, Archway is generally pretty low on the fun scale. Most of the pubs are of the "old man" variety and not terribly exciting. But, it's not all bad and if nothing else there's at least some good eatin' around. RRC Thai never disappoints and the meze at Archgate Café is simply spectacular.

Banks

• **Lloyds** • 19 Highgate Hill

Coffee

• **Cafe Metro** • 4 Junction Rd

O Landmarks

• **Banksy's Hitchhiking Charles Manson** • Tally Ho Corner (off Highgate Hill)
• **Dick Whittington's Cat** • Highgate Hill

Libraries

• **Archway Library** • Highgate Hill

Nightlife

• **Archway Tavern** • 1 Archway Close
• **The Mother Red Cap** • 665 Holloway Rd

Restaurants

• **Archgate Café** • 5 Junction Rd
• **Junction Café** • 61 Junction Rd
• **Kingfisher** • 657 Holloway Rd
• **Mosaic Café** • 24 Junction Rd
• **Nid Ting** • 533 Holloway Rd
• **RRC Thai Café** • 36 Highgate Hill
• **St Johns** • 91 Junction Rd
• **The Toll Gate** • 6 Archway Close

Shopping

• **Pure Groove Records** • 679 Holloway Rd

Supermarkets

• **Co-Op** • 11 Junction Rd
• **Sainsbury's** • 643 Holloway Rd

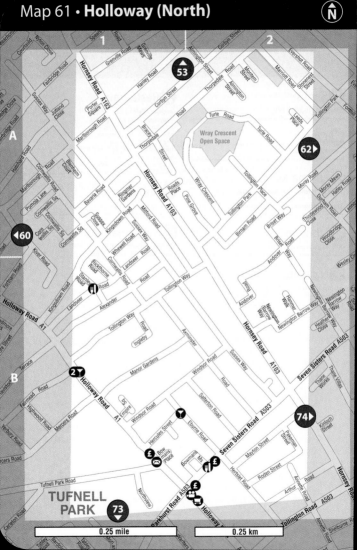

Map 61 · **Holloway (North)**

Holloway (North)

The borough of Islington, in which north Holloway sits, is supposed to be either a byword for liberal middle class cosiness or else grim inner city deprivation, depending on who you talk to. This bit has neither. Instead it's got one very nice pub, (The Swimmer), a slightly pretentious pub (Nambucca), and lots of very ordinary residential streets.

Map 61

£ Banks

- **Barclays** • 403 Holloway Rd
- **Halifax** • 19 Seven Sisters Rd
- **NatWest** • 490 Holloway Rd

Cinemas

- **Odeon Holloway** • 419 Holloway Rd

Nightlife

- **Nambucca** • 596 Holloway Rd
- **The Quays** • 471 Holloway Rd
- **The Swimmer** • 13 Eburne Rd

Post Offices

- **Halloway** • 482 Holloway Rd

Restaurants

- **The Landseer** • 37 Landseer Rd
- **Pasteleiro** • 22 Seven Sisters Rd

Shopping

- **Michael's Fruiterers** • 56 Seven Sisters Rd

Supermarkets

- **Iceland** • 442 Holloway Rd

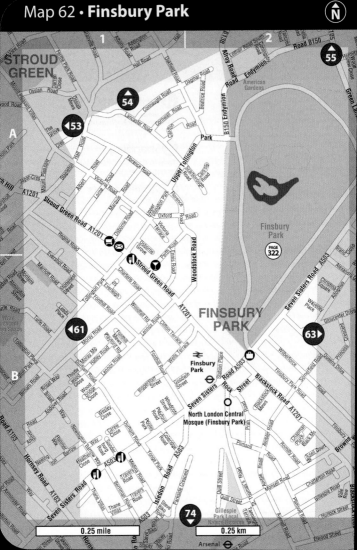

Map 62

'Let's move to Finsbury Park,' newcomers say, 'why it's so near a park, a tube, AND a station.' Then they get here. But there are twinkles—the park café, and the infamous mosque now doing community outreach. Head to the Faltering Fullback for a pint, Petek for Turkish, the Happening Bagel Bakery for—well you know—or run the gauntlet of Blackstock Road for bundles of mint and tasty lamachun.

O Landmarks
- **North London Central Mosque (Finsbury Park)** • 7 St Thomas's Rd

Nightlife
- **Faultering Fullback** • 19 Perth Rd

Post Offices
- **Stroud Green Rd** • 97 Stroud Green Rd

Restaurants
- **Fassika** • 152 Seven Sisters Rd
- **Le Rif** • 172 Seven Sisters Rd
- **Petek** • 96 Stroud Green Rd

Shopping
- **The Happening Bagel Bakery** • 284 Seven Sisters Rd

Supermarkets
- **Tesco** • 105 Stroud Green Rd

Map 63 · **Manor House**

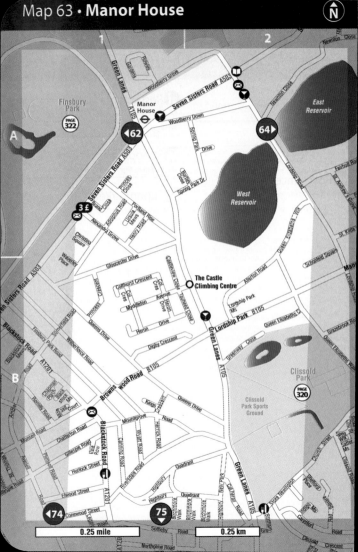

Don't hang out near the 'scummy round the edges' station as it can get pretty gruesome at night, particularly round the horrific Manor Club. You might chance upon a warehouse party round here, but walk south, dodge the rats around the reservoir, admire the faux turrets of the Castle Climbing Centre and head to the New River Cafe for great fry ups with views over the leafy oasis of Clissold Park.

 Banks

• **Abbey** • 304 7 Sisters Rd
• **Barclays** • 254 7 Sisters Rd
• **HSBC** • 312 7 Sisters Rd

o Landmarks

• **The Castle Climbing Centre** • Green Lanes

 Libraries

• **Woodberry Down Library** • 440 7 Sisters Rd

 Nightlife

• **The Blarney Stone** • 89 Woodberry Grove
• **The Brownswood Park Tavern** • 271 Green Lanes
• **Manor Club** • 277 Seven Sisters Rd

⊠ Post Offices

• **Blackstock Rd** • 149 Blackstock Rd
• **Finsbury Park** • 290 7 Sisters Rd
• **Woodberry Grove** • 107 Woodberry Grove

🍴 Restaurants

• **Il Bacio** • 178 Blackstock Rd
• **New River Café** • 271 Stoke Newington Church St

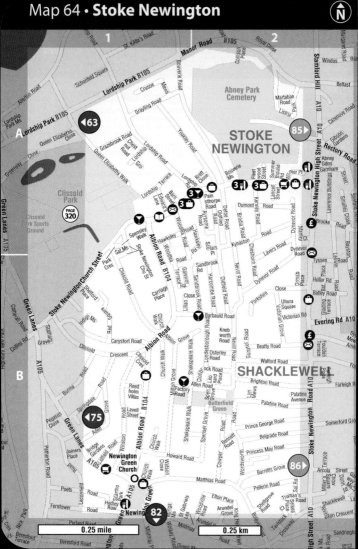

Famed for its high square footage of creative types and three-wheeled buggies, this buzzing villagey 'hood has lost a lot of its Hackney edge but still has the odd shooting to keep locals on their toes. Perfect Guinness (Auld Shillelagh), curry (Rasa), Sunday roast (Rose and Crown), and silver jewelry (Metal Crumble) to be found along mainly chain-free Stoke Newington Church Street.

£ Banks

• **Abbey** • 139 Stoke Newington Rd
• **Lloyds** • 133 Stoke Newington High St

O Landmarks

• **Newington Green Church** • 39 Newington Green

Libraries

• **Stoke Newington Library** • Stoke Newington Church St

Nightlife

• **Auld Shillelagh** • 105 Stoke Newington Church St
• **The Lion** • 132 Stoke Newington Church St
• **Londesborough** • 36 Barbauld Rd
• **Rose and Crown** • 199 Stoke Newington Church St
• **Ryan's Bar** • 181 Stoke Newington Church St
• **The Shakespeare** • 57 Allen Rd

Post Offices

• **Church Street** • 170 Stoke Newington Church St
• **Stoke Newington** • Stoke Newington High St
• **Stoke Newington Rd** • 133 Stoke Newington Rd

Restaurants

• **56** • 56 Newington Green
• **Anglo Asian** • 60 Stoke Newington Church St
• **Blue Legume** • 101 Stoke Newington Church St
• **Rasa N16** • 55 Stoke Newington Church St
• **Three Crowns** • 175 Stoke Newington Church St
• **Yum Yum** • 187 Stoke Newington High St

Shopping

• **Ark** • 161 Stoke Newington High St
• **The Beaucatcher Salon** •
  44 Stoke Newington Church Street
• **Belle Epoque Boulangerie** • 37 Newington Green
• **Bridgewood & Neitzert** • 146 Stoke Newington Church St
• **Metal Crumble** • 13 Stoke Newington Church St
• **Ribbons and Taylor** • 157 Stoke Newington Church St
• **Route 73 Kids** • 92 Stoke Newington Church St
• **S'graffiti** • 172 Stoke Newington Church St
• **Sacred Art** • 148 Albion Rd
• **The Spence** • 161 Stoke Newington Church St

Supermarkets

• **Fresh & Wild** • 32 Stoke Newington Church St
• **Iceland** • 17 Green Lanes

Map 65 · **West Hampstead**

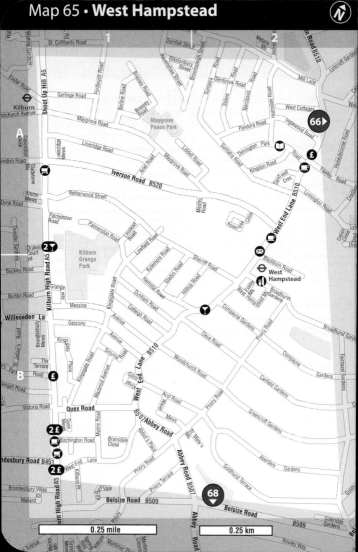

Hampstead's ugly sister, West Hampstead is a leafy suburb that has absorbed some of Kilburn's grittiness. Young urban nomads make up much of the population, as rent is moderate by London standards. Like the rest of London, West Hampstead has its fair share of Caffe Neros and Costa Coffees, but check out the Green Room for atmosphere and The Good Ship for music.

£Banks

- **Barclays** • 83 Kilburn High Rd
- **Barclays** • 208 W End Ln
- **Halifax** • 149 Kilburn High Rd
- **Lloyds** • 106 Kilburn High Rd
- **NatWest** • 74 Kilburn High Rd

Coffee

- **Caffe Nero** • 101 Kilburn High Rd
- **Costa** • 203 W End Ln
- **Starbucks** • 201 W End Ln

Libraries

- **West Hampstead Library** • Dennington Park Rd

Nightlife

- **The Czech and Slovak Club** • 74 West End Lane
- **The Good Ship** • 289 Kilburn High Rd
- **The Luminaire** • 311 High Rd

Post Offices

- **West Hampstead** • 128 W End Ln

Restaurants

- **The Green Room** • 182 Broadhurst Gardens

Supermarkets

- **Sainsbury's** • 88 Kilburn High Rd
- **Sainsbury's** • 377 Kilburn High Rd

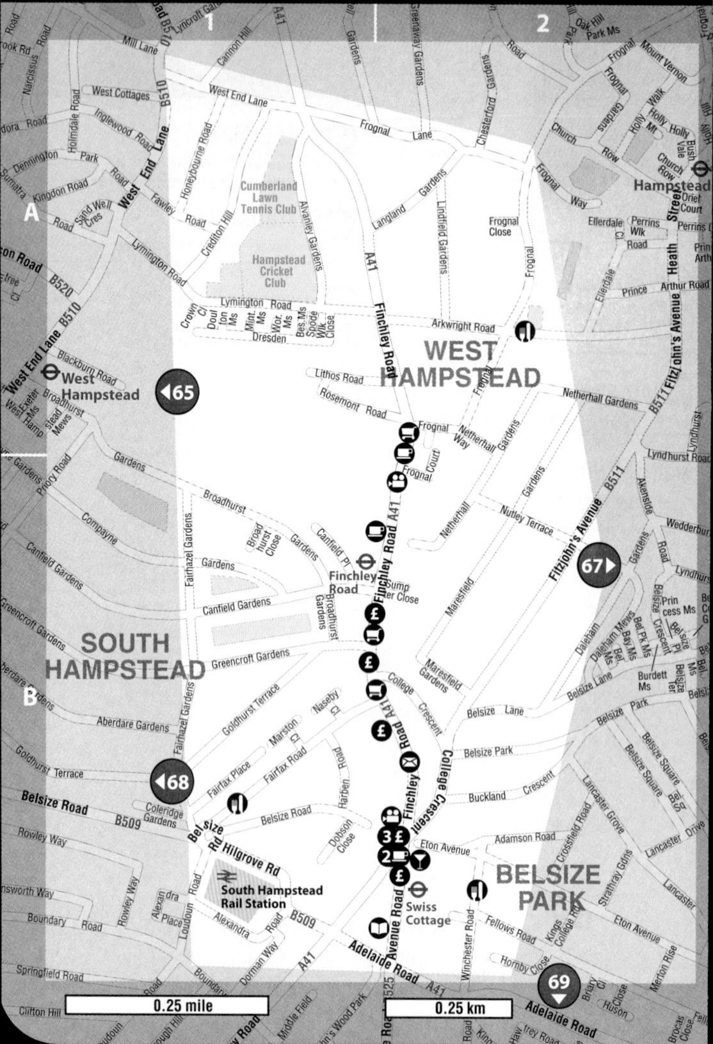

Map 66 · **Finchley Road / Swiss Cottage**

WEST HAMPSTEAD

SOUTH HAMPSTEAD

BELSIZE PARK

West Hampstead

South Hampstead Rail Station

Swiss Cottage

Cumberland Lawn Tennis Club

Hampstead Cricket Club

◀65

67▶

◀68

69▼

0.25 mile

0.25 km

Map 66

Finchley Road / Swiss Cottage

Although it is sandwiched between West Hampstead and Primrose Hill, this is simply not a great spot unless you're seeking bargains in the local pound shop. Finchley Road has a range of mediocre restaurants. Swiss Cottage has a good library and sports centre. The Camden Arts Centre and Freud Museum are jewels in this battered crown—it's worth braving the traffic to see them.

£ Banks

- **Abbey** • 8 Finchley Rd
- **Barclays** • 131 Finchley Rd
- **Halifax** • 169 Finchley Rd
- **HSBC** • 122 Finchley Rd
- **Lloyds** • 145 Finchley Rd
- **NatWest** • 106 Finchley Rd

Cinemas

- **Odeon Swiss Cottage** • 96 Finchley Rd
- **Vue Finchley Road** • Finchley Rd & Blackburn Rd

Coffee

- **Cafe Express** • 25 Finchley Rd
- **Costa** • 149 Finchley Rd
- **Costa** • 255 Finchley Rd
- **Starbucks** • 255 Finchley Rd

Libraries

- **Swiss Cottage Library** • 88 Avenue Rd

Nightlife

- **Ye Olde Swiss Cottage** • 98 Finchley Rd

Post Offices

- **Swiss Cottage** • 18 Harben Parade

Restaurants

- **Bradleys** • 25 Winchester Rd
- **Camden Arts Centre** • Arkwright Rd
- **Singapore Garden** • 83 Fairfax Rd

Shopping

- **Yeomans Grocers** • 152 Regent's Park Rd

Supermarkets

- **Sainsbury's** • 241 Finchley Rd
- **Waitrose** • 199 Finchley Rd

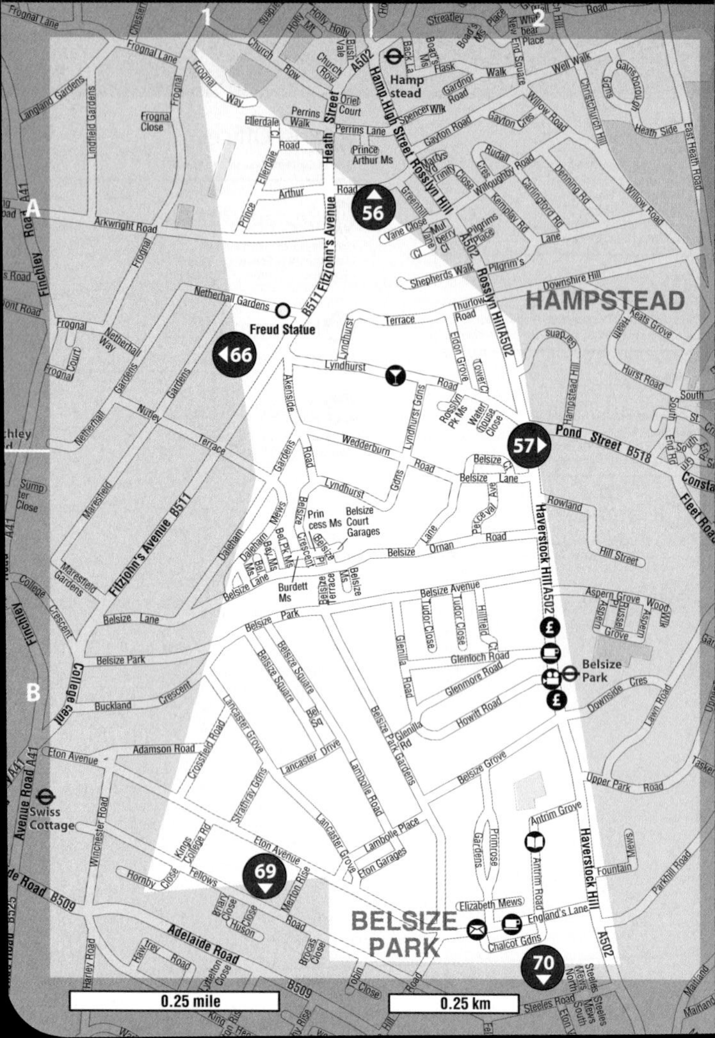
HAMPSTEAD
BELSIZE PARK
Freud Statue
Hampstead
Belsize Park
Swiss Cottage
56
66
57
69
70
1
2
A
B
0.25 mile
0.25 km
Frognal Lane
Church Row
Holly Bush Vale
Holly Mt
Hamp. High Street
Back La
Streatley Place
New End Square
Well Walk
Christchurch Hill
Gainsborough Gdns
Heath Side
East Heath Road
Flask Walk
Gardnor Road
Gayton Road
Gayton Cres
Willow Road
Langland Gardens
Lindfield Gardens
Frognal Close
Frognal Way
Ellerdale Road
Perrins Walk
Perrins Lane
Oriel Court
Heath Street
Spencer Wlk
Prince Arthur Ms
Prince Arthur Road
Rosslyn Hill
Rudall Cres
Willoughby Road
Denning Rd
Carlingford Rd
Kemplay Rd
Pilgrims Place
Pilgrim's Lane
Downshire Hill
Vane Close
Mulberry Cl
Greenhill
Shepherds Walk
Arkwright Road
Finchley Road
A41
Netherhall Gardens
Netherhall Way
Fitzjohn's Avenue
B511
Thurlow Road
Lyndhurst Terrace
Lyndhurst Road
Lyndhurst Gdns
Eldon Grove
Tower Cl
Rosslyn Pk Ms
Waterhouse Close
Keats Grove
Hampstead Hill Gdns
Hurst Road
South End Rd
Pond Street
B518
Wedderburn Road
Akenside Road
Belsize Lane
Belsize Ct
Percival Ave
Rowland Hill Street
Haverstock Hill
A502
Nutley Terrace
Maresfield Gardens
Daleham Gardens
Daleham Mews
Belsize Crescent
Princess Ms
Belsize Court Garages
Bel Pk Ms
Bay Ms
Belsize Pl
Ornan Road
Burdett Ms
Belsize Terrace
Belsize Ms
Belsize Avenue
Tudor Close
Hillfield Ct
Aspern Grove
Russell Grove
Wood Wlk
Belsize Park
Belsize Park Gardens
Belsize Square
Glenilla Road
Glenloch Road
Glenmore Road
Howitt Road
Downside Cres
Lawn Road
College Crescent
Buckland Crescent
Eton Avenue
Adamson Road
Crossfield Road
Lancaster Grove
Lancaster Drive
Lambolle Road
Lambolle Place
Belsize Grove
Upper Park Road
Strathray Gdns
Winchester Road
Kings College Rd
Eton Garages
Antrim Grove
Antrim Road
Primrose Gardens
Fountain Mews
Parkhill Road
Hornby Close
Fellows Road
Merton Rise
Briary Close
Huson Close
Elizabeth Mews
England's Lane
Chalcot Gdns
Adelaide Road
B509
Hawtrey Road
Lyttelton Close
Harley Road
Tobin Close
Steeles Road
Steeles Mews North
Steeles Mews South
Maitland

Aggressively affluent, Belsize Park is awash with celebrities and salaries bigger than the budgets of small countries. Quaint old streets and the poshness of Finchley road make this a nice place to stalk Gwyneth Paltrow, but you probably wouldn't want to live here. Check out Freud's statue or drink yourself into an upper-middle class stupor in the Washington.

£ Banks

- **HSBC** • 147 Haverstock Hill
- **NatWest** • 185 Haverstock Hill

Cinemas

- **Screen on the Hill** • 203 Haverstock Hill

Coffee

- **Starbucks** • 57 England's Lane
- **Starbucks** • 202 Haverstock Hill

O Landmarks

- **Freud Statue** •
  Fitzjohn's Ave, opposite Maresfield Gardens Junction

Libraries

- **Belsize Library** • Antrim Rd

Nightlife

- **The Washington** • 50 England's Lane

Post Offices

- **Englands Lane** • 28 England's Ln

Map 68 · Kilburn High Road / Abbey Road

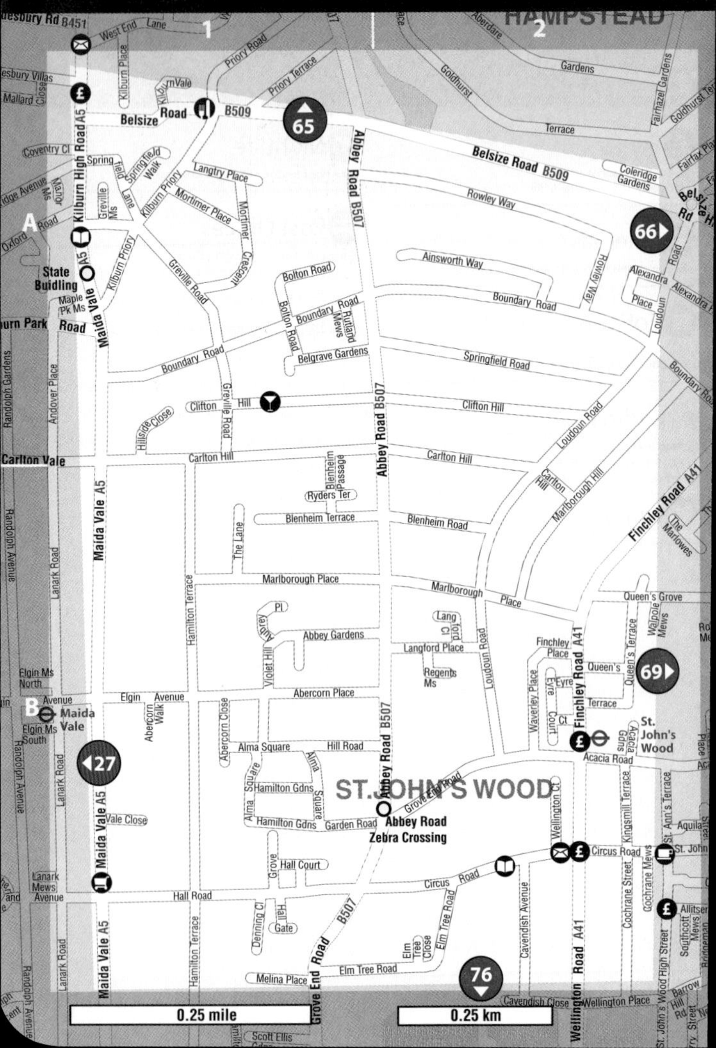

HAMPSTEAD

1

2

Priory Terrace

esbury Rd B451

West End Lane

Kilburn Place

Priory Park

Goldhurst

Gardens

esbury Villas

KilburnVale

Priory Road

Fairfax Gardens

Mallard

Belsize

Road

B509

65

Coventry Ct

Spring

Langtry Place

Belsize Road B509

Coleridge Gardens

idge Avenue

Oxford

A

Greville Ms

Spring field Walk

Mortimer Place

Kilburn Priory

Mortimer Crescent

Abbey Road B507

Rowley Way

Belsize Rd

66

State Buidling

Greville Road

Ainsworth Way

Alexandra Place

Loudoun

urn Park Road

Maple Pk Ms

Boundary Road

Boundary Road

Bolton Road

Bolton Road

Boundary Road

Rudolf Road

Belgrave Gardens

Springfield Road

Boundary Road

Andover Place

Boundary Road

Hillgate Close

Clifton

Grville Hill

Clifton Hill

Loudoun Road

Carlton Vale

Carlton Hill

Carlton Hill

Marlborough Hill

Finchley Road A41

The Marlowes

Maida Vale A5

Carlton Hill

Abbey Road B507

Carlton Hill

Blenheim Passage

Ryders Ter

Blenheim Terrace

Blenheim Road

Queen's Grove

Walpole Mews

The Lane

Hamilton Terrace

Marlborough Place

Marlborough Place

69

Violet Hill

Pl

Abbey Gardens

Lang

Loudoun Road

Finchley Place

Queen's

St. John's Wood

Langford Place

Regents Ms

Finchley Road A41

Abercorn Place

Waverley Place

Queen's Terrace

B

Elgin Ms North

Maida Vale

Avenue

Elgin Avenue

Abercorn Walk

Abercorn Place

Abbey Road B507

Eyre Ct

Acacia Road

St. John's Wood

Elgin Ms South

Lanark Road

27

Maida Vale

Abercorn Close

Alma Square

Hill Road

Alma

Alma Square

ST. JOHN'S WOOD

Grove End Road

Wellington Ct

Randolph Avenue

Maida Vale A5

Vale Close

Hamilton Gdns

Hamilton Gdns

Garden Road

Abbey Road Zebra Crossing

Circus Road

Circus Street

Cochrane Mews

Lanark Mews

Hall Road

Grove

Half Court

Circus Road

Cavendish Avenue

Kingsmill Terrace

Cochrane Street

St. Ann's Terrace

Lanark Road

Hamilton Terrace

Denning Cl

Gate

Abbey Road B507

Elm Tree Close

Elm Tree Road

Cavendish Avenue

Wellington Road A41

St. John's Wood High Street

Allitsen Mews

Lanark Mews Avenue

Melina Place

76

Cavendish Close

Wellington Place

Scott Ellis

0.25 mile

0.25 km

Kilburn High Road / Abbey Road

Opposites attract: to the east Abbey Road and dull suburbia beckon, while the west is dominated by grime and urban decay. For pockets of somethin' somethin' try The Clifton for drinkies or pig out at the delightful Little Bay. Better still, look up to the faded Art Deco grandeur of the State Building. Oh yeah, and remember it's just another bloody zebra crossing.

Map 68

£ Banks

- **Barclays** • 40 Wellington Rd
- **HSBC** • 50 Kilburn High Rd
- **HSBC** • 1 Finchley Rd
- **NatWest** • 102 St John's Wood High St

Coffee

- **Starbucks** • 79 St John's Wood High St

O Landmarks

- **Abbey Road Zebra Crossing** • 3 Abbey Rd
- **State Buidling** • 195 Kilburn High Road

Libraries

- **Kilburn Library** • 12 Kilburn High Rd
- **St John's Wood Library TEMPORARY LOCATION!** • 20 Circus Rd

Nightlife

- **The Clifton** • 96 Clifton Hill

Post Offices

- **Kilburn** • 79 Kilburn High Rd
- **St Johns Wood** • 32 Circus Rd

Restaurants

- **Little Bay** • 228 Belsize Rd

Supermarkets

- **Tesco** • 115 Maida Vale

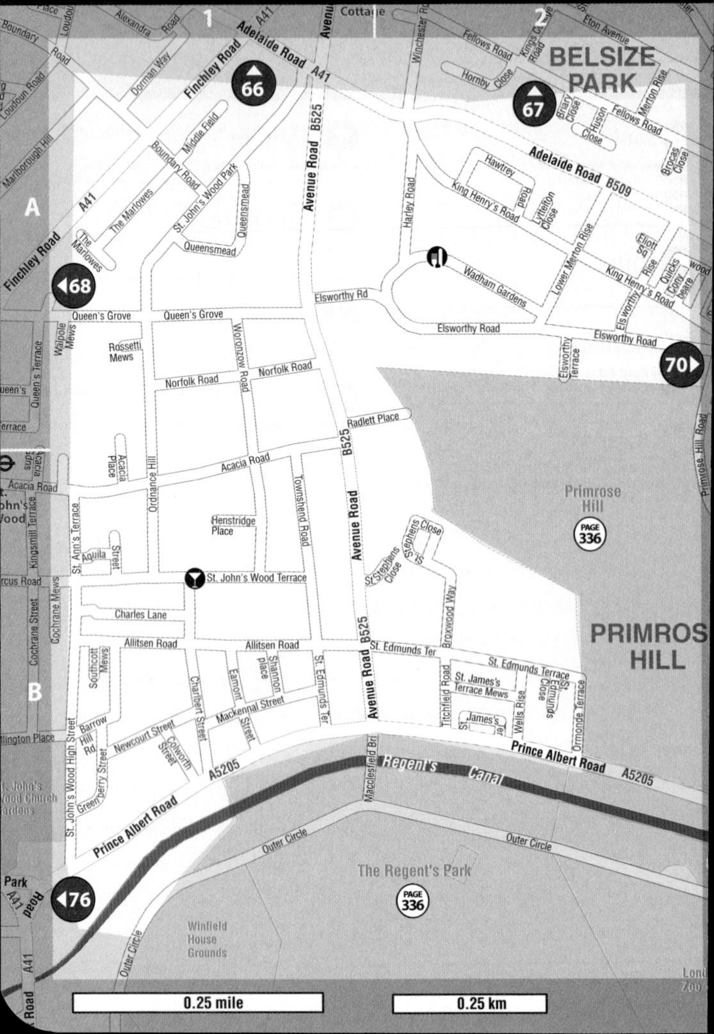

Map 69 · St. John's Wood

N

1 2

Cottage

Eton Avenue

Winchester Rd

Fellows Road

BELSIZE
PARK

Alexandra Rd

Loudoun Place

Boundary Rd

London Road

Adelaide Road A41

Dorman Way

Finchley Road

Hornby Close

66

Brassy Close

Fellows Road

Knox Court

Belsize Rd

Maresfield

Merton Rise

Brooks Close

Eton College Rd

Marlborough Hill

A41

Middle Field

Boundary Road

The Marlowes

St. John's Wood Park

Queensmead

Queensmead

Avenue Road B525

67

Harley Road

Hawtrey

King Henry's Road

Peel

Lyttelton Close

Adelaide Road B509

Eldon

Grove

Lower Merton Rise

King Henry's Road

Elsworthy Rd

Chalcots

Road

A

Finchley Road

A41

68

Queen's Grove

Queen's Grove

Wadham Gardens

Elsworthy Road

Walton St

Queen's Terrace

Rossetti
Mews

Wordsworth Road

Norfolk Road

Norfolk Road

Elsworthy Road

Elsworthy
Terrace

70

Acacia Gardens

Acacia Road

Ordnance Hill

B525

Radlett Place

Acacia Road

Townshend Road

Primrose
Hill

PAGE
336

Henstridge
Place

Acacia Road

St. Ann's Terrace

St. Aquila Street

Avenue Road

St. Stephen's Close

St. Stephen's Close

Kingsmill Terrace

St. John's
Wood

Acacia Road

St. John's Wood Terrace

Charles Lane

Allitsen Road

Allitsen Road

B525

Barrowgate Road

Henstridge Place

Boxwood Way

PRIMROSE
HILL

B

Cochrane Mews

Cochrane Street

Marcus Road

Southcott
Mews

Newcourt Street

MacKennal Street

Eamont Street

Charlbert Street

Salisbury St

St. Edmunds Ter

Titchfield Road

St. Edmunds Terrace

St. James's
Terrace Mews

James's
Close

Ormonde Terrace

Wells Rise

Prince Albert Road

Ellington Place

St. John's Wood High Street

Barrow Hill Rd

Queen's Terrace

Green

Berry Street

Charlbert Street

Cockspur Street

A5205

Prince Albert Road

Macclesfield Bri

Regent's Canal

Prince Albert Road A5205

St. John's
Wood Church
Gardens

Park
Road
A41

76

Outer Circle

Outer Circle

The Regent's Park

PAGE
336

Outer Circle

Long
Zoo

Winfield
House
Grounds

Outer Circle

| 0.25 mile | 0.25 km |

St. John's Wood

A leafy suburb for shy, retiring super-rich types. There's not much to do here (especially if you discount spotting hungover celebrities), but the leisure centre on Adelaide road is pretty swish with its climbing wall. To the west, Primrose Hill (and its hyper-bourgeois shops) is like Valhalla in North London and should be flocked to as soon as the sun shines.

Nightlife

• **The Star** • 38 St. Johns Wood Terrace

Restaurants

• **Tupelo Honey** • 27 Parkway, Camden [Arlington Road]

Map 69

Map 70 · **Primrose Hill**

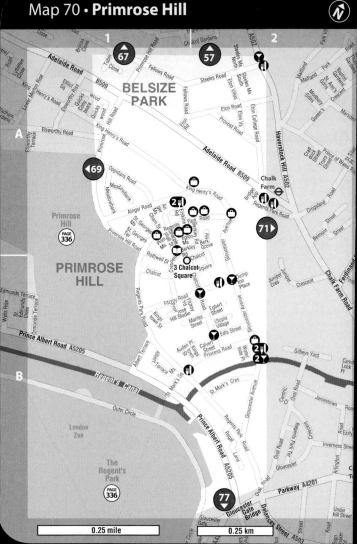

The debauched Primrose Hill set, a gang of famous drug-taking, booze-swilling, partner-swapping models and actors, has upped sticks for St. John's Wood, but Primrose Hill retains a trendy appeal. Home of yummy mummies and their spouses and a few (older) artistic types, it has an excess of wonderful and expensive shops (Miss Lala's Boudoir, Shikasuki), restaurants (Odette's) and coffee shops (Cafe 79, Primrose Bakery).

O Landmarks

• **3 Chalcot Square** • 3 Chalcot Sq

Libraries

• **Chalk Farm Library** • 11 Sharples Hall St

Nightlife

• **The Albert** • 11 Princess Rd
• **The Engineer** • 65 Gloucester Ave [Princess Road]
• **The Lansdowne** • 90 Gloucester Ave [Regent's Park Road]
• **Princess of Wales** • 22 Chalcot Rd
• **Queens No. 1** • 1 Edis St
• **Sir Richard Steele** • 97 Haverstock Hill

Restaurants

• **Cafe Seventy Nine** • 79 Regents Park Rd
• **Fishworks** • 57 Regents Park Rd
• **The Honest Sausage** • Inner Circle, Regent's Park
• **J restaurant** • 148 Regents Park Rd
• **Legal Cafe** • 81 Haverstock Hill
• **Lemonia** • 89 Regents Park Rd
• **Manna** • 4 Erskine Rd [Regent's Park Road]
• **Melrose and Morgan** • 42 Gloucester Ave
• **Odette's** • 130 Regents Park Rd
• **Primrose Bakery** • 69 Gloucester Ave [Edis Street]
• **Trojka** • 101 Regents Park Rd
• **Two Brothers** • 297 Regents Park Rd

Shopping

• **Miss Lala's Boudoir** • 148 Gloucester Ave
• **Nicolas (off licence)** • 67 Regents Park Rd
• **Press** • 3 Erskine Rd
• **Primrose Newsagent** • 91 Regents Park Rd
• **Shepherd Foods** • 59 Regents Park Rd
• **Shikasuki** • 67 Gloucester Ave
• **Tann Rokka** • 123 Regent's Park Rd

Map 71 • Camden Town / Chalk Farm / Kentish Town (West)

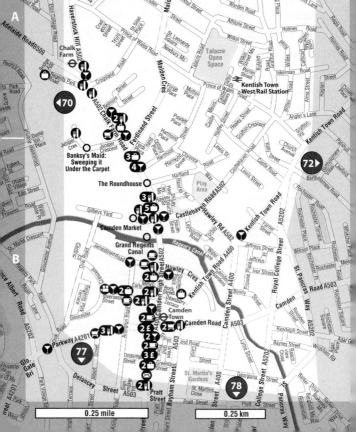

Map 71

Music central, where every skinny jean-wearing kid on the block's got a guitar, gigs are played, legends made—try Barfly and Dingwalls for guitar angst and heavy rock, Camden Underworld for metal, the Lock Tav for eye-candy. Brave Saturday's heaving Camden Lock for a psychedelic crowd of punks 'n Emos and top-notch brekkie at Camden Kitchen. Fashionistas hit the market, foodies Parkway, yoofs Regent's Canal.

£ Banks

- **Abbey** • 121 Camden High St
- **Barclays** • 193 Camden High St
- **HSBC** • 176 Camden High St
- **Lloyds** • 140 Camden High St
- **Royal Bank of Scotland** • 189 Camden High St

Cinemas

- **Odeon Camden Town** • 14 Parkway

Coffee

- **Cafe Metro** • 180 Camden High St
- **Caffe Nero** • 7 Jamestown Rd
- **Costa** • 181 Camden High St
- **Eat.** • 185 Camden High St
- **Pret A Manger** • 157 Camden High St
- **Pret A Manger** • 261 Camden High St
- **Starbucks** • Parkway Camden & Arlington Rd

O Landmarks

- **Banksy's Maid: Sweeping it Under the Carpet** • Chalk Farm Rd
- **Camden Market** • Camden Lock Pl
- **Grand Regents Canal** • Grand Regents Canal
- **The Roundhouse** • Chalk Farm Rd

Libraries

- **Queen's Crescent Library** • 165 Queen's Crescent

Nightlife

- **At Proud** • Chalk Farm Rd
- **Bar Vinyl** • 6 Inverness St
- **Barfly** • 49 Chalk Farm Rd
- **The Barfly** • 49 Chalk Farm Rd
- **Bartok** • 78 Chalk Farm Rd
- **The Camden Tup** • 2 Greenland Pl
- **Dingwalls** • Middle Yard
- **The Dublin Castle** • 94 Parkway
- **Electric Ballroom** • 184 Camden High St
- **The Enterprise** • 2 Haverstock Hill
- **Good Mixer** • 30 Inverness St
- **The Hawley Arms** • 2 Castlehaven Rd
- **Jazz Cafe** • 5 Parkway
- **Koko** • 1 Camden High St
- **Lock Tavern** • 35 Chalk Farm Rd
- **Oxford Arms** • 265 Camden High St
- **Quinn's** • 65 Kentish Town Rd
- **The Underworld** • 174 Camden High St
- **The World's End** • 31 Jamestown Rd

Post Offices

- **Camden High Street** • 112 Camden High St
- **Queen's Crescent** • 139 Queen's Crescent

Restaurants

- **Bar Gansa** • 2 Inverness St
- **Bar Solo** • 20 Inverness St
- **Bento Cafe** • 9 Parkway
- **Camden Bar And Kitchen** • 102 Camden High St
- **Camden Kitchen** • 102 Camden High St
- **Cotton's** • 55 Chalk Farm Rd
- **Gilgamesh** • The Stables Market, Chalk Farm Rd
- **Haché** • 24 Inverness St
- **Kim's Vietnamese Food Hut** • Unit D, Camden Lock Palace
- **Limani** • 154 Regents Park Rd
- **Marathon Cafe** • 87 Chalk Farm Rd
- **Marine Ices** • 8 Haverstock Hill
- **Market** • 438 Parkway
- **Muang Thai** • 71 Chalk Farm Rd
- **My Village** • 37 Chalk Farm Rd
- **Than Binh** • 14 Chalk Farm Rd
- **Viet-anh Cafe** • 41 Parkway
- **Woody Grill** • 1 Camden Rd
- **Yumchaa Tea Space** • 91 Upper Walkway, West Yard, Camden Lock Market
- **Zorya Imperial Vodka Room** • 48 Chalk Farm Rd

Shopping

- **Acumedic** • 101 Camden High St
- **Black Rose** • The Stables Market, Chalk Farm Rd
- **Cyberdog** • Stables Market, Chalk Farm Rd
- **Episode** • 26 Chalk Farm Rd
- **Escapade** • 150 Camden High St
- **Eye Contacts** • 10 Chalk Farm Rd
- **Graham and Green** • 164 Regents Park Rd
- **Know How Records** • 3 Buck St
- **Music & Video Exchange** • 208 Camden High St
- **Ray Man Music** • 54 Chalk Farm Rd
- **Rokit** • 225 Camden High St
- **Rough Sleepers** • 43 Chalk Farm Rd
- **Sounds That Swing** • 46 Inverness St
- **Up The Video Junction** • Middle Yard, Camden Lock Pl
- **Village Games** • 65 The West Yard

Supermarkets

- **Fresh and Wild** • 49 Parkway
- **Sainsbury's** • 77 Chalk Farm Rd
- **Sainsbury's** • 17 Camden Rd
- **Sainsbury's** • 10 Camden Rd

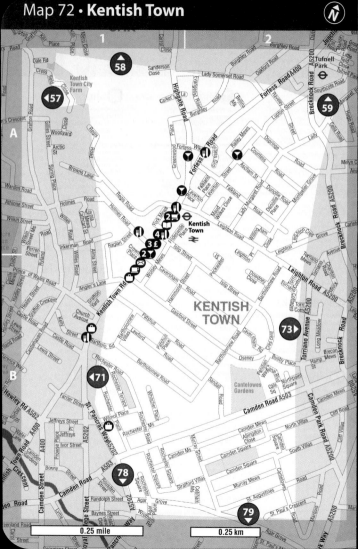

Map 72 · Kentish Town

Kentish Town

Sitting contentedly between the mad scrum of Camden and genteel Hampstead, Kentish Town is a usually amicable mix of all day drinkers, winos, and junkies all being politely ignored by Guardian-reading media types. By night indie kids pour into legendary live venue the Bull and Gate, but avoid the grubby high street and head for the superb Pineapple pub; one of London's quirky gems.

Map 72

Banks

- **Abbey** • 121 Kentish Town Rd
- **Barclays** • 230 Kentish Town Rd
- **HSBC** • 246 Kentish Town Rd

Coffee

- **Cafe Metro** • 180 Camden High St

Libraries

- **Kentish Town Library** • 262 Kentish Town Rd

Nightlife

- **The Abbey Tavern** • 124 Kentish Town Rd
- **Bull & Gate** • 389 Kentish Town Rd
- **The Forum** • Highgate Rd
- **Monkey Business** • 289 Kentish Town Rd
- **The Pineapple** • 51 Leverton St

Post Offices

- **Kentish Town** • 212 Kentish Town Rd

Restaurants

- **Bintang Cafe** • 93 Kentish Town Rd
- **Café Euro Med** • 225 Kentish Town Rd
- **Eat Zone** • 18 Fortess Rd
- **Le Petit Prince** • 5 Holmes Rd
- **Mario's Cafe** • 6 Kelly St
- **The Oxford** • 256 Kentish Town Rd
- **Pane Vino** • 323 Kentish Town Rd
- **Phoenicia** • 186 Kentish Town Rd

Shopping

- **Dots** • 132 St Pancras Way
- **Fish** • 161 Kentish Town Rd
- **Phoenicia** • 186 Kentish Town Rd

Supermarkets

- **Co-Op** • 250 Kentish Town Rd
- **Iceland** • 301 Kentish Town Rd

Map 73 • Holloway

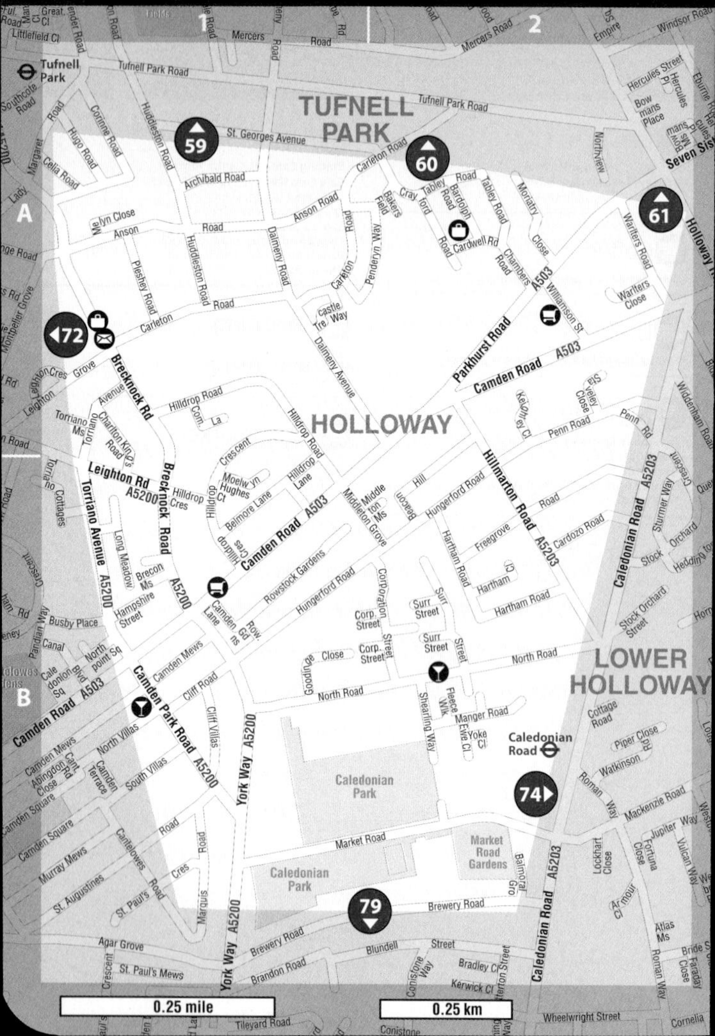

TUFNELL PARK
HOLLOWAY
LOWER HOLLOWAY
Tufnell Park
Caledonian Road
Caledonian Park
Market Road Gardens
Tufnell Park Road
Mercers Road
St. Georges Avenue
Archibald Road
Anson Road
Carleton Road
Huddleston Road
Dalmeny Road
Dalmeny Avenue
Corinne Road
Hugo Road
Celia Road
Margaret Road
Melyn Close
Pleshey Road
Carleton Road
Castle Tre Way
Penderyn Way
Bakers Field
Crayford Road
Tabley Road
Bardolph Road
Cardwell Rd
Moriatry Close
Chambers Road
Williamson St
Warlters Road
Warlters Close
Hercules Street
Hercules Pl
Bowmans Place
Bowmans Ms
Northview
Seven Sisters
Holloway Road
Parkhurst Road
Camden Road
A503
Hillmarton Road
A5203
Penn Road
Keleley Cl
Stavely Close
Widdenham Road
Hilldrop Road
Hilldrop Crescent
Hilldrop Lane
Hilldrop Cres
Hilldrop Ct
Moelwyn Hughes Ct
Belmore Lane
Middleton Grove
Middleton Ms
Beacon Hill
Hungerford Road
Hartham Road
Hartham Cl
Freegrove Road
Cardozo Road
Caledonian Road
Stock Orchard Crescent
Stock Orchard Street
Sturmer Way
Brecknock Rd
Brecknock Road
A5200
Leighton Rd
Leighton Grove
Leighton Cres
Torriano Avenue
Torriano Ms
Torriano Cottages
Charlton King's Road
Long Meadow
Brecon Ms
Hampshire Street
Busby Place
Camden Gdns
Camden Row
Rowstock Gardens
Corporation Street
Corp. Street
Surr Street
North Road
Goodinge Close
Fleece Wlk
Shearling Way
Manger Road
Ewe Cl
Yoke Cl
Camden Mews
Camden Park Road
Cliff Road
Cliff Villas
York Way
North Villas
South Villas
Caledonian Sq
North Point Sq
Camden Square
Camden Terrace
Abingdon Close
Cantelowes Road
Murray Mews
St. Augustines Road
St. Paul's Cres
Marquis Road
Market Road
Balmoral Gro
Brewery Road
Agar Grove
St. Paul's Mews
Brandon Road
Blundell Street
Bradley Cl
Kerwick Cl
Tiverton Street
Conistone Way
Tileyard Road
Wheelwright Street
Cottage Road
Piper Close
Watkinson Rd
Roman Way
Mackenzie Road
Jupiter Way
Vulcan Way
Lockhart Close
Fortuna Close
Armour Cl
Atlas Ms
Bride Street
Faraday Close
Cornelia
59
60
61
72
74
79
A
B
1
2
0.25 mile
0.25 km

Holloway is best known for its women's prison and not much else. To the west of Holloway Road it feels a bit like a sprawling backyard to gentrified Camden, Islington, and King's Cross. Nevertheless bars like The Lord Stanley and Shillibeers have gone all gastro, so it doesn't quite have the gritty vibe that it once had.

Nightlife

- **The Lord Stanley** • 51 Camden Park Rd
- **Shilibeers** • 1 Carpenter's Mews, North Rd

Post Offices

- **Brecknock Rd** • 20 Brecknock Rd

Shopping

- **Bumblebee Natural Foods** • 33 Brecknock Rd
- **DOC Records** • 5 Cardwell Terrace, Cardwell Rd

Supermarkets

- **Sainsbury's** • 4 Williamson St
- **Tesco/Esso** • 196 Camden Rd

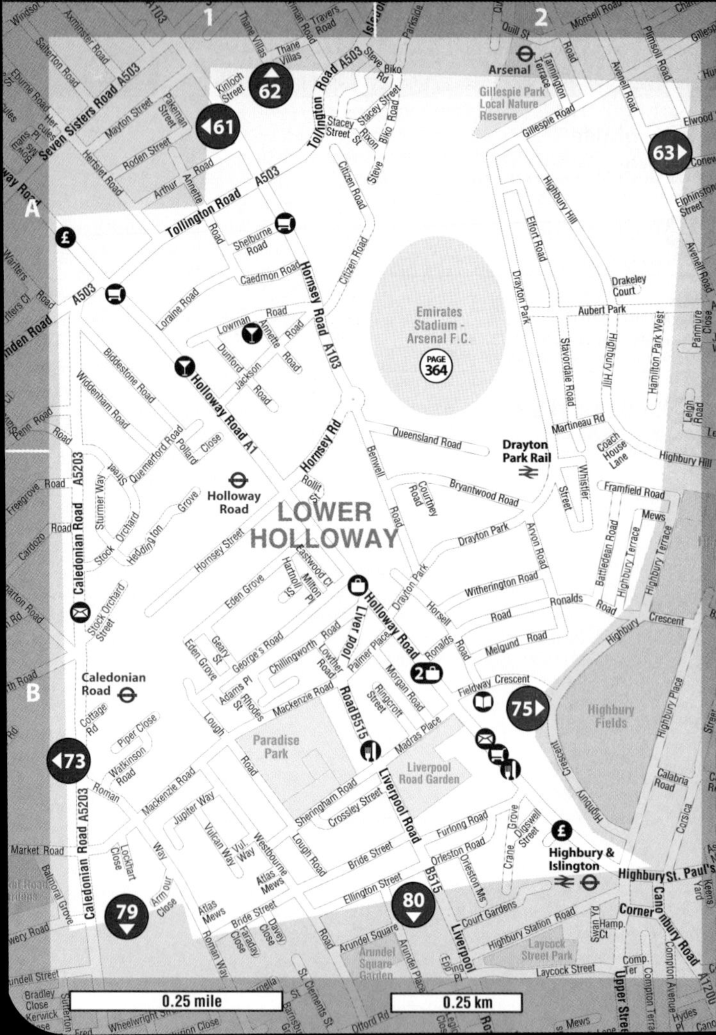

Map 74 · **Holloway Road / Arsenal**

N

1
2

Thane Villas
Thane Road
Travers Road
Isledon Road
Patricia

Quill St
Monsell Road
Pimlico Road
Gillespie Road

Salterton Road
Xmander Road A503
Pakeman Street
Kinloch Street
Tollington Road A503
Steve Biko Road
Stacey Street
Stacey Street

62

Arsenal

Quill St
Tennyson Road
Conewood

Gillespie Park
Local Nature
Reserve

Elwood

Seven Sisters Road A503
Mayton Street
Roden Street
Arthur Road
Annette Road
Arthur Road

61

Gillespie Road
Highbury Hill

63

Elphinstone
Street
Arvell Road

A

£

Tollington Road

Shelburne Road
Caedmon Road
Hornsey Road A103
Citizen Road

Effort Road
Drayton Park
Drakeley
Court

Hamilton Park West

Widdenham Road
Biddestone Road
Loraine Road
Lowman Road
Dunford Road
Jackson Road

**Emirates
Stadium -
Arsenal F.C.**
PAGE
364

Aubert Park

Shavedale Road

Freegrove Road
Penn Road
A503
Caledonian Road A5203
Quemerford Road
Pollard Close

**Holloway
Road**

Hornsey Rd
Benwell

Queensland Road

**Drayton
Park Rail**

Martineau Rd
Coach
House
Lane
Highbury Hill

Framfield Road
Whistler Street

Mews

Caledon Road
Stock Orchard
Sturmer Way
Orchard
Heddington Grove
Hornsey Road
Eden Grove
Hartnoll St.

**LOWER
HOLLOWAY**

Courtney Road
Bryantwood Road
Drayton Park
Avon Street

Witherington Road

Battledean Road
Highbury Terrace
Highbury Crescent

Stock Orchard
Street

**Caledonian
Road**

Piper Close
Cottage
Rd.
Watkinson Road
Roman Way
Mackenzie Road
Eden Grove
Geary's
Road
George's Road
Chillingworth Road
Palmer Place
Lowelle Rd
Adam's Pl
Rhodes

B

173

Horsell
Road
Ronalds
Road
Melgund Road

Ronalds Road

Highbury

Highbury
Fields

Market Road
Caledonian Road A5203
Lough Road
Jupiter Way
Vulcan Way
Vul. Way
Mackenzie Road
Adams Pl
Sheringham Road
MacKenzie Road
Moray Place
Fieldway Crescent

75

Calabria
Road

**Paradise
Park**

Westbourn Road
Lough Road
Crossley Road

Liverpool
Road Garden
2

Corsica
Street

Roman Way
Lockhart Close
Lough Road
Bride Street
Furlong Road
Liverpool Road B515

Caledonian Road A5203
Armour Close
Atlas
Mews
Bride Street
Davey
Close
Bride Street Close
Ellington Street
Orleston Street
Orleston Mews
Crane Road
Chapwell
Road

**Highbury &
Islington**
Highbury Corner
Highbury St. Paul's
Canonbury

79

80

Arundel Square
Roman Way
St Clements St
Court Gardens
Highbury Station Road
Liverpool Road

Laycock
Street
Park

Comp. Tech
College
Compton Ter
Compton Avenue

0.25 mile

0.25 km

One of the universe's biggest football stadiums has been shoe-horned into this area of tidy terraces---red guttering anyone?---and on match days the streets make a sardine tin look roomy. This area also includes the first grotty stretch of Holloway Road. For something different try House of Harlot for fetish fashion, El Comandante for drinks, and Tblisi for cheap eastern European eats.

Banks

- **Abbey** • 408 Holloway Rd
- **Lloyds** • 31 Holloway Rd

Libraries

- **Central Library** • 1 Fieldway Crescent

Nightlife

- **The Coronet** • 338 Holloway Rd
- **El Comandante** • 10 Annette Rd

Post Offices

- **Caledonian Rd** • 492 Caledonian Rd
- **Holloway Rd** • 118 Holloway Rd

Restaurants

- **Morgan M** • 489 Liverpool Rd
- **Tbilisi** • 91 Holloway Rd

Shopping

- **21st Century Retro** • 162 Holloway Rd
- **Fettered Pleasures** • 90 Holloway Rd
- **House of Harlot** • 90 Holloway Rd

Supermarkets

- **Sainsbury's** • 104 Holloway Rd
- **Sainsbury's** • 89 Hornsey Rd
- **Waitrose** • 366 Holloway Rd

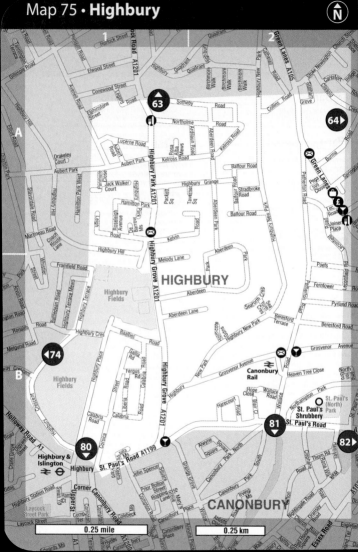

Highbury

A quiet residential area in the main, blessed with the marvellous Highbury Fields for a hit of green and a thriving gay bar (Oak Bar). Bordered by busy St Paul's Road and bustling Green Lanes—great for Turkish seafood (Sariyer Balik) and the best auto parts shop in the world (Cabbies Delight). All gets packed on match day, but try the Snooty Fox for a quiet drink or San Daniele Del Friuli for classic Italian.

£ Banks

• **Abbey** • 517 Green Lanes

O Landmarks

• **St Paul's Shrubbery** • St Paul's Rd

Nightlife

• **Alwyne Castle** • 83 St. Pauls Road
• **Oak Bar** • 79 Green Lanes
• **Snooty Fox** • 75 Grosvenor Avenue

Post Offices

• **Green Lanes** • 137 Green Lanes
• **Grosvenor Avenue** • 91 Grosvenor Ave
• **Highbury Park** • 12 Highbury Park

Restaurants

• **San Daniele Del Friuli** • 72 Highbury Park
• **Sariyer Balik** • 56 Green Lanes

Shopping

• **Cabbies Delight Auto Parts** • 9 Green Lanes

Map 76 • Edgeware Road / Marylebone (North)

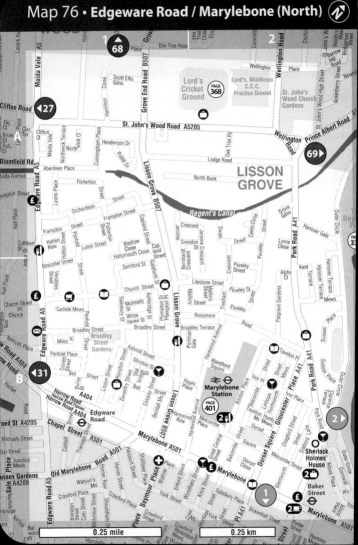

Marylebone Road is noisy enough to have you running for the taps of the Cellars Bar straight away. Things get calmer (meaning duller) further north, but Mandalay's inexpensive Burmese treats save the north end of Edgeware Road, while the Sea Shell of Lisson Grove does fine fish. And did we mention the great detective? Baker Street, dear Watson, Baker Street.

Banks

- **Abbey** • 388 Edgeware Rd
- **HSBC** • 186 Baker St
- **Lloyds** • 185 Baker St
- **NatWest** • 508 Edgeware Rd
- **Royal Bank of Scotland** • 119 Marylebone Rd

Coffee

- **Costa** • 124 Baker St
- **Pret A Manger** • 120 Baker St

Emergency Rooms

- **Western Eye Hospital** • 173 Marylebone Rd

O Landmarks

- **Sherlock Holmes' House** • 221 Baker St

Libraries

- **Church Street Library** • Church St
- **London Business School Library** • 25 Taunton Pl
- **Marylebone Library** • 109 Marylebone Rd

Nightlife

- **Cellars Bar** • 222 Marylebone Road
- **The Feathers** • 43 Linhope Street
- **Perseverance** • 11 Shroton Street
- **Volunteer** • 245 Baker St

Post Offices

- **Edgware Rd** • 354 Edgware Rd

Restaurants

- **Mandalay** • 444 Edgeware Rd
- **Sea Shell Of Lisson Grove** • 49 Lisson Grove
- **Zen Spice Market** • Melcombe Place

Shopping

- **Alfie's Antiques Market** • 25 Church St
- **Archive Secondhand Books & Music** • 83 Bell St
- **Beatles London Store** • 231 Baker St
- **Elvisly Yours** • 233 Baker St
- **J Michael & Daughter** • 78 Park Rd
- **Lord's Cricket Shop** •
  Lord's Cricket Ground, Lisson Grove

Supermarkets

- **Tesco** • 94 Church St

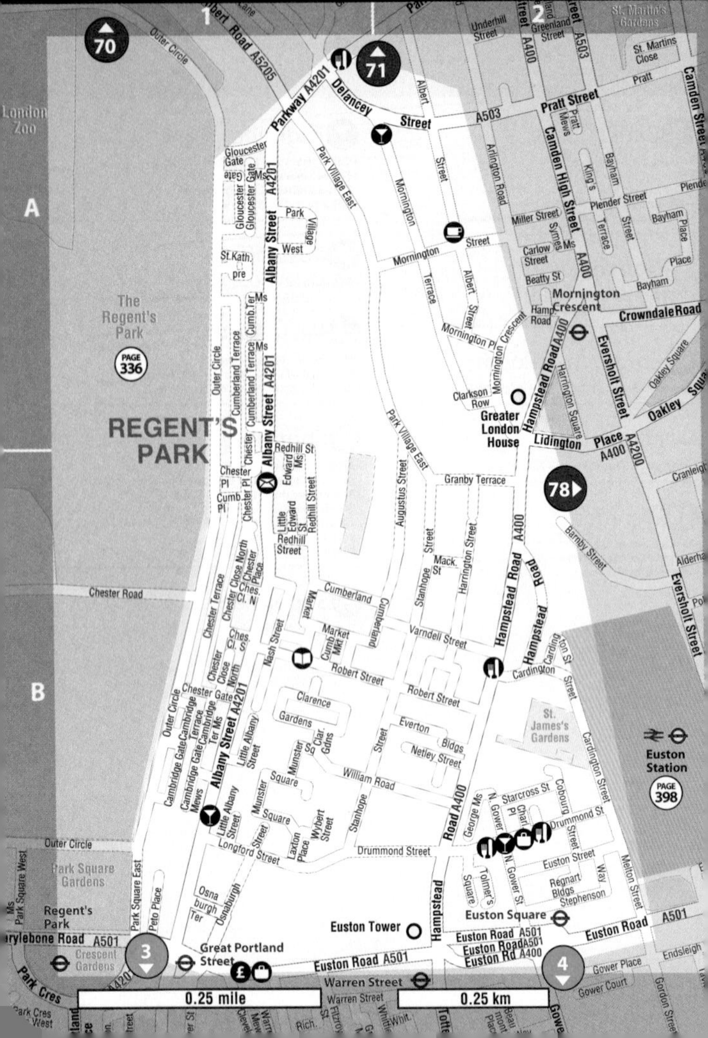

Map 77 • Mornington Crescent / Regent's Park

70

Outer Circle

Albert Road A5205

71

Delancey Street

Gloucester Gate

Gloucester Gate

Gloucester Gate

St. Kath
pre

London Zoo

Park West

Park Village East

Parkway A4201

Albany Street A4201

Park Village East

The Regent's Park

PAGE 336

REGENT'S PARK

Outer Circle

Chester PI
Cumb. PI

Chester Terrace

Cumberland Terrace

Cumberland Terrace A4201

Cumb. Ter

Redhill St.
Edward Ms

Chesters

Little Steward Ms

Redhill Street

Augustus Street

Chester Road

Chester Close North
CCI. N.

Little Redhill Street

Cumberland Market

Neath Street

Market Street

Cumberland

Mornington Terrace

Mornington Place

Mornington Street

Albert Street

Mornington Street

Mornington Crescent

Clarkson Row

Greater London House

Granby Terrace

Mack. St

Harrington Street

Stanhope Street

Harrington Square

Mornington Crescent

Crowndale Road

Hampstead Road

Arlington Road

Camden High Street A400

Pratt Street

Pratt Mews

King's Terrace

Plender Street

Miller Street

Carlow Street Ms

Carlow Street

Beatty St

Bayham Place

Bayham Street

Bayham Place

Eversholt Street

Oakley Square

Oakley Place A400

Lidington Place A400

Barnby Street

Eversholt Street

Cranleigh

Alderha

78

Chester Terrace

Chester Close North

Chester Gate

Cambridge Gate

Cambridge Gate Mews

Cambridge Terrace

Outer Circle

Little Albany

Albany Street A4201

Clarence Gardens

Minster Square

Laxton Place

Minster Square

Robert Street

Clarence Gardens

Everton Bldgs

Netley Street

William Road

Wybert Street

Drummond Street

Longford Ter

Osna
Burgh
Ter

Varndell Street

Robert Street

Cardington Street

Hampstead Road A400

Hampstead Road

St. James's Gardens

Cardington Street

Colburg Street

Starcross St

George Ms

Drummond St

Euston Street

Euston Street

Cobourg Street

Drummond Street

Chal

Regnart Bldgs

Melton Street

≠ ⊖ **Euston Station**

PAGE 398

Park Square East

Park Square Gardens

Regent's Park

rylebone Road A501

Park Cres West

Peto Place

Ulster

Marylebone Road A501

3

⊖ Great Portland Street

£

Euston Tower ○

Hampstead Road A400

Drummond Street

George Ms

Starcross St

Tolmer's Square

Euston Road A501

Warren Street ⊖

Euston Road A501
Euston Road A501
Euston Rd A400

Euston Square ⊖

4

Gower Place

Gower Court

Euston Road

Gordon St

Gower

0.25 mile   0.25 km

Mornington Crescent / Regent's Park

Hemmed in by Regent's Park and Euston, this patch combines pretty streets with tower-block thoroughfares. Skip the din of Euston underpass for Drummond Street, Camden's 'little India'—decent dosas in Bhel Poori, Chutneys for veggies, the Crown & Anchor for mugs of Black Sheep ale. Chow on tofu cheesecake with beatnik slam poets in Green Note. Mingle al fresco with Edinboro Castle's yuppier folk.

Map 77

£ Banks
• **NatWest** • 350 Euston Rd

☕ Coffee
• **Cafe La Cigale** • 47 Albert St

O Landmarks
• **Euston Tower** • 286 Euston Rd
• **Greater London House** • Hampstead Rd

📖 Libraries
• **Regents Park Library** • Robert St [Compton Close]

🍸 Nightlife
• **Crown and Anchor** • 137 Drummond St
• **Edinboro Castle** • 57 Mornington Terrace
• **Queen's Head and Artichoke** • 30 Albany St

✉ Post Offices
• **Albany Street** • 6 Chester Ct

🍴 Restaurants
• **Chutneys** • 124 Drummond St
• **Diwana Bhel Poori** • 121 Drummond St
• **The Green Note** • 106 Parkway
• **Mestizo** • 103 Hampstead Rd

🛍 Shopping
• **Chess & Bridge** • 369 Euston Rd
• **Greens and Beans** • 131 Drummond St

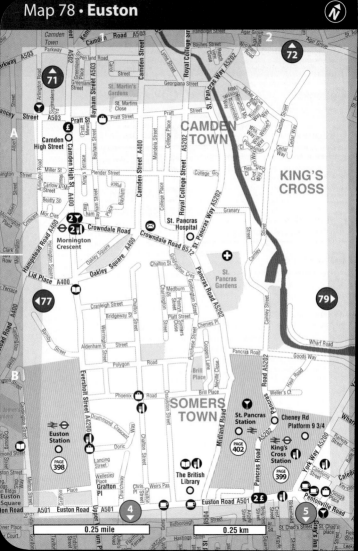

Map 78 · Euston

Euston

Euston's first port of call for thousands of people each day, be it city workers from the Shires or pilgrims to the many erotic bookshops by the railway. Look beyond the station---an ugly grey cube that dominates the area---and you find few gems. Students and bookish types head to the outstanding library (British that is), hipsters to the Rock'n'Roll Jumble Sale, and nobody to the in-station barber.

Banks

- **Barclays** • 23 Euston Rd
- **Halifax** • 96 Camden High St
- **HSBC** • 31 Euston Rd

Coffee

- **Pret A Manger** • 296 Pentonville Rd
- **Pret A Manger** • 117 Euston Rd
- **Starbucks** • 296 Pentonville Rd
- **Starbucks** • 93 Euston Rd

O Landmarks

- **The British Library** • 96 Euston Rd
- **Camden High Street** • Camden High St
- **Cheney Road** • Cheney Rd
- **Euston Station** • Euston Rd
- **Platform 9 3/4, King's Station** • St Pancras •
- **St. Pancras Hospital** • 4 St Pancras Way

Libraries

- **The British Library** • 96 Euston Rd
- **Camden Town Library** • 218 Eversholt St
- **Wellcome Library** • 183 Euston Rd

Nightlife

- **The Champagne Bar at St Pancras** • Pancras Rd
- **The Crown & Goose** • 100 Arlington Rd
- **Purple Turtle** • 61 Crowndale Rd
- **Scala** • 275 Pentonville Rd

Post Offices

- **Crowndale Rd** • 18 Crowndale Rd

Restaurants

- **Asakusa** • 265 Eversholt St
- **Camino** • 3 Varnisher's Yard
- **Chop Chop Noodle Bar** • 1 Euston Rd
- **El Parador** • 245 Eversholt St
- **Great Nepalese** • 48 Eversholt St
- **Kitchin** • Caledonia St
- **Last Word Cafe** • 96 Euston Rd, St. Pancras
- **The Somerstown Coffee House** • 60 Chalton St

Shopping

- **All Ages Records** • 27 Pratt St
- **Housmans** • 5 Caledonian Rd
- **Rock'n'roll Jumble Sale** • 15 Phoenix Road
- **Transformation** • 52 Eversholt St

Map 78

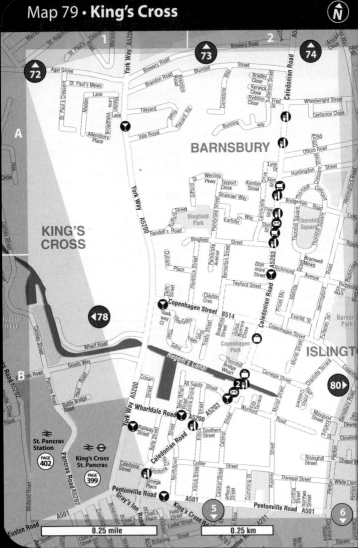

Map 79 · King's Cross

From St Pancras Station, restored to its full former glory, to the futuristic new campus of Central St Martins—this wasteland-turned-construction site-turning-super hub is changing so fast it's hard to keep track. For now, most things worth your while still centre on Caledonian Road (for eating and shopping) and York Way (for the slowing nightlife). As for tomorrow, we'll see.

Nightlife

- **Big Chill House** • 257 Pentonville Rd
- **Canal 125** • 125 Caledonian Rd
- **Central Station** • 37 Wharfdale Rd
- **Cross Kings** • 126 York Way
- **EGG** • 200 York Way
- **Lincoln Lounge** • 52 York Way
- **The Tarmon** • 270 Caledonian Rd

Post Offices

- **Caledonian Rd** • 100 Caledonian Rd
- **Caledonian Rd** • 320 Caledonian Rd

Restaurants

- **Addis** • 42 Caledonian Rd
- **Dallas Burger Bar** • 257 Caledonian Rd
- **Euro Café** • 299 Caledonian Rd
- **Marathon** • 196 Caledonian Rd
- **Menelik** • 277 Caledonian Rd
- **The New Didar** • 347 Caledonian Rd
- **Oz** • 53 Caledonian Rd
- **Tony's Natural Foods** • 10 Caledonian Rd
- **Yum Yum** • 48 Caledonian Rd

Shopping

- **Continental Stores** • 26 Caledonian Rd
- **Cosmo Cornelio** • 182 Caledonian Rd

Supermarkets

- **Co-Op** • 303 Caledonian Rd
- **Iceland** • 259 Caledonian Rd

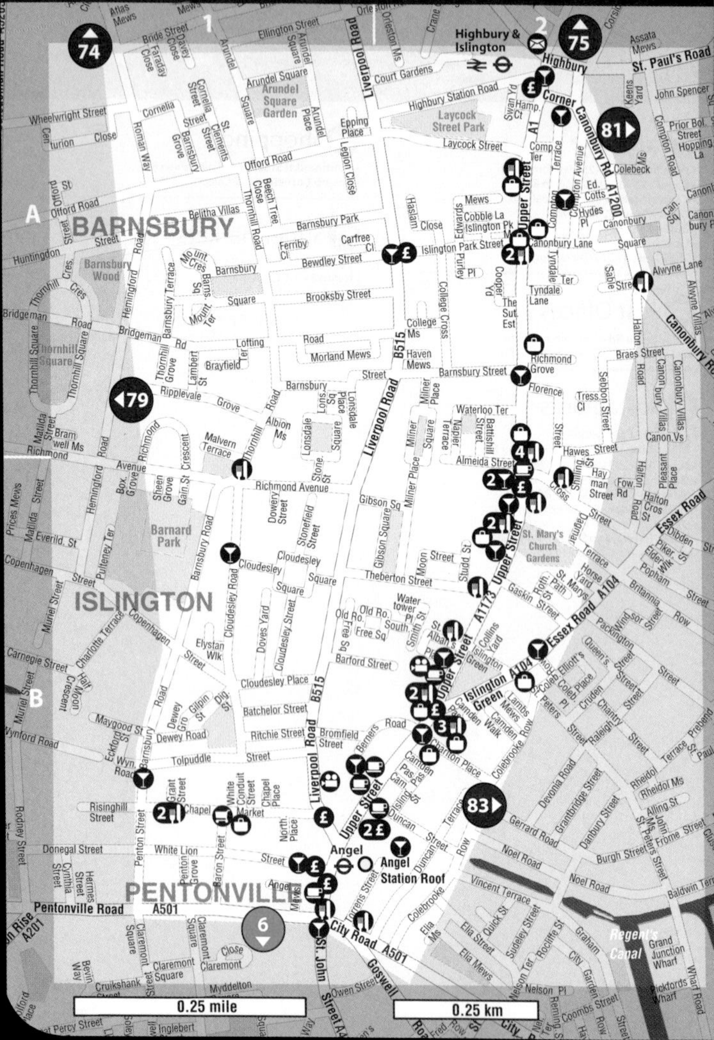

Map 80 · **Angel / Upper St**

74

75

81▶

BARNSBURY

79

ISLINGTON

83▶

PENTONVILLE

6

Highbury & Islington

Highbury Corner

St. Paul's Road

Assata Mews

John Spencer Square

Canonbury

Essex Road A104

St. Mary's Church Gardens

Islington Green

Angel

Angel Station Roof

Pentonville Road A501

City Road A501

Regent's Canal

Grand Junction Wharf

0.25 mile

0.25 km

Angel / Upper St

Map 80

This area has everything. Welcoming bars full of lovely young things (Upper Street), antique shops full of lovely old things (Camden Passage), romance (Mem & Laz), passion (Cuba Libre), chilled Sunday mornings (The Breakfast Club), and a great mix of shops. And if all that sounds a little too cheerful, even whingers are catered for at the Carling Academy's Feeling Gloomy club night. Perfection!

£ Banks

- **Abbey** • 15 Islington Park St
- **Barclays** • 38 Islington Green
- **Barclays** • 2 Highbury Corner
- **Barclays** • 14 Upper St
- **Halifax** • 1 Liverpool Rd
- **HSBC** • 25 Islington High St
- **Lloyds** • 19 Upper St
- **NatWest** • 218 Upper St
- **Royal Bank of Scotland** • 40 Islington High St

Cinemas

- **Screen on the Green** • 83 Islington Green
- **Vue Islington** • 36 Parkfield St

Coffee

- **Pret A Manger** • 27 Islington High St
- **Starbucks** • 71 Upper St
- **Starbucks** • 30 Upper St
- **Starbucks** • 7 High St
- **Starbucks** • 250 Upper St
- **Tinderbox** • 21 Upper St

O Landmarks

- **Angel Station Roof**

Nightlife

- **25 Canonbury** • 25 Canonbury Lane
- **The Angel** • Islington High St
- **Barrio North** • 45 Essex Rd
- **Buffalo Bar** • 259 Upper St
- **Camden Head** • 2 Camden Walk
- **Carling Academy** • 16 Parkfield St
- **The Cedar Room** • 235 Upper St
- **Compton Arms** • 4 Compton Ave
- **The Crown** • 116 Cloudesley Rd
- **Cuba Libre** • 72 Upper St
- **Electrowerkz** • 7 Torrens St
- **The Florence** • 50 Florence St
- **The Garage** • 20 Highbury Corner
- **Hope And Anchor** • 207 Upper St
- **Keston Lodge** • 131 Upper St
- **King's Head Theatre Pub** • 115 Upper St
- **Old Red Lion** • 418 St John St
- **Salmon & Compass** • 58 Penton St
- **Union Chapel** • Compton Terrace

Post Offices

- **Highbury** • 5 Highbury Corner

Restaurants

- **Afghan Kitchen** • 35 Islington Green
- **The Albion** • 10 Thornhill Rd
- **Alpino** • 97 Chapel Market
- **The Breakfast Club** • 31 Camden Passage
- **Candid Café** • 3 Torrens St
- **Desperados** • 127 Upper St
- **Elk in the Woods** • 39 Camden Passage
- **Fig and Olive** • 151 Upper St
- **Gem** • 265 Upper St
- **House** • 63 Canonbury Rd
- **Indian Veg Bhelpoori House** • 93 Chapel Market
- **Isarn** • 119 Upper St
- **Itsuka** • 54 Islington Park St
- **La Forchetta** • 73 Upper St
- **La Porchetta** • 141 Upper St
- **Le Mercury** • 140 Upper St
- **Masala Zone** • 80 Upper St
- **Mem & Laz** • 8 Theberton St
- **Olive Grill** • 61 Upper St
- **Ottolenghi** • 287 Upper St
- **Pizzeria Oregano** • 19 St Alban's Pl
- **Rodizo Rico** • 77 Upper St
- **Tortilla** • 13 Islington High St
- **The Trawlerman Fish Shop** • 205 Upper St
- **Zaffrani** • 47 Cross St

Shopping

- **After Noah** • 121 Upper St
- **Annie's** • 12 Camden Passage
- **Camden Passage** • Camden Passage
- **Cass Art** • 66 Colebrooke Row
- **Gill Wing Kitchen Shop** • 194 Upper St
- **Monte's Deli** • 23 Canonbury Lane
- **Palette London** • 21 Canonbury Ln
- **Paul A Young chocolate shop** • 33 Camden Passage
- **Raymond Roe Fishmonger** • Chapel Market
- **Salvation Army Islington** • 284 Upper St
- **Twentytwentyone** • 274 Upper St

Supermarkets

- **Iceland** • 62 Chapel Market

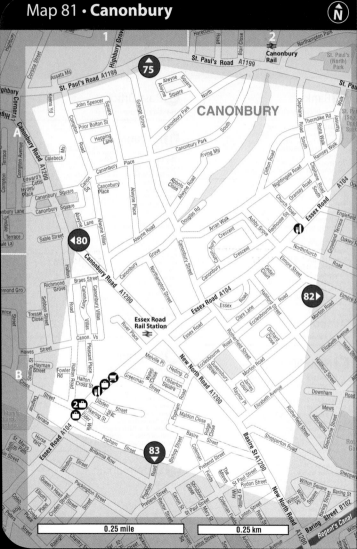

Map 81 · **Canonbury**

Canonbury

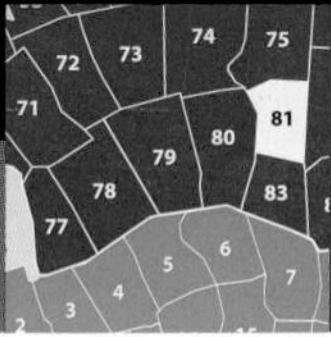

Heady mix of leafy spacious streets with multi-million pound mansions, right next to some of London's poorest estates—London in a nutshell. Essex Road has cracking shops including the eccentric Get Stuffed for all your taxidermy needs. Foodies are well catered for with real butchers (James Elliot), bakers (Raab's), and great ethnic eateries (Zigni House and Sabor).

🍴 Restaurants

- **Sabor** • 108 Essex Rd
- **Zigni House** • 330 Essex Rd

🛍 Shopping

- **Get Stuffed** • 105 Essex Rd
- **Handmade and Found** • 109 Essex Rd
- **James Elliot Master Butcher** • 96 Essex Rd
- **Raab's The Baker's** • 136 Essex Rd

🛒 Supermarkets

- **Co-Op** • 132 Essex Rd

Map 81

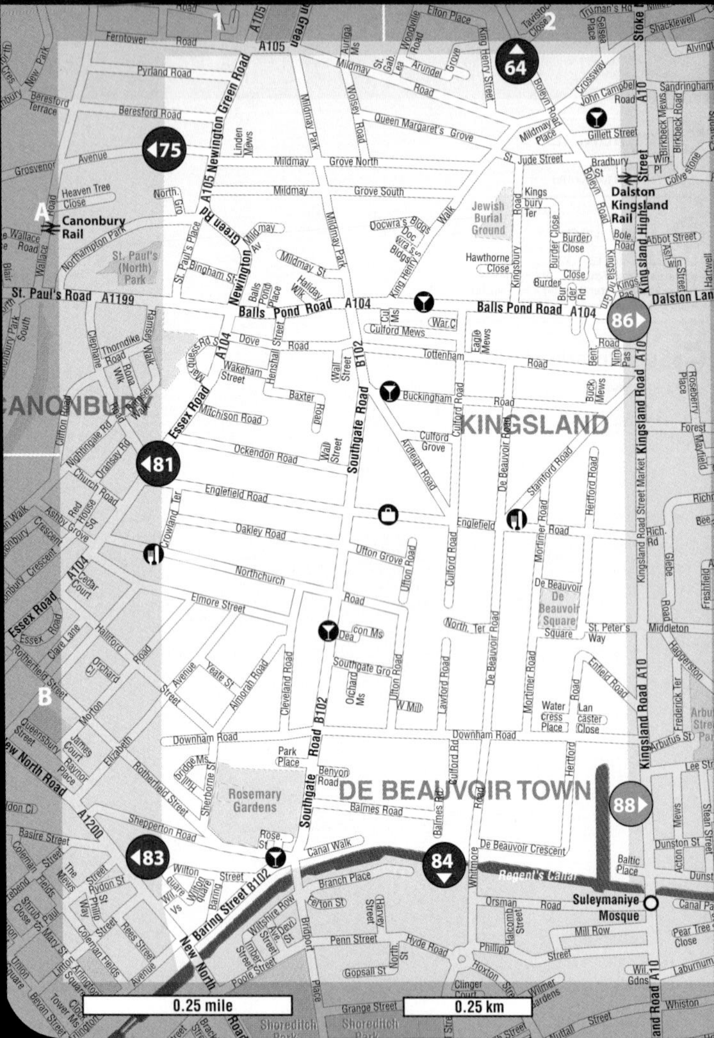

Map 82 · **De Beauvoir Town / Kingsland**

N

1 2

Ferntower Road A105

Pyrland Road

Beresford Road

Beresford Terrace

Grosvenor Avenue

Heaven Tree Close

64

Elton Place

Mildmay

Arundel

Queen Margaret's Grove

St. Jude Street

Trolman's

Crossway

John Campbell Road

Gillett Street

Bradbury St

Colvestone

Sandringham

Alving

75

Canonbury Rail

St. Paul's (North) Park

North Gr

Newington Green Rd A105

Linden Mews

Mildmay Park

Mildmay

Mildmay

Mildmay St

Grove North

Grove South

Oocwra's Bldgs

Kings bury Ter

Jewish Burial Ground

Hawthorne Close

Kingsbury Rd

Burder Close

Burder Close

Dalston Kingsland Rail

Burder

Bole Ter

Abbot Street

Win

Dalston Lane

Dalston Kingsland High Street

St. Paul's Road A1199

Wallace Blair

A

Northampton Grove

St. Paul's Place

Bingham

Mildmay Av

Hadlay Wk

Newington Green Rd

Balls Pond Road

Balls Pond Road A104

Cul

Mews

War C

Balls Pond Road A104

Eagle Mews

Bentl

Kings

Kingsland Road A10

Ridley

CANONBURY

Thornhill Road

Nightingale Rd

Dranies Rd

Church Road

Red Rose Grove

A104

Dove Road

Jacques Rd

Wakeham Street

Henshall Wall

Baxter

Southgate Rd B102

Buckingham

Tottenham

Culford Mews

Culford Road

Culford Grove

Road

Stamford Road

KINGSLAND

Buck Mews

Forest

Rich-Rd

81

Mildson Road

Ockendon Road

Englefield Road

Oakley Road

Wall Street

Ufton Grove

Culford Road

Englefield

Mortimer Road

Hertford Road

Freshfield

Richm

Halton Walk

Nightingale Rd

Culford Road

Northchurch

Elmore Street

Road

Ufton Grove

De Beauvoir Square

St. Peter's

Middleton

Hagg

Essex Road

Essex Road A104

Baldwin Court

Cave Lane

Orchard

Halmord

Tealle St

Avenue

Morton

icon Ms

Dea

(North Ter)

De Beauvoir Road

Mortimer Road

Enfield Road

Haberston

Arbutus St

B

New North Road

Queensbridge

James Street

Rotherfield Street

Bridge Ms

Sherborne St

Southgate Road B102

Park Place

Benyon Road

Balmes Road

Downham Road

Clifford Road

Downham Road

Water cress Place

Lancaster Close

Hertford Road

Frederick Ter

Lee Str

Dunston St

Baltic Place

Dunst

83

Shepperton Road

A1200

Wilton Street

Baring Street B102

Rose St

Canal Walk

Branch Place

Rosemary Gardens

Southgate Road B102

DE BEAUVOIR TOWN

De Beauvoir Crescent

84

Regent's Canal

88

Suleymaniye Mosque

Canal Pa

Win Gdns

New North Road

Basire Street

Coleman Fields

Rydon St

Phillipp St

Wilmer

Whiston

0.25 mile   0.25 km

Shoreditch Park

Shoreditch

De Beauvoir Town / Kingsland

Map 82

De Beauvoir is the buffer zone where swanky Islington merges into manic Hackney. As such it's the best of both worlds. To the west, there's quiet squares and gastropubs. But turn to the eastern edge for up-till-dawn boozing sessions. Bizarrely, it's also home to thousands of palm trees---so sit in de Beauvoir Square and pretend you're on a tropical holiday.

O Landmarks

• **Suleymaniye Mosque** • 212 Kingsland Rd

Nightlife

• **The Northgate** • 113 Southgate Rd
• **The Rosemary Branch** • 2 Shepperton Rd
• **Vortex** • 11 Gillett Sq
• **The Wellington** • 119 Balls Pond Rd

Restaurants

• **Casaba** • 162 Essex Rd
• **Huong Viet** • Englefield Rd

Shopping

• **North One Garden Centre** • 25 Englefield Rd

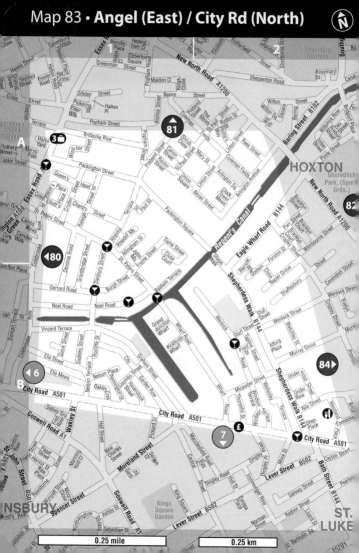

For anyone bored of the bars of Upper Street or the ironic chic of Hoxton, the streets in between (along Essex Road or by the canal) are a better bet. There's a more laidback atmosphere in most of the pubs, although it's advisable to avoid The Island Queen, where NFT writers are violently debating whether Chiswick deserves to be in the next guide.

Banks
• **Barclays** • 146 City Rd

Nightlife
• **The Duke of Cambridge** • 30 St Peter's St
• **Earl of Essex** • 25 Danbury St
• **The Island Queen** • 87 Noel Rd
• **Narrow Boat** • 119 St.Peters St
• **Offside Bar and Gallery** • 271 City Rd
• **Old Queen's Head** • 44 Essex Rd
• **The Wenlock Arms** • 26 Wenlock Rd

Restaurants
• **Fifteen** • 15 Westland Pl

Shopping
• **Flashback** • 50 Essex Rd
• **Haggle Vinyl** • 114 Essex Rd
• **Past Caring** • 76 Essex Rd

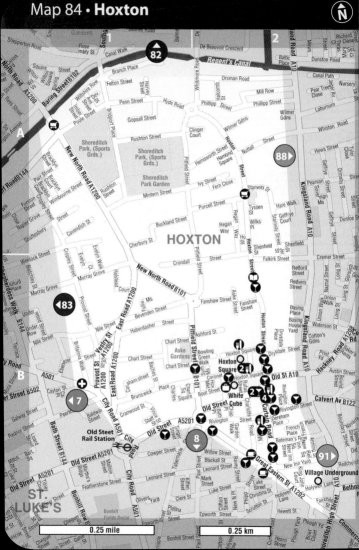

Map 84 · **Hoxton**

With more bars than Brixton prison, Hoxton is so happening anything we say here will probably be out of date within the next two minutes. Most of the good stuff radiates out from Hoxton Square and Curtain Road---follow wherever the skaggy (skintight yet baggy-arsed) jean clad youngsters lead. Find modern art (White Cube), cheap Thai (Yelo), clubs (333, Cordy House), and bars (Troy, Cocomo).

Coffee

- **Apostrophe** • 42 Great Eastern St
- **Eat.** • 59 Great Eastern St

Emergency Rooms

- **Moorfields Eye Hospital** • 162 City Rd

O Landmarks

- **Hoxton Square** • Hoxton Sq
- **Village Underground** • 54 Holywell Ln
- **White Cube** • 48 Hoxton Square

Libraries

- **Shoreditch Library** • 80 Hoxton St

Nightlife

- **333** • 333 Old St
- **Bar Music Hall** • 134 Curtain Rd
- **Bedroom Bar** • 62 Rivington St
- **The Bricklayers Arms** • 63 Charlotte Rd
- **The Cantaloupe** • 35 Charlotte Rd
- **Cargo** • 83 Rivington St
- **Charlie Wright's International Bar** • 45 Pitfield St
- **Club Aquarium** • 256 Old St
- **Cocomo** • 323 Old St
- **Comedy Cafe** • 66 Rivington St
- **Cordy House** • Curtain Rd
- **East Village** • 89 Great Eastern St
- **The Elbow Room** • 97 Curtain Rd
- **Electricity Showroom** • 39 Hoxton Sq
- **Favela Chic** • 91 Great Eastern St
- **The Foundry** • 84 Great Eastern St
- **The Griffin** • 93 Leonard St
- **Hoxton Square Bar and Kitchen** • Hoxton Sq
- **The Legion** • 348 Old St
- **The Macbeth** • 60 70 Hoxton St
- **The Old Blue Last** • 39 Great Eastern St
- **Plastic People** • 147 Curtain Rd
- **Pool Bar** • 104 Curtain Rd
- **The Red Lion** • 41 Hoxton St
- **Strongroom Bar** • 120 Curtain Rd
- **Troy Bar** • 10 Hoxton St

 Restaurants

- **The Bean** • 126 Curtain Rd
- **The Diner** • 128 Curtain Rd
- **Macondo** • Hoxton Sq
- **Rivington Bar and Grill** • 28 Rivington St
- **Yelo** • Hoxton Sq

Shopping

- **Sh!** • 57 Hoxton Sq

Supermarkets

- **Co-Op** • 136 New North Rd
- **Iceland** • 209 Hoxton St

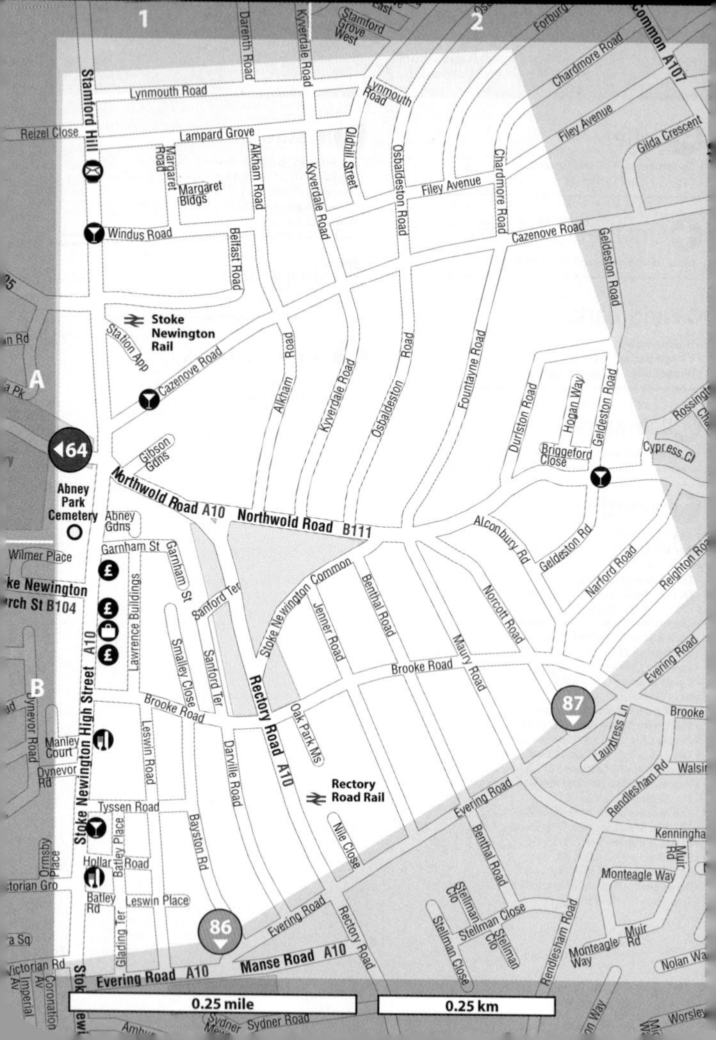

Map 85 · **Stoke Newington (East)**

N

1

Darenth Road

Stamford Hill

Stamford Grove West

2

Stamford Grove East

Forburg Road

Common A107

Chardmore Road

Lynmouth Road

Lynmouth Road

Filey Avenue

Gilda Crescent

Reizel Close

Lampard Grove

Oldhill Street

Osbaldeston Road

Filey Avenue

Chardmore Road

Margaret Road

Margaret Blggs

Alkham Road

Kyverdale Road

Cazenove Road

Geldeston Road

Windus Road

Belfast Road

✈ **Stoke Newington Rail**

Station App

Cazenove Road

Alkham Road

Kyverdale Road

Fountayne Road

Osbaldeston Road

Durlston Road

Hogan Way

Geldeston Road

Rossington

Cypress Cl

a Pk

A

◄64

Gibson Gdns

Briggeford Close

Abney Park Cemetery

Abney Gdns

Northwold Road A10

Northwold Road B111

Alconbury Rd

Geldeston Rd

Narford Road

Reighton Ro

Wilmer Place

Garnham St

Garnham St

Stoke Newington Common

Benthal Road

Norcott Road

ke Newington rch St B104

£ £ £ ① £

Lawrence Buildings

Sanford Ter

Smalley Close

Jenner Road

Brooke Road

Maury Road

Evering Road

Brooke

87 ▼

B

Stoke Newington High Street A10

Brooke Road

Leswin Road

Sanford Ter

Rectory Road A10

Oak Park Ms

Launtress Ln

Rendlesham Rd

Walsin

Manley Court

Dynevor Road

Tyssen Road

Batley Place

Darville Road

Bayston Rd

Rectory Road Rail

Evering Road

Benthal Road

Kenningha

Muir Road

Hollar Rd

Batley Ter

Gladinng Ter

Leswin Place

Nile Close

Stellman Close

Monteagle Way

86 ▼

Evering Road A10

Manse Road A10

Rectory Road

Stellman Close

Hendesham Road

Muir Rd

Monteagle Way

Nolan Wa

Worsley

0.25 mile

0.25 km

Sydner Road

Sydner Road

Stoke Newington (East)

A health food shop next to a neon-lit 24hr Turkish supermarket, a thriving mosque in the heart of the Orthodox Jewish community, cemetery/nature reserve/ cruising zone (Abney Park cemetery), and a lesbian bar (Blush) thrown in for extra measure—this is Hackney at its best. Also check out great bagels (Bagel House) and the world's biggest beer garden (White Hart).

 Banks

• **Halifax** • 173 Stoke Newington High St
• **HSBC** • 150 Stoke Newington High St
• **NatWest** • 196 Stoke Newington High St

 Landmarks

• **Abney Park Cemetery** • Stoke Newington High St

Nightlife

• **The Birdcage** • 58 Stamford Hill
• **Blush** • 8 Cazenove Rd
• **Royal Sovereign** • 64 Northwold Rd
• **White Hart** • 69 Stoke Newington High St

Post Offices

• **Stamford Hill** • 82 Stamford Hill

Restaurants

• **Bagel House** • 2 Stoke Newington High St
• **Café Z Bar** • 58 Stoke Newington High St
• **Testi** • 38 Stoke Newington High St

Shopping

• **Hamdys** • 167 Stoke Newington High St

Map 86 · **Dalston / Kingsland**

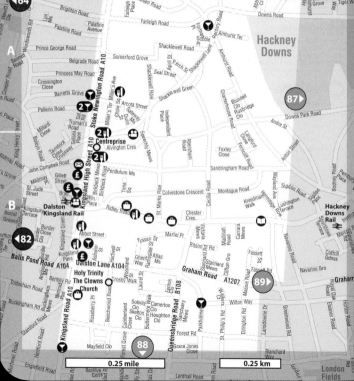

1

2

85

Scolars Place

Harcombe Road

Oldfield Road

Nevill Road

Cheshom Rd

Lavers Road

Dynevor Road

Manley Court

Tyssen Road

Leswin Rd

Oak Park Clo

Jenner Road

Benthal Road

Maury Road

Norcott Road

Brooke Rd

Laurestan Lane

Walsingham Rd

Knebworth Road

Osterley Road

Barbauld Road

York shire Clo

Uhura Sq

Victorian Grove

Victorian Rd

Victorian Road

Rectory Rd

Shelford Pl

Batley Pl

Glading Terr

Lesvin Place

Holra Rd

Evering Road

Rectory Road

Nile Road

Stellman Close

Stellman Rd

Montague Way

Clapton Way

Muir Rd

Della Path

Nolan Way

Worsley Grove

Monro Way

Tiger Way

Gloddon

64

Gunstor Rd

Beatty Road

Walford Road

Brighton Road

Foulden Road

Foulden Terrace

Farleigh Place

Evering Road A10 **Manse Road** A10

Sydner Rd

Sydner Road

Farleigh Road

Downs Road

Lyn Rd

Palatine Road

Palatine Avenue

Prince George Road

Princess May Road

Cressington Close

Barretts Grove

Truman's Road

Pellerin Road

Belgrade Road

Somerford Grove

Palatine Avenue

A

Wordsworth Rd

Bennett Rd

Cowper Road

82

Milton Grove

King Henry Street

Midway Road

Boleyn Road

Tavistock Crescent

Clissold Crescent

John Campbell Rd

Mildmay Rd

St. Jude Street

Bramp

Brunner Rd

Dumont Rd

Tyssen Rd

Millard Clo

Solander Rd

Selsea Pl

Stoke Newington Road A10

Miller's Ave

Vine Sq

Arcola Street

Gateway

Dunn St

Shacklewell Row

Seal Street

St Jude St

Perch St

Shacklewell Lane

Shacklewell Road

Sable Pl

Frimmer's

Pl

Amhurst Ter

Amhurst Road

Somerford Grove

Shacklewell Green

Independent Place

Aberstan Road

Blundell Clo

Rusbridge Clo

Clartermouse Road

Landford Close

Ferncott Road

Foxley Close

Sandringham Road

Andre St

Downs Park Road

Anton Street

87

Wayland Ave

Montague Road

Kreedmann Walk

Sigdon Road

Seldon Pass

Lushington Terrace

Hermitage Terrace

Pembury Rd

Hackney Downs

Hackney Downs Rail

Cottrill Gdns

Centreprise

Alvington Cres

Speechly Mews

Pendulum Ms

Birkbeck Mews

Time St

Colvestone Crescent

St Marks Rise

Cecilia Road

Victoria Mews

Chester Cres.

Madinah Road

Carrara Mews

Navarino Gro

Dalston Kingsland Rail

Win

Ridley Road

Martel Pl

Ritson Rd

Stannard Rd

Fassett

Rd

Fassett Rd

89

Abbot Street

Kingsland Green

Kingsland Pass

Balls Pond Road

Burder Close

Burder Rd

Angus St

Kingsland

Abbot St

Hartwell St

Tyssen St

Gheurg Way

Atlas Ms

Graham Road A1207

Graham

Kingsland Pass

Dalston Lane A104

Woodland St

Sandford St

Laurel St

Eglinton Rd

Massie Road

Wilton Way

Greenwood Road

Horton Road

Eleanor Road

Tottenham Road

Bentley Rd

Kingsland Mews

Buckingham Rd

Buckingham Mews

Holy Trinity The Clowns Church

Crosby Walk

Roseberry Rd

Beechwood Road

Cumberland Clo

Sketon Clo

Solway Clo

Butterfield Clo

Camerton Clo

Houghton Clo

Forest Road

St. Philip's Rd

Parkholme

Ellingford Rd

Lansdowne Dr

Royal Oak Rd

Stamford Rd

Mortimer Rd

Englefield Road

Mayfield Clo

Beehive Close

88

Queensbridge Road B108

Sanctuary Clo

Grace Jones Close

Lenthall Road

Blanchard Way

London Fields

0.25 mile

0.25 km

Map 86

The length of Kingsland Road provides a catwalk for London's bright young creative things sporting the latest 'dos (and frankly referee, some serious don'ts). Sit and watch the show with a coffee at Evin before the waft of Turkish barbeque entices you to Mangal 2. Fall down the stairs of Barden's Boudoir for sweaty, scuzzy noise and entertainment. Hungover shopping at the market on Saturdays is a local tradition.

£ Banks

- **Abbey** • 86 Kingsland High St
- **Barclays** • 3 Kingsland High St
- **Halifax** • 81 Kingsland High St

Cinemas

- **Lux Salon** • 18 Shacklewell Ln
- **Rio Cinema** • 107 Kingsland High St

O Landmarks

- **Centreprise** • 136 Kingsland High St
- **Holy Trinity, The Clowns Church** • Beechwood Rd & Kirkland Walk

Libraries

- **CLR James Library** • 30 Dalston Ln

Nightlife

- **Bar 23** • 23 Stoke Newington Rd
- **Barden's Boudoir** • 38 Stoke Newington Rd
- **Café Oto** • 18 Ashwin St
- **The Haggerston** • 438 Kingsland Rd
- **Jazz Bar** • 4 Bradbury St
- **Marquis of Lansdowne** • 48 Stoke Newington Rd
- **Passion** • 251 Amhurst Rd
- **The Prince George** • 40 Parkholme Rd

Post Offices

- **Kingsland High Street** • 118 Kingsland High St

Restaurants

- **19 Numara Bos Cirrik** • 34 Stoke Newington Rd
- **The Best Turkish Kebab** • 125 Stoke Newington Rd
- **Evin Bar and Café** • 115 Kingsland High St
- **Mangal 1** • 10 Arcola St
- **Mangal 2** • 4 Stoke Newington Rd
- **Mr Bagel's** • 15 Ridley Rd
- **Peppers and Spice** • 20 Kingsland High St
- **Shanghai** • 41 Kingsland High St
- **Somine** • 131 Kingsland High St
- **Stone Cave** • 111 Kingsland High St

Shopping

- **Dalston Mill Fabrics** • 69 Ridley Rd
- **Oxfam Dalston** • 570 Kingsland Rd
- **Party Party** • 9 Ridley Rd
- **Ridley Road Market** • Ridley Rd
- **Turkish Food Centre** • 89 Ridley Rd

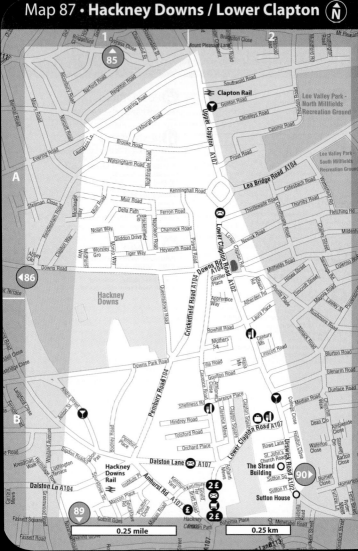

Hackney Downs / Lower Clapton

Map 87

Ok, the place looks like a foul dump, but it's pretty happening. As Dalston's budget brother the Downs are a breeding ground for secret gigs (see Hugo's), warehouse raves, and the occasional blud with a shank. Lower Clapton is an eccentric area in mid-boom; check out the grand Orphan Asylum before a pint with the pissheads in Biddle Brothers. *Then* try and talk sense with Umit.

£ Banks

- **Abbey** • 392 Mare St
- **Barclays** • 298 Mare St
- **Halifax** • 402 Mare St
- **HSBC** • 283 Mare St
- **NatWest** • 20 Amhurst Rd

O Landmarks

- **London Orphan Asylum** • Linscott Rd
- **The Strand Building** • 29 Urswick Rd
- **Sutton House** • 2 Homerton High St

Nightlife

- **Biddle Brothers** • 88 Lower Clapton Rd
- **Crooked Billet** • 84 Upper Clapton Rd
- **Hugo's Speaker Palace** • 14 Andre St

Post Offices

- **Dalston Lane** • 244 Dalston Ln
- **Hackney** • 382 Mare St
- **Lower Clapton Road** • 235 Lower Clapton Rd

Restaurants

- **India Gate** • 75 Lower Clapton Rd
- **Parioli** • 90 Lower Clapton Rd
- **Pogo Café** • 76 Clarence Rd

Shopping

- **Umit & Son** • 35 Lower Clapton Rd

Supermarkets

- **Iceland** • 150 Mare St

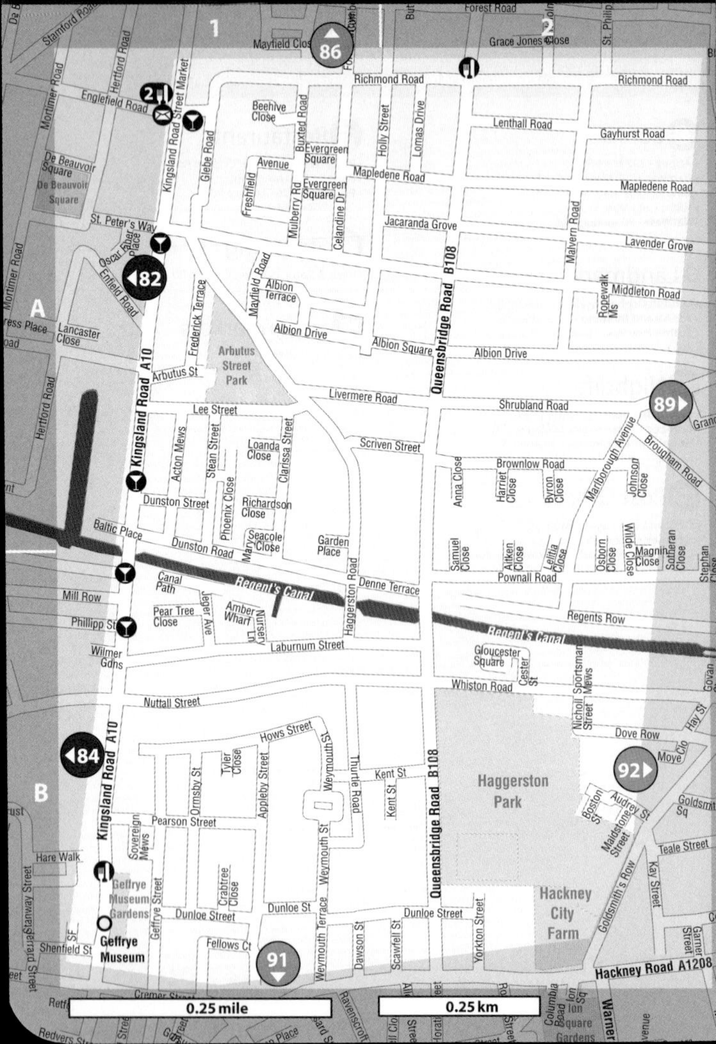

Map 88 · **Haggerston / Queensbridge Rd** Ⓝ

1

2

De B

Mayfield Close

86

Forest Road

Grace Jones Close

St. Philip

Stamford Road

Hertford Road

Englefield Road

Mortimer Road

De Beauvoir
Square

De Beauvoir
Square

St. Peter's Way

Oscar Faber

Enfield Road

Kingsland Road Street Market

Glebe Road

Richmond Road

Richmond Road

Beehive
Close

Buxted Road

Evergreen
Square

Avenue

Freshfield

Mulberry Rd

Evergreen
Square

Celandine Dr

Holly Street

Lomas Drive

Lenthall Road

Mapledene Road

Jacaranda Grove

Gayhurst Road

Mapledene Road

Lavender Grove

2

82

St. Peter's Way

Frederick Terrace

Mayfield Rd

Albion
Terrace

Albion Drive

Albion Square

Queensbridge Road B108

Malvern Road

Middleton Rd

Rosewalk
Ms

Albion Drive

A

ress Place

Lancaster
Close

Hertford Road

Kingsland Road A10

Arbutus St

Arbutus
Street
Park

Lee Street

Acton Mews

Sean Street

Dunston Street

Baltic Place

Mill Row

Livermere Road

Shrubland Road

89

Brougham Road

Loanda
Close

Clarissa Street

Phoenix Close

Richardson
Close

Marcon Court

Scriven Street

Anna Close

Harriet Close

Brownlow Road

Byron Close

Marlborough Avenue

Johnson
Close

Grand

Dunston Road

Seacole Close

Garden
Place

Denne Terrace

Haggerston Road

Samuel
Close

Aitken
Close

Pownall Road

Letitia
Close

Osborn
Close

Wide Close

Magninan
Close

Sultan Street

Stephan

Canal
Path

Pear Tree
Close

Phillipp St

Amber
Wharf

Jay Mews

Nursery

Regent's Canal

Laburnum Street

Regent's Canal

Gloucester
Square

Whiston Road

Regents Row

Cester
St

Sportsman
Mews

Nichol
Street

Govan

Hay St

Clio

Wilmer
Gdns

Nuttall Street

Dove Row

84

Hare Walk

B

Kingsland Road A10

Hows Street

Tyler
Close

Ormsby Street

Sovereign
Mews

Pearson Street

Appleby Street

Weymouth St

Kent St

Weymouth St

Thurtle Road

Kent St

Weymouth Terrace

Haggerston
Park

Hackney
City
Farm

Boston

Audrey St

Maldon Close

Goldsmiths Row

Moye

92

Goldsmith
Sq

Teale Street

Key Street

Carter

rust

Geffrye
Museum Gardens

Geffrye Street

Crabtree
Close

Dunloe Street

Fellows Ct

Dunloe St

Dawson St

Scawfell Street

Dunloe Street

Yorkton Street

Sharman Railway Street

Shenfield St

Geffrye
Museum

91

Hackney Road A1208

Columbia

Warner

Redvers Street

Cremer Street

Retf

0.25 mile

0.25 km

Subsumed by the Hackney/Dalston/Stokey axis of cool, this area is a fashionable rash on a dirty backside. There are delicate highs in the Geffrye Museum but the place belongs to seedy, trendy joints like Melange and the Russian Bar. You can really be 'artistic' round Kingsland Road or at least get pissed with a bunch of people you're going to despise come daylight.

○ Landmarks

• **Geffrye Museum** • 136 Kingsland Rd

Nightlife

• **A10 (aka The Russian Bar)** • 267 Kingsland Rd
• **The Fox** • 372 Kingsland Rd
• **Melange** • 281 Kingsland Rd
• **Passing Clouds** • 440 Kingsland Rd
• **Plaza** • 161 Kingsland Rd

Post Offices

• **Kingsland Road** • 416 Kingsland Rd

Restaurants

• **Faulkner's** • 424 Kingsland Rd
• **LMNT** • 316 Queensbridge Rd
• **Usha** • 428 Kingsland Rd
• **Viet Hoa Café** • 70 Kingsland Rd

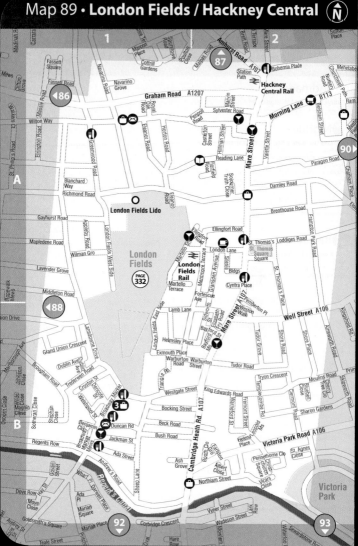

Map 89 · **London Fields / Hackney Central**

Map 89

London Fields is Hackney showing off. Join the area's arty warehouse residents and VW van-driving young families in their cracking park, before browsing Broadway Market's cute delicatessen and quirky shops. Hackney Central is either annoyingly busy or refreshingly vibrant. Up to you. Thirsty? The Dove for Belgian brews, The Pub on the Park for its sunny terrace, The Dolphin for debauched late-nighters.

Coffee

• **Caffe Nero** • 22 London Lane

O Landmarks

• **London Fields Lido** • London Fields Westside

Libraries

• **Hackney Central Library** • 1 Reading Lane

Nightlife

• **Baxter's Court** • 282 Mare St
• **The Dolphin** • 165 Mare St
• **The Dove** • 24 Broadway Market
• **Pub on the Park** • 19 Martello St
• **The Ship** • 2 Sylvester Path

Post Offices

• **London Fields** • 39 Broadway Market
• **Wilton Way** • 67 Wilton Way

Restaurants

• **Buen Ayre** • 50 Broadway Market
• **Cafe Bohemia** • 2 Bohemia Pl
• **Cat and Mutton** • 76 Broadway Market
• **Corner Deli** • 121 Mare St
• **Hai Ha** • 206 Mare St
• **R Cooke and Sons** • 9 Broadway Market
• **The Spurstowe Arms** • 68 Greenwood Rd

Shopping

• **Artvinyl** • 20 Broadway Market
• **Broadway Market** • Broadway Market
• **Burberry Factory Shop** • 29 Chatham Pl
• **Candle Factory** • 184 Mare St
• **L'eau a la Bouche** • 49 Broadway Market London
• **Lazy Days** • 21 Mare St

Supermarkets

• **Tesco** • 55 Morning Ln

Map 90 · Homerton / Victoria Park North

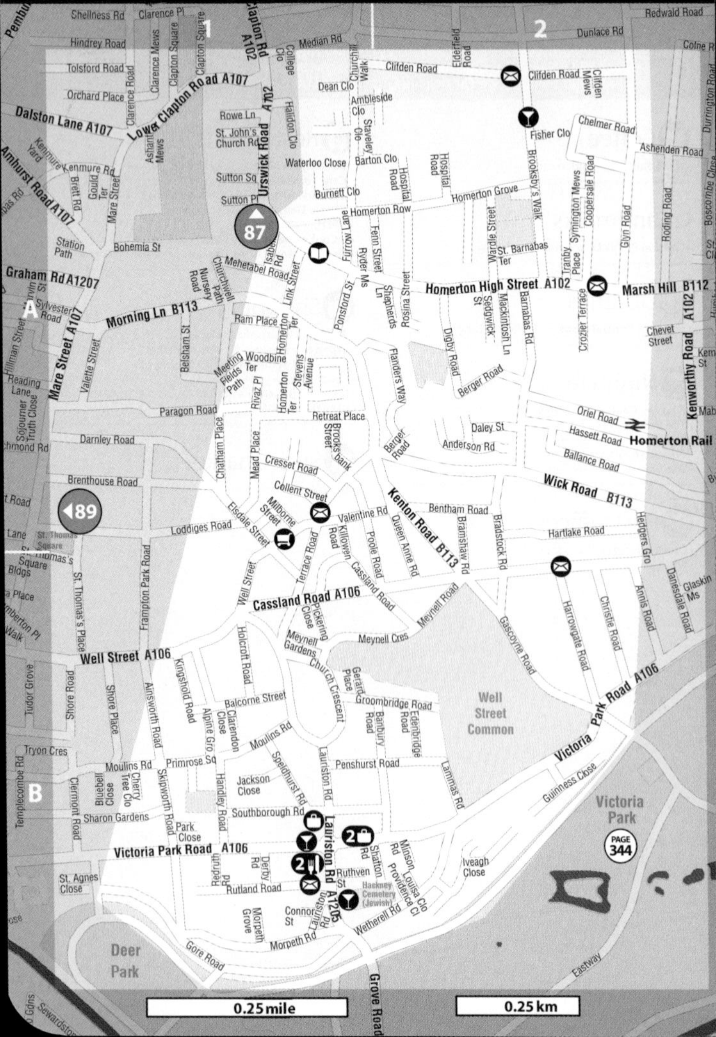

Shelliness Rd
Clarence Pl
Redwald Road
Hindrey Road
Tolsford Road
Clarence Mews
Clapton Square
Dunlace Rd
Colne Rd
Orchard Place
Clapton Rd A102
Median Rd
Clifden Road
Elderfield Rd
Clifden Road
Cliff Vill
Dean Clo
Chelmer Road
Dalston Lane A107
Lower Clapton Road A107
Ambleside Clo
Fisher Clo
Ashenden Road
Amhurst Road A107
Asham Mews
Rowe Ln
Staveley Clo
Blooksby's Walk
Symington Mews
Coopersdale Road
Glyn Road
Roding Road
Kenmure Yard
Brett Rd
St. John's Church Walk
Waterloo Close
Barton Clo
Hospital
Homerton Grove
Gould Rd
Mare Street
Unswick Road A102
Sutton Sq
Burnett Clo
Wardle Street
St. Barnabas Ter
Tranby Place
Sutton Pl
Barnabas Rd
Mackintosh Ln
Crozier Terrace
Marsh Hill B112
Station Path
Bohemia St
Fenn Street
Ryde Ms
Shepherds
Sedgwick St
Chevet Street
Kenworthy Road A102
Kem
Graham Rd A1207
Mehetabel Road
Link Street
Ponsford St
Rosina Street
Homerton High Street A102
A
Sylvester Road
Morning Ln B113
Churchwell
Nursery
Ram Place
Belsham St
Merino Pl
Woodbine Ter
Stevens Avenue
Flanders Way
Berger Road
Daley St
Oriel Road
Hassett Road
Homerton Rail
Reading Lane
Valette Street
Paragon Road
Rivaz Pl
Anderson Rd
Ballance Road
Richmond Rd
Darnley Road
Chatham Place
Mead Place
Retreat Place
Brooksbank Street
Cresset Road
Bentham Road
Wick Road B113
Hartlake Road
Brenthouse Road
Loddiges Road
Collent Street
Valentine Rd
Poole Road
Bramshaw Rd
Bradstock Rd
Gascoyne Road
St. Thomas's Square
Frampton Park Road
Elsdale Street
Milborne Street
Terrace Road
Killowen Road
Queen Anne Rd
Cassland Road
Meynell Road
Harrowgate Road
Christie Road
Annis Road
Glaskin Ms
Danesdale Road
St. Thomas's Pl
Cassland Road A106
Well Street A106
Kingshold Road
Ainsworth Road
Holcroft Road
Meynell Gardens
Church Crescent
Gerald Road
Groombridge Road
Edenbridge Road
Well Street Common
Victoria Park Road A106
Tudor Grove
Shore Place
Clarendon Close
Moulins Rd
Banbury Road
Lammas Rd
Guinness Close
Tryon Cres
Clermont Road
Moulins Close
Agnes Gro
Primrose Sq
Lauriston Road
Penshurst Road
Minson Louisa Clo
Victoria Park
B
Cherry Tree Clo
Skipworth Road
Jackson Close
Speldhurst Road
Providence Row
Retreat
Iveagh Close
PAGE 344
Sharon Gardens
Southborough Road
Park Close
Derby Grove
Hackney Cemetery (Jewish)
Victoria Park Road A106
St. Agnes Close
Rutland Road
Ruthven St
Connor St
Wetherell Rd
Morpeth Grove
Gore Road
Morpeth Rd
Deer Park
Grove Road

87

89

189

0.25 mile   0.25 km

Hackney Heartlands with rows of terraces that get posher the nearer Vicky Park you go. The gentrification fairy has sprinkled lots of magic dust on village Lauriston Road—head to Sublime for lux goods, Work Shop for pottery, Empress of India to stuff your face, the Royal Inn on the Park for a breezy pint, and slightly further north to the mighty Chats Palace for entertainment.

Emergency Rooms
- **Homerton University Hospital** • Homerton Row

Libraries
- **Homerton Library** • Homerton High St

Nightlife
- **Chats Palace Arts Centre** • 42 Brooksby Walk
- **The Lauriston** • 162 Victoria Park Rd
- **Royal Inn on the Park** • 111 Lauriston Rd

Post Offices
- **Cassland Road** • 142 Cassland Rd
- **Chatsworth Road** • 11 Chatsworth Rd
- **High Street** • 226 Homerton High St
- **Victoria Park** • 112 Lauriston Rd
- **Well Street** • 188 Well St

Restaurants
- **The Empress of India** • 130 Lauriston Rd
- **The Fish House** • 126 Lauriston Rd

Shopping
- **Cheech Miller** • 227 Victoria Park Rd
- **Sublime** • 225 Victoria Park Rd
- **Work Shop** • 77 Lauriston Rd

Supermarkets
- **Tesco** • 180 Well St

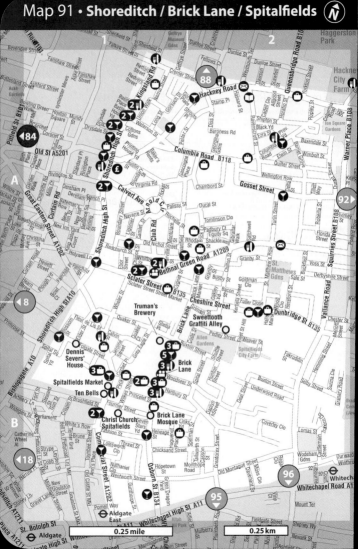

Map 91 • Shoreditch / Brick Lane / Spitalfields

So achingly hip you wonder why this golden triangle of neighbourhoods doesn't get itself off to the doctors for some ointment. Brick Lane for curries (Le Taj), bars (Vibe or Loungelovers), clubs (93 Feet East), and leather by the yard. Shoreditch for more boozers (Bar Kick or Anda de Bridge) and Spitalfields for the spangley tarted-up market and the best lunch stalls in the City.

£ Banks

• NatWest • 180 Shoreditch High St

Cinemas

• Rich Mix Centre •
  34 Bethnal Green Rd
• Short & Sweet • 91 Brick Ln

O Landmarks

• Brick Lane Mosque • 59 Brick Lane
• Christ Church Spitalfields •
  2 Fournier St
• Dennis Severs' House • 18 Folgate St
• Spitalfields Market •
  105 Commercial St
• Sweettooth Graffiti Alley • Pedley St
• Ten Bells • 84 Commercial St
• Truman's Brewery • Brick Lane

Libraries

• Dorset Library • Ravenscroft St

Nightlife

• 93 Feet East • 150 Brick Ln
• Anda De Bridge • 42 Kingsland Rd
• The Archers • 42 Osborn St
• Bar Kick • 127 Shoreditch High St
• Bethnal Green Working Men's
  Club • 44 Pollard Row
• The Big Chill Bar •
  Dray Walk off Brick Lane
• Café 1001 • 91 Brick Lane
• The Carpenter's Arms • 73 Cheshire St
• Casa Blue • 228 Brick Lane
• Catch • 22 Kingsland Rd
• Club In a Toilet! • 82 Commercial St
• The Commercial Tavern •
  142 Commercial St
• Ditch Bar • 145 Shoreditch High St
• Exit • 174 Brick Lane
• The George & Dragon • Hackney Rd
• The Golden Heart • 110 Commercial St
• The Gramaphone Bar •
  60 Commercial St
• Green and Red • 51 Bethnal Green Rd
• Herbal • 10 Kingsland Rd
• Jaguar Shoes • 32 Kingsland Rd
• Joiners Arms • 116 Hackney Rd
• Loungelover • 1 Whiteby St

• On the Rocks • 25 Kingsland Rd
• Owl And The Pussycat •
  34 Redchurch St
• Prague • 6 Kingsland Rd
• Pride of Spitalfields • 3 Heneage St
• Public Life • 82 Commercial St
• Redchurch • 107 Redchurch St
• The Royal Oak • 73 Columbia Rd
• Shoreditch House • Ebor St
• T Bar • 56 Shoreditch High St
• Vibe Bar • 91 Brick Ln
• The Water Poet • 9 Folgate St
• Ye Olde Axe • 69 Hackney Rd

Post Offices

• Bethnal Green •
  223 Bethnal Green Rd
• Hackney Road • 198 Hackney Rd

Restaurants

• Beigel Bakery • 159 Brick Lane
• Brick Lane Clipper Restaurant •
  104 Brick Ln
• Café Bangla • 128 Brick Lane
• Drunken Monkey •
  222 Shoreditch High St
• Ethiopian Food Stall •
  Sunday Upmarket, Truman's Brewery,
  Brick Lane
• Green and Red • 51 Bethnal Green Rd
• Hackney City Farm •
  1 Goldsmiths Row
• Hanoi Café • 98 Kingsland Rd
• Hawksmoor • 157 Commercial St
• Jones Dairy Cafe • 23 Ezra St
• Le Taj • 96 Brick Ln
• Les Trois Garcons • 1 Club Row
• Noodle King • 185 Bethnal Green Rd
• The Premises • 201 Hackney Rd
• Rootmaster • Elys Yard
• Song Que • 134 Kingsland Rd
• St John Bread and Wine •
  94 Commercial St
• Story Deli • 91 Brick Ln
• Viet Grill • 58 Kingsland Rd

Shopping

• A Butcher of Distinction • 91 Brick Ln
• Absolute Vintage • 15 Hanbury St
• Arckiv • 37 Heneage St
• Bangla City • 86 Brick Lane
• Beats Workin' • 93 Sclater St
• Bernstock Speirs • 234 Brick Lane
• Beyond Retro • 112 Cheshire St
• Blackman's Shoes • 42 Cheshire St
• Brick Lane • Brick Lane
• Caravan • 11 Lamb St
• Columbia Road Market • Columbia Rd
• Duke of Uke • 22 Hanbury St
• FairyGothMother • 15 Lamb St
• The Grocery • 54 Kingsland Rd
• The Laden Showrooms •
  103 Brick Lane
• Luna and Curious • 198 Brick Lane
• No One • 1 Kingsland Rd
• Nudge Records • 20 Hanbury St
• Rough Trade East • 91 Brick Ln
• Scooter Emporium •
  10 Dray Walk, Brick Lane,
• Second Tread • 261 Hackney Rd
• Taj Stores • 112 Brick Lane
• Tatty Devine • 236 Brick Ln
• Taylor Taylor • 137 Commercial St
• Treacle • 110 Columbia Rd

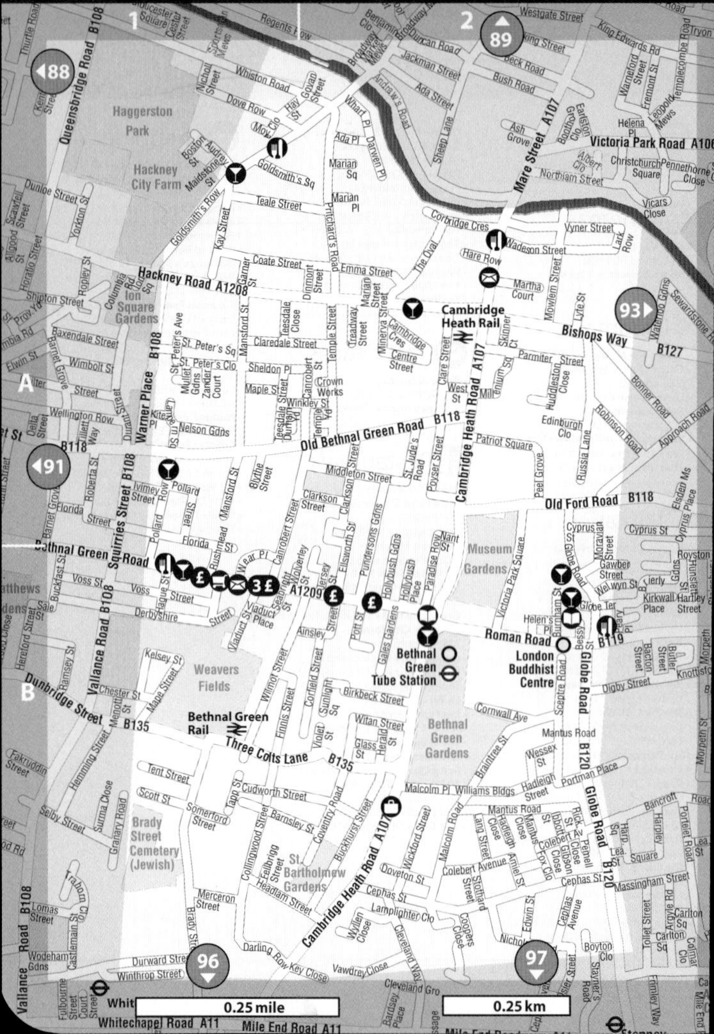

Map 92 · **Bethnal Green**

Regents Row

Westgate Street

King Edwards Rd

Thirle Street

B108

B108

Hackman Street

Bush Road

88

Queensbridge Road

Whiston Road

Dove Row

Mow

Ada St

Wharf Pl

Sheep Lane

Ash Grove A107

Victoria Park Road A106

89

Haggerston Park

Goldsmith's Row

Teale Street

Goldsmith's Sq

Marian Pl

Darwen Pl

Ada Pl

Helena St

Northiam Street

Christchurch Pennethorne Square Close

Hackney City Farm

Coate Street

Marian Sq

Marian St

Corbridge Cres

Vyner Street

Vicars Close

Hare Row

Emma Street

Martha Court

Law Row

Dunloe Street

Goldsmith's Row

Wimbolt St

Hackney Road A1208

Pownall Rd

Squares Gardens

Baxendale St

St. Peter's Ave

Claredale Street

St. Peter's Clo

Teesdale Street

Sheldon St

Crown Works

Temple Street

Cranwork Centre Street

Minerva Street

Cambridge Heath Rail

93

Bishops Way

B127

Parmiter St

Pritchards Rd

Warner Place B108

Mansford St

Muldit Sts

Zander Court

Maple Street

Winkley St

St. Jude's Road

West St

Clare Street

Old Bethnal Green Road

Cambridge Heath Road A107

Patriot Square

Huddleston Close

Edinburgh Clo

Russia Lane

Robinson Road

Approach Road

91

Ivimey St

Pollard

Mansford St

Florida Street

Blythe St

Clarkson Street

Middleton Street

B118

Old Ford Road B118

Cyprus St

Cyprus St

Royston

Wellington Row

Squirries Street B108

Pollard St

Bethnal Green Road B108

Voss St

Voss St

Derbyshire St

Rushmead

Wilmot Pl

Carnegie St

A1209

Viaduct St

Ainsley St

Port St

Gales Gardens

Hollybush Gdns

Wilmot St

Three Colts Lane

BT35

Witan Street

Sunlight St

Violet

Glass St

St

Brady Street Cemetery (Jewish)

Dunbridge Street B135

Kelsey St

Chester St

Weavers Fields

Bethnal Green Rail

Three Colts Lane

Scott St

Somerford Street

Cudworth Street

Barnsley St

Coventry Rd

Blackthorn Street

St. Bartholomew Gardens

Collingwood Street

Headlam Street

Cephas Street

Buckhurst St

Digby St

Roman Road

London Buddhist Centre

Bethnal Green Tube Station

Bethnal Green Gardens

Cornwall Ave

Mantus Road

Wessex St

BT20

Malcolm Pl

Williams Bldgs.

Hadleigh Clo

Portman Place

Globe Road B120

Museum Gardens

Victoria Park Sq

Helen St

Sceptre Rd

Morpeth Street

Gawber Street

Cyprus St

Kirkwall Harley Place Street

Bonner Road

Globe Road

Cambridge Heath Road A107

Mantus Road

Cephas Avenue

Coleberry Av

Darling St

Durward St

Winthrop St

Whit

Whitechapel Road A11

Mile End Road A11

Mercer Road

Mace Street

Massingham St

Mape Street

Carlton

Vawdrey Clo

Cleveland Gro

96

97

0.25 mile

0.25 km

Ah, you've got to love it. Blossoming from a caricature inner-city ghetto into glorious yummy-mummy media-worker land, you can sate pretty much any desire here, dark or quaint. The Columbia Road Flower Market is genuinely 'nice,' with retro shops lining its fringes and the Working Men's Club is full of ideas. Drink in The Camel and then go on a pissed psychogeographical meander.

Banks

- **Abbey** • 450 Bethnal Green Rd
- **Barclays** • 412 Bethnal Green Rd
- **Halifax** • 376 Bethnal Green Rd
- **HSBC** • 465 Bethnal Green Rd
- **Lloyds** • 404 Bethnal Green Rd
- **NatWest** • 403 Bethnal Green Rd

O Landmarks

- **Bethnal Green Tube Station** •
  Bethnal Green Tube Station
- **London Buddhist Centre** • 51 Roman Rd

Libraries

- **Bethnal Green Library** • Cambridge Heath Rd
- **Idea Store Bow** • Roman Rd

Nightlife

- **The Albion** • 94 Goldsmiths Row
- **Backyard Comedy** • 231 Cambridge Heath Rd
- **Bethnal Green's Working Men's Club** • 44 Pollard Row
- **The Camel** • 277 Globe Rd
- **Florist** • 255 Globe Rd
- **Images** • 483 Hackney Rd
- **The Star of Bethnal Green (DUP)** •
  359 Bethnal Green Rd

Post Offices

- **Bethnal Green Road** • 365 Bethnal Green Rd
- **Cambridge Heath** • 481 Cambridge Heath Rd

Restaurants

- **Bistrotheque** • 23 Wadeson St
- **E Pellicci** • 332 Bethnal Green Rd
- **Little Georgia** • 87 Goldsmiths Row
- **Wild Cherry** • 241 Globe Rd

Shopping

- **AP Fitzpatrick** • 142 Cambridge Heath Rd

Supermarkets

- **Tesco** • 361 Bethnal Green Rd

Map 93 · **Globe Town / Mile End (North)**

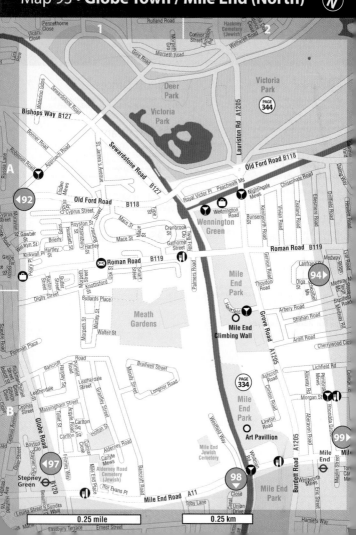

Globe Town / Mile End (North)

Map 93

Victoria Park in the north might get all the attention but, friends, there are some pleasant surprises in this unassuming stretch of east London. And, no, we don't mean Mile End Hospital. We mean the up-for-it vibe at The Approach Tavern, the pizza-and-cocktail menu of the Fat Cat, the glorious seafood at Winkles, and the purple-coloured dance hole that is Club E3.

Landmarks

- **Art Pavillion** • 221 Grove Rd
- **Mile End Climbing Wall** • Haverfield Rd

Nightlife

- **The Approach Tavern** • 47 Approach Rd
- **Club E3** • 562 Mile End Rd
- **The Fat Cat** • 221 Grove Rd
- **Jongleurs (Bow Wharf)** • 221 Grove Rd
- **The Morgan Arms** • 43 Morgan St
- **Palm Tree** • 1 Haverfield Rd

Post Offices

- **Roman Road** • 138 Roman Rd

Restaurants

- **L'Oasis** • 237 Mile End Rd
- **Matsu** • 558 Mile End Rd
- **The Morgan Arms** • 43 Morgan St
- **Winkles** • 238 Roman Rd

Shopping

- **Massage Table Store** • Bow Wharf, Grove Rd
- **Paul Mark Hatton** • 65 Roman Rd

Map 94 · **Bow**

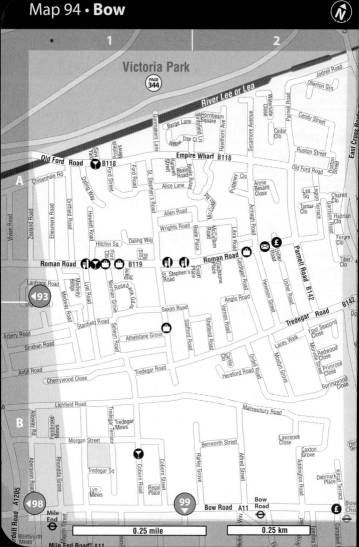

What have the Romans ever done for us? Not much, you might think, walking down Roman Road. But look closer and you'll find not only one of the oldest, most authentically East End jellied eels and mash eateries of the city, but also a market so cheap it'll knock even the most die-hard bargain hunters right out of their Centurion sandals. Pint? The Young Prince.

Banks
• **Barclays** • 92 Bow Rd
• **Barclays** • 611 Roman Rd

Nightlife
• **The Coborn Arms** • 8 Coborn Road
• **The Lord Morpeth** • 402 Old Ford Road
• **The Young Prince** • 448 Roman Road

Post Offices
• **Roman Road (603)** • 603 Roman Rd

Restaurants
• **Chicchi** • 516 Roman Rd
• **G.Kelly Pie & Mash shop** • 526 Roman Rd
• **The Roman Tandoori** • 432 Roman Road

Shopping
• **Pure** • 430 Roman Rd
• **Roman Road Market** • Roman Rd
• **Sew Amazing** • 80 St Stephens Rd
• **South Molton Drugstore** • 583 Roman Rd

Map 95 • **Whitechapel (West) / St Katharine's Dock** ⊗

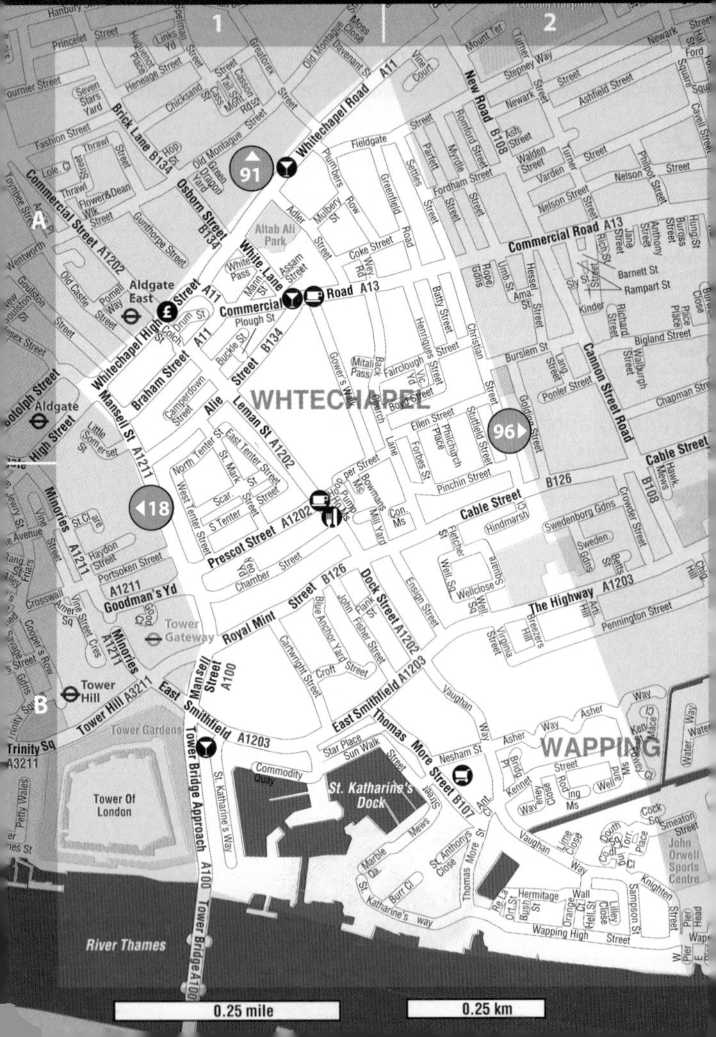

WHTECHAPEL

WAPPING

St. Katharine's Dock

Tower Of London

River Thames

0.25 mile   0.25 km

St. Katherine's Dock is full of floating gin palaces and nondescript dockside dining. If you like your gin wrapped in a brown paper bag, try the grimier Whitechapel and Commercial Roads. Local notables include The Rhythm Factory for chaotic nights, The Empress for Indian and cheesy Prohibition for drinkers dumb enough to believe it when you claim to captain one of the on-looking yachts.

Banks
• **Lloyds** • 35 Whitechapel High St

Coffee
• **Fresco Café Bar** • 11 Hooper St
• **Oi Bagel** • 45 Commercial Rd

Nightlife
• **The Castle** • 44 Commercial Rd
• **Prohibition** • 1 St. Katherine's Way
• **Rhythm Factory** • 16 Whitechapel Rd

Restaurants
• **The Empress** • 141 Leman St

 Supermarkets
• **Waitrose** • Thomas More St & Nesham St

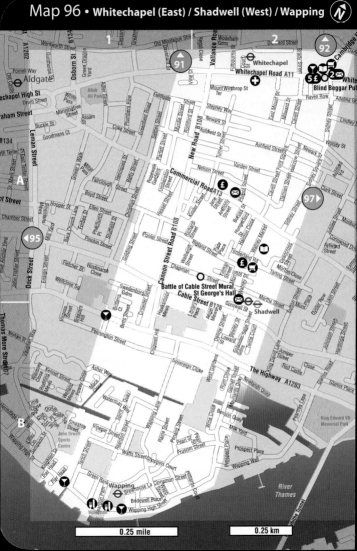

Map 96 • **Whitechapel (East) / Shadwell (West) / Wapping**

Map 96

Ex-dockland Wapping now imports yuppies into its converted warehouses, less gleaming Shadwell and Whitechapel keep more of the East End spirit alive. Wapping High Street is mainly residential, Whitechapel Road is more lively. Drink at Indo if you're boho, stick with the Captain Kidd if not. Tayyab's is cracking--stick out the queues or if curry's not your thing head to Il Bordellos.

£ Banks

- **Abbey** • 40 Watney Market
- **Barclays** • 240 Whitechapel Rd
- **HSBC** • 75 Whitechapel Rd
- **Lloyds** • 210 Commercial Rd
- **NatWest** • 130 Whitechapel Rd
- **NatWest** • 45 Whitechapel Rd
- **NatWest** • 331 Whitechapel Rd

Emergency Rooms

- **Royal London Hospital** • Whitechapel Rd

O Landmarks

- **Battle of Cable Street Mural, St George's Hall** • 236 Cable St
- **Blind Beggar Pub** • 337 Whitechapel Rd

Libraries

- **Idea Store Whitechapel** • 321 Whitechapel Rd
- **Watney Market Library** • 30 Watney Market

Nightlife

- **The Captain Kidd** • 108 Wapping High St
- **Caxtons** • 50 The Highway
- **Indo** • 133 Whitechapel Rd
- **Town of Ramsgate** • 62 Wapping High St

Post Offices

- **Eastern** • 206 Whitechapel Rd
- **Philpot Street** • 12 Philpot St
- **Watney Street** • 81 Watney St
- **Whitechapel** • 75 Whitechapel Rd

Restaurants

- **Il Bordello** • 81 Wapping High Street
- **Tayyabs** • 83 Fieldgate St

Supermarkets

- **Iceland** • Watney St & Tarling St
- **Sainsbury's** • 1 Cambridge Heath Rd

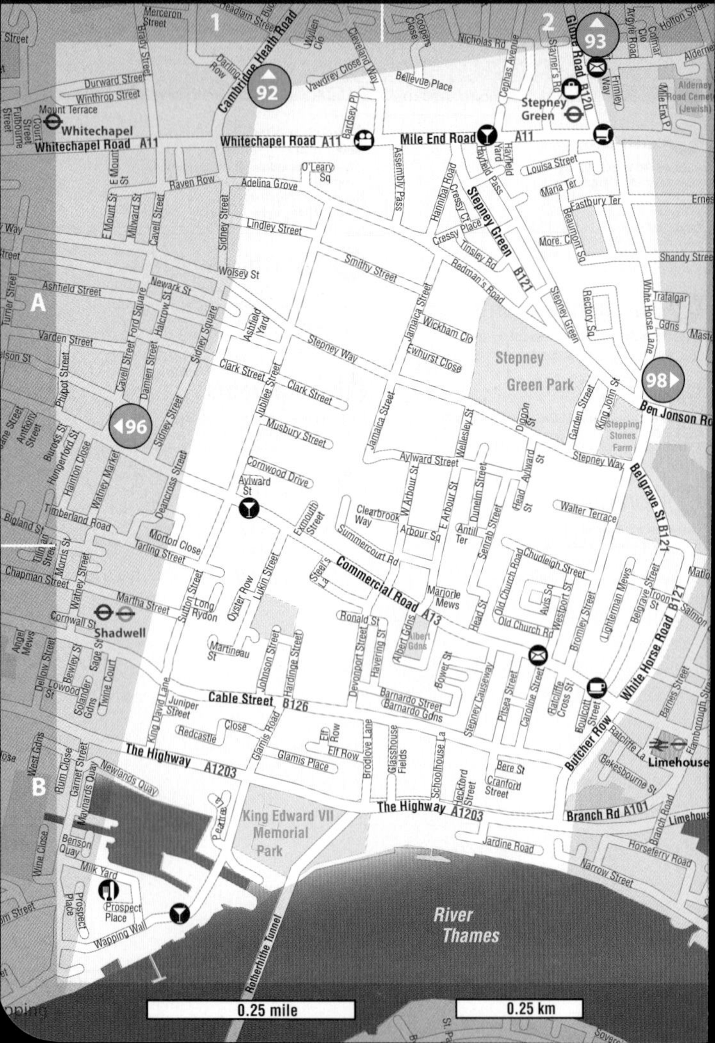

Map 97 · **Stepney / Shadwell (East)**

1

2

93

N

Merceron Street
Deadman Street
Nelson Cro
Nicholas Rd
Coshan Close
Argyle St Rd
Cornwall
Alderney
Durward Street
Winthrop Street
Cambridge Heath Road
92
Darling Row
Vawdrey Close Way
Bardsley Ln
Bellevue Place
Cephas Avenue
Stayner's Rd
Gloss Road B120
Turner's
Stepney Way
Alderney Rd
Mile End Rd
Alderney Road
(Jewish)
Mount Terrace
Whitechapel
Whitechapel Road A11
Whitechapel Road A11
Mile End Road
Stepney Green
A11
Louisa Street
Maria Ter
Eastbury Ter
Ernes
O'Leary Sq
Adelina Grove
Assembly Pass
Hannibal Rd
Cressy Place
Tinsley Rd
Redman's Road
More. Cerot St
Shandy
Raven Row
Lindley Street
Wolsey St
Smithy Street
Wickham Cro
Stepney Green B121
Rectory Sq
White Horse La
Trafalgar
Gdns
Mash
A
Ashfield Street
Newark St
Ashfield Yard
Stepney Way
Elmhurst Close
Stepney
Green Park
98
Ben Jonson Ro
Varden Street
Ford Square
Sidney Square
Clark Street
Clark Street
Jubilee Street
Jamaica Street
Stepping
Stones
Farm
Garden St
96
Musbury Street
Stepney Way
Belgrave St B121
Cornwood Drive
Aylward
St
Aylward Street
W Arbour St
Dunstan Street
Walter Terrace
Clearbrook
Way
Summercourt Rd
Arbour Sq
E Arbour St
Antill Ter
Smith Street
Chudleigh Street
Ligatherman Mews
Troon St B121
Salmon
Commercial Road A13
Ronald St
Marjorie
Mews
Old Church Road
Old Church Rd
Bromley Row
White Horse Road B121
Shadwell
Martha Street
Long Rydon
Oyster Row
Lukin Street
Devonport Street
Havering St
Barnardo Street
Barnardo Gdns
Albert Gdns
Steney Causeway
Plaza
Caroline St
Sutcliffe
Cross Sq
Westport St
Limehouse
Cable Street B126
Juniper
Street
Close
Redcastle
Elf Row
Brodlove Lane
Glamis Place
Schoolhouse La
Bere St
Cranford
Street
Bekesbourne St
Horseferry Road
The Highway A1203
Glasshouse
Fields
Bickford Street
The Highway A1203
Branch Rd A101
Narrow Street
West Gdns
Rum Close
Garnet Street
Newlands Quay
Pesria
King Edward VII
Memorial
Park
Jardine Road
Wina Close
Benson Quay
Milk Yard
Prospect
Place
Wapping Wall
Rotherhithe Tunnel

River
Thames

ping

0.25 mile   0.25 km

Stepney / Shadwell (East)

Cockney geezers run into hipsters and smart new developments sit next to run-down estates. No one quite knows where this area is going. We know where we're going, though---to the George Tavern, mainly, for impromptu theatre, blue-collar poetry and other arty madness, or the Prospect of Whitby, if we're feeling nostalgic. Wapping Food, meanwhile, serves great fare inside a century-old power station.

Cinemas
• **Genesis Mile End** • 93 Mile End Rd

Coffee
• **Popular Café** • 536 Commercial Rd

Nightlife
• **The Black Horse** • 168 Mile End Rd
• **The George Tavern** • 373 Commercial Rd
• **The Prospect of Whitby** • 57 Wapping Wall

Post Offices
• **Globe Road** • 34 Globe Rd
• **Stepney** • 502 Commercial Rd

Restaurants
• **Wapping Food** • Wapping Wall

Shopping
• **John Lester Wigmakers** • 32 Globe Rd

Supermarkets
• **Co-Op** • 193 Mile End Rd

Map 98 · **Mile End (South) / Limehouse**

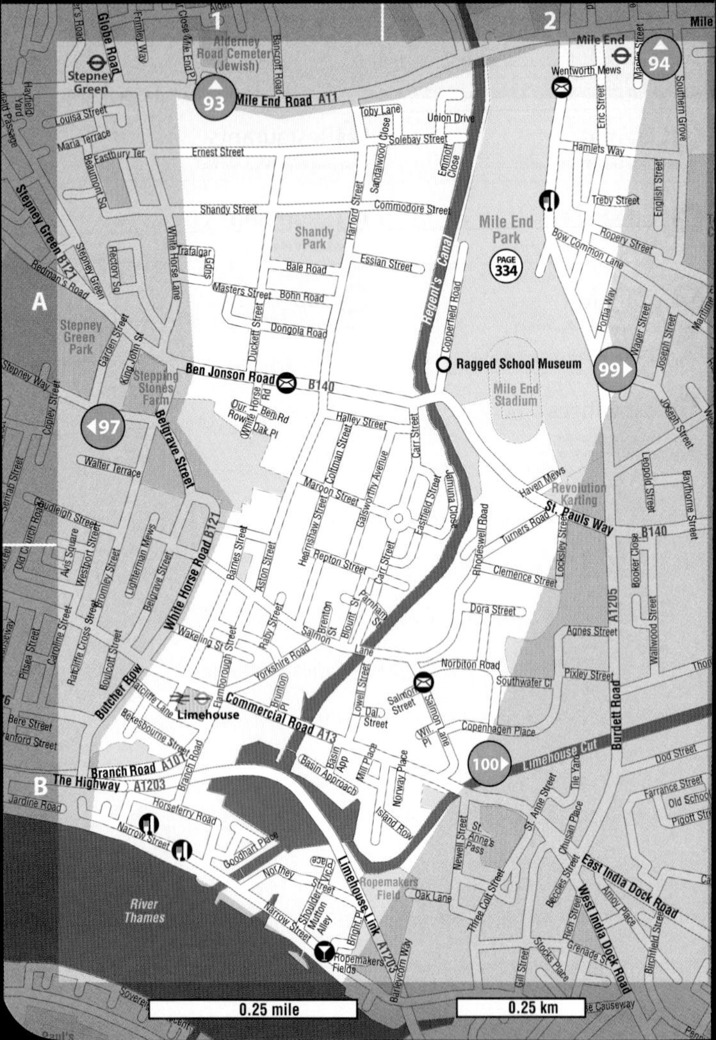

Globe Road
Stepney Green
Louisa St
Maria Terrace
Eastbury Ter
Beaumont St
Stepney Green
Rectory Sq
Aston St
Trafalgar Gdns
King John St
Redmans Rd
Stepney Green Park
Stepney Way
Copley St
Oxley Square
Walter Terrace
Cleveland Way

Aldeney Road Cemetery (Jewish)
93
Mile End Road A11
Toby Lane
Ernest Street
Sandilawood Close
Solebay Street
Union Drive
Mile End
Wentworth Mews
94
Southern Grove
Eric Street
English Street

Shandy Street
Harford Street
Commodore Street
Hamlets Way
Treby Street
Ropery Street
Bow Common Lane

Shandy Park
Bale Road
Essian Street
Mile End Park
PAGE 334

Masters Street
Bohn Road
Dongola Road
Ben Jonson Road
Copperfield Road
Ragged School Museum
99

Portia Way
Joseph Street

97
Stepping Stones Farm
Belgrave Street
White Horse Road B121

Our Lady &
St Joseph
RC
Halley Street
Beth Rd
Oak Pl
Carr Street

Mile End Stadium

Clemson Street

Haven Mews
Revolution Karting
Turners Road
St Pauls Way
B140

Maroon Street
Colman Street
Repton Street
Aston Street
Bromley St
Barnes Street
Hermitage Mews
Trenton Street
Salmon
Blount St
Piggotts Lane
Rhodeswell Road
Clemence Street
Dora Street
Lockesley Street

Butcher Bow
White Horse Lane
Belgrave Street
Ratcliffe Cross Street
Bromley Hall
Caroline Mews
Westport St
Wakeling St
Yorkshire Road

Agnes Street
Pixley Street
Norbiton Road
Southwater Cr
Burdett Road A1205
B140
Booker Close
Wallwood Street
Josseline Street
Bowthorne Road

Commercial Road A13
Limehouse

Lowell Street
Salmon Lane
Dod Street

Pelling St
Dial Street
Saint Anne St
Will Pl
Mill Place
Norway Place
Copenhagen Place
100
Limehouse Cut
Farrance Street
Old School Road
Pigott Street

Branch Road A10
The Highway A1203
Bekesbourne Street
Spert Street
Horseferry Road
Basin Approach
Boothart Place
Island Row
Newell St
St James Pass
Newell St
Three Colt Street

Jardine Road
Narrow Street
Limehouse Link Road
Barleycorn Way
Ropemakers Field
Oak Lane
Amoy Place
Grenade St

East India Dock Road
West India Dock Road

River Thames
Narrow Street
Shoulder of Mutton Alley
Roper Street
Ropemakers Fields

0.25 mile   0.25 km

Mile End (South) / Limehouse

Map 98

Classic east end with a heady mix of poverty-stricken bleakness around the tail of Mile End park and a Docklands developer's wet dream by the river. But cheer up—great eats and drinks along the Thames on Narrow Street (The Grapes, The Narrow, and La Figa) and the illuminating Ragged School Museum and Lebanese tastiness (Orange Room) near Mile End.

O Landmarks
• **Ragged School Museum** • 45 Copperfield Rd

Nightlife
• **The Grapes** • 76 Narrow Street

Post Offices
• **Ben Jonson Road** • 52 Ben Jonson Rd
• **Mile End** • 1 Burdett Rd
• **Salmon Lane** • 127 Salmon Ln

Restaurants
• **La Figa** • 45 Narrow St
• **The Narrow** • 44 Narrow Street
• **Orange Room Café** • 63 Burdett Rd

Map 99 · **Bow Common**

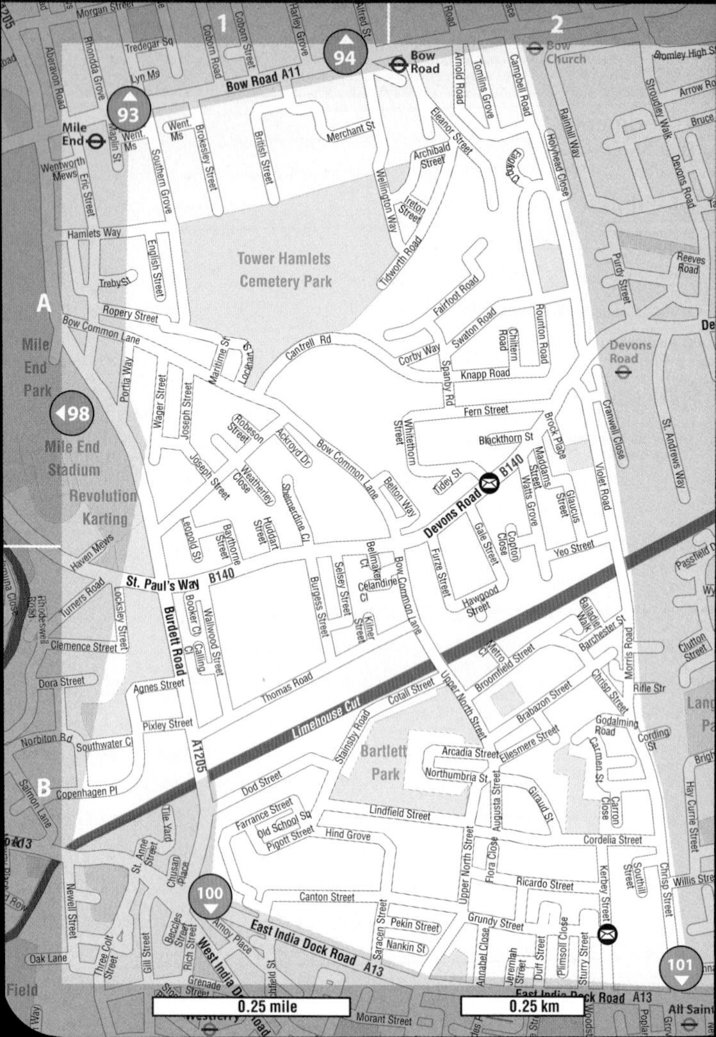

Map 99 · Bow Common

N

1

2

94

Bow Road

Bow Church

Tredegar Sq

Bow Road A11

93

Mile End

Tower Hamlets
Cemetery Park

A

Mile End Park

98

Mile End Stadium

Revolution Karting

Devons Road

B140

Devons Road

St. Paul's Way

B140

Burdett Road

Limehouse Cut

B

Bartlett Park

100

East India Dock Road

A13

East India Dock Road A13

101

All Saints

0.25 mile

0.25 km

There's not a whole lot to do or see here. Countless old housing estates and boarded up pubs is about as exciting as it gets. If for some reason you need to visit, The Tower Hamlets Cemetery Park is a nice place to spend half an hour. Keep alert after dark in these parts.

Post Offices

- **Devons Road** • 159 Devons Rd
- **Poplar** • 22 Market Sq

Map 100 · **Poplar (West) / Canary Wharf (West)**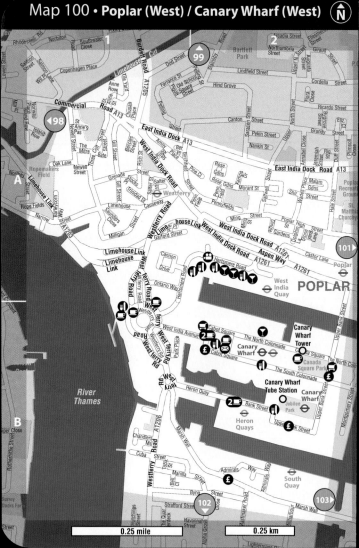

Finance's new engine room, wander the Wharf and marvel at the 'scrapers, straight streets and starched suits. Shop at the malls under Cabot Square and Jubilee Place; just don't expect independent boutiques or much soul. Best lunch options are Nicolas or Tiffin Bites. If you've got a bonus to spend, Plateau will relieve you of half of it, if you haven't, what are you doing here?

£ Banks

- **Halifax** • 350 Cabot Pl E
- **HSBC** • Canary Wharf
- **HSBC** • 45 Bank St
- **NatWest** • 54 Marsh Wall
- **NatWest** • 20 Canada Sq

Cinemas

- **Cineworld West India Quay** • 11 Hertsmere Rd

Coffee

- **Bagel Factory** • 7 Westferry Circus
- **Café Brera** • 45 Bank St
- **Café Brera** • 12 Cabot Sq
- **Café Brera** • 31 Westferry Circus
- **Coffee Republic** • Canary Wharf
- **Coffee Republic** • Hertsmere Rd
- **Fresco Café Bar** • 15 Cabot Sq
- **Fresco Café Bar** • Cabot Sq & N Colonnade
- **Starbucks** • 1 Canada Sq
- **Starbucks** • 45 Bank St
- **Starbucks** • 7 Westferry Circus

O Landmarks

- **Canary Wharf Tower** • 1 Canada Sq
- **Canary Wharf Tube Station** • Canary Wharf

Nightlife

- **Bar 38** • West India Quay
- **Davy's at Canary Wharf** • 31 Fisherman's Walk
- **Dion Canary Wharf** • Port East Building, West India Quay
- **Via Fossa** • 18 Hertsmere Rd

Post Offices

- **Canary Wharf** • 5 Chancellor Passage

Restaurants

- **1802 Bar** • Hertsmere Rd
- **Beluga Café** • West India Quay
- **Browns** • Hertsmere Rd
- **la tasca** • Hertsmere Rd
- **Nicolas** • 480 One Canada Sq
- **Plateau** • Canada Pl
- **Tiffin Bites** • 22 Jubilee Place
- **Ubon by Nobu** • 34 Westferry Circus

Supermarkets

- **Tesco** • 15 Cabot Sq
- **Waitrose** • N Colonnade & Canada Sq

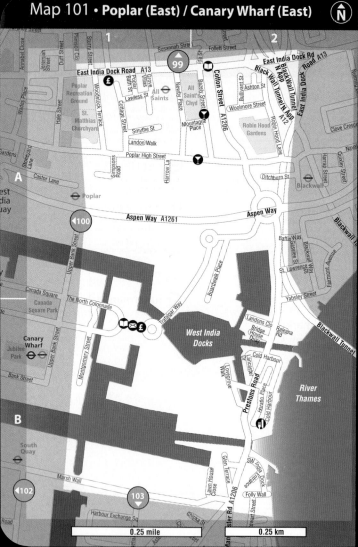

Map 101 · **Poplar (East) / Canary Wharf (East)**

Poplar (East) / Canary Wharf (East)

Let's be honest, there's not much to do here unless you like gazing up dull glass towers (and ugly council estates) or enjoy squeezing past investment bankers talking credit derivatives in chain bars. That said, Gun, tucked away on Coldharbour, is an excellent British restaurant-cum-pub that's enjoyed by docklands veterans and office workers alike. After real East End boozing? Try Poplar's Greenwich Pensioner.

Map 101

£ Banks
- **Barclays** • 2 Churchill Pl
- **Barclays** • 159 E India Dock Rd

Libraries
- **Idea Store Canary Wharf** • Churchill Pl
- **Idea Store Chrisp Street** • East India Dock Rd

Nightlife
- **The Greenwich Pensioner** • 28 Bazely Street
- **The Resolute** • 210 Poplar High Street

Post Offices
- **Churchill Place** • 2 Churchill Pl

Restaurants
- **Gun** • 27 Coldharbour

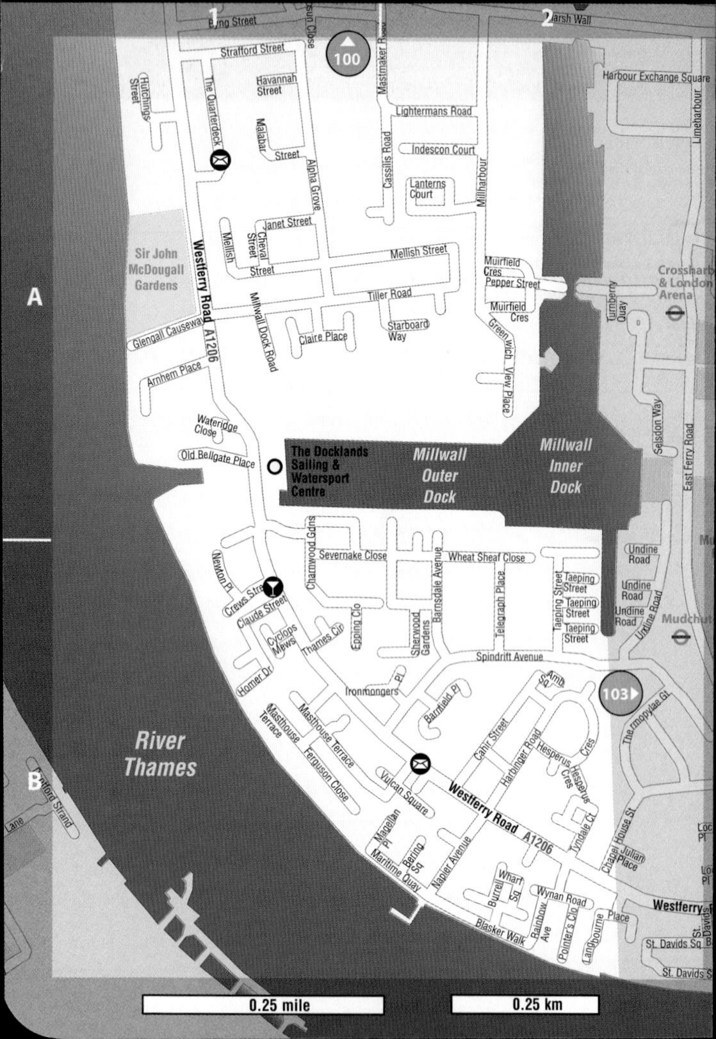

Map 102 · **Millwall**

N

Long Street

Marsh Wall

Strafford Street

100

Hutchings Street

The Quarterdeck

Havannah Street

Malabar Street

Alpha Grove

Harbour Exchange Square

Lightermans Road

Cassilis Road

Indescon Court

Mastmaker Road

Lanterns Court

Millharbour

Janet Street

Cheval Street

Mellish Street

Mellish Street

Muirfield Cres

Pepper Street

Crossharbour & London Arena

Sir John McDougall Gardens

Westferry Road A1206

Millwall Dock Road

Tiller Road

Muirfield Cres

A

Glengall Causeway

Arnhem Place

Claire Place

Starboard Way

Greenwich View Place

Turnberry Quay

East Ferry Road

Selsdon Way

Wateridge Close

Old Bellgate Place

The Docklands Sailing & Watersport Centre

○

Millwall Outer Dock

Millwall Inner Dock

Mudchut

Newton Pl

Severnake Close

Chartwood Gdns

Wheat Sheaf Close

Undine Road

River Thames

Crews Street

Claude Street

Cyclops Mews

Thames Circ

Epping Clo

Barnsdale Avenue

Sherwood Gardens

Telegraph Place

Taeping Street
Taeping Street
Taeping Street
Taeping Street

Undine Road

Linsey Road

Homer Dr

Ironmongers Pl

Spindrift Avenue

Amb

Sq

103 ▶

The Quarrles Gt

Masthouse Terrace

Maltings Close

Ferguson Close

Vulcan Square

Barnfield Pl

Cahir Street

Harbinger Road

Hesperus Cres

Cres

Westferry Road A1206

B

Stalford Strand

Lane

Magellan Pl

Baring St

Maritime Quay

Wharf St

Burrells Wf

Midland Avenue

Bandbox Ave

Wynan Road

Pointer's Clo

Lindisfarne

Pl

Lockesfield Pl

Chapel House St

Julian Place

Westferry

St. Davids Sq S.

St. Davids S

Blasker Walk

0.25 mile

0.25 km

Map 102

Though Millwall has award winning Docklands Sailing Centre and decent community venue The Space (Hubbub Café and Bar), it doesn't really have much else. Bereft of tube, overground, or DLR, it doesn't even have Millwall FC anymore. Despite the potential of Canary Wharf on the doorstep and flush of luxury riverside apartments, it's still tainted with the whiff of BNP and football hooliganism. Buy now.

O Landmarks

• **The Docklands Sailing & Watersport Centre** •
235 Westferry Rd

Nightlife

• **Hubbub** • 269 Westferry Rd

Post Offices

• **The Quarterdeck** • 3 The Quarterdeck
• **Westferry Rd** • 367 Westferry Rd

Map 103 · **Cubitt Town / Mudchute**

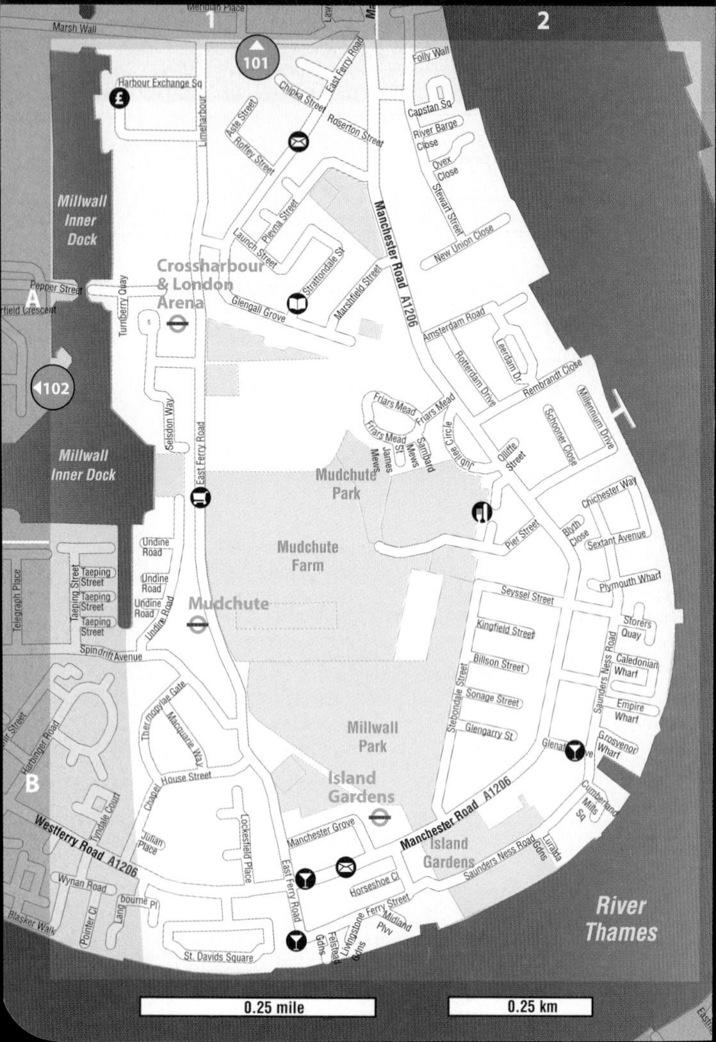

Marsh Wall

Mendian Place

1

2

101

Harbour Exchange Sq

£

Folly Wall

East Ferry Road

Limeharbour

Chipka Street

Roserton Street

Capstan Sq

River Barge Close

Oyer Close

Stewart Street

Agas Street

Roffey Street

Pierpoint Street

Launch Street

Pienna Street

Manchester Street

A1206

Millwall Inner Dock

New Union Close

Pepper Street

field Crescent

A

Turnberry Quay

Crossharbour & London Arena

Strattondale St

Stratton Grove

Mastsford Road

Amsterdam Road

Rotterdam Drive

Leerdam Dr

Rembrandt Close

Millennium Drive

102

Selsdon Way

Friars Mead

Friars Mead

Friars Mead

Friars Mead Mews

St James

Saffbild

Castalia Sq

Clare Light

Qilette Street

Schooner Close

Chichester Way

Mudchute Park

Pier Street

Blyth Close

Sextant Avenue

Millwall Inner Dock

Undine Road

Undine Road

Undine Road

Teaping Street

Teaping Street

Teaping Street

Teaping Street

Spindrift Avenue

Mudchute

Mudchute Farm

Seyssel Street

Plymouth Wharf

Kingfield Street

Storers Quay

Billson Street

Caledonian Wharf

Saunders Ness Road

Telegraph Place

Harbour Road

Stebondale Street

Sonage Street

Empire Wharf

Thermopylae Gate

Macquarie Way

Chapel House Street

Glengarry St

Grosvenor Wharf

Glenaff

Luralda

Millwall Park

B

Cahir Street

Tobago Street

Juban Place

Cockerell Place

Island Gardens

Manchester Grove

Manchester Road A1206

Island Gardens

Cumberland

Mills Sq

Westferry Road A1206

East Ferry Road

Horseshoe Cl

Saunders Ness Road

Wynan Road

Bourne Pl

Lang

Pointer Cl

Blasker Walk

Livingstone Ferry Road

Felstead Gdns

Midland Pl

River Thames

St Davids Square

| 0.25 mile | 0.25 km |

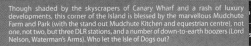

Cubitt Town / Mudchute

Map 103

Though shaded by the skyscrapers of Canary Wharf and a rash of luxury developments, this corner of the Island is blessed by the marvellous Mudchute Farm and Park (with the stand out Mudchute Kitchen and equestrian centre), not one, not two, but three DLR stations, and a number of down-to-earth boozers (Lord Nelson, Waterman's Arms). Who let the Isle of Dogs out?

Banks
• **Lloyds** • 24 Harbor Exchange

Libraries
• **Cubitt Town Library** • Strattondale St

Nightlife
• **Ferry House** • 26 Ferry St
• **Lord Nelson** • 1 Manchester Road
• **Waterman's Arms** • 1 Glenaffric Avenue

Post Offices
• **Cubitt Town** • 15 Castalia Sq
• **Isle Of Dogs** • 159 Manchester Rd

Restaurants
• **Mudchute Kitchen** • Pier Street,

Supermarkets
• **ASDA** • 151 E Ferry Rd

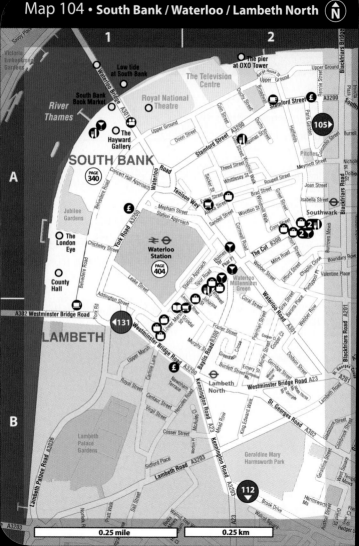

South Bank / Waterloo / Lambeth North

Map 104

Hug the riverbank and you can culture 'till you puke. But you'll need stamina to survive; with such densely populated institutions your brain will give up long before your body. When it does, head for The Cut and get rid of some of those bothersome brain cells at Cubana (great happy hour) or The Young Vic's Cut Bar (best chips in town).

£ Banks

- **HSBC** • 22 Stamford St
- **Lloyds** • 2 York Rd
- **NatWest** • 91 Westminster Bridge Rd

Cinemas

- **BFI London IMAX** • Waterloo Rd & York Rd
- **BFI Southbank** • Belverdere Rd

Coffee

- **Costa** • Belvedere Rd
- **Eat.** • Belvedere Rd
- **Eat.** • Barge House St
- **Pret A Manger** • 58 Stamford St
- **Starbucks** • 3 Belvedere Rd

O Landmarks

- **County Hall** • Riverside Walkway
- **The Hayward Gallery** • Southbank Centre
- **The London Eye** • Westminster Bridge Rd
- **Low tide at South Bank** • South Bank
- **National Theatre** • South Bank
- **The pier at OXO Tower** •
- **South Bank Book Market** •
  Southbank (under Waterloo Bridge, opposite BFI)
- **Waterloo Bridge** • Waterloo Bridge

Libraries

- **Poetry Library** • Belvedere Rd
- **Waterloo Library** • 114 Lower Marsh

Nightlife

- **Anchor & Hope** • 32 The Cut
- **Cubana** • 48 Lower Marsh
- **The Cut Bar** • 66 The Cut
- **Da Vinci's** • 6 Baylis Rd
- **The Fire Station** • 150 Waterloo Rd
- **The Pit Bar at the Old Vic** • The Cut
- **Royal Festival Hall** • Belvedere Rd
- **Skylon** • Belvedere Rd

Restaurants

- **Anchor & Hope** • 32 The Cut
- **Canteen** • Belvedere Rd
- **The Cut Bar** • 66 The Cut
- **Giraffe** • Southbank
- **Livebait** • 45 The Cut
- **Marie's Cafe** • 90 Lower Marsh
- **Oxo Tower Wharf** • Barge House St
- **RSJ** • 33 Coin St
- **Skylon** • Belvedere Rd
- **Studio 6** • Gabriels Wharf

Shopping

- **The Bookshop Theatre** • 51 The Cut
- **Calder Bookshop** • 51 The Cut
- **I Knit London** • 106 Lower Marsh
- **Konditor & Cook** • 22 Cornwall Rd
- **Oasis** • 84 Lower Marsh
- **Radio Days** • 87 Lower Marsh
- **Scooterworks** • 132 Lower Marsh
- **Top Wind** • 2 Lower Marsh
- **Waterloo Camping** • 37 The Cut
- **What The Butler Wore** • 131 Lower Marsh

Supermarkets

- **Iceland** • 112 Lower Marsh
- **Marks & Spencer** • Waterloo Station
- **Sainsbury's** • 101 Waterloo Rd

Map 105 · **Southwark / Bankside (West)**

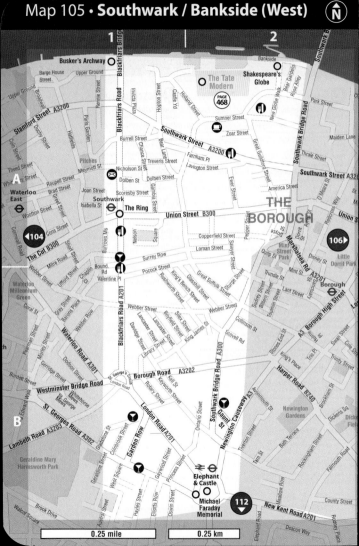

The Tate Modern, ladies and gents. This is where it is and it deserves all the praise it gets. Next door, there's the reconstruction of Shakespeare's famous playhouse, making this looked-after stretch of the Thames embankment a treasure for those hungry for culture. For those hungry for something else: Baltic for Polish hunter's stew, The Table for fresh salads, Amano for stone-baked pizza..

Coffee

• **Eat.** • Bankside
• **Pret A Manger** • 2 Canvey St

O Landmarks

• **Buskers' Archway** • Southbank
• **Elephant & Castle** • Elephant & Castle
• **Michael Faraday Memorial** • Elephant & Castle
• **The Ring** • 72 Blackfriars Rd
• **Shakespeare's Globe** • 21 New Globe Walk
• **Tate Modern** • Bankside

Nightlife

• **Albert Arms** • 1 Gladstone St
• **Imbibe** • 173 Blackfriars Rd
• **Ministry of Sound** • 103 Gaunt St
• **Prince of Wales** • 51 St George's Rd

Post Offices

• **Blackfriars Road** • 52 Blackfriars Rd

Restaurants

• **Amano** • 20 Sumner St
• **Baltic** • 74 Blackfriars Rd
• **Blackfriars Cafe** • 169 Blackfriars Rd
• **The Table** • 85 Southwark St
• **Tapas Brindisa** • 18 Southwark St
• **Tate Modern Restaurant** • Sumner St

Shopping

• **Elephant & Castle Market** • Elephant & Castle

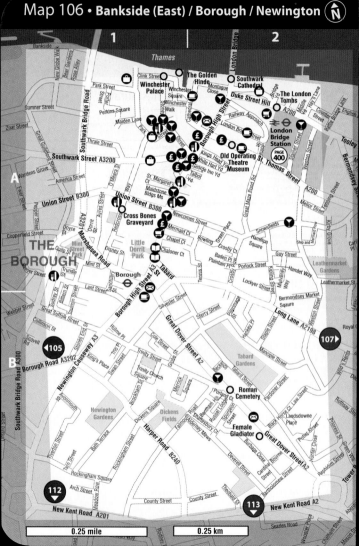

Map 106 • Bankside (East) / Borough / Newington

Bankside (East) / Borough / Newington

Map 106

A Shoreditch for grown-ups, of sorts, these parts have become a bit sutified lately. Still, there's plenty of fun around. Gourmet-minded Borough Market draws the crowds on Saturdays, while the pubs and bars lining Borough High Street keep the party-minded happy throughout the week. Don't miss The Rake if you like (unusual) beer, Brindisa for Spanish tapas, and Roast if meat's your thing.

£ Banks

• **Abbey** • 9 Southwark St
• **Barclays** • 29 Borough High St
• **HSBC** • 28 Borough High St
• **Lloyds** • 69 Borough High St
• **NatWest** • St Thomas St
• **NatWest** • 10 Southwark St

Coffee

• **Caffe Nero** • 3 Cathedral St
• **Costa** • 134 Borough High St
• **Pret A Manger** • 8 London bridge st
• **Starbucks** • 21 St. Thomas St

O Landmarks

• **Cross Bones Graveyard** • Red Cross Way
• **Female Gladiator** • Great Dover St
• **The Golden Hinde** • Clink St
• **The London Tombs** • Tooley St
• **Old Operating Theatre Museum** • 9 St Thomas St
• **Roman Cemetery** • 165 Great Dover St
• **Southwark Cathedral** • London Bridge
• **Winchester Palace** • Clink St

Libraries

• **John Harvard Library** • 211 Borough High St
• **Local History Library** • 211 Borough High St

Nightlife

• **Belushi's** • 161 Borough High St
• **The Blue-Eyed Maid** • 173 Borough High St
• **Brew Wharf** • Brew Wharf Yard, Stoney St
• **The George Inn** • 77 Borough High St
• **The Globe** • 8 Bedale St
• **La Cave** • 6 Borough High St
• **The Market Porter** • 9 Stoney St
• **The Rake** • 14 Winchester Walk
• **The Roebuck** • 50 Great Dover St
• **The Rose** • 123 Snowfields
• **Roxy Bar and Screen** • 128 Borough High St
• **The Royal Oak** • 44 Tabard St
• **Shunt Lounge and Vaults** • 20 Stainer St
• **Southwark Tavern** • 22 Southwark St
• **Wine Wharf** • Stoney St

Post Offices

• **Borough** • 239 Borough High St
• **Great Dover Street** • 159 Great Dover St
• **London Bridge** • 19 Borough High St

Restaurants

• **Amano** • Clink St
• **Boot and Flogger** • 10 Redcross Way
• **Brew Wharf** • Brew Wharf Yard, Stoney St
• **Cantina Vinopolis** • 1 Bank End
• **Champor-Champor** • 62 Weston St
• **El Vergel** • 8 Lant St
• **Feng Sushi** • 13 Stoney St
• **Fish!** • Cathedral St
• **Fusebox** • 12 Stoney St
• **Hing Loon** • 159 Borough High St
• **Roast** • The Floral Hall, Stoney St
• **Silka** • Southwark St
• **Tas** • 72 Borough High St
• **Wright Bros Oyster Bar** • 11 Stoney St

Shopping

• **German Deli** • 8 Southwark St
• **Paul Smith** • 13 Park St
• **Richer Sounds** • 2 London Bridge Walk
• **Vinopolis** • 1 Bank End

Supermarkets

• **Marks & Spencer** • London Bridge Station
• **Sainsbury's** • 116 Borough High St

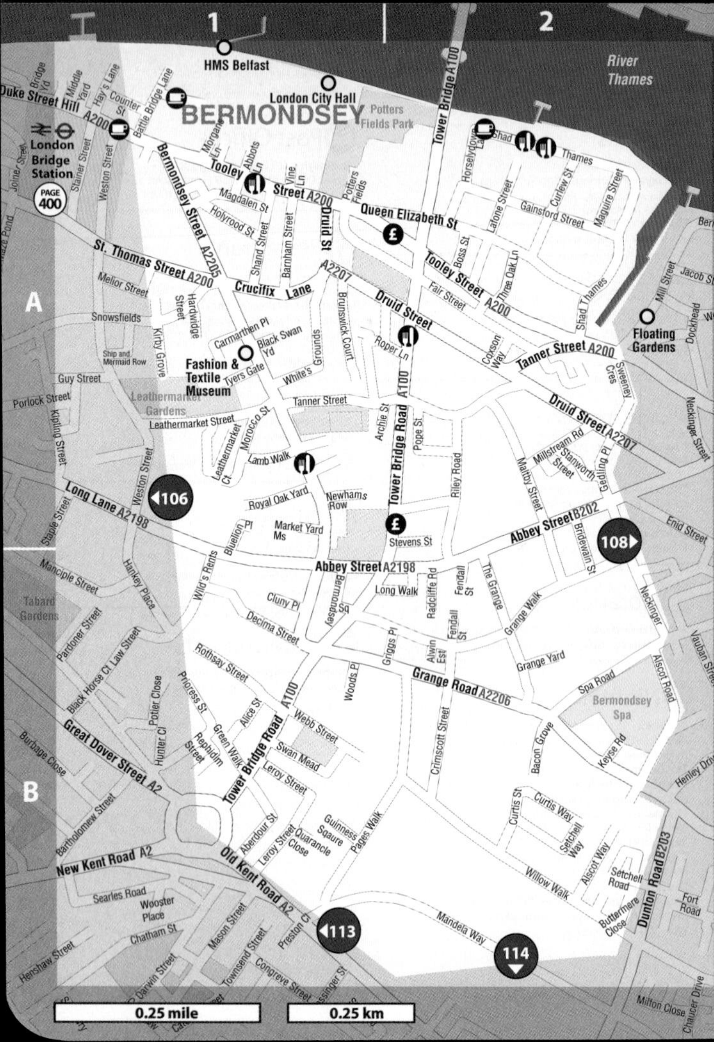

Map 107 · **Shad Thames**

N

River Thames

HMS Belfast

London City Hall

BERMONDSEY

Potters Fields Park

Duke Street Hill A200

London Bridge Station

PAGE 400

Tooley

Street A200

Queen Elizabeth St

£

Tooley Street A200

1

2

Shad Thames

Gainsford Street

Maguire St

Curlew St

Lafone St

Horselydown Ln

St. Thomas Street A2205

Bermondsey Street

Crucifix Lane

Druid Street

Fair Street

Snowsfields

Fashion & Textile Museum

Tanner Street

A

Floating Gardens

Roper Ln

Tanner Street A200

Druid Street A2207

Black Swan Yd

Lamb Walk

◀106

Market Yard Ms

Tower Bridge Road A100

Abbey Street

£

Stevens St

Abbey Street B202

108▶

Long Lane A2198

Abbey Street A2198

Long Walk

The Grange

Grange Walk

Grange Yard

Bermondsey Spa

Decima Street

Grange Road A2206

Great Dover Street A2

Tower Bridge Road A100

Spa Road

B

Tabard Gardens

New Kent Road A2

Old Kent Road A2

◀113

Dunton Road B203

114▼

0.25 mile   0.25 km

Shad Thames

Map 107

The elitist's Bermondsey, Shad Thames is an ultra-hip jumble of glass balconies and converted warehouses, emanating an excited-to-be-in-London buzz. Stroll the capital's answer to the Riviera between the Mayor's offices and the Design Museum. Try Bermondsey Street for affluent hipsters (clustered around the Fashion & Textile Museum) and Butler's Wharf Chop House for grey squirrel and rook's pie. Seriously.

£ Banks

- **Barclays** • 104 Tower Bridge Rd
- **NatWest** • 201 Tooley St

Coffee

- **Caffe Nero** • 6 More Pl [Tooley Street]
- **Pret A Manger** • 49 Tooley St
- **Starbucks** • 49 Shad Thames

O Landmarks

- **City Hall** • Queen's Walk, More London Development
- **Fashion and Textile Museum** • 83 Bermondsey St
- **Floating Gardens** • 31 Mill St
- **HMS Belfast** • Morgan's Lane, Tooley St
- **London City Hall** • Greater London Authority, City Hall, The Queen's Walk

Nightlife

- **The Hide** • 39 Bermondsey St
- **Village East** • 171-173 Bermondsey St

Restaurants

- **Butlers Wharf Chop House** • 36 Shad Thames
- **Delfina** • 50 Bermondsey St
- **Le Pont de la Tour** • 36 Shad Thames
- **M Manze Pie and Mash** • 87 Tower Bridge Rd
- **Magdalen** • 152 Tooley St
- **Village East** • 171-173 Bermondsey St

Shopping

- **The Design Museum Shop** • Shad Thames

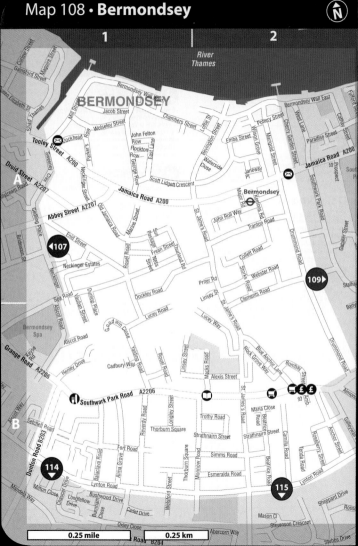

With its mixed bag of winding cobbled streets, council estates and posh new builds, you can imagine the awkwardness when the new-to-the-neighbourhood clean shirt steps into the adamantly local Bermondsey local. The old-timers are sticking to their guns, and there is a definite dirty side to this on-the-cusp part of town. For pasta, try Arancia on Southwark Park Road.

£ Banks

• **Barclays** • 264 Southwark Park Rd
• **Lloyds** • 255 Southwark Park Rd

Libraries

• **Blue Anchor Library** • Southwark Park Rd

Post Offices

• **Dockhead** • 31 Dockhead
• **Jamaica Road** • 158 Jamaica Rd

Restaurants

• **Arancia** • 52 Southwark Park Rd

Supermarkets

• **Co-Op** • 193 Southwark Park Rd
• **Iceland** • 222 Southwark Park

221

Map 109 · **Southwark Park**

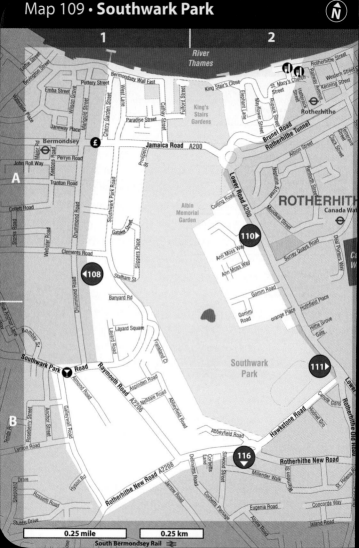

It might look a little runty compared to its Royal Park rivals, but if you want green without getting on a tube then Southwark Park is a lovely option. Well-spent investment has given it a boating lake, wildlife area, an inspiring artist-led café and the Dilston Grove gallery. For drinks, head to the river for an ale in the Mayflower—the pub of dreams.

Banks
• **Abbey** • 210 Southwark

Nightlife
• **Ancient Foresters** • 282 Southwark Park Rd

Restaurants
• **Mayflower** • 117 Rotherhithe St
• **Simplicity** • 1 Tunnel Rd

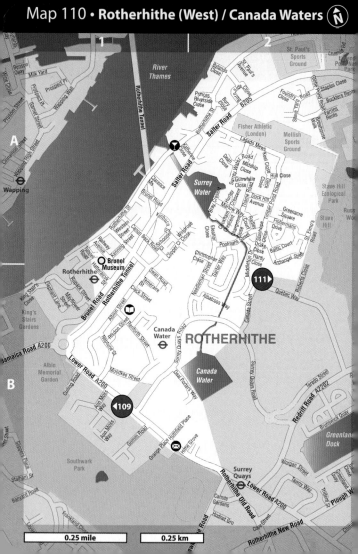

Map 110 · Rotherhithe (West) / Canada Waters

If residential flats are your thing you'll love Rotherhithe West. Not if pubs are your thing though. Or shops. Or life. But among the warren of apartments you can drink on the fabulous Thameside patio at Old Salt Quay, entertain your dad at the Brunel Museum, and stroll the enchantingly serene stretch of the Thames Path (if you can stand the joggers and the snoggers).

O Landmarks
• **Brunel Museum** • Railway Ave

Libraries
• **Rotherhithe Library** • Albion St

Nightlife
• **Old Salt Quay** • 163 Rotherhithe St

Post Offices
• **Lower Road Rotherhithe** • 142 Lower Rd

Map 111 · **Rotherhithe (East) / Surrey Quays**

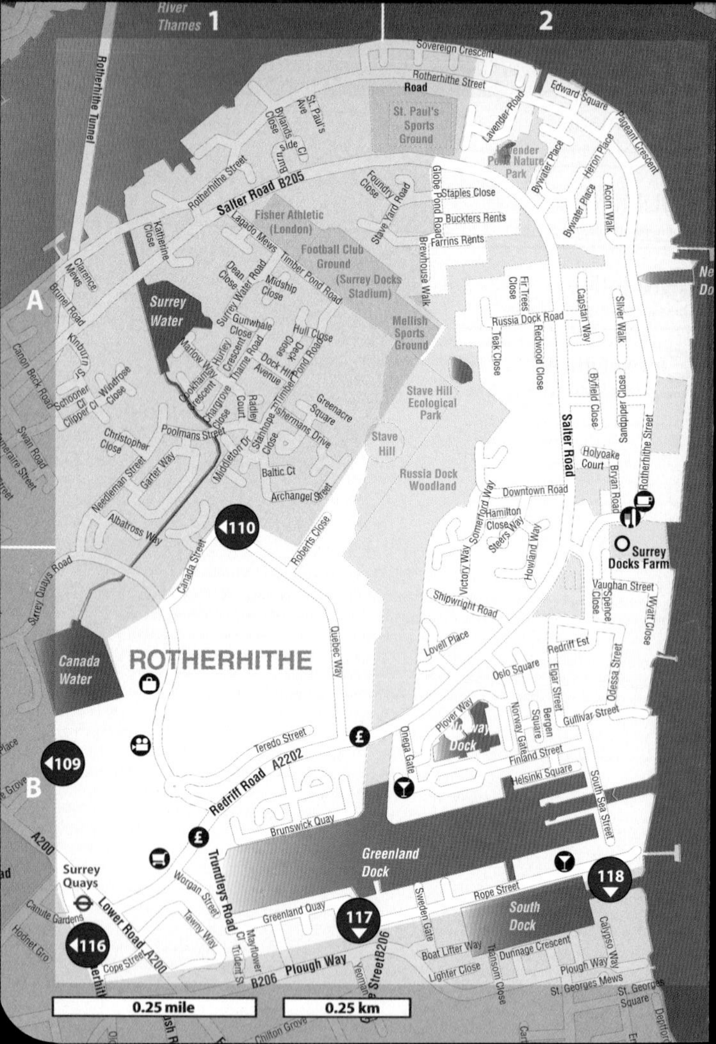

River Thames **1** **2**

Sovereign Crescent

Rotherhithe Street

Edward Square

Rotherhithe Street

Road

Lavender Road

St. Paul's Ave

St. Paul's Sports Ground

St. Paul's Close

Brandside

Heron Place

Pilgrim Crescent

Lavender Pond Nature Park

Byward Place

Acorn Walk

Bywater Place

Rotherhithe Street

Saller Road B205

Foundry Close

Staples Close

Globe Pond Road

Stave Yard Road

Bucklers Rents

Silver Walk

Fisher Athletic (London)

Lagado Mews

Timber Pond Road

Farrins Rents

Captain Way

Brewhouse Walk

Fir Trees Close

Russia Dock Road

Redwood Close

Byfield Close

Sandpiper Close

Rotherhithe Street

Football Club Ground (Surrey Docks Stadium)

Dean Close

Midship Close

Surrey Water Road

Teak Close

Mellish Sports Ground

Gumwhale Close

Marlow Way

Hurley Crescent

Hull Close

Holyoake Court

Johnathan
St.
Bailey St.
Dock Hill Avenue

Dog & Duck

Surrey Water

Kinburn St.
Clipper Ct.
Windrace Close

Schooner

Glasgow Court

Acorn Way

Greenacre Square

Stave Hill Ecological Park

Saller Road

Downtown Road

Radley Court

Rotherhithe Street

Canon Beck Road

Sweet Road

Christopher Close

Poolmans Street

Middleton Dr.

Baltic Ct.

Stanhope Drive

Tradesmans Drive

Stave Hill

Russia Dock Woodland

Hamilton Close Alley

Steers Way

Bryan Road

Sunfield Way

A

Clarence Mews

Brunel Road

Surrey Quays Road

Needleman Street

Gater Way

Albatross Way

Archangel Street

Somerford Way

Surrey Docks Farm

Vaughan Street

Spence Close

Wyatt Close

Jessop Close

Victory Way

Hothfield Way

Lovell Place

Shipwright Road

Redriff Est

◀110

Canada Gate

Roberts Close

Quebec Way

Osio Square

Edgar Street

Bergen Square

Gullivar Street

Norway Gate

South Sea Street

Finland Street

Helsinki Square

B

ROTHERHITHE

Canada Water

🛍

Teredo Street

£

Plover Way

Onega Gate

Norway Dock

109▶

🏛

Redriff Road A2202

£

🛒

Worgan Street

Brunswick Quay

Greenland Dock

Rope Street

Surrey Quays

Lower Road A200

Trundleys Road

Greenland Quay

Steelyard Close

117▼

118▼

South Dock

Calypso Way

A200

Tanny Way

Mayflower St.

Plough Way

Boat Lifter Way

Lighter Close

Dunnage Crescent

Plough Way

◀116

Cope Street

Yeoman Street B206

Trident Street

B206

Lifesmann Close

St. Georges Mews

St. Georges Square

Chiffon Grove

Canute Gardens

Hobart Gro

Place

Surrey Grove

0.25 mile **0.25 km**

Rotherhithe (East) / Surrey Quays

Map 111

It still has some dodgy estates, but Rotherhithe East is blossoming in a clean-cut city-worker kind of way. The docks are delightful and have resisted the chain bars, instead allowing great little independents like Wibbley Wobbley and Moby Dick to flourish. Trying to be healthy? Enjoy lunch among the goats at wholesome Café Nabo in Surrey Docks Farm, and visit Decathlon for sport equipment paradise.

£ Banks

- **Halifax** • 28 Redriff Rd
- **HSBC** • Redriff Rd

Cinemas

- **Odeon Surrey Quays** • Redriff Rd & Surrey Quays Rd

O Landmarks

- **Surrey Docks Farm** • Rotherhithe St

Nightlife

- **Moby Dick** • 6 Russell Place, off Greenland Dock
- **Wibbley Wobbley** • South Dock Marina, Rope St

Restaurants

- **Café Nabo** • Surrey Docks Farm, Rotherhithe St

Shopping

- **Decathlon** • Surrey Quays Road

Supermarkets

- **Tesco** • Redriff Rd

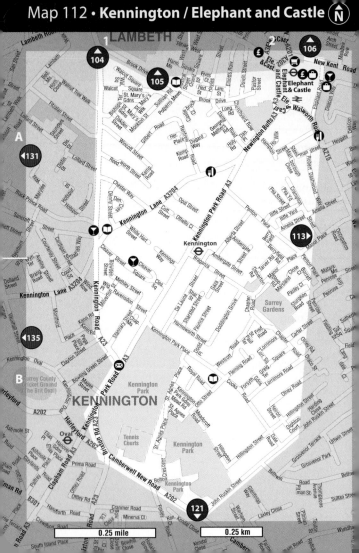

Kennington / Elephant and Castle

Map 112

Overly-keen "battlefield recreation" contractors at the Imperial War Museum forgot to stop at the museum gates. The resultant concrete crime-fest is the dystopian 'Clockwork' Elephant. True, it has something of Berlin about it—but that's Berlin 1945. Bunker down in Dragon Castle with resigned LCC media lecturers for surprisingly good Chinese food, or tunnel out to Kennington's Prince of Wales as you salute the budding redevelopers' optimism.

 Banks

• **Abbey** • 335 Elephant & Castle
• **Lloyds** • 245 Elephant and Castle

 Libraries

• **Brandon Library** • Cooks Rd [Maddock Way]
• **Durning Library** • 167 Kennington Ln
• **Imperial War Museum** • Austral St

 Nightlife

• **Corsica Studios** • 5 Elephant Rd
• **Dog House** • 293 Kennington Rd
• **Prince of Wales** • 43 Cleaver Sq

 Post Offices

• **Kennington Park** • 410 Kennington Park Rd

Restaurants

• **Dragon Castle** • 100 Walworth Rd
• **Lobster Pot** • 3 Kennington Ln

Shopping

• **Pricebusters Hardware** • 311 Elephant & Castle Shopping Centre
• **Recycling** • 110 Elephant Rd

Supermarkets

• **Iceland** • 300 Elephant & Castle
• **Tesco** • Elephant & Castle

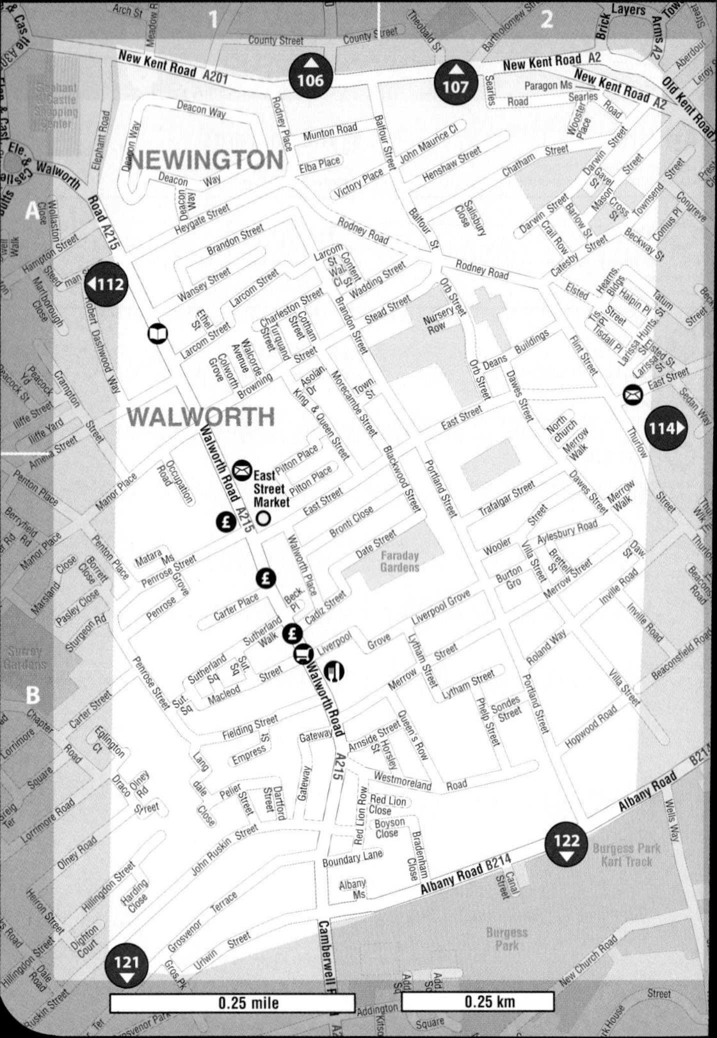

Map 113 · **Walworth**

1　2

N

County Street　County Street

Theobald St　Bartholomew St

Brick　Layers

Arch St

New Kent Road A201

106

New Kent Road A2

Searles Road

107

New Kent Road A2

New Kent Road A2

Old Kent Road

Aberdour

Paragon Ms

Searles Road

Wooster Place

Deacon Way

Rodney Place

Munton Road

Balfour Street

John Maurice Cl

Chatham Street

Darwin Street

St Georges

Elephant & Castle Shopping Center

NEWINGTON

Deacon Way

Elba Place

Henshaw Street

Salisbury Close

Townsend Street

Mason Cross St

Beckway St

Congreve St

Comus Pl

Elephant & Castle

Victory Place

Darwin Court

Barlow Street

Walworth Road A215

Heygate Street

Rodney Road

Balfour St

Crail Row

Catesby Street

Elsted Street

Hearns Buildings

Hapin Pl

Haldane Pl

Larissa

A

112

Brandon Street

Larcom Street

Wansey Street

Larcom St

Colworth Grove

Chapter Rd

Charleston Street

Cobham St

Turquand Street

Brandon Street

Wadding Street

Stead Street

Rodney Road

Nursery Row

Orb Street

Deans Buildings

Dawes Street

Flint Street

Thurlow St

Theobald St

Larissa Haw

Sandys Rd

Longley St

East Street

Sedan Wk

114

WALWORTH

Ethel St

Browning

Avenue

Kings & Queens St

Apoler Dr

Morecambe Street

Town St

East Street

Orb Street

North church

Merrow Walk

Dawes Street

Merrow Walk

Penton Place

Pilton Place

Pilton Place

East Street

Bronti Close

Blackwood Street

Portland Street

Trafalgar Street

East Street Market

Occupation Road

Manor Place

Walworth Road A215

Date Street

Faraday Gardens

Wooler

Aylesbury Road

Villa Street

Dawes Street

Merrow Street

Invilie Road

Surrey Gardens

Matara Ms

Penrose Grove

Carter Place

Beck St

Cadiz Street

Liverpool Grove

Burton Gro

Roland Way

Beaconsfield Road

B215

Penton Place

Penrose

Sutherland Walk

Sutherland Sq

Sol St

Macleod

Liverpool

Liverpool Grove

Grove

Urham Street

Lytham Street

Merrow Street

Portland Street

Villa Street

B

Carter Street

Eglinton Rd

Larcom Ct

Fielding Street

Empress St

Gateway

Walworth Road A275

Arnside Street

Dawes Row

Horsley St

Merrow Street

Lytham Street

Sondes Street

Philip Street

Hopwood Road

Olney Road

Draco St

Pelier Street

Dartford Street

Red Lion Row

Red Lion Close

Boyson Close

Westmoreland

Road

Albany Road

Wells Way

B215

John Ruskin Street

Boundary Lane

Bradinham Street

122

Burgess Park Kart Track

121

Grosvenor Terrace

Albany Ms

Albany Road B214

Canal Street

Burgess Park

New Church Road

Camberwell

0.25 mile　0.25 km

Oh, Walworth. With all this about the Elephant and Castle redevelopment, why do we get the funny feeling you will never change? From the excessive amount of Gregg's bakeries along Walworth Road, to the 'who really buys these things?' tat at East Street Market, Walworth's lack of motivation is somehow endearing. La Luna for pizza is a find, as is the Newington Library.

 ## Banks

- **Abbey** • 347 Walworth Rd
- **Barclays** • 260 Walworth Rd
- **NatWest** • 290 Walworth Rd

O Landmarks

- **East Street Market** • East Street

 ## Libraries

- **Newington Library** • 157 Walworth Rd

 ## Post Offices

- **East Street** • 221 East St
- **Walworth Road** • 234 Walworth Rd

 ## Restaurants

- **La Luna** • 380 Walworth Rd

Supermarkets

- **Iceland** • 332 Walworth Rd

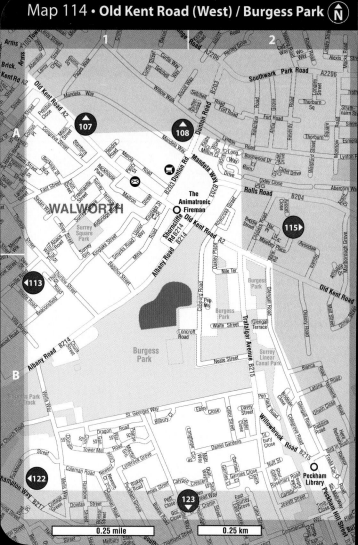

Map 114 • **Old Kent Road (West) / Burgess Park** N

0.25 mile   0.25 km

Old Kent Road (West) / Burgess Park

With the actually-not-that-bad Burgess Park at its heart, this bustling bit of Old Kent Road is probably most famous for its Tesco—trust us, it's pretty f'ing brilliant. But oddest of all is the animatronic fireman in the fireplace shop across the way. Cycle the ex-canal walkway towards Peckham and hover around people fishing in the Burgess Park pond.

O Landmarks

- **The Animatronic Fireman** • Old Kent Road
- **Peckham Library** • 122 Peckham Hill St

Post Offices

- **Old Kent Road** • 240 Old Kent Rd

Supermarkets

- **Tesco** • 107 Dunton Rd

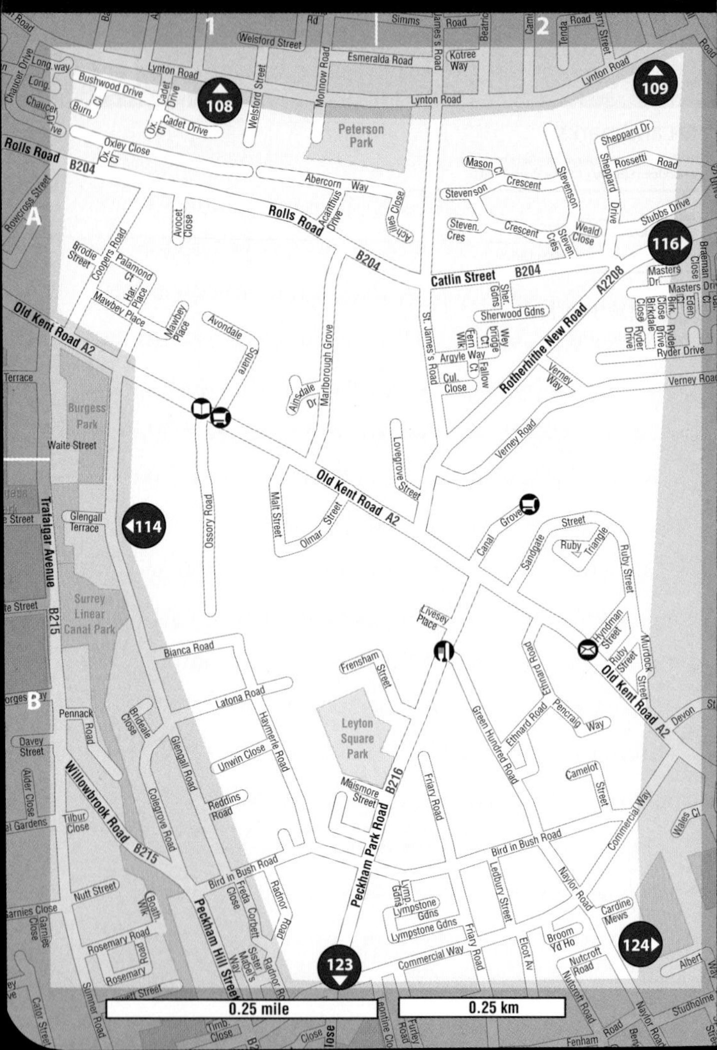

Map 115 · **Old Kent Road (East)**

N

1 | 2

Welsford Street
Simms Road
Beatrice
Esmeralda Road
Kotree Way
Lynton Road
Lynton Road

Chaucer Dr Long. way
Bushwood Drive
Cadet Drive
Cadet Drive
Chaucer
Burn
108
109

Oxley Close
B204
Rolls Road

Peterson Park

Sheppard Dr
Rossetti Road
Sheppard Drive
Abercorn Way
Mason
Crescent
Stevenson
Stubbs Drive

Avocet Close
Rolls Road
Garnies Drive
B204
Stevenson Crescent
Steven Cres
Weald Close
Stephen Cres

A

Brodia Street
Cooper's Road
Palamond Ct
Mawbey Place
Catlin Street B204
St. James's Road
Sherwood Gdns
Fenn Ct
Masters Dr
116
Masters Drive
Eden Close
Ryder Drive
Birkdale Close
Close Ryder Drive

Old Kent Road A2
Avondale Square
Marlborough Grove
Alsdale Dr
Argyle Way
Fallow Way
Fem Way
Cul. Close
Rotherhithe New Road
Verney Way
Verney Road
Verney Road

Terrace

Burgess Park
Waite Street

Ossory Road
Matt Street
Olmar Street
Longrove Street
Old Kent Road A2
Canal Grove
Sandgate Street
Ruby Triangle
Ruby Street

114
Glengall Terrace
Surrey Linear Canal Park

Trafalgar Avenue B215

Bianca Road
Frensham
Linsey Place
Hornsman Street
Fuller Close
Ruby Street
Murdock Street
Old Kent Road A2
Devon
St

B

Pennack Road
Brayards Close
Gatenall Road
Latona Road
Hammett Road
Unwin Close
Reddins Road
Leyton Square Park
Green Hundred Road
Ethnard Road
Pencraig Way
Camelot

Davey Street
Tilbut Close
Willowbrook Road B215
Cobergue Road
Bird in Bush Road
Frida Corbett
Radnor Maismore Street
Peckham Park Road B216
Friary Road
Bird in Bush Road
Naylor Road
Commercial Way

Gardens
Nutt Street
Rosemary Road
Peckham Hill Street
Lyndhurst Way
Lympstone Gdns
Lympstone Gdns
Commercial Way
Eliot Av
Cardine Mews
Nutcroft Road
124

Rosemary
Summer Road
123
Bird in Bush Road
Broom Yd Ho

0.25 mile | 0.25 km

There must be something to this portion of Old Kent Road, as the Pearly Kings and Queens won't shut up about the whole thing. As far as we can tell, it's not that much more than a giant Asda. Walk along Bird In Bush Road to laugh at its name and over to Peckham Park Road for a damn good fry-up at Roma Cafe.

Libraries
• **East Street Library** • 168 Old Kent Rd

Post Offices
• **Old Kent Road (654)** • 654 Old Kent Rd

Restaurants
• **Roma Café** • 21 Peckham Park Rd

Supermarkets
• **ASDA** • Old Kent Rd & Ossory Rd
• **Sainsbury's** • 2 Canal Grove

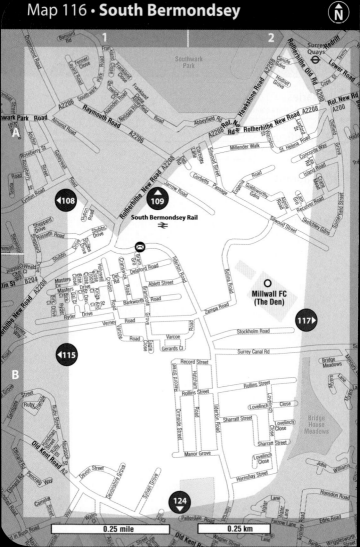

Map 116 · **South Bermondsey**

South Bermondsey plays home to one of the more over-looked London football clubs, Millwall FC, and this might be the only landmark. But they are proposing cool cycle lanes on the disused rail bridges, so watch this space. Population-wise, it's an odd slurry of Surrey Quay/Old Kent Road/Rotherhithe overspill but probably home to some of London's last real estate deals.

○ Landmarks

• **Millwall FC Stadium** • The Den, Zampa Road

Post Offices

• **Ilderton Road** • 1 Ilderton Rd

Map 117 · Deptford (West)

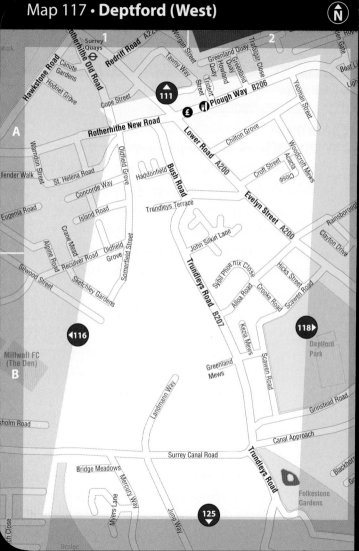

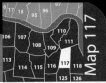

Apparently, developers have their eye on Deptford West. You've really got to hope so. The Blitz did its best, but the area came back with hastily built and charmless '60s tower blocks. Still, like the rest of Deptford it's going through a gradual regeneration as young buyers move in to make their money stretch. The Yellow House offers salvation for eating out.

 Banks

• **Barclays** • 1 Plough Way

 Restaurants

• **Yellow House** • 37 Plough Way

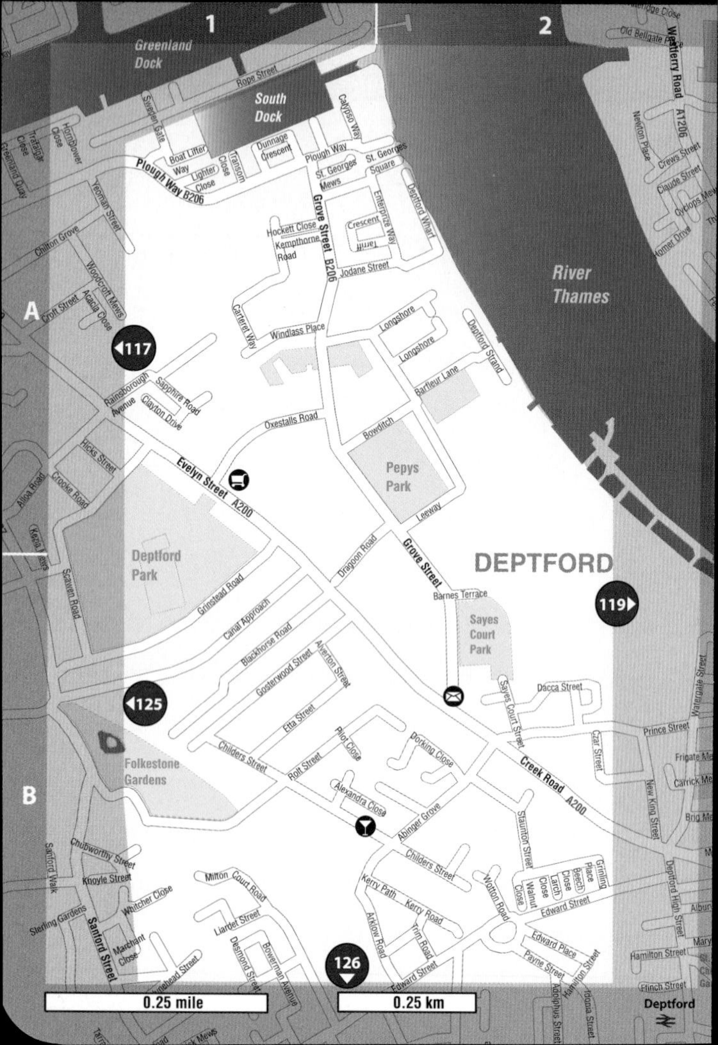

Map 118 · **Deptford (Central)**

N

1   2

Greenland
Dock

South
Dock

Rope Street

Capstan Way

Boat Lifter
Way
Lighter
Close

Plough Way B206

Dunnage
Crescent

Plough Way

St. Georges
Mews

St. Georges
Square

Deptford Wharf

Hockett Close

Kemthorne
Road

Crescent
Alley

Grove Street B206

Jodane Street

Clifton Grove

Woodcroft Mews

Croft Street

Aqua Close

Sargeant Way

Gerrard Way

Windlass Place

Crescent
Way

A

Ramasarough
Avenue

Sargeant Road

Clarion Drive

◀117

Longshore

Longshore

Barfleur Lane

Deptford Strand

*River
Thames*

Ropes Street

Hicks Street

Croasia Road

Abinger Road

Oxestalls Road

Bowditch

Evelyn Street A200

Pepys
Park

Lovelace

Deptford
Park

Grinsead Road

Canal Approach

Dragoon Road

Grove Street

Barnes Terrace

DEPTFORD

119▶

Sanford Road

Scawen Road

Blackhorse Road

Gosterwood Street

Trundleys Road

Etta Street

Prior Close

Sayes
Court
Park

Sayes Court Street

Decca Street

Prince Street

◀125

Folkestone
Gardens

Childers Street

Rolt Street

Alexandra Close

Perking Close

Abinger Grove

Staunton Street

Creek Road A200

Car Street

Frigate Mews

Carrick Mews

New King Street

B

Chubworthy Street

Khoyle Street

Milton Court Road

Whitcher Close

Sterling Gardens

Liardet Street

Childers Street

Kerry Path   Kerry Road

Abinew Road

Ashnew Road

Watson Street

Edward Street

Grinling
Place

Beach
Close

Latch
Close

Walnut
Close

Edward Street

Deptford High Street

Safford Road

Deptford Broadway

Meakham
Close

Resenmead Avenue

Deimord Road

Edward Place

Payne Street

Hamilton Street

Elverson Road

Alburt Mews

Mary

Etinch Place

Ashgrove Street

126
▼

0.25 mile   0.25 km

Deptford
≷

Deptford (Central)

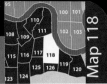

Map 118

When Christopher Marlowe was murdered in a Deptford tavern, Deptford hit its nightlife peak. That was 1593. Today, while the rest of London turns everything into a pub, Deptford turns its pubs into churches. Without beer, you may want to drown your sorrows in the Thames, but even that is thwarted: here the Thames path breaks to take you through neglected residential areas instead. Escape!

Nightlife
• **The Lord Palmerston** • 81 Childers Street

Post Offices
• **Evelyn Street** • 301 Evelyn St

Supermarkets
• **Sainsbury's** • 101 Evelyn St

Map 119 · Deptford (East)

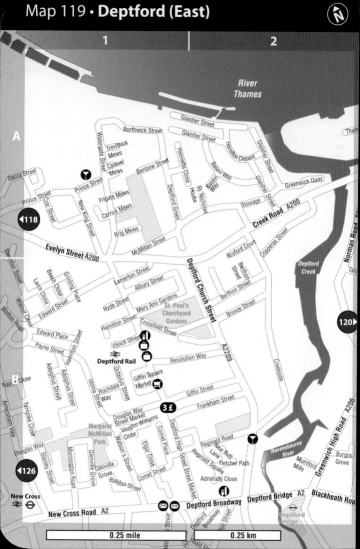

As you arrive you may think twice about stepping out the comforting folds of the bendy bus. But toughen up: it's not all bad. Even if the clothes are nicked from your back, you can buy replacements from Deptford Market and still have change for pie & mushy peas from Manzes. The Dog & Bell is a rare local gem for a comforting pint.

£ Banks

- **Barclays** • 80 Deptford High St
- **Halifax** • 93 Deptford High St
- **HSBC** • 90 Deptford High St

Nightlife

- **Bird's Nest** • 32 Deptford Church St
- **Dog & Bell** • 116 Prince Street

Post Offices

- **New Cross** • 500 New Cross Rd
- **New Cross Gate** • 500 New Cross Rd

Restaurants

- **Kaya House** • 37 Deptford Broadway
- **Manzes** • 204 Deptford High St

Shopping

- **Deptford Market** • Deptford High St
- **El-Khadijat International Grocer** • 147 Deptford High St

Supermarkets

- **Iceland** • 112 Deptford High St

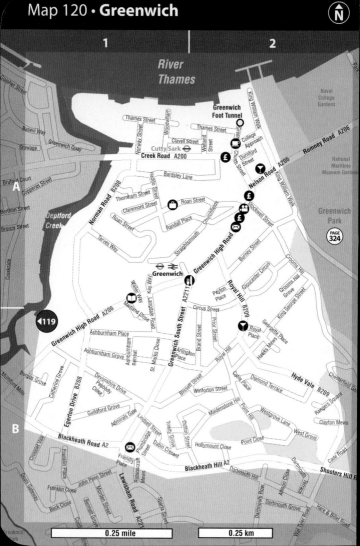

Map 120 · Greenwich

N

1

2

River Thames

Greenwich Foot Tunnel

Thames Street
Woodwharf
King William Walk
College Approach
Thames Street
Clavell Street
Welland Street
Durnford Street
Church Street

Creek Road A200

Cutty Sark

Romney Road A206

Naval College Gardens

Nelson Road A206

National Maritime Museum Gardens

Norway Street

Bardsley Lane

Roan Street

Thornham Street

Claremont Street

Roan Street

Randall Place

Churchfields

Rockwell Street

Greenwich High Road A2211

Greenwich Park

PAGE 324

Burney Street

Straightsmouth

Greenwich

Greenwich

Kay Way

Welling Street

Lambarde Road

Maitland Close

Greenwich High Road A206

Peyton Place

Circus Street

Prior Street

Royal Hill B209

Gloucester Circus

Grooms Hill

Grooms Hill Grove

King George Street

Gerdette Place

Hawks Mews Grove

Chesterfield Gardens

Normal Road B209

Deptford Creek

Coopers Street
Bruford Court
Berthion Street
Bronze Street
Creekside

Glaisher Street
Basevi Way
Greenwich Quay
Stowage

◀ 119

Ashburnham Place
Ashburnham Grove
Ashburnham Retreat
St. Marks Close

Devonshire Drive
Peabody Close

Guildford Grove

Admirals Gate

Lindsell Street

Arlington Place

Brand Street

Blissett Street

Royal Hill

Cade Place

Royal Place

Winforton Street

Maidenstone Hill

Diamond Terrace

Hyde Vale B209

Westgrove Lane

West Grove

Rangers Square

Clayton Mews

Burgos Grove
Catherine Grove
Egerton Drive B208

Blackheath Road A2

Friendly Place

Plumbridge Street

Dabin Crescent

Trinity Grove

Dutton Street

Hollymount Close

Point Close

Blackheath Hill A2

Dartmouth Hill

Dartmouth Row

Allison Close

Shooters Hill R

Cresswell Way
Franklin Place
John Penn Street
Franklin Close
Beck Close

Lewisham Road A20

Rokisnicroft Mews

Morden Street
Bennet Street
Sparta Street

Dartmouth Grove

Hare & Billet Road

Wat Tyler Road

0.25 mile   0.25 km

Greenwich

Host of the mighty O2 Arena and one of the most charming village markets in London, don't forget to set your watch and give thanks to the birthplace of Greenwich Mean Time (GMT). Most head to the bustling market for quirky art and authentic Spanish chorizo. Stock up on old fashioned sweets at Mr Humbug before a visit to the Greenwich Picturehouse; French bistro Bar du Musee and world food restaurant Inside also measure up.

£Banks

- **HSBC** • 275 Greenwich High Rd
- **Lloyds** • 6 Crescent Arcade
- **NatWest** • 2 Greenwich Church St

Cinemas

- **Greenwich Picturehouse** • 180 Greenwich High Rd

Coffee

- **Starbucks** • 54 Greenwich Church St

O Landmarks

- **Greenwich Foot Tunnel** • Greenwich Church St

Libraries

- **West Greenwich Library** • Greenwich High Rd

Nightlife

- **Bar du Musee** • 17 Nelson Rd
- **Greenwich Union** • 56 Royal Hill

Post Offices

- **Blackheath Hill** • 11 Blackheath Hill
- **Greenwich** • 261 Greenwich High Rd

Restaurants

- **Inside** • 19 Greenwich South St

Shopping

- **Mr Humbug** • Greenwich Market

245

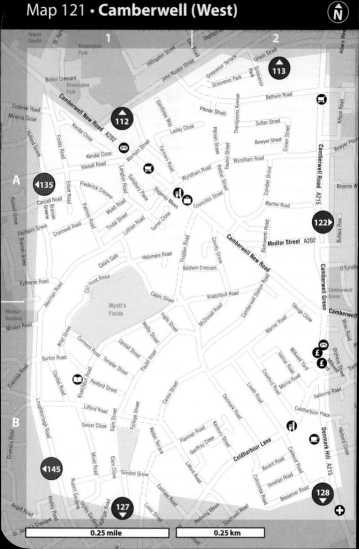

Map 121 · **Camberwell (West)**

0.25 mile 0.25 km

This tired segment of Camberwell brings together a minority of polite arty types in the crumbling yet quaint townhouses of Camberwell New Road with take-no-prisoners urbanites as seen in the chaos of Denmark Hill and its pointless Butterfly Shopping Centre (why?). The neighbourhood good stuff includes music bargains (Rat Records), killer Indian (New Dewaniam), and phenomenal Thai food (Su-Thai).

Banks
- **HSBC** • 23 Denmark Hill
- **NatWest** • 70 Denmark Hill

Coffee
- **Kings Cafe** • 120 Denmark Hill

Emergency Rooms
- **King's College Hospital** • Denmark Hill

Libraries
- **Minet Library** • 52 Knatchbull Rd

Post Offices
- **Camberwell Green** • 25 Denmark Hill
- **Camberwell New Road** • 163 Camberwell New Rd

Restaurants
- **New Dewaniam** • 225 Camberwell New Rd
- **Su-Thai** • 16 Coldharbour Lane

Shopping
- **Rat Records** • 348 New Camberwell Rd

Supermarkets
- **Co-Op** • 177 Camberwell New Rd
- **Iceland** • 120 Camberwell Rd

Map 122 · **Camberwell (East)**

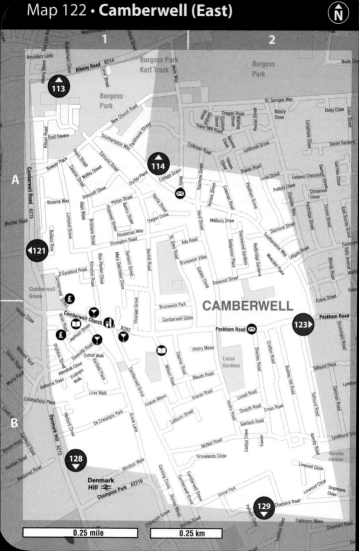

Camberwell (East)

Map 122

This lucky dip of a neighbourhood is home to a few gangs, art students, and the occasional Time Out editor. Anyone who wrinkles their nose at Camberwell has never experienced the bohemian opulence of Camberwell Grove (which does fade rather quickly into the familiar dodginess of Camberwell Church Street). For posh, sip cocktails at The Dark Horse, for nosh, try Caravaggio.

£ Banks
• **Barclays** • 1 Butterfly Walk
• **Lloyds** • 25 Camberwell Green

Libraries
• **Camberwell Library** • 17 Camberwell Church St
• **Education Library Service** • Wilson Rd

Nightlife
• **The Castle** • 65 Camberwell Church St
• **Dark Horse** • 16 Grove Lane
• **Funky Munky** • 25 Camberwell Church St

Post Offices
• **Peckham Road** • 46 Peckham Rd
• **Southampton Way** • 156 Southampton Way

Restaurants
• **Caravaggio** • 47 Camberwell Church St

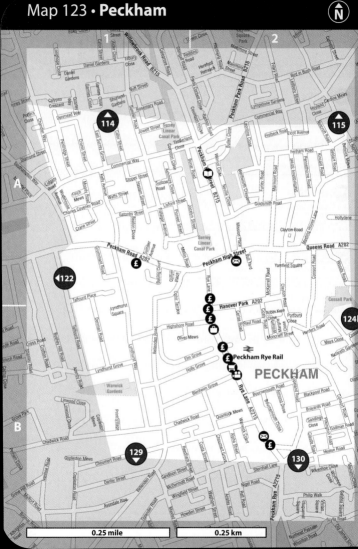

Map 123 · **Peckham**

Peckham

Map 123

Peckham: so many gang wars, so little time. Though it tries hard with such overly-enthusiastic delights as the cheery Peckham Library set on spindly post-modern stilts or those palm trees planted down Queen's Road to 'reflect the multi-cultural diversity of Peckham'. Not that anyone notices. Rye Lane's the real hub, with its disconcertingly affordable Peckham Multiplex cinema and classic Primark.

Banks

- **Abbey** • 97 Rye Ln
- **Barclays** • 28 Rye Ln
- **Barclays** • 223 Rye Ln
- **Halifax** • 24 Rye Ln
- **HSBC** • 20 Rye
- **Lloyds** • 76 Rye Ln
- **NatWest** • 65 Peckham High St

Libraries

- **Peckham Library** • 122 Peckham Hill St

Movie Theaters

- **Peckham Multiplex** • 95 Rye Ln

Post Offices

- **Peckham** • 121 Peckham High St
- **Rye Lane** • 199 Rye Ln

Shopping

- **Primark** • 51 Rye Lane

Supermarkets

- **Iceland** • 74 Rye Lane

Map 124 · **Peckham East (Queen's Road)**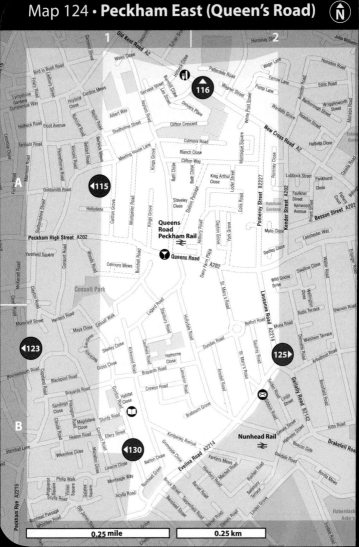

Never one to be cheery, the eastern side of Peckham surrounding the Queen's Road is a rather bleak landscape of monolithic tower blocks and sprawling council estates. But there is something refreshingly gritty and nonplussed about the area and its dedicated locals. For instance, the 805 Bar and Restaurant has excellent African food and is a culinary oasis in an urban desert.

 Libraries

• **Nunhead Library** • Gordon Rd

 Post Offices

• **Nunhead Nr Station** • 6 Gibbon Rd

 Restaurants

• **805 Bar Restaurant** • 805 Old Kent Rd

Map 125 · **New Cross Gate**

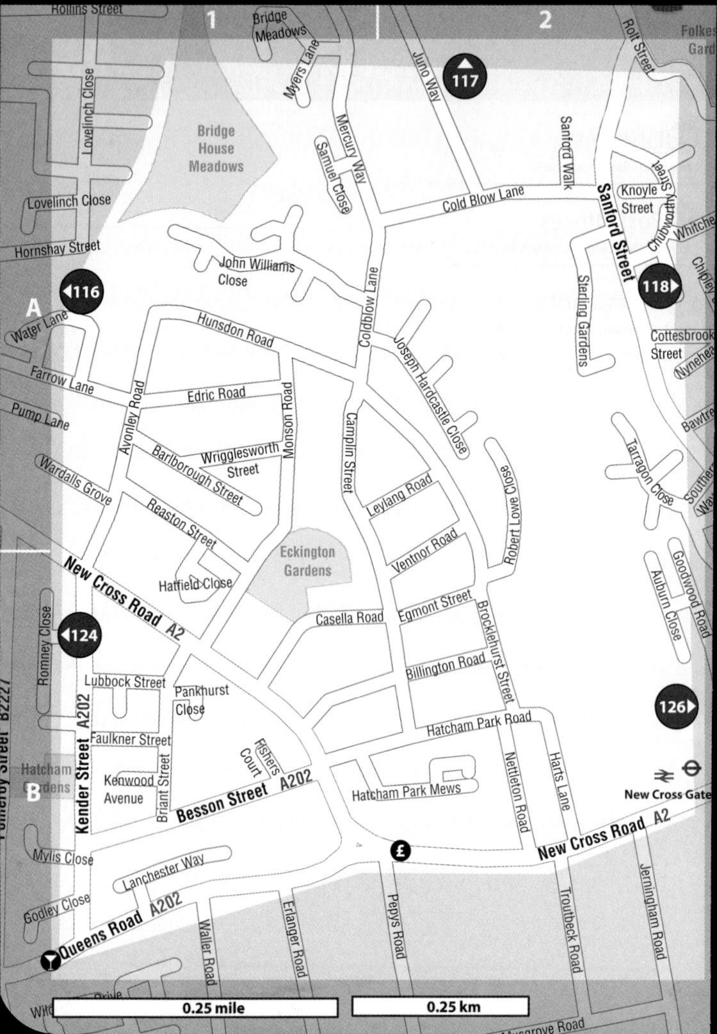

Ⓝ

Rollins Street

Bridge Meadows

Myers Lane

1

2

Rott Street

Folkes Gard

Lovelinch Close

Juno Way

▲ 117

Mercury Way

Samuel Close

Sanford Walk

Knoyle Street

Chubworthy Street

Whitche

Lovelinch Close

Bridge House Meadows

Cold Blow Lane

Sanford Street

Chidle

Hornshay Street

◀ 116

John Williams Close

Coldblow Lane

118 ▶

A

Water Lane

Hunsdon Road

Sterling Gardens

Cottesbrook Street

Nyneheo

Farrow Lane

Avonley Road

Edric Road

Monson Road

Joseph Hardcastle Close

Pump Lane

Barlborough Street

Wrigglesworth Street

Camplin Street

Tarragon Close

Baxtron

Southe Wa

Wardalls Grove

Reaston Street

Leyland Road

Robert Lowe Close

Goodwood Road

Auburn Close

New Cross Road A2

Hatfield Close

Eckington Gardens

Ventnor Road

Pomeroy Street B2227

◀ 124

A202

Lubbock Street

Casella Road

Egmont Street

Brocklehurst Street

Billington Road

126 ▶

Romney Close

Pankhurst Close

Fisher's Court

Hatcham Park Road

Netherton Road

Harts Lane

⇌ ⊖
New Cross Gate

Kender Street A202

Faulkner Street

Kenwood Avenue

Briant Street

Besson Street A202

Hatcham Park Mews

Hatcham Gdens

B

Mylis Close

£

New Cross Road A2

Godley Close

Lanchester Way

Waller Road

Pepys Road

Erlanger Road

Troutbeck Road

Jerningham Road

✈ Queens Road A202

Drive

Witc

Musgrove Road

| 0.25 mile | 0.25 km |

New Cross Gate

There used to be an urban myth that there are no cash machines in New Cross because of the muggings. Since then it's gone all art-student-cool but this bit is still quite rugged. Its biggest claim to fame is the fantastic Montague Arms, which looks like it was furnished by a drunken sailor-turned-taxidermist waking up and bellowing "bring me. . .stuff!"

Banks

• **Barclays** • 197 New Cross Rd

Nightlife

• **The Montague Arms** • 289 Queen's Rd

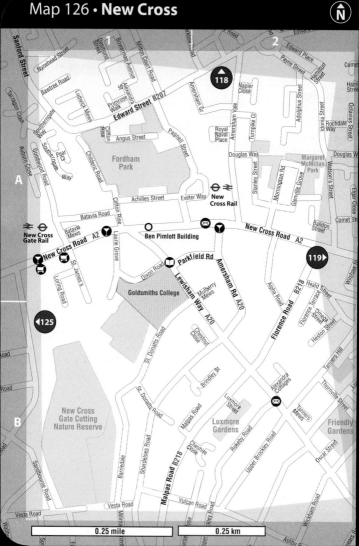

Around here, the art student is King. In the shadow of the rather ugly Goldsmiths College Ben Pimlott Building, trendy young students enthralled to debauchery live out their art-school fantasies. Join them in the Hobgoblin for booze or try the decrepit New Cross Inn for your mate's band. The Amersham Arms is a great, spanking new palace to destroy your brain cells in.

O Landmarks

• **Ben Pimlott Building** • University of London, New Cross

Libraries

• **Goldsmiths Library** • Lewisham Wy

Nightlife

• **Amersham Arms** • 388 New Cross Rd
• **Hobgoblin** • 272 New Cross Rd
• **New Cross Inn** • 323 New Cross Rd

Post Offices

• **Lewisham Way** • 150 Lewisham Way
• **New Cross Road** • 405 New Cross Rd

Supermarkets

• **Iceland** • 277 New Cross Rd
• **Sainsbury's** • 263 New Cross Rd

Map 127 · **Coldharbour Lane / Herne Hill (West)**

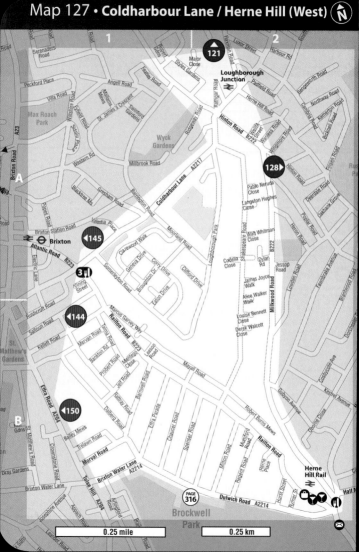

Coldharbour Lane / Herne Hill (West)

There don't seem to be as many shootings on Coldharbour Lane as there used to be. Maybe the crack dealers are just quietly selling the stuff, as somebody on The Wire once sensibly advised. Or maybe they've all left the buzzing bars of Brixton, like the infamous Dogstar, for much more laidback Herne Hill and famous outdoor swimming pool The Brockwell Lido.

Nightlife
- **The Commercial** • 210 Railton Rd
- **Escape Bar and Art** • 214 Railton Rd

Post Offices
- **Herne Hill** • 31 Norwood Rd

Restaurants
- **Café Prov** • 2 Half Moon Ln
- **Ichiban Sushi** • 58 Atlantic Rd
- **The Lounge** • 56 Atlantic Rd
- **New Fujiyama** • 5 Vining St

Shopping
- **Blackbird Bakery** • 208 Railton Rd

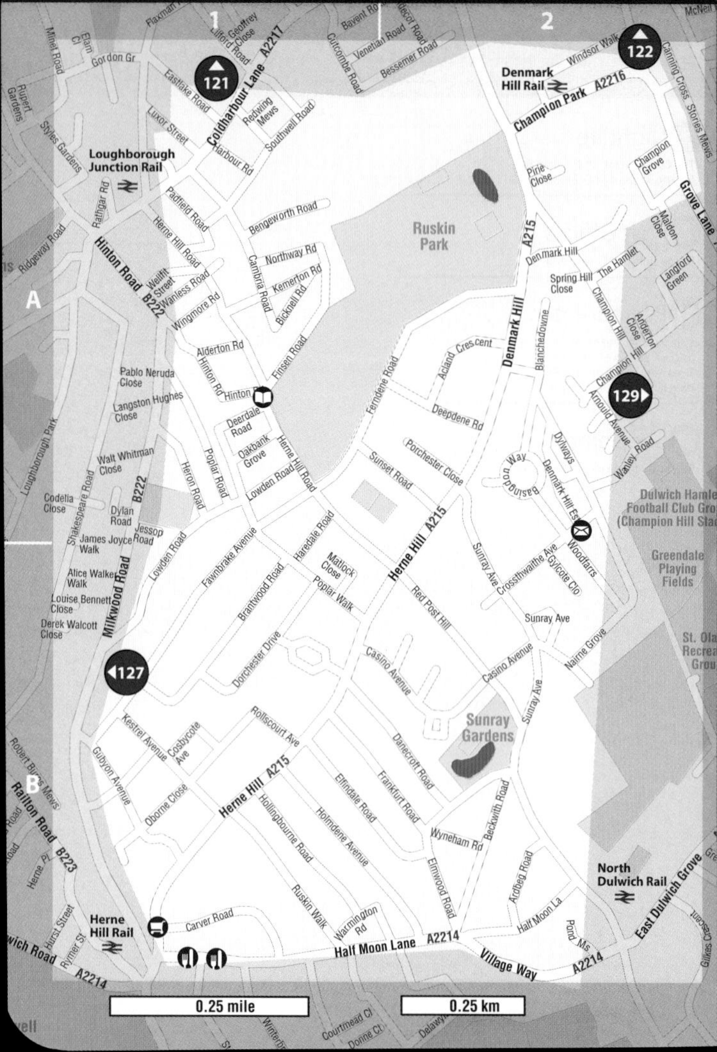

Map 128 · **Denmark Hill / Herne Hill (East)** Ⓝ

1   **2**

▲ **122**

▲ **121**

McNeil

Paxman
Mirl Road   Gordon Gr   Elm
Cross
Rupert
Gardens   Stiles Gardens   Ridgway Road
Gordon Gr
Eastlake Road   A2217   Lilford Close   Geoffrey
Close
Bavent Rd   Venetian Road
Kincaid Road   Clitconda Road
Bessemer Road

Denmark Hill Rail ⭲

Champion Park A2216

Windsor Walk

Cross Shores Mews   Grove Lane
Champion Grove
Mellow Close
Madeira Green   Langford
Green

Loughborough Junction Rail ⭲

Reiving Mews   Southwell Road
Harbour Rd   Coldharbour Lane

Herne Hill Road

Rathgar Rd   Padfield Road   Bengeworth Road

Pirie Close
A215   Denmark Hill

Ruskin Park

Northway Rd   Cambria Road
Kemerton Rd   Bickell Rd

Spring Hill Close   The Hamlet   Champion Hill
Alderton Close

Blanchedowne

A   Wingmore Rd
Wanless Road   Wolfe Cr   Hinton Road B222

Alderton Rd   Finsen Rd

Hinton 🏛

129▶

Knatchbull Road

Deerdale Road   Oakbank Grove
Herne Hill Road

Acland Crescent   Deepdene Rd   Dylways

Way   Bastion

Denmark Hill Est   Woodfarrs

Dulwich Hamlet Football Club Gro (Champion Hill Sta

Greendale Playing Fields

Walt Whitman Close   Lowden Road   Poplar Road
Ferndene Road   Porchester Close

Sunset Road   Sunray Ave   Crossthwaite Ave   Gipcycle Clo

Codella Close   Shakespeare Road   B222   Jessop Road   Dylan Road
James Joyce Walk
Alice Walker Walk
Louise Bennett Close
Derek Walcott Close

Heron Road   Lowden Road   Milkwood Road
Fawnbrake Avenue   Hardale Road   Matlock Close   Red Post Hill   Sunray Ave   Narine Grove

St. Ola Recrea Grou

127◀

Brantwood Road   Dorchester Drive   Poplar Walk
Casino Avenue   Casino Avenue   Sunray Ave

Sunray Gardens

Kestrel Avenue   Cosbycote Ave
Rollescourt Ave   Danecroft Road

B   Gubyon Avenue   Osborne Close   Herne Hill A215
Hollingbourne Road   Effingdale Road   Holmdene Avenue   Frankfurt Road   Wyneham Rd   Beckwith Road   Archbishop Road   Elmwood Road

Ruskin Walk   Warmington Road   Elmwood Road

North Dulwich Rail ⭲

East Dulwich Grove

Herne Hill Rail ⭲   Carver Road

🍴 🍴   **Half Moon Lane** A2214   Half Moon La   Village Way   A2214   Pond Ms

wich Road   A2214   Railton Road B223   Hurst Street   Mayall Rd

Courtmead Cl   Donne Ct   Delawyk

0.25 mile	0.25 km

There's something quaintly grounded about the leafy Victorian suburb of Herne Hill where funky neo-hippies settle into dreadlocked nuclear families. Denmark Hill sits at its top, with the fascist-esque Salvation Army training grounds, following on to Ruskin Park for ornamental ponds and Edwardian ruins. Half Moon Lane plays main drag—try Number 22 for tapas and Lombok for a good ol' stir-fry.

Libraries
• **Carnegie Library** • 188 Herne Hill Rd

Post Offices
• **Crossthwaite Avenue** • 6 Crossthwaite Ave

Restaurants
• **Lombok** • 17 Half Moon Ln
• **Number 22** • 22 Half Moon Ln

Supermarkets
• **Sainsbury's** • 132 Herne Hill

Map 129 · **East Dulwich**

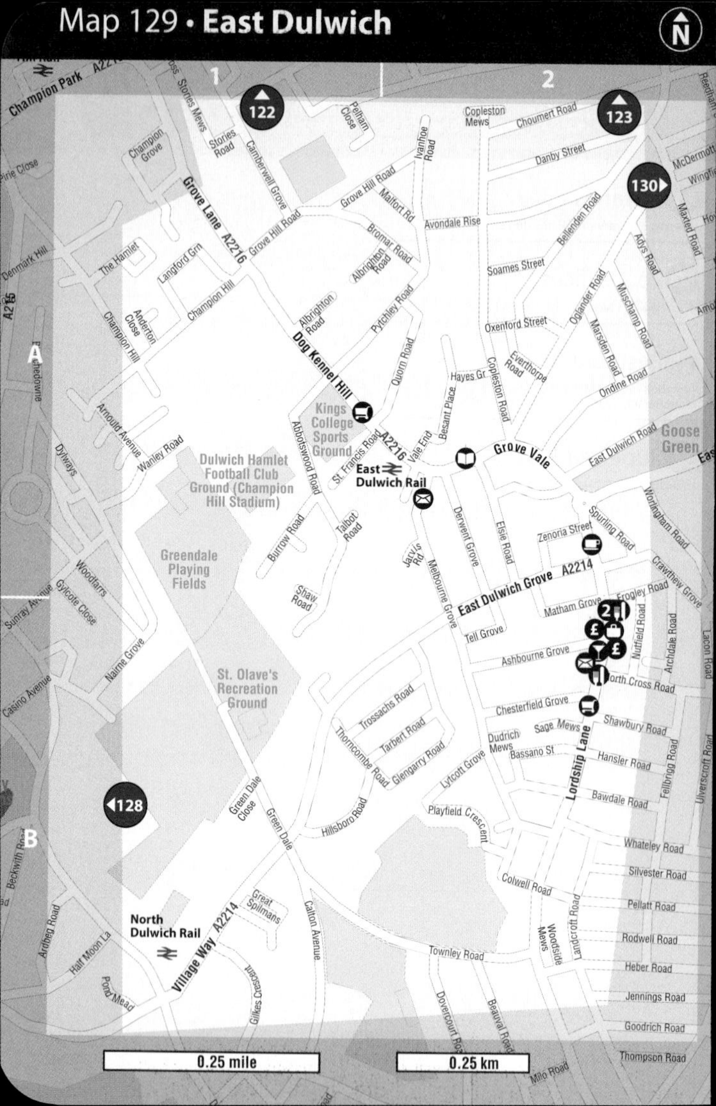

N

1   2

Champion Park A2214

122

123

130

Champion Grove

Stories Road

Camberwell Grove

Grove Hill Road

Pelham Close

Ivanhoe Road

Copleston Mews

Chourmert Road

Danby Street

Pine Close

Grove Hill Road

Malfort Rd

Avondale Rise

Denmark Hill

The Hamlet

Langford Grn

Grove Hill Road

Bromar Road

Ads's Road

McDerm

Wright

A216

Champion Hill

Anderson Close

Champion Hill

Albrighton Road

Pytchley Road

Soames Street

Bellenden Road

Oglander Road

Marsden Road

Moschung Road

Maxted Road

A216

Grove Lane A2216

Dog Kennel Hill

Albrighton Road

Oxenford Street

Everthorpe Road

Ondine Road

A
Archbishop

Arnould Avenue

Warley Road

Abbotswood Road

Quorn Road

Dog Kennel Hill A2216

Hayes Gr.

Besant Place

Copleston Road

East Dulwich Road

Goose Green

D'Eynsford

Grecian Close

Woodfarrs

Kings College Sports Ground

St Francis Road

Vale End

Grove Vale

Spurling Road

Worlingham Road

Crawthew Grove

Sunray Avenue

Narnie Grove

Dulwich Hamlet Football Club Ground (Champion Hill Stadium)

Burrow Road

East Dulwich Rail

Derwent Grove

Elsie Road

Zenoria Street

130

Casino Avenue

Greendale Playing Fields

Shaw Road

Talfourd Road

Lucy's Rd

Melbourne Grove

East Dulwich Grove A2214

Frogley Road

Matham Grove

Nutfield Road

Arcadian Grove

Worlingham Road

St. Olave's Recreation Ground

Trossachs Road

Tarbert Road

Glengarry Road

Tell Grove

Ashbourne Grove

2

£

£

North Cross Road

Universoft Road

128

Green Dale Close

Green Dale

Hillsborough Rd

Thorncombe Road

Lytcott Grove

Chesterfield Grove

Dudrich Mews

Sage Mews

Bassano St

Shawbury Road

Hansler Road

Fellbrigg Road

Tappesfield Road

B
Beckwith Rd

Ardbeg Road

Half Moon La.

North Dulwich Rail

Village Way A2214

Calton Avenue

Great Spilmans

Hillsborough Rd

Playfield Cresc.ent

Colwell Road

Lordship Lane

Dovercourt Road

Beauval Road

Whateley Road

Silvester Road

Pellatt Road

Rodwell Road

Heber Road

Jennings Road

Goodrich Road

Plaza Mead

Gilkes Cres.

Townley Road

Woodside Mews

Landcroft Road

Milo Road

Thompson Road

0.25 mile   0.25 km

East Dulwich

Map 129

East Dulwich is where your ex-flatmate finally settled down and now won't shut up about taramasalata, babies, and how he's only fifteen minutes from London Bridge by train. Dodge baguettes, pushchairs, and delis along Lordship Lane, just don't get sucked in. Try the Sea Cow for fish & chips, the Cheeseblock for cheese, a pint at the Palmerston, and a night out at Inside 72.

Banks

• **Barclays** • 68 Lordship Ln
• **HSBC** • 66 Lordship Ln

Coffee

• **Caffe Nero** • 8 Lordship Lane

Libraries

• **Grove Vale library** • 25 Grove Vale

Nightlife

• **Inside 72** • 72 Lordship Lane

Post Offices

• **East Dulwich** • 74 Lordship Ln
• **Melbourne Grove** • 7 Melbourne Grove

Restaurants

• **The Palmerston** • 91 Lordship Lane
• **Sea Cow** • 37 Lordship Lane

Shopping

• **The Cheeseblock** • 69 Lordship Lane

Supermarkets

• **Iceland** • 84 Lordship Ln
• **Sainsbury's** • 80 Dog Kennel Hill

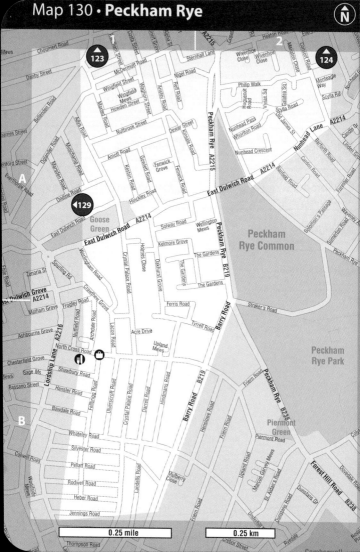

A noticeboard on Peckham Rye Common alleges that ancient British Queen Boudicca was finally defeated by the Romans here. Anyone suggesting that the very middle class streets around North Cross Road, with its market, independent sweet shop, and numerous gastropubs, are anything to do with Peckham might get the same treatment. But this area, despite Peckham's rough reputation, is actually a very nice place indeed.

Restaurants

• **Thai Corner Cafe** • 44 Northcross Rd

Shopping

• **Hope And Greenwood** • 20 North Cross Rd

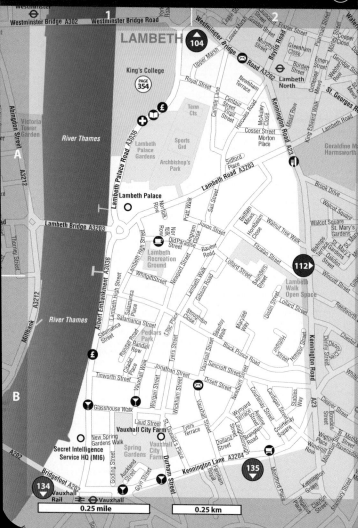

Map 131 · **Vauxhall / Albert Embankment** N

LAMBETH

104

York Road

Westminster Bridge A302   Westminster Bridge Road

Westminster Bridge Road A3202

Lambeth North

St. Georges Rd

King's College

PAGE
354

Royal Street

Lambeth North

Victoria
Tower
Garden

River Thames

Lambeth Palace Gardens

Sports Grd

Archbishop's Park

A2212

Abingdon Street

Lambeth Palace Road A3036

Tenn Cts

Upper Marsh

Carlisle Lane

Centaur Street

Virgil Street

Hercules Road

Cosser Street
Morton Place

Newnham Terrace

McAuley Close

Mead Row

Cottesloe Mews

Kennington Road A23

King Edward Walk

Geraldine M
Harmsworth

Lambeth Road A3203

Sidford Place

Brook Drive

Walcot Square

Walcot Square

St. Mary's Gardens

Lambeth Palace

Lambeth Bridge A3203

Norfolk Row

Pratt Walk

Sail Street

Juxon Street

Bishops Ter

Lane Oaken Street

Wincott Street

Thorney Street

A2212

Lambeth High Street

Old Paradise Street

Ravent Road

Lollard Street

Bastan
Mews

Hornbeam
Close

Walnut Tree Walk

Fitzalan Street

112

Lambeth Recreation Ground

Whitgift Street

Newport Street

Lambeth Walk

Gibson Road

Saunders

Lollard Street

Lambeth Walk Open Space

Dixon Street

Reedworth

River Thames

Albert Embankment A3036

Salamanca Place

Salamanca Street

Salamanca Street

Pedlars Park

Bandal Road

Randall Row

Clac Place

Tyers Street

Lambeth Walk

Vauxhall Street

Stoughton Close

Black Prince Road

Baalbey Walk

Marlee Way

Kennington Road

Denny Street

A23

Chester

White

Millbank

A202

Citadel Place

Tinworth Street

Jonathan Street

Wickham Street

Wirgman Street

Laud Street

Glasshouse Walk

New Spring Gardens Walk

Secret Intelligence Service HQ (MI6)

Bridgefoot A202

Vauxhall Rail

Vauxhall

Sancroft Street

Orsett Street

Newburn Street

St Oswald's Place

Tyers Terrace

Spring Gardens

Vauxhall City Farm

Auckland Street

Glyn Street

Durham Street

Dolland Street

St Oswald's Place

Wynyard Terrace

Brangton Road

Courtenay Street

Kennington Lane A3204

Cardigan Street

Courtenay Square

Stables Way

Cleaver Street

Bowden Street

Wigton Place

Methley

A23

Windmill Row

Ravensdon

Montford Place

Kennington Green

Kennington

Clayton Street

Peasley Stree

134
Vauxhall

135

0.25 mile   0.25 km

Vauxhall / Albert Embankment

Map 131

Despite being sliced up by busy roads, major rail tracks and infested with millionaire riverside apartments, there is life to be found here. Around Spring Gardens, where the IRA allegedly fired a rocket at the MI6 building, is a great local (The Lavender) and the ponies of Vauxhall City Farm. Hunt down tasty Thai (Thai Pavillion East) and trashy cabaret (The Royal Vauxhall Tavern).

Banks
- **HSBC** • 20 Albert Embankment
- **NatWest** • Lambath Palace Rd

Coffee
- **Costa** • 34 Old Paradise St

Emergency Rooms
- **St Thomas' Hospital** • Lambeth Palace Rd

O Landmarks
- **Lambeth Palace Rd** • Lambeth Palace Rd
- **Secret Intelligence Service HQ (MI6)** • Vauxhall Cross
- **Vauxhall City Farm** • 165 Tyers St

Libraries
- **Lambeth Palace Library** • Lambeth Palace Rd

Nightlife
- **Area** • 67 Albert Embankment
- **The Lavender** • 112 Vauxhall Walk
- **The Royal Vauxhall Tavern** • 372 Kennington Ln
- **South Central** • 349 Kennington Ln

Post Offices
- **Lambeth Walk** • 34 Vauxhall St
- **Westminster Bridge Road** • 125 Westminster Bridge Rd

Restaurants
- **Thai Pavillion East** • 82 Kennington Rd

Supermarkets
- **Tesco** • Kennington Ln

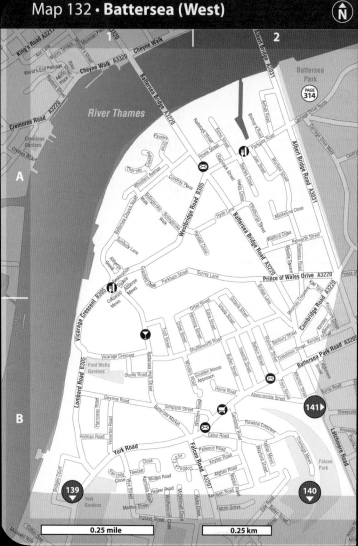

With no tubes or trains to attract the Hoi Polloi, Battersea West is a slightly smug area, happily cut off from the rest of London. Other than an enviable riverside location, it's rather dull. Battersea Square, a European style 'piazza' offers some al fresco action. Try La Tosca for people watching over pasta or head to the Woodman for a nice pint of badger ale.

Nightlife

• **The Woodman** • 60 Battersea High St

Post Offices

• **Battersea Bridge Road** • 72 Battersea Bridge Rd
• **Battersea Park Road (268)** • 268 Battersea Park Rd
• **York Road** • 583 Battersea Park Rd

Restaurants

• **Ransom's Dock** • 35 Parkgate Rd
• **La Tosca** • 31 Battersea Square

Supermarkets

• **Sainsbury's** • 326 Battersea Park Rd

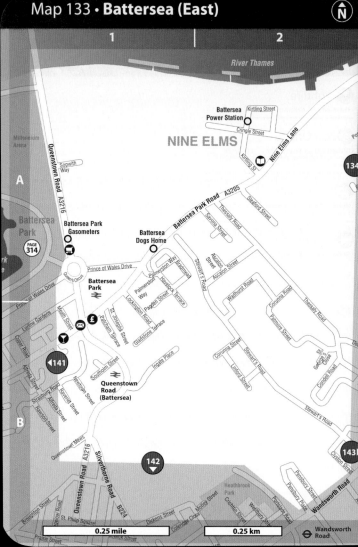

Map 133 · **Battersea (East)**

Battersea (East)

An odd slice of post-industrial London dominated by the derelict Battersea Power Station, there's naff all here until someone decides what to do with the old hulk and its surrounding domain. In the meantime, try registering for a new pooch at the Dogs' Home or escaping to nearby Battersea Park from where you can rue the slow death of the crumbling giant.

Map 133

£ Banks

• **Barclays** • 278 Queenstown Rd

O Landmarks

• **Battersea Dogs' Home** • 4 Battersea Park Rd
• **Battersea Park Gasometers** • Queenstown Rd
• **Battersea Power Station** • 188 Kirtling St

Libraries

• **Battersea Park Library** • 309 Battersea Park Rd

Nightlife

• **The Chelsea Reach** • 181 Battersea Park Rd

Post Offices

• **Battersea Park Road** • 20 Battersea Park Rd

Supermarkets

• **Sainsbury's** • 326 Queenstown Rd

Map 134 · South Lambeth

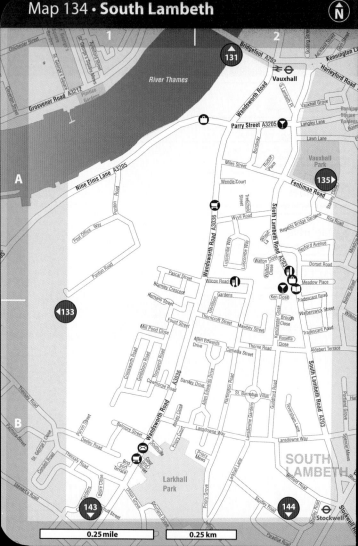

South Lambeth

Map 134

This neighbourhood ain't glamorous but it still has a lot to offer. The area around Vauxhall has a buzzing gay scene – not for the faint hearted. 'Little Portugal,' around South Lambeth Road boasts a number of great, traditional tapas bars and restaurants; try Estrella for an authentic, Mediterranean vibe. Join the traders and head to New Covent Garden Market for fresh flowers, fruit and veg but you'll need to be early!

Libraries
• **South Lambeth Library** • 180 S Lambeth Rd

Nightlife
• **Bar Estrella** • 115 Old South Lambeth Rd
• **Fire** • 38 Parry St

Post Offices
• **South Lambeth** • 347 Wandsworth Rd

Restaurants
• **Bar Estrella** • 115 Old South Lambeth Rd
• **Hot Stuff** • 19 Wilcox Rd

Shopping
• **New Covent Garden Market** • Nine Elms Lane

Supermarkets
• **Sainsbury's** • 62 Wandsworth Rd

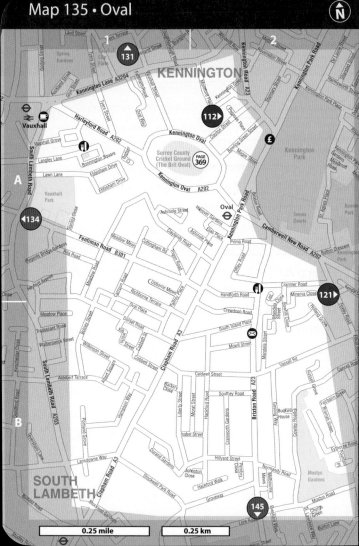

Oval

Posh mansions rub shoulders uneasily with housing estates. The Oval cricket ground draws the crowds but usually people just pass through here en route to somewhere more interesting. It's the kind of place that doesn't have a cashpoint. Make of that what you will. Hippy loving veggies will love The Bonnington Café but meat eaters head to Adulis for Eritrean delicacies.

Posh mansions rub shoulders uneasily with housing estates. The Oval cricket ground draws the crowds but usually people just pass through here en route to somewhere more interesting. It's the kind of place that doesn't have a cashpoint. Make of that what you will. Hippy loving veggies will love The Bonnington Café but meat eaters head to Adulis for Eritrean delicacies.

Banks

- **Barclays** • 414 Kennington Rd

Coffee

- **Starbucks** • 2 South Lambeth Rd

Post Offices

- **Brixton Road** • 82 Brixton Rd

Restaurants

- **Adulis** • 44 Brixton Rd
- **The Bonnington Café** • 11 Vauxhall Grove

Map 135

Map 136 · **Putney**

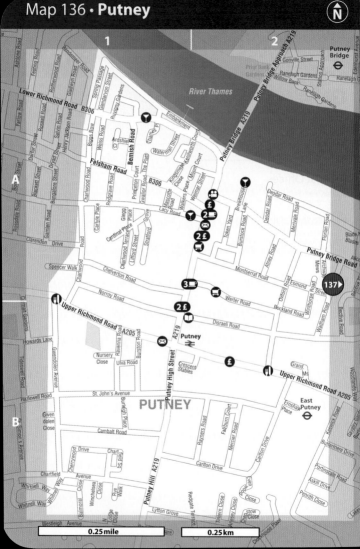

Ah, Putney—a bi-polar place with an air of suburban middle England. Maybe it's all the Rugby and Rowing types. The high street is bland and genteel but by night a generally young, up-for-it crowd descend. Chakalaka offers up a taste of home to hordes of South Africans and the Jolly Gardeners is a great spot for beer tasting and funky tunes.

£ Banks

- **Abbey** • 88 Putney High St
- **Barclays** • 159 Putney High St
- **Barclays** • 60 Putney High St
- **Halifax** • 171 Putney High St
- **HSBC** • 172 Upper Richmond Rd
- **Lloyds** • 110 Putney High St

Coffee

- **BB's Coffee and Muffins** • Putney High St & Chelverton Rd
- **Caffe Nero** • 95 Putney High St
- **Costa** • 86 Putney High St
- **Pret A Manger** • 121 Putney High St
- **Starbucks** • 117 Putney High St

Libraries

- **Putney Library** • 5 Disraeli Rd

Movie Theaters

- **Odeon Putney** • 26 Putney High St

Nightlife

- **The Boathouse** • Brewhouse Lane
- **Duke's Head** • 8 Lower Richmond Rd
- **Jolly Gardeners** • 61 Lacey Rd

Post Offices

- **Putney** • 214 Upper Richmond Rd
- **Putney Bridge Road** • 279 Putney Bridge Rd

Restaurants

- **Chakalaka** • 136 Upper Richmond Rd
- **Talad Thai** • 320 Upper Richmond Rd

Supermarkets

- **Sainsbury's** • 2 Werter Rd
- **Waitrose** • Putney High St & Lacy Rd

Map 137 · **Wandsworth (West)**

Wandsworth (West)

Dissected by the busy Upper and Lower Richmond Roads, this bit of Wandsworth is a bit lifeless though pleasant enough. The pretty, riverside Wandsworth Park is a huge plus and heaves with locals with the first sniff of sunshine. Head to the Queen Adelaide or the Cats Back (Map 138) for a spot of liquid refreshment after a hard day's Frisbee chucking.

Nightlife

• **The Queen Adelaide** • 35 Putney Bridge Rd

Restaurants

• **Miraj** • 123 Putney Bridge Road
• **Yia Mas** • 40 Upper Richmond Rd

279

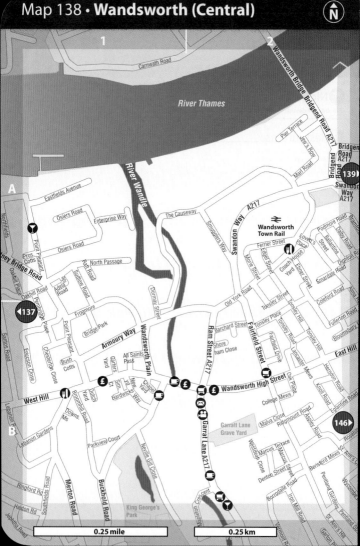

Map 138 · **Wandsworth (Central)**

Wandsworth (Central)

Pity poor Wandsworth Central. Not only is it lumbered with an ugly shopping centre but a four lane gyratory system brings constant traffic and pollution. On the plus side, plenty of chain stores (GAP, Uniqlo etc) and a multi-screen cinema make life a little easier. Old York Road offers a pleasant escape from the madness—try the retro Brady's for great fish and chips.

Map 138

 ## Banks

- **Barclays** • 83 Wandsworth High St
- **HSBC** • 73 Wandsworth High St
- **Lloyds** • 159 Wandsworth High St

Cinemas

- **Cineworld Wandsworth** •
  Wandsworth High St & Ram St

 ## Coffee

- **BB's Coffee and Muffins** •
  Buckhold Rd & Wandsworth High St
- **Caffe Nero** • Southside Shopping Centre
- **Coffee Republic** • Wandsworth High St

Nightlife

- **The Cat's Back** • 88 Point Pleasant
- **GJ's** • 89 Garratt Lane

 ## Post Offices

- **Wandsworth** • 1 Arndale Walk

Restaurants

- **Brady's** • 513 Old York Rd
- **Kathmandu Valley** • 5 West Hill

Supermarkets

- **Iceland** • Wandsworth High St & Buckhold Rd
- **Sainsbury's** • 45 Garratt Ln
- **Waitrose** • 66 Wandsworth High St

281

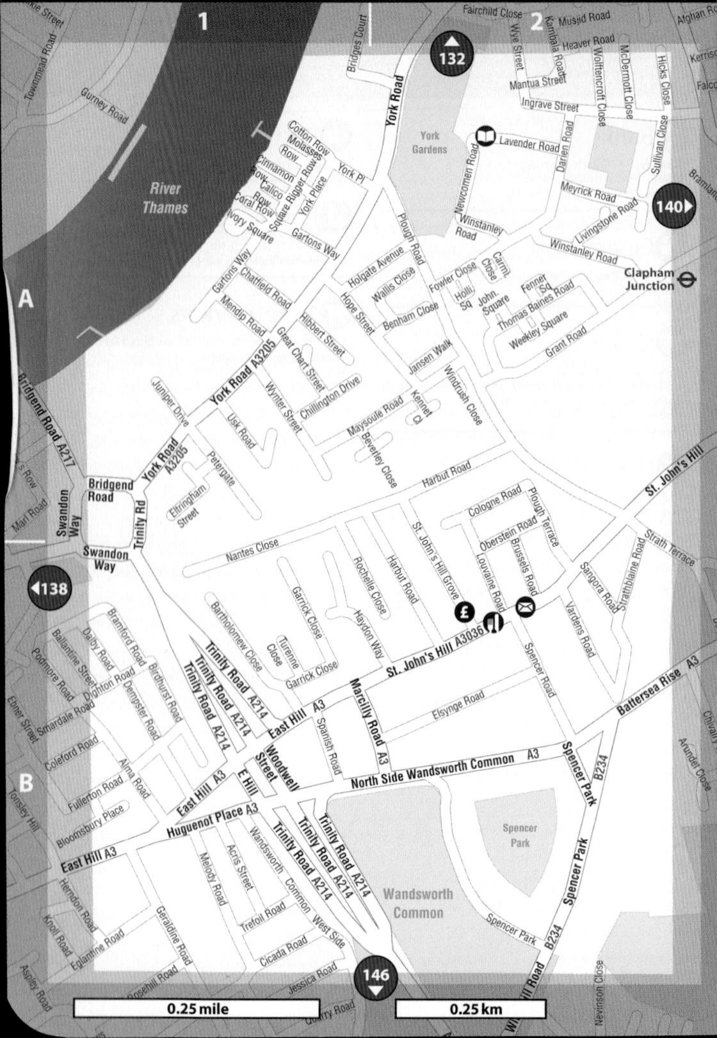

Map 139 · **Wandsworth (East)**

N

1

2

132

Fairchild Close

Musjid Road

Kambala Road

Hraver Road

McDermott Close

Afghan Rd

West Street

Wolftencroft Close

Mantua Street

Ingrave Street

Hicks Close

Kerrison

Sullivans

Falcon

Bridges Court

York Road

York Gardens

Lavender Road

Darien Road

Meyrick Road

Livingstone Road

Bramah

140

Gurney Road

Towns Road

Ave Street

Alfre

River Thames

Cotton Row

Molasses Row

York Pl

York Place

Rope Street

Ragwort St

Cardamon Row

Cinnamon Row

Calico Row

Ivory Square

Canal Row

Gartons Way

York St

A

Gartons Way

Chatfield Road

Mendip Road

Hope Street

Hibbert Street

Great Church Street

Wallis Close

Holgate Avenue

Benham Close

Fowler Close

Holly St

John Sq

Cairn Close

Newcomen Road

Winstanley Road

Winstanley Road

Thomas Baines Road

Fenner Sq

Weekley Square

Grant Road

Clapham Junction

Junger Drive

York Road A3205

York Road A3205

Usk Road

Wynter Street

Chillington Drive

Jansen Walk

Maysoule Road

Kerral Ct

Windrush Close

Beverley Close

Harbut Road

St John's Hill

Bridgend Road

Swandon Way

Trinity Rd

Ellingham Street

Nantes Close

Rochelle Close

Harbut Road

St John's Hill Grove

Coleman Road

Oberstein Road

Plough Terrace

Russells Road

Govanne Road

Sangora Road

Strathmore Road

Strath Terrace

Strathblaine Road

138

Bridgend Road A217

Sr's Row

Marl Hill

Balvernie Street

Dighton Road

Bramford Road

Dempster Road

Dalby Road

Birchlands Avenue

Podmore Road

Smardale Road

Coleford Road

Alma Road

Fullerton Road

Bloomsbury Place

Bartholomew Close

Turenne Close

Garrick Close

Garrick Close

Haydon Way

Hayton Close

St. John's Hill A3036

£

✉

⛽

Spencer Road

Vardens Road

Battersea Rise

B

Eglantine Road

Trinity Road A214

Trinity Road A214

East Hill A3

E Hill

Wardwell Street

Spanish Road

Marcilly Road A3

St. John's Hill A3036

Elsynge Road

North Side Wandsworth Common A3

Spencer Park

Spencer Park

East Hill A3

Huguenot Place A3

Trinity Road A214

Trinity Road A214

Wandsworth Common West Side

Acris Street

Mexfield Road

Trefoil Road

Cicada Road

Spencer Park

Spencer Park

Wandsworth Common

Spencer Park

B234

Arundel Close

Tonsley Hill

Herndon Road

Geraldine Road

Jessica Road

Quarry Road

Knoll Road

Ashley Road

Neville Close

146

Superstores, gas works, swanky apartment blocks, some of London's most deprived housing estates; Wandsworth East has it all! St John's Hill to the s outh is more promising, offering a bustling strip of boutique shops, bars, and restaurants. Grab a great curry at the Spice of Life and work it off with a brisk Frisbee session on Wandsworth Common.

 ## Banks
• **Halifax** • 6 St John's Hill Grove

 ## Libraries
• **York Gardens Library** • 34 Lavender Rd

 ## Post Offices
• **St Johns Hill** • 7 St John's Hill

 ## Restaurants
• **Spice of Life** • 147 St. Johns Hill

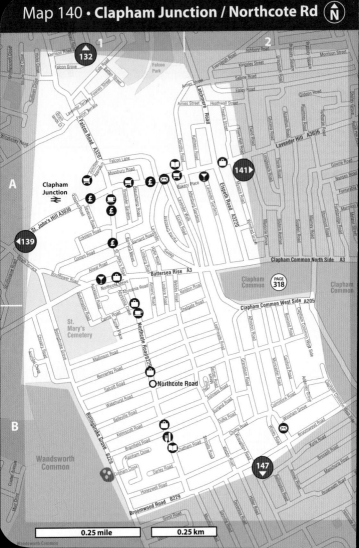

Map 140 · **Clapham Junction / Northcote Rd**

Yummy mummies rule by day when fancy pushchairs, laden with organic groceries from Fresh and Wild, cram the pavement. Hedonistic party people invade at night. With direct rail links to 'the provinces,' Clapham Junction buzzes with out-of-towners while locals hang at the bars on Northcote Road. Try B@1 for drinks, tunes, and bright young things. RUPERT RABY

Banks

- **Abbey** • 24 St John's Rd
- **Barclays** • 7 St John's Hill
- **HSBC** • 240 Lavender Hill
- **NatWest** • 66 St John's Rd

Coffee

- **Caffe Nero** • 20 St John's Rd
- **Starbucks** • 33 Northcote Rd

O Landmarks

- **Northcote Road** • Northcote Rd

Libraries

- **Battersea Library** • 265 Lavender Hill
- **Northcote Library** • 155 Northcote Rd

Nightlife

- **adventure bar and lounge** • 91 Battersea Rise
- **b@1** • 85 Battersea Rise
- **Jongleurs (Battersea)** • 49 Lavender Gardens

Post Offices

- **Alfriston Road** • 99 Alfriston Rd
- **Battersea** • 202 Lavender Hill

Restaurants

- **I Sapori di Stefano Cavallini** • 146 Northcote Rd

Shopping

- **Anita's Vintage Fashion Fair** •
  Battersea Arts Centre, Lavender Hill
- **Huttons** • 29 Northcote Rd
- **Lighthouse Bakery** •
- **QT Toys and Games** • 90 Northcote Rd
- **Russ** • 101 Battersea Rise
- **Sweaty Betty** • 136 Northcote Rd

Supermarkets

- **ASDA** • 204 Lavender Hill
- **Fresh & Wild** • 305 Lavender Hill
- **Sainsbury's** • Clapham Junction

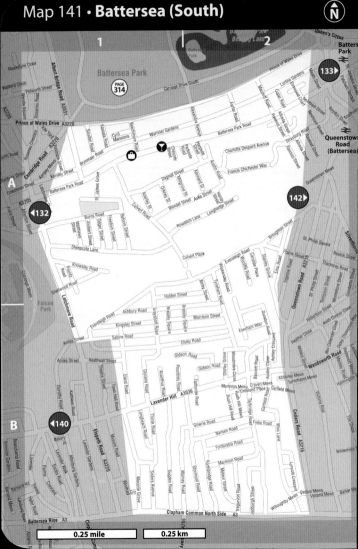

Map 141 · Battersea (South)

No one goes to Battersea South. You either live there, congratulating yourself on your nice Victorian conversion, or, you pass through on the way to Clapham or one of the lively bits of Battersea. Any of the 'action' happens around Lavender Hill. Dusk is a fancy (and decent) cocktail bar that would rather be a mile east or west.

Nightlife

• **Dusk** • 339 Battersea Park Rd

Shopping

• **Battersea Car Boot Sale** •
  401 Battersea Technical College, Battersea Park Rd

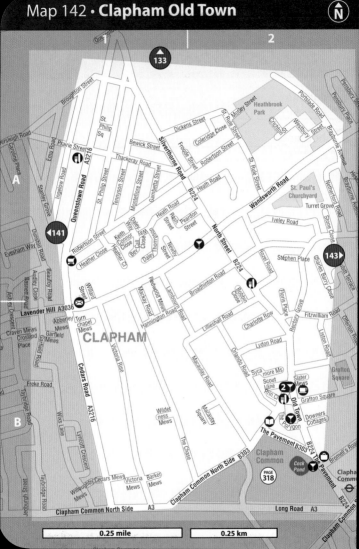

Map 142 · **Clapham Old Town**

The more genteel side of Clapham, Old Town hosts some fine restaurants (Trinity, Mooli), good watering-holes (The Prince of Wales, Frog, and Forget-Me-Not) and one of London's best butchers (Moens), all bordered by the green of Clapham Common. If you need more, and can resist Fish & Chips with free banter (Benny's), head to Queenstown Road for further fine dining establishments.

Coffee

• **Starbucks** • 40 Old Town

Libraries

• **Clapham Library** • 1 Clapham Common North Side

Nightlife

• **Frog and Forget-Me-Not** • 32 The Pavement
• **Lost Society** • 697 Wandsworth Rd
• **Prince of Wales** • 38 Old Town
• **Rose and Crown** • 2 The Polygon
• **The Sun** • 47 Clapham Old Town

Post Offices

• **Cedars** • 833 Wandsworth Rd

Restaurants

• **Benny's** • 30 North St
• **Mooli** • 36 Old Town
• **Tom Ilic** • 123 Queenstown Rd
• **Trinity** • 4 The Polygon

Shopping

• **M. Moen & Sons** • 24 The Pavement

Supermarkets

• **Sainsbury's** • 646 Wandsworth Rd

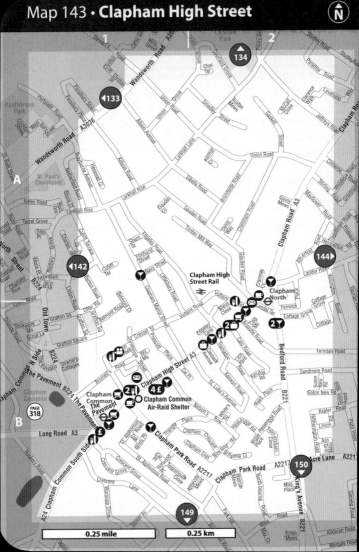

Map 143 · **Clapham High Street**

Filled with young pros spending too much on rent, look past the nobs on the main drag, Clapham High Street, to enjoy decent drinking (The Bread & Roses) and even better eating (Tsunami, Pepper Tree, Café Wanda). Alternatively, if you are a nob, try one of the High Street's brash bars or The Falcon, where everyone else will be talking too loudly and wearing shades.

Banks

- **Abbey** • 164 Clapham High St
- **Barclays** • 188 Clapham High St
- **HSBC** • 154 Clapham High St
- **Lloyds** • 12 Clapham Common South Side
- **NatWest** • 145 Clapham High St

Cinemas

- **Clapham Picturehouse** • 76 Venn St

Coffee

- **Café Delight** • 19 Clapham High St
- **Caffe Nero** • 186 Clapham High St

Landmarks

- **Clapham Common Air-Raid Shelter** • Clapham High St

Nightlife

- **The Alexandra** • 14 Clapham Common South Side
- **Bread and Roses** • 68 Clapham Manor St
- **The Clapham North** • 409 Clapham Rd
- **The Falcon** • 33 Bedford Rd
- **Green & Blue** • 20 Bedford Rd
- **Infernos** • 146 Clapham High St
- **The Railway** • 18 Clapham High St
- **The Two Brewers** • 114 Clapham High St
- **The White House** • 65 Clapham Park Rd

Post Offices

- **Clapham Common** • 161 Clapham High St
- **Clapham High Street** • 16 Clapham High St

Restaurants

- **Café Wanda** • 153 Clapham High St
- **The Fish Club** • 57 Clapham High St
- **The Pepper Tree** • 19 Clapham Common South Side
- **The Rapscallion** • 75 Venn St
- **San Marco Pizzeria** • 126 Clapham High St
- **Tsunami** • 5 Voltaire Rd

Shopping

- **Apex Cycles** • 40 Clapham High St
- **Paws** • 62 Clapham High St
- **Today's Living** • 92 Clapham High St

Supermarkets

- **Iceland** • 4 The Pavement
- **Sainsbury's** • Clapham High St
- **Sainsbury's** • 33 Clapham High St

Map 144 · **Stockwell / Brixton (West)**

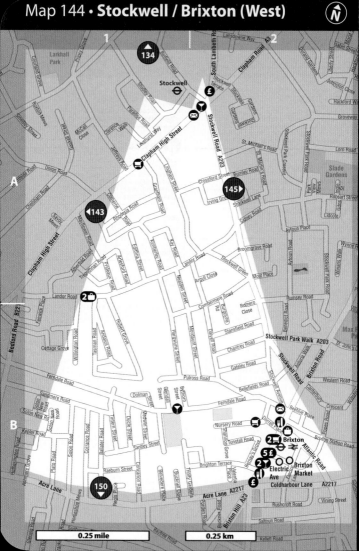

Stockwell / Brixton (West)

Stockwell has turned from dodgy to lively without losing character. If you can ignore the crack dealers outside KFC then the same can be said of Brixton. Brixton Market is an institution and a great taste of Caribbean flavour. At night, avoid the sweaty, heaving Swan at Stockwell unless desperate. Plan B is a decent option but you might need ear plugs.

£ Banks

- **Abbey** • 498 Brixton Rd
- **Barclays** • 463 Brixton Rd
- **Halifax** • 393 Brixton Rd
- **HSBC** • 512 Brixton Rd
- **NatWest** • 358 S Lambeth Rd
- **NatWest** • 395 Brixton Rd

O Landmarks

- **Brixton Market** • Electric Ave
- **Electric Avenue** • Electric Ave

Nightlife

- **Duke of Edinburgh** • 204 Ferndale Rd
- **Plan B** • 418 Brixton Rd
- **The Prince** • 469 Brixton Rd
- **The Swan** • 215 Clapham Rd

Post Offices

- **Frendale Road** • 250 Ferndale Rd
- **Stockwell** • 225 Clapham Rd

Restaurants

- **Speedy Noodle** • 506 Brixton Rd
- **SW9 Bar Cafe** • 11 Dorrell Pl

Shopping

- **Continental Delicatessen** • 3 Atlantic Rd
- **Lisa Stickley London** • 74 Landor Rd
- **The Old Post Office Bakery** • 76 Landor Rd

Supermarkets

- **Iceland** • 441 Brixton Rd
- **Iceland** • 314 Clapham Rd
- **Sainsbury's** • 425 Brixton Rd
- **Tesco** • 330 Brixton Rd

Map 144

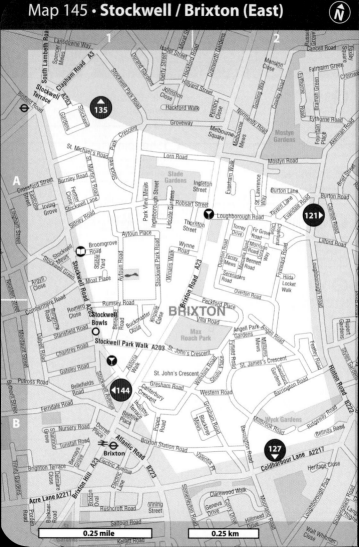

Map 145 · **Stockwell / Brixton (East)**

0.25 mile

0.25 km

Stockwell / Brixton (East)

Map 145

Things have changed a bit since The Clash sang 'The Guns of Brixton' in '79 and race riots were a regular occurrence. While the middle classes have infiltrated most parts of Brixton, this neighbourhood still retains a defiant edge. Community spirit and close-knit neighbourhoods take precedence over trendy bars and pricey restaurants. Live music rules here; the legendary Brixton Academy still draws the hordes but a new pretender, Jamm, is making waves.

O Landmarks
• **Stockwell Bowls** • Stockwell Rd

Libraries
• **Anti-Slavery International Library** • Broomgrove Rd

Nightlife
• **Brixton Academy** • 211 Stockwell Rd
• **Jamm** • 261 Brixton Rd

Map 146 · **Earlsfield**

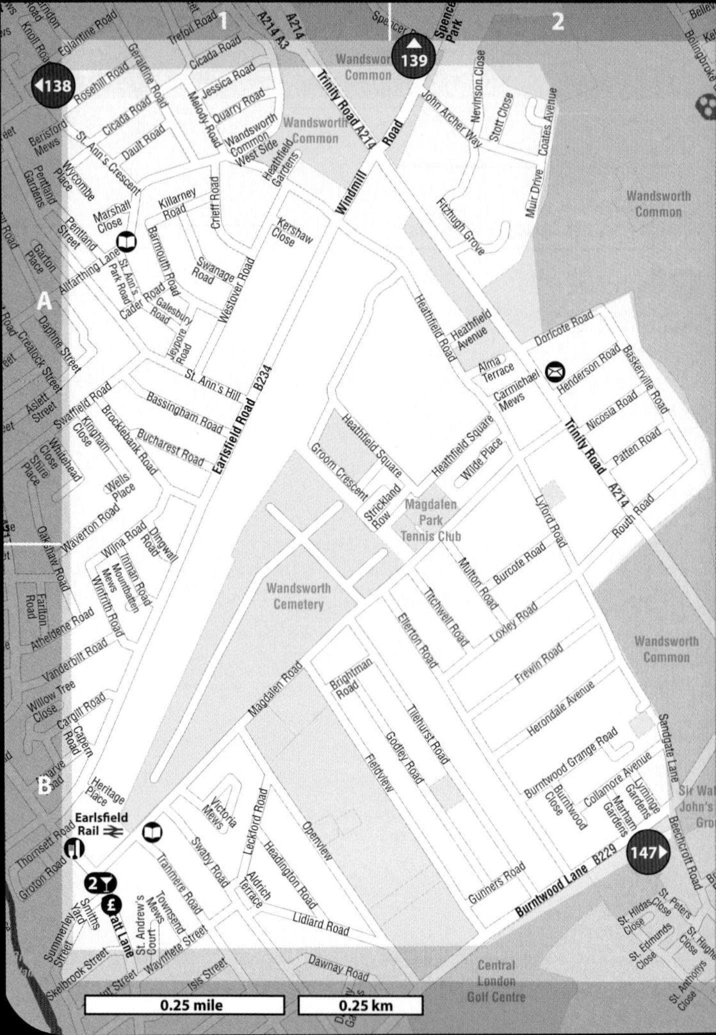

N

◄138

◄139▲

147►

Eglantine Road
Geraldine Road
Trefoil Road
Cicada Road
Spencer Road
Science Park
A214 A3
A214
Wandsworth Common
Rosehill Road
Cicada Road
Jessica Road
Quarry Road
Nevinson Close
Stott Close
Coates Avenue
Belle
Billingbroke
Dault Road
Maldy Road
Wandsworth Common West Side
Heathfield Gardens
John Archer Way
Muir Drive
Berisford Mews
St Ann's Crescent
Wiscombe
Pentland Gardens
Wandsworth Common A214
Windmill Road
Trinity Road A214
Fitzhugh Grove
Wandsworth Common
Garton Street
Pentland Street
Marshall Close
Killarney Road
Barmouth Road
Chieft Road
Kershaw Close
Allfarthing Lane
Cadet Road
Galesbury Road
Westover Road
Swanage Road
Heathfield Road
Heathfield Avenue
Dorlcote Road
Henderson Road
Besseville Road
A
Asfelt Street
Cracklock Street
Daphne Street
St. Ann's Road
Jessore Road
St. Ann's Hill
B234
Earlsfield Road
Bassingham Road
Bucharest Road
Brocklebank Road
Heathfield Square
Groom Crescent
Alma Terrace
Carmichael Mews
Nicosia Road
Patten Road
Trinity Road A214
Swaffield Road
Kinham Close
Wells Place
Whitnash
Stone Close
Strickland Row
Heathfield Square
Wilde Place
Magdalen Park Tennis Club
Lyford Road
Routh Road
Waterton Road
Dingwall Road
Wilna Road
Mountearl Mews
Immah Road
Wimbledon Road
Wandsworth Cemetery
Melton Road
Burcote Road
Wandsworth Common
Oakhaw Road
Vanderbilt Road
Atheldene Road
Magdalen Road
Thornwell Road
Ellerton Road
Loxley Road
Felton Road
Willow Tree Close
Cargill Road
Caistor Road
Brightman Road
Trewin Road
Herondale Avenue
B
Dove Road
Heritage Place
Thornsett Road
Groton Road
Victoria Mews
Leckford Road
Tilehurst Road
Godley Road
Fieldview
Burntwood Grange Road
Collamore Avenue
Lyming Gardens
Burntwood Close
Meham Gardens
Sandgate Lane
Sir Wa
John's L
Gro
Beechcroft Road
Earlsfield Rail
2
Earl Lane
Summerley
Yard
Smith's
Swaby Road
Trammere Road
Townsend
Mews
St. Andrew's Court
Openview
Headington Road
Aldrich Terrace
Aldrich Terrace
Lidiard Road
Guiness Road
Burntwood Lane B229
147►
St. Hildas Close
St. Peters Close
St. Esmonds Close
St. Antholins
Swinbrook Street
Isis Road
Waynflete Street
Dawnay Road
Central London Golf Centre

| 0.25 mile | | 0.25 km |

Sleepy little Earlsfield tends to mind its own business. It's a pretty sedate kind of place, slightly cut off by the lack of a tube stop. The well-heeled locals seem happy enough and make the most of what's on offer. Try the Thai Café for great noodles before moving on to Bar 366 a few doors down for some chilled boozing.

£ Banks

• **Barclays** • 376 Garratt Ln
• **Halifax** • 87 Wandsworth High St

Libraries

• **Alvering Library** • 2 Allfarthing Lane
• **Earlsfield Library** • 276 Magdalen Rd

Nightlife

• **Bar 366** • 366 Garratt Ln
• **Box Bar** • 537 Garratt Lane

Post Offices

• **Trinity Road** • 318 Trinity Rd

Restaurants

• **Thai Cafe and Noodle Bar** • 346 Garratt Ln

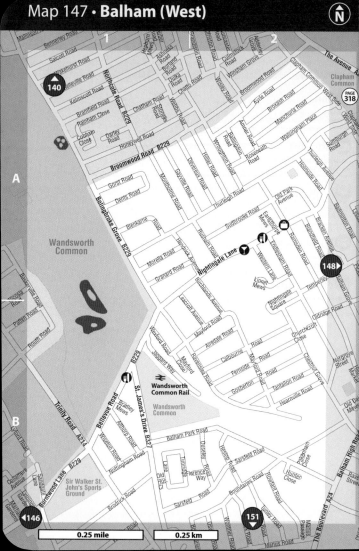

Ensconced between the livelier Clapham and Tooting, this is a gentle slice of residential south west London. Bellevue Road offers a number of places to eat and drink overlooking Wandsworth Common, climaxing with the stupendous Chez Bruce. Nightingale Lane is terribly twee and hosts a few opportunities to shop organically and, you know, locally, or to stuff yourself silly at the Bombay Bicycle Club.

Nightlife

• **The Nightingale** • 97 Nightingale Lane

Restaurants

• **The Bombay Bicycle Club** • 95 Nightingale Lane
• **Chez Bruce** • 2 Bellevue Rd

Shopping

• **Bon Vivant** • 59 Nightingale Lane

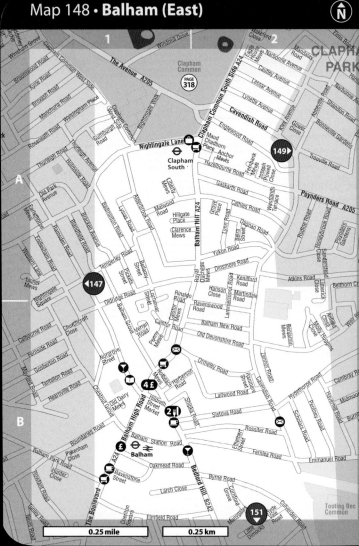

The gentrification of Balham proceeds at pace but it hasn't yet killed off its character. Illegal all-nighters are a thing of the past but once the baby buggy crowds have finished their Waitrose run, Balham really comes alive. Diverse eating options (try Dish Dash for Persian treats) great pubs (Balham Bowling Club rules) and swanky bars (Harrison's darhling) all vie for your hard earned nuggets.

£ Banks

- **Abbey** • 200 Balham High Rd
- **Barclays** • 169 Balham High Rd
- **Halifax** • 160 Balham High Rd
- **HSBC** • 117 Balham High Rd
- **Lloyds** • 125 Balham High Rd

Coffee

- **Caffe Nero** • 137 Balham High Rd
- **Starbucks** • 41 Bedford Hill

Libraries

- **Balham Library** • 16 Ramsden Rd

Nightlife

- **Balham Bowls Club** • 79 Ramsden Rd
- **The Bedford** • 77 Bedford Hill

Post Offices

- **Balham** • 92 Balham High Rd
- **Cavendish Road** • 273 Cavendish Rd

Restaurants

- **Dish Dash** • Bedford Hill
- **Harrison's** • 15 Bedford Hill

Shopping

- **Moxon's** • Westbury Parade

Supermarkets

- **Sainsbury's** • 149 Balham High Rd
- **Sainsbury's** • 19 Balham Hill
- **Waitrose** • Balham High Rd & Ramsden Rd

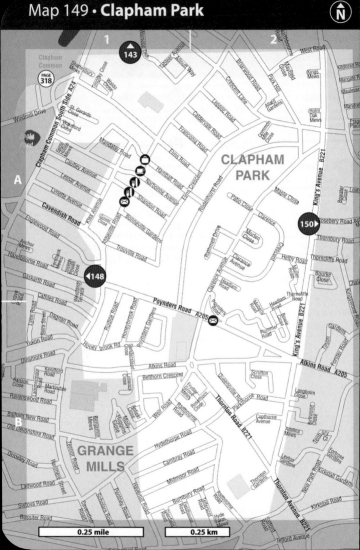

Largely a residential rat run, Clapham Park has its moments. After a day out on Clapham Common it's far less hectic and boozy than its tube served neighbours. Head to Abbeville Road for a wide selection of bars and restaurants. Fill up on hearty Italian at Antipasto and Pasta or for Dexter's for a lazy brunch.

Coffee

• **Starbucks** • 39 Abbeville Rd

Post Offices

• **Abbeville Road** • 34 Abbeville Rd
• **Clapham Park** • 49 Poynders Rd

Restaurants

• **Dexter's** • 36 Abbeville Rd
• **Grissini** • 31 Abbeville Rd

Shopping

• **MacFarlanes** • 48 Abbeville Rd

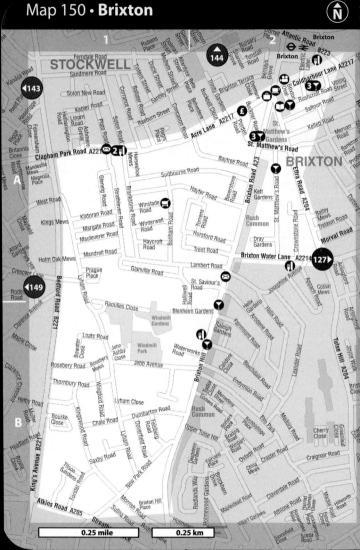

Map 150 · Brixton

Believe the hysteria and Brixton is a nest of gun-toting crack heads. Yes, it has its problems but Brixton is also one of London's most diverse and vibrant neighbourhoods popular with a young, cool crowd. The Brixton Ritzy is a brilliant art house cinema offering bars and interesting food as well as great films. Clubbers gravitate towards the Brixton Fridge (sweaty) and Mass (funky); a sprawling multi-purpose venue housed in a church.

£ Banks

• **Lloyds** • 18 Acre Ln

Coffee

• **Rosie's Deli Cafe** • 14 Market Row

Libraries

• **Brixton Library** • Brixton Oval

Movie Theaters

• **Ritzy Cinema** • Coldharbour Ln & Brixton Oval

Nightlife

• **The Brixton Fridge Club and Bar** • 1 Town Hall Parade
• **The Dogstar** • 389 Coldharbour Ln
• **The Effra** • 38 Kellet Rd
• **The Fridge** • 1 Town Hall Parade, Brixton Hill
• **Mango Landin'** • 40 St Matthews Rd
• **Mass** • Brixton Hill
• **Prince Albert** • 418 Coldharbour Ln
• **Ritzy Café** •
   Brixton Oval, Coldharbour Lane (above Ritzy cinema)
• **St Matthews Church** • Brixton Hill
• **The Windmill** • 22 Blenheim Gardens

✉ Post Offices

• **Acre Lane** • 154 Acre Ln
• **Brixton Hill** • 104 Brixton Hill

🍴 Restaurants

• **Asmara** • 386 Coldharbour Ln
• **Khan's** • 24 Brixton Water Lane
• **Negril** • 132 Brixton Hill
• **Opus Café** • 89 Acre Ln
• **Upstairs Bar and Restaurant** • 89 Acre Ln

🛍 Shopping

• **Traid** • 2 Acre Ln

🛒 Supermarkets

• **Iceland** • 13 Winslade Rd

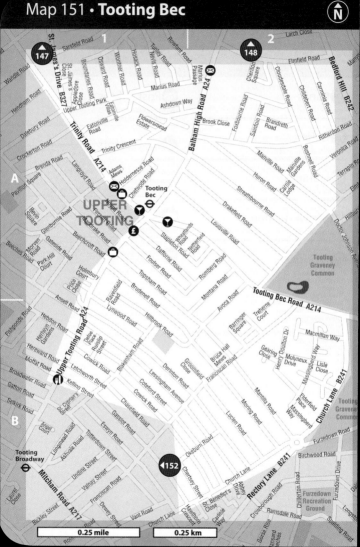

Map 151

Not quite the Bec of beyond, the home of Europe's largest lido has a plethora of Asian snack bars for post-pub munchies. Generally you're going to have to travel to work up that hunger though, maybe trot over the border to Balham. But for midweek (or for the lazy), try daiquiris at the Bec Bar, cocktails at Smoke, or top drawer curry at Mirch Masala.

Banks

• **Barclays** • 29 Upper Tooting Rd

Nightlife

• **The Bec Bar** • 26 Tooting Bec Rd
• **Smoke Bar** • 14 Trinity Rd

Post Offices

• **Balham High Road** • 258 Balham High Rd
• **Upper Tooting** • 63 Trinity Rd

Restaurants

• **Mirch Masala** • 213 Upper Tooting Rd

Shopping

• **Russell's Hardware & DIY** • 46 Upper Tooting Rd
• **Wandsworth Oasis HIV/AIDs Charity Shop** •
  40 Trinity Rd

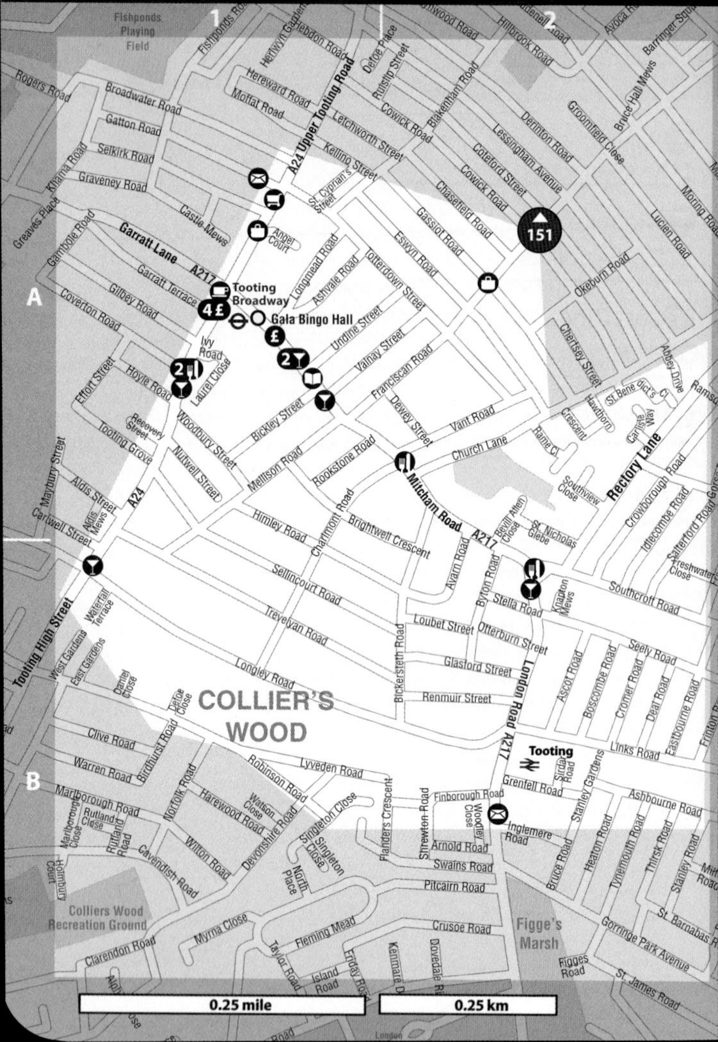

Map 152 · **Tooting Broadway**

N

Fishponds
Playing
Field

1

2

Fishponds Road

Hertwood Garfield Road

Broadwater Road

Chillerton Place

Chillerton Road

Hillgrove Road

Avoca Ro

Barmore

Rogers Place

Hereward Road

Cricklade Street

Brudenell Road

Blackenham Road

Dennison Road

Groomfield Close

Bruce Hall Mews

Moffat Road

Cowick Road

Lessingham Avenue

Morina Ro

Gatton Road

Knollys Road

Greaves Place

Selkirk Road

Letchworth Street

Coteford Street

Lucien Ro

Graveney Road

Kellino Street

Chasefield Road

Okeburn Road

Castle Mews

St Cyprian's Street

Gassiot Road

Garratt Lane **A217**

Angel
Court

Upper Tooting Road **A24**

Ashvale Road

Esporta Road

151

Abbey Dri

Chelsea Street

St Bene'dict's Gle

Camfield

Coverton Road

Gilbey Road

Garratt Terrace

Longmead Road

Totterdown Street

Undine Street

Vainay Road

Vant Road

Crescent

Rectory Lane

Ramse

Effort Street

Hoyle Road

A

Tooting
Broadway

4 £

Ivy
Road

Gala Bingo Hall

£

2

Bickley Street

Laurel Close

Franciscan Road

Dewey Street

Church Lane

Rang Cl.

Crowborough Road

Crowford Road

Freshwater Close

St Bene'dict's Ro

Tooting Grove

Aldis Street

Recovery
Street

Woodbury Street

Nutwell Street

Mellison Road

Rookstone Road

Mitcham Road **A217**

St. Nicholas
Glebe

Southcroft Road

Marbury Street

Carlwell Street

Tooting High Street

Himley Road

Charlmont Road

Brightwell Crescent

Adam Road

Byron Road

Stella Road

Southey Close

Garden Mews

Illecombe Road

West Gardens

Carr Gardens

Daniel
Close

Longley Road

Sellincourt Road

Loubet Street

Otterburn Street

Seely Road

Boscombe Road

Ascot Road

Cromer Road

Deal Road

Eastbourne Road

B

Marlborough Road

Warren Road

Clive Road

Bloxhurst Road

Rutland
Close

Norton Close

Watson
Close

Harewood Road

Wilton Road

Devonshire Close

Singleton Close

Flanchers Crescent

Trevelyan Road

Glasford Street

Renmuir Street

Lyveden Road

Shrewton Road

Finborough Road

Arnold Road

Grenfell Road

Tooting

Inglemere
Road

Woolley
Close

Stanley Gardens

Ashbourne Road

Heaton Road

Truro Road

Tynemouth Road

Stanley Road

St. Barnabas

Cavendish Road

Singleton Close

North
Place

Swains Road

Pitcairn Road

Bruce Road

Hillery
Court

Marlborough Close

Rutland
Close

**COLLIER'S
WOOD**

Robinson Road

Bickersteth Road

London Road **A217**

Colliers Wood
Recreation Ground

Clarendon Road

Myrna Close

Fleming Mead

Taylor Road

Island
Road

Crusoe Road

Kenmare
Road

**Figge's
Marsh**

Figges
Road

St. James Road

Gorringe Park Avenue

0.25 mile

0.25 km

Tooting Broadway

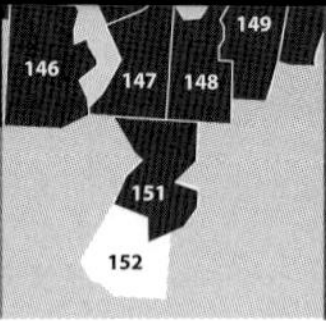

Decent rent, a Northern Line station, and a grade one listed bingo hall, there's not much here not to like. Hit the High Street for curries and halal everything, Mitcham Road should supply you with anything else required. Local eat treats include Radha Krishna Bhavan and Rick's Café, whereas Garden House, Tooting Tram, and Social show that trendy pubs can survive this far south.

£ Banks

- **Abbey** • 266 Upper Tooting Rd
- **Barclays** • 262 Upper Tooting Rd
- **Barclays** • 14 Mitcham Rd
- **Halifax** • 50 Tooting High St
- **HSBC** • 56 Tooting High St

O Landmarks

- **Gala Bingo Hall** • 50 Mitcham Road

Libraries

- **Tooting Library** • 75 Mitcham Rd

Nightlife

- **Garden House** • 196 Tooting High St
- **Jack Beard's** • 76 Mitcham Rd
- **The Ramble Inn** • Amen Corner
- **Spirit** • 94 Tooting High St
- **Tram and Social** • 46 Mitcham Rd
- **The Tramshed** • 48 Mitcham Rd

Post Offices

- **London Road** • 47 London Rd
- **Tooting** • 2 Gatton Rd

Restaurants

- **Jaffna House** • 90 Tooting High St
- **Radha Krishna Bhavan** • 86 Tooting High St
- **Rick's Cafe** • 122 Mitcham Rd
- **Sette Bello** • 8 Amen Corner
- **Urban Coffee** • 74 Tooting High St

Shopping

- **Tooting Market** • 21 Tooting High St

Supermarkets

- **Iceland** • 27 Tooting High St

Map 152

(309)

General Information

Website: www.alexandrapalace.com
Phone: 020 8365 2121

Overview

Usually overshadowed by its north London neighbours Hampstead Heath and Primrose Hill, Alexandra Palace Park is one of the most overlooked gems in the capital. Nearby, Muswell Hill's well-to-do residents would probably prefer that this 197-acre parkland remained somewhat of a secret rarely found in a guide, but too bad! Designed by Alexander Mackenzie in 1873 with many diverse attractions within its grounds, the park's historic status is most assured by the venue lying within its grounds, Alexandra Palace itself. Often referred to as the home of television on account of the BBC broadcasting the world's first public high definition TV transmissions there in 1936, it is now mainly an exhibition and conference

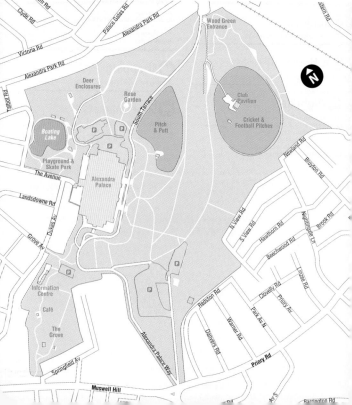

centre, although in recent years its use as a concert venue has been revived as well.

Practicalities

The park can be easily accessed by various modes of transport: there is a rail station called Alexandra Palace station located at the Wood Green entrance to the park, and you can also take the underground to Wood Green, catching a W3 bus outside the station which stops outside the Palace. You could also take advantage of the 2000 free parking spaces in the park itself if driving, though it's only a short walk from Muswell Hill town centre.

Nature

No doubt tempted by the reservoirs, 155 species of birds have been spotted in the park over the last 30 years. Nature fetishists should take in the two-hectare conservation area, which includes a wide array of animals including deer, donkeys, foxes and rabbits. In 1998, there was even a rare water vole sighting. There he was, large as life, like he owned the bloody place.

Architecture

Seen as the main focal point of the park by many, Alexandra Palace (affectionally known as "Ally Pally") is a prime example of stunning Victorian architecture, having undergone much restoration work following a severe fire in 1980. Alas, much of architectural interest within the park has gone by the wayside, with the old banqueting venue Blandford Hall having burnt down in 1971. What is it about this place and fire?

Open Spaces

It's safe to say that Alexandra Park has more than enough grass to keep Cheech & Chong happy, being typified by the diverse range of landscaped grounds that can be found within. The Grove Garden actually pre-dates the park itself and there's also a good little café here if you fancy a quick bite. The Rose Garden is to the east side of the Palace and is even more aesthetically pleasing. Many newer small woodlands have been developing over the last few decades owing to the planting of large numbers of trees, producing an environment pleasing to both the rambler and runner.

Performance

The park often plays host to funfairs and circuses, but the Palace itself will usually be used at night for concerts. Its revival over recent years as a gig venue has led to the likes of the Arctic Monkeys and Paul Weller playing there, with its capacity being around 8,500, making it ideal for bands who've outgrown the Brixton Academy. Other parts of the Palace, such as the Great Hall, are used for classical music recitals. Of course, none of these performances will compare to Barry Manilow live at the Palace in 1988. Probably.

The Palace also houses a theatre, which was dormant for over sixty-five years until a performance took place in 2004. It is still being restored and should be re-opened to the public for performances in the near future.

Sports

An indoor ice rink is housed within the Palace with a capacity of 1,250, with all manner of ice sports catered for (you can get further information by ringing 020 8365 4386). There is also a large boating lake with its own islands and fishing place (and even a smaller area for kids to boat on their own), with pedalos and rowing boats available for hire; being a seasonal facility, it's best to ring the operators Bluebird Boats Ltd. (020 7262 1330) beforehand. The boating pond is adjacent to a children's playground as well. At the time of writing, the pitch and putt course (golf for people who don't like golf) was due to reopen, with Heritage Lottery Fund money enabling this popular attraction to be refurbished. Alexandra Palace Park is also popular with cyclists, with the Parkland Walk a particular favourite, being a disused railway line that links up with Finsbury Park. You can also see countless spontaneous games of football and Frisbee, as well as the ubiquitous joggers. For those with a more sedentary approach to sport, last year saw the return of the World Darts Championship to the Palace, which means that Londoners and tourists alike can strive to understand the appeal of watching half-drunk, beer-bellied men throw sharply tipped missiles at a circular target ("Darts, Keith, darts...").

General information

NFT Map: 7

Address: Barbican Centre, Silk St, London, EC2Y 8DS.

Phone: Box Office & Membership: 020 7638 8891 (9 am-8 pm daily); Switchboard: 020 7638 4141

Centre opening times: Mon-Sat: 9 am-11 pm; Sun & Public Holidays: 12 pm-11 pm (although different parts of the centre may open at different times)

Website: www.barbican.org.uk

Overview

As terrifying as it is impressive, the Barbican Centre is a one-stop shop for all things cultural. At its best, the Barbican is utterly brilliant: a rambling collection of cinemas, galleries, bars, theatres, even a housing estate and a school. But stay after dark, when the culture vultures have left, and you can find yourself alone and lost in this city-within-a-city.

That the centre is brutally ugly makes what's inside even more splendid. The gallery space hosts world-class exhibitions and the cinemas show both mainstream and arthouse films. There's a world, classical and jazz music programme catering for everyone from scruffy backpackers to bearded professors. Most are sensible enough to leave before it gets too spooky. But plan your exit route in advance just in case.

Music

The heart of the Barbican monster is its music hall. Its near-2,000 capacity has become a mecca for lovers of cerebral music, hosting major festivals in the thinking genres. Each summer the Barbican holds the Mostly Mozart festival, a celebration of the composer that reaches sci-fi convention levels of fanaticism. In 2006, 250 years since he was born, the festival claimed to be the biggest birthday bash held for him in the capital. The music centre's resident band

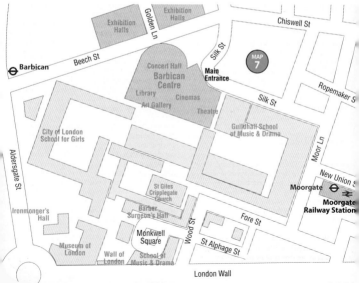

is the London Symphony Orchestra, classical heavyweights who play year-round. Come winter, though, and it's elbow patches that take centre stage as the Barbican hosts the London Jazz Festival. But it's not all polite serenity in the hall—the world music programme delves into the lairiest parts of Africa and Latin America for its own noisy festival.

Film

In keeping with its creed as a cultural hotspot, the Barbican's film programme is suitably arty. The three-screen cinema is home to two permanent showcases—the London Australian and London Children's film festivals—and the centre curates its own programmes. The listings constantly change, but you can generally stick to the following rule: silent films, in; Sly Stallone, out; subtitles, in; J Lo, out; indy award-winners, in; the Mighty Ducks trilogy, out. But they do offer the screens for private hire—so, if you really want to, you can stick it to 'em and have your own showing of Snakes on a Plane.

Theatre and Dance

Don't be fooled by the Barbican's hulking exterior—the centre dabbles in the more delicate arts rather well. Its two theatres cater for both ends of the performance spectrum. The main room, a shared home for acting and dance, seats over 1,000 punters and attracts some of the biggest names in high culture. Deep in the Barbican's bowels the smaller Pit theatre is home to experimental and new acts. But be warned: with just 200 seats the Pit is small enough for anyone dozing off to be highly visible.

Art

Nowhere else at the Barbican is the idea of making art accessible for all more apparent than their art spaces. The main gallery hosts temporary exhibitions, mixing all types of art into one cultural hot pot. In 2007, under the umbrella of Art and Sex from Antiquity to Now, erotic Roman cutlery—that's right: erotic cutlery— shared a stage with impressionist paintings and an 11-minute film of someone's face as she was,

ahem, attended to. Every first Thursday of the month the gallery opens for a nocturnal viewing, with talks, performances—burlesque dancers for the art and sex exhibition—and a themed bar. A second space, The Curve, winds its way round the ground floor where the exhibitions are generally free.

The Library

Libraries often get a bad press. They've got stuck with an image of frumpy, middle-aged women peering down their spectacles and telling youths to be quiet. But this couldn't be further removed from the reality of the Barbican Library. Alongside a decent array of books, there's a dazzling collection of live musical recordings. Some of these tracks are so rare that they can't be heard anywhere else in the world. Put some headphones on and rock out. Just don't get carried away and smash up the children's section.

How To Get There

By car: The Barbican's well signposted in surrounding areas and, once there, there are four car parks to choose from. Two are off Beech Street (with westbound access only) and two are off Silk Street, near the main entrance. Parking is around £2.20 an hour (depending on how long you stay), although there's a flat weekend and evening (post-5.30 pm) fee of £5.
By bus: The 153 (which runs from Liverpool Street to Finsbury Park) stops directly outside the Barbican at Silk Street; the following buses run nearby: 8, 11, 23, 26, 35, 42, 43, 47, 48, 55, 56, 76, 78, 100, 133, 141, 149, 172, 214, 242, 243, 271, 344 (seven days a week); 4, (Mon-Sat); 21, 25, 521 (Mon-Fri). If none of these buses can take you home then consider yourself extremely unlucky.
By tube: Barbican stations runs on the Circle, District and Hammersmith & City lines. Other stations nearby are Moorgate, St Paul's, Bank, Liverpool Street and Mansion House.
By train: The nearest overland stations are Liverpool Street, Farringdon and Blackfriars. City Thameslink services run through Barbican, Moorgate and Cannon Street.

Parks & Places · **Battersea Park**

Practical Information

NFT Map: 132, 133, & 141

Official opening time is 8 am, although the gates are usually unlocked a little earlier than this. The park closes at dusk.

Friends of Battersea Park:
www.batterseapark.org

Zoo: www.batterseaparkzoo.co.uk

Local council: www.wandsworth.gov.uk
(see also for information on the Pump House Gallery)

Cycle hire:
www.londonrecumbents.co.uk

Blue bird boat hire:
www.wandsworth.gov.uk

Overview

Opened in 1858 with the aim of giving the Victorian working classes something to do other than drinking gin, Battersea Park has developed to become one of London's prettiest, most popular and most usable parks. Squeezing a range of gardens, cafes, animals, walks, sports and cultural facilities into its diminutive 200 acres, the park is popular with everyone from hordes of snotty little kids to wandering dog-walkers. It is also centrally located enough to be easy to get to but still far enough from Central London to retain a local feel.

The park is about two miles southwest from Westminster and occupies the spot on the south bank of the Thames between Albert and Chelsea bridges. Originally used for duelling, the Duke of Wellington famously discharged upon the Earl of Winchelsea on the site in 1829. Rather than the vast open and flat spaces that many London parks offer, Battersea is neatly divided into a number of features and sections, making it feel much larger than it is.

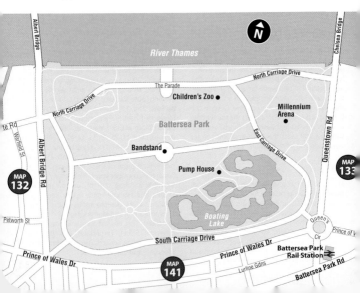

Sporting Activities

Battersea has an incredibly good array of sporting facilities. The 'Millennium Arena' is a 400m 8-lane running track situated in the northeast corner of the park; it hosts athletic meets and training sessions and it benefited from an expensive overhaul in, you guessed it, 1999. Next to the arena are ten tennis courts and an all-weather football pitch whilst there are further all-weather astro-turf pitches in the south east corner of the park marked for both hockey and football. The park also boasts cricket pitches and practice nets, a bowling green, a number of routes for jogging and enough spare open spaces to invite impromptu sessions of pretty much any other sport. If you consider attacking fish a sport, and have a permit and rod licence, the park's lake offers fishing for nine months of the year. Rowing boats and pedaloes can also be taken out on to the lake during July and August (adults £4.50/hour, children £2.50). Bicycles can be hired from the London Recumbents shop, which is next to the Millennium Arena on the park's East Carriage Drive.

Art

Battersea has fostered a creative relationship with the arts and has a number of sculptures dotted about, its own public gallery and a biannual art fair. Taking pride of place next to the lake are two large Henry Moore and Barbara Hepworth sculptures, both of which are well worth rooting out. The Pumphouse Gallery is a grade II-listed building, originally used to power the park's water works, which has been restored and converted into a gallery and information centre with six exhibitions throughout the year. The Gallery, located northeast of the lake, is also available for private hire and even has a licence to hold civil weddings. The park has hosted the Affordable Art Fair since 1999, which has become a leading showcase for art priced under £3,000.

Nature and Children's Zoo

The varied landscapes of the park ensure that you stand a decent chance of seeing more than a rat or a pigeon whilst sauntering around the park. Squirrels, ducks and Canada geese are all too plentiful. More interesting potential sightings include woodpeckers, cormorants, Peregrine falcons, terrapins and, according to the RSPB, Pochards (whatever they are). If you don't come across any interesting wildlife, your only option is to cheat and visit the park's zoo. A 5-minute stroll from the Park's Chelsea Gate entrance, the zoo is aimed at children and has a cool collection of small mammals, including lemurs, as well as small farm animals and some excitingly named birds, such as some 'Peach-faced Love birds'. In case you do fall in love with any of the zoo's inhabitants, most are available for adoption. Mice start at £10 for six months, pay-up and claim it's for your kid. The zoo is open throughout the year.

How To Get There

By tube: Sloane Square (on the Circle and District lines) is the nearest Underground station at just under a mile away. From the station walk down Lower Sloane Street, which becomes Chelsea Bridge Road and leads to the Thames. Walk over Chelsea Bridge and you will see the park on your right. Alternatively take bus no 319.

By bus: From central London, buses run to the park from Liverpool Street (number 344), Notting Hill (452), Oxford Circus (137), Sloane Square (319, 137), Victoria Station (44) and Vauxhall (344).

By train: Battersea Park station is within sight of the park, trains run to both Clapham Junction and Victoria at high frequency. Queenstown Road is around 300m from the park. Trains from this station run to Waterloo and Clapham Junction and depart less often than from Battersea Park.

Chaucer Rd
Spenser Rd
Shakespeare Rd
Milton Rd
Regent Rd
Railton Rd
Milkwood Rd
Lubron Av
Woodquest Av

Brixton Water Ln

Herne Pl

Herne

Herne Hill
Railway Station

Carve

**MAP
127**

Hurst St

Rymer St

Half Me

Railton Rd

Dulwich Rd

Brailsford Rd

Arlington Rd

Sport
Pitches

Wildflower
Meadows

Brockwell
Lido

Pool

Sport
Pitches

Play
Area

BMX
Track

Sport
Pitches

Sport
Pitches

Bowling
Pavilion

**Brockwell
Park**

Wildflower
Meadows

Bascome St

Community
Greenhouses

Walled
Garden

Sport
Pitches

Tulse Hill

Temple

**Wet Play
Area**

Café

Brockwell
Hall

Stables

Norwood Rd

Rosendale

Guer

Wildflower
Meadows

Norwood
Lodge

Peabody Estate

Tulse Hill

Brockwell Park Gdns

Trinity Rise

Norwood

Bello Close

General Information

NFT Map: 127
Brockwell Park: www.brockwellpark.com
Brockwell Park Lido: www.brockwelllido.com
020 7274 3088

Overview

Much loved by the local residents of Herne Hill and surrounds, Brockwell Park has 128 acres of history, views and plenty to do. Not quite amazing in any way, it's still surprisingly good. Tilting towards ragged and unconventional, it's also family-friendly and cool. The park and its regular events draw a nice eclectic selection of locals.

History

By the end of the 19th century the local population was large, growing and in need of a serious park. Brockwell was secured for use by the public after MP Thomas Bristowe got wind of a private country estate that seemed just the ticket. Still, he might have over-exerted himself in the process: having taken a Bill through Parliament to convert the land, led a committee to negotiate the price, and raised funds from across the community, Bristowe himself promptly collapsed and died on the steps of Brockwell Hall, moments after the opening ceremony in 1892.

Café

If that doesn't put you off your scones, nowadays, the ground floor of Brockwell Hall is a café where refreshments have been served ever since. Located at the top of the hill, it's a great place to stop for inexpensive cake, drinks etc. after some...

Activities!

There's heaps to do. A BMX track, tennis courts, bowling green, football and cricket pitches, basketball courts, a children's play area and a paddling pool. Or you could chill by the ponds, in the walled garden, under the clock tower, at the picnic area, near the flower gardens, etc.

Brockwell Lido

Built in 1937, Brockwell Lido is essentially an (unattractive) art deco building that replaced an old bathing pond. After experiencing financial difficulty it was restored and reopened in 2007. As well as a large outdoor pool, there is a gym and classes are held in yoga, pilates, tai-chi and meditation. For the under 5s, Whippersnappers have everything from acrobatics to puppets and African drumming. A Miniature Railway runs between Herne Hill Gate and the Lido. Run by a local enthusiast on a not-for-profit basis; it's only £1 for a round trip.
May–Sept, Sat–Sun, 11am–5pm.
There is also a community greenhouse project which is open to volunteers. Or you could get yourself involved in the...

Annual events!

July: Lambeth Country Show in is always good fun and involves medieval jousting, farm animals, live reggae/dub and rides, and there are homemade cake and jam contests too. The Alternative Vegetable Animal Competition requires fruit and veg be crafted into a famous person or building with a very entertaining adult category.
September: The first Urban Green Fair was held in 2007.
November: The big fireworks show on Guy Fawkes Night is worth braving the cold for.

How to Get There

By rail/tube/foot: The park is a short walk from the following overland and underground stations:

Herne Hill Rail Station—5 mins
Tulse Hill Rail Station—15 mins
Brixton Tube —20 mins
Clapham North Tube —30 mins
By bus: The following all stop at Brockwell Park—2, 3, 37, 68, 196, 322, 468, P15

Overview

Lively and happening; youngish, professional, and trendy (in a safe way). Clapham Common reflects the area well.

Popular all year round, the Common truly comes alive in summer. On a warm weekend you'll find the park overflowing with picnickers sipping champagne and just plain lookin' good. It's a lovely scene made better by the relaxed, friendly atmosphere. And, when the sun finally sets, you're left with a seriously impressive choice of bars close by.

As well as drawing the usual funky sophisticates, the park is also family-friendly with lots of little ones enjoying the space. Although in parts, there are well-known cruising spots for the gay sophisticates.

Plenty of organised (or not) sport, kite-flying, model boating, Ultimate Frisbee, and even a spot of fishing, happens here.

History

Clapham began as a Saxon village. Back then it was called Clopp Ham, meaning the village (ham) by the short hill (clopp). The common was used by villagers to graze their livestock and as a source of firewood.

In the late 17th century the population began to grow as refugees arrived from the Great Plague of London (1665) and the fire of 1666. During this time, the rich gentry of London built a number of fine country houses around the common. When the railways were developed there was a sudden influx of commuters, driving the upper class away to somewhere less, um, common.

Today, the surrounding area is one of the more expensive in South London, partly because of its excellent transport links.

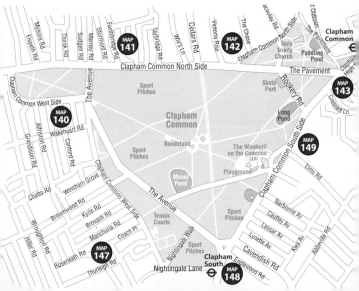

Clapham Sect

On the common is the Holy Trinity Church. This was a meeting place of the Clapham Sect, a group of 19th-century Evangelical Anglicans who fought for social reform. "Ugh" you say, but wait…

The Clapham Sect played a significant part in the abolition of slavery in England. They didn't stop there, going on to campaign for the eradication of slavery worldwide. They also fought for reform in the penal system, focusing on unjust sentencing and the dire prison conditions of the time.

The Bandstand

For many years this was thought to have been built in 1861, which would have made it the oldest surviving cast-iron bandstand in Europe. However it was recently discovered to have been erected in 1890, reducing its claim to be the oldest in London. Oh well, good enough. Three cafés

Cicero's on the Common (vegetarian)
2 Rookery Road, SW49QN, 020 7498 0770

Cafe Des Res (English/ Carribean)
8 The Pavement, SW4 0HY, 020 7622 6602

The Bowling Green Café (sandwiches, pasta etc) Clapham Common West Side, SW4 9AN, 020 7801 0904

Three ponds

Mount Pond – is a fishing park pond about three acres in size. It contains carp, roach, gudgeon and eels. Suggested baits include pellet, maggot, meat, and boilies, it says here.

Eagle Pond – is a smaller pond with a little island. This one is also fishable. Stocks include carp, tench, bream, roach, rudd, perch, chub and gudgeon. Best baits are bread, pellet, maggot, hemp and castor, it goes without saying.

Long Pond - has a century-old tradition of use for model boating.

Activities

These days there are still some nice leafy pathways lined by mature trees left for the strollers to enjoy.

Sporty types can go for the football, rugby, cricket, softball, tennis, basketball, Aussie rules football, croquet (!) or bowling.

Events

Some of the annual highlights include:

May: A Country Affair—is kinda interesting. There are rides, bands, Morris dancing and lots of cleaner than usual farm animals.

June/July: The Sprite Urban Games—Showcases pro skateboarding, BMXing and breaking, with (mostly hip hop) DJs providing the beats.

July: Ben 'n Jerry's Sundae On The Common—also goes down well. If it sounds horribly corporate, it's worth noting that a full restoration of the bandstand in '05/'06 was partly funded by proceeds from this festival. Or, just think of the free ice-cream…

August: The Clapham Common Metro Weekender—Two successful, quality festivals have joined forces. South West Four (progressive house, trance, and breaks) and Get Loaded In the Park (indie/dance) now happen side by side at the end of August.

November: The Bonfire Night Fireworks—it's as good as it gets here.

How to Get There

By train: Wandsworth Road Station (12 minutes), Clapham High Street Station (12 minutes)

By tube: Clapham Common (4 minutes), Clapham South (13 minutes)

By bus: 4, 35, 37, 88, 137, 155, 255, 345, 355, 417, G1

Overview

A lot is packed into this 54 acre park. Mostly people. On a sunny day Clissold throngs with Stokenewingtonites; yummy mummies and three wheeled buggies; gaggles of youths, with or without hoods; lads playing football; and assorted dog walkers. Visitors can see deer and goats in the animal enclosure, diamond doves and love birds in the aviary, and coots and moorhens in the nature ponds. Parents take little ones to the paddling pool (summer months only), toddlers group at the One O'clock Club or the well-equipped children's playground. The park hosts the usual hodgepodge of circuses and steam fairs as well as the famous arts festival, StokeFest, in the summer. On grey days, chilly days, or in the early hours, peace can be found - in the rose garden perhaps, or underneath one of the ancient trees.

Clissold Park Café

Phone:	0207 923 9797
Email:	info@clissoldparkcafe.com
Website:	www.clissoldparkcafe.com
Hours:	9 am–5.30 pm (winter)
	7.30 pm (summer)
Admission:	FREE

Clissold Mansion, the Grade II listed building just visible from Stoke Newington Church Street, is home to a large, child friendly cafe (that is, the cafe is large and child friendly, not friendly only to the larger child). Herbal tea drinkers jostle with dripping ice-cream cone lickers on the sun trap front veranda and circular lawn. The large inside rooms are best avoided if you find children's chatter grating, but otherwise a lively spot to tuck into a plate of egg and chips. The building was constructed in the late 18th century on behalf of a Quaker family whose daughter was courted by a local reverend—Augustus Clissold. He wooed, then married her, and swiftly changed the name

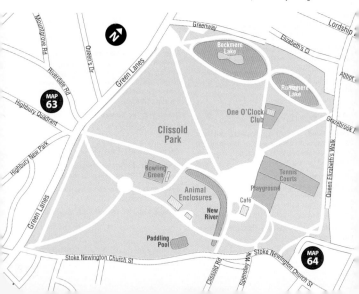

Parks & Places • **Clissold Park**

of the estate to Clissold Place. Where is Catherine Cookson when you need her? A hundred years later when the land was up for redevelopment, two influential campaigners persuaded the Metropolitan Board of Works to create a public space, and Clissold Park was born on 24 July 1889. Now run by the London Borough of Hackney, Clissold is kept in check by the Clissold Park User Group, who recently secured a multi-million pound lottery bid to spruce the place up a bit and return it to its former 19th century splendour.

Sport in the Park

Year round you can hear the yells of football players churning up mud, the whine of iPods as joggers run in ever decreasing circles, the thwack of cricket ball against cricket bat, and the crunch of misthrown Frisbees hitting the litter bins. There is a basketball court and 10 tennis courts (two kiddies' sized) which are bookable by contacting the Park rangers (020 7254 4235) though they are impossible to get your hands on around Wimbledon—and they say TV doesn't affect our behaviour.

But one of the delights of this park is the more unusual sport that takes place. On misty mornings you can watch cotton-clad figures practice tai chi, and on warm weekends you can nearly always spot a group of hotties from the London School of Capoeira circling around each other. Then there is the occasional father/ daughter pair practising Taekwondo, or two dreadlocked crusties slinging up a line to get some tightrope practice in. Most recent addition to watchable sports in the park is run by 'Pushy Mothers'- groups of mums exercising with buggies. The buggy, with child on board, is pushed hither and thither by the panting parent. It's the ultimate in resistance training.

Nature and The Ponds

Hackney is one of the greenest inner-city boroughs and though relatively small, Clissold Park is still an important green, shady and watery spot for local wildlife, particularly waterfowl. The two nature ponds are named Beckmere and the Runtzmere in honour of the two principal founders (Beck and Runtz, in case you were wondering). The third pond in front of the cafe

is more of a 'canalette' and actually used to be part of the New River built in the early 1600s to supply drinking water to London.

The animal enclosure with its fuzzy-nosed deer, fluffy rabbits and bearded mini-goats are popular with visitors who stand stuffing chips and handfuls of poisonous leaves from nearby bushes through the fence directly under the signs saying: 'Please don't feed the animals—it will make them ill.'

Note: the paddling pool is not a nature pond and though you still can't let your dog in, hours spent gazing at its inhabitants are not looked on kindly.

How to Get There

By car: Don't. There isn't much in the way of parking. But if you really need to, from Newington Green head north along Green Lanes until you see a large green space with trees on your right. Or from the A10 turn left onto Stoke Newington Church St past all the cute shops and inviting pubs, until you get to the large church on your left. The park is on your right.

By tube: From Manor House, take exit 4 and walk south down Green Lanes for 10 minutes. The park is on your left.

By train: From Stoke Newington station, head south down the High St and turn right up Stoke Newington Church St, walk for 10 minutes until you see the park on your left just past Stoke Newington Town Hall.

By bus: The 341, 141, 73, 393, and 476 all stop at various entrances to the park

Additional Information

London Borough of Hackney
www.hackney.gov.uk/cp-community-park.htm

Clissold Park User Group
www.clissoldpark.com

Stokefest
www.stokefest.co.uk

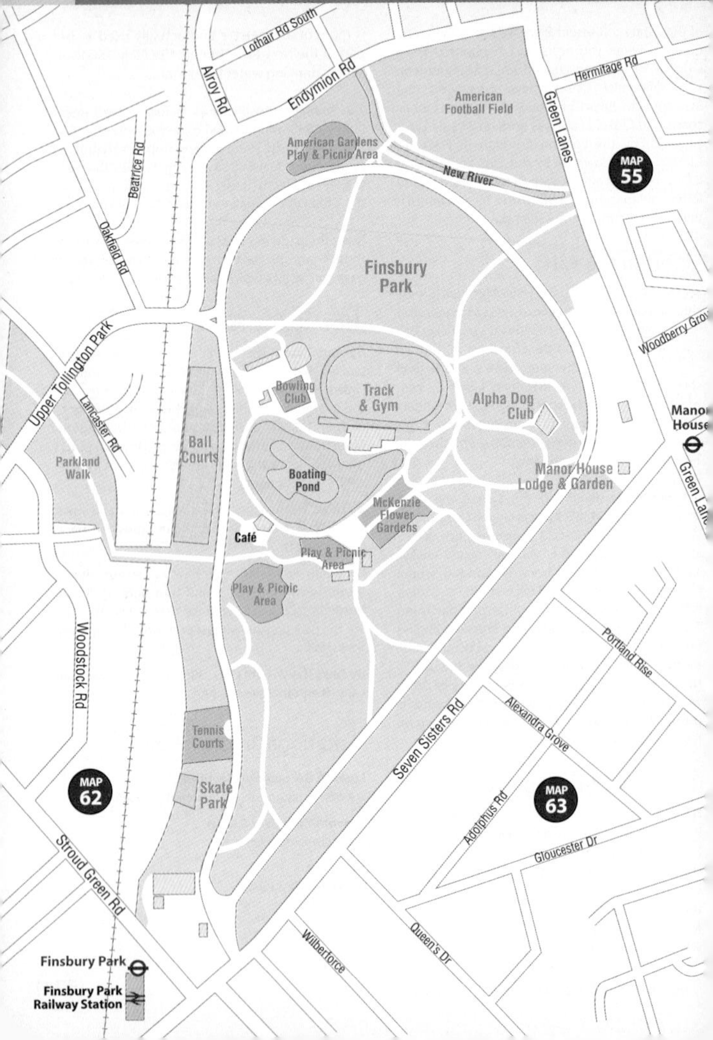

Lothair Rd South

Alroy Rd

Endymion Rd

Hermitage Rd

Beatrice Rd

Oakfield Rd

American
Football Field

Green Lanes

American Gardens
Play & Picnic Area

New River

MAP 55

Finsbury
Park

Woodberry Grove

Upper Tollington Park

Lancaster Rd

Bowling
Club

Track
& Gym

Alpha Dog
Club

Manor
House

Green Lanes

Ball
Courts

Parkland
Walk

Boating
Pond

Manor House
Lodge & Garden

Café

McKenzie
Flower
Gardens

Play & Picnic
Area

Play & Picnic
Area

Portland Rise

Woodstock Rd

Tennis
Courts

Seven Sisters Rd

Alexandra Grove

MAP 62

Skate
Park

Adolphus Rd

MAP 63

Gloucester Dr

Stroud Green Rd

Wilberforce

Queen's Dr

Finsbury Park

**Finsbury Park
Railway Station**

General Information

NFT Map: 55, 62, & 63
Website: www.haringey.gov.uk/
              finsbury_park_leaflet.pdf

Overview

Sculpted from what was once a large woodland area on the fringes of London, Finsbury Park was baptized officially in the mid 19th Century as a green escape for increasingly urbanized North Londoners. Today's Finsbury Park has been revamped to the tune of £5 million in an attempt to shake off the cloak of urban grime which descended during the 1970s. Though it certainly has cleaned up its act, the park is still a barren tundra-esque plain compared to Hyde or Regent's Park. More of a green scab on the city landscape that surrounds it, the sparse shrubbery and token trees are more suitable for football or running away from Staffordshire Terriers. Delve a little deeper, however and there are quaint eccentricities and little gems dotted around.

Practicalities

You can enter this veritable urban Oz at Endymion Road, Seven Sisters Road, Green Lanes and Stroud Green Road. Two tube stops serve Finsbury Park: Manor House and the eponymous Finsbury Park. There are also overland trains at Harringey Green Lanes (grab an opulent Turkish meal on the way) and at Finsbury Park Stroud Green Road. Buses 4, 19, N19, 29, N29, 106, N106, 253, N253, 254, N279, W3 and W7 all touch the park at some point. Bear in mind that if you wish to travel in the area during an Arsenal match day you'd better take a stun gun and a red scarf to navigate the crowds!

Attractions

Quaint Englishness and sweaty sporting pursuits abound within the perimeters of Finsbury Park. There are many activities you can partake in from tennis (seven courts are available on a turn up and play basis) to running in the Heathside Athletics Club (020 8802 9139). There are even two American Football pitches. For a more twee time stroll up to the tiny boating pond and spend an hour in a beat-up boat circling the aviary island—home to exotic birds like ducks, some swans and, uh, ducks again. The kidz are catered for in the form of a skate park. Best of all is the amazing Parkland Walk, which snakes out from Finsbury Park to Alexandra Palace via Highgate.

Nature

The Arboretum and the Avenue of Mature Trees are the two main spots for tree watching. Granted, experienced botanists may find little to fire them up here, but on a mild Autumn day there are plenty of rich colours and textures that enrich any stroll through the park. There are no real 'wild' areas in the park, unlike Hampstead Heath, but there are some lovely quiet spots in the American Gardens which have been landscaped according to the original 19th century plans, with added kiddie play areas. There are some shrubs planted around the boating pond which Harringey Council calls the 'McKenzie Flower Garden' with capital letters which are barely merited.

Festivals

Recently the vast open spaces of the park have been used for music festivals and various other fairs. The Rise, Fleadh, and FinFest festivals are all fairly regular events. The park is also a popular venue for one off special music events—both the Sex Pistols and Morrissey have played controversial shows here. The steam and fun fairs are also worth going to for nostalgic or regressive fun.

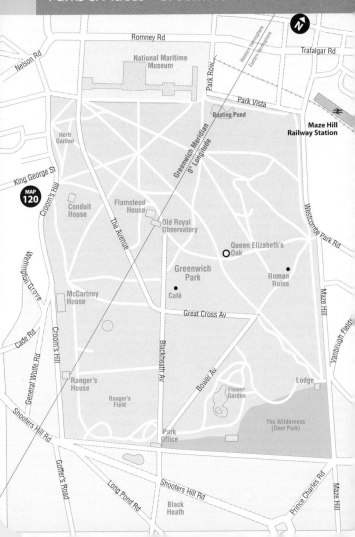

Romney Rd

Trafalgar Rd

Nelson Rd

National Maritime
Museum

Park Row

Park Vista

Boating Pond

Western Hemisphere

Eastern Hemisphere

**Maze Hill
Railway Station**

Herb
Garden

King George St

MAP
120

Croom's Hill

Conduit
House

Flamsteed
House

Old Royal
Observatory

Greenwich Meridian
0° Longitude

Queen Elizabeth's
Oak

Roman
Ruins

Westcombe Park Rd

Wellington Grove

Greenwich
Park

The Avenue

McCartney
House

Café

Great Cross Av

Maze Hill

Cade Rd

Croom's Hill

Ranger's
House

Ranger's
Field

Blackheath Av

Bower Av

Flower
Garden

Lodge

Vanbrugh Fields

The Wilderness
(Deer Park)

General Wolfe Rd

Park
Office

Shooters Hill Rd

Gaffer's Road

Long Pond Rd

Shooters Hill Rd

Black
Heath

Prince Charles Rd

Maze Hill

Overview

Greenwich Park is the oldest enclosed Royal Park in Britain and has been an integral part of London life for centuries. Saxons built mounds here; Romans worshipped here; King Henry VIII and Anne Boleyn flirted here, and Charles II even built an observatory here. It's now a playground for ageing eccentrics escaping London, yuppie families with new puppies, and heaps of tourists trekking up the staggeringly steep hill towards the iconic Royal Observatory.

And it's worth the trek. The sweeping views from the highest point are spectacular and beat the London Eye hands down. London is revealed in all its glory, from the jutting skyline of Canary Wharf, to the sinuous turns of the Thames and the seemed-like-a-good-idea-at-the-time Millennium Dome. All in stark contrast with the neoclassical architecture of the Old Royal Observatory, Royal Naval College, National Maritime Museum and the Queen's House in the immediate foreground.

A well sought-after spot throughout history, the park has belonged to the Royal Family since 1427. In the early 1600s, under James I, the park was given a makeover in the French style, which gave it its well-groomed tree-lined pathways. He then had Inigo Jones build the missus the stately Queen's House.

The Royal Observatory and Flamsteed House

Address:	Greenwich Royal Park, Greenwich, London SE10
Phone:	020 8858 4422
Website:	www.nmm.ac.uk
Hours:	10 am-5 pm daily
Admission:	Free

Time begins, rather arbitrarily, here—on the Prime Meridian of the World, or Longitude 0°. Time all over the earth is based on a place's distance east or west from this imaginary line, outlined in metal so throngs of tourists can gawp at it. Thanks to Charles II's interest in science, Sir Christopher Wren was commissioned to build the Royal Observatory and Flamsteed House, the living quarters for the first Royal Astronomer. It is the imaginary axis of the Meridian, which runs through Greenwich Park from the Royal Observatory, which gives this World Heritage site its fame.

Also notable is the Camera Obscura, which sits in a small building next to Flamsteed House. A predecessor to the modern camera, this small dark room displays a live image of the distant National Maritime Museum, projected using only a small hole in the roof.

National Maritime Museum

Address:	Greenwich, London SE10 9NF
Phone:	020 8858 4422
Website:	www.nmm.ac.uk
Hours:	10 am-5 pm daily
Admission:	Free

Adjacent to the park's boundaries, this is a museum dedicated to all things nautical. It comprises the Royal Observatory, as well as the Queen's House, but its main components are the Maritime Galleries. Highlights include a collection of ships' figureheads, navigational charts, maps, medals, flags and models. They also host relics from Sir John Franklin's ill-fated Northwest Passage expedition (1845-1848) including a pair of his very old-school sunglasses.

Nature

Amongst the well-mowed green are trees of infinite varieties. The scented herb garden is best enjoyed in the summer time. The fallen remains of the 900 year-old Queen Elizabeth Oak can still be viewed and lie as proof of Henry VIII's passion for these grounds, he was said to have danced around the younger tree with Anne Boleyn (before he had her executed, obviously).

How to Get There

The Docklands Light Railway provides a good public transport link into Greenwich. It's fun too. You can sit in the front and pretend to be the driver. The nearest DLR station is Cutty Sark. By bus, take the 199 or 188 bus. From North Greenwich Station take the 188 or 129. You can also take the Greenwich Foot Tunnel (very cool and quite short, actually) from the Isle of Dogs.

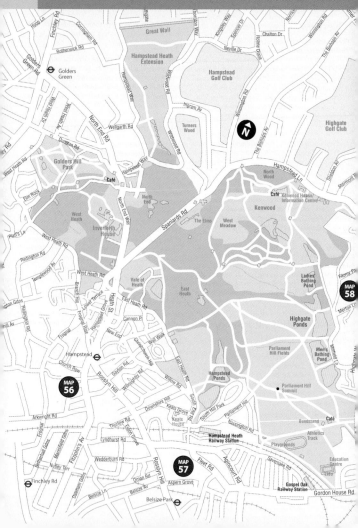

Overview

Hampstead Heath is 791 acres of rambling woods and idyllic meadows worthy of much frolicking. It's the fact that its wilderness seems so, well, wild that makes this London park deceptive. You can be merrily re-enacting the Brothers Grimm, only to be spat out rather rudely onto Parliament Hill and confronted with gob-smacking views of St Paul's and the Gherkin. The Heath is truly nothing short of heaven—until you stumble over George Michael up to no good in the bushes. You can swim naked in its ponds, stroll amongst its tall grasses without seeing another living soul for twenty minutes or more and engage in a little sex scandal amongst the greenery. The park's common theme is one of a hidden countryside retreat right in the middle of it all.

Most likely because it *is* countryside. It's just the rest of London that's gone all urban around it. Long-established hedgerows and ancient trees attest to its lengthy history. The range of wildlife on show is impressive—kingfishers, parakeets, 300 species of fungi and several types of bat, to name a few. All sorts of famous people have enjoyed its leafy company through the years. Boudicca's Mound near the men's bathing pond (hmm... sounds dirty), is said to mark the ancient queen's burial chamber. Karl Marx and his family had a picnic here every Sunday while he lived in London and writer Wilkie Collins used the park as a backdrop for *The Woman in White*. All in all, the Heath has been a much-loved place of social gathering and strolling for centuries, a place of peace and perspective amongst the greater hustle and bustle of the Big Smoke.

Ponds, Ponds and... Oh Yeah, More Ponds…

It might be argued that losing your Heath virginity consists of swimming in one of its famous outdoor bathing ponds. These are open throughout the year and attract throngs of dedicated swimming fans. On the eastern side—closer to Highgate—are a series of eight 17th and 18th century reservoirs dotted between Parliament Hill Fields and Kenwood House. Amongst these is one swimming pond for guys, another for gals, a toy boat pond, a wildlife reserve pond, and a lake for fishing. On the western side of the Heath are three more, including the 'mixed pond', where you can have some underwater flirtations, should you wish.

Kenwood House

Address:	Hampstead - NW3 7JR
Phone:	0208 348 1286
Website:	www.english-heritage.org.uk
Hours:	April-October: 11 am-5 pm, Monday-Sunday, November-March: 11 am-4 pm, Monday-Sunday
Admission:	Free

Kenwood House, a 17th century manor in the middle of the park, adds very nicely to the Heath's countryside effect. Its striking classically white walls and landscaped grounds play backdrop to summer jazz festivals as well as a few scenes in the movie Notting Hill. Purchased by brewing magnate Edward Cecil Guinness in 1925, Kenwood House is more than just a pretty façade. Thanks to Guinness's fortune and interest in art, the manor house is also a very noteworthy art gallery.

Golders Hill Park

Golders Hill Park is the younger brother to the bigger Hampstead Heath, adjoining it on the western side. Where the latter is an icon of epic proportions, the former is more of a good ol' neighbourhood park. Its large expanse of grass was created rather suddenly when a house that stood on the grounds was bombed during the Blitz. It has a lot to offer for its size though, with a formal flower garden, a deer park and a small zoo (with alpacas no less). If you're feeling sporty, there are tennis courts, putting greens and plenty of jogging paths.

How to Get There

The closest tube stations are Hampstead, Golder's Green and Archway on the Northern Line. Nearby overland stations include Hampstead Heath and Gospel Oak. Bus numbers running to the park are the 168, 268 and 210, which cuts through on Spaniard's Road (where you may want to stop for a pint at the historic Spaniard's Inn).

Additional Information

City of London
www.cityoflondon.gov.uk
Information and booking tickets for swimming:
020 7485 5757
Heath and Hampstead Society:
www.heathandhampsteadsociety.org.uk

Highgate Cemetery
General Info

NFT Map: 51 & 59
Web: www.highgate-cemetery.org
Phone: 020 8340 1834

West Cemetery

The West Cemetery opened in 1839 and most of the original pathways and structures still exist. The only way you can access this side is by taking the guided tour, but don't let this put you off, it's a spectacular place and a bargain at five pounds. Tour places are limited to 15 visitors per day and you should phone in advance to book a place. The hour-long tour starts daily at 2 pm between March and November. From December to February there are no weekday tours.

East Cemetery

The newer East Cemetery is located on the opposite side of the road to the West entrance. This side is open daily and for three pounds you get to roam unsupervised for as long as you please. It may not be as impressive as the West side, but it's still a place of breathtaking beauty. Although there are some well-trodden paths and proper walkways, large parts of the cemetery are almost completely overgrown, making it a wonderful place to go for a stroll.

East Cemetery Opening hours

1st April to 31st October
Mon-Fri: 10 am-5 pm
Sat-Sun: 11 am-5 pm

1st November to 31st March
Mon-Fri: 10 am-4 pm
Sat-Sun: 11 am-4 pm

Famous Occupants

Quite a few notable people are buried here. The caretakers will be more than willing to inform you of the whereabouts of the following graves and plenty of others.

Douglas Adams, author. Most famous for the *Hitchhiker's Guide To The Galaxy* series of books.

George Eliot, English author and poet; also actually a woman.

Christina Rossetti, English poet.

Karl Marx. Philosopher; considered the father of communism.

Alexander Litvinenko, Russian ex-spy, famously murdered by radiation poisoning in a Soho sushi restaurant in 2006.

The Highgate Vampire

There have been numerous accounts of shapes, ghosts and supernatural figures seen on the cemetery grounds. In the early 70s the media picked up on a theory involving a vampire and the legend of The Highgate Vampire was born. It caused quite a stir and soon mobs of 'vampire hunters' descended on the place (imagine something like the Thriller video, but with flares and tank tops). Finally, Sean Manchester, president and founder of the Vampire Research Society, claimed to have killed the fiend in 1973, which he tracked to a nearby house. Manchester was also, in his spare time, patron of the Yorkshire Robin Hood society, and remains, in this publication's estimation, the single most compelling reason not to wander around Highgate Cemetery after dark.

Waterlow Park Overview

Waterlow Park is a beautifully landscaped park located just next to the cemetery, making it a perfect spot for a pre or post-gravespotting picnic. Often overlooked and overshadowed by nearby Hampstead Heath it is a charming and peaceful alternative. You can feed the ducks in one of the three ponds, hire tennis courts by the hour, admire the awesome view of London, wander in the rose garden, or just go and look at the cool hollow tree at the bottom of the park.

Lauderdale House

Address: Highgate Hill, Waterlow Park
London N6 5HG
Tel: 020 8348 8716
Web: www.lauderdalehouse.co.uk

Lauderdale House operates independently from the park, but is located on its grounds. The original house was built in 1582, but has gone through major alterations and restorations since then. In 1963 a major fire destroyed much of the old building and it was left untouched and unoccupied for 15 years. In 1978 it was finally repaired and reopened in its current incarnation. The house runs classes, concerts and exhibitions by local artists. There's also a small café. The House and the galleries are usually open Tue-Fri 11 am-4 pm, Sat 1.30 pm-5 pm & Sun 12 pm-5 pm, but you can always phone in advance to avoid disappointment.

How to Get There

Nearest tube station is Archway. Exit the station and turn left up Highgate Hill. Waterlow Park is about five minutes walk on your left hand side. To get to the cemetery, cross the park down to the Swain's Lane exit, which is adjacent to the East Cemetery gates.

General Information

Website: www.royalparks.org.uk
Phone: 020 7298 2000

Overview

Hyde Park serves as the 'lungs of London'. For over 370 years it has been *the* place to go for oxygen-starved Londoners to take a breath of fresh air. As the city's grown, so has the desire to preserve this 350-acre mass of parkland and thankfully, Hyde Park has never been in better shape.

Eating

Perambulating through the park is bound to get that metabolism going, so stop off at one of the numerous food stalls to quench your thirst or down a plasticky hot-dog. Yum. For a more civilised affair check out one of the park's seated joints - **Lido** (which also has a paddling pool), **Dell Restaurant** or the **Cumberland Café**.

Nature, Architecture & Sculpture

The Serpentine Lake attracts the usual assortment of ducks and insects as well as some exotic additions, such as Egyptian Geese. **The Lookout Education Centre** holds informative talks about the park's wildlife. **The Grand Entrance** at Hyde Park Corner is an awe-inspiring arched construction of Greek influence, whilst the **Albert Memorial**, erected by Queen Victoria after her husband's death, is a true show of love. The **Diana, Princess of Wales Memorial Fountain**, remains one of the most visited areas in Hyde Park and is worth a look to satisfy curiosity, as is the **Peter Pan Memorial**.

Performance

The park attracts big musical events, and by big we mean Live 8 big. It's only the musical deities that get their own special Hyde Park treatment—The Stones, Queen, The Police, but Summer means

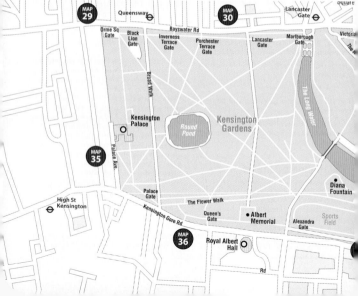

festival time and the annual 02 Wireless Festival and Capital FM Party In The Park. Brass band concerts are held throughout the summer at **The Bandstand**. **Speakers' Corner** is guaranteed to entertain. Since 1872 it's been the site of a verbal free-for-all stemming from the activities of the Reform League who marched for manhood suffrage in 1866. These days the topics aren't quite as revolutionary. Heather Mills sounded off here recently…ah, the injustice of having too much cash.

Sports

There are ample jogging paths, designated bike routes (see www.companioncycling.org.uk) and great paths for roller-blading and walking. Even more fun is boating on The Serpentine Lake from March to October. Informal games of rugby, football or cricket can be played on the **'Sports Field'** while **Hyde Park Tennis & Sports Centre** does exactly

what it says on the tin. There's also a bowling green and horse riding at the **Manege**.

Kensington Gardens

The 111 hectares west of the Western Carriage Drive are known as Kensington Gardens. Annexed from the main park in 1689, the area retains a slightly more formal air, with regular tree-lined avenues to stroll down and less spaces for rambunctious sporting displays. This makes the Gardens an ideal spot for a picnic or a quiet ponder. Kensington Gardens also boasts the **Serpentine Gallery** (in between the Diana Fountain and the Albert Memorial), a toy-sized venue for renowned modern and contemporary art exhibitions, and the rather stunning **Kensington Palace**. Still a royal residence, the palace majestically overlooks some of the most well ordered green spaces London has to offer.

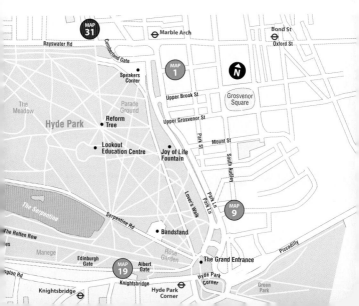

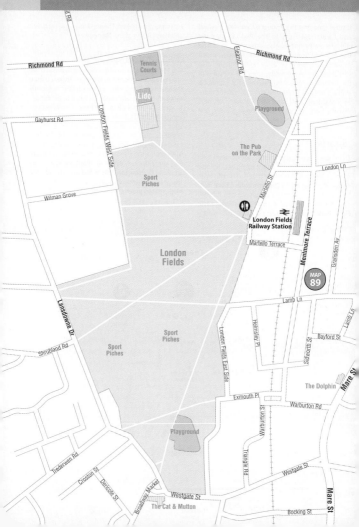

Overview

Best green space of the northeast? Victoria Park might still bag the accolade, but this relaxed, mid-sized park in the middle of Hackney is catching up. And quickly. It's lush and it's spacious and its latest addition, a smashing 50-metres Lido (see below), is hard to beat. Just off busy Mare Street and minutes from Regent's Canal, the park is easily reachable and easily manageable. There are two tennis courts, football, basketball and cricket pitches, and two well-equipped and well-maintained playgrounds, if you have kids in tow. London Fields does a nice job of attracting a pleasantly diverse mix of people, from Hoxton-refugee artists and rollie-smoking would-be philosophers, to pram-pushing mums and East End geezers with no teeth and big dogs. The architecture framing the tree-studded space is just as varied: bland high rises, pretty Victorians, depressing brick estates and fancy new developments, all modern Hackney is there.

The park's own drinking spot, imaginatively called Pub on the Park, is good for a relaxed outside pint, simple pub food or the footie. If you're after a slightly more refined meal, check the gastropub-ish Cat and Mutton at the park's bottom. This is also where Broadway Market begins, a traditional East End market street, now brimming with nice little shops, several pubs and original eateries. If the red wine you shared with your painter friends on their picnic blanket got you into serious party mood, head to the close-by (and late-night) Dolphin on Mare Street. Or just fall asleep in the shadows of those massive oak trees. Chances are, one of the dogs will lick you back to reality.

London Fields Lido

Address:	London Fields Westside, London E8 3EU
Phone:	020 7254 9038
Website:	www.gll.org
Hours:	Mon-Fri 6.45 am-6 pm; Sat-Sun 8 am-5 pm
Admission:	£3.85

You might say that in a city where, essentially, you have the choice between stomach-turningly grotty leisure centre pools and hopelessly overpriced member gym versions, any new public swimming basin would be a winner. Fair enough. But WHAT a winner. Having mouldered closed for almost two decades, a £2.5m effort has restored this art deco gem to its former glory. In fact, it's probably better than ever: the 50-metre basin is nicely heated all year round (25C when we last checked), the changing rooms are modern and clean, admission's okay. Come during the week for a few pre-work lanes, when steam mysteriously hangs over the water, or jump in on the weekend, followed by a Sunday roast in one of the pubs close-by or a picnic in the park. Sounds nice? We know.

Sports

There's no shortage of things to do. The park's two tennis courts can be booked for hourly slots (open 8.30 am-dusk; £5.50/h during peak times, £2.50/h off-peak; call 020 7254 4235 for more info). The Hackney Tennis Club (www.hackneycotytennisclub.co.uk) also offers classes and joint sessions. The football pitch (just come and play) is located in the middle, the basketball space (ditto) towards the south. Follow the sound of children for the playgrounds, one in the north, one in the south. If cricket is your cup of tea, get in touch with the London Fields Cricket Club (londonfieldscc@gmail.com), who keep the park's long-standing tradition as a cricket pitch alive (which, incidentally, is said to go back to 1800).

How to Get There

By bus: Most buses stop on Mare Street (get off at the London Fields stop), a few minutes walk from the actual park. From Liverpool Street Station, take 48 and 55, from Mile End or Bethnal Green grab the D6. The 106 takes you here from Finsbury Park, the 277 from Highbury & Islington. Two buses stop directly at the bottom of the park: the 236 (connecting to Dalston, Newington Green, Finsbury Park) and the 394 (Hackney Central, Homerton Hospital, Hoxton, Angel).

By train: The train is a great option, since London Fields station is located right next to the park. Train operator National Express East Anglia (formerly known as One Railway) serves the central Liverpool Street Station (via Cambridge Heath and Bethnal Green) and connects the Victoria Line tube stations Seven Sisters and Tottenham Hale further north. You can travel using your Oyster Card, for timetables check www.nationalexpresseastanglia.com.

Overview

Bordered at the north by the chain-ridden fake-a-rama, Bow Wharf, to the east and south by rat runs, and to the west by the dank waters of the Regent's Canal, this strange elongated park doesn't appear to have a lot going for it. However, this 32-hectare wiggle of green is more a string of mini parks—divided up by roads and railway lines—and each segment has hidden treasures worth digging for. There is an adventure playground, an arts pavilion with weird orange-and-white sculptural seats by Leona Matuszczak, an ecology park with moths and all sorts, a terraced garden and a sheltered children's playground. Clever landscaping and inventive use of space creates pockets of peace, and when the sun comes out, sparkling on the canal, bouncing off of the reflective jackets of the cyclists bombing past or laying its beams on giggling young couples, the park of many parks comes into its own.

It was created following the Second World War after the area was destroyed in the Blitz. The idea of Lord Abercombie, who envisioned a creepy-sounding 'finger of green' in amongst the rubble, Mile End really came into being in 1999 with Millennium Commission funding providing new areas, strange metal cross signage and an amazing green bridge—known by locals as the Banana. It actually has grass and shrubs taking walkers and cyclists over Mile End Road.

The remains of the Victorian terraces sit on the west side of the park, and one resilient pub, The Palm Tree, squats alone in the middle of a grey car park, a testament to the rows of two-up-two-downs which no longer flank the pub. This great local boozer is filled most nights with a mix of climbers and locals tucking into doorstep sandwiches and draft beer.

For those who want a bit more local history, The Ragged School Museum (www.raggedschoolmuseum.org.uk) on Copperfield St overlooks the southern tip of the park: a canal side slum that was transformed into a school for the local urchins by philanthropist Dr Barnado. It now has a mocked-up Victorian classroom and clunky little cafe. Only open Wednesday and Thursday and the occassional Sunday—check before you go.

Sports in the Park

The southern end of the park is a haven for sporty types with a refurbished stadium and 10 all weather pitches made from recycled car tyres, a go-kart track and the large Ikea-like Mile End Leisure Centre with all the usual sauna, gym, pool and verruca infested changing rooms.

Mile End Climbing Wall is housed in an old pipe engineering works in the middle of the park, and is one of London's 'big three' (The Castle and the Westway are the others). It was opened in the 80's and some of the users of the centre seem unaware of time's passage, judging by their fetching leggings. Like the other large walls, Mile End, inspires fierce loyalty—said to be more edgy and 'real' (aka scruffy) where even in the freezing winter months the toned climbers scale the walls bare chested (lads) or in tiny tops (lasses), undoubtedly for their own fine reasons.

How to Get There

By tube: Turn left out of Mile End station, cross Grove Rd and you'll find yourself at one of the entrances to the middle section of the park.

By car: The park can be easily accessed from Bow Road, Grove Rd, or Mile End Rd, though according to London Borough of Tower Hamlets, 'The local streets operate a resident's parking permit system and are regularly patrolled by traffic wardens. Limited parking is available at Bow Wharf.'

By bus: The, D6, D7, 25, 205, 277, 323, 339 and all take you to various entrances around the park.

Additional Information

London Borough of Tower Hamlets
www.towerhamlets.gov.uk/data/discover/data/parks/mile-end/the-park-map.cfm

Mile End Climbing Wall
www.mileendwall.org.uk

General Information

Website: www.royalparks.org.uk/parks/
                     regents_park
Park Tel: 020 7486 7905
London Zoo: www.zsl.org
Open Air Theatre: www.openairtheatre.org

Overview

Whenever your quaint and backward country-dwelling friends are telling you the virtues of rural life, you can silence them with two words: Regent's Park. Let the yokels have their cleaner lungs, their maypoles and their children running barefoot and

feral, because London may have its city drawbacks but it knows how to do a good park. When you stroll in Regent's Park, you're strolling on nothing less than Property of the Crown—you can see tigers and gorillas, play on the largest outdoor sports area in London, take in some Shakespeare, or, on a very good day, watch girls playing volleyball in bikinis. With 410 acres of parkland, you will always find a spot away from the (many thousands of) fellow visitors. It is the perfect space to take stock, step back and refresh, to sit in a deckchair with a good book, picnic with friends, breathe better air. Moreover, the same obnoxious people who wouldn't move down the tube to let you on or

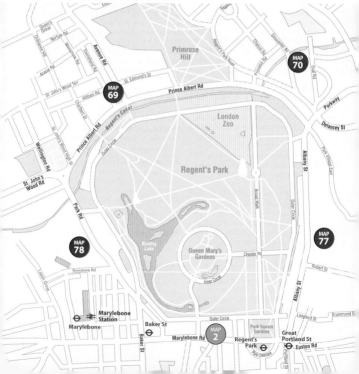

who pushed in the sandwich queue, are here relaxing with their families, lazing over a paper in a patch of sun, falling in love, throwing a Frisbee: it can be just what you need to re-bond with London when you're becoming jaded, and to get away from it all without leaving Zone One.

How to Get There

By tube:
Regent's Park – Bakerloo.
Great Portland St – Hammersmith & City, Circle, Metropolitan.
Baker St – Hammersmith & City, Jubilee, Metropolitan, Bakerloo.
St John's Wood – Jubilee.
Camden Town – Northern.

The Park is served by bus routes 2, 13, 18, 27, 30, 74, 82, 113, 139, 189, 274, 453 and C2.

Nature

The Park is a haven for the city's wildlife, thanks to a biodiversity which includes grassland, woodland, wetland, lakes and scrubs, as well as beautifully-tended and fragrant gardens. Over 200 species of birds have been spotted in the Park, along with favourite garden mammals such as hedgehogs, squirrels and foxes. But if that's all just a bit too Beatrix Potter, you can get your fix of the more badass species at London Zoo in the Park's north-east end, where in addition to the normal enclosures, visitors can get closer to some of the animals with events like "Meet the Monkeys" or even help as a volunteer.

The Park's size and calm makes it a choice hangout for celebrities (not strictly nature, but dandelion schmandelion: spotting A-Listers doing Tai Chi in oversized sunglasses will impress more down the pub, and can there be a nobler calling?).

Performances and Events

The Park's permanent outdoor theatre is an absolute treat. The shows have a Shakespearian bias, but the venue also puts on non-bard performances, comedy nights and concerts. It is the experience more than the performance which will likely stay in your memory. Among the atmospheric trees of the park in the evening, with a bottle of wine and a blanket to snuggle up in (it is Britain after all—how many other theatres have an official "weather policy"?), it is a magical way to spend an evening. Outdoor does not mean free however: prices range from £10–£42 (Saturdays are the most expensive), and you pay theatre prices for food and drink. Cheaper to bring a picnic to enjoy in front of the theatre before the performance.

Regent's Park also hosts a number of big outdoor events. Notable regulars include Taste of London, the Innocent Smoothies Festival, and the Frieze art show. Check the website for one-off listings.

Primrose Hill

To the north of Regent's Park sits Primrose Hill, boasting corking views of much of Central and East London.

The former hunting ground for playboy king Henry VIII has a murky history, becoming the scene of a political feud in 1678, when magistrate Edmund Berry Godfrey was found dead there after being implicated in a plot to kill Charles II. In later generations Primrose Hill became the setting for duels: London lovers fought there over their ladies, while fops found it a good place to settle literary disagreements ("I say Dryden is naught but a one-trick satirist sir!" "Well then I say you are a cad and a scoundrel! Die you maggot!").

Celebrity voyeurs should keep 'em peeled for the likes of Kate Moss and, uh, writer Alan Bennett, while Primrose Hill in winter is the ideal spot to check out panoramic views of fireworks across the city on Guy Fawkes' night (5 November).

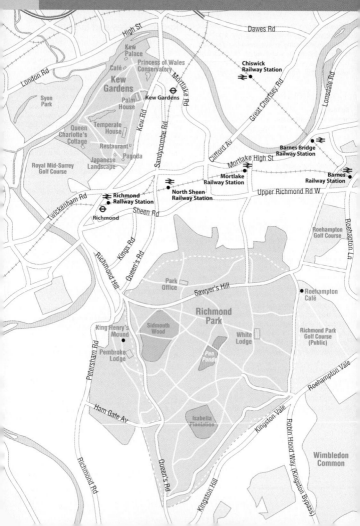

Overview

In 1625 Charles I brought his court to Richmond. He subsequently, with quite heroic selfishness, built a wall 'round a large expanse of open grassland, and created Richmond Park. These days the park is thankfully accessible to the public, opening at 7 am (or 7.30 in the winter) and closing at dusk every day. It's the biggest of the Royal Parks in London, and is an obvious choice for long bike rides, picnics, informal sports and other wholesome pursuits for your golden, happy days of youth.

Attractions

The park has a number of gardens and wooded areas, the most beautiful of which is probably the Isabella Plantation, an organic woodland garden that blooms with azaleas and rhododendrons. The Pen Ponds is another popular feature, as is Pembroke Lodge, the park's Georgian mansion, which can be rented out for weddings and conferences (www.pembroke-lodge.co.uk or call 020 8940 8207). The adjacent café also does a mean cream tea, if that's not a contradiction in terms.

Sports

There are three rugby pitches near the Roehampton Gate that are available for rental on weekdays during winter (contact the Rosslyn Park Rugby Club at 020 8948 3209), and two eighteen hole, pay and play golf courses (call 020 8876 1795 for info. and booking). Between 16 June and 14 March you can purchase a fishing permit for the Pen Ponds (call 020 8948 3209 for information) and for more extreme park-goers there is the option of Power Kiting, whatever the hell that is (www.kitevibe.com).

Kew

The Royal Botanic Gardens at Kew, begun in 1660, are not only easy on the eyes but an important centre for horticultural research and a UNESCO world heritage site. The gardens are still going strong, with record amounts of visitors. The Gardens are a hugely popular day trip destination for schoolchildren and adults alike and contain such a surplus of sights and attractions that repeat visits are always surprising.

Attractions

Of course the main attractions here are the Gardens themselves. Between the formal gardens, smaller themed collections of plants and wildlife and conservation areas, there is enough walking and cooing to be done to justify any length of cake and sandwich sessions at one of the Gardens' eateries. There are also 39 Grade I and II listed buildings, all of which have some kind of historic significance. The 17th century Kew Palace (www.hrp.org.uk), is one of the most interesting of these, having previously been home to the notoriously 'mad' King George III. Other buildings in the gardens include the Chinese Pagoda of 1762, a traditional Japanese 'Minka' house and a number of museums. Decimus Burton's glasshouses (The Palm House and the Temperate) are iconic examples of this quintessentially Victorian architectural theme, and an essential part of any visit to Kew.

Events

Kew Gardens is run with great enthusiasm and has a packed programme of events throughout the year. These occur and change frequently so it's best to check the Kew website, which has comprehensive listings of everything that is going on in the Gardens, down to the blooming or blossoming of individual plant species: www.kew.org.

Several of the historic buildings, most spectacularly the Temperate Glasshouse, are available to rent for corporate and private parties.

How to Get There

Richmond station (overland trains, District Line) is a 20 minute walk from Richmond Park, or buses 371 and 65 both go from the station to the pedestrian gate at Petersham. Kew Gardens is (surprisingly) the closest station for Kew Gardens, London Overground trains stop here from across North and North West London. Trains from Waterloo stop at Kew Bridge station, a ten- minute walk from the gardens.

A large number of buses go from Hammersmith, Fulham, Clapham Junction, Wandsworth and Ealing to Richmond Park and to Kew Gardens.

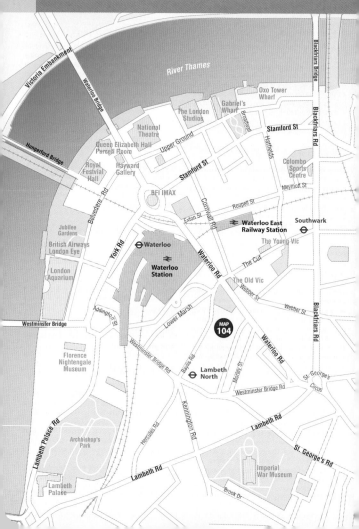

River Thames

Victoria Embankment

Waterloo Bridge

Blackfriars Bridge

Hungerford Bridge

Oxo Tower Wharf

Gabriel's Wharf

The London Studios

Stamford St

National Theatre

Broadwall

Upper Ground

Queen Elizabeth Hall Purcell Room

Hatfields

Stamford St

Blackfriars Rd

Royal Festival Hall

Hayward Gallery

Colombo Sports Centre

Meymott St

BFI IMAX

Roupell St

Cornwall Rd

Belvedere Rd

Exton St

Waterloo East Railway Station

Southwark

Jubilee Gardens

York Rd

Waterloo

Waterloo Rd

The Young Vic

British Airways London Eye

Waterloo Station

The Cut

The Old Vic

London Aquarium

Webber St

Webber St

Blackfriars Rd

Addington St

Lower Marsh

MAP 104

Westminster Bridge

Florence Nightengale Museum

Westminster Bridge Rd

Baylis Rd

Lambeth North

Morley St

Kennington Rd

St. George's Circus

Hercules Rd

Westminster Bridge Rd

Lambeth Rd

St. George's Rd

Archbishop's Park

Lambeth Palace Rd

Lambeth Rd

Lambeth Rd

Imperial War Museum

Lambeth Palace

Brook Dr

Overview

A pedestrianised quarter formed of venues for theatre, music, cinema, art and various other artistically orientated entities, the South Bank is the realisation of a post-war dream of an arts-for-all hub in London. The area has its roots in 1951's Festival of Britain, a technicoloured marvel designed to showcase an optimistic future for Britons used to coal, Spitfires and fake mashed potato. The legacy of the Festival ensured that the surrounding area went on to grow into the playground that it has become today.

The South Bank Centre

The actual 'South Bank Centre' is officially formed of the Royal Festival Hall, the Queen Elizabeth Hall, the Purcell Room, the Hayward Gallery and the Saison Poetry Library, which are all concentrated in the centre of the South Bank. The Royal Festival Hall hosts a variety of musical and dance performances from its auditorium, whilst the Hall's foyer is an enormous and relaxed open-plan area with a bar, performance spaces and shop. The Queen Elizabeth Hall and Purcell Room offer further stages for musical recitals whilst the Saison Poetry Library houses a vast collection of poetry dating from 1912 onwards. The Hayward Gallery has an exterior of frightening ugliness, which shields a surprisingly spacious interior, devoted to exhibitions of the visual arts.

The National Theatre

The National Theatre is next-door to the South Bank Centre complex and is another gaping example of uncompromising architecture. Opened in 1963, it still looks slightly unhinged. The building consists of three theatres and puts on a range of productions from the established to the experimental. It also features an inviting foyer, and in the open spirit of the South Bank, offers back-stage tours, workshops, talks and costume and prop hire to Joe Schmo.

British Film Institute and IMAX

Nestling under Waterloo Bridge, the BFI promotes film and television through its archives, cinema screens, talks and festivals. It's a great alternative to the disgustingly over-priced and sticky-floored chain cinemas of central London and promotes an all-encompassing program from its three screens. The Film Café and Benugo Bar & Kitchen do good pre and post-flick munch. The BFI IMAX is the separate, rotund glass building situated around 200m south of the BFI. It shows films on Britain's biggest cinema screen accompanied by sound pumped from a gargantuan 11,600 watt sound system.

Everything Else

Beyond its theatres, music halls, galleries and cinemas, the South Bank has spawned a number of other attractions. The London Eye is an enormous Ferris wheel built in 2000 on the banks of the Thames adjacent to Westminster Bridge, it revolves at a leisurely 0.5 mph and offers brilliant views from its 135m high peak. The London Aquarium is just opposite but with ticket prices roughly similar to the Eye, seeing big fish in small tanks starts to look a distinctly lame option. Less expensive attractions around South Bank include the open-air book market tucked under Waterloo Bridge and Gabriel's Wharf, a dinky enclave of small shops, bars and restaurants that offer succour to those cultured-out.

Getting There

By tube: Nearest stations are Waterloo (Northern, Bakerloo, Jubilee and Waterloo & City lines) and Embankment (Circle, District, Northern & Bakerloo lines). From Waterloo, head 50m towards the river. Embankment station is at the foot of Hungerford footbridge.

By train: Nearest stations are Waterloo & Charing Cross. For directions from Waterloo, see 'By Tube'. From Charing Cross, walk 100m down Villiers Street towards the river and then walk across the Hungerford footbridge.

By bus: The South Bank is on numerous bus routes. Buses stop on nearby Waterloo Bridge, York Road, Belvedere Road, Stamford Street and Waterloo Station. Most coming from the North get to South Bank via Holborn, The Strand or Victoria. From the South they come via Elephant and Castle or Lambeth North.

By boat: Festival Pier is adjacent to the London Eye. Pleasure boats dock here on cruises, as do riverboat services which sail west as far as Tate Britain and east as far as Woolwich Arsenal.

General Information

NFT Maps: 9 & 23
Website: www.royalparks.org.uk
Free guided walks: 020 7930 1793
Inn the Park Café and Restaurant (St. James's Park): 020 7451 9999

Overview

With Trafalgar Square at one end and Buck Palace at the other, both St. James's and Green Park are slap-bang in the heart of picture-postcard London. When the belching fumes of bendy buses and hordes of Oxford Street shoppers threaten both health and sanity, there's only one place to go. Zip past the crowds and pigeons in Trafalgar Square and head under the grand curve of Admiralty Arch into the stately calm of St. James's Park. Stand yourself on the bridge that crosses the lake, take a deep breath and marvel at the history surrounding you in the city's oldest Royal Park, dating back to the days of Henry VIII.

The views: fairytale Buckingham Palace to the west, Downing Street, the seat of Parliament and Big Ben jutting out over Horse Guards' Parade to the east and the towers of Westminster Abbey to the south. There ain't nowhere else in London where you can view the icons of Church, State and Monarchy in one quick spin on your heels. Impressive. And when you're done marvelling, join the families, office workers, joggers and tourists in taking a stroll round the lake for pelican-spotting, duck-feeding, lunching and romancing.

A hop across the Mall and you'll find yourself in the rolling green of, yup, Green Park. Flowerbed free, this 53-acre patch of park with its aged plane trees is the more meditative of the two. A refuge from the noisy thoroughfare of Piccadilly and Hyde Park corner, its grounds soon fill with picnicking office-workers at the slightest suggestion of sun while the tree-lined Mall is the nearest you'll get to a Parisian boulevard.

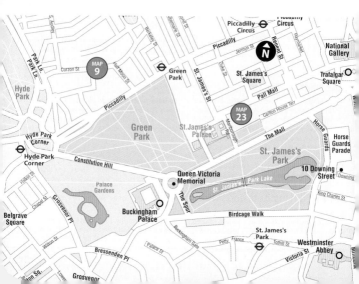

Nature

The curving lake of St. James's park runs the length of the grounds and is perfect for indulging in some casual bird-spotting. Ever since the days of James I, the park has been home to an exotic menagerie, once including elephants, camels and even crocs.

While the crocs and ellies might be long gone, both Duck Island and the smaller West Island remain home to an impressive array of water birds. Beyond the humble duck and gulls, there are suitably stately black swans, rare golden eyes and the rather less-illustrious sounding shovelers, a close relative of the time-starved office-worker on lunch, we believe. But, with their gentlemanly swagger and mighty beaks, the five resident pelicans unquestionably steal the show. A gift from the Russian Ambassador in 1664, feeding time is worth a gander at 3pm daily. Known for their entertaining antics—like flying to Regent's Park Zoo on fish-stealing sprees—one caused a media storm when, clearly lusting after a menu change, it swallowed a live pigeon whole, flapping feathers 'n' all.

Take some old bread and the park's tame, tubby squirrels will feast from your hand. Hang around 'til dusk and the bats come out to play.

Architecture & Sculpture

As if housing ol' Queenie's Buckingham Palace wasn't enough, the parks are surrounded by two more palaces—Westminster, now the Houses of Parliament, and St. James's. From the Regency elegance of the Mall's Carlton House, home to the Institute of Contemporary Arts (ICA), to the impressive frontage of Horse Guard's Parade, the parks are hemmed in by grandeur.

Once a swampy wasteland for grazing pigs, it's a tale with humble beginnings for London's most royal park. While each passing King and Queen slowly improved St. James's Park, it was Charles II that really put the work in, getting trees planted, lawns laid and then opening it up for the first time to us commoners.

Sobering war memorials in St. James's Park abound, including world war icons Mountbatten and Kitchener in Horse Guards' Parade, and an overblown marble statue of Queen Victoria complete with glitter and gates. Oh, and that grand old Duke of York, best-known for marching his men up and down some hill? He's here too, in bronze atop a mighty pillar by the ICA.

The Parks in Season

St. James's in spring is carpeted with crocuses and daffodils. Come summer, they're quickly replaced with a carpet of sun-starved Tom, Dick and Sallys, laid bare as they dare to catch some rays. For an instant upgrade from the rabble, head to Green Park by the tube and hire a stripy deck-chair at £1.50 a pop from April to September.

Between May and August, add a dash of high-brow culture to your day with free concerts at the bandstand every lunchtime and early evening.

Autumn days might be chilly but clear skies make for impressive sunsets while wintry strolls are all the more head-clearing, especially after a night on the Soho tiles.

Sports

With cycling and ball-games banned—*entirely inappropriate in such stately surrounds!*—jogging, morning tai chi, leisurely strolls and pigeon chasing are as energetic as it gets. Sundays are best for strolling when Constitution Hill is closed to traffic.

The Mall and Constitution Hill are cycle-friendly and make a pleasant cut through the West End. Join the Serpentine running club for regular jaunts through St. James's. (www.serpentine.org.uk).

Enjoy the sedate pace with free lunch-time guided walks twice a month, discussing anything from horticulture to royalty (booking line: 020 7930 1793).

General info

NFT Map: 90, 93, & 94
Website: www.towerhamlets.gov.uk
Information: 020 8985 1957

Overview

Look at all the joggers, skaters, cricketers and picnickers swarming in Victoria Park on any given weekend, and it seems hard to continue calling this 218-acres green space one of London's best-kept secrets. Yet, to many Londoners not living east, it still is. Lined by Regent's Canal in the south, London's third-largest green space is a nice blend of Regent's Park's beauty and the wilderness found in Hampstead Heath. It's also far enough off the Central London map to stay virtually tourist-free, while, at the same time, feeling reassuringly inner city urban, with the Gherkin and Canary Wharf's skyscrapers all in sight.

Divided into two handy bits by Grove Road, Victoria Park has much of what makes a park more than just grass and trees: excellent sporting facilities, ranging from athletics to rugby, several lakes, a deer enclosure, a secret garden—and plenty of decent drinking holes nearby. Designed in the 1840s to bring much needed greenery and breathing space to a soul-destroyingly grim East End, the "people's park" can also look back on an intriguing past of dissent, non-conformist rallying and all sorts of political mischief-making. And it's home to the oldest model boat racing club in the country. Come now, before the Olympics do. Once the squirrels start digging out amphetamines, the secret will be gone forever.

Nature

Ducks, swans, birds and god knows what else live around The Lake in the west, while deer and goats graze slightly further north. You're allowed to fish in the Old Lake, although we're not at all sure that there are really many fish in there. Pretty oak trees and hawthorns stud the whole place; colourful flowers and perfectly-groomed shrubs grow in the Old English Garden. It's a beautifully landscaped gem of a garden and one of this city's most peaceful spots—if you don't mind the odd greying philosopher, mumbling to himself.

Sports

Jogging and skating are popular and, thanks to wide pathways, possible throughout the park. There's a

Parks & Places · **Victoria Park**

rugby pitch, a large dedicated football area, four tennis courts (call 020 8986 5182) and three all-weather cricket pitches, run by the esteemed Victoria Park Community Cricket League (www.vpccl.co.uk). The children's playgrounds are decent enough, and the athletic field is excellent. Get in touch with the park's own athletics association (www.vphthac.org.uk) for access to changing rooms, showers and its indoor training hall.

Architecture & sculpture

Rising in the middle of the park is a Grade-II listed drinking fountain erected by Baroness Angela Burdett-Coutts (England's wealthiest woman at some point, we're told), adorned by several half-naked marble boys, smiling cheekily. The Hackney Wick Great War Memorial, in the east part of the park, is a reminder that this part of London was hit especially hard by the bombings of the Second World War. Close-by, you'll find two alcove-type fragments that survived the demolition of the old London Bridge Station. Fairly unremarkable, but good shelter when it's raining. Let's face it, no one comes here for architecture.

Festivals

The hazy days when The Clash whipped up a beer-can-throwing frenzy in the park—heralding a new area called punk along the way—might be over, but Victoria Park has kept its musical tradition alive. Slightly more tamed and organised, the festivals taking place these days range from the trendy, village-feel Fields Day to the indie-and-electro-blending Lovebox Weekender, while big names (Radiohead for one) have also discovered a liking for the park's scenery and music-appreciating attitude.

Eat & drink

The park's café, next to The Lake, is tiny, but the organic cakes are a tasty lot. That aside, you have to venture to the park's fringes for food and drink, but fear not: a tap is never far. Leave behind the bog-standard, soulless pub that is The Victoria and opt instead for the East End earthiness of the Top of the Morning, near the Cadogan Gate. Good Ales, a real fireplace, and up-marketish pub food make The Royal Inn on the Park, near the Royal Gates, the usually busy favourite. The Fat Cat, a few minutes south of the park along Grove Road, is more restaurant than pub, a bit pricey but a good choice for high-quality pasta, burgers and steaks.

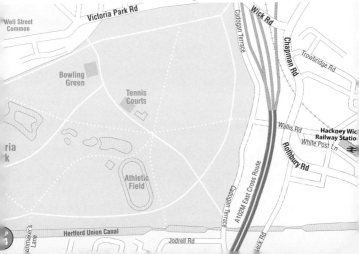

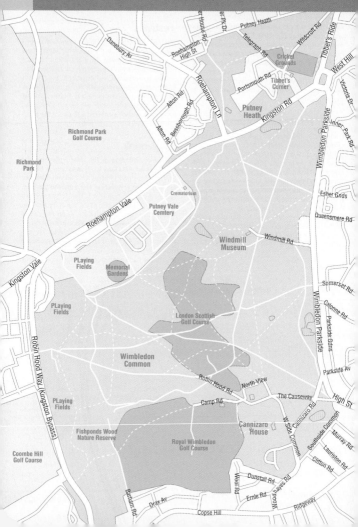

General Information

www.wpcc.org.uk

Overview

If London life starts to get you down, but trekking to the countryside is too much hassle, then Wimbledon Common provides the best of both worlds. Incorporating Putney Heath to the north, Wimbledon Common offers over 1000 acres of wild woodland, scrubland, heathland, ponds and well-tended, mown areas for sports and recreation. Bordered by the urban sprawls of Wimbledon, Putney and Richmond, the common has offered Londoners an escape from city life for centuries. Although thousands visit every weekend, the scale of the place is so vast that you can easily find a private haven for reading a book or a romantic picnic.

Unlike the micro-managed and perfectly structured central London parks, Wimbledon feels much more natural and random. Paths are unpaved and often little more than a muddy track leading off in unlikely directions. The untamed beauty of the common and the lack of traffic noise, or any noise for that matter, make it hard to believe you are still in London.

After a hard day of outdoor activity, or sunbathing, there are plenty of historic pubs to retire to in Wimbledon village. If you prefer your nature tamed or don't want to get your shoes dirty, head to the southeast corner of the common for Cannizaro House and gardens, a grand mansion converted into a boutique hotel and restaurant, with elegantly manicured gardens open to the public. In the summer, the friendly hotel bar opens onto a patio overlooking the grounds and makes a good spot for a sun-downer as you imagine being Lord or Lady of the Manor for the day.

Nature

The common is home to many animals including bats, badgers, and muntjac deer. It's also an important breeding ground for dragonflies and damselflies. For anyone wanting to find out more about the flora and fauna, the London bat group organises 'bat walks' while the London Wildlife Trust organises guided walks. You can also take a self-guided wander along The Windmill Nature Trail. 800 metres long, the trail has been created with accessibility in mind and begins right next to the Windmill car park. The visitors' centre behind the Windmill has wildlife exhibits and also tells the history of the common. It also sells maps and booklets giving the low down on the nature on offer.

Recreation

There is loads of space on the common for pick-up games of rugby, football, Frisbee and cricket. If you fancy a 'real game', you can hire tennis courts by the hour, cricket pitches by the day (from as little as £100) or enjoy a round of golf on the two available courses. The common is very popular with runners and steeplechase events have been held here since 1867. Various running clubs such as the South London Harriers and Hercules Wimbledon use the Common. If you've ever fancied trying horse riding, there are a number of stables that make use of the 16 miles of trails—or bring your own nag with you.

Golf
www.wcgc.co.uk
www.londonscottishgolfclub.co.uk

Horse Riding
Wimbledon Village Stables: 020 8946 8579
Ridgway Stables: 020 8946 7400

Rugby, Football and Cricket Pitch Hire
020 8788 7655

How to Get There

By public transport:
The Northern Line goes to South Wimbledon where you can take a bus to central Wimbledon then change or walk to the village and common. Wimbledon station is much closer. Take the District Line from central London or over ground trains from Waterloo or London Bridge. If you are feeling fit, a ten-minute walk up Wimbledon Hill takes you to Wimbledon village and beyond that, the edge of the common. Regular buses serve the village. Alternatively, you can access Putney Heath which joins up with Wimbledon Common. To do this, take the District Line to Putney Bridge or East Putney overground to Putney mainline station and take a bus up Putney Hill.

It's likely that at some point during your London residence, you've been seized with the romantic notion of floating your way round a London market—savouring the smells, laughing with a vendor, flirting your way to some freebies. If you have, then your attempts to live that dream almost certainly resulted in you silently fuming as you crawled among a crowd of thousands, trekking for a cashpoint because you forgot that stalls don't accept cards, and getting crapped on by a pigeon. Don't be put off!

At the markets you can buy some of the most unique, quirky, fresh, stylish, grungy, exquisite, unusual items in London. Sometimes you'll get brilliant bargains, sometimes you'll pay high for something you fall in love with. And sometimes, yes, you'll be driven near to homicidal rampage. But they're one of London's great strengths: use them while you can, because the developers have their evil, dollar-signed eyes on them.

For groceries

The food in markets isn't necessarily locally grown, but you get a much more tempting choice than in most supermarkets. Expect fruit, veg, breads, cheeses, meats, spices and pastries, as well as stalls concocting irresistible snacks from around the world.

Borough (Map 106)

You don't come here for bargains: you come for ambiance, exquisite international foods, and to impress the person you woke up with. If you're rich and like the finer things in life, then here your weekly shop can consist of some of the freshest vegetables, plumpest fruit, sweetest patisseries and sockiest cheeses in London. If you're poor and just fancy a change from Saturday morning repeats of *Friends*, then head here for a hearty hog roast sandwich and to snaffle some free samples.

Broadway (Map 89)

As gorgeous as Borough, for a third of the price and a fifth of the crowds. It's a pain to get to, stuck in one of the city's remaining quaintly retro spots not closely served by the tube (London Fields), but you'll want to move here by the end of your visit.

Ridley Road (Map 86)

If the gourmet markets are too poncey for you, with their Bavarian organic rye bread and Malaysian honey from breast-fed bees, then get down the Ridley Road. Here, in a market which is bright, chaotic, grubby and bouncing to reggae, you can pick up an incredible array of Jamaican, Turkish, African, Indian and Chinese foodstuffs (and possibly e-coli).

For market-chic

You won't necessarily pay less than at the high street, but you will have a choice of original and irresistible items sold with passion and knowledge. Expect to leave these markets with a lighter pocket (though try to make sure it's not because of the pickpockets…).

Spitalfields (Map 91)

Mecca for anyone looking for ethnic-hip and well-priced clothes, bags and jewellery. Here you can often chat to the maker of the clothes you're eyeing up and learn the story behind their designs. Which is all very inspiring, until you try on their beloved creations, realise you're too fat for it, and reject it having slightly stretched it. Because then it's just awkward.

Greenwich (Map 120)

Craft-tastic: a great place to go for beautiful handmade gifts which people love to receive and then put in a cupboard for the rest of their useful life. Here you'll find a gorgeous range of items for home and lifestyle: pictures, antiques, candles, pottery, soft furnishings and clothes, as well as some great food stalls, and an above-average number of beautiful rich people than at most markets.

Portobello Road (Map 29)

Although famed for being the World's Largest Antique's Market, Portobello Road seems to sell *everything*. You'll need patience to work around its sprawling size and the crowds, but just about anything you're looking for is there somewhere or can be sourced by speaking to the right vendor. Stalls include clothes (from classy-vintage to student-cheap), jewellery, fabric, food, as well as 1500 antique stalls selling maps, medals, silverware, and things you never thought you needed (and which, after you've got them home, you realise you didn't).

Camden (Map 71)

Camden is actually home to six markets, though "chic" doesn't do any of them justice. Here you'll find a purse-emptying range of alternative fashions, vintage clothes, accessories, gifts, t-shirts, comedy hot water bottle covers, tie-dyed hippies, teeny-punks and chaps asking if you'd care for a nice bit of crack. Anything goes, and this open, free atmosphere makes it a major and exciting draw. Hit Camden Stables for brilliant international food stalls.

Fer findin a bit o Laaandon prop'a.

If you're a Londoner who "just adores the city! But oh dear *no*, wouldn't *dream* of bringing kids up here", then chances are you don't mingle much with the Prop'a Laandoner. This hardy breed whose family history is a Dickensian yarn of blitzes, TB and chimney sweeps are the core of this city, and the gradual nudging out of their jellied eels and pub sing-songs is tantamount to ethnic cleansing. Find them at London's Propa Markets before they vanish.

Smithfield (Map 15)

Smithfield Market is in full swing at 4 am, which makes it the perfect place to stumble into on your way home from clubbing. Unless you're vegetarian, because while frying bacon may have you yearning for looser morals, the smell of this 800 year old meat market will have you retching over your recycled sandals. It's the best place in London to pick up any meat you could hope for, including, in the 1500s, a barbecued Protestant or a topside of William Wallace, this being the site of hundreds of executions in its time. Some of the local pubs hold special early licenses, so on your way to the office you can swing in for breakfast over a pint with some of the meat porters: they'd just *love* it if you did.

Columbia Road (Map 91)

There's something deeply touching about an exquisite flower market being manned by some of the burliest Cockneys you'll see outside a Guy Ritchie film. Get there first thing on Sundays for the best choice, or in a low-cut top for the best bargains. And if the crowds and cries of the "daffs, dahlin'?" become too much, just slip into the enchanting boutiques lining Columbia Road.

Billingsgate (Map 101)

For the largest selection of fish in London, outside the London Aquarium (where they frown on you if you try to fry the fish. Bloody bureaucracy.), head to Billingsgate. People were buying their fish here long before London went all yuppie, and much the same stock is available—winkles, cockles, potted shrimp and things which smell ungodly. Today you'll find alongside them almost any fish you could hope for (though don't ask for goldfish), as well as poultry, oils and snacks.

Colleges & Universities · **Central St Martins**

General info

Address: Southampton Row, London,
WC1B 4AP
Phone: 020 7514 7022
Website: www.csm.arts.ac.uk

Overview

Though hyped to infinity, and often lazily editorialised as the one vital source of all things up-and-coming in London, Central St Martins nevertheless has an undeniable history of producing graduates that tend to rocket to international fame upon leaving. The frequently-cited list of alumni reads like a Who's Who of European art-and-design talent, and includes past superstars such as Alexander McQueen, Gilbert and George, and Anthony Gormley, as well as recent fashion darlings Christopher Kane, Gareth Pugh and Kim Jones, to name a few.

The school as it is today was formed in 1989 through the amalgamation of two prestigious 19th century institutions, the Central School of Arts and Crafts and St Martins School of Art. Since then it has annexed the Drama Center and the Byam Shaw School of Art in Archway, and as a result offers a huge range of courses covering most areas of the visual and performing arts. St Martins has a particularly formidable reputation for fashion design—it is the only university to show student collections as part of London Fashion Week—but it is well-respected in all departments for its hyper-progressive ethos (expect to

hear words like 'challenging,' and 'risk-taking' liberally thrown around on open days). The college has recently revealed plans to move to a swish new building in King's Cross in 2011, where student activity will be centralised and everyone will no doubt be even more fabulous than before. Consequently, whether you find the whole thing pretentious and overrated or are waiting in breathless anticipation for the next St Martins wunderkind, it's going to be very difficult to ignore the place in the coming years.

Campuses

Central St Martins
The majority of teaching for fine art, fashion and design students takes place in the very centre of London, with one building on Southampton Row (nearest tube Holborn) and one on Charing Cross Road (near Tottenham Court Road). This means many of sensitive creative souls find themselves struggling against tides of tourists, but on the plus side they also get to inflict their frequently baffling artwork upon a large section of the general public, who, on their way to Wetherspoons, are treated to installations of varying quality in the front windows of the Charing Cross site. Of course, being in the heart of Soho, most St Martins students are a moment away from a cornucopia of incredibly trashy bars where they can lubricate their inner muses.

Drama Centre

The theatre types are based in Clerkenwell, home of Sadler's Wells and the Barbican, and mount public performances at the university-owned Cochrane Theatre in Holborn. The Drama Centre runs courses ranging from set design to classical acting, but also has a programme specifically designed for those wanting to act, direct or write in the film and television industries, and to this end is equipped with various studio and recording facilities. Pierce Brosnan went there but there's no need to let that put you off.

Byam Shaw

The Byam Shaw School of Art in Archway is a fairly recent addition (2003) to Central St Martins, the 'Central' tag here being somewhat misleading as it's a good 20 minutes by tube from the other sites. Devoted solely to fine art, it runs a BA and a more skills-based 2 year FdA as well as a variety of short and post-graduate courses.

College Culture

As is the case with most London institutions, the university community is massively subsumed by the bright lights of the city itself, but this is no bad thing. Though the college puts on frequent exhibitions, talks and events, there is no independent bar or central hub—students will instead inevitably find themselves taking advantage of the central location (which is, after all, a short walk from the National Gallery and ICA). The Student Union is not particular to Central St Martins but provides services for and represents all the art colleges in London (University of the Arts London) as a whole, and various services and societies (such as sports clubs) are run at this level. As far as the education part goes, it's not always easy being in the midst of the constant search for the next-big-thing, but at the same time the idiosyncratic slant of the teaching makes for a unique experience, and the generally high talent level of the students fosters a fantastic creative and social atmosphere.

Tuition

Fees vary between courses and change all the time, but most BA degrees cost in the region of £3,000 a year for home students and run for three years, though you may pay less if you receive support from your local authority. Fees for international students are about three times as much.

Short Courses

Central St Martins also runs a large number of short courses for all aspirational (and rich) non-students wanting a piece of the action. Prices are high but the courses very popular, partly because of the college's reputation and partly because there are many interesting options to choose from. The courses run in evenings, weekends, or can be taken intensively as a Summer, Easter or Christmas school. Information: www.csm.arts.ac.uk or call 020 7514 7015.

Phone Numbers:

Charing Cross Road site: 020 7514 7190

Southampton Row site: 020 7514 7037

Drama Centre: 020 7514 8778

Byam Shaw School of Art: 020 7281 4111

Admissions—degree courses:
020 7514 7023

Admissions—short courses: 020 7514 7015

International Office: 020 7514 7027

Charing Cross Road Shop: 020 7514 7612

Southampton Row Shop: 020 7514 7017

Back Hill Shop: 020 7514 6851

University of the Arts Students' Union:
020 7514 6270

General info

Address: Northampton Square, London,
EC1V 0HB
Phone: 020 7040 5060
Website: www.city.ac.uk

Overview

In London, a place rich with academia, City University often gets overlooked. Unlike King's or LSE it has no grand halls, secret-handshakes or old-boys' networks. Its facilities are modest and its library short on fusty books. But it's carved out a reputation as a supplier of professionals, cementing its place in the top five for graduate employment in recent years.

Located on a pretty park on the edge of the City of London—the 'Square Mile' that's fast becoming the centre of the global economy— the university is overwhelmingly diverse. Ethnicities make up over half the student body, with young Chinese and wealthy Russians flocking to the business school. It's that section of the university that churns out workers for the finance industry—students who are so hell-bent on business success that they go to school in suits.

The university's first incarnation came in 1894 as an industrial college for the working classes. The on-site swimming pool was used when London hosted the 1908 Olympics, although it wasn't until 1966 that it gained full university status. It's maintained strong links with industry, with alumni including the founding father of budget Euro-travel, easyJet's Stelios (like Sting and Madonna he chooses to use only one name). Students at City may be lined up for good jobs when they graduate; but it comes at the cost of having to explain what their less well-known university is whenever they mention it.

Tuition

In line with most British universities, undergraduate fees for EU students were £3,070 in the 2007-2008 academic year. International fees range from £7,750 (law) to £9,850 (informatics). There are three undergraduate-only uni digs, starting at £3,497.

Culture

Culture in the traditional sense is a little thin on the ground. There are no museums or galleries to speak of, although one department did exhibit photos of prisoners at work last year. But as it included a con making sandwiches for 16p an hour this could've just been to get the wayward students to knuckle down.

Instead, the uni hosts some heavyweight lectures. Although it sounds a little dull, some top speakers in the uni's specialised fields—like journalism, or business—address City pretty frequently. If you're lucky enough to love asset management or food policy then congratulations! You'll be thoroughly entertained.

Departments

Admissions office (undergrad and postgrad):
.... 020 7040 8716
Library........................ 020 7040 8191
Saddler's Sports Centre...... 020 7040 5656
Student Union 020 7040 5600

1 Gloucester Building
2 Innovation Centre
3 School of Social Sciences
4 College Building
5 Centenary Building
6 Drysdale Building
7 Refectory Building
8 University Building
9 Tait Building
10 Goswell Place
11 Myddelton Building
12 Parkes Building
13 Health Centre
14 Walmsley Building
15 Paramount House
16 Saddlers Sports Centre
17 Finsbury Residence Hall
18 Heyworth Residence Hall
19 Peartree Court Residence Hall

General info

Address: Imperial College London
             South Kensington Campus
             London SW7 2AZ
Phone: 020 7589 5111
Website: www3.imperial.ac.uk

Overview

Imperial College is London's specialist college of science, engineering and medicine. It consistently ranks in the top five British universities; usually third, although a few years ago it beat Oxford to come in second. Students come from far and wide and it is super-selective; undergraduate applications to admissions are approximately 7:1. Formerly a constituent college of the University of London, Imperial became independent in 2007 (the 100th anniversary of its founding). Students now receive Imperial College degrees awarded by the university.

Departments

The pride and soul of the college are three faculties, each headed by a principal: engineering, medicine and natural sciences. The Tanaka Business School doesn't offer undergraduate degrees, but does allow undergraduate students to study management modules towards their degrees. The main purpose of the Humanities department is to provide elective subjects and language courses for the science students.

Campus Culture

Students come here to study. There are many clubs and societies, but it's hardly a party place. Live! is an online student news source and forum run by the City and Guilds College Union. (http://live.cgcu.net/). Felix is a free weekly student newspaper which aims to be independent of both the College itself and also the Student Union. Stoic TV (Student Television of Imperial College) is Imperial College Union's TV station: Programmes are available to watch on their website. ICRadio broadcasts on www.icradio.com and on 1134 AM.

Facilities

The main campus in South Kensington is surrounded by museums and other lovely cultural institutions, there are also smaller campuses and in Berkshire and Kent. The college is associated with various hospitals in Greater London, including St. Mary's Hospital, Charing Cross Hospital, Northwick Park & St. Mark's Hospital, and Hammersmith Hospital.

The main campus has impressive facilities. The sports centre has a boathouse, 60-acre athletic ground and a swimming pool. There is a large central library and several smaller departmental libraries for specialisation. There is also a language laboratory. The College has a range of on-campus shops, including a bookshop, restaurants, a newsagent, a shop for general provisions, a travel agent and a bank.

Tuition

£3,070 per year for full-time UK and EU undergraduate students in (2007).

General Information

Address:	Too many campuses to list!
Phone:	020 7836 5454
Website:	www. kcl.ac.uk

Overview

The University of London, with its 19 colleges, sprawls over the city. King's College London is part of it. King's (or KCL, as otherwise known) has nearly 20,000 students and five campuses—the Strand, Guy's, Waterloo, St. Thomas' and Denmark Hill. It has an excellent academic reputation and ranks in the top ten UK universities. Unlike some of the other University of London colleges, King's is equally well known for its arts and science courses.

Its religious affiliation is now less central, but back in 1829 King's was founded as a Church of England institution to counter University College London, or "the godless college in Gower Street." The beautifully designed chapel at the Strand campus testifies to its pious beginnings, though few students

would consider it a motivation for attending the college. The student body is diverse, as the societies list reflects—it includes a Catholic society, a Christian Union, a Krishna Consciousness group, and a Nomads society, amongst a myriad others.

King's boasts a number of famous alumni. Keats studied apothecary there (he didn't like it much), and Florence Nightingale set up the world's first school of nursing at St. Thomas' Hospital, now the Florence Nightingale School of Nursing and Midwifery. In the 1960s, Archbishop Desmond Tutu spent time in its halls. The KCL student union nightclub, Tutu's—a pretty grungy place but one of the few open past 2 am in the Strand on a Saturday—is named after him.

London prices may take their toll on the student purse, but King's students at least benefit from a prime location. As well as the nightclub, the college has two bars, one at Guy's Campus and one at the Strand. The Waterfront bar at the Strand looks directly onto the Thames, giving a view of everything from Westminster to the

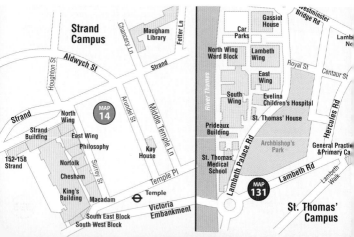

Oxo Tower. It's also a great gig venue—Alanis Morissette, Richard Ashcroft, and Beth Orton have all played there.

Sports

The college's sports facilities are impressive. It caters to almost anything—it has a swimming pool, gym, and even rifle range. Although King's cannot rival the Oxbridge rowing tradition, its sports do have a history—two of the men's rugby clubs, Guy's and St. Thomas', are the oldest in the world. To access the sports grounds students must leave Zone 1; the grounds are in Dulwich, Surrey, and South London.

Culture

King's has numerous dramatic societies where amateur thesps can hone their skills. More unusually, its classics department stages a play in ancient Greek every year, and is the only classics department in the UK to do so. The college's religious origins are evident in its wonderful choral music. 25 choral scholars uphold this tradition.

Tuition

Fees were controversially introduced in the UK in 1997 and increased in 2001. King's undergrads can expect to pay £3,070 a year, though overseas students pay between £10,980 and a whopping £25,600 (for clinical programs). Postgraduate study is at around the £3,500 mark for most courses (about £11,000 for overseas students).

Contact details

General Enquiries 020 7836 5454
Social Science and Public Policy .020 7848 1495
Physical Sciences and Engineering . . . .
. . . . .020 7848 2267/2268
Nursing and Midwifery 020 7848 4698
Medicine .020 7848 6501
Law. 020 7836 5454
Institute of Psychiatry 020 7836 5454
Humanities 020 7848 2350
Dental Institute . . . .020 7848 6512 (undergrad),
. . . . .020 7848 6703 (postgrad)
Biomedical and Health Sciences . . . .
. . . . 020 7848 6400 (Guy's)
. . . . .020 7848 4172 (Waterloo)

Libraries:
Maughan Chancery Lane 020 7848 2430
Waterloo. 020 7848 3000
St. Thomas. 020 7188 3740
Guy's .020 7848 6900
Denmark Hill 020 7848 5740
Student Union 020 7848 1588

MAP 104

Waterloo Campus

Doon St
Cornwall Rd
Franklin-Wilkins Building
Waterloo Bridge Wing
K4 Fitness Centre
Stamford St
Stamford Street Apartments
James Clark Maxwell Building
Secker St
aterloo
Waterloo Rd
Waterloo Station
Exton

General Information

Address: Houghton Street,
          London WC2A 2AE
Phone: 020 7405 7686
Website: www.lse.ac.uk

Overview

The London School of Economics and Political Science, or LSE as it is commonly known, is a single faculty college focused on the social sciences; world-renowned for its highly prestigious programmes and distinguished alumni. Located amidst a hub of academic activity with UCL, Kings College, SOAS and Birkbeck nearby, the college is affiliated with the University of London and stands apart due to its high proportion of postgraduate students. LSE was founded in 1895 by the intellectual socialist movement, the Fabian Society, with the aim of bettering society through the education of Britain's business and political elite. Today it remains a strongly political institution, with considerable influence in government through both its research programmes and campaigns. Its alumni are also highly represented in business and law spheres. While best known for its economics and politics degrees, the broad range of social science programmes offered complements the international ethos of the school and it remains at the cutting edge in terms of research.

The college enrolls around 8,000 students who represent over 140 different countries; over half of these are postgraduates who

rarely leave the library unless attending high-brow seminars on globalization and inequality. Its starry alumni includes Nobel laureates, international Heads of State, outstanding academics, and a notable proportion of British MP's. And of course Mick Jagger.

Culture On Campus

Despite its reputation for academic excellence, LSE's social activities are mainly fuelled by a lively undergraduate population who also know how to enjoy themselves. With over 170 eclectic student societies, ranging from 'Catalan' to 'Taiwanese'; from 'United Nations' to 'Anti-Authoritarian' and from 'Maths&Stats' to good old fashioned 'Lager&Real Ale', the broad international and diverse facets of the student population is encompassed. An atmosphere of work hard/play hard prevails and nightly events lure the undergraduates from the libraries and keep the campus buzzing. The large postgraduate population tends to shuffle by however, books in hand; the days of cheesy music, luminous drinks in shot glasses and ill-conceived experimental fashions behind them while they actually do some work.

Sports

Not to be let down by its central, and somewhat geographically limited campus, LSE manages to maintain a thriving sports culture through the Athletics Union. Football and rugby seem to top the bill, with provision for some of the less mainstream athletic pursuits such as capoeira and ultimate Frisbee. The college makes use of its affiliation with the University of London Union, which broadens the scope for sports participation alongside students of other universities.

Tuition

2008-2009 undergraduate fees are £3,145 for home students and £12,360 for international students. Graduate fees are varying from around £3,000 to £17,000. Add on books, accommodation and personal expenses.

Departments

Undergraduate Admissions Office . . . .
. . . . 020 7955 7125
. . . . 020 7955 7757
Graduate Admissions Office . . . .
. . . . 020 7955 7160
Library 020 7955 6733
Students' Union 020 7955 7158

General Information

Address: Gower Street
London WC1E 6BT
Phone: 020 7679 2000
Website: www.ucl.ac.uk

Overview

UCL, a constituent college of the University of London, has been a place of diversity from the word go—living very much up to its status as London's Global University. University College London was founded in 1826 by Jeremy Bentham as a progressive alternative to Oxford and Cambridge's social exclusivity and religious restrictions. Thus, it was the first university in England to admit students of any race, class or religion and welcome women on equal standing with men. International students have been a part of the college's fabric since day one and it was the first English university to offer the systematic teaching of law, architecture and medicine. Bentham even requested in his will that his body be preserved in the name of science and stored in a wooden cabinet, which is on display to this day in the main building of the College. Creepy.

UCL consistently ranks among the top five universities in Britain and is currently in the top ten universities globally. To this day, the science, law and medical departments are still some of its strongest. 20 Nobel prizes have been awarded to UCL academics and students, ten of which were in Physiology & Medicine alone. However, UCL degrees in anthropology, history and the arts are also very highly regarded in their fields.

UCL's many networks of libraries are impressive and an easy place to get lost. The Main Library, designed by William Wilkins, who also

designed the similar National Gallery building, focuses on arts and humanities, history, economics, public policy and law. The Special Collections include medieval manuscripts and first editions of works by George Orwell, James Joyce's *Ulysses*, Newton's *Principia* and Darwin's *Origin of the Species*.

There's no such thing as a typical UCL student, as it's such a diverse place. The only thing students have in common is their intelligence and London. Because it's a university with great academics right in the heart of Bloomsbury, it makes for some pretty interesting alums. Where else can you have such diverse graduates as Alexander Graham Bell, Mahatma Gandhi, Ricky Gervaise, and all four members of Coldplay?

Tuition

Fees vary, but for a resident of the EU, the maximum fee payable is £3,145 per year. If you're an international student who is not a resident of the EU, fees are quite a bit more expensive at £11,360 - £22,170. You should expect to pay between £90-£95 a week for accommodation. Other costs to consider are entertainment, travel, books, TV licence and clothes. Remember that you'll be living in London, where everything is that much more expensive generally.

Sports

UCL's sports are as diverse as its students—everything from hockey, rowing and women's rugby to Kung Fu, skateboarding and water polo. The UCLU (University College London Union) is your one-stop shop for campus sports teams and clubs. If you're looking for football, The 90-acre UCL sports ground at Shenley, Hertfordshire, has very high quality pitches. Watford football club even train there. The Union gym (Bloomsbury Fitness) offers facilities for activities such as basketball and personal fitness programmes.

Culture

Being right in the centre of London means that you're never short of something cultural to do. However, UCL stands up quite well. It even has its own museum—the Petrie Museum of Egyptian Archaeology—accessible from the Science Library. Here you're even given your own torch to explore the collection of over 80,000 rare objects DIY (or Indiana Jones) style. UCL also has its own West End theatre, the UCL Bloomsbury, wedged into the maze of main buildings. It's a must-stop for top comedian tours. Jimmy Carr and Ricky Gervaise have been known to shoot their stand-up DVDs there. The UCL Union has access to the theatre for at least ten weeks a year, where it is dedicated to student drama and music society performances. Although neither drama, music nor dance are formally taught at UCL, this does not stop the Union's drama club from making it to the Edinburgh Fringe Festival. At UCL, despite the fact that students can really go out just about anywhere in London, many stay loyal to the bars within the Union, and it's usually a great place to meet before a bigger night out.

Departments

Undergraduate & Postgraduate Admissions
.... 020 7679 7742
Student Information Centre . 020 7679 3000
UCL Union 020 7387 3611
UCL Bloomsbury Theatre 020 7388 8822
Petrie Museum. 020 7679 2884

General Information

Address: Thornhaugh Street, Russell Square, London WC1H 0XG
Phone: 020 7637 2388
Website: www.soas.ac.uk

Overview

The School of African and Oriental Studies is a specialist college which focuses on the languages, cultures, law and social studies of Africa, Asia, and the Near and Middle East. SOAS, as it is commonly known, is part of the University of London and is the only institution of its kind in the United Kingdom. It has an excellent reputation as one of the leading authorities on African and Asian studies in the world and ranks highly in university charts on the strength of its programmes Originally founded in 1916 to educate and inform British citizens bound for overseas postings, the school began with an Oriental studies' focus and later incorporated African studies. SOAS is nestled in the corner of Russell Square, with another campus up close to King's Cross; its diversity complements the hotbed of academic activity that makes up this part of London.

The college enrolls over 4,000 students and nearly half of the postgraduates are from countries outside of the UK or the EU. They are often seen sitting in Russell Square eating their organic lunch, and chatting (in Swahili or Taiwanese) about their UNICEF internships. SOAS's alumni include members of parliament and royalty of a range of countries from Ghana to Burma. The Crown Princess of Norway went here. Well of course she did. The Norwegians are so PC. Except for whale hunting.

Culture On Campus

One thing to be said about SOAS students is: they are serious. The Students Union has a reputation of leaning heavily to the left and is very politically active. SOAS students have been a notable presence at anti-war protests, and they are also now rather concerned with environmental causes—campaigning for the reduction of carbon footprints, among other issues. Societies at the college, unsurprisingly, have a very international, 'right-on' flavour, and include the obvious 'Amnesty International Society', 'Campaign for Human Rights in the Philippines Society', 'Model United Nations' and of course the 'Natural Remedies Society' for when these guys need to let their hair down and knock back an entire bottle of Echinacea.

Tuition

2008-2009 undergraduate fees are £3,145 for home students and £11,460 for international students. Graduate fees vary from around £4,090 to around £12,000. Add on books, accommodation and personal expenses.

Departments

Undergraduate Admissions Office
020 7898 4301/ 4306

Graduate Admissions office
020 7898 4300/ 4311/ 4322/ 4361

Library
020 7898 4197

Students Welfare Office
020 7074 5014

General Information

University of London Students Union (ULU),
Malet Street, WC1E 7HY
www.ulu.co.uk
www.thebarflyclub.com/ulu (The Venue)

Overview

Students are the same the world over and in London they ain't no different. In amongst the banter over Bronte and misunderstandings about Marx stands beer, boogying and burgers. Luckily, for over 100,000 of the University of London's students there's a central place to go to make your university years active and sociable—ULU.

You will need to be a member of ULU to get into some of the events, although grabbing a cheeky cheap sarnie in the café shouldn't pose too much of a problem for clued-up Londoners. There are 20 University of London colleges that are eligible for ULU membership, so if you're a student at one of these then you've got it made. If not, use your powers of persuasion to get the gold dust of cheap beer and food.

Practicalities

There's a plethora of nearby tube stations on various lines:

Piccadilly Line – Russell Square
Central Line/Northern Line (Charing Cross Branch) – Tottenham Court Road.
Victoria Line – Euston or Warren Street
Circle Line/Metropolitan Line/Hammersmith & City Line – Euston Square

ULU is also a 5 minute stroll from the numerous buses of Oxford Street.

Clubs & Societies (non-sport)

ULU offers more extra-curricular activities than Micky J's had nose jobs. What's on offer is somewhat subject to annual change which is more reason to get down there and sign up.

Now. Yes, there's the usual suspects such as Drama Club et al but it's easy to be tempted by some of ULU's more obscure offerings such as the Revelation Rock Gospel Choir. Hell, yeah.

Sports

Sports are big at ULU. Again, there's the usual—tennis, football, cricket, and swimming clubs etc. There are also opportunities to master a martial art at Shorinji Kempo (may come in handy for students living in Seven Sisters). Amongst other things you can also participate in Salsa, Break Dancing, Mountaineering, Fencing, Lifesaving or Rifle Club. Now there's one for the CV…

Food & Bars

Lunch Box is ULU's coffee shop, perfectly located on the ground floor for those who want to grab a quick (Fair Trade) coffee or a bargain meal deal—you even get fruit—how healthy. The aptly named **Duck 'n Dive** bar is, erm, a bit of a dive in that usual charming student way, but does have a lively atmosphere and loads of events. There's also **The Gallery Bar** which, despite the rather odd sheets hanging from the ceiling, serves up some wallet and taste bud satisfying treats until 11pm.

Facilities

The **Student Print Centre** will resolve all your reprographics and binding troubles. Wander into the **Student Union Shop** with a clear conscience to grab a Fair Trade snack or a recycled notepad. Open until 7pm on weekdays.

Events

You'll never be without events at ULU. You've got the **Duck 'n Dive** for regular events but there's also live music at **The Venue** hosting up and coming unsigned bands as well as the odd better-known act. For gigs enter ULU on Byng Place.

Learning in the capital has a long and venerable history. University College London (UCL) was the third university founded in England after Cambridge and Oxford and the first to admit students of any race or religion. It even let women in, showing scant regard for their swooning nature and feeble minds. Now there are hundreds of universities, colleges and adult education centres offering a mind-boggling array of courses.

The first port of call for those with a lust for learning or even an empty Tuesday night to fill is Floodlight (www.floodlight.co.uk), which lists 40,000 courses. Fancy brushing up your motorbike maintenance skills at Hackney Community College, getting an NVQ in sugar modelling at the National Bakery School, learning how to create the ultimate kitchen garden at the English Gardening School or studying the nonsense verse of Lear and Carroll at City Lit? The sky is your oyster.

Continuing Education and Professional Development

University College London
Gower Street, WC1E 6BT
020 7679 2000
www.ucl.ac.uk

City University
Northampton Square, EC1V 0HB
020 7040 5060
www.city.ac.uk

London South Bank University
103 Borough Road, SE22 0HU
020 7815 7815
www.lsbu.ac.uk

London Metropolitan University
31 Jewry Street, EC3N 2EY
020 7423 0000
www.londonmet.ac.uk

University of East London
4 University Way, E16 2RD
020 8223 2420
www.uel.ac.uk

University of Greenwich
Park Row, SE10 9LS
020 8331 8000
www.gre.ac.uk

A Little Bit of Everything…

Birkbeck
26 Russell Square, WC1B 5DQ
0845 601 0174
www.bbk.ac.uk/ce/aboutus

Open University
Your home
0845 300 60 90
www.open.ac.uk

Bishopsgate Institute
230 Bishopsgate, EC2M 4QH
020 7392 9200
www.bishopsgate.org.uk

Arts and Lifestyle

University of the Arts London
65 Davies Street, W1K 5DA
020 7514 6000
www.arts.ac.uk

Leiths School of Food and Wine
16-20 Wendell Road, W12 9RT
020 8749 6400
www.leiths.com

The London School of Journalism
126 Shirland Road, W9 2BT
020 7289 7777
www.lsj.org

Glass Blowing Courses
15 Forest Trading Estate, E17 6AL
020 8418 5900
www.glassblowingcourses.co.uk

English Gardening School
66 Royal Hospital Road, SW3 4HS
020 7352 4347
www.englishgardeningschool.co.uk/

London School Of Beauty & Make-Up
47-50 Margaret Street, W1W 8SB
020 7636 1893
www.lond-est.com

Institute Francais
17 Queensbury Place SW7 2DT
020 7073 1350
www.institut-francais.org.uk

London Buddhist Centre
51 Roman Road, E2 0HU
084 5458 4716
www.lbc.org.uk

Athletics and Dance

Circus Space
Coronet Street, London, N1 6HD
020 7613 4141
www.thecircusspace.co.uk

Tokei Martial Arts
28 Magdalen Street, SE1 2EN
020 7403 5979
www.tokeicentre.org

Jump and Dance
400 York Way, N7 9LR
020 7700 7722
www.jumpanddance.com

Regents Canoe Club
Regents Canal, Graham Street, N1
www.regentscanoeclub.co.uk

Docklands Sailing & Watersport Centre
235a Westferry Road, E14 3QS
020 7537 2626
www.dswc.org

London School of Capoeira
1 & 2 Leeds Place, N4 3RF
020 7281 2020
www.londonschoolofcapoeira.co.uk

General Information

NFT Map:	74
Website:	www.arsenal.com
Phone:	020 7704 4000
Box office:	020 7704 4040
Location:	Highbury House, 75 Drayton Park, London N5 1BU

Overview

On the British sporting landscape, few other institutions continue to dominate proceedings more than Arsenal Football Club. With almost limitless economic wealth and a seemingly unending supply of hot foreign talent, the Gunners (or Gooners to the hardcore) rightly earned the alternate nickname 'The Invincibles' in the mid noughties. The club holds numerous national records and has a trophy room packed with more silver than any other, save Manchester United. T'was not always thus of course. From humble beginnings south of the river, Arsenal built themselves up from roots level, with glory years seeming to come in waves. The mid 80s saw the instatement of George Graham, a hugely popular former player, who begat a powerful, muscular side captained by local hero Tony Adams. The Gunners are currently managed by Arsene Wenger, who has brought a continental flavour to the team and an invigorating playing style—once a byword for boring defensive football. Following Arsenal is not always an easy ride. It's surprising that so many people still flock to the new Emirates stadium in Holloway given the stupendous ticket prices (anywhere between £30 and £75), and that's if you can even get one, given the six year Membership waiting list. If you're lucky enough to have the £1000s needed for a decent season ticket then you get to sit in a huge, soulless stadium named after an airline company to watch what are ostensibly a bunch of bloody foreigners. On the plus side, those bloody foreigners play some of the most dazzling football in Europe.

How to Get There

By Car: The Arsenal website states: 'Supporters are strongly advised not to drive to Emirates Stadium. The ground is situated in a mainly residential area with an extensive Event Day Parking Scheme in operation. Only car owners with resident's permits will be allowed to park on-street in the designated areas and any cars parked illegally will be towed away'. In other words, don't bother bringing a car.

By Public Transport: Arsenal (Piccadilly Line) is the nearest tube station, around three minutes walk from the ground. Finsbury Park (Victoria, Piccadilly Lines and Great Northern rail) and Highbury & Islington (Victoria Line, North London Line and Great Northern rail) stations are around a 10-minute walk - these should be slightly less crowded.

How to Get Tickets

As Arsenal play some damn sexy football, tickets are not easy to come by. However, in the new, swanky Emirates stadium there is always going to be one or two no-shows or corporate tickets that have slipped into the wrong hands. Members have first dibs on tickets and snap them up but the less scrupulous ones sell them on to make a fast buck. Try Gumtree or matchday touts if you really must. To be honest, it's probably one of the rare instances where it really is worth the hassle.

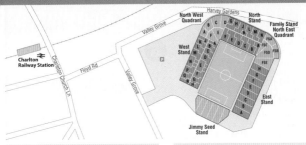

General Information

Phone: 0871 226 1905
Website: www.cafc.co.uk
Location: The Valley, Floyd Road,
Charlton, London SE7 8BL

Overview

"Valley Floyd Road,
Oh mist rolling in from the sea,
My dream is always to be here
Oh Valley Floyd Road".

Well, it's one of the cleaner football songs you'll hear at this ground sung by the Charlton faithful, referring to their nomadic existence at Crystal Palace and West Ham's grounds for eight seasons from 1985. Based in Charlton (funnily enough) within the borough of Greenwich, the team's fortunes have been mixed over the years, having had its share of financial troubles. As if to invite further woes, the club's chairman (in a seemingly foolish act of bravado) stated in 2007 that anyone taking a season ticket would get a free one the following season if Charlton were promoted from the Football League Championship to the Premiership; at the time of writing, Charlton lie 6th in the league table and the chairman will probably not be in danger of soiling himself. Also known as The Addicks, they pride themselves on being viewed as a family-orientated club with a strong relationship with its supporters, and even go as far as to have an elected adult season ticket holder on the club's board of directors. Easy to reach from central London, it's certainly well worth a day out with its engaging atmosphere making it popular with "away" fans from other visiting teams. Well, it beats going to watch Millwall play…

How to Get There

By Car: You can leave the M25 at Junction 2 in order to access the A2, heading towards London. When the A2 becomes the A102 (M), take the right hand exit at the roundabout into the A206 Woolwich Road. After passing the major set of traffic lights at the junction of Anchor and Hope Lane and Charlton Church Lane, turn right at the second roundabout into Charlton Lane. Go over the railway crossing then take the first right into Harvey Gardens, with the road leading to the ground. From central London, travel along the A13 until it becomes the East India Dock Road, then take the A102 through the Blackwall Tunnel. Come off at the second junction and take the first exit at the roundabout, then go along the A206 Woolwich Road into Charlton Lane as detailed above. Thanks to the local residents' parking scheme, you'll be hard pushed to find a parking space; try Westmoor Street, Eastmoor Street, Warspite Road and Ruston Road.

By Public Transport: The ground is within walking distance of Charlton railway station, with the Southeastern line running services from mainline stations Charing Cross and London Bridge and services from Cannon Street on Saturdays. You can also take the Jubilee Line to North Greenwich, and then a short ride on buses 161, 472 or 486 to get to the Valley. Moderate masochists can walk from the tube station.

How to Get Tickets

Unless the unlikely event arises of a successful cup run, getting to see a match shouldn't be an issue. Tickets can be ordered by phone from the Box Office, via the internet at the club's website or in person at The Valley.

General Information

NFT Map: 43
Phone: 0871 984 1905
Website: www.chelseafc.com
Location: Stamford Bridge,
             Fulham Road,
             London, SW6 1HS

Overview

Stamford Bridge, home to one of the Premiership's 'big four' clubs, is now one of Europe's most glamorous stadiums. However, 'The Bridge' was once an unappealing and daunting shit-hole more used to hosting pitch invasions and fighting hooligans than the well-heeled city types and Russian oligarchs of today. In the '70s and '80s, it was the violent 'headhunters' that made the club unpopular, but as 'The Blues' never won anything, no one took much notice. In recent years, Chelsea have succeeded in wrestling the mantle of most-hated team in England away from Manchester United, largely due to winning things with the never-ending supply of money from Roman Abramovich. The hooligans have all but gone, either priced out or grown up, but the antics of Prima Donna players and managers, who have often been less than graceful in defeat, hasn't exactly helped the club's public profile. With money to burn, Chelsea have attracted some of the world's great names over the years, such as Gianfranco Zola and Marcel Desailly, as well as some big flops (anyone remember Veron?). With the club able to cherry-pick (and steal) the biggest stars, many believe the back-to-back Premiership wins in 04/05 and 05/06 were inevitable, but that would be unfair. Many other clubs have tried to 'buy' success and got nowhere; so Chelsea, under the recently departed manager and larger-than-life 'character' José Mourinho, should be applauded. With regular qualifications for the Champions League, Chelsea often play twice a week, with Premiership fixtures on the weekend and European football mid-week.

How to Get There

By Car: It is possible to drive to Stamford Bridge on match days but it's pretty pointless to do so.

Traffic snarls up badly and the effects are felt throughout South West London. If you do brave the traffic, remember that Fulham Road is closed off on match days. Parking is a nightmare with most zones given over to residents. Gangs of eager traffic wardens are on hand to make your Saturday afternoon miserable.

By Public Transport: Stamford Bridge is a two-minute stroll from Fulham Broadway tube station. Regular district line underground trains deliver the hordes from central London in a matter of minutes. If the idea of a packed train full of sweaty football fans isn't your idea of heaven, many fans descend at Ealing Broadway and take the ten-minute walk to the stadium instead.

How to Get Tickets

With so many competitions and cups, getting tickets is easier than you might think. The 'big' fixtures—London derby's, Man U, Liverpool and the later cup stages are either impossible to get or crazily priced, but tickets for the less glamorous ties can be picked up from the Chelsea website or box office. Otherwise, cheeky geezers will be on hand to fleece you on match day. You will probably end up in the new West Stand alongside Japanese and American tourists, but that might be preferable to a fat skinhead in the 'Shed.'

General Information

NFT Map: 47
Tickets: 0870 442 1222
Website: www.fulhamfc.com
Location: Craven Cottage, Stevenage Road,
London SW6 6HH

Overview

You have to feel a bit sorry for Fulham. The likes of George Best and Rodney Marsh once graced the pitch at Craven Cottage. These days you'd be lucky to find a non-Fulham fan who could name a current squad player, let alone the first eleven. In the shadow of rich and successful Chelsea a mile or so down the road, Fulham have not had an easy ride. Failure to find a new site for a multi-million stadium and reluctance by Harrods owner and royal conspiracy accuser, Mohamed Al Fayed, to dip his hand too deeply in his very large pockets suggest they are a club that might never win anything. An aura of resignation hangs over the place, not helped by Craven Cottage resembling a crumbling throwback to the '70s. The stadium, with a capacity of under 25,000, seems tiny compared to monsters like Arsenal's majestic ground. However, in the new football world of playboy millionaires and fans taken to the cleaners for an hour and a half of entertainment, there is something nostalgic and noble about a day at the Cottage. The ground was one of the last in the country to be made all-seated and some fans defiantly act as if the terraces still exist. As the wind blows off the Thames and you chomp down on a dodgy meat pie and cup of tea, things don't seem so bad. Part you can't help harking back to 'the good old days' and mourning the loss of football's soul to the corporate beast. Or maybe it's the cheap tickets that numb the pain.

How to Get There

By Car: Craven Cottage sits in a leafy, riverside suburb of Fulham. Parking is relatively easy around the ground with plenty of parking meters, although reaching the ground could be difficult as weekend traffic in London is never fun to negotiate.

By Public Transport: Putney Bridge on the District Line is your best bet. Putney also has a mainline station with connections from Clapham Junction and direct trains from Waterloo. Cross the road opposite Putney station and hop on any passing bus. Alternatively, a ten minute walk down the high street and over the river will get you to the ground.

How to Get Tickets

One of the 'joys' of watching Fulham is that tickets are easy to get your hands on. Many games are available on general sale through the club website. For the biggest matches, priority is given to members but persevere and you should be rewarded. If you can't get a ticket legitimately, you can always take your chance with a tout on match day. Try haggling; due to Fulham's fortunes, you could get lucky.

General Information

NFT Map: 76
Main switchboard: 020 7616 8500
Ticketline: 020 7616 8700
Lord's website: www.lords.org
England Cricket Board website:
www.ecb.co.uk
Middlesex CCC website:
www.middlesexccc.com
Location: St John's Wood,
            London, NW8 8QN.

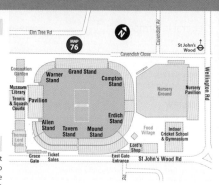

Overview

Even if you know nothing about cricket, don't be put off coming to Lord's. Yes, some games last for five days, and yes, it can still be a draw at the end of it. But as much as anything else Lord's is a fabulous place to come and have a drink. On a hot day the ground is paradise. The sunburnt crowd get slowly boozed up and by the time the players break for tea—yes, tea—few people are concerned at what's going on in the middle. With the polite hum of chatter building up to full-blown drunken singing, it's worth going to Lord's for the atmosphere alone. But when the rabble have calmed down, Lord's is a very genteel place. It's widely seen as the Home of Cricket, and used to house the international governing body. It hosts a heap of England games every year and it's the home ground of county side Middlesex. There's also a year-round gym—you don't even have to be posh to use it—and an indoor training centre. There's even a museum to amuse you when rain stops play. And, rest assured, at some point rain WILL stop play. At the moment Lords holds two Test matches (the marathon international five-dayers) and a handful of England one-day games. These are the ground's showpiece events, where the crowd are at their most boisterous. Middlesex games rarely attract many spectators, and unless you're an old man or a dog you may be in a minority.

How to Get There

By Car: There's little parking around Lord's so, as you'll be parked up all day, public transport will always be cheaper. If you must drive, the ground is off the A4, which turns into the M4.

By Public Transport: The nearest station is St John's Wood (Jubilee Line). Marylebone (Bakerloo) and Baker Street (Bakerloo, Jubilee, Hammersmith and City, Metropolitan and Circle) are both nearby. Marylebone mainline station serves the north and west of the country. London Paddington is a short bus ride away. Dozens of buses run to Baker Street, many of which stop right outside the ground: 13, 82, 113, 139, 189, 755, 757, 758, 768, 771, 772, 773, 797

How to Get Tickets

Getting your hands on England tickets can be tricky. The first few days of a Test match tend to sell out months in advance, though tickets for the last day never go on pre-sale (as the game could be over by then). Similarly, One Day Internationals are normally sell-outs, so it does take a little planning to get in. Check the website over the preceding winter and you might get lucky. If there are less than ten overs in a day due to rain, or if the game's already over, you can claim the full ticket price back. If the weather limits play to between 10.1-24.5 overs (in English, that's up to 149 balls played) you get a 50 per cent refund. Any more than that and you're deemed to have got your money's worth. Middlesex games rarely sell out, however, so you can just rock up on the day, beers in hand, and enjoy the Lord's village.

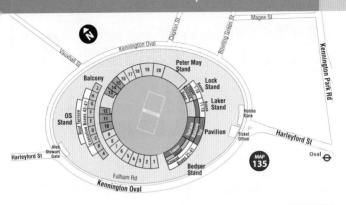

General Information

NFT Map: 135
Telephone: 020 7582 6660
Website: www.surreycricket.com
             the-brit-oval
Location: The Brit Oval, Kennington,
             London, SE11 5SS

Overview

What better way to while away a sunny summer's day than at The Oval cricket ground, typically alongside hundreds of other shirkers who also called in sick? The Oval is one of London's twin icons of the game, alongside Lord's in North London, and boasts a rich history stretching all the way back to 1846, when it was converted from cabbage patch to cricket pitch. It now plays host to Surrey County and international test matches, including the biennial England-Australia slugfest "The Ashes." Live international cricket remains a boozy, good natured affair with English fanbase 'The Barmy Army' typically belting out salty chants and cheering occasional streakers. County cricket is a mellower, no less enjoyable event, with readily available tickets and a good portion of the crowd more interested in today's paper than the action in front of them. Taxing it ain't.

How to Get There

By Car: Driving to the Oval is not ideal, because parking is near impossible. Should you be willing to risk it, it's situated on the A202, near the junction with the A3 and A24, south of Vauxhall Bridge. As ever with London driving, you'll need your A to Z and nerves of steel.

By Public Transport: The Oval boasts its own, eponymous tube stop on the Northern Line, from which the stadium is a few hundred yards walk. Determinedly overground travellers should alight at Vauxhall, from which Oval is a ten minute jaunt, tops. Buses 36, 185 and 436 stop right outside the ground too.

How to Get Tickets

Tickets for Surrey county matches are relatively easy to get hold of, though seats for some fixtures can only be bought on site on the day of the match. Check www.surreycricket.com/tickets/domestic for a list of fixtures and availability. International matches tend to sell out very quickly indeed—touts or online sales sites like eBay and Gumtree are usually the best option, at a price. Check out www.surreycricket.com/tickets/international for more info. Ticketmaster also offers tickets to all Oval fixtures at www.ticketmaster.co.uk/venue/147862.

General Information

NFT Map: 32
Telephone: 020 8743 0262
Ticket hotline: 08444 777 007
Website: www.qpr.
                premiumtv.co.uk
Location: Loftus Road Stadium,
                South Africa Road,
                Shepherds Bush,
                W12 7PA

Overview

Once-itinerant football club Queen's Park Rangers have called Loftus Road—based, confusingly, in Shepherd's Bush—home since 1917, give or take a few seasons. Their footballing fortunes have yo-yoed through the decades: once a whisker away from winning Division One in the years before it became the Premiership; they now scuffle about in the Championship (or second division, in layman's terms), with one eye fixed anxiously on the precipitous drop to Football League One (or third division, it says here). New ownership, including Formula One oligarch Bernie Ecclestone, promises better times and a serious injection of cash, though a rabid fanbase would dispute times had ever been sour. Pundits reckon the Hoops, as partisans know them, could see a Chelsea FC-style resurgence in 2009 if owner money is spent, as expected, on new blood.

How to Get There

By Car: Whether you're approaching Loftus Road from the North (from the M1 through the A406 and A40), East (via the A40(M)), South (from the A3 and A219) or West (up the M4 via the A315 and A402

on a wing and a prayer), all routes lead through White City. Once there, turn right off Wood Lane into South Africa Road. Don't even set off without your NFT London, or emergency rations. For the brave, full details of all journeys are available at QPR's official website listed above.

By Public Transport: The majority of QPR fans are local and rely either on nearby tube stops (White City on the Central Line, Shepherd's Bush on the Hammersmith and City Line), any of buses 72, 95, or 220 to White City Station, or overground train to Acton Central, followed by a quick bus ride.

How to Get Tickets

As long as QPR are knee deep in the Championship, tickets are relatively easy to get hold of, either via the Rangers' ticket website (eticketing.co.uk/qpr) or phone numbers listed above, or by visiting the Loftus Road box office on game days. They're around £25 per person.

General Information

Ticketline: 0844 499 5000
Website: www.spurs.co.uk
Location: Bill Nicholson Way,
748 High Road,
London, N17 OAP

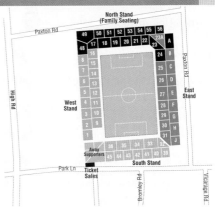

Overview

Even the Spurs die-hard would admit that White Hart Lane is a little scruffy. The team moved into the stadium over a century ago, and it's been growing slowly more dog-eared ever since. Few grounds in the capital are located further from a tube stop, and it's in a corner of London where even the police dogs walk in pairs. But that's part of the old ground's charm. More than most fans, the Spurs faithful have a tight grasp of history (which could be because there's been no league title there since 1961). And it shows at the stadium—supporters even chant about what a grand old team Spurs are. But that song only gets sporadic outings. Most of the chants that ring around White Hart Lane are about how much the fans hate Arsenal. It's a rivalry that's as intense as any in football—and as Arsenal started out in the south of the city, only moving across the river in 1913, Spurs claim of being Kings of North London isn't such a wild one. And the division has grown deeper since Arsenal moved into their corporate-branded Emirates Stadium. While Spurs have remained in touch with their Jewish roots—old ladies still sell bagels inside the ground—Arsenal have become the bourgeoisie of football. Their fans may sneer down their lattes at the Spurs supporters who piss in the sinks, but be honest—the queue's huge, the game's kicking off: wouldn't you?

How to Get There

By Car: The area's congested at the best of times; on match days, traffic can grind to a standstill. But if you don't mind a bit of gridlock, White Hart Lane is on the Tottenham High Road (A1010) a mile south of the North Circular (A406). This is easily accessible from junction 25 of the M25, in itself a temple to traffic.

By Public Transport: The nearest tube is Seven Sisters (Victoria Line), which is a 25 minute walk away. But at least if you work up a hunger from all that walking there's hundreds of kebab shops en route. White Hart Lane overland station, which runs from Liverpool Street through Seven Sisters, is a five-minute walk from the ground. Bus routes 279, 349, 149, 259 run closest to the stadium, but many more pass nearby.

How to Get Tickets

Although home games normally sell out, tickets are fairly easy to get hold of. Club members get first refusal at tickets (it costs £32 to join), ten days before going on sale to the public. But few games sell out before this stage, and if you're savvy about the on-sale dates, snapping up tickets is reasonably simple. To get on the season ticket waiting list, you have to become a One Hotspur Bronze Member. This costs £47; but as the club's fortunes are on the rise, the wait could be some time.

(371)

General Information

Website: www.rfu.com
Phone: 0870 405 2000
Location: Twickenham Stadium,
Rugby Road, Twickenham, TW1 1DZ

Overview

The home of English rugby, Twickenham is a behemoth of a stadium. An ugly chunk of concrete seemingly dumped from a great height onto a quiet London suburb, Twickenham lacks the charm and character of Ireland's Landsdowne Road and Scotland's Murrayfield, and has been all but pushed to the sidelines by the magnificent Millennium Stadium in Wales. However, the stadium has largely remained a fortress when it comes to England Internationals. Cheered on by 82,000 well-spoken, white-shirted fans booming out 'Swing Low Sweet Chariot' probably helps. Maybe the England players absorb the unfussy and uncompromising nature of their surroundings into their psyche on match days. Critics would argue that their style of rugby is as ugly and bland as the stadium they play in. This would be harsh if England hadn't consistently under-performed after carrying off the Rugby World Cup in 2003. Twickenham also hosts a series of Rugby tournaments and exhibition matches, including the famous 'Sevens', in addition to the occasional Premiership fixture. Outside the Rugby season, the stadium is given over to rock concerts for international bands like Bon Jovi and R.E.M.

How to Get There

By Car: Twickenham is very accessible by road - if you live in the South. The M3 motorway turns into the A316 that passes the stadium, carrying on into central London. Certain roads get closed down on match days so drivers should allow plenty of time. Parking at the stadium is extremely limited and should be booked in advance. Resident permits are helpfully required for all roads bordering the stadium so the best thing to do is park in the general vicinity and walk the rest of the way.

By Public Transport: Mainline trains run to Twickenham station from Waterloo and Reading. London Underground runs to Richmond on the District Line where shuttle buses will take

fans to the stadium (50p outbound. Free return) Hounslow is an alternative Underground station but shuttle buses only run from Twickenham to Hounslow station so you will have to make it to the stadium under your own steam. Bus numbers 281, 267 and H22 all have regular services passing close to the stadium.

How to Get Tickets

England rugby tickets are hot property, commanding higher prices than top football games. As competition games are relatively infrequent, tickets sell out well in advance so keep checking the website for updates on ticket releases. Premiership tickets and friendly matches are easier to come by but will generally sell out. If you don't get lucky in advance, rugby touts (slightly less aggressive than their football cousins) will happily make your wallet lighter for you. Ticketmaster is the best option for concerts or Gumtree and Craigslist for re-sales and swaps.

General Information

Website: www.whufc.com
Phone: 020 8548 2794
Location: Boleyn Ground,
Green Street,
London E13 9AZ

Overview

Perennial under-achievers, West Ham's most recent pursuit of glory saw them knocked out of the 2007 FA Cup Final by Liverpool in one of the best matches in memory. Sadly, their heroic endeavours are rarely translated into decent Premiership runs—flirtations with relegation are a more common event. A lack of finance seems to be the main problem, with the talented products of West Ham's famous 'Academy' getting nicked by richer rivals. Flirtations with money men have seen the club's fingers get seriously burnt—something the fiercely loyal supporters don't deserve. Hammers fans are as vocal as any and the club makes up for its recent lack of success with passion and a gleeful hatred of the 'bigger' London clubs. 35,000 'Irons' fans singing the Hammer's anthem, 'I'm forever blowing bubbles,' is some spectacle. Over the years, West Ham has been unfairly tainted by association with the ICF hooligan firm. Largely active in the '70s and '80s, a 2005 film, 'Green Street' did its best to rekindle unwanted memories. The drama was undermined slightly by giving the lead role to a hobbit. These days, thanks to CCTV and high ticket prices, the Premiership is a largely peaceful affair. Under the stewardship of current manager Alan Curbishley, it should only be a matter of time before West Ham find their feet again and start a serious league challenge.

How to Get There

By Car: Driving in London is a waste of time even on the best of days, but try it on match days and you are asking for trouble. East London is a warren of one way streets, dead ends and no through roads. You are likely to either miss kick-off or get a parking ticket or both.

By Public Transport: The district line will 'whisk' you from central London to Upton Park in half an hour or so. The Boleyn Ground is 5 minutes walk from the underground station.

How to Get Tickets

Unless you want to pay through the nose for tickets against the big clubs, you should be able to find spares for the smaller fixtures. West Ham is a relatively small ground with a dedicated, hardcore following. Being less glamorous than Chelsea et al means that casual fans have a better chance of watching a game for a decent price.

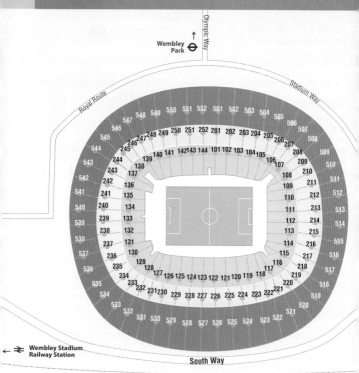

General Information

Phone: 0844 980 8001
Website: www.wembleystadium.com
Location: Wembley Stadium,
           Wembley HA9 0WS

Overview

Wembley Stadium enjoys a strange position in the British psyche. For football fans it's most significant as the scene of England's only World Cup win back in 1966, as well as numerous pitch invasions by angry / jubilant Scottish fans whenever their national team came down to play. Plus, a generation of British bands have grown up dreaming of the day they'd bellow: "hello Wem-ber-ley, are you ready to rock?!!" to tens of thousands of people who've just paid a fiver for a chewy patty of minced spleen 'n' testicles in a dry bun. For these sentimental reasons, then, very few people complained that the National Stadium was a bit of a crap-hole stuck in an inaccessible suburb of West London. By the late '90s the place was looking a bit battered, so they knocked it down and then very, very slowly, and at tremendous, tabloid-scandalising expense, built a replacement on the same site. The result is, just about, worth it. There are none of the blind spots for spectators that the old stadium used to have, plus it has far greater leg-room for 90-thousand-plus people and much more comfortable seating. It also looks fantastically imposing as you walk out of Wembley Park tube with its massive arch curving into the sky. A trip here might not make your knees go "all trembly" as fans used to sing but for football lovers it's one of the world's great venues. They also have a special removable running track for athletics and, to the disgust of "soccer" purists, they've even let American "football" teams play here, too.

How to Get There

By Car: Short of hiring snipers to pick drivers off as they approach the mighty arch, the Stadium could hardly do more to discourage visitors from driving. "Wembley Stadium is a public transport destination. Please leave your car behind," the website primly advises. However, if you are some kind of die-hard, planet-raping petrol-head you'll see signs pointing to the stadium from Great Central Way

onwards. There are very few parking spaces at the Stadium itself and these need to be booked in advance for £25 or £12 for disabled users and, despite the prices, they often sell out. On match days, or when there's anything else happening, the local area becomes residents' parking only, too. Yes, they really don't want you to bring your car.

By Public Transport: The nearest Tube is Wembley Park on the Metropolitan and Jubilee line. Wembley Central (on the Bakerloo line) is about 10–15 minutes walk and there's also Wembley Stadium mainline train station with links all over the country. If you're travelling from outside London there are National Express coaches from 43 different towns and cities.

How to Get Tickets

Easier said than done. 'Club Wembley' have kindly created a 'ten year seat licence'—no doubt to re-coup the massive overspend that accompanied completion of the stadium. These licences give owners access to all major events hosted at Wembley and its worth going on the website to laugh at the ridiculous prices. A 'one-off licence fee' costs from £1,650 to £19,226. Annual season tickets are on top of that. Cloud Cuckoo Land. 'Normal' people can buy tickets to England games through the FA (you need to be a member), for football and rugby cup games through the respective clubs and tickets for one off events and shows through Ticketmaster. It's always worth checking Gumtree.com as you never know who might be flogging off a golden ticket to the highest bidder.

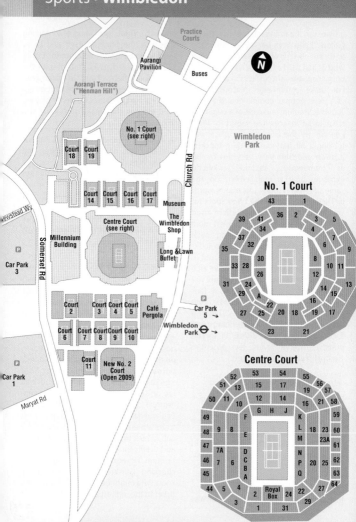

Practice Courts

Aorangi Pavilion

Buses

Aorangi Terrace ("Henman Hill")

No. 1 Court (see right)

Court 18   Court 19

Court 14   Court 15   Court 16   Court 17

evstead Wy

Millennium Building

Centre Court (see right)

Somerset Rd

Church Rd

Wimbledon Park

Museum

The Wimbledon Shop

Long & Lawn Buffet

P Car Park 3

Court 2   Court 3   Court 4   Court 5

Café Pergola

P Car Park 5 →

Court 6   Court 7   Court 8   Court 9   Court 10

Wimbledon Park →

P Car Park 1

Court 11

New No. 2 Court (Open 2009)

Maryat Rd

No. 1 Court

43 1
39 41 36 2 3 5
37 34
35 32 30 8 7 9
33 28 26 12 10 11
31 24 A 14 15 13
29 22 16
27 25 20 18 19 17
23 21

Centre Court

53 54
51 52 13 15 17 55 56
50 11 10 12 14 19 21 57 58
49 G H J K 59
48 9 8 F L 18 23 61
47 7A E M 23A
46 7 6 D C B A N P 20 25 62
45 Q 63
44 5 4 Royal Box 24 22 27 64
3 1 31 29

General Information

Telephone: 020 8944 1066
Website: www.wimbledon.org
Location: The All England Lawn
Tennis and Croquet Club,
Church Road, Wimbledon,
SW19 5AE

Overview

New balls please! If it's not pissing it down—which is a big if—Wimbledon's All England Tennis and Croquet Club is the place to witness the world's finest tennis players do battle on rye grass courts, home as it is to the oldest major Championship in the game each June/July. But this is also a place to be seen and to be merry—sure, it's about the tennis, but it's also about strawberries and cream (of which 62,000 pounds and 1,540 gallons worth are sold each year respectively), the free flowing champagne, the celebrity crowd, and the Ralph Lauren-designed ballboy and ballgirl outfits. And if you can't actually get a ticket for the tournament—and the All England Club makes approximately 1,500 of them available each day, if you're prepared to camp out overnight in the queue—you can always sit yourself on Henman Hill at the northern end of the complex, where a vast television screen allows you to watch British players systematically eliminated in typically heartbreaking fashion. Really, we should stick to darts.

How to Get There

By Car: During the tournament, traffic and parking are nightmarish propositions, and you're better off using public transport. Nonetheless, the determined will need to take the A219 from the A3, and turn off left onto Church Road once in Wimbledon itself.

By Public Transport: Wimbledon railway station is a short journey from both Waterloo and Clapham Junction, and is otherwise serviced (Vicar!) by trains from towns right across the South of England. From here, board the London General shuttle bus straight to the grounds; they depart every five minutes or so during the tournament. Tube users should head for Southfields on the District Line, from where a London General shuttle also operates. Those who prefer to saunter can mosey on down Wimbledon Park Road heading south for ten minutes or so, and you can also walk it from Wimbledon Park tube station, heading north-west.

How to Get Tickets

You can (legally) come by tickets to Wimbledon in two ways—one, apply in advance to the public 'ballot', via the website above, in the hope you are selected at random to purchase tickets (closing date end of December). Two, join the serpentine, overnight queues for on-the-day tickets, of which five hundred are usually made available for each of Centre, Number One and Number Two Courts. Then, of course, there are all the other methods of which you're already no doubt aware.

Overview

Any bowling buff will tell you that there are two types of bowling in this country. Ten Pin Bowling, the ghastly Americanized import, is by far the most popular among Londoners and the generally disrespectful 'Youth Of Today'. Crown Green Bowling is a far more serene, (elderly) gentlemanly pursuit complete with its own rules and rituals. Of course, bowlers of both persuasions are served in London, ensuring that violent confrontations between the two groups are kept to a minimum.

London's Ten Pin bowlers have been spoiled rotten of late. With the opening of new bowling lanes like 'All Star Lanes' (in Bayswater, Holborn and soon Brick Lane) the onset of yuppie money and boho style has transformed this past-time into an aesthetically pleasing but financially painful experience. At a peak time rate of £8.50 per person per game (your average game is a mere 10 minutes!) it's no wonder these shiny palaces of faux vintage design and Americana are populated largely by corporate parties and big spenders. Even cooler and slightly cheaper is the Bloomsbury Bowling Lanes (Holborn) which boasts an American diner and rates of £36 per lane per hour—doable if you have a large posse. It's even become a hip live music venue for indie gigs!

For families and the penniless, London has plenty of more 'traditional' British bowling lanes. By this, of course, we mean cavernous warehouses with pumping chart music, scary underage drinkers and sticky air hockey tables. Try the classic Rowans (Finsbury Park) which at its priciest is a mere £3.70 per person per game or Queens (Bayswater) which has also has an ice rink to cool off those skittle blues.

And what of Green Bowling? Well, being an outdoor pursuit in Britain, it's safe to say it is primarily a Summer affair. When the sun is out you'll find bowling greens in all the major parks; Hyde Park offers a set of woods for £5 (with no time limit) May till October.

After suffering at the hands of boho and cheapo Ten Pin bowling facilities you may find that there can be no better way to waste an afternoon than to sit around a bowling green in Finsbury Park with a beer in hand, laughing at your idiot friends' attempts to hit the 'jack'. Maybe those elderly gentlemen are on to something...

Bowling	Address	Phone	Map
All Star Lanes	Victoria House, Bloomsbury Pl	020 7025 2676	4
All Star Lanes	6 Porchester Gardens	020 7313 8363	30
Bloomsbury Bowling Lanes	Bedford Way	020 7183 1979	4
Hyde Park	Hyde Park	020 7262 3474	n/a
Queens	17 Queensway	020 7229 0172	30
Rowans	10 Stroud Green Rd	020 8800 1950	62

Overview

Nothing combines relaxation and hypertension quite like golf, nor indeed knee-length socks, spats and flat caps. For golfing Londoners, opportunities to play must be sought towards the outskirts of the capital, where the city shore is lapped once more by greenery and open space. You can, of course, take your one wood out onto London's pavements and practise your fade drive there, but you're odds on to be arrested if you do.

You'll be better received moving clockwise around London from the North, at establishments such as the Highgate Golf Club and Muswell Hill Golf Club. Both are highbrow member institutions with epic fairways, open nonetheless to the public, as long as that public is wearing a decent shirt. Eighteen holes at each are in the £30-40 range, which is also the case at the Hampstead Golf Club, home of one of England's toughest front nines. Nearby Finchley Golf Club is similarly priced for visitors but also offers some neat specials such as winter green fees in the £25 range and knockdown prices for twelve holes of 'twilight golf'. A little further north, Mill Hill Golf Club is a shade cheaper though no less satisfying.

In the south-east, the Royal Blackheath Golf Club positions itself as the oldest in the world, which might be why playing eighteen holes as a visitor requires a small trust fund, at £50 during summer weekdays. Moving further west, the Central London Golf Centre is a no-nonsense 'pay-and-play' establishment offering nine full-length holes to golfers of all standards for a little more than a tenner. The Wimbledon Park Golf Club is another quality members club open to visitors, while nearby Royal Wimbledon Golf Club terms itself a 'very private' club—visitors are welcome but will be required to apply in writing, prove handicap and, in all likelihood, undergo some kind of permanently scarring initiation ritual. Access to each of these Wimbledon clubs kicks off at a chokingly high £70 for eighteen holes. You could buy a second hand Playstation for that. The London Scottish Golf Club on Wimbledon Common is much more like it, at £20 a round, though a pillar-box red top is compulsory for all. Out west, Dukes Meadows Golf Club in Chiswick offers nine three-par holes, a driving range and function rooms, all at a reasonable price.

For golfers who really are determined not to leave Zone One, there is one option after all. Urban Golf, with venues in Soho (W1) and Smithfield (EC1), is the last word in golf simulation, with the chance to play, virtual-style, some of the world's top courses. It also boasts well-stocked bars and chic lounge areas. You just know the purists will loathe it.

Golf Clubs	Address	Phone	Map
Central London Golf Centre	Burntwood Ln	020 8871 2468	n/a
Dukes Meadows Golf Club	Dukes Meadow	020 8995 0537	n/a
Finchley	Frith Ln	020 8346 1133	n/a
Hampstead Golf Club	82 Winnington Rd	020 8455 0203	n/a
Highgate Golf Club	Denewood Rd	020 8340 3745	n/a
Holland Park	Ilchester Pl	020 7602 2226	34
London Scottish Golf Club	Windmill Rd	020 8788 0135	n/a
Mill Hill Golf Club	100 Barnet Way	020 8959 2339	n/a
Muswell Hill Golf Club	Rhodes Ave	020 8888 1764	n/a
Royal Blackheath Golf Club	Court Rd	020 8550 1795	n/a
Urban Golf	33 Great Pulteney St	020 7434 4300	10
Urban Golf	12 Smithfield St	020 7248 8600	15
Wilbledon Park Golf Club	Home Park Rd	020 8946 1250	n/a

Overview

Remember the Levi's ad in the pool hall? The one which had The Clash's *Should I Stay Or Should I Go?* as the soundtrack? Yeah, that one. It conjured up a pretty cool image, right? Unfortunately London's pool halls have not had the retro revamp (is that an oxymoron?) that bowling is currently enjoying (All Star Lanes, Bloomsbury Bowling) so it's rare to actually find a place where you can stand around looking like James Dean, kissing your teeth, chewing on a tooth pick, and generally inviting any hustler to take you on without like, really being taken on by someone from the Russian/Turkish mafia. Of course, if you just want to chill, have a few beers and play some 8-ball with your buddies there is the ever reliable Elbow Rooms (Shoreditch/Islington/Westbourne Grove) and the slightly less groovy but no less functional Riley's (Victoria/Clapham/Lewisham). The Islington Elbow Room has experienced a couple of shootings of the gun variety in recent years, so try not to spill your pint on anyone as you go from bar to pool table. The Shoreditch Elbow Room has a ping pong table in the summer. Why it is a seasonal attraction is uncertain but us Brits tend to associate sports according

to weather it seems. We also inextricably link shooting some pool with having a drink or two, but it is often the lesser red and yellow-balled "pub" pool table (funnily enough) rather than the greater spotted (and striped) genuine American pool table which is found within the confines of the few remaining non-chain traditional pubs in London. The Westbury Bar in Kilburn however, has three American pool tables in a rather swank environment of leather Chesterfields, parquet flooring and red lampshades. Food is pan-Asian and roasts are served on Sundays, adding to a pub vibe. 19:20 in Clerkenwell has more of a pool hall feel with media types taking their game a little more seriously at the end of the working day. If you do fancy something a little more louche, there are many a pool and snooker hall to be found on the edges of central London which can offer a grittier atmosphere. Bomonti on the Kingsland Road is a Russian Bar where various art "happenings", poetry readings and live music nights occur as well as being a near-open all hours venue to play pool. The fact that Pete Doherty has been known to frequent the premises will either pique your interest or put you right off.

Pool & Snooker	Address	Phone	Map
19:20	20 Great Sutton St	020 7253 1920	6
Bomonti	340 Kingsland Rd	020 7923 1548	88
The Elbow Room	97 Curtain Rd	020 7613 1316	84
The Elbow Room	89 Chapel Market	020 7278 3244	80
The Elbow Room	103 Westbourne Grove	020 7221 5211	30
Riley's	638 Wandsworth Rd	020 7498 0432	142
Riley's	16 Semley Pl	020 7824 8261	19
Rowans	10 Stroud Green Rd	020 8800 1950	62
The Westbury	34 Kilburn High Rd	020 7625 7500	68

Tennis

Ah…the other beautiful game, beloved of park fence jumpers and upper class grunters alike. Like many popular sports, tennis may have originated in Britain, but we're pretty consistent in our ineptitude at it. This is not for the lack of trying: the country's capital is packed full of tennis clubs, outdoor park courts and large sports complexes.

Tennis is certainly not as exclusive as it once was, with an hour's playing a lot cheaper than ten-pin bowling, for example. You can mince about amidst leafy surroundings in Hyde Park (Hyde Park Sports Centre, 020 7262 3474), flail in the dark depths of Finsbury Park on a turn-up-and-play basis, or in the luxury of the historic Queens Club (www.queensclub.co.uk, 020 7386 3429 for membership information). Also commendable are the Paddington Sports Club (020 7286 8448) in Maida Vale and the courts in Regent's Park: go to www.tennisintheparks.co.uk for information on, uh, playing tennis in parks. Indicative of the new equalitarian nature of the game are Tennis London International (www.tennislondon.com) who take pride in being 'the largest gay and lesbian tennis group in the UK.' But it's not all democratic: there's always Wimbledon (www.wimbledon.org, which due to the jaw dropping ticket prices, still is as exclusive as it's always been. If you still want to get caught up in the annual tennis frenzy, head to Henman Hill, or Murray Mound, or whatever it's called these days. Essentially a hill outside Centre Court, here you can sit on the grass and watch the action on video screens with all the other poor proles who don't have any kidneys left to trade for a ticket.

Squash

Like some weird secret society, squash players spend their time locked indoors, organised into little private clubs and engaged in an activity which will eventually mess them up. Squash is hard—just ask your poor knees. The squash court is a high-octane containment tank swimming in adrenalin, which explains why Londoners have taken to it with such gusto. A court at Sobell Center (020 7609 2166) in Finsbury Park for example, is near impossible to book at peak times. In Shepherd's Bush, there's the exclusive squash club New Grampians (020 7603 4255) which is lush, but there are sizeable membership fees to match. Be warned—a lot of sports centres don't have squash facilities, but somewhere like the Oasis Sports Centre (0207 831 1804) in Tottenham Court Road is a church to all things sweaty and squashy…and you can go for an outdoor swim afterwards too. For a quirkier court try Maiden Lane (020-7267 9586)—a community centre in a housing estate, which has one beat-up court for £6 an hour. If there isn't a yoga class in progress, that is.

Badminton/Table Tennis

They may be worlds apart in many ways, but badminton and table tennis are usually offered in the same place, and both are 'genteel' sports in which it is almost acceptable to be beaten by the opposite sex (whichever sex you are). Badminton is especially popular across the board, with almost all sizeable sports centres offering courts and equipment. However, if you've any experience in attempting to book a court at most public sports complexes you'll know of the often depressing amount of phone wrangling and frustration that arises from these exchanges. Chief perpetrator is Kings Hall Sports Centre (020 8985 2158) in Lower Clapton, who will test your patience to inhumane limits. The Brixton Recreation Centre (020 7926 9779) caters for badminton and squash players but always sound like they can't wait to get you off the phone; their rates are around £7 for badminton, which is pretty competitive. The Sobell Centre, as mentioned above, also caters for table tennis (doesn't ping pong sound nicer?) and badminton. The best strategy is to phone your local centre to ascertain which racquet sports they cater for and then prepare yourself to be either double-booked, misinformed or given a free session depending on the ability of the desk assistant!

Sports • Yoga

Overview

As the nascent city of 'Londinium' was being named by the Romans in AD 43, in Asia the practice of yoga was entering its third or fourth millennium. Nineteen hundred years on, at last it found its way out west, and London's yoga establishments have flourished ever since. Essentially, the capital's schools can be divided into those concerned primarily with physical fitness—often the larger institutions offering a range of styles—and those with a more spiritual bent. Of the former, Go Yoga in Shepherd's Bush is a fine example, offering yoga and pilates for adults and kids alike, while the popular Triyoga centres in Primrose Hill and Covent Garden are one-stop holistic shops for the upwardly mobile set. More specialised centres include Bikram Yoga College of India in Kentish Town, and its partner Bikram Yoga City—

bring water and a towel for hard wearing, specially heated sessions—and the Iyengar Yoga Institute in Maida Vale, which offers a free introductory class. Special mention also goes to Fulham Yogashala, a newish venture offering all sorts including, unnervingly, 'power yoga'. Still, entering the peaceful surroundings of Yogashala is, according to one client, like getting a hug. Those more spiritual schools include the wonderful Sivanada Yoga Centre, an oasis of serenity in the midst of Putney boasting resident yogi teachers, and the Satyananda Yoga Centre in Clapham with its deep focus on yoga-meditation techniques. Shanti Sadam, out west, is also more concerned with inner stillness than downward dogs. And hidden away in Archway, the Kriya Centre runs a series of kundalini yoga classes in humble but hospitable surroundings—Ohm tastic!

Yoga Centers	Address	Phone	Website	Map
Alchemy	Stables Market	020 7267 6188	www.alchemythecentre.co.uk	71
Battersea Yoga	152 Northcote Rd	020 7978 7995	www.batterseayoga.com	140
Bikram Yoga City	6 Vestry St	020 7336 6330	www.bikramyoga.co.uk/studio_city.html	84
Bikram's Yoga College Of India	173 Queen's Crescent	020 7692 6900	www.bikramyoga.co.uk/studio_north.html	71
Fulham Yogashala	11 Lettice St	079 5609 1696	www.fulhamyogashala.co.uk	48
Go Yoga	140 Percy Rd	020 8740 1989	www.go-yoga.co.uk	n/a
The Hidden Space	93 Falkland Rd	020 8347 3400	www.thehiddenspace.co.uk	55
Islington Yoga	357 City Rd	020 7704 6796	www.islingtonyoga.com	83
Iyengar Yoga Institute	223 Randolph Ave	020 7624 3080	www.iyi.org.uk	27
Jamyang Buddhist Centre	43 Renfrew Rd	020 7820 8787	www.jamyang.co.uk	112
The Kriya Centre	25 Bickerton Rd	020 7272 5811	www.karamkriya.com	59
The Lotus Exchange	Black Prince Rd	020 7463 2234	www.lotusexchange.com	131
North London Buddhist Centre	72 Holloway Rd	020 7700 1177	www.northlondonbuddhistcentre.com	74
Satyananda Yoga Centre	70 Thurleigh Rd	020 8673 4869	www.syclondon.com	147
Shanti Sadan Yoga Centre	29 Chepstow Villas	020 7727 7846	www.shantisadan.org	29
Shoreditch Studio	49 Curtain Rd	020 7012 1238	www.shoreditchstudio.co.uk	8
Siddha Yoga Sangham Of Europe	63 Collier St	020 7278 0567		79
Sivanada Yoga	51 Felsham Rd	020 8426 9795	www.sivananda.co.uk	136
Surya Yoga Studio (CLOSED TILL JULY 09)	9 Park Hill	020 7622 4257	www.suryayoga.co.uk	149
Templeton House Yoga Studio,	34 Chiswell St	020 7074 6000	www.templetonhouse.co.uk	7
Triyoga	6 Erskine Road	020 7483 3344	www.triyoga.co.uk	70
Urban Bikram	24 Shacklewell Ln	020 7254 3060		86
Yoga Place	449 Bethnal Green Rd	020 7739 5195	www.yogaplace.co.uk	92
Yoga Therapy Center	92 Pentonville Rd	020 7689 3040	www.yogatherapy.org	80

There's nothing quite like an obesity epidemic to make a city sporty. We're constantly being told that we're swelling to huge new levels. The message is worrying: buck up fatties, or you won't even fit into your own coffin. But with a London Olympics on the horizon, grassroots sport has been thrust into the spotlight. Part of the package that won the Games was to build a sporting legacy. And in the hope that we won't all be housebound when the Olympics rolls into town, lower-level sport is seeing increased investment. London's sizeable ethnic communities have also brought weird and wonderful games with them (American Football? In London? Not in our lifetimes). Dozens of leagues, in dozens of sports, gather every evening to try and beat the bulge.

General tips

A good starting point is the Gumtree website (www.gumtree.com). Their sports and community section is full of ads trying to fills gaps in sports teams. And as it was started by born-to-sweat Aussies, it never lets up in sheer quantity of athletic opportunities. The local press is also a decent bet. All London boroughs have their own newspapers, who cover amateur sports with as much enthusiasm as the professionals. You may never make it in the big leagues, but at least you can be a hero in Camden. But one area where London struggles is with the concept of pick-up games. Perhaps it's part of our reserved nature, but it's unusual to just rock up at a park and challenge whoever's there. By all means try, but you may get rebuked by a stiff upper lip.

Football

Sunday league football in London used to have a reputation of being rough. For many years it was the preserve of hungover builders, who wanted ninety minutes letting off steam by kicking people around. But it's moved on slightly from those days, with a more general acceptance of skill and less emphasis placed on pain. The spiritual home of recreational football is Hackney Marshes. The east London site has a whopping 87 pitches—so many leagues and teams play there that it's worth just turning up and asking around. If you draw a blank there, then the FA website (www.thefa.com) has a club locator search. Regardless of where you live, you'll get a mammoth list of clubs. The hardest part of finding a team in London is narrowing down who it is you want to play for. Five-a-side football is also booming in London. In the city centre, where space is at a premium, it's often the only way of getting in a game. Powerleague (www.powerleague.co.uk) organise leagues around the capital, though these can be pricey. A cheaper option is to head to a leisure centre with a five-a-side pitch. They often run leagues and are less profit-driven than the private companies. Lists of leisure centres can be found on specific borough's website (such as Islington's www.islington.gov.uk).

Rugby

Don't mind drinking pints of your team-mates' urine? Enjoy a good eye-gouging? Then you must be a rugby fan! The Rugby in London website (www.rugbyinlondon.co.uk) is a Bible for lovers of casual violence, as it lists hundreds of clubs, contact details and even training venues and times. Female fans of egg chasing are also well represented. Most teams play around south-west London, though there's a few more dotted around the city. A full list is on the RFU Women's website (www.rfuwlonse.co.uk). If you don't fancy the full-on ear-biting code of the sport there's a flourishing touch rugby scene in London. In this form of the game tackling is represented by tagging your opponent. It's an altogether less bloody type of rugby, although you're still allowed to indulge in the booze-fuelled rituals that the contact players enjoy. In2Touch (www.in2touch.com) lists a few of these leagues.

Cricket

As a sport that takes up plenty of space, you have to head slightly out of town to play cricket. Most London clubs play in either the Essex, Middlesex or Surrey leagues, in the outskirts of the capital. The Play-Cricket website (www.play-cricket.co.uk) has a full rundown on London clubs.

Athletics and the London Marathon

Every spring, London's runners dust down their gorilla costumes and tackle the London Marathon. If you feel up to it then you have to plan ahead; places are limited and dished out via a ballot. If you need a helping hand in the run up to the race, there's a list of jogging and road-running clubs at www.onesite.co.uk/find/running. As well as getting you in shape, so you don't die after 20 miles, they can help you get a spot in the starting line-up. And if you catch the bug of competitive athletics, there are six clubs who compete in the London Inter Club Challenge (www.licc.co.uk).

Miscellaneous

For fans of all things Irish, there's the London Gaelic Sports Association (www.londongaa.org); American footballers can get their fix with the British American Football League (www.bafl.org.uk); and if tight shorts and sleeveless shirts are your thing there's the British Aussie Rules Association (www.barfl.co.uk; or you could just join the navy).

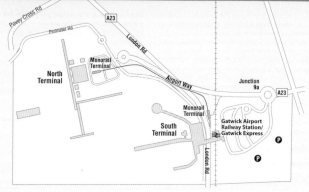

Airline	Terminal	Phone Number
Adria Airways	North	020 7437 0143
Aer Lingus	South	0870 876 5000
Afriqiyah	South	0870 242 2267
Air Algerie	South	020 8750 3300
Air Baltic	South	0870 607 2772
Air Comet	North	020 7290 7887
Air Malta	South	0845 607 3710
Air Namibia	North	0870 774 0965
Air Southwest	North	0870 240 8202
Air Transat	South	020 7616 9187
Atlas Blue	North	020 7307 5803
Aurigny	South	0871 871 0717
Azerbaijan Airlines	South	0870 760 5757
Belavia Belarusian Airlines	South	020 7393 1201
BH Air (Balkan Holidays)	South	0845 130 1114
bmi	South	0870 60 70 555
British Airways	North	0844 493 0787
British Jet	South	0800 091 4444
Brussels Airlines	North	0870 735 2345
Bulgaria Air	South	
Centralwings	South	+48 22 558 0045
Clickair	North	00 800 25425247
Continental Airlines	North	0845 607 6760
Croatia Airlines	South	020 8563 0022
Cubana	South	020 7537 7909
Daallo Airlines	North	
Delta Air Lines	North	0800 414 767
easyJet	both	
Emirates	North	0870 243 2222
Estonian Air	South	020 7333 0196
Eurocypria	South	
First Choice Airways	North	0870 750 0001
Flybe	South	0871 700 2000
flyglobespan	South	0871 987 1687
flyLAL Lithuanian Airlines	North	01293 579 900

Airline	Terminal	Phone Number
Flystar Astraeus	North	01293 819 800
Ghana International Airlines	South	020 7100 1165
Karthago	South	
KD Avia	South	0871 423 5741
Kibris Turkish Airlines	North	020 7930 4851
Malev	North	0870 909 0577
Meridiana Airlines	South	0845 355 5588
Monarch Airlines Charter	South	0870 066 1472
Monarch Airlines Scheduled	South	0870 040 5040
Montenegro Airlines	South	
Northwest Airlines	South	0870 507 4074
norwegian.no	South	01279 680 500
Olympic Airways	South	0870 606 0460
Oman Air	South	0870 7707 319
Onur Air	South	
Pakistan International Airlines	South	0800 587 1023
Qatar Airways	South	020 7896 3636
Rossiya Airlines	South	
Ryanair	South	
SAS	South	0870 607 2772
SATA International	South	
Sterling	South	0870 787 8038
TAP Air Portugal	South	0845 601 0932
Tarom	North	020 7224 3693
Thomas Cook	South	0870 111 1111
ThomsonFly	North	0870 190 0737
Ukraine International Airlines	South	01293 596 609
US Airways	South	0845 600 3300
Virgin Atlantic Airways	South	0870 574 7747
Virgin Nigeria	North	0844 412 1788
Wizz Air	South	+48 22 351 9499
XL Airways	South	0870 169 0169
Zoom Airlines	South	0870 240 0055

General Information

West Sussex
RH6 0NP
General enquiries: 0870 000 2468
Lost property: 01293 503 162
www.gatwickairport.com

Overview

"Gatwick is the busiest single-runway airport in the world." No shit. And they say that like it's a good thing. Basically if you've ever had to go to Spain in high summer, you know the reasons why you shouldn't go to Gatwick: it's not on the Tube and, more importantly, the check-in zone is a sweat-filled free-for-all. Realistically, if being in an airport really was some kind of holiday, you wouldn't need to fly out of the place. Gatwick, though clunkier than some of the bigger, flashier airports, is not so bad to deal with if you have patience. Just don't be there when all the transatlantic flights arrive at the same time.

As far as amenities go, the usual suspects are all present, with convivial times available at Britain's premier diluting station, J.D. Wetherspoons, and the glamour of Knightsbridge miraculously squeezed into one of those little airport branches of Harrods—just in case you feel the need to inflict one of their god-awful teddy bears on another country. As far as eating's concerned, you could try something apart from McDonald's but then again why pretend to yourself that you're having a nice time when it's clearly not on the cards for the next few hours?

Which Terminal?

Trains arrive at the South Terminal, and there are more shops here – but if your flight is from the North Terminal, a free automated train will take you on the five minute transfer.

Getting There

A refreshingly good train service—the creatively-titled Gatwick Express (www.gatwickexpress.com) —runs from Victoria every 15 minutes 5.20 am–12:50 am; and hourly during the night. It takes 30 minutes and if you're near the rail hubs it is by far the most pleasant way to get there—though a single journey is going to set you back around £16. First Capital Connect run trains to Gatwick from St Pancras International and London Bridge which costs closer to £8 and take only about 45 minutes. Easybus coaches from Victoria Coach Station get to Gatwick in 40 minutes, and cost around £2–6 for a single.

To drive to Gatwick from the M25 you need to leave at Junction 7 and carry on southwards along the M23, following the signs. Leave the M23 at junction 9 and again, follow those handy signs to get to the appropriate terminal.

Parking

The short stay car park is recommended for up to five hours at a time, and is incremented every hour, with a maximum charge of £19.50 per 24 hours (or part thereof). For long stays there are several parks located 5-15 minutes away (via bus transfers) from the airport. These are best booked in advance. For the official Gatwick car park, charges are £8.60 per day 1–5 days and £8.20 for six days and over.This can be done through the BAA Gatwick website.

Car Hire

All the big names are represented, or you can try generic websites such as www.travelsupermarket.com/carhire.

Shops

There is the usual wide range of shops ranging from chemists to food/drink to fashion. Retail stores include Harrods, Monsoon, Nike, Quiksilver, Ray Ban, and Yo! Sushi.

Hotels

Alexander House	Langshott Manor
Arora International	Moathouse Hotel
Cambridge Hotel	Premier Travel Inn
Clarion Hotel	Ramada Plaza
Copthorne Hotel	Renaissance Hotel
Corner House Hotel	Russ Hill
Effingham Park Hotel	Skylane Hotel
Europa Hotel	Sofitel Hotel
Express	Thistle
Felbridge Hotel	Travelodge
George Hotel	Whitehouse
Hilton	Worth Hotel
Holiday Inn	
Ibis Hotel	

385

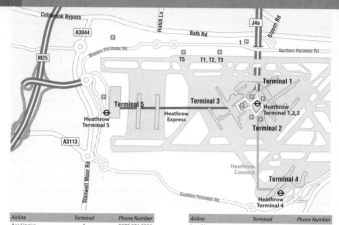

Airline	Terminal	Phone Number
Aer Lingus	1	0870 876 5000
Aeroflot	2	020 7355 2233
Air Algerie	2	020 8750 3300
Air Astana	2	01293 596 622
Air Canada	3	0871 220 1111
Air China	3	020 7630 0919
Air France	2	0870 142 4343
Air India	3	020 8560 9996
Air Malta	4	0845 607 3710
Air Mauritius	3	020 7434 4375
Air New Zealand	3	0800 028 4149
Air Seychelles	2	01293 596 656
Alitalia	2	0870 544 8259
All Nippon Airways	3	0870 837 8811
American Airlines	3	0845 778 9789
Asiana Airlines	1	020 8990 9880
Atlas Blue	2	020 7307 5803
Austrian Airlines	2	0845 601 0948
Azerbaijan Airlines	2	0870 760 5757
Bellview Airlines	2	020 7372 3770
Biman Bangladesh Airlines	3	020 7629 0252
Blue1 (SAS Group)		
bmi	1	0870 60 70 555
British Airways	1, 4, 5	0844 493 0787
Bulgaria Air	2	
Cathay Pacific Airways	3	020 8834 8888
China Eastern	2	020 7935 2676
Clickair	2	00 800 25425247
Continental Airlines	4	0845 607 6760
Croatia Airlines	2	020 8563 0022
CSA Czech Airlines	2	0870 444 3747
Cyprus Airways	1	020 8359 1333
Delta Air Lines	4	0800 414 767
Egypt Air	3	020 8759 3635
El Al Israel Airlines	1	020 7957 4100
Emirates	3	0870 243 2222
Ethiopian Airlines	3	020 8745 4235
Etihad Airways	3	0870 241 7121
Eva Air	3	020 7380 8300
Finnair	3	0870 241 4411
GB Airways	1	
Gulf Air	3	0870 777 1717
Iberia	2	0870 609 0500
Icelandair	1	0870 787 4020

Airline	Terminal	Phone Number
Iran Air	3	020 8759 0921
Japan Airlines	3	0845 774 7700
JAT Airways	2	020 8745 0899
Jet Airways	3	0800 026 5626
Kenya Airways	4	01784 888 222
Kibris Turkish Airlines	3	020 7930 4851
KLM Royal Dutch Airlines	4	0870 507 4074
Korean Air	3	0800 413 000
Kuwait Airways	3	020 8745 7772
Libyan Arab Airlines	2	020 8750 4066
LOT Polish Airlines	1	0845 601 0949
Lufthansa	2	0870 837 7747
Luxair	2	0800 389 9443
Malaysia Airlines System	3	0870 607 9090
MEA Middle East Airlines	3	020 7467 8000
Northwest Airlines	4	0870 507 4074
Olympic Airlines	2	0870 606 0460
Pakistan International Airlines	3	0800 587 1023
Qantas	4	0845 774 7767
Qatar Airways	3	020 7896 3636
Rossiya Airlines	2	
Royal Air Maroc	2	020 7439 4361
Royal Brunei Airlines	3	020 7584 6660
Royal Jordanian	3	020 7878 6300
SAS	3	0870 607 2772
Saudi Arabian Airlines	3	020 7798 9898
Singapore Airlines	3	0844 800 2380
South African Airways	1	0870 747 1111
Sri Lankan Airlines	3	020 8538 2000
Swiss International Airlines	2	0845 601 0956
Syrianair	2	020 7493 2851
TAM	4	020 8897 3700
TAP Air Portugal	2	0845 601 0932
Tarom	2	020 7224 3693
Thai Airways International	3	0870 606 0911
Transaero Airlines	1	0870 850 7761
Tunisair	2	020 7734 7644
Turkish Airlines	3	020 7766 9300
Turkmenistan Airlines	3	020 8577 2211
United Airlines	3	0845 844 4777
US Airways	1	0845 600 3300
Uzbekistan Airways	3	020 7935 4775
Virgin Atlantic Airways	3	0870 574 7747
Virgin Nigeria	3	0844 412 1788
Yemenia Yemen Airways	2	0870 732 3213

General Information

234 Bath Road, Hayes, Middlesex, UB3 5AP
General enquiries: 0870 000 0123
Lost property: 020 8745 7727
www.heathrowairport.com

Overview

We all hate airports—especially Heathrow. It's way overcrowded and has tiresome security checks; delays; queues; overpriced shops; terrible food and a tendency to lose baggage. Our ex-mayor Ken Livingstone has accused Heathrow of keeping people "prisoner" in its "ghastly shopping mall." There does seem to be slow, gradual improvement but it's still a long way from what it should be, and gives a poor first impression of the UK.

Often said to be the busiest in the world, there are a few contenders for this title. Heathrow definitely has the largest number of international passengers.

For years its facilities have been stretched beyond capacity, but Heathrow now has some large-scale and controversial expansion plans. The expansion began with T5 and an unsurprisingly chaotic luggage-losing launch in 2008. T5 will provide capacity for an additional 30 million people, taking the total number of passengers to 90 million annually. Next steps are to replace terminals 1 and 2 with Heathrow East, although this won't be ready until 2012 . A third runway and a sixth terminal are also grinding inexorably through the planning process—to the dismay of local residents.

Which Terminal?

Heathrow is in a seemingly constant state of flux, so confirm before you travel.

Terminal 1 is for domestic flights, most UK airline departures to Europe plus EL AL and South African Airways. **Terminal 2** is for most non-UK carriers' flights to Europe and some long haul destinations. **Terminal 3** is the long haul terminal for Asian and Asia Pacific airlines, US and South American, plus most African carriers. **Terminal 4** is for most British Airways long haul flights and some European services. KLM and Qantas also use T4. **Terminal 5** will be used exclusively by British Airways, though a small number of their flights will depart from T3.

Terminals 1-3 are within walking distance of each other (up to 15 minutes) so just follow the signs. You can transfer (for free) to T4 on the Heathrow Connect train and T5 on the Heathrow Express. There is also a free bus which connects T4 and T5, every 6 minutes.

Getting There

The London Underground's Piccadilly Line can get you to central London in less than an hour for only about £4. The wait time for a train is generally no more than 10 minutes. Heathrow has three underground stations; one servicing terminal 1, 2 & 3, and one each for terminals 4&5.

Heathrow Express is a non-stop train between the airport and Paddington station, "In 15 minutes—every 15 minutes". It stops at Heathrow Central Station (T1-3) and the new T5. £15.50 one way

Heathrow Connect follows the same route into west London, but serves intermediate stations making its journey time 25 minutes. Trains depart Paddington every 30 minutes from Platform 12, stopping at Heathrow Central (T1,2,3) and Terminal 4. £6.90 one way. Passengers arriving at T5 may catch the Heathrow Express free of charge to Central station if they wish to use Heathrow Connect into town.

Both these trains run between approx 5 am–12 am. There are also three tube stations—a cheaper and slower option. Roughly £4 for an hour's journey to central London. During rush hour it gets packed with commuters.

National Express run a bargain bus from London Victoria station which only costs £4 one way. It takes anywhere from 45-75 minutes and drops you off at Heathrow Central bus terminal (T1,2,3)

Driving from Central London takes about 45-60 minutes—well anything really—depending on traffic. When leaving Terminals 1–3, follow exit signs to the access/exit tunnel. Then follow signs to the M4 motorway, which will eventually bring you into London. A taxi to central London takes 45-60 minutes and costs £35+.

Car Parking

There are short-term and long-term car parks, both are expensive. An hour at the short stay is £3.90, 48 hours is £89. The long stay car park is about 10 minutes away by courtesy bus and the drive-up price is £15.40 per day.

General Information:

Royal Docks,
London, E16 2PX
General Enquiries: 020 7646 0000/88
www.londoncityairport.com

Overview

With its one wee runway squeezed over the water between the old George V and Royal Albert Docks, City is London's smallest and most central airport (6 miles from the City of London). Where once stevedores ate pie and mash, stockbrokers are now whisked off to lunchtime meetings on dinky short take-off jets. Primarily used by business types, its small size and short runway means City only serves European destinations (33 in total, although British Airways do have a flight to New York in the pipeline) from its single terminal and 22 check-in desks. Still, this means much faster check-in times and fewer delays than at the comparative behemoths of Heathrow and Gatwick.

Getting There

In 2005 someone, somewhere, saw the light and extended the DLR (Docklands Light Railway) to City. The airport now couldn't be simpler to get to by public transport: get on the DLR at Bank; make sure you take a train destined for the King George V branch (these are marked "via City Airport"); and you'll arrive at the airport's station in 25 minutes. A slightly quicker route is to take the Jubilee Underground line to Canning Town and take the DLR a mere three stops westbound from there. There is a taxi rank directly outside the terminal exit, expect to pay at least £30 for a black cab to go to or from the West End. Don't expect the journey to be much faster than on the DLR/Underground. Pre-booked cabs should be a little cheaper, try Airport Executive (020 8838 3333) or the trusty Addison Lee (020 7387 8888).

If you're driving—given its central location—there's no obvious route to City. A useful general rule is to point your wheels at the eastern end of Central London and then keep going that way from Tower Hill on the A1203 (East Smithfield/The Highway). The airport is signposted from this road. If you're getting there from the South East, head through the Blackwall tunnel and follow signs once you emerge into the daylight. If you're near the M25 and like traffic jams, crawl your way to junction 30 and

take the Thames Gateway to the airport from there.

Parking

Short stay is directly next to the terminal and rates start at £7 for one hour going up to £80 for 48 hours.

You can also have your car valet-parked for no extra cost (apart from having to tip the man entrusted with not scratching your pride and joy).

The long stay carpark is a short walk from the terminal and will relieve you of £5 for an hour or £32 per day if you stay two or more days.

So parking is expensive. If you still feel the need to park and can book in advance, get in touch with BCP airport parking for a (slightly) cheaper option at www.parkbcp.co.uk.

Car Hire

Avis 020 7646 0832
Europcar................ 020 7646 0844
Hertz 020 7476 9646

Hotels

Etap Hotel London City Airport,
North Woolwich Road, Silverstown,
London, E16 2EE
020 7474 9106

Custom House Hotel Excel Docklands,
272-283 Victoria Dock Road, London,
E16 3BY
020 7474 0011

Premier Travel Inn
Excel East, Royal Victoria Docks, Canning Town, E16 1SL
0870 238 3322

Novotel London Excel
7 Western Gateway Royal Victoria Dock,
London, E16 1AA
020 7540 9700

Ibis London Excel
9 Western Gateway, London, E16 1AB
020 7055 2300

Sunborn Yacht Hotel
1 Royal Victoria Dock, London, E16 1SL
020 70599100

Holiday Inn Express
1 Silvertown Way, Docklands, London,
E16 1EA
020 75404040

Airlines:

Air France

Air One

Austrian Airlines

British Airways

Euromanx

KLM

Lufthansa

Luxair

SAS

ScotAirways

Swiss International Air Lines

VLM

General Information

London Luton Airport
Navigation House
Airport Way
Luton, Bedfordshire LU2 9LY
General enquiries including lost property:
01582 405100
www.london-luton.co.uk

Overview

To call Luton Airport a 'London' airport is surely one HUGE marketing scam. The same tragedy happens everyday: the unsuspecting traveller smugly enters their credit card details as they book their £2.99 easyJet flight to some godforsaken club 18-30 resort on the Spanish coast, thinking they got the best deal *ever*. One big problem. The flight's from Luton Airport—which should stop any celebrating London traveller dead. Unless you live in North London, getting to and from Luton by public transport is awful. It consists of taking an unreliable half-hour train service from St Pancras or London Bridge to Luton Parkway. After your train journey, if you're lucky, you'll be met at Luton Parkway by a shuttle bus. Be sure to purchase your rail tickets with London Luton Airport as your final destination. If your plane is delayed past midnight, which most budget airlines tend to be, God help you. Where's the Luton Express you might wonder? Ha ha. Good question…

Once you get to the one-terminal airport, your travelling companions will be the kind of people who hunt down the absolute cheapest airfares for their raucous stag or hen nights. Inside security, the few shops and cafés of the Pret a Manger and Dixons variety, will be teeming with these unsavoury characters. So next time you select 'all London airports' when booking your weekend getaway—think carefully!

Getting There

This can be extremely tricky and there's really no easy way. What with a Tube journey to St Pancras or London Bridge station, a train journey, and finally a shuttle bus, you better pack light. Also, you really don't want to get stuck sleeping in the airport when the shuttle bus stops at midnight.

Coach services, such as the 757 Greenline (collaborating with Terravision), easyBus and National Express are good alternatives that will at least get you home if your flight comes in late. Greenline & Terravision are probably your best bet (0990 747 777) with pick-up and drop-off points on Buckingham Palace Road, Marble Arch and Baker Street. Prices are from £10 and it takes about an hour, but it runs pretty regularly through the night. The National Express (08705 80 80 80) service 421 also operates between Luton, Heathrow Airport and London Victoria.

London Luton Airport is somewhat accessible from both the M1 and M25. If you have a choice, go for the M1, as the airport is only about five minutes from junction 10. Without traffic, it can take c. 45 minutes from central London. This can sometimes be longer when there are extensive road works, which tends to be always. When using Sat Nav systems, use the postcode LU2 9QT.

How To Get There – Really

Seriously. You've paid next to nothing for your airfare, splash out on a private cab. If you book a licensed mini-cab ahead of time, the service is often cheaper than the equivalent black cab fare and definitely easier, as they'll meet you at the arrivals hall. A consistently cheap company is Simply Airports (020 7701 4321) which is usually under £50, but you may want to get a quote from your own local company. If you leave it to the last minute, and must take a black cab, get ready to shell out at least £80 (with their meters, this can increase with traffic) plus a meeting fee if you want them to wait for you. Cab rides from central London usually take about an hour.

Parking

Short Term Parking is pricier but situated closest to the terminal, with prices ranging from £2.50 for 15 minutes, to £160 for 16 days. Mid-term is ideal for stays of around five days and is about a five-minute transfer by bus. Prices can vary from £11.25 to £17.00 per day dependent on length of stay. Long-term parking is about 10 minutes from the terminal by bus, and can be booked ahead of time online (www.ncp.co.uk) to save money. Prices range from £12.50 per day for up to four days to £90 for eight days. NCP can be reached on 01582 395484 (9 am–4 pm) and 07734 595560 in an emergency.

Rental Cars

Hertz Rent A Car 01582 450333
Avis Rent A Car Ltd 01582 454040
Thrifty Car Rental 01582 416222
National Car Rental. 01582 454554

Shops

Luton has a small selection of shops, but don't expect too much. There is a Boots (chemist/drugstore), a newsagent, and somewhere to eat/drink.

Hotels

Chiltern Hotel Luton
73 Beechwood Road; 01582 575911

Days Hotel Luton
Regent Street; 01582 878 090

Express by Holiday Inn Hotel
2 Percival Way; 01582 589 100

Holiday Inn Luton South
London Road; 0870 443171

Menzies Strathmore Hotel Luton
The Luton Arndale Centre; 01582 734199

Airlines

Aer Arann

easyJet

Flybe

Monarch

Ryanair

Silverjet

SkyEurope

Thomas Cook

Thomson

Wizz Air

XL.com

General Information

Address: Stansted Airport,
Essex CM24 1QW
General enquiries: 0 870 000 0303
Lost property: 0 1279 663 293
Left luggage: 0 1279 663 213
Police: 0 1245 452 450
Website: www.stanstedairport.com

Overview

It might be tucked away in the middle of the dull Essex countryside, but Stansted Airport has one thing going for it—it's amazingly simple. One terminal (and quite a nice one too, Norman Foster saluted), one check-in area, one security gate. Take that, Heathrow. Around 20 airlines, most of them budget, fly more than 20 million passengers from here to a growing list of mainly domestic and short-haul destinations. If you're budget-crazy enough to fly in the middle of the night, there are several breakfast opportunities. Eating options are generally better before security—unless you like tiny, overpriced ciabatta baguettes or the sugar-drenched fare offered by the big coffee chains. But once through, you can settle for a few surprisingly average-priced pints at Est Bar Est and grab a sandwich on the run once you hear your name being called for the third time. On the downside, the ridiculously long walk to your gate is often obstructed by screaming children or singing hen-night crowds. And the queue at border

control is, at most times, long enough to make you reconsider the whole affair and just run back to your plane.

Getting There

Public Transport

Stansted might seem a long way from London, but getting there by public transport is surprisingly easy. All you have to do is choose between the train (fast) and the bus (cheap). Several train operators serve the airport from Liverpool Street Station. But before you start struggling with too many timetables for trains that stop at too many stops, opt for the dedicated Stansted Express (www.stanstedexpress.com; 08456 007 245). The service runs every 15 minutes and takes you to the airport in 45 minutes straight. Tickets start at £15 and can be bought online, from the ticket office or a ticket machine. Buses will take an hour to take you to the airport, and longer if there's a lot of traffic, but single tickets start at £8. Three operators fight for your custom: Terravision (01279 680 028; www.terravision.eu) leaves from Liverpool Street Station and Victoria Station. The slightly more expensive National Express (08705 747 777; www.nationalexpress.com) connects to the same stations but some buses also stop in Stratford and Golders Green. Easybus (www.easybus.co.uk) gives you the intimacy of a small mini-van, stopping in Baker Street and Victoria Station. If you're traveling during the rush

hour, take a book. Whitechapel Road is one of London's most bustling streets, but it will get boring at some point.

Driving

If you're fortunate enough to have a car, or managed to convince your dad-in-law to lend you his, find your way out of the city via Stratford and hit the M11. It's a straight drive from here and amid Essex' greenery, the airport is hard to miss. Cab drivers will know how to get you to the airport, but will probably charge you a small fortune for it.

Parking

Daily parking rates start at £1.50 for the first half-hour and rise in steps to £23 for 24 hours. Long-term parking, in the intriguingly christened Pink Elephant car park, will cost you £8.30 a day. If you're in for a weekend trip, opt for the mid-stay car park, which is closer to the terminal than the Elephant and charges £14.20/day. The airport recently introduced valet parking, which can be pre-booked on 08708 502 825. Once there, drop your car at the end of Set Down Lane; the pick-up point is next to the Fast Track car park. For discounts on all Stansted parking options, call BAA Advance on 0121 410 5228 and book your parking lot before you head off.

Car Rental

Hertz, Check-In Concourse	0 8708 460 005
Budget, Check-In Concourse	0 1279 681 396
Avis, Check-In Concourse	0 8706 086 364
Europcar, Check-In Concourse	0 1279 680 240
National, International Arrivals Concourse	0 1279 506 534

Shops

Stansted has the usual selection of 'small airport shops', more aimed at passing the time than serious purchases.

Hotels

Hilton National Hotel, Enterprise House, Bassingbourne Road, Essex CM24 1QW , 0 08700 000 303

Radisson SAS Hotel, Waltham Close, London Stansted Airport, Essex CM24 1PP, 0 1279 661 012

Express by Holiday Inn, Thremhall Avenue, Stansted, Essex CM24 1PY, 0 1279 680 015

Airlines

Aegean Airlines	Iceland Express
Air Berlin	Norwegian Air Shuttle
Air Malta	Ryanair
Air Moldova	TACV Cabo Verde Airlines
American Airlines	transavia.com
Atlantic Airways	Turkish Airlines
Aurigny Air Services	Wizz Air
Albanian Airlines	(There's only one terminal)
Cyprus Airways	
Cyprus Turkish Airlines	
easyJet	
Eastern Airways	
El Al Israel Airlines	
Eos Airlines	
Germanwings	

Overview

If the Underground had a motto it wouldn't be "Mind the gap" but "Sorry for any inconvenience caused." But as we grumble and ponder if anyone is ever actually sorry for squeezing you 30m below the surface, in a sweat-box held together by dust, and expensive fares, the magnificence of the 'Tube' network should really be appreciated. Across its 250-odd miles of track the Underground will take you to 275 stations spread the length and breadth of London (although with disproportionately few lines reaching into south London). The system is well integrated with the bus and overground train networks and—with the advent of the Oyster card—most of these share a common ticketing system.

When fully functioning, the Underground will get you across town quicker than the bus and without the complicated timetables and schedules of overground trains. When it is struck by signal failures and breakdowns, which is very often, it can be excruciatingly slow and get very overcrowded, very quickly. In conclusion: the Underground won't necessarily get you anywhere on time, in style or in comfort, but it will (eventually) get you pretty much anywhere.

Fares

The vast majority of the network is divided into concentric fare rings or zones (1-6). Zone 1 covers central London, zone 6 covers the outskirts of London. Fares are dependent on how many zones your journey includes and there's a premium for travelling in zone 1. Peak fares (Monday to Friday from 4.30-9.30 am) are from 50p to a few pounds more than off-peak, although journeys limited to zone 1 do not benefit from the off-peak discount. Your best bet is to get an Oyster Card—single fare is £1.50 off-peak (£2 peak) instead of £4 if you pay by cash. Oyster Cards are available for jsut £3 from vending machines. It's a total no-brainer. The total amount that can be deducted from your Oyster card is also capped over a 24-hour period to match the equivalent cost of a one day travel card.

So the fare system is complicated, but if you take £1.50 (which will get you a single journey within zone 1 with an Oyster card) as a base rate, and add to this the further out of zone 1 you travel, things become clearer. If you feel the need to marvel at the full intricacy of the fares and ticketing system, give yourself eye-strain at Transport for London's website www.tfl.gov.uk.

Frequency and Quality of Service

The vast majority of centrally-located stations will have a train at least every three minutes most of the day. At the very beginning and end of the day service frequency tails-off and can get as low as eight minutes between trains. Trains are also much less frequent at the further reaches of some lines—the Metropolitan line has trains only every 20 minutes from its most north-western stations, even during peak times. Almost all lines have a reduced frequency on Sundays. First trains are 05:00-05:30, last trains are between midnight and 12.30. Last trains are generally safe; expect a slightly raucous mix of pickled after-workers and overly obsequious rough-sleepers rather than any real troublemakers. The whole network is currently having £5bn thrown at it to try to get things ship-shape for the 2012 Olympics. As a result, line closures are common at weekends, so check before you travel.

Lines

Bakerloo: (Brown coloured on maps) Runs from Harrow & Wealdstone in the north west to Elephant & Castle in the south east.

Central: (Red) Runs from West Ruislip in the east to Epping in the far north east. The central section is buried under Oxford Street and has four stops on the street, the quietest usually being Bond Street.

Circle: (Yellow) Circles the circumference of the city centre. Shares almost all of its track and stations with other lines so don't necessarily bother waiting specifically for a dedicated Circle Line train. Look out for the 'Platform for Art' as you pass Gloucester Road station.

District: (Green) One of the few lines to serve deepest south London, branches run into Richmond and Wimbledon in the southwest and also to Ealing. The line continues up to Upminster in the northeast. Almost all of the branches of this fragmented line come together at Earls Court station into an infuriating mess, so plan ahead if changing there.

East London: (Orange) Still features on maps but is now closed. Due to re-open in 2010 as part of the London Overground network. Until then you'll have to plump for a limited rail-replacement bus service.

Hammersmith & City: (Pink) Starts at Hammersmith in the west of the city before heading north to Paddington and continuing east to Barking. Take it to Ladbroke Grove if heading to the Portobello market.

Jubilee: (Silver) Silver coloured as it opened in the year of the Queen's Silver Jubilee in 1977, the line serves northwest, central and east London, including the Canary Wharf business district. The section east of Green Park is the most recent addition to the network (it opened in 1999) and has a number of architecturally exemplary stations.

Metropolitan: (Dark Purple) The oldest of all the lines, this granddaddy of metropolitan underground railways strikes far out in the suburbs and countryside northwest of the city from its central root at Aldgate.

Northern: (Black) Presumably given black as its colour to reflect the dark mood of anyone unlucky enough to have to commute on it, the Northern line is the overcrowded spine of London, covering vast swathes of the city centre, the north and the south.

Piccadilly: (Dark Blue) From Cockfosters in the far northeast this line trundles all the way to Heathrow airport, with some of the most popular tourist spots in between. It's a very cheap way to the airport but is also the slowest. Southgate and Arnos Grove stations are both 1930s modernist brilliance.

Victoria: (Light Blue) Runs from Walthamstow in the north to Brixton in the south. This musty line is currently undergoing refurbishment and will feature new trains and track by 2011. In the meantime, check for early closing and shutdowns, particularly during weekends.

Waterloo & City: (Turquoise) No-one has ever met anyone who has been on this line. Erm, it has two stations, Waterloo and Bank, and is designed for suited and booted commuters coming in by train from Waterloo. No trains on Sundays.

Bicycles

Bicycles are generally only allowed on the tube outside peak hours and only from stations outside central London. They are not permitted on the Victoria or Waterloo and City lines at all. Folding bicycles can be taken on all sections of the Tube free of charge.

General Info

Website: www.tfl.gov.uk/dlr
Phone: 020 7363 9700
Lost property: 020 7363 9550

Overview

Not quite a tram, tube or train, it's simply the Docklands Light Railway, a nifty little thing that makes getting to places like Greenwich Village and City Airport easy and cheap. Launched in 1987 with a modest 11 trains and only 15 stations, the regeneration of the Docklands area has seen it grow to 94 trains covering 38 stations and counting. Serving the east and Southeast of the city, it is pretty much as pleasant as London public transport gets. It's reliable, less noisy than the tube, generally less crowded and it's pretty well air-conditioned. The DLR is also fully-automated and most of the time there is no driver, meaning that you can take the front seat and pretend that you're actually driving the thing.

The DLR provides a key service for London's suits, with the Bank to Canary Wharf journey taking just over ten minutes. For normal people, Canary Wharf also makes an interesting/unusual weekend destination. Almost completely deserted, a stroll amongst the abandoned skyscrapers is a strangely satisfying way to spend a Sunday afternoon.

With the Olympic games invading East London in 2012, there's quite a bit of engineering work going on. Stations are being adapted to cope with longer trains and they're also building an extension to the new Stratford International Station and the nearby Olympic Park. Expect some disruptions to the service over the next few years and check the website before you travel.

Fares

As on the rest of London's public transport you're best off with an Oyster card. One thing to remember is that there are no barriers at DLR stations and instead Oyster readers are located at station exits and entrances. To avoid getting slapped with a fine and to ensure you're charged the right amount, remember to touch in and out correctly. The prices are the same as on the tube, so between zones 1 and 2 you'll be charged £1.50 for a single journey. Cash tickets are ridiculously pricey and that same journey would set you back four quid.

Hours

The DLR runs 5.30 am–12.30 am, with train frequencies depending on the time of day. During peak hours, there's usually a train every three minutes or so, but even on Sundays you shouldn't have to wait more than 10 minutes.

Transport · **Overground Trains**

General Information

National Rail Enquiries 08457 48 49 50
Tickets . . . . www.thetrainline.com;
. . . . also websites of individual franchisees
Eurostar . . . . 08705 186 186 or
. . . . 0 1233 617 575
. . . . www.eurostar.com

Overview

The railways are one of the great British inventions
but, unfortunately, the Victorians who built the
network in this country did slightly too good a job.
Every generation since has taken one look at the
massively expensive task of modernising them
and scuttled back into their Ford Fiestas. So, while
France, Germany and Japan got on with building
super-speed bullet trains Britain was stuck with an
uneasy compromise between the technologies of
1950 and 1850. This doesn't mean that you shouldn't
use them. It just means that it's probably best to
avoid them at peak times. That's when London
plays a cruel trick on people who choose to live in
places with names like 'Gravesend' and 'Slough' by
making them lurch home slowly with less personal
space than the legal minimum for cattle. During off-
peak times train travel can, in contrast, be positively
pleasant. It's a great way to see the countryside, every
city and major town in the country is connected,
and, if you book far enough in advance and shop
around on sites like www.megatrain.com it can be
less expensive than you'd think.

Stations

Broadly speaking, Euston and King's Cross stations
serve the north of the country, Liverpool Street
the east, Victoria the south, Paddington and
Marylebone the west.

Eurostar

The King's Cross area is also home to the splendid St
Pancras—the terminal for the Eurostar train service
which connects Britain with the rest of Europe.
Since November 2007 it's been possible to get from
here to Paris or Brussels in around two hours—with
connecting trains to Siberia and beyond.

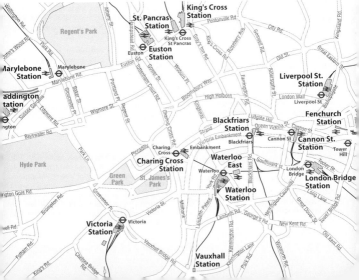

Charing Cross Station

NFT Map:	24
Address:	12-30 The Strand, London WC2N 6RQ
General enquiries:	020 7839 2576
South Eastern Trains:	08706 030405
Southern Trains:	0845 123 7770

Overview

Perched at the top of the Strand amidst popular tourist attractions such as Trafalgar Square and with the majestic 1865 Charing Cross Hotel being part of the station, you may presume that a cornucopia of ornate delights lies within. Well, it's a dump; the chances of "Brief Encounter" being remade here are pretty slim. But your chances of being barged by a curmudgeonly office worker are very good, what with it being the fifth busiest rail terminal in London. Still, can you blame them for wanting to get out of the place so quickly?

With services to south London and Kent, even the pigeons give the concourse here a wide berth. It's also home to possibly the worst station pub in the country; "The Boadicea" excels in the areas of soullessness and morbidity, likely to satisfy only the hardened alcoholic on their third liver and with a preference for pubs that reek of urine. If only Dante had been able to sample this place…

Tickets

There is a small ticket office open some 20 hours per day, and three banks of ticket machines on or around the concourse.

Services

If you're in need of a quick bite, there's a decent variety of food outlets to cater for all tastes, whether burger-lover (Burger King) or health food freak (Cranberry). Indulge your Schadenfreude by watching the beleaguered information guy having to dispense a plethora of poor excuses as to why the 17.34 to Margate was cancelled. And those kinky souls with a tie fetish will love Tie Rack.

Natwest and Bank of Scotland cash machines can be found on the concourse, as well as a Barclays in the front entrance.

Public Transport

The station is easily accessible by Charing Cross station (Northern & Bakerloo lines) and also the adjoining Embankment station (Circle & District lines). The nearby Trafalgar Square is a major hub for buses—especially night buses for post-West End madness—which inch their way out to places as far apart as Harrow and Crystal Palace.

Euston Station

NFT Map:	78
Address:	Euston Road NW1 2RT
General enquiries:	020 7922 6482
Lost property:	020 7247 4297
Virgin Trains :	08457 222 333

Overview

Easily the ugliest station in London, Euston creeps up as you nervously edge along Euston Road. The first inter-city terminal built in London, it was originally constructed in 1837, but the lovely original was demolished to make way for the monstrous concrete-and-glass coffin which now squats next to the mail depot. Since privatisation the interior has become an identi-kit British rail station with more chain businesses per head than is morally decent. Thanks Network Rail.

It's not all doom and gloom, however. Within this architectural eyesore you'll find a scarily concise summation of human nature. Like most busy stations, there's plenty of eccentricity and electricity here: abandoned Tube tunnels; stressed-out coffee guzzling power-commuters; fresh-faced backpackers sprawled out on the floor ; and the infamous beggar who — to the delight of football lovers everywhere except in Manchester — was arrested for punching Manchester Utd manager Sir Alex Ferguson.

The station is London's gateway to the north west of England and Scotland, and also North Wales. As such it is the point of entry for Scousers, Mancunians, Glaswegians and more. Virgin trains (www.virgintrains.co.uk) to Glasgow can take a measly 4.5 hours, but to make the trip in style take the Caledonian Sleeper (www.firstgroup.com/scotrail/content/caledoniansleeper/index.php).

Tickets

The ticket cashiers may have the glazed look of Kafka-esque zombies but the cleaning staff are often more helpful. Just use the Fasttrack machines!

Services

There's plenty of eating and drinking options, all of the 'chain' variety. Of this motley crew Paul and Upper Crust are as good as it gets. If you're determined to hang around, check out the Doric Arch (1 Eversholt St; 020 7388 2221) which is a shoddy little boozer with a cool 'end of the world' vibe. The left luggage office is at the top of the ramp to platforms 16–18 and is open between 7 am–11 pm.

Public Transport

As an actual railway station it is adequate. Served by two Tube lines and nine bus routes, it's nothing if not convenient.

King's Cross Station

NFT Map:	78
Address;	Euston Rd & Pancras Rd N1 9AP
General enquiries:	0207 922 4931
Lost property:	0207 2783310
National Express East Coast	0457 225 225
First Capital Connect	0845 676 9904

Overview

Previously a dingy playground for prostitutes, drug dealers, and all sorts of similarly bad kids, King's Cross Station has scrubbed up a bit in recent years, thanks to lots of chin scratching and typically panicked spending on the government's part. Built in 1852 on the site of a former smallpox hospital, it is one of the busiest and most well-connected stations in the country: running trains to Edinburgh; Newcastle; the East coast; as well as six Tube lines. Zany trivia about the station includes the fact that it is supposedly built on top of legendary Fembot-Queen Boudicea's grave (most probably a total lie) and that it has a tacky little shrine to Harry Potter at what has been designated 'Platform 9 3/4' (oh God).

All long distance train services leave from the overground platforms under the arches straight ahead of you as you enter from Euston Road. The Tube is also accessible from steps at this entrance and at what used to be the Thameslink station next to the Scala on Pentonville Road. From the main Tube entrance there is a pedestrian subway that comes up on the other side of Euston road just outside Macdonald's. This is handy for crossing the road at busy times, and of course for getting chips.

Tickets

Tube tickets, including Oyster top ups and season tickets, can be purchased from the machines in front of the Tube entry gates, located just at the bottom of both sets of stairs at the station. For railcard discounts and more specific enquiries you'll have to queue at the manned ticket desks next to the machines. For all other tickets go to the upstairs ticket hall which is to the left of the main Euston Road entrance.

Services

Food options are pretty poor, consisting of a small array of chain stores with prices hiked just enough so that people in a rush will not notice they're being ripped off. If you're not one of those people, it's probably best to just pop across the road and get some noodles from Chop Chop, which is fast, cheap and dirty, like the best rail travel.

Public Transport

King's Cross crosses more Tube lines (six) than any other station, and is serviced by at least twice as many buses, many of which run all night. For full details of bus routes look at the bus maps for Camden on the Transport for London website: http://www.tfl.gov.uk/tfl/gettingaround/maps/buses/.

Liverpool Street Station

NFT Map:	8
Address:	EC2M 7QH
General enquiries:	020 7295 2789
Lost property:	020 7247 4297
One Railway:	0845 6007245.

Overview

It's not that Liverpool Street is particularly ugly, but if it's architectural beauty you're after, you're much better off heading to Paddington or the newly re-opened St. Pancras International. In comparison to these two icons of British station design, Liverpool Street is extremely modest, boring even. Clean, modern and easy to navigate around, it is simply a good train station. With the markets, bars and restaurants of Spitalfields and Brick Lane just around the corner, the station is the perfect starting point to explore east London. First opened to the public in 1874, it is now the second-busiest station in London (after Waterloo) with an estimated 123m visitors each year. With 18 platforms, the station mainly serves destinations in the east of England, including daytrip favourites such as Cambridge and Southend on Sea.

It is also the home of the Stansted Express, providing easy airport access with departures every 15 minutes. If you're travelling with a group of people a taxi might work out slightly cheaper, but the tube is much quicker and more reliable. The Tube station, with its main entrance centrally located on the main concourse, makes all of London easily accessible with the Central, Hammersmith & City, Circle and Metropolitan lines all passing through. Being the fifth busiest station on the underground network, rush hour can get nasty and is best avoided.

Tickets

The ticket office is located on the main concourse, on your left hand side if entering from Bishopsgate. Ticket windows are open for immediate travel 24/7 with advance ticket purchases available between 7.30 am–7.30 pm. There are also several express ticket machines scattered throughout the station. Tickets for the Stansted Express can be purchased from designated ticket machines opposite platforms 5-6. A cluster of cash machines can be found by the stairs leading up to the Old Broad Street exit. There are payphones on both levels and most are located on the Bishopsgate side of the station.

Services

With Brick Lane just around the corner, eating, drinking and shopping here should really be a last resort. The regular big-chain fast food joints are scattered (some of them repeatedly) throughout the station with the usual selection of coffee, burgers, sandwiches and sweets. The main shopping area is on the lower level around the Broadgate and Exchange Square exits, offering everything from toiletries and birthday cards to Italian silk ties and double-glazed windows.

Passengers are invited to wait for their trains in the so-called "food court," which really isn't much more than a few cramped tables between Burger King and The Wren, one of the station's two shitty pubs. There's a small but nicer waiting lounge located adjacent to platform 10. Here you also find the left luggage, a bureau de change, a less-busy cash machine and access to the main taxi rank. Smoking is prohibited at all times throughout the station.

Public Transport

The main bus station is located on the upper level of the station (Broadgate end), and provides a large number of services to destinations throughout London. Plenty of buses also stop on the street just outside the Bishopsgate exit.

London Bridge Station

NFT Map:	106
Address:	Station Approach SE1 9SP
General enquiries:	020 7234 1209
Lost property:	020 7234 1247
Southern Trains	0845 123 7770
South East Trains	0845 000 2211
First Capital Connect	0845 026 4700
South Eastern disabled contact:	0800 783 4524

Overview

Around in one form or other since 1836, when steam trains filled the air with smoke, London Bridge is the city's oldest station. Sounds romantic? It's anything but. Hopelessly overcrowded, with 42 million people elbowing their way through the tunnel-like walkways every year, and crumbling on its grey concrete edges, London Bridge has long been SCREAMING for a makeover. Someone finally heard the call, and £3.5m is earmarked to get this vital commuter hub (connecting south London, Sussex and Kent) up to scratch. The ambitious revamp will also see the construction of one of Europe's highest skyscrapers—a massive arrowhead of a building, hosting 7,000 people once completed.

It's a good starting point for weekend trips to Kent's countryside or days on Brighton's beach. Operators Southeastern and Southern cover the south east, while First Capital Connect operates (little-known) connections to the airports Gatwick and Luton.

The station couldn't be better connected to public transport, with two Tube lines and a plethora of buses at the doorstep. The catacombs underneath the station—said to be haunted—have been turned into the museum-cum-gore-fest London Bridge Experience, adding to the spooky entertainment already provided by the London Dungeon next door—just in case a cancelled or delayed train leaves you with too much time on your hands. Does happen, we're told.

Tickets

The main office is located next to the main entrance (London Bridge Street) or there are machines situated throughout the station. Jump the queues by booking online at www.nationalrail.co.uk.

Services

The main concourse is lined with eating and shopping options. Grab Cornish pasties, sandwiches, donuts; and the usual burgers from the usual chains. Bodyshop, M&S and WH Smith lead the list of practical, but terribly unexciting shop names. There are toilets on platforms 1-2 and 5-6.

Public Transport

Connections are excellent. London Bridge Station is served by the Jubilee Line and the Bank branch of the Northern Line. Escalators take you down from the main concourse. Step outside the main entrance for the massive bus station, where buses leave in all directions of the city, except its far western reaches.

Marylebone Train Station

NFT Map;	76
Address:	Great Central House Melcombe Place NW1 6JJ
Central number:	08456 005165

Overview

Despite Monopoly-board notoriety, Marylebone railway station fell into neglect in the mid to late-twentieth century, spurned as a rundown piggy-in-the-middle wedged haplessly between neighbours Paddington and Euston. But it's an aimless drifter no more. A refurb' in the 90s and again in 2006 saw Marylebone reinvigorated, with a thorough sprucing up and two new platforms. Servicing the Midlands, it now threads as far as Birmingham, Shakespeare's Stratford-Upon-Avon, Leamington Spa, Aylesbury, and High Wycombe, amongst others. It remains the runt of the London train station litter, but is a popular location for television filming (Doctor Who; Magnum PI; Green Wing; Peep Show) at a mere £500 per hour—half the price of King's Cross. In its bowels, Bakerloo Line trains rumble through an underground station of the same name.

Tickets

Rail ticket windows are to the north of Marylebone's relatively petite concourse and open from 06.30 am–11:10 pm Monday to Saturday, and 7.30 am-10.15 pm Sundays. As with all mainline train stations, self-service ticket machines are in abundance should ticket offices be closed or queues too long. Sturdy padded-barriers ensure buying tickets on board the train, or getting away without them, is not an option. Underground tickets can be purchased from windows or machines alike within the Tube station itself.

Services

The usual plethora of railway station chains are on hand: newsagent WH Smith, baguette bakers Upper Crust, supermarket Marks & Spencer, and pasty purveyors the West Cornwall Company among them. More individually, Marylebone also hosts AMT Coffee, a café with a seating area at the centre of the concourse, the nifty Chiltern Flowers on the south wall, and The V&A free house in the west passageway—an old man's boozer in the classic, wood panelled style. Cash points and payphones are in this same walkway, and toilets are situated on the south wall.

Public Transport

Marylebone underground station lies directly beneath Marylebone overground, and is serviced (Matron!) by the Bakerloo Line, while buses 2, 205 and 453 stop directly outside the main entrance. A taxi stand is also situated out front. Baker Street and Edgware tube stations are a short walk away.

Paddington Station

NFT Map:	31
Address:	Paddington, London, W2 1HQ
General enquiries:	020 7922 6793
Lost property:	020 7247 4297
First Great Western:	084 5700 0125
Heathrow Express:	084 5600 1515
Chiltern Railways:	084 5600 5165

Overview

If you're in that small minority of people who love stations, then Paddington's paradise. Designed by engineering legend Isambard Kingdom Brunel—his middle name is Kingdom for God's sake, of course his work's going to be magnificent—this barn-like structure harks back to an era when train travel retained a little glamour. If it wasn't for the on-site Burger King you could easily imagine tearful ladies waving silk handkerchiefs at dapper gents.

The station also occupies a unique place in literary heritage. Every British child in the last half-century knows the tales of Paddington Bear. From "deepest darkest Peru", he was left unattended at the station; but a kind family picked him up, took him in, and named him after it. No other station name can inspire such genuine warmth. It certainly wouldn't have worked if he'd been found at Clapham Junction.

Heathrow Express

The super-fast link to Heathrow runs from Paddington. Be warned, though; it's far from cheap. At £29 return it could end up being more than your flight (and works out at £22 more than taking the tube). Ouch.

Tickets

A ticket office and machines are located near platforms 9-10, and there are other machines and an information point near the Eastbourne Terrace entrance and also underneath the mezzanine.

Services

If you have any money left from your ticket—unlikely at today's prices—there are plenty of sharks who can take it off you. Burger King and Upper Crust will overcharge you for burgers or baguettes and there's an 'offie' (off-license) for expensive booze. There's also a pub that resembles a building site (Portakabin). If you find yourself drinking in there you've got some serious questions to ask yourself.

There are other ways of staying amused; as it's the main portal for commuters entering London from the west and Wales there's WiFi, a supermarket, a bookshop and curiously, a lingerie shop. Just what sort of a job do you have if you get to the station and realise: "Bollocks! No suspenders!"? Certainly not one compatible with Paddington's place in children's lit, that's for sure.

Public Transport

The Bakerloo, Circle, District, and Hammersmith & City Tube lines all stop at Paddington. Buses serve west and north west London.

St Pancras International

NFT Map;	78
Address:	Pancras Road, London, NW1 2QP
Central number:	020 7843 4250
Eurostar:	08705 186 186
Midland Mainline:	08457 125678

Overview

The newly souped-up St Pancras station has been generating waves of breathless excitement ever since its opening ceremony in 2007, which was by all accounts a pretty histrionic affair. This "Cathedral of Transport" situated next door to King's Cross station, is now home to the Eurostar international train service and has domestic connections (via First Capital Connect's Thameslink trains) to Luton Airport, Bedford and Brighton; as well as Midland Mainline connections to places like Leicester and Sheffield. As the first major project of a huge scheme to redevelop the area, St Pancras has been marketed as so-much-more-than-a-station. Alongside its rail platforms it features Europe's longest Champagne bar, a farmers market, and an arcade of pointedly-classy shops. All this is housed within beautiful listed buildings dating from 1868, with an extension for the long Eurostar trains designed by British starchitect Norman Foster—presumably on time out from his usual business of making pleasure domes for the world's nastiest totalitarian governments.

Tickets

The Eurostar ticket office and travel centre is located at the Euston Road end of the long arcade, while self-service machines (for collecting pre-booked tickets) can be found outside the Eurostar departure lounge further along the arcade and to the right. Opening times for the Eurostar ticket office are 4.30 am–9 pm (Mon-Fri), 5.30 am–9 pm (Sat) and 6.30 am–9 pm (Sun). For National Rail services, you will need to buy tickets from machines, or a manned ticket desk at the designated area at the far end of the Arcade, next to that horrific kissing statue.

Services

At St Pancras International there are more than 40 places to eat, drink and shop, with a fair number of chain stores as well as some exclusives, such as the Champagne Bar and Gastro Pub. The station has its own dedicated shopping arcade with branches of classic London stores Hamleys and Foyles, as well as a market area and another brace of shops at the north end of the station ('The Circle'). Everything is shiny, new and upmarket, so expect your money to vanish pretty damn quickly.

Public Transport

St Pancras can be reached by Tube (via adjacent King's Cross station) on the Victoria, Hammersmith & City, Circle, Piccadilly, Northern and Metropolitan Lines. A large number of buses also stop along Euston Road day and night. For route details check the bus maps for Camden borough at www.tfl.gov.uk/tfl/gettingaround/maps/buses/.

Victoria Station

NFT Map:	20
Address:	Buckingham Palace Road SW1V 1JU
General enquiries:	020 7922 6214
Lost property:	020 7963 0957
Gatwick Express	0845 850 1530
Southern	08451 27 29 20
Southeastern	0845 000 2222

Overview

80 million people use London Victoria per year, making it one of the UK's busiest stations. Hit it at rush hour and it will feel like those 80 million are all there with you. Built a century ago for a less populous, less rushed and less demanding city, it struggles with crowds of commuters who jostle

for platform space. Now it enforces crowd-control measures at peak times: prepare to be patient. Nevertheless, it is well laid-out with services clearly sign-posted, and a major upgrade is planned to improve its capacity.

Victoria's main train operators are Southeastern, Southern and Gatwick Express, who between them will whisk you to Brighton, Portsmouth, Hastings and Gatwick, among other south eastern towns. Or if you're looking for a romantic break and the Victoria route to Bognor Regis is just a little too obvious for you, you can earn yourself brownie points and a hefty overdraft by taking the Orient Express from this station.

The building itself is impressive: look above the modern shop fascias to enjoy century-old architecture. But if that is all a little too high-brow, look up anyway, as the entrance to the South East building sports four caryatids: columns shaped like women, whose tunics saucily hang open so a gratuitous nipple can pop out to cheer the commuters. Rule Britannia!

Tickets

If you haven't booked in advance (why? Why?!), then head for the 24 hour ticket office in the central concourse, where you will queue for anything up to a year to buy your journey for much more money than you'd have paid online a week earlier. If you don't require assistance from a ticket officer, use the automated machines dotted round the concourse: their queues always move faster (unless the person in front of you is a newbie who can't figure out the buttons, which is guaranteed if you have less than five minutes to catch your train). Keep your ticket handy as all platforms are guarded by ticket barriers, and add a few extra minutes to reach platforms 15–19.

Services

All the predictable station fare is available in the main concourse for your journey's usual sandwich, loofah and tie needs. Food options have mercifully diversified so in addition to the obligatory artery-cloggers you can now grab sushi from the Wasabi stand or maintain your body's temple-status at the Camden Food Co. If it's a meal you're after and you must remain at the station, head up to the food court via Victoria Place for a choice of what could charitably be described as restaurants. Victoria Place itself boasts the ubiquitous high street shops to help you kill time or for any last minute gifts (as long as you don't really like the person you're buying for). Station loos are 20p—even up in the food court you can't pee for free—and showers are available if you're getting a bit ripe. Victoria also has a left luggage service, WiFi (charged) and photo booths.

Public Transport

Victoria is on the Victoria, Circle and District lines; entrance to the underground is opposite platform 7. The bus terminus is just outside the main entrance. It is also next door to London's national bus depot for cheapo travel to/from other parts of the UK. The main taxi rank is outside the main entrance, but if it has a heart-sinking queue then head up to the Plaza exit for an alternative rank.

Waterloo Station

NFT Map;	104
Address:	Waterloo, London, SE1 8H
Train company:	South West Trains
General enquiries:	020 7922 2545
Lost property:	0845 330 9882
	0845 6000 650
Website:	www.southwesttrains.co.uk

Overview

Until 2007, Waterloo was the first port of call for 'Europeans' arriving by train. Thousands of chic foreigners, clutching manbags and sporting huge sunglasses, would arrive at the station every week. But not any more. Nearly 200 years after the British triumphed in the first battle of Waterloo—a town in Belgium—the French got their revenge. Last November Eurostar gave the two fingers to the British Waterloo and promiscuously buggered off to St Pancras. Rumour has it that ex-PM Margaret Thatcher had specifically ordered that Eurostar terminate at a station named after a famous French defeat; but things have moved on a little since the "Iron Lady" left office. We're all Europeans now...

In truth, perhaps it's not that bad a thing. Even though no other British station covers as much space, Waterloo feels like it's at bursting point. Even without the Eurostar it has a whopping 19 platforms—in almost constant use—and four

Tube lines. It's calmed down slightly since the international terminal was put out to stud, but it's still pretty manic.

The station services London's south western suburbs (as can be seen by the swathes of well dressed commuters) and, further afield, the towns south west of the capital.

Waterloo East

NFT Map;	104
Address:	Sandell St, SE8 8H
Central number;	0871 200 49650

Overview

If the south west isn't your bag, you can disappear to England's south east—Kent, Sussex and SE London—from Waterloo East. There's an escalator next to Burger King, opposite platform 12, that makes a trip to the south east look far more alluring than it really is.

Tickets

The main office is opposite platforms 16–17. And it's open 24 hours—so why not charm them into giving you a free ticket after a few drinks? They can't have heard it before, right?

Services

A delay is just unplanned "me time", so make the most of it by buying a newspaper, eating your own weight in overpriced pasties and cookies; then wash it down with a few pints of generic football-sponsor lager in Bonaparte's pub before buying your loved-one a novelty tie/'cute' socks to make up for being late. And drunk. And flatulent. And tasteless. There's a left luggage office between platforms 11-12.

Public Transportation

Waterloo is served by four underground lines: Bakerloo, Jubilee, Northern, Waterloo & City; and approximately 20 bus routes. See tfl.gov.uk for details.

Overview

If there's one thing that screams London, it's big red buses—loads of 'em—preferably passing beneath Big Ben for maximum iconic impact. The furore that greeted the withdrawl of the old style Routemasters continues to rumble on years after their replacement by hi-tech bendy buses.

Whether you view the latter as characterless boxes and a fare-dodger's paradise, or whether you think the Routemaster was a diesel-breathing dinosaur: you're going to spend a lot of time in buses, around them, dodging them or talking about them. As a Londoner, your list of hobbies and interests now includes transport. Deal with it.

Ken Livingstone always had a thing for buses and we make 6m journeys every day. There are a variety of different operating companies, but to us they're all the same, all the way out to the frontiers of Zone 6. Get on at the front, get off at the middle.

If you can't find the middle door, you're on a single-decker bus. It's the half-the-height thing that gives it away on the outside. Most single-deckers can drop to kerb level and most double-deckers have a disabled ramp at the rear door. Retro is in, so show your old-school ways by queuing. Most people don't, but manners maketh the (wo)man and you might even start a trend.

Fares

In an effort to make the city more efficient and to cut down on theft-based attacks on drivers, Transport for London (TfL) introduced the Oyster card. Now people only beat up drivers for fun. The Oyster ("The world's your..."—geddit?) is an electronic swipe card that can be bought at all 275 Tube stations and at 2,200 other outlets such as newsagents.

The card can carry a mixture of travel passes (often referred to as travelcards in a nod to the pre-electronic age of cardboard); and pay-as-you-go cash value. Note that if you choose pay-as-you-go, and you end up making more journeys than you anticipated; once it reaches the equivalent cost of a one-day travelcard, it will cap itself so you don't spend more.

Unless you are making a small number of journeys it usually works out cheaper to get a travelcard. In a further move towards the cashless society, coins are still accepted—but you will pay more for a journey. A single ticket costs 90p with Oyster or £2 with cash. Or you can buy a book of 6 single tickets for £6 at selected locations. On some bus routes you will not be allowed to purchase a ticket on the bus, but instead there will be a roadside ticket machine. Believe us, Oyster's just easier…

When you get on, don't forget to push your card against the scanner by the drivers' window. Sure, you're on camera 300 times per day, and every journey you make is recorded. But if you're paranoid, try another city, because they are watching you here.

You can buy a bus-only pass (£13 p/w), or you can buy a bus/tube travelcard (prices vary by zones). If you don't work or socialise in the centre, and you only buy, let's say a Zone 2-3 bus travelcard, you can still use this on all buses in Zones 1-6. Which is nice. An Oyster card costs £3 to get, but you'll soon recoup that. Concessions are also available for the unemployed and for full-time students.

24-Hour Services

You'll not hear London referred to as "the other city which never sleeps". Partly because it's unwieldy, but mostly because it's not true. After a hard night's binge-drinking and fighting in taxi ranks, we like our kip.

But for those of you that are hardcore no-sleep-till-Brockley types, there is a network of 24-hour services. There are also a large number of night buses. They're just like day buses, except the route number is prefixed by a large 'N' and the view is less interesting.

Information

TfL's website (tfl.gov.uk) is an essential reference. Fare information and travel updates are available, plus PDFs of routes and timetables. As you get closer to central London, many routes operate on a frequency—basis rather than at fixed times.

The main reason to visit TfL's site is the Journey Planner. Enter your start and end points and it will (usually) calculate the best options. A word of warning though, computers are fallible and some route maps are schematics—so do check your own map and use common sense. Like those idiots that follow their GPS even when it tells them to drive into a river, it's frustrating to take three buses in a big circuit then realise you could have walked it in five minutes…

If you do want to live out your 1940s film fantasies, you can still catch the quaint old Routemasters doddering along 'Heritage Routes' 9 and 15. If you're wondering who this guy is that keeps bugging you at the door-less rear step, it's the conductor and he only wants your money. It's the silent guy in the corner who wants your soul that you have to watch out for…

Safety

Like all big cities, London has its fair share of oddballs and criminals. And then a few institution-loads more in case things ever get boring. But CCTV in every bus and the creation of Safer Transport teams is having an effect—and not just on the share price of video camera manufacturers. TfL claimed an 11% reduction in reported crime at the end of 2007 and a ratio of 15 crimes per million journeys. Also, bus crime is concentrated in particular areas on particular routes. And you'll soon get to know the 'usual suspects' so don't worry. Night buses can get a bit lairy, so follow a few tips below to make sure the only stress you suffer is traffic-related. Gangsters may wish to laugh at the following; Mother Theresas may wish to tattoo it on the inside of their eyelids:

Avoid the top deck when possible. Sit on the left so the driver can see you (he has a radio link to base). Don't fall asleep. Use the same stop at night and know your surroundings so you can be confident. Keep your belongings close to you and be switched on. Get to know the 'hot spots' so you can be aware.

For more info, see our fabulous fold out bus map.

Overview

Coaches are traditionally associated with the grimier side of travel. But London's biggest coach company, National Express, are desperately trying to shake their image as a purveyor of seedy transport. They're rebranding themselves as quick, comfortable and green. Their fleet of coaches are shiny and the drivers slightly less grumpy than they used to be.

Then there's the Megabus. In comparison to their coaches, just walking where you wanted to go would be more comfortable. It's no surprise that the repositioning of National Express as a classy operator is linked to the rise of Megabus. Faced with a company who reroute you so your journey takes an extra week, anything else is 'luxury'. But you know what? They're dirt cheap. Literally. With fares from £1 you can ignore the garish buses and the man being sick in the back. They're the cheap version of the cheap version of transport.

The main coach hub is near Victoria train station. You can buy tickets for both Megabus and National Express—the two main operators who run from Victoria Coach Station—from the same booths just inside the station. But, like plane tickets, (only without that last shred of glamour that air travel still has) if you buy in advance, you can get some super-cheap prices. National Express has an office on the road between the train and bus stations.

London's other main hub is Golder's Green. This is the last stop for services heading north (or the first stop for buses coming down into London). If you live in north London, it's worth jumping off here, as it's on the Northern Line and can shave an hour off the trip.

There's also a healthy trade in coaches to Oxford. The Oxford Tube competes with National Express on the route from Victoria; travelling via Marble Arch, Notting Hill and Shepherd's Bush. Tickets normally cost about £10 and you can buy on board. They also run through the night—so if you get drunk and have the urge to go on an impromptu holiday—well, Oxford it is.

National Express

Unit 6/7 Collonades Walk
123 Buckingham Palace Road, SW1W 1SH
08717 818181
www.nationalexpress.com

Megabus
0900 160 0900
www.megabus.co.uk

Oxford Tube
01865 772250
www.oxfordtube.com

There's a war going on out there, one with real casualties and collateral damage. When Tory leader David Cameron was spotted going through a red light on his bicycle, it threw into sharp relief a low level conflict which has been going on for decades. Bikes v. Cars: with hapless pedestrians caught in the middle.

Cycling around London is not for the faint-hearted, but recent improvements—like Ken's Congestion Charge and the hard work of the London Cycling Campaign (www.lcc.org.uk) are encouraging people to drop their Oyster cards and jump on their bikes. Some of the routes highlighted in the brilliant (and free) maps produced by LCC and Transport for London have become so popular, cycling along them is like taking part in the Tour de France (albeit slower and with slightly fewer drugs).

But cycling does hold some risks. As well as the nightmare of walking around all day with 'helmet hair' you've got accidents and theft. LCC's website has details of road-confidence training and lists local cycling groups who run social events and cycle maintenance classes. They will sometimes cycle your new route to work with you to help you negotiate the difficult bits. Aren't they nice?

For those new to cycling on London's roads, basic rules include: stay a door length (or stride) away from the pavement or parked cars; watch out for distracted office drones leaping into the road and into black cabs; don't undertake bendy-buses or HGVs; don't use your phone while moving; and if in doubt on a tricky junction—transform yourself into a pedestrian—get off and push your bike wherever you need to go. For debates around riding on pavements, wearing helmets and jumping red lights check out www.cyclechat.co.uk/forums.

Bolt-cutting 'tea-leaves' steal thousands of bikes every year. You have three options to reduce this particular risk. One, buy a rubbish bike that no-one would want to steal and lock it with one lock. Two, get a decent bike, carry around a D-lock and two other locks and spend 20 mins each time you stop. Three, get a shit-hot bike and never take it out.

Where to Ride Bikes

There are plenty of great rides around town and a happy cyclist is one who has been able to incorporate one into their commute. The cycling maps mentioned above give colour-coded help, look for the brown routes (separate from the traffic) or even better the green routes (separate from the traffic and passing through parks, beside canals or rivers.)

Good options are the short but scenic Parkland Walk Nature Reserve, which links Finsbury Park to Highgate via an abandoned railway line; a Saturday morning cycle takes you to one of Highgate's wonderful pubs for lunch and a lazy pint. The City, normally snarled with cabs, buses and kamikaze pedestrians, is a dream on a Sunday morning.

Though not continuous, the path along the Regent's Canal linking Paddington with Canary Wharf takes cyclists away from traffic and along some surprisingly gorgeous stretches of canal (which also sport some top notch graffiti)—as well as some godawful, festering dumps. A useful section of the canal links the west side of Regent's Park with Paddington via Lisson Grove and Warwick Avenue. Watch out for super-fast cyclists determined to slice a second off their PB, especially where the path narrows under bridges or around ramps. Also recent yellow crime signs around London Fields spoke of a gang of youths pushing cyclists into the canal for fun. Watch out for them too.

A jaunt through any of the capital's great parks seems an obvious choice, but beware, some parks (notably Hampstead Heath) ban bikes on almost all paths, thanks to selfish cyclists of the past who went too fast and frightened the jumpy pedestrians.

The new anarchic FreeWheel Event is a real highlight, where great swathes of normally packed roads along the Embankment and up to St James's Park are closed to all but cyclists every September (we fervently hope this will remain forever). And the London Critical Mass meet at 6 pm on the last Friday of the month by the National Film Theatre, if you can't wait that long.

Bike Shops	Address	Phone
Apex Cycles	40-42 Clapham High St, SW4 7UR	020 7622 1334
Bicycle Magic	6 Greatorex St, E1 5NF	020 7375 2993
Bikefix	48 Lamb's Conduit St, WC1N 3LJ	020 7405 1218
Brick Lane Bikes	118 Bethnal Green Rd, E2 6DG	020 7033 9053
Brixton Cycles	145 Stockwell Rd, SW9 9TN	020 7733 6055
Condor Cycles	51 Gray's Inn Rd, WC1X 8PP	020 7269 6820
Evans (Spitalfields)	The Cavern, 1 Market St, E1 6AA	020 7426 0391
Holloway Cycles	290 Holloway Rd, N7 6NJ	020 7700 6611
London Fields Cycles	281 Mare St, E8 1PJ	020 8525 0077
Mosquito	123 Essex Rd, N1 2SN	020 7226 8765
ReCycling	110 Elephant Rd, SE17 1LB	020 7703 7001

To consider taking a taxi in London you either need (a) a trust fund, or (b) to be drunk. If you are both, congratulations: prepare to be taken for a ride in more ways than one.

Dating back to the mid-17th Century (kind of), London's 'black cabs' (www.londonblackcabs.co.uk), or 'Hackneys', are the world's oldest taxi service and are as representative of London as Routemasters, Big Ben and robbery. They are the most visible, the most iconic and probably the most expensive taxi service in London. While this flag-down option is great (they are the only company licensed to pick up on the street) budgeting for a black cab is tricky. Their prices are designed to confuse passengers into parting with huge wads for what often feels like a round-the-block trip. A whole range of metaphysical problems contribute to that huge sum waiting to be paid at jouney's end; all fares start at £2.20 and then go up according to the time of day, speed, and the time spent in the cab. There's also an airport surcharge and the 'puke charge' of £40. Keep it in!

Black cabs are operated by many different companies who are all regulated and licensed by the Public Carriage Office (PCO). Generally speaking, the service you receive doesn't vary much from company to company, though some boast little add-ons to capture your fare. Big, well organized companies like Dial-A-Cab (www.dialacab.co.uk; 020 7253 5000) and Radio Taxis (www.radiotaxis.co.uk; 020 7272 0272) offer online booking, carbon neutral trips, and friendly service. All black cab drivers must pass 'The Knowledge' test to get their license, so every driver will have a labyrinthine understanding of London and most will not be shy in sharing this with you.

Though a cheaper option, going private can be a minefield. Since 2001 all taxi services in London are required by law to be licensed by the PCO: this includes the city's thousands of private-hire minicabs. Private hire companies are everywhere you look and often take the form of nicotine-stained, shoddily-built little offices with lots of bored men milling about. Every neighbourhood has plenty of local services and it's really trial and error to find one that doesn't rip you off or drive barely roadworthy chariots of rust. The drivers of these little companies can be pretty eccentric; you can be regaled by tales of times past, given essential life advice or simply receive the disdainful silent treatment. The website www.taxinumber.com offers a list of local minicabs for every postcode in the UK.

The 'private taxi sector' does do upmarket, however. By far the most efficient and elegant service is that offered by Addison Lee, (www.addisonlee.com; 020 7387 8888) who text you twice, have huge gleaming six-seaters, and perfectly-manicured drivers. Fares are pretty cheap over longer distances but the minimum is around £8. E-london Cars are almost as good (www.elondoncars.co.uk; 020 7494 4004). Of course, you can also sup from the cup of bad taste by ordering a stretch hummer or pink limo at Book A Limo (www.booklimo.co.uk; 020 8965 1724).

A word of warning: London is awash with rogue taxi-drivers who are not licensed and who will attempt to pick you up from outside a club or theatre. These guys will either charge you more than you agreed upon, not know where they are going, or they will be driving beat-up death-traps. There are also many stories of attacks on women, so if in doubt, don't get in!

Helicopter Services

Westland Heliport
020 7228 0181 www.helipad.co.uk

SW11's very own heliport! Aerial tours of London can be made online with Helipad running from Westland Heliport in Battersea, Elstree and London City Airport. The nearest tube is Clapham Junction.

EBG Helicopters
01737 823 282 www.ebghelicopters.co.uk

Running helicopter tours of London and charter flights from Redhill Airport in Surrey, 10 minutes by car from Gatwick Airport. £140 will get you 35 minutes over London, the only downside is getting to Surrey. Flights are between 10-4pm. Also offers charters for weddings and corporate events. Flying from Heathrow? Take a 20 minute sky ride for a cool £1,200.

Helicopter Days
08704 430 555 www.helicopterdays.co.uk

Operating out of Biggin Hill, 30-minute flights over Canary Wharf and Westminster start at £119 per person and you can cram up to 5 friends in with you. Lessons are available for £165. For drivers the helipad's close to M25 or you can be picked up by a helicopter from another location!

Elstree Aerodrome
020 8953 7480 www.egtr.net

A variety of charters operate out of Elstree offering sky tours, as well as flight academies for those who want to take the wheel. On site is The Elstree Bar & Café, plus it's close to M1.

Ferries/Boat Tours, Rentals & Charters

London River Services (LRS)
020 7222 1234
www.tfl.com/gettingaround

Provides commuter river transportation on the Thames. This runs in the East from Masthouse Terrace Pier to Savoy Pier at Embankment. In peak hours extensions on the Eastern service runs to Woolwich Arsenal with a further peak service from Blackfriars Pier in the City to Putney Pier in the west costing £13.50 return. WiFi is available on Eastern services. Services run every 20 minutes. All are wheelchair friendly.

Thames Clippers
0870 7815049
www.thamesclippers.com

London's answer to the NYC water taxis, primarily serving the O2 stadium from Waterloo, Embankment and Tower Bridge. Conveniently runs later than the Tube meaning you can actually stay right to the end of a show

without the worry of being stranded on the south side of the river. Single tickets cost between £2.60-4 with Oyster Card holders getting 1/3 off. Boats leave every 15 minutes.

Bateux London
020 7925 2215
www.bateuxlondon.com.

Dinner, lunch and charter cruises from Embankment Pier. Yes, there's even a jazz cruise.

Westminster Passenger Services Association
020 7930 2062
www.wpsa.co.uk

One of the only popular charters to offer services upriver to Kew, Richmond and Hampton Court.

City Cruises
020 7740 0400
www.citycruises.com.

Hop on hop off services primarily aimed at tourists and with tourist prices. Tickets start from £9.80

return for adults from Greenwich to Westminster/Waterloo Pier.

Heritage Boat Charters
01932 224 800
www.heritageboatcharters.com

For something different, try messing about on the river in one of these historic wooden numbers. On offer are skippered cruises down the Thames starting at £825. Formal dinner on board is available.

Silver Fleet Woods River Cruises
020 7481 2711
www.silverfleet.co.uk

Luxury chartered boats. Particularly good at putting on top-notch corporate events.

Thames Cruises
020 7928 9009
www.thamescruises.com

Two words—disco cruise. Hot pants are not required for dinner cruises.

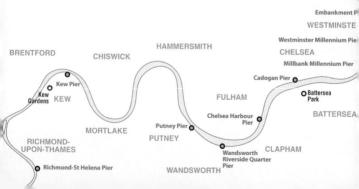

Marinas/Passenger Ship Terminal

Chelsea Marina
07770 542 783
www.chelseaharbourmarina.com

Despite being in upmarket Chelsea, the prices for mooring your boat here are incredibly generous—£2 per metre a night or £300 a year with space for 60 boats. Secure subterranean parking also available.

Chiswick Quay Marina
020 8994 8743
www.chiswickquay.com/marina

Great, secluded spot for West Londoners near Chiswick Bridge. A little far from a tube station, yet Chiswick overland station is within walking distance with services to Waterloo. Prices are on an annual basis at £162 per metre including a resident harbourmaster, shower block, mains water and electricity.

Gallions Point Marina
020 7476 7054
www.gallionspointmarina.co.uk

In London's Docklands and therefore perfect for those working in the city.

St Katharine Haven
020 7481 8350
www.stkaths.co.uk

One of London's best marinas. Great location by Tower Bridge, close to the quayside bars and restaurants and reasonable London prices—£3.60 per metre, per day.

Welcome Floating Terminal in Greenwich
01474 562 200
www.portoflondon.co.uk

Built in 2004 and believed to be the world's first floating terminal. Welcome has on-site immigration and custom services for cruise ship passengers entering or leaving London.

London Cruise Terminal at Tilbury
01375 852 360
www.londoncruiseterminal.com

The most popular regional departure point for passenger liners is 25 miles from Central London in Essex. Its close proximity to the M25 makes it easy for Londoners to get to. Current destinations from here include Scandinavia and continental Europe.

With London's Congestion Charge, Low Emission Zone, pricey parking, kamikaze bus drivers, dreaded speed bumps, speed cameras and a road layout that would give Spock the night terrors—"it's so illogical Captain"—driving around town is something to be avoided. Combine this with over 7.5 million people who just want to get from A to B without anyone getting in their frickin' way, and you can see where problems arise.

But, there are times when a four-wheeler is the only option, and for those times here are some things to watch out for:

Pedestrians love to stride purposefully into the road with nary a thought for their safety. Keep a weather eye out, one foot over the brake and one hand over the horn.

Cyclists are ever-increasing in number—give them plenty of space and remember for the one speedhound jumping the lights there are hundreds of law abiders that you just don't notice. Try to focus on them.

Motorbikes and Scooters are not all ridden by leather clad Hells Angels or Jamie Oliver clones; most just want get about and avoid the Congestion Charge. As with cyclists, give plenty of space and check your blind spots.

Black Cabs, these roving London landmarks have been known, on occasion, to pull up to the curb, do a 'U-ie' and even advertise the FT without sufficient warning.

Traffic Wardens A.K.A. 'council revenue generating units'. Make sure you avoid illegal parking—unless you are an ambassador.

Driving Statistics

Speed Limit: **30 mph**

Average speed in rush hour: **6 mph** (estimates vary)

Amount stolen from Westminster parking meters: **Over £50,000 a week**

Increase in congestion predicted by 2015: **25%**

Amount of UK Carbon emissions coming from road traffic: **21%**

Worst day of the week for accidents: **Friday**

Ways to make it bearable

Most of the stress caused by driving in London, apart from the sheer volume of traffic, is caused by lack of consideration for others—usually as drivers are running late. So make sure you leave PLENTY of time for your journey, try not to block junctions, and let people out if you have a chance.

Get a tiny car that you can park sideways. Ha! That'll show 'em.

Join a car club like Street Car or WhizzGo– then you can drive whenever you want at a fraction of the cost of owning a car.

Try and avoid rush hour. Morning rush lasts from 7 am to 10.30 am, lunch rush from 11 am to 2.30 pm, school run rush from 2.45 pm to 4.15 pm and afternoon rush from 4.30 pm to 8.45 pm. Bonne chance…

Driving in the Congestion Charge Zone and the Low Emission Zone

The Congestion Zone, introduced in 2003, meant the centre of town was remarkably less congested—for about twenty minutes if the Daily Mail is to be believed. The charge is currently £8 if you enter the zone between 07:00 and 18:00, Monday to Friday. Bank Holidays don't count. If you pay a day late the charge goes up to £10. After that, hefty fines apply. Huge red Cs in circles alert drivers to the start of the zone, if you miss them you should consider a swift visit to your optician. Check the website for exemptions. There is ongoing debate over the actual impact of the charge, and whether the zone will expand, or be removed altogether.

The Low Emission Zone (LEZ) was introduced in February 2008 to deter large lorries, buses, coaches and vans from dragging their belching exhausts through town. It covers a much larger area than the Congestion Charge: almost all of London within the M25 and applies 24/7. The charge varies between £100 and £200. A DAY.

Key Roads

A1
Running straight north from St Paul's Cathedral in the City through Islington, Archway, Highgate and beyond, this old Roman Road has some freer stretches allowing the frustrated drive to accelerate to 43 mph for 3 seconds, get a speeding ticket and then slam on the brakes. Ends (eventually) in Princes Street, Edinburgh, Scotland.

North Circular/South Circular (A406)
This is the M25's angrier and twisted little brother. Circling Outer London it has some of the busiest stretches of road in London and even includes a ferry across the river at Woolwich. The way dwindles to one exhausted lane in certain sections, causing great clots of traffic every day in rush hour. See left for rush hour times.

Euston Rd/Marylebone Road (A501)
Running east-west past King's Cross and Euston, this wide road skirts the northern edge of the congestion zone. It gets very crowded, because it's a feeder road to the relatively breezy start of the A40 heading out of London.

Embankment
The view as you drive along the Embankment along the north bank of the Thames is breathtaking. It needs to be to keep you occupied as you inch forward for hours. Runs from Chelsea (A4) to Tower Bridge.

Vauxhall Bridge Rd/Grosvenor Place/Park Lane/Edgware Rd (A5)
Running roughly north-west from Vauxhall Bridge Rd, around Victoria, past Hyde Park Corner and Marble Arch and out to join the A40, this route is a free corridor through the Congestion zone – free from charge rather than free from traffic. Be prepared—it's rammed.

Old Kent Rd / New Cross Rd / Lewisham Way / etc. (A2/A20)
Running south-west from The Bricklayers Arms roundabout and eventually down to Dover, where you catch the ferry to France; the Old Kent Rd, despite being the cheapest Monopoly property, is totally free from traffic at all times. No wait—that can't be right.

A3
Starting at London Bridge, this road eventually ends up in Portsmouth, but you have to struggle past Elephant and Castle, Clapham Common and Wimbledon Common along with everyone else trying to get to Guildford.

Traffic Hot Spots
Angel, Elephant and Castle, Hanger Lane Gyratory, Vauxhall Gyratory, Trafalgar Square, Parliament Square, Hammersmith Gyratory, everywhere else.

Useful links

TfL Interactive Traffic Map:
trafficalerts.tfl.gov.uk/microsite

Capital FM for traffic news from the Flying Eye 95.8 FM

Parking for Cars
www.park-up.com

Parking for Motorbikes and Scooters:
www.parkingforbikes.com

Route Planner:
www.theaa.com/travelwatch/planner_main.jsp

Congestion Charge:
www.tfl.gov.uk/roadusers/congestioncharging

Parking Ticket Appeals:
www.ticketbusters.co.uk

The great thing about being a Londoner is there's really no need to have a car. Except on those few occasions where you're cursing yourself for hauling a flat-packed Ikea coffee table on the shitty Croydon tram service. This is where joining a membership-based carsharing company, such as Streetcar (www.streetcar.co.uk; 0845 644 8475), Zipcar (www.zipcar.co.uk; 0800 011 2555) or City Car Club (www.citycarclub.co.uk; 0845 330 1234) comes in handy.

Streetcar and Zipcar are your best bet, as they offer self-service cars and vans to members, billable by the hour, day, week or month. The beauty of this service is there's probably either a Zipcar or Streetcar parked around the corner from wherever you are in central London, which means you don't have to hike to a car rental centre, stand in a queue or deal with annoying upselling at a counter. Plus,

if you get thrown out of your girlfriend's flat at 2 am and need a ride, you're in luck. Both offer a 24/7, 365 day a year self-service. For a membership fee of £50 a year, you have access to a fleet of cars, where all you have to do is enter the PIN, grab the keys from the glovebox and away you go.

On top of the membership fee, prices vary from £5.95 to £7.50 p/h depending on the company. The difference between Streetcar and Zipcar is the car. Streetcar offers only Volkswagens but their prices are pretty standardised. With Zipcar, you can have fun varying the car, with Minis, environmentally-friendly hybrids and BMWs on offer—but this means prices can vary too.

If you must go the conventional route, there are, of course, Hertz, National, and Avis centres aplenty, but for a smart Londoner who only wants a car sometimes—go for a carshare.

Company	Address	Phone	Map
Avis	8 Balderton St	0870 153 9104	002
Avis	88 Eversholt St	0840 010 7967	078
Avis	20 Seagrave Rd	0870 010 7968	043
Avis	86 St Katharines Wy	0207 423 8875	095
Avis	33 York Rd	0870 608 6369	104
Easy Car	Elms Mews	0871 0500 444	030
Easy Car	20 Seagrave Rd	0871 0500 444	043
Easy Car	88 Eversholt St	0871 0500 444	078
Easy Car	77 Britannia Rd	0871 0500 444	043
Easy Car	37 Munster Rd	0871 0500 444	048
Easy Car	68 Clapham Rd	0871 0500 444	135
Easy Car	136 Pentonville Rd	0871 0500 444	079
Easy Car	1 Brewery Rd	0871 0500 444	073
Easy Car	7 Bryanston St	0871 0500 444	001
Easy Car	171 Battersea Park Rd	0871 0500 444	133
Easy Car	43 York Rd	0871 0500 444	104
Easy Car	131 Belsize Rd	0871 0500 444	068
Easy Car	8 Balderton St	0871 0500 444	002
Easy Car	12 Semley Pl	0871 0500 444	019
Easy Car	33 York Rd	0871 0500 444	104
Easy Car	245 Warwick Rd	0871 0500 444	034
Enterprise	145 Bow Rd	02089805600	094
Enterprise	131 Belsize Rd	02073280200	068
Enterprise	200 King St	02085637400	040
Enterprise	59 Royal Mint St	02076809944	095
Enterprise	202 Ilderton Rd	02077323838	116
Enterprise	49 Woburn Pl	02076314700	094
Hertz	156 Southampton Row	087 0850 2664	004
Hertz	200 Buckingham Palace Rd	0870 8460002	020
Hertz	35 Edgware Rd	0870 8460011	001
Hertz	79 Clapham Rd	0207 582 5775	135
Hertz	713 Old Kent Rd	020 76392121	116
National	68 Clapham Rd	44 207 8200202	135
National	150 Pentonville Rd	44 20 72782273	079
National	7 Bryanston St	44 207 4081255	001
National	12 Semley Pl	44 207 2 59 16 00	019
National	43 York Rd	44 207 9282725	104
Thrifty	131 Belsize Rd	44 20 76253556	068
Thrifty	Sloane Ave	44 02072622223	046
Thrifty	178 Tower Bridge Rd	44 02074033458	107

Petrol Stations	Address	Map
Total	170 Marylebone Rd	002
Jet	30 Clipstone St	003
BP	Russell Ct & Woburn Pl	004
Shell	198 Old St	007
BP	Park Ln & Mount St	009
BP	Vauxhall Bridge Rd & Udall St	021
Esso	115 Sutherland Ave	027
Shell	104 Bayswater Rd	030
Texaco	383 Edgware Rd	031
BP	383 Edgware Rd	031
BP	1 Westwick Gardens	033
BP	Shepherds Bush Green & Rockley Rd	033
Total	137 Chiswick High Rd	038
Total	372 Goldhawk Rd	039
BP	Great West Rd & Oil Mill Ln	039
BP	372 Goldhawk Rd	039
Jet	182 Goldhawk Rd	040
BP	Talgarth Rd & Gliddon Rd	041
Tesco	459 Fulham Rd	043
Shell	49 Tadema Rd	044
Shell	106 Old Brompton Rd	045
Tesco	601 King's Rd	049
Total	31 N Rd	051
Esso	640 Holloway Rd	060
Texaco	73 Stapleton Hall Rd	062
Jet	314 7 Sisters Rd	063
Total	409 Kilburn High Rd	065
BP	Finchley Rd & College Crescent	066
BP	Haverstock Hill & Oman Rd	067
BP	Wellington Rd & Wellington Pl	068
Tesco	115 Maida Vale	068
Esso	33 Chalk Farm Rd	071
BP	142 Camden Rd	072
Tesco	196 Camden Rd	073
Sainsbury's	4 Williamson St	073
Total	109 York Wy	073
Sainsbury's	104 Holloway Rd	074
Sainsbury's	89 Hornsey Rd	074
BP	Hampstead Rd & Cardington St	077
BP	Goodsway & Camley St	078
Shell	276 Upper St	080
Jet	43 Stamford Hill	083
BP	144 Stoke Newington Rd	086
Texaco	168 Shoreditch High St	091

Petrol Stations	Address	Map
Total	112 Vallance Rd	091
BP	Cambridge Heath Rd & Paradise Row	092
Sainsbury's	1 Cambridge Heath Rd	092
Texaco	51 Grove Rd	093
Texaco	127 Bow Rd	094
Texaco	77 The Highway	095
Texaco	102 The Hwy	096
Shell	139 Whitechapel Rd	096
ASDA	151 E Ferry Rd	103
Shell	101 Southwark Bridge Rd	106
Shell	137 Walworth Rd	113
BP	New Kent Rd & Balfour St	113
Total	234 Old Kent Rd	114
Tesco	107 Dunton Rd	114
Total	272 St James Rd	115
Jet	747 Old Kent Rd	116
Sainsbury's	101 Evelyn St	118
Jet	179 Creek Rd	119
Jet	25 Greenwich High Rd	120
BP	Camberwell Rd & Albany Rd	121
BP	Peckham Rd & Southampton Wy	122
Total	38 Peckham Rd	122
BP	New Cross Rd & Pomeroy St	125
Sainsbury's	263 New Cross Rd	125
Jet	42 Hinton Rd	127
Jet	13 E Dulwich Rd	130
Texaco	213 Kennington Rd	131
BP	238 Kennington Ln	131
Shell	326 Queenstown Rd	133
Sainsbury's	326 Queenstown Rd	133
Esso	2 Battersea Park Rd	133
Esso	54 Wandsworth Rd	134
Sainsbury's	62 Wandsworth Rd	134
Esso	77 Clapham Rd	135
Total	257 Upper Richmond Rd	136
BP	Swandon Wy & Smugglers Wy	138
Texaco	474 Wandsworth Rd	142
Tesco	330 Brixton Rd	144
Esso	243 Brixton Rd	145
Total	39 Nightingale Ln	147
Total	40 Balham Hill	148
BP	124 Brixton Hill	150
BP	Marius Rd & Rowfant Rd	151

General Information • **Calendar of Events**

January

- **New Year's Day Parade** • Big Ben to Piccadilly Circus • Marching band and thousands of kids. How better to cure a hangover?
- **London Boat Show** • ExCel Exhibition Centre • Like we always say: you can never have too many yachts.
- **Russian Winter Festival** • Trafalgar Square • Magical Russian Winterland replaces the normal Pigeon-Crap Land.
- **London Art Fair** • Business Design Centre • Pick up something to hide that patch of mould.
- **Destinations: Holiday and Travel Show** • Earls Court Exhibition Centre • Chase away the January Blues.
- **Chinese New Year** • West End • Party like it's 4707.
- **London International Mime Festival** • Southbank Centre • Even weirder when you see it for real.
- **Charles I Commemoration Ceremony** • Trafalgar Sq - St James' Palace • Thousands of uniformed Cavaliers confuse the tourists.

February

- **London Fashion Week** • Natural History Museum • Far Too Thin.
- **National Wedding Show** • Olympia • Perfect day out for a first date.
- **Lifted** • Harrods • A bizarre annual exhibition inside Harrod's lifts.
- **The Great Spitalfields Pancake Race** • Old Truman Brewery • Pancake race in wacky clothes. No, London. Just, no.
- **Blessing the Throats** • St Etheldreda's Church, Ely Place • Lemsip not working? Sore throats cured by holy candle.
- **Clowns' Service** • Holy Trinity, Dalston • Because God likes clowns too.

March

- **Affordable Art Fair** • The Marquee, Battersea Park • Now

even The Great Unwashed can buy art!
- **Ideal Home Show** • Earls Court Exhibition Centre • Make your home ideal (or a bit less grotty).
- **St Patrick's Day Parade** • Park Lane • Shamrocks, river-dancing, big fluffy Guinness hats: true Irish tradition.
- **East Festival** • East London • Because East London isn't just for muggers.

April

- **Oxford & Cambridge Boat Race** • River Thames • Hole up in a pub by the river and cheer over a beer.
- **Careers and Jobs Live** • ExCel Exhibition Centre • Career ideas and thousands of vacancies.
- **Flora London Marathon** • Greenwich – The Mall • 35,000 pairs of bleeding nipples.
- **London Book Fair** • Earl's Court • The publishing industry's main event. Occasionally stuff for free.
- **Camden Crawl** • Throughout Camden • If you're not crawling by the end, you haven't done it right.
- **Alternative Fashion Week** • Old Spitalfields Market • Huge range of cutting edge fashion. And fetishwear.
- **BAFTAs** • London Palladium • Ten points per autograph.
- **Queen's Birthday Gun Salute** • Hyde Park • Who said the monarchy is archaic?
- **St George's Day** • Covent Garden / Cenotaph / Shakespeare's Globe • Brush up your Morris dancing skills.
- **The Real Food Festival** • Earl's Court Exhibition Centre • Real Food: much nicer than fake food.
- **Hot Cross Bun Service** • St Bartholomew-the-Great, Smithfield • Widows get a free hot cross bun. Worth losing the husband.

May

- **Sci-Fi Festival** • London Apollo • The UK's only Sci-Fi Festival. Thank god.
- **Baishakhi Mela** • Brick Lane • Celebrate the Bengali New Year in

the British tradition: vindaloo.
- **Mind, Body, Spirit Festival** • Royal Horticultural Halls • Make up for all the time in the pub.

June

- **Start of Open Air Theatre season** • Regent's Park • Ignore the climate and take in an outdoor play.
- **Taste of London** • Regent's Park • The best picnic in the world.
- **O2 Wireless Festival** • Hyde Park • Big names vibrate the Serpentine.
- **Wimbledon** • All England Lawn Tennis and Croquet Club • Short skirts and grunting. Marvellous.
- **Trooping the Colour** • Horse Guard's Parade • Hundreds of chaps in uniforms. Ohhhhh yes.
- **Meltdown Festival** • Southbank Centre • Eclectic music festival curated by major musicians.
- **Chelsea Flower Show** • Royal Hospital Chelsea • You'll go for the flowers. You'll stay for the Pimms.
- **Royal Academy Summer Exhibition** • Royal Academy • Lots and lots and LOTS of art.
- **Big Sexy Festy Party** • Finsbury Park • So good-natured you'll want to hug a tree. And it's FREE!

July

- **The Big Dance (biennial: even years)** • Various around London • London learns to dance.
- **The Drag Olympics** • The Way Out Club • Drag Queens are put through their pedicured, high-heeled paces.
- **Dogget's Coat & Badge Race** • Thames: London Bridge to Chelsea • Intense boat race to win a badge. Hardly seems worth it.
- **Pimms Urban Regatta** • Finsbury Square • People full of Pimms race on land in bottomless boats. Bloody Ozzies.
- **Pride of London** • Trafalgar Square • One of Britain's biggest, funnest street parties.
- **The British 10k London Run** • Hyde Park - Whitehall • Work off the pies.
- **Hampton Court Palace Show** • Hampton Court • Stock up your

garden / flowerpot / imagination.
- **The Chap Olympics** • Bedford Square Gardens • Olympics for gentleman—no sportswear please.
- **Rise Festival** • Finsbury Park • Celebrating the best of multicultural London, for free.
- **Swan Upping** • River Thames • Census of swans. For goodness sake.
- **Opening of Buckingham Palace** • Buckingham Palace • The Plebeians allowed in to see how their taxes (and steep entrance fees) are spent.

August

- **Innocent Smoothies Festival** • Regent's Park • You wouldn't think fun could be this wholesome.
- **Great British Beer Festival** • Earls Court Exhibition Centre • A festival that puts the Great in Britain.
- **Trafalgar Square Festival** • Trafalgar Square • 3 weeks of music, theatre, dance and art.
- **Carnaval del Pueblo** • Burgess Park • Thousands of Latino lovelies. That's all you need to know, right?
- **London Triathlon** • Docklands • Marathons are for pussies.
- **London Mela** • Gunnersbury Park • Partaaaay, Asia-style.
- **Metro Weekender** • Clapham Common • Dance music Saturday, bands on Sunday, chilled all weekend.
- **Notting Hill Carnival** • Ladbroke Grove • Party till your wallet gets nicked.
- **Kids Week** • West End • West End shows free for kids. Soooo unfaaaaaiiiiir.
- **Shoreditch Festival** • Shoreditch. • Because you can never have too many local festivals. Apparently.
- **Bathing the Buddha** • Leicester Square • Buddha gets a birthday bath.

September

- **The Great British Duck Race** • The Thames • Like the Oxbridge boat race. But with 165,000 rubber ducks.

- **Horseman's Sunday** • Hyde Park Crescent • London's horses say their Hail Maries. Yes, really.
- **Oyster & Seafood Fair** • Hays Galleria • The romance of oysters with the unholy stink of kippers.
- **Thames Festival** • Tower Bridge - Westminster • Fireworks, costumes, river races, carnivals. Kids like it.
- **Last Night of the Proms** • Royal Albert Hall • Camp overnight if you want tickets.
- **Spitalfields Show & Green Fair** • Buxton Street • Who has the biggest marrow?
- **Open House Weekend** • Various around London • Over 600 architectural landmarks open for a nosey.

October

- **The Big Draw** • Museum of Childhood • Pencils, not guns. Unfortunately.
- **Cockney Pearly Kings & Queens** • Church of St Martin-in-the-Fields • British eccentricity at its best.
- **London Tattoo Convention** • Old Truman Brewery • Who cares if it looks crap when you're 80?
- **International Halloween Festival** • Queen Mary College • Witches, druids and shamans unite for Europe's biggest Pagan festival.
- **Halloween** • London Dungeon • Trick Or Treating is for pussies.
- **Frieze Art Fair** • Regent's Park • Air kisses all round.
- **London Film Festival** • BFI Southbank • Two weeks of the best new films and lectures from A-Listers.
- **Metro Ski & Snowboard Show** • Olympia • London hosts the world's biggest winter sport show. Naturally.
- **Shell Wildlife Photographer of the Year (exhibition opens, for 6mths)** • Natural History Museum • Puts your arty market photos to shame.
- **The Yoga Show** • Olympia • Bendy people upon bendy people. Literally.

November

- **London's Christmas Ice Rinks** • Venues across London • Much more romantic in your head than in reality.
- **London-Brighton Car Race** • Starts Hyde Park • Century-old bangers potter their way to Brighton.
- **Erotica Show** • Olympia • 31,000 horny adults pretend they're just browsing.
- **Bonfire Night** • Venues across London • Hundreds of thousands of pounds go pop.
- **Royal British Legion Festival of Remembrance** • Royal Albert Hall • Take tissues.
- **Lord Mayor's Show** • Central London • Running for over 800 years and yet still a bit crap.
- **London Jazz Festival** • South Bank Centre • Start practising your jazz hands.

December

- **Satan's Grotto** • London Dungeon • Tortured elves and spit-roasting robins.
- **Trafalgar Square Christmas Tree** • Trafalgar Square • The only thing everyone knows about Oslo.
- **Blackrock Masters Tennis** • Royal Albert Hall • Former World No.1s wheeze their way through a tournament.
- **Peter Pan Cup** • Serpentine Lido, Hyde Park • Freeze your nipples off on Christmas morning.
- **Christmas Pudding Race** • Covent Garden • We're mad, us! What are we like? Crazy!
- **Christmas Carol Sing-along** • Royal Albert Hall • Belt out your favourites and get in the mood.
- **International Horse Show** • Olympia • Not just for posh people. But mostly.
- **Midnight Mass at St Paul's** • St Paul's • Eats the other Midnight Masses for breakfast.
- **New Year's Eve Fireworks** • Jubilee Gardens • Ooooooh. And, of course, aaaaaaah.

(419)

Tactics

Finding somewhere to live in London is a ruthless and cutthroat business. Make sure you have plenty of red bull, cigarettes and patience. Also take a week off. And hire a driver, maybe.

Ok, so these precautions aren't completely necessary, but you will have to work in mysterious and multifarious ways if you don't want to spend the next six months paying through your gullible nose for mice and verrucas. A good place to start is everywhere you can think of. Estate agents (see below for a list) will invariably try and rip you off but, then again, so will everyone else, so it's worth registering with all the big ones, as well as any whose office you see in the street, or you spot in newspapers, on TV or the internet. After uncovering a fair few completely brazen lies in the property listings on www.gumtree.com you will find that many of the smaller businesses place adverts for (sometimes fake) properties here. Don't be put off by the lies though, because this can be a good way of finding an agent (or getting in direct contact with a landlord) who is keen to make a deal with you, or who will try and match the prices advertised, even if they have nothing that fits the bill at the exact moment of lying. Of course, some of these listings are also genuine, and a good way to find rooms/apartments at lower than usual rates. Just bare in mind that a LOT of people use this site.

General sites

www.gumtree.com
www.findaproperty.co.uk
www.craigslist.org
www.rightmove.co.uk
www.propertyfinder.com

Estate Agents

There are hundreds of Estate Agents and Letting Agents across the city, some of the larger players (good and bad) include:

www.foxtons.co.uk - Offices all over London.
www.keatons.co.uk - Bow, Hackney, Harringey, Kentish Town, Stratford.
www.black-katz.com - Lettings only agency, numerous offices.
www.fjlord.co.uk - Numerous offices, specialise in uncooperative staff.
www.nelsonslettings.com - South and central London.
www.atkinsonmcleod.com - City and Docklands.

If you do end up using an agent, they will of course want to charge you an additional fee beyond any deposits or advance rent required by the landlord. But, as many of the agents in central London are close together, it's possible that they may be competing with each other to sell/rent the same properties. This will enable you to get a better deal. So shop around, be devious, and backstab as much as possible.

Council Tax

Council Tax is an annoying hidden cost that always comes as a bit of a surprise. It is worked out by your local council and is based on the value of your house/flat, which the council will already have placed in to one of 8 tax bands (bands are A–G, G covering the most valuable properties).There are several ways to determine the value of a property, but the easiest is probably to go to the website of the valuation office at www.voa.gov.uk. Having done that, it's possible to weigh up the benefits of different areas by comparing the council tax in equivalent bands charged by different local councils. It's fairly laborious, but worth it in the long run, if you can be bothered.

Because council tax is based on the property, not the people inside it, the rate is constant no matter how many people live in the house. This means that it's much cheaper to live in a big house with lots of people to split the tax with, than on your own, when you are liable for the full amount. Students do not have to pay council tax at all, but if they are sharing with one or more non-students then there will still be council tax to pay. A single non-student in a house full of students receives a 25% discount on his/her council tax bill, but if there is more than one non-student then all non-students are liable to pay full whack.

Alternative Options

In a city where house prices have been soaring through the roof for some time now (although it's calmed down somewhat recently), of course people do things like squat, have dreadlocks and go vegan. If you're not willing to go the whole way but fancy an adventure, or simply don't have much money, then it might be worth taking a look at being a guardian for Camelot. This company aims to fill vacant properties with responsible people who will prevent them from being abused. You must have good references, a job, and be over eighteen, as well as be ok with sharing with an indeterminate number of strangers, but the benefits are the unusual properties (e.g. schools, disused churches), the often large spaces and the ridiculously cheap rent (£25–60 pw inclusive of all bills). Of course loads of people want to do this and properties in London are not always available, but it's nevertheless a good idea to keep an eye on their site if the idea excites you: www.camelotproperty.co.uk.

The best of the best

London is full of interactive children's pursuits, and nothing beats discovering all the joys that the city has to offer to the little ones, so we thought we'd give you some inside tips on what there is!

- **Best Rainy Day Activity:** The Science Museum (Exhibition Road, SW7 2DD, 0870 870 4868) is great fun and one of London's most interactive museums. Don't miss the Launchpad gallery, which is full of hands-on exhibits to tinker with, simulators and a face morphing machine. The museum's occasional Science Nights are activity filled, with overnight camping in the building included. Entry is free. Open 7 days a week from 10am to 6pm.

- **Coolest Cinema:** The BFI London IMAX Cinema (1 Charlie Chaplin Walk, SE1 8XR, 020 7902 1234) has the largest screen (20 metres) in the country, as well as an 11,600-watt digital surround sound system with which to deafen your children. With most of the cinema's 3D programming dedicated to children's films, they'll be spoilt rotten by the whole experience; even the entrance to the place is cool, with futuristic blue lighting paving your way through the tunnels.

- **Goriest Tourist Haunt:** The London Dungeon (28-34 Tooley Street, SE1 2SZ, 020 7403 7221) specialises in the darker side of English history and has a preponderance of gruesome waxworks, theme rides and costumed staff to scare the bejesus out of your children, which they'll love (unless you've brought them up to be soft). Open all week from 11am to 5pm.

- **Best Tour For Budding Media Moguls:** The BBC Television Centre Tour (Wood Lane, W12 7RJ, 0870 603 0304) provides a chance for children 9 and over to take a behind the scenes look at the world of TV, as well as a chance to play in an interactive studio. A separate tour (ages 7 and over) entitled "The CBBC Experience" is based on the BBC's kids' channel and offers visitors the chance to roam around the Blue Peter garden, amongst other things. Regular tours are conducted every day except Sunday.

- **Best Ice Cream:** It's no secret that kids love ice cream, but the plethora of dodgy "Mr Whippy" vans selling their frozen wares in London can be improved upon. For outstanding homemade gourmet sorbets and exotic ice cream cones, there is no better place than the kiosk to the side of Golders Hill Park Refreshment House (North End Road, NW3 7HD, 020 8455 8010); prices are very reasonable and the park is a gorgeous setting within which to consume such tasty delights.

- **Best One To Keep The Boys Happy:** The Arsenal Emirates Stadium Tour (Ashburton Grove, N7 7AF, 020 7704 4504). Surely even Spurs fans would appreciate a look behind the scenes at London's newest and most aesthetic football venue. Poke around the first team dressing room, walk down the player's tunnel and sample a unique pitchside view of the stadium; under 5s get in free.

- **Best For Halloween Costumes:** Escapade (150 Camden High Street, NW1 0NE, 020 7485 7384) has been kitting kids out in all manner of costumes since 1982, and offers wigs (maybe one for Dad?), hats, masks, make-up, jokes and magic tricks. Perfect for trick or treat, or for those already bored of their child's ugly face.

- **Best Eatery For Families:** Maxwell's (8-9 James Street, WC2E 8BH) lies deep in the heart of Covent Garden and specialises in burgers (does any child not like burgers?) which won't break parents' banks. A kids' menu is provided, as well as activities and games.

Rainy day activities

Especially for when the infamous London weather puts a dampener on outdoor activities…

- **Cartoon Museum** (35 Little Russell Street, WC1A 2HH, 020 7580 8155) This fascinating place archives the development of cartoon art in Britain, from the 18th century through to the present day; best of all, the Young Artists' Gallery lets children try their hands at animation and claymation.

- **London Aquarium** (County Hall, Westminster Bridge Road, SE1 7PB, 020 7967 8000) One of the largest aquariums in the world, over 400 species of aquatic life (including the only zebra sharks in the U.K.) can be found within this building. With three floors, piranhas, and pools where you can prod things, there's more than enough to keep even the most jaded parent happy.

- **London Eye** (Jubilee Gardens, South Bank, SE1 7PB, 0870 500 0600) This 135-metre high riverside Ferris wheel offers breathtaking views of London in up to 25 miles in each direction, all from the vantage point of an air-conditioned glass pod. Book online to beat the queues.

- **Natural History Museum** (Cromwell Road, SW7 5BD, 020 7942 5000) Ever wanted to see a replica skeleton of a 26-metre long Diplodocus dinosaur? It's one of the 70 million items housed within this excellent museum, which also includes the Darwin Centre, a must for any budding paleontologists; non-nerds should love it too.

- **Madame Tussaud's** (Marylebone Road, NW1 5LR, 0870 999 0046) Infamous exhibition of waxworks, with recently introduced interactive exhibits giving you the chance to score a goal for England or sing with Britney Spears (she'll be the one lip-syncing). Worth booking online to avoid the often long queues.

- **Museum Of London** (150 London Wall, EC2Y 5HN, 0870 444 3852, some galleries undergoing renovation and due to re-open late 2009) Explains the history of London in vivid detail; the innovative layout consists of a chain of chronological galleries (no skipping to 1945, OK?) Also has fragments of the old London Wall in the grounds.

- **Peter Harrison Planetarium** (Royal Observatory Greenwich, Greenwich Park, SE10 9NF, 020 8312 8565) Open since 2007 and the only planetarium in London seats 120 and uses the latest technology to take you on an armchair tour of the universe. Children aged 4 and under will not be admitted.

- **Queens Ice And Bowl** (17 Queensway, W2 4QP, 020 7229 0172) An ice rink, ten pin bowling alleys and a pizza restaurant, it's the perfect opportunity for kids to stuff their faces whilst watching their Dad break a bone on the rink. Children's skating classes available.

- **Topsy Turvy World** (Brent Cross Shopping Centre, Prince Charles Drive, NW4 3FP, 020 8359 9920) A huge indoor playground in the middle of one of London's busiest shopping centres. There's more to this place than just bouncy things and over-excitement, it also offers baking activities (might as well get your children cooking for you early) and various classes.

- **Tower Of London** (Tower Hill, EC3N 4AB, 0870 756 7070) A cornucopia of royal history and English culture lies within the Tower's ancient walls, with royal jewels aplenty. Good for the whole family, and under 5s get in free. Avoid the queues by booking ahead.

- **The V&A Museum Of Childhood** (Cambridge Heath Road, E2 9PA, 020 8983 5200) This lesser known gem of the Victoria & Albert Museum houses the national childhood collection, which basically means it's full of toys, games, dolls, dollhouses, nursery antiques and children's costumes. There's no shortage of activities and events going on here to keep your kids occupied, and it's free.

Classes

A recent resurgence in the amount of out of school programmes being implemented in the capital means that there's more for your kids to do than ever before.

- **Art Club** (Orleans House Gallery, Riverside, TW1 3DJ, 020 8831 6000) A rare opportunity for 5-10 year olds to work with practicing artists and explore new techniques and materials. Every Wednesday and Thursday from 3.45-5pm.

- **Barnsbury One O'Clock Club** (Barnard Park, Hemingford Road, N1 0JU, 020 7278 9494) Fun and games for the under 5s.

- **Brixton Recreation Centre** (27 Brixton Station Road, SW9 8QQ, 020 7926 9779) Recently refurbished, this centre includes The Energy Zone (ages 5-15) for ball games and The Fitness Zone (ages 8-15) with SHOKK fitness equipment specifically designed for the younger body builder/steroid abuser.

- **Camden Square Play Centre** (Camden Square, NW1 9RE, 020 7485 6827) After school (and school holiday) centre with fun activities for children aged 4-12.

- **Camden Swiss Cottage Swimming Club** (Swiss Cottage Leisure Centre, Winchester Road, NW3 3NR, 020 7974 5440) Swimming lessons for children aged 4 and upward.

- **Chang's Hapkido Academy** (Topnotch Health Club, 3 Tudor Street, EC4Y 0AH, 07951 535876) Martial arts school with classes for ages 12 and upward.

- **The Circus Space** (Coronet Street, N1 6HD, 020 7613 4141) Prepare your children for a life in the circus with The Circus Space's variety of classes and workshops for all ages.

- **Crazee Kids** (Jackson Lane Community Centre, Archway Road, N6 5AA, Tuesdays), (Union Church & Community Centre, Weston Park, N8 9TA, Saturdays) 020 8444 5333. Weekly term-time dance, drama and music classes. Summer workshops.

- **Harringay Club** (Hornsey YMCA, 50 Tottenham Lane, N8 7EE, 020 8348 2124) A range of things to do for those aged up to 15, including a pre-school programme, gymnastics, ballet, street dance and kickboxing.

- **The Kids' Cookery School** (107 Gunnersbury Len W3 8HQ, 020 8992 8882) Get your kids cooking at this fine venue which offers classes and workshops for those aged 3 and upwards.

- **Kite Art Studios** (Priory Mews, 2B Bassein Park Road, W12 9RY, 020 8576 6278) Courses and workshops on painting, pottery and jewellery making amongst other fun activities for kids of all ages. Mother and toddler sessions too.

- **London Irish Centre** (50-52 Camden Square, NW1 9XB, 020 7916 7222) Irish dancing classes for beginners upwards, every Monday at 6pm, courtesy of the Barrett Semple-Morris School.

- **The Little Angel Theatre** (14 Dagmar Passage, Cross Street, N1 2DN, 020 7226 1787) Children's theatre offering after-school courses in puppet making, the art of puppetry performance and a Saturday Puppet Club.

- **The Little Gym** (Compass House, Riverside West, Smugglers Way, SW18 1DB, 020 8874 6567) Gymnastics and skills development within a relaxed environment for children aged up to 12.

- **Music House For Children** (Bush Hall, 310 Uxbridge Road, W12 7LJ, 020 8932 2652) Whether it's instrumental or singing lessons, this wonderful place can provide individual and group tuition and even caters for 1 year olds!

- **Painted Earth** (Arch 65, The Catacombs, Stables Market, NW1 8AH, 020 7424 8983) Ceramic arts classes supervised by staff. Children can make their own mugs and plates.

- **Richmond Junior Chess Club** (ETNA Community Centre, 13 Rosslyn Road, TW1 2AR, 07720 716336) Chess classes with a mixture of instruction and play for those up to the age of 18.

- **Sobell Leisure Centre** (Hornsey Road, N7 7NY, 020 7609 2166) No need to book, just turn up for coached sessions in basketball, badminton, football and ice hockey amongst other sports.

Children aged 7 and under must be accompanied by an adult.

- **Tricycle Theatre** (269 Kilburn High Road, NW6 7JR, 020 7328 1000) Not just a theatre/cinema/gallery, the Tricycle also runs term-time workshops in drama, storytelling and music.

- **Triyoga** (6 Erskine Road, NW3 3AJ, 020 7483 3344) Let the kids get their Zen on at after school yoga classes for ages 5 and over.

- **Westway Stables** (20 Stable Way, Latimer Road, W11 6QX, 020 8964 2140) Horse riding lessons for the over 5s in the heart of Notting Hill.

Babysitting/nanny/services,

- **Nannies Unlimited** 11 Chelveton Road, SW15 1RN, 020 8788 9640

- **Nanny Search** 1st Floor, 1 Shepherds Hill, N6 5QJ, 020 8348 4111

- **Sleeptight Nannies** 20 Nursery Road, N14 5QB, 020 8292 2618

- **Top Notch Nannies** 49 Harrington Gardens, SW7 4JU, 020 7259 2626

Where to go for more info

www.kidslovelondon.com

Shopping essentials

- **Baby Dior** 6 Harriet Street, SW1X 9JW, 020 7823 2039 – Encourage label envy as soon as possible.

- **Baby Munchkins** 186 Hoxton Street, N1 5LH, 020 7684 5994 – Baby wear.

- **Balloonland** 12 Hale Lane, NW7 3NX, 020 8906 3302 – Balloons and party supplies.

- **Benjamin Pollock's Toyshop** 44 The Piazza, Covent Garden WC2E 8RF, 020 7379 7866 – Toys.

- **Biff** 43 Dulwich Village, SE21 7BN, 020 8299 0911 – Designer and street brands.

- **Boomerang** 69 Blythe Road, W14 0HP, 020 7610 5232 – Clothes and necessities for tots.

- **Bonpoint** Chic clothes.
  17 Victoria Grove, W8 5RW – 020 7584 5131
  197 Westbourne Grove, W11 2SE – 020 7792 2515
  256 Brompton Road, SW3 2AS – 020 3263 5057
  35B Sloane Street, SW1X 9LP – 020 7235 1441
  38 Old Bond Street, W1S 4QW – 020 7495 1680

- **Burberry** 21-23 New Bond Street, W1S 2RE, 020 7839 5222 – Clothes.

- **Caramel** 291 Brompton Road, SW3 2DY, 020 7589 7001 – Cool clothes.

- **Catamini** – Babies and children's clothes. 33C King's Road, SW3 4LX – 020 7824 8897, 52 South Molton Street, W1Y 1HF – 020 7629 8099

- **Cheeky Monkeys** – Mainly wooden toys. 202 Kensington Park Road, W11 1NR – 020 7792 9022, 94 Kings Road, SW6 4UL – 020 7731 3037

- **Children's Book Centre** 237 Kensington High Street, W8 6SA, 020 7937 7497 – Books.

- **Coco Children's Boutique** 27A Devonshire Street, W1G 6PN, 020 7935 3554 – Children's boutique (fancy that!).

- **D2 Leisure** 201-203 Roman Road, E2 0QY, 020 8980 4966 – Bicycle shop.

- **Daisy & Tom** 181 King's Road, SW3 5EB, 020 7352 5000 – Clothes, toys and a carousel.

- **Davenports Magic Shop** 7 Adelaide Street, WC2N 4HZ, 020 7836 0408 – Magic shop.

- **Early Learning Centre** 36 King's Road, SW3 4UD, 020 7581 5764 – Educational toyshop.

- **Disney Store** – Disney merchandise.,

  Unit 10, The Piazza, WC2E 8HD – 020 7836 5037

  22A & 26 The Broadway Shopping Centre, W6 9YD – 020 8748 8886

  360-366 Oxford Street, W1N 9HA – 020 7491 9136

- **Eric Snook's Toyshop** 32 Covent Garden Market, WC1 8RE, 020 7379 7681 – Toys and teddies.

- **Escapade** 150 Camden High Street, NW1 0NE, 020 7485 7384 – Costumes and masks.

- **The Farmyard** 63 Barnes High Street, SW13 9LF, 020 8878 7338 – Toys for younger children and babies.

- **GapKids/Baby Gap**

  35 Hampstead High Street, NW3 1QE – 020 7794 9182

  146-148 Regent Street, W1B 5SH – 020 7287 5095

  Brent Cross Shopping Centre, NW4 3FB – 020 8203 9696

  122 King's Road, SW3 4TR – 020 7823 7272

  4 Queens Road, SW19 8YE- 020 8947 9074

  101-111 Kensington High Street, W8 5SA – 020 7368 2900

  260-262 Chiswick High Road, W4 1PD – 020 8995 3255

  47-49 St John's Wood High Street, NW8 7NJ – 020 7586 6123

  151 Queensway, W2 4YL – 020 7221 8039

  330-340 Cabot Place East, E14 4QT – 020 7513 0241

  121-123 Long Acre, WC2E 9PA – 020 7836 0646

- **Green Rabbit** 20 Briston Grove, N8 9EX, 020 8348 3770 – Contemporary kids' wear.

- **Hamley's** 188-196 Regent Street, W1B 5BT, 020 7153 9000 – Toys galore, tourists galore.

- **Happy Returns** 36 Rosslyn Hill, NW3 1NH, 020 7435 2431 – Toys again!

- **Honeyjam** 267 Portobello Road, W11 1LR, 020 7243 0449 – Retro and vintage toys and rocking horses.

- **Igloo Kids** Wide range of kids' clothes. 300 Upper Street, N1 2TU – 020 7354 7300, 80 St John's Wood, NW8 7SH – 020 7483 2332

- **Infantasia Unit 103** Wood Green Shopping City, N22 6YA, 020 8889 1494 – Furniture and bedding.

- **International Magic** 89 Clerkenwell Road, EC1R 5BX, 020 7405 7324 – Magic shop.

- **Joujou & Lucy** 32 Clifton Road, W9 1ST, 020 7289 0866 – Children's boutique.

- **Kent & Carey** 154 Wandsworth Bridge Road, SW6 2UH, 020 7736 5554 – Classic children's clothes.

- **Little Stinkies** 15 Victoria Grove, W8 5RW, 020 7052 0077 – Dolls' houses, toys and puppet theatres.

- **Marie Chantal** 148 Walton Street, SW3 2JJ, 020 7838 1111 – Children's fashion.

- **MIMMO** 602 Fulham Road, SW6 5PA, 020 7731 4706 – Designer duds.

- **Mothercare** – The leading chain for baby stuff in the UK; will sell you everything but the baby.

  Brent Cross Shopping Centre, NW4 3FD – 020 8202 5377

  416 Brixton Road, SW9 7AY – 020 7733 1494

  Unit 7, The Waterglade Centre, 1-8 The Broadway, W5 2ND – 0208 579 6181

  Ravenside Retail Park, Angel Road, N18 3HA – 020 8807 5518

  146 High Street, SE9 1BJ – 020 8859 7957

  4 Palace Gardens, EN2 6SN – 020 8367 1188

316 North End Road, SW6 1NG – 020 7381 6387

Kings Mall Shopping Centre, W6 0PZ – 020 8600 2860

448 Holloway Road, N7 6QA – 020 7607 0915

112 High Street, TW3 1NA – 020 8577 1767

Unit 1A, Richmond Retail Park, Mortlake Road, Kew – 020 8878 3758

41 Riverdale High Street, SE13 7EP – 020 8852 2167

526-528 Oxford Street, W1C 1LW – 0845 365 0515

Unit 2, Aylesham Centre, Rye Lane, SE15 5EW – 020 7358 0093

33-34 The Mall, E15 1XD – 020 8534 5714

BHS Surrey Quays Shopping Centre, Redriff Road, SE16 7LL – 020 7237 2025

Unit 59, Southside Shopping Centre, SW18 4TF – 020 8877 4180

Unit Lsu4, Centre Court, SW19 8YA – 020 8944 5296

38-40 High Road, N22 6BX – 020 8888 6920

62 Powis Street, SE18 1LQ – 020 8854 3540

- **Never Never Land** 3 Mildhurst Parade, Fortis Green, N10 3EJ, 020 883 3997 – Toys and dolls.

- **Olive Loves Alfie** 84 Stoke Newington Church Street, N16 0AP, 020 7241 4212 – Children's lifestyle boutique.

- **Patrick's Toys & Models** 107 Lillie Road, SW6 7SX, 020 7385 9864 – Outdoor games and equipment.

- **Patrizia Wigan** 19 Walton Street, SW3 2HX, 020 7823 7080 – Clothing boutique.

- **Petit Bateau** 62 South Molton Street, W1K 5SR, 020 7491 4498 – Luxurious baby wear.

- **Petite Ange** 6 Harriet Street, SW1X 9JW, 020 7235 7737 – Exclusive clothing.

- **Please Mum** 85 Knightsbridge, SW1X 7RB, 020 7486 1380 – Expensive clothing.

- **Pom D'Api** 3 Blenheim Crescent, W11 2EE, 020 7243 0535 – Classy shoes.

- **QT Toys** 90 Northcote Road, SW11 6QN, 020 7223 8637 – Toys, games and gifts.

- **Rachel Riley** 14 Pont Street, SW1X 9EN, 020 7935 7007 – Clothes.

- **Rainbow** 253 Archway Road, N6 5BS, 020 8340 9700 – Toys, games and clothes.

- **Showroom** 64 Titchfield Street, W1W 7QH, 020 7636 2501 – Funky children's clothes.

- **Soup Dragon** 27 Topsfield Parade, Tottenham Lane, N8 8PT, 020 8348 0224 – Toys and clothes.

- **The Shoe Station** 3 Station Approach, Kew Gardens, TW9 3QB, 020 8940 9905 – Shoes and footwear.

- **Their Nibs** 214 Kensington Park Road, W11 1NR, 020 7221 4263 – Designer clothes and bedding.

- **Tots** 39 Turnham Green Terrace, W4 1RG, 020 8995 0520 – Clothes boutique.

- **Toys R Us** - Toys, toys, toys.

Tilling Road (opposite Brent Cross Shopping Centre), NW2 1LW – 020 8209 0019

Great Cambridge Road, EN1 3RN – 020 8364 6600

Hayes Road, UB2 5LN – 020 8561 4681

760 Old Kent Road, SE15 1NJ – 020 7732 7322

- **Traditional Toys** Chelsea Green, 53 Godfrey Street, SW3 3SX, 020 7352 1718 – Timeless toys.

- **The Little White Company** 261 Pavillion Road, SW1X 0BP, 020 7881 0783 – Clothing, bed linen and furniture.

For many, the Internet is *the* key to the city. Before the dawning of the Internet, we Dickensian scamps had to scurry around in the filth foraging for information in 'books' and by talking to actual 'people'. Now that the future is here, Londoners can navigate their city's streets, explore its dark history, organise a debauched weekend in Chiswick or, as is more likely, peer over the shoulder of men in raincoats in Internet Cafes.

Internet Cafes are *everywhere*. In fact you probably live in one. They can range from the dimly lit 'Money Transfer' shacks that have an air of illegality, to the over-orange **Easyeverything** chain that dominated the market before home internet use skyrocketed in the late 90s. In between the grim DIY flea-pits and the huge destitute hangouts are places like **Helen Cafe (124A Dalston Lane Tel No – 020 7241 2800)** which are both friendly and serve great coffee. **Cyberia Cafe** near Goodge Street (**39 Whitfield Street Tel No – 020 7209 0984**) claims to have been the first Internet Cafe in the world and is still very plush. To be fair, internet use in these places is usually criminally cheap : as low as 50p per hour in the non-tourist areas. For a large list of London internet cafes check out **http://www.allinlondon.co.uk/directory/1166.php.**

London was recently crowned WiFi capital of the world, owing to its astronomical rate of increase in WiFi networks. It is becoming more and more difficult to move in your local cafe without catching the sharp edge of a laptop. The **Apostrophe Cafe** chain is efficient, expensive and has WiFi as standard. Like many WiFi-compatible eateries, wireless access is limited to an hour and they give out passwords to paying customers only. If you wish to cook your internal organs with your PowerBook you can do so in hundreds of cafes in London; for a decent online map of WiFi locations check out http://londonist.com/2007/05/free_wifi_in_lo.php. **Of course there is always the pirate option—dodging the Community Officers and fiendishly stealing a neighbours connection.** Beware however, in 2007 a man was arrested in what was the first case of WiFi theft—he was balancing his laptop on his garden wall!

Useful And/Or Fun London Links:

www.fedbybirds.com
www.royalparks.org.uk
www.tfl.gov.uk
www.londonist.com
www.londonfreelist.com
www.davehill.typepad.com
www.shadyoldlady.com
www.derelictlondon.com
www.walk-london.blogspot.com
www.hiddenlondon.com
www.londonbloggers.iamcal.com
www.london-underground.blogspot.com
www.fancyapint.com
www.dailycandy.com/london
www.gumtree.com
www.timeout.com
www.brickads.blogspot.com
www. wildinlondon.blogspot.com
www. westlondonblogger.blogspot.com
www. dalstonoxfamshop.blogspot.com
www.viewlondon.co.uk
www.lecool.com/cities/london

There have been worries recently that Gayhood in London is in sad decline. **Heaven** (London's self-proclaimed most-famous gay club) may be facing closure after 27 years, whilst many other nights, including popular indie discos **Popstarz** and **Rebel Rebel**, have been relocated, downsized or retired. Thankfully, all these worries are unfounded—yes, things are changing, nights are ending, but, as they say, every time one door (read: gay club) closes, another one opens, and let's face it, the latter will probably open later and sell you even cheaper Red Bull and vodka.

One of the most exciting developments in the past few years has been the advent of what has been dubbed London's new 'Gay Village'—the cluster of clubs, saunas and after-hours hangover incubators that have sprung up in Vauxhall. Now it's possible, though still just as unadvisable, to party from Thursday through to Tuesday without stopping to reapply deodorant, or think about the consequences of what you're doing—hooray. The small outcrop of gay and 'polysexual' nights in the East End, (which until recently included the notoriously wonderful, but necessarily short-lived 'Boombox') is still thriving, and offers another refreshing alternative to Soho for those in search of an aggressive fashion consciousness and a less cruisy atmosphere. This said, if you can handle bright lights, pop music, tight t-shirts and a lot of hair gel, you'll still have massive amounts of fun around Soho and Old Compton Street, the traditional central London gay epicentre. This area is always buzzing, day and night, and is a great place to sit back and do some people watching as well as to go out and, y'know, go crazy.

For girls, the options are fewer and less centralised, but the recent opening of two new women-only nights in Soho (at **Village** and **Element** on Wednesdays) suggests that the scene is very much alive and full of possibilites. Many mixed and polysexual nights (such as Motherfucker at **Barden's Boudoir**) also draw large female crowds, and though dedicated lesbian bars and clubs are few and far between, there is enough going on in the city to make any day of the week a possible night out.

Websites

www.dirtydirtydancing.com - Super-airbrushed photos from many of the trendier Soho and east London nights.

http://scene-out.com - Comprehensive mainstream scene guide.

www.gaylondon.co.uk - Online gay and lesbian community for London.

www.gingerbeer.co.uk - Lesbian guide to London.

www.girlguidelondon.co.uk - Does what it says on the tin.

www.gmfa.org.uk - Gay men's health charity.

www.pinkdate.com - Speed dating events for gay men and women in central London.

Publications

The following are all free listings/scene magazines that can be found in most gay shops and venues (anywhere on Old Compton Street should have some copies lying around):

Boyz Magazine - Weekly scene news and listings, out Thursdays. www.boyz.co.uk

G3 Magazine - Lesbian scene, monthly. www.g3mag.co.uk

Out in the City Mag - Monthly London lifestyle magazine for gay men. www.outmag.co.uk

Qx Magazine - Gay men's mag. www.qxmagazine.com

Shops

Gay's the Word, 66 Marchmont Street, WC1N 1AB, 020 7278 7654, http://freespace.virgin.net/gays.theword/, The only dedicated Gay and Lesbian Bookshop in London, recently threatened by rising rent. Visit whilst it's still there!

Foyles, 113–119 Charing Cross Road, WC2H 0EB, 020 7437 5660, www.foyles.co.uk, Huge bookshop with large gay and lesbian section.

Prowler, 5–7 Brewer Street, W1F 0RF, 020 7734 4031, The ultimate gay men's shop, stocking everything from (skimpy) clothes to sex toys plus mountains of lube, pornography, and the other usual suspects.

Sexual Health

A comprehensive list of London clinics that offer same day HIV testing and PEP treatments for gay/bisexual men is available at www.gmfa.org.uk/londonservices/clinics. CLASH, below, is particularly recommended.

CLASH (Central London Action on Street Health), 11 Warwick Street, W1B 5NA, 020 7734 1794, Friday night clinic for gay men, with incredibly friendly staff who will offer comfort and advice. Same day (often instant) HIV testing, PEP treatment. Fridays, 5 - 8.30pm, call for an appointment.

Support Organizations

Again, a more comprehensive list can be found at the GMFA website: www.gmfa.org.uk/londonservices/support-groups/index

Stonewall, Tower Building, York Road, SE1 7NX, www.stonewall.org.uk, Gay rights charity and lobbying group.

PACE Youthwork Service, 34 Hartham Road, N7 9LJ, 020 7700 1323, www.outzone.org, Support organization for gay and lesbian youths under 25. Organizes regular social events and offers one to one consultations with advisors: phone or visit the website to get involved.

London Friend, 86 Caledonian Road, N1 9DN, 020 7833 1674, www.londonfriend.org.uk, Voluntary organization which runs several helplines, group workshops and social events, as well as offering advice on reporting hate crime.

London Lesbian and Gay Switchboard, 020 7837 7324 (helpline), 020 7689 8501 (Volunteers), Counselling and information service.

Kairos in Soho, Unit 10, 10-11 Archer Street, W1D 7AZ, 020 7437 6063, www.kairosinsoho.org.uk, Gay and lesbian charity that organises a variety of recreational events to promote the health, well being and development of the LGBT community.

Naz Project London, Palingswick House, 241 King Street, W6 9LP, 020 8741 1879 www.naz.org.uk, Charity that organizes support and sexual health services for black and ethnic minority communities in London. Various services, including free one-on-one counselling and support groups are available, phone or check website for details.

GALOP, PO Box 32810, N1 3ZD, 020 7704 6767, www.galop.org.uk, Charity specialising in advice about reporting hate crime.

Annual Events

Pride London, www.pridelondon.org, Large pride festival, takes place every July.
London Lesbian and Gay Film Festival, www.bfi.org.uk/llgff, Film festival at the BFI on South Bank, March–April.
Bistrotheque Annual Drag Ball, www.myspace.com/trannylipsync or www.bistrotheque.com, Annual team-based drag contest. Open entry but fierce competition!
London LGBT History Month, www.lgbthistorymonth.co.uk, Nationwide awareness month, with various talks and events staged in London, every February.

Gay/mixed venues

Soho:
79CXR, 79 Charing Cross Road, WC2H 0NE, 020 7734 0769, Dingy bar with middle aged crowd.
The Admiral Duncan, 54 Old Compton Street, W1D 4UB, 020 7437 5300
Barcode Soho, 3-4 Archer Street W1D 7AT, 020 7734 3342
Box, 32–34 Monmouth Street, WC2H 9HA, 020 7240 5828, Civilised bar and eatery.
Comptons, 53–57 Old Compton Street, W1D 6HN, 020 7479 7961, Crammed gay pub.
Duke of Wellington, 77 Wardour Street, W1D 6QA
The Edge, 11 Soho Square, W1D 3QF, 020 7439 1313
G-A-Y Bar, 30 Old Compton Street, W1D 5JX, 020 7494 2756, Poptastic bunker. Video walls and cheap drinks.
G-A-Y Late, 5 Goslett Yard, WC2H 0ER, 020 7734 9858, Cheap drinks and pop videos wipe out brain functions 'til 3am.
Ghetto, Falconberg Court, W1D 3AB, 020 7287 3726, Loud electro at this busy gay club. Thursday is ladies night.
Halfway to Heaven, 7 Duncannon Street, WC2N 4JF, 020 7321 2791.
Heaven, Under the Arches, Villiers Street, WC2N 6NG, 020 7930 2020, Legendary gay club. An institution.
Ku Bar, 30 Lisle Street, WC2H 7BA, 020 7437 4303, Newly relocated bar for the young and clueless.
Kudos, 10 Adelaide Street, WC2N 4HZ, 020 7379 4573
Profile, 56–57 Frith Street, W1D 3JG, 020 7734 8300
Shadow Lounge, 5 Brewer Street, W1F, 020 7439 4089, Supposed to be a shi-shi cocktail lounge. Hmmmm.
Soho Revue Bar, 11 Walkers Court, Brewer Street, W1F 0ED, Cabaret acts followed by dancing 'til late.

The Village, 81 Wardour Street, W1D 6QD, 020 7434 2124, Tacky, flirtatious bar spread across two floors.

Trash Palace, 11 Wardour Street, W1D 6PG, 020 7734 0522, Bratty queer indie bar.

North:

Cosmo Lounge, 43 Essex Road, N1 2SF, 020 7688 0051, Subdued bar, normally full of regulars.

Central Station, 37 Wharfdale Road, N1 9SD, 020 7278 3294. Pub/club with ominously blacked out windows.

The Green, 74 Upper Street N1 0NY, 0871 971 4097, Innocuous gay bar/restaurant frequented by many unsuspecting straight couples.

King Edward VI Pub, 25 Bromfield Street, N1 0PZ

The Black Cap, 171 Camden High Street, NW1 7JY, 020 7428 2721, Slightly crummy gay pub.

East:

Bistrotheque, 23–27 Wadeson Street, E2 9DR, Jonny Woo's restaurant, great food and drag acts.

The Black Horse, 168 Mile End Road, E1 4LJ, 020 7790 1684

George and Dragon, 2 Hackney Road, E2 7NS, Small, atmospheric pub full of trendy boys and girls.

Joiners Arms, 116–118, Hackney Road, E2 7Q, Late opening free-for-all with a wonderfully mixed crowd. ('til 2/3am most nights)

South:

Area, 67–68 Albert Embankment, SE1 7TP

Barcode Vauxhall, 69 Albert Embankment, 020 7582 4180

The Two Brewers, 114 Clapham High Street, SW4 7UJ, 020 7498 4971

Depot, 66 Albert Embankment, SE11 7TP, Sister club of Area, with a more cruisy vibe.

Fire, South Lambeth Road, SW8 1RT, 020 7434 1113, The quintessential Vauxhall club. Open pretty much forever, bulging muscles everywhere.

The Fort, 131 Grange Road, Bermondsey, SE1 3AL - Themed cruising/fetish/sex bar.

Kazbar Clapham, 50 Clapham High Street, SW4 7UL, 020 7622 0070

Little Apple Bar, 98 Kennington Lane, SE11 4XD Mixed/lesbian bar.

Man Bar, 82 Great Suffolk Street, SE1 0BE, 020 7928 3223, Cruise bar.

The Powder Monkey, 22 King William Walk, SE10 PHU, 020 8293 5928, thepowdermonkey.net

Royal Vauxhall Tavern, 372 Kennington Lane, SE11 5HY, 020 7820 1222

South Central, 349 Kennington Lane, SE11 5QY, 020 7793 0903

Substation South, 9 Brighton Terrace, SW9 8DJ, 020 7737 2095

XXL, 51–53 Southwark Street, SE1 1TE, www.fatsandsmalls.com. Busy bear club.

West:

Bromptons, 294 Old Brompton Road, SW5 9JF, 020 77370 1344

The Coleherne, 261 Old Brompton Road, SW5 9JA 020 7244 5951

Recommended Nights

Club Motherfucker, second Saturdays @ Barden's Boudoir, 38 Stoke Newington Road, Dalston, N16 7XJ, Polysexual band night. Sweaty, noisy, very much about the music.

Circus, Fridays @ Soho Revue Bar, 11 Walkers Court, Brewer Street, W1F 0ED, Drag Queen Jodie Harsh's long running night attracts its fair share of celebrities from both on and off the scene. Get there early or be prepared to queue.

DTPM, www.myspace.com/dtpm, Legendary event, no longer with a fixed location. See site for details of upcoming parties.

For3ign, Saturdays @ Bar Music Hall, 134 Curtain Road, EC2A 3AR, 020 7613 5951, Outlandish costumes and, of course, thumping electro.

Horsemeat Disco, Sundays @ South Central, Italo and 70s Disco bring all sorts to this fantastic night, originally a bear love club.

Icon, Sundays @ Essence, 562a Mile End Road, E3 4PH, 0208 980 6427, mob 07843 440 443 (weekly), New night in the East End. Yet to prove itself.

Issue, monthly (check site for details) @ Electricity Showrooms, 39a Hoxton Square, N1 6NN, issueclub.blogspot.com. Polysexual parties to coincide with the launch of this scene/fashion magazine.

Matinee, monthly (check site) @ Fabric, 77a Charterhouse Street, EC1M 3HN, 020 7335 8898, www.matineelondon.com, Irregular gay night at this enormous club in Farringdon.

Popstarz, Fridays @ Sin, 144 Charing Cross Road, WC2H 0LB, 020 7240 1900, Gay indie institution, recently relocated.

Trailer Trash, Fridays @ On the Rocks, 25 Kingsland Road, E2 8AA, 020 7688 0339, The dirtiest electro and the drunkest you've ever been. Crammed with sweating fashionistas.

Wet Yourself, Sundays @ Aquarium, 256–264 Old Street, EC1V 9DD, 020 7251 6136, This used to be the place to be after Boombox. It's lost only a little of its charm since (mixed polysexual crowd).

Lesbian Venues

Blush Bar, 8 Cazenove Road, Stoke Newington N16, 020 7923 9202, www.blushbar.co.uk

Candy Bar, 23-24 Bateman Street, W1V 5HR, 020 7437 1977, The reluctant epicentre of the Lesbian scene in Soho.

First Out Café Bar, Soho - 52 St Giles High St, WC2H 8LH, 020 7240 8042, Cafe with nightly events. All girls on Friday.

Oak Bar, 79 Green Lanes, N16, www.oakbar.co.uk, 020 7354 2791,

The Star At Night, 22 Great Chapel Street, Soho, W1 8FR, 020 7434 3749, Mixed cocktail bar with a predominantly female crowd.

Recommended Nights

100% Babe, Bank Holiday Sundays @ The Roxy, 3 Rathbone Place, W1P 1DA, 020 7636 1598, Irregular party for fans of funky house, R&B, old skool and electropop.

Blue Light, last Saturdays @ Bar Med, Triton Court, 14 Finsbury Square, EC2, 020 7588 3056

Club Wotever, first Saturday of the month @ The Masters Club, 12 Denman Street, Piccadilly, W1D 7HH, 020 7734 4243, Draggy night with a large 'King' quota.

Code, irregular night @ the Enclave, 25–27 Brewer Street, W1F 0RR, www.club-code.net - check website for details.

Girls on Girls, Wednesdays @ Village, 81 Wardour Street, W1D 6QD, 020 7434 2124

Lounge, second Thursdays @ Vertigo, 1 Leicester Square, WC2H 7NA, 020 7734 0900, Relaxed cocktail night at this swish Leicester Square club.

Miss Shapes, Thursdays @ Ghetto, Falconberg Court, W1D 3AB, 020 7287 3726, Popular girls-only indie night.

Pink, Wednesdays @ Element, 4-5 Greek Street, W1D 4DD, 020 7434 3323.

Play, irregular night @ Bar Rumba, 35 Shaftesbury Ave, W1D 7EP, 020 7287 2715, www.myspace.com/_clubplay

Rumours, last Saturday of the month @ 64–73 Minories, EC3, 07949 477 804

Smack, irregular night @ various venues, check website, www.myspace.com/smackclub

Wish, first Saturdays @ Gramophone, 60–62 Commercial Street, E1 6LT, Style conscious night for young techno-heads and indie girls.

Women's Anarchist Nuisance Cafe, Penultimate wednesdays @ the RampART Creative Centre and Social Space, Rampart St, Aldgate, E1 2LA, Social group and cooperative vegan women's cafe.

Stickier Options

Club Fukk, second Fridays @ Central Station, 37 Wharfdale Road, N1 9SD, 020 7278 3294, www.centralstation.co.uk or www.wotewerworld.com/id12.html, Predominantly Lesbian fetish/play club. One of many sex/cruising nights at the venue – check site for details.

Chariots, www.gaysauna.co.uk, Popular chain of gay saunas, with branches at the following locations: *Shoreditch*: 1 Fairchild Street, EC2A 3NS, *Waterloo*: 101 Lower Marsh, SE1 7AB, 020 7401 8484, *Limehouse*: 574 Commercial Road, E14 7JD, 020 7791 2808, *Streatham*: 292 [rear of] Streatham High Road, SW16 6HG, 020 8696 0929, *Farringdon*: 57 Cowcross Street, EC1M 6BX, 020 7251 5553, *Vauxhall*: 63-64 Albert Embankment, SE1, 020 7247 5333

The Fort, 131 Grange Road, Bermondsey, SE1 3AL , Themed cruising/fetish/sex bar.

Hard On, monthly @ Hidden, 100 Tinworth Street, SE11 5EQ, www.hardonclub.co.uk, Rubber and fetish sex club for gay and bisexual men and women.

The Hoist, Arch 47b & 47c, South Lambeth Road, SW8 1RH, 020 7735 9972, www.thehoist.co.uk, Fetish sex club with strict dress codes, check website for details.

Man Bar, 82 Great Suffolk Street, SE1 0BE, 020 7928 3223, www.manbar.info, Cruise bar.

Nudity, first Fridays @ Hidden, 100 Tinworth Street, SE11 5EQ, Nude men's dance/play club.

Purrrr, 87 Fortess Road, Kentish Town NW5, www.purrrr.co.uk, Monthly S&M play club for Lesbians.

London Timeline

A timeline of significant events in London's history.

50: The Romans found Londinium, building the first London Bridge.

61: Queen Boudicca burns Londinium down.

100: Londinium becomes the capital of Roman Britain.

200: The Romans build the London Wall.

410: Roman occupation ends and Londinium is largely abandoned for many years.

604: King Aethelbert of Kent completes the first St Paul's Cathedral.

700: The Saxons build Lundenwic a mile to the west of old Londinium.

851: The Vikings burn Lundenwic down (starting to see a pattern, here?)

878: Alfred The Great defeats the Vikings and establishes a new settlement within the Roman Walls.

1013: The Viking King Canute besieges London.

1066: William The Conqueror becomes the first king to be crowned at Westminster Abbey.

1088: William The Conqueror builds the Tower Of London.

1097: William Rufus builds Westminster Hall—later part of the Houses Of Parliament.

1176: The wooden London Bridge is replaced by a stone structure.

1343: 'The Canterbury Tales' author Geoffrey Chaucer is born in London.

1348: The Black Death wipes out between a third and half of London's population in 18 months.

1381: Peasants revolt, storming the Tower Of London.

1599: William Shakespeare's theatre company The Chamberlain's Men build the Globe Theatre.

1605: Guy Fawkes' Gunpowder Plot fails to blow up the Palace Of Westminster.

1635: Hyde Park opens to the public.

1649: King Charles I is beheaded at Whitehall.

1665: The Great Plague kills a fifth of London's population (starting to see another pattern, here?)

1666: The Fire of London destroys 60% of the city, including St Paul's Cathedral, but wipes out the plague. This really must have been a great year.

1708: The new St Paul's Cathedral is completed by Sir Christopher Wren.

1732: Downing Street becomes the home of the Prime Minister.

1750: Westminster Bridge is built.

1814: Lord's Cricket Ground is opened.

1829: Robert Peel establishes the Metropolitan Police force, policemen known as 'Bobbies' or 'Peelers'.

1831: London becomes the world's biggest city.

1834: The Houses Of Parliament are built.

1843: Nelson's Column is completed in Trafalgar Square.

1851: Six million people gawp at newfangled technology and design at The Great Exhibition.

1858: The Great Stink inspires the 19th century's biggest civil engineering project—London's sewerage system.

London Timeline

1863: The first London Underground line is built.

1876: The Albert Memorial to Queen Victoria's husband Prince Albert is completed.

1884: An imaginary line through Greenwich Royal Observatory is internationally accepted as the Prime Meridian. Except by the French.

1887: Arthur Conan Doyle publishes the first Sherlock Holmes story 'A Study In Scarlet.'

1888: Jack The Ripper's first victim, Mary Ann Nichols, is murdered.

1908: London hosts the Olympics for the first time.

1915: German Zeppelin airships launch first air raids on London, ultimately killing over 700 people.

1923: Wembley Stadium is built in 300 days, costing £750,000.

1940: The Blitz begins—German bombs kill over 30,000 Londoners by the end of WW2 and destroy large areas of the city.

1946: Heathrow Airport opens for commercial flights.

1948: The second London Olympics is held.

1951: The Royal Festival Hall is built as part of the Festival Of Britain.

1952: The Great Smog, caused by a combination of fog and coal smoke, kills 4000 people in five days.

1956: The Clean Air Act puts an end to London's smog problems.

1965: The Notting Hill Carnival is established by West London's Caribbean community.

1969: The Beatles play their last ever gig on the roof of the Apple building.

1976: The Sex Pistols play at the first 'International Punk Festival' at the 100 Club on Oxford Street.

1981: The first London Marathon.

1983: Six people are killed when the IRA bombs Harrods.

1991: London's tallest building, One Canada Square (better known as Canary Wharf), is completed.

2000: Ken Livingstone becomes London's first directly-elected Mayor.

2005: 52 people are killed by four suicide bombers on Underground trains and a bus.

2007: The rebuilt Wembley Stadium is completed after four years, costing £778 million.

2012: London's third Olympics to be held, expectations of a bumper haul of medals remains low.

London is an egotist—it just *loves* to talk about itself. As you might expect, there's a vast array of print and online publications, not to mention radio stations, designed to let the city do exactly that. Single-handedly forcing the environmental movement back twenty years are freebie dailies **The London Paper, Metro** and **London Lite**. Each a celeb-focused quasi-tabloid, distributed and discarded in the millions. The more substantial, twice-daily **Standard** is the preferred news-roundup du jour of suburbanites and city types alike, if only for the sudoku and quick crossword puzzles. Online, **www.thisislocallondon.co.uk** condenses forty local newspapers into 'one online voice'. On the wireless, **Capital Radio** broadcasts an irksome parade of popular hits and frenetic DJs, whilst **Heart** and **Magic** corner the market on lip-trembling power ballads, mid-paced chart rock and wacky quizzes. All of the British Broadcasting Corporation's national radio stations—including the snazzy, young(ish) **Radio 1** and ovaltine-drinkers' choice **Radio 2**—are based in London, as is (surprisingly) **BBC London**, a decent option for weekend sports coverage. Cooler, urban types are more likely to be tuning into **Kiss FM** (dance, hip hop), **Smooth FM** (jazz, soul) or **Choice** (dancehall, roots), while alternative rockers tune their dials anguishedly over to **XFM**, and the talkative indulge in unreserved subjectivity over at **LBC**. Un-licensed and illegal pirate radio stations offer a slightly un-hinged ear into the fringes of London's musical society. Twiddle your dials around the extreme ends of the FM spectrum for pirate stalwarts **Rude FM** and **Kool FM**. On the goggle-box, the latest news is spoon-fed to you on ITV's **London Tonight** show and delivered in short slots at the end of the BBC and ITV national news programs. For those actually risking going outside, **Time Out** remains the socialite's sacred text.

Print

The London Paper 1 Pennington Street, E98 1XY, 020 7782 4835, Free, gossipy daily.

The Evening Standard Northcliffe House, 2 Derry Street, W8 5TT, 020 7938 6000, Scaled down Daily Mail, leaning to the right.

London Lite Northcliffe House, 2 Derry Street, W8 5TT, 020 7938 6000, Free, mini Standard.

Metro Northcliffe House, 2 Derry Street, W8 5TT, 020 7651 5200, Free underground daily from same stable.

City AM New London Bridge House, 25 London Bridge St, SE1 9SG, 020 7015 1200, Free morning business bulletin for city-goers.

My Free Sport Third Floor, Courtyard Building, 11 Curtain Road, EC2A 3LT, 0207 375 3175 Free sports overview every Friday.

TimeOut London 251-255 Tottenham Court Road, Universal House, W1T 7AB, 0207 813 3000, Listings & reviews across the city. Pretty damned comprehensive.

London Gazette PO Box 7923, SE1 5ZH, 020 7394 4517, Capital's oldest paper—official journals record of the government.

London Literary Review 44 Lexington Street, W1 0LW, 020 7437 9392, Fortnightly publication for the bookish.

The London Magazine 32 Addison Grove, W4 1ER, 020 8400 5882, Bi-monthly Arts reviews.

TNT London 14-15 Childs Place, Earls Court, SW5 9RX, 020 7373 3377, Info and opinion for the antipodean set.

Loot 31 John Street, WC1N 2AT, 0871 222 5000, Classifieds: flats, bought/sold and lonely hearts.

The Voice GV Media Group Ltd, Northern & Shell Tower, 6th Floor, 4 Selsdon Way, E14 9GL, 020 7510 0340, African-British national.

London Bichitra Bangalink Media, 272 Holton Road, Barry, CF63 4HU, Bengali monthly.

Polish Express 603 Cumberland House, 80 Scrubs Lane, NW10 6RF, 020 8964 4488 , News and info for the Polish community.

Reflect Magazine 130 Stroud Green Road, N4 3RZ, 020 7272 8502, For 'thinking, young Muslims'.

Live Listings Magazine Keith Villa (House), 102 Mallinson Rd, SW11 1BN, 020 7207 2734 Guide to what's on in multicultural London.

Public Radio

FM

89.1 BBC Radio Two: Middle-aged music and chat.
91.3 BBC Radio Three: Classical.
93.5 BBC Radio Four: Current affairs, comfort listening.
94.9 BBC London: Chat, sport.
95.8 Capital FM: Chart, capers.
96.9 Choice FM: Hip hop, R&B.
97.3 LBC: Phone in, chat.
98.8 BBC Radio 1: Pop, rock, more pop.
100.0 Kiss FM: Dance, urban.
100.9 Classic FM: Classical.
102.2 Smooth FM: Jazz, soul.
102.6 Essex FM: Audible in East London.
103.3 London Greek Radio: Um, Greek.
103.5 BBC Essex: Audible out East.
104.9 Xfm: Alternative, rock.
105.4 Magic: Pop, slush.
105.8 Virgin Radio: Pop, rock.
106.2 Heart: Chart, pop.
106.6 Time: West London only.
107.3 Time: South East London only.

AM

252 Atlantic: Rock.
558 Spectrum International: Multi-ethnic.
648 BBC World Service: Global.
720 BBC Radio Four: Spoken word.
909 BBC Radio Five Live: Sport, phone in.
963 Liberty Radio: 70s, 80s pop.
1035 Ritz: Country.
1089 talkSPORT: Sports phone in.
1152 LBC News: News, weather.
1215 Virgin Radio: Pop, rock.
1305 Premier Radio: Christian.
1458 Sunrise: Asian.
1548 Capital Gold: Rock 'gold', sport.
1584 London Turkish Radio: Turkish community.

Essential London Books

London – The Biography, and *Illustrated London*, Peter Ackroyd: definitive, eight hundred page mother lode of remarkable city history, and lavish pictorial version.

The Clerkenwell Tales, Peter Ackroyd: corking murder mystery set in the time of Chaucer.

Oliver Twist; Hard Times; Great Expectations, Charles Dickens: any Dickens novel paints Victorian London at its most exacting.

Intimate Adventures of a London Call Girl, Belle de Jour: steamy, real-life shenanigans ahoy.

Brick Lane, Monica Ali: award winning coming-of-age tale centred on Brick Lane's Muslim community.

The Diary of Samuel Pepys, Samuel Pepys: eyewitness accounts of the Restoration, Great Plague and Fire of London from noted sixteenth century scribbler.

Secret London: Exploring the Hidden City, with Original Walks and Unusual Places to Visit, Andrew Duncan: an explorer's dream.

Around London with Kids – 68 Great Things to See and Do, Eugene Fodor: should keep the little rascals from breaking into cars.

The London Encyclopaedia, Ben Weinreb and Christopher Hibbert: London's history and culture documented in minutest detail

London's Disused Underground Stations, JE Connor: documenting forgotten, ghostly tube stations beneath the pavements.

From Here to Here, Simmons, Taylor, Lynham, Rich: 31 top notch short stories about Circle Line destinations, includes Simon Armitage.

The Adventures of Sherlock Holmes; The Hound of the Baskervilles, Arthur Conan Doyle: classic whodunits featuring Holmes and Watson.

The Strange Case of Dr. Jekyll and Mr. Hyde, Robert Louis Stevenson: the book that enthralled a city unnerved by Jack the Ripper.

The Inimitable Jeeves, P.G. Wodehouse: prewar upper-class tomfoolery in London Town.

London Fields, Martin Amis: post-modern jaunt through London at the end of the millennium.

The London Bombings: An Independent Inquiry, Nafeez Mosadeq Ahmed: balanced, subtle overview of 2005 Underground bombings.

General Information · **Media**

Essential London Songs

Lambeth Walk, Noel Gay/Douglas Furber (1937): All together! *Doing the Lambeth Walk! Oi!*

A Nightingale Sang in Berkeley Square, Judy Campbell (1940): Wartime cheer made famous by Vera Lynn.

London Pride, Sir Noel Coward (1941): Written during the Blitz, this sensational ballad gave comfort to Londoners being bombed nightly.

Maybe It's Because I'm a Londoner, Hubert Gregg (1944): Pearly Queen favourite crammed with WWII spirit.

A Foggy Day (In London Town), Ella Fitzgerald (1956): Definitive recording of Gershwin classic.

Waterloo Sunset, The Kinks (1967): Timeless paean to the nation's capital.

Consider Yourself, Lionel Bart (1968): Oliver Twist hoodwinked into a life of crime by the Artful Dodger, the rascal.

Baker Street, Gerry Rafferty (1978): Feel that sax line, air that guitar.

London Calling, The Clash (1979): Joe Strummer paints an apocalyptic vision of a city in post-punk transition.

Electric Avenue, Eddy Grant (1983): Roots-rock champion name checks 80s Brixton scene.

London, The Smiths (1983): Morrissey lugubriously debates a trip south. Miserable shite.

West End Girls, Pet Shop Boys (1986): East London working class meets West London affluence in electro-pop classic.

Parklife, Blur (1994): Home counties-boys get cockney makeover while eyeing London's jogging scene.

Essential London Films

The 39 Steps (1935): Hitchcock adaptation of John Buchan novel.

Pygmalion (1938): Leslie Howard as Henry Higgins and Wendy Hiller as Eliza Doolittle prove Shaw's classic comedy does very well without music.

Great Expectations (1946): Rare Richard Attenborough acting outing in classic Dickens adaptation.

The Ladykillers (1955): Superb black comedy from the Ealing canon, with pre-Obi Wan Alec Guinness.

Oliver! (1968): Sprightly musical adaptation of Dickens classic.

One Hundred and One Dalmations (1961): Innocent pelt-seeker tortured by 101 belligerent pups. For shame.

Mary Poppins (1964): Notable for Dick Van Dyke's confounding, lanky turn as cockney chimney sweep.

A Hard Day's Night (1964): Classic, swinging 60s comedy from the Fab Four.

Alfie (1966): Caine in much-lauded role as audience-addressing lothario.

Carry On Doctor (1967): Critically-panned, guilty-pleasure raunchfest from Pinewood Studios.

The Elephant Man (1980): John Merrick 'accepted' by London's polite Victorian-era society in David Lynch masterpiece.

An American Werewolf in London (1981): US student attacked on moors; gets haunted; romps with Jenny Agutter; becomes werewolf; slaughters innocents; is shot in alley; credits roll.

My Beautiful Launderette (1985): Hanif Kureishi's controversial depiction of cross-culture, same-gender love in the Thatcher-era.

Muppet Christmas Carol (1992): That Michael Caine, he sure can act. But he sure can't play.

Lock, Stock and Two Smoking Barrels (1998): East End crime capers from Madonna's (not from the East End) husband.

Notting Hill (1999): Hugh Grant as mumbling, bumbling, lovesick fop.

Bridget Jones's Diary (2001): Rene Zellweger goes Sloane in adaptation of Helen Fielding novel.

Love Actually (2003): Expansive Richard Curtis romcom with Grant in slightly-less mumbly, slightly-more bumbly form.

Shaun of the Dead (2003): Fighting off zombies at the local pub. Hilarious.

There can't be anything worse than the inconvenience of trying to find a convenience when nature takes an unexpected hold of your nether regions; you may choose to follow the lead of many a Saturday evening reveller and pee in a public doorway, but is it really worth the £80 fine that will be levied if caught in the act (and let's face it, it's hard to conceal the evidence)?

Unfortunately, London has seen a recent decline in the provision of public toilet facilities, as local councils seem to have decided that they are under no obligation to provide such a service; you'll also be hard pushed to find a toilet attendant manning a lavatory these days, and the dubious goings-on in some loos may not be quite what you had in mind, unless your name has a "Michael" in it. Most surviving public toilets seem also to emit their own particular aroma of…well, you don't really have to use your imagination. But don't get down in the dumps!

The most obvious place to go when in need is McDonald's. Despite what some may say about their food, their outlets are the place to go when caught short and not wishing to pay to pee. Usually maintained and cleaned throughout opening hours, they can also be used inconspicuously and without purchasing anything; and let's face it, you can't move for McDonalds in London. It's also a safe bet to use Starbucks, Caffe Nero and Costa Coffee bars, although they often have a policy of access to toilets by key only, which can be a bit of a bummer (groan).

It may seem like a good idea to visit pubs or bars solely for their toilets, but you might find yourself being hauled out by an irked landlord mid-act. Furthermore, don't expect luxury; pub toilets are usually fairly scummy and often not furnished with toilet paper. It's also unlikely to find a men's cubicle that will have a working lock in it; do you really wish to have an unwanted visitor whilst on the throne? Exceptions are the Wetherspoon's chain, which prides itself on having toilets cleaned on the hour, and the nicest of gastro pubs, which can offer commodious and clean facilities (at least during the day). Otherwise, if desperate, at least go for a pub or bar that's busy.

Also bear in mind that if you find yourself in need in the City of Westminster, you can use a toilet text service from your mobile phone! Known as SatLav, texting the word 'Toilet' to 80097 will result in a message being sent to your phone informing you of the nearest public convenience. It may prove to be the most relieving 25p you'll ever spend in London…

A good and extensive list of London public toilets can be found at www.lastrounds.co.uk/public_toilets.html.

If none of the afore-mentioned places are available, there are other options:

Other street public toilets—yes, those bizarre futuristic looking structures on some of London's central streets are toilets. Known as sanisettes or "superloos", there is a charge to use them and once in, you've got 15 minutes before the door automatically opens (don't get extended stage-fright). They're self-cleaning, which usually means that they're in a right state, and are also quite popular with junkies and prostitutes, so best saved for when extremely desperate.

There are also a few pop-up toilets which, intended for night use, disappear underground during the day. These are only suitable for (drunk) men and rise to the challenge of channelling away an evening's excesses from 7pm to 6am. Located at notorious 'wet spots' in the West End, they are linked to the main sewerage system; taking the piss, indeed…

Stations—including almost all large railway stations and a few central London tube stations. There will usually be a cost for these facilities though (around 20p).

Department Stores—All the large ones, including John Lewis, Selfridges, Debenhams and Harrods. Smaller shops rarely have toilets for public use.

Supermarkets—many larger branches of Sainsbury's and Marks & Spencer.

Museums—the majority of London's large museums and galleries are free to enter (erm, and have toilets).

Libraries—most libraries will have an area of salvation for the needy.

Universities and Colleges—and you get to pass yourself off as a student or lecturer (in need of loo).

Hospitals—you can also drop in on that relative that you always meant to visit, or maybe leave a stool sample; just try not to leave with a superbug.

Parks—not on the grass, please.

Hotels—larger hotels shouldn't pose a problem.

General Information · **Hospitals**

London has some of the finest hospitals in the world, attracting top-notch specialists who carry-out state-of-the-art procedures—the trick is, getting in to see one of them. An appointment at a specific hospital, or with a specialist, requires a referral from your GP and plenty of patience. In an emergency go to your nearest A&E—bring a book and some earplugs. On the weekends after eleven, waiting times for non-urgent problems can be measured in aeons, but rest assured, if something is seriously wrong you'll be seen very quickly—lucky ol' you. For non serious injuries or illnesses, find your nearest Minor Injuries Unit or Walk-in Centre on www.nhs.uk. You'll spend less time hanging around and free up A&E for critical cases and over-cidered teens needing stomach pumps. The ever-friendly 24 hr NHS Direct 0845 4647 is also always available for advice.

If you have the money, numerous private sector hospitals and clinics are available to cure what ails you, or to pander to your hypochondriacal needs. You won't necessarily get better treatment, but there'll be less waiting, more pampering and more grapes by your bedside. For information, start at www.privatehealth.co.uk.

A & E	Address	Phone	Map
Charing Cross Hospital	Fulham Palace Rd	020 8846 1234	047
Chelsea and Westminster Hospital	369 Fulham Rd	020 8746 8000	043
Homerton University Hospital	Homerton Row	020 8510 5555	090
King's College Hospital	Denmark Hill	020 3299 9000	121
Moorfields Eye Hospital	162 City Rd	020 7253 3411	084
Royal Free Hospital	Pond St	020 7794 0500	057
Royal London Hospital	Whitechapel Rd	020 7377 7000	096
St Mary's Hospital	Praed St	020 78866666	031
St Thomas' Hospital	Lambeth Palace Rd	020 7188 7188	131
University College Hospital	235 Euston Rd	0845 155 5000	004
Western Eye Hospital	173 Marylebone Rd	020 7886 6666	002
Whittington Hospital	Magdala Ave	020 7272 3070	059

Other Hospitals	Address	Phone	Map
Bolingbroke Hospital	Bolingbroke Grove	020 7223 7411	140
Capio Eye	114 Harley St	0800 169 2020	002
Capio Nightingale Hospital	11 Lisson Grove	020 7535 7700	076
Capio Nightingale Hospital	1 Radnor Walk	020 7351 7098	045
Charing Cross Hospital	Fulham Palace Rd	020 8846 1234	047
Chelsea and Westminster Hospital	369 Fulham Rd	020 8746 8000	043
Cromwell Hospital	162 Cromwell Rd	020 7460 2000	035
Eastman Dental Hospital	256 Gray's Inn Rd	020 7915 1000	005
Elizabeth Garrett Anderson Hospital	Huntley St	0845 155 5000	004
Gordon Hospital	Bloomsbury St	020 8746 8733	021
Great Ormond St Hospital	Great Ormond St	020 7405 9200	005
Guy's Hospital	Great Maze Pond	020 7188 7188	106
Heart Hospital	16 Westmoreland St	020 7573 8888	002
Highgate Private Hospital	17 View Rd	020 8341 4182	051
Homerton University Hospital	Homerton Row	020 8510 5555	090
Hospital For Tropical Diseases	Mortimer Market	0845 155 5000	004
Hospital of St John and St Elizabeth	60 Grove End Rd	020 7806 4000	068
King Edward VII Hospital For Officers	5 Beaumont St	020 7486 4411	002
King's College Hospital	Denmark Hill	020 3299 9000	121
Lambeth Hospital	108 Landor Rd	020 3228 6000	144
Lister Hospital	Chelsea Bridge Rd	020 7730 7733	020

Other Hospitals	Address	Phone	Map
London Bridge Hospital	27 Tooley St	020 7407 3100	106
London Chest Hospital	Bonner Rd	020 7377 7000	093
London Independent Hospital	1 Beaumont Sq	020 7780 2400	097
London Welbeck Hospital	25 Welbeck St	020 7224 2242	002
Mildmay Mission Hospital	Hackney Rd	020 7613 6309	091
Mile End Hospital	Bancroft Rd	020 7377 7000	093
Moorfields Eye Hospital	162 City Rd	020 7253 3411	084
National Hospital for Neorology and Neurosciences	Queen Sq	0845 155 5000	005
Portland Hospital For women and Children	209 Great Portland St	020 7580 4400	003
Princess Grace Hospital	42 Nottingham Pl	020 7486 1234	002
Royal Brompton Hospital	Sydney St	020 7352 8121	045
Royal Free Hospital	Pond St	020 7794 0500	057
Royal London Homeopathic Hospital	60 Great Ormond St	0845 155 5000	005
Royal London Hospital	Whitechapel Rd	020 7377 7000	096
Royal Marsden Hospital	Fulham Rd	020 7352 8171	045
Royal National Orthopaedic Hospital	51 Bolsover St	020 8954 2300	003
Royal National Throat, Nose and Ear Hospital	330 Gray's Inn Rd	020 7915 1300	005
St Bartholomew's	West Smithfield	020 7377 7000	015
St Luke's Hospital For The Clergy	14 Fitzroy Sq	02073884954	003
St Mary's Hospital	Praed St	020 78866666	031
St Pancras Hospital	4 St Pancras Way	020 7530 3500	078
St Thomas' Hospital	Lambeth Palace Rd	020 7188 7188	131
University College Hospital	Grafton Wy	0845 1555 000	004
University College Hospital	235 Euston Rd	0845 155 5000	004
Wellington Hospital	8 Wellington Pl	020 7483 5148	076
Western Eye Hospital	173 Marylebone Rd	020 7886 6666	002
Whittington Hospital	Magdala Ave	020 7272 3070	059

Overview

Librarians love nothing more than a warm cardigan and a complex cataloguing system, nevertheless, they've done themselves proud with London's libraries. London boasts an enormous, if somewhat eccentric and confusing, network of over 360 libraries. NFT have tried to make things a little clearer with a starter guide below, but check www. londonlibraries.org for a great searchable database to match your needs with the right library.

London's libraries vary enormously in subject, range and facilities, with some accessible for free, some for a fee, some with an appointment and some only if you are very very nice and give the curator a chocolate digestive. But the treat of such a large network, apart from the world-class breadth, depth and quality of collections, is that many of the libraries have a unique personality to make them a treasured part of London. For example, £10 will get you a day's membership to the **London Library (Map 23)**, an atmospheric labyrinth where you can browse alongside ghosts of past members including Dickens, Tennyson and Darwin, and feel several IQ points higher than before you went in. In Tower Hamlets, libraries are now **"Ideas Stores" (Map 92, 101, 96)**, because Tower Hamlets is, like, cool. In addition to the books, magazines, music and internet facilities which are available at most public libraries, these superb spaces also offer activities such as free PopLaw legal advice clinics, homework clubs and jazz classes. The borough has built four of these wonders; find them in Bow, Whitechapel, Canary Wharf and on East India Dock Road. London linguists are spoiled with the excellent **French Institute (Map 36)**, **Instituto Cervantes (Map 19)** and the **Goethe Institut (Map 37)**, while more cunning linguists may prefer the eye-opening gynaecological collection among the 2.5 million medical-related works in the **Wellcome Library (Map 4)**. Poets should meander their way to the **Saison Poetry Library (Map 104)**, ensconced within the South Bank Centre, for a little inspiration. Artists will enjoy the **National Art Library (Map 36)**, which nestles within the V&A Museum. You can use many of London's academic and specialist libraries through the Inspire London scheme, which grants one-day reference access to collections throughout London; ask your local library to refer you.

However, the Daddy of them all is the **British Library (Map 78)**. This behemoth receives a copy of every publication printed in the UK and Ireland, and requires 625km of shelving space to accommodate its 150million items. But it's just such a tease. You cannot borrow books, and to even access the collections you need to obtain a Reader Pass, via an introductory discussion to establish why you need it and whether you're likely to doodle on the books. This requires two forms of ID, no compromise: refer to www.bl.uk for the latest guidelines. Once you have your pass you can access the Reading Rooms, albeit with your personal belongings in a clear plastic bag (or stored in a locker). But if you just fancy seeing the Magna Carta, Shakespeare in Quarto or some Beatles manuscripts, you can access the book-free visitor areas without appointment and still gain an impressive look at one of the world's greatest information resources.

General Information

Important phone numbers:
All emergencies: 999
Non-emergencies: 101
Anti-terrorism hotline: 0800 789 321
Crime Stoppers: 0800 555 111
Neighbourhood Watch: 020 79934709
Missing Persons: 0500 700 700
Complaints: 08453 002 002
Websites:
www.met.police.uk
www.cityoflondon.police.uk (Separate police force specifically covering the Square Mile).
www.btp.police.uk (Separate police force specifically covering public transport).

Statistics* (Greater London)

	2007/08	2007/06	2006/05	2005/04
Murder	123	142	142	155
Rapes	1,558	1,977	2,001	2,035
GBH	3,785	4,380	4,702	4,496
Burglary (res)	49,946	50,193	53,939	52,693
Vehicle Crime	100,678	109,436	114,501	114,698

* taken from a report from the Metropolitan Police Performance Directorate

Police Stations

	Address	Phone	Map
Albany Street Police Station	60 Albany St	020 7404 1212	77
Battersea Police Station	112 Battersea Bridge	020 7350 1122	132
Belgravia Police Station	203 Buckingham Palace Rd	020 7730 1212	20
Brixton Police Station	367 Brixton Rd	020 7326 1212	144
Camberwell Police Station	22 Camberwell Church St	020 7378 1212	122
Cavendish Road Police Station	47 Cavendish Parade	020 7326 1212	149
Charing Cross Police Station	Agar St & Strand	020 7240 1212	24
Chelsea Police Station	2 Lucan Pl	020 7376 1212	46
Chiswick Police Station	209 Chiswick High Rd	020 8577 1212	38
Deptford Police Station	114 Amersham Vale	020 8297 1212	126
East Dulwich Police Station	173 Lordship Ln	020 7378 1212	129
Greenwich Police Station	31 Royal Hill	020 8853 1212	120
Hampstead Police Station	26 Rosslyn Hill	020 7404 1212	56
Harrow Road Police Station	325 Harrow Rd	020 7402 1212	26
Holborn Police Station	10 Lamb's Conduit St	020 7404 1212	5
Holloway Police Station	284 Hornsey Rd	020 7704 1212	61
Hornsey Police Station	98 Tottenham Ln	020 8808 1212	54
Islington Police Station	2 Tolpuddle St	020 7704 1212	80
Kennington Police Station	49 Kennington Rd	020 7326 1212	131
Kensington Police Station	72 Earl's Court Rd	020 7376 1212	35
Kentish Town Police	12 Holmes Rd	020 7404 1212	72
Lavender Hill Police Station	176 Lavender Hill	020 7350 1122	140
Marylebone Police Station	1 Seymour St	020 7486 1212	1
Notting Hill Police Station	100 Ladbroke Grove	020 7376 1212	28
Paddington Green Police Station	2 Harrow Rd	020 7402 1212	31
Peckham Police Station	177 Peckham High St	020 7378 1212	123
Rotherhithe Police Station	99 Lower Rd	020 7378 1212	110
Southwark Police Station	323 Borough High St	020 7378 1212	106
St John's Wood Police Station	20 Newcourt St	020 7486 1212	69
Tooting Police Station	251 Mitcham Rd	020 8807 1212	152
Walworth Police Station	12 Manor Pl	020 7378 1212	113
Wandsworth Police Station	146 Wandsworth High St	020 7350 1122	138
West End Central Police Station	27 Savile Row	020 7437 1212	10

Overview

London hotels can be sources of hopelessly romantic creativity. In 1899 Claude Monet painted the Houses of Parliament from his balcony at the Savoy hotel. About 100 years later, Fay Weldon moved in with her typewriter as writer in residence. If you've got visitors in town, fancy giving Claude a run for his money, or just can't face going back to your dump of a flat, you'll need the services of a hotel. When choosing your hotel, think carefully about what kind of London you're looking to experience and whom the room is for. We've identified a few of the usual suspects for whom you may find yourself booking a hotel room, and heartily offer you our best suggestions for each. Just don't expect to emerge from any of them clutching a masterpiece penned overnight.

Only the best, Daah-ling

So you need to find a hotel for a VIP client who will accept nothing but the best. Where to start? Since you don't have to cover the bill yourself, here is where you can really dig into London hospitality at its most deluxe. Start by trying to book **The Ritz (Map 9)**, with its amazing views of Green Park, Rococo detailing and killer high tea. **Brown's (Map 9)** is a stunning five-star and was the first hotel in London to have a lift. There is also the **Dorchester (Map 9)**, and its neighbour the **Hilton Park Lane (Map 9)**, where you may see a celebrity stumbling back to their quarters at four in the morning, if you're very, very lucky. **The Landmark (Map 76)** is a wonderfully Victorian retreat in the centre of ritzy Marylebone and has a rather fine atrium. But the granddaddy of luxury London must be the **Savoy (Map 24)**. This elegant old-timer stunk of old money until its temporary closure in 2007 for a £100 million spruce-up. It was built on the location of the Savoy Palace, which burned down during the Peasants' Revolt in 1381. We say let them eat cake (and tea).

A Dirty Weekend

This can be any weekend where a Londoner decides booze-goggled sex and/or quick-to-bed access after a night of clubbing is worthy of dishing out the dosh on an über-chic central hotel. It's one (giant) step up from splurging on a taxi and is the realm of the London boutique hotel where location is everything. **Hazlitt's (Map 12)** is right in the middle of Soho yet still wonderfully intimate. **Andaz Hotel (Map 8) (formerly Great Eastern Hotel)** is in the heart of the City, with funky Shoreditch on its doorstep, whilst the 'modern English' style of the **Charlotte Street Hotel (Map 3)** is painfully hip and sophisticated.

The Tea-and-Crumpet Tourist

Then there's the hotel for your sweetly naïve cousin that sees London through rose-tinted Ray Bans: full of scones, Mary Poppins and the chimes of Big Ben. You wouldn't want to burst her cute little bubble, would you? Not to worry, there are plenty of hotels to satisfy the Harrods tourist. **San Domenico House London (Map 46)** is a Chelsea boutique hotel that is about as warm and cuddly as a cup of sugary tea. **The Rookery (Map 15)**, built amongst a warren of once derelict Georgian townhouses in Clerkenwell, is cluttered with museum-worthy furniture, open fires and ye oldey worldey frippery. Or, if she just can't bear to be too far away from Buckingham Palace, there's the nearby **Windermere (Map 20)**.

Parents in Town?

If your parents have spent their nest egg on bailing you out of your London-induced debt, they will probably want to get the most out of London for the least money possible. But if the hotel you pick for their stay is anything short of perfect, you'll never hear the end of it. If they have loyalty cards with any of the bigger hotel chains, now is a good time to use them. **The Sheraton Park Lane (Map 10)** is a glamorous choice; it has an entire floor for its reward cardholders, plus its Art Deco Palm Court is worth a gin and tonic or two. **The London Bridge Hotel (Map 106)** is an independent four-star that usually has good deals and is conveniently close to Borough Market and London Bridge station. Gower Street has a wealth of small family-run hotels at reasonable prices, including the **Cavendish (Map 23)** and **Jesmond (Map 4)**, both within stumbling distance of the British Museum. There's also the nearby **Crescent Hotel (Map 4)**, next to Russell Square.

In Lieu of a Couch to Crash On

Then you get your university friend still in strong denial of the real world, who refuses to get a real job. The amount of times this sponger has crashed on your sofa has been enough to send your might-be-the-one girl/boyfriend packing. Instead of blaming him/her for your future life of loneliness, banish them from the flat and call in the services of one of London's cheapies. They do exist, you just have to look hard. Sometimes short-term rental companies, like **Best London Rent**, offer shared-facility flats at very cheap prices. This is perfect if it's going to be for a week or more, and although the locations aren't too central, this can be a good alternative to endless weeks of friends imposing on your hospitality. Otherwise, London does have one or two great youth hostels. Decent choices include **St Christopher's Inn (Map 106)** on Borough High Street, the **Alhambra (Map 5)** by King's Cross, and a number of reasonable choices by Paddington Station, such as **Europa House (Map 31)**. If your visitor can't be separated from Camden, escort them to the **Hampstead Britannia Hotel (Map 70)** on Primrose Hill Road.

Where to Stick Your Best Friend From School
(And Her Husband, Two Perfect Kids and a Dog)

Unfortunately, for some people visiting London, a dodgy guesthouse isn't going to cut it. You want to show them how your city can be just as perfect as their countryside home and how not jealous you are of them! Of course, they don't see the point in paying tons either. This is where the few and far between bed and breakfasts come out of the woodwork. Most of these are small, so book in advance. London's best is the warm and welcoming **Bay Tree House and Annex B&B (Out of coverage)**. Great for families or singletons alike, it's in New Southgate (about 25 minutes by tube from central London) but can be a relaxing retreat. **Barclay House (Map 43)** is a hidden gem in Fulham Broadway (make sure you write down the address as it's not signposted and can blend in). **Aster House (Map 45)** is a bit pricier but close enough to posh High Street Kensington to give a glimpse of how the other half live.

With all these hotels, compare prices online, ask for their best rate and/or call for last minute deals, you may be surprised at the reductions available. Good offers mean you can pay less than you'd think for the best, and London does really have the best.

Map 1 • Marylebone (West)	Address	Phone	Price in £
22 York St	22 York St	020 7224 2990	89
Boston Court Hotel	26 Upper Berkeley St	020 7723 1445	89
The Cumberland	Marble Arch	087 1376 9014	110
Edward Lear	28 Seymour St	020 7402 5401	50
Hadleigh Hotel	24 Upper Berkeley St	020 7262 4084	81
Hotel 82	82 Gloucester Pl	020 7486 3679	110
The Leonard	15 Seymour St	020 7935 2010	100
Sherlock Holmes Hotel	108 Baker St	020 7486 6161	117
Thistle Marble Arch	Bryanston St Marble Arch	0871 376 9027	149

Map 2 • Marylebone (East)	Address	Phone	Price in £
Claridges	Brook St	020 7629 8860	167
Hotel La Place	17 Nottingham Pl	020 7486 4335	99
Jury's Clifton Ford	47 Welbeck St	020 7486 6600	120
The Langham	1 Portland Pl	020 7636 1000	198
No. 5 Maddox	5 Maddox St	020 7647 0200	270

Map 3 · Fitzrovia

	Address	Phone	Price in £
Grange Fitzrovia Hotel	20 Bolsover St	020 7467 7000	101
Sanderson Hotel	50 Berners St	020 7300 1400	214

Map 4 · Bloomsbury (West)

	Address	Phone	Price in £
Academy	19 Gower St	020 7631 4115	200
Ambassadors Hotel	12 Upper Woburn Pl	020 7693 5400	112
Arosfa	83 Gower St	020 7636 2115	55
Bloomsbury Park Hotel	126 Southampton Row	087 1376 9006	99
Crescent Hotel	49 Cartwright Gardens	020 7387 1515	100
Hotel Cavendish	75 Gower St	020 7636 9079	95
Hotel Russell	1 Russell Square	020 7837 6470	119
The Montague	15 Montague St	020 7637 1001	135
Myhotel Bloomsbury	11 Bayley St	020 7667 6000	186
Radisson	97 Great Russell St	020 7637 3477	142
St Giles	Bedford Ave	020 7300 3000	88

Map 5 · Bloomsbury (East)

	Address	Phone	Price in £
Comfort Inn	2 St Chad's St	020 7837 1940	98
Generator Hostel	37 Tavistock Pl	020 7388 7666	17

Map 7 · Barbican / City Road (South)

		Phone	Price in £
Barbican Hotel	120 Central St	087 1376 9004	71
Citadines Hotel	7 Goswell Rd	020 7566 8000	99

Map 8 · Liverpool Street / Broadgate

		Phone	Price in £
Andaz Hotel	8 Liverpool St	020 7961 1234	160

Map 9 · Mayfair / Green Park

	Address	Phone	Price in £
Athenaeum Hotel	116 Piccadilly	020 7499 3464	153
Brown's Hotel	1 Albemarle St	020 7493 6020	239
Chesterfield	35 Charles St	020 7491 2622	116
The Connaught	Carlos Pl	020 7499 7070	188
Curzon Plaza Hotel	56 Curzon St	020 7499 4121	122
The Dorchester	53 Park Ln	020 7629 8888	245
Flemings Mayfair Hotel	7 Half Moon St	020 7493 2088	134
Grosvenor House	86 Park Ln	020 7499 6363	175
Hilton Park Lane	22 Park Ln	020 7493 8000	226
The Intercontinental	1 Hamilton Pl	020 7409 3131	198
May Fair Hotel	Stratton St	020 7629 7777	173
Metropolitan	Old Park Lane	020 7447 1047	191
Millennium Hotel	44 Grosvenor Square	020 7629 9400	145
The Ritz	150 Piccadilly	020 7493 8181	265

Map 11 · Soho (Central)

	Address	Phone	Price in £
The Shaftesbury	65 Shaftesbury Ave	020 7871 6000	164
The Soho Hotel	4 Richmond Mews	020 7559 3000	240

Map 12 · Soho (East)

	Address	Phone	Price in £
Hazlitt's Hotel	6 Frith St	020 7099 3190	159

Map 13 · Covent Garden

	Address	Phone	Price in £
Covent Garden Hotel	10 Monmouth St	020 7806 1000	235
Fielding	4 Broad Ct	020 7836 8305	85
The Radisson	20 Monmouth St	020 7836 4300	150

General Information · **Hotels**

Map 14 · Holborn / Temple	Address	Phone	Price in £
Citadines Hotel	94 High Holborn	020 7395 8800	99
One Aldwych	1 Aldwych	020 7300 1000	240
Renaissance Chancery Court	252 High Holborn	020 7829 9888	340

Map 15 · Blackfriars / Farringdon	Address	Phone	Price in £
Club Quarters	24 Ludgate Hill	020 7451 5800	84
Malmaison	18 Charterhouse Sq	020 7012 3700	225
The Rookery	12 Peter's Ln	020 7336 0931	128

Map 17 · Square Mile (East)	Address	Phone	Price in £
Club Quarters	7 Gracechurch St	020 7451 5800	79
Threadneedles Hotel	5 Threadneedle St	020 7657 8080	153

Map 18 · Tower Hill / Aldgate	Address	Phone	Price in £
Apex Hotel	1 Seething Ln	020 7702 2020	86
Chamberlain	130 Minories	020 7680 1500	94
Novotel Tower Bridge	10 Pepys St	020 7265 6000	145

Map 19 · Belgravia	Address	Phone	Price in £
B&B Belgravia	64 Ebury St	020 7259 8570	99
The Berkeley	Wilton Pl	020 7235 6000	255
The Halkin	Halkin St	020 7333 1000	390
Morgan Guest House	120 Ebury St	020 7730 2384	52
Sheraton Belgravia	20 Chesham Pl	020 7235 6040	178

Map 20 · Victoria / Pimlico (West)	Address	Phone	Price in £
41	41 Buckingham Palace Rd	020 7300 0041	255
Caswell Hotel	25 Gloucester St	020 7834 6345	63
Central House	39 Belgrave Rd	020 7834 8036	122
Days Hotel	80 Belgrave Rd	020 7828 8661	102
Dover Hotel	42 Belgrave Rd	020 7821 9085	63
Durrants Hotel	26 St George's Dr	020 7935 8131	153
Elizabeth Hotel and Apartments	37 Eccleston Square	020 7828 6812	85
Enrico Hotel	77 Warwick Way	020 7834 9538	56
Goring	Beeston Pl	020 7396 9000	279
Hart House Hotel	51 Gloucester St	020 7935 2288	85
Hesperia London Victoria Hotel	2 Bridge Pl	087 0225 4134	114
Windermere	144 Warwick Way	020 7834 5163	90

Map 21 · Pimlico (East)	Address	Phone	Price in £
Best Western	85 Belgrave Rd	020 7828 9279	76
City Inn Westminster	30 John Islip Street	020 7630 1000	140
Corbigoe Hotel	101 Belgrave Rd	020 7834 9790	46
Dolphin House Hotel	Chichester St	020 7798 8000	52
Wellington	71 Vincent Square	020 7834 4740	62

Map 22 · Westminster	Address	Phone	Price in £
51 Buckingham Gate	51 Buckingham Gate	020 7769 7766	326
London Bridge Hotel	8 Bridge St	020 7855 2200	172
Vandon House Hotel	Vandon St	020 7799 6480	45

Map 23 • St. James's

	Address	Phone	Price in £
The Cavendish Hotel	81 Jermyn St	020 7930 2111	142
Dukes Hotel	35 St James's St	020 7491 4840	185
Radisson	3 St Martin's St	020 7930 8641	167
Radisson Edwardian Hampshire	31 Leicester Square	020 7839 9399	160
The Stafford	16 St James's Pl	020 7493 0111	290
Thistle Trafalgar Hotel	Whitcomb St	087 1376 9037	114

Map 24 • Trafalgar Square / The Strand

	Address	Phone	Price in £
Guoman Charing Cross	The Strand	087 0333 9105	111
The Savoy	Strand	020 7420 2405	TBD
The Strand Palace	372 Strand	020 7836 8080	115

Map 27 • Maida Vale

	Address	Phone	Price in £
Colonade	2 Warrington Crescent	020 7286 1052	270
The Royal Park	3 Westbourne Terrace Rd	020 7479 6600	140

Map 29 • Notting Hill Gate

	Address	Phone	Price in £
Guesthouse West	165 Westbourne Grove	020 7792 9800	155
The Lennox	34 Pembridge Gardens	087 0850 3317	190
The Main House	6 Colville Rd	020 7221 9691	50
Miller's Residence	111 Westbourne Grove	020 7243 1024	150
The Portobello Hotel	22 Stanley Gardens	020 7727 2777	145

Map 30 • Bayswater

	Address	Phone	Price in £
Bayswater Inn	8 Princes Square	020 7727 8621	91
Best Western	27 Devonshire Terrace	020 7745 1200	102
Best Western Mornington	12 Lancaster Gate	020 7262 7361	130
Best Western Phoenix Hotel	1 Kensington Gardens Sq	020 7229 2494	91
Blakemore Hotel	30 Leinster Gardens	020 7262 4591	102
Caesar Hotel	26 Queen's Gardens	020 7262 0022	91
Central Park Hotel	49 Queensborough Terrace	020 7229 2424	61
Comfort Inn	19 Craven Hill Gardens	020 7262 6644	72
Commodore Hotel	50 Lancaster Gate	020 7099 3190	102
Craven Gardens Hotel	16 Leinster Terrace	020 7262 3167	56
Duke of Leinster Hotel	20 Leinster Gardens	014 8039 4138	89
Dylan House	14 Devonshire Terrace	020 7723 3280	117
Garden Court	30 Kensington Gardens Square	020 7229 2553	48
Hempel Hotel	31 Craven Hill Gardens	020 7298 9000	173
Henry VIII Hotel	19 Leinster Gardens	020 7262 0117	101
Hyde Park Premier	14 Craven Hill	020 7262 0111	132
Paddington Court Hotel	27 Devonshire Terrace	020 7262 2204	113
Pembridge Palace Hotel	52 Princes Square	020 7229 6262	87
Princes Square Hotel	23 Prince's Sq	020 7229 9876	115
Royal Lancaster Hotel	1 Lancaster Terrace	086 6539 8063	145
Vancouver Studios	30 Prince's Square	020 7221 8678	85
Whites Hotel	90 Lancaster Gate	0871 376 9022	86

Map 31 • Paddington

	Address	Phone	Price in £
Castleton	164 Sussex Gardens	020 7706 4666	76
Chrysos Hotel	25 Norfolk Square	020 7262 2417	102
The Delmere	130 Sussex Gardens	020 7262 1863	99
Edward Hotel	1 Spring St	020 7262 2671	95
Hilton	225 Edgware Rd	020 7402 4141	117
Hilton	146 Praed St	020 7850 0500	153
Pavilion Hotel	36 Sussex Gardens	020 7262 0905	60
Queensway Hotel	147 Sussex Gardens	020 7723 7749	61

Map 35 · Kensington

	Address	Phone	Price in £
Ambassadors Hotel	16 Collingham Rd	020 7693 5400	104
Best Western	33 Hogarth Rd	020 7370 6831	119
Comfort Inn	22 West Cromwell Rd	020 7373 3300	68
Copthorne Tara Hotel	Scarsdale Place	020 7937 7211	117
Derby Hotel	155 Cromwell Rd	020 7262 0022	103
Exhibition Court Hotel	109 Warwick Rd	020 7244 9750	67
Exhibition Court Hotel	25 Collingham Pl	020 7370 7788	124
Majestic	160 Cromwell Rd	020 7373 3083	57
The Milestone Hotel	1 Kensington Ct Pl	020 7917 1010	265
Radisson	68 W Cromwell Rd	020 7761 9000	98
The Rockwell	181 W Cromwell Rd	020 7244 2000	120

Map 36 · South Kensington / Gloucester Rd

		Phone	Price in £
Baglioni Hotel	60 Hyde Park Gate	020 7368 5700	357
Best Western	4 Queens Gate	020 7808 8400	122
Citadines Hotel	35 Gloucester Rd	0207 543 7878	107
Eden Plaza Hotel	68 Queens Gate	020 7370 6111	74
Fraser Place Hotel	39 Queen's Gate Gardens	020 7969 3555	115
Gainsborough Hotel	7 Queensberry Pl	020 7957 0000	91
Gallery Hotel	8 Queensberry Pl	020 7915 0000	112
The Gore	190 Queen's Gate	020 7584 6601	178
Grange Hotel	41 Queen's Gate Gardens	020 7584 0512	90
Grosvenor Kensington Hotel	2 Harrington Rd	020 8859 3333	119
Holiday Inn	97 Cromwell Rd	870 400 9100	99
Millennium Hotel	140 Gloucester Rd	020 7373 6000	110
Park International Hotel	117 Cromwell Rd	020 7370 5711	101

Map 37 · Knightsbridge

	Address	Phone	Price in £
Cadogan Hotel	75 Sloane St	020 7235 7141	178
The Capital Hotel and Apartments	22 Basil St	020 7589 5171	230
Durley House Hotel	115 Sloane St	020 7235 5537	459
The Franklin Hotel	22 Egerton Gardens	020 7584 5533	200
The Knightsbridge	10 Beaufort Gardens	020 7584 6300	170
Knightsbridge Green Hotel	159 Knightsbridge	020 7584 6274	150
The Rembrandt Hotel	11 Thurloe Pl	020 7589 8100	142

Map 42 · Barons Court

	Address	Phone	Price in £
Holiday Inn Express	295 North End Rd	020 7384 5151	109

Map 43 · West Brompton / Fulham Broadway / Earl's Court

			Price in £
Barclay House	21 Barclay Rd	020 7384 3390	66
Best Western	18 Barkston Gardens	020 7373 3151	74
City Continental London	11 Penywern Rd	020 7373 6514	106
Enterprise Hotel	15 Hogarth Rd	020 7373 4502	68
Garden View Hotel	29 Nevern Square	020 7244 6466	68
Mayflower Hotel	26 Trebovir Rd	020 7370 0991	170
Rushmore	11 Trebovir Rd	020 7370 3839	164
Twenty Nevern Square	20 Nevern Square	020 7565 9555	79

Map 44 · Chelsea

	Address	Phone	Price in £
Astons Apartments Hotel	31 Rosary Gardens	020 7590 6000	97
Blakes Hotel	33 Roland Gardens	020 7370 6701	175

Map 45 · Chelsea (East)	Address	Phone	Price in £
Aster House	3 Sumner Pl	020 7581 5888	99
Myhotel Chelsea	35 Ixworth Pl	020 7225 7500	222
Regency	100 Queens Gate	020 7373 7878	114
Sydney House	9 Sydney St	020 7376 7711	160

Map 46 · Sloane Square	Address	Phone	Price in £
Draycott Hotel	22 Cadogan Gardens	020 773 06466	306
San Domenico House	29 Draycott Pl	020 7581 5757	210

Map 56 · Hampstead Village	Address	Phone	Price in £
Hampstead Village Guesthouse	2 Kemplay Rd	020 7435 8679	65

Map 69 · St. John's Wood	Address	Phone	Price in £
Marriott	128 King Henry's Rd	020 7722 7711	127

Map 70 · Primrose Hill	Address	Phone	Price in £
Hampstead Britannia Hotel	Primrose Hill Rd	087 1222 0043	76

Map 76 · Edgeware Road / Marylebone (North)		Phone	Price in £
Danubius Hotel	18 Lodge Rd	0207 722 7722	84
Dorset Square Hotel	39 Dorset Sq	020 7723 7874	160
Four Seasons Hotel	173 Gloucester Pl	020 7723 5978	96
Landmark	222 Marylebone Rd	020 7631 8000	210

Map 77 · Mornington Crescent / Regent's Park		Phone	Price in £
Melia White House Hotel	Albany St	207 391 3000	109

Map 91 · Shoreditch / Brick Lane / Spitalfields		Phone	Price in £
City Hotel	12 Osborn St	020 7247 3313	102
Hotel St Gregory	100 Shoreditch High St	020 7613 9800	137

Map 98 · Mile End (South) / Limehouse		Phone	Price in £
Holiday Inn Express	The Highway	020 7791 3850	133

Map 100 · Poplar (West) / Canary Wharf (West)		Phone	Price in £
The Hilton	Marsh Wall	020 3002 2350	104
International Hotel	163 Marsh Wall	086 6539 8063	81
Marriot	22 Hertsmere Rd	020 7093 1000	119

Map 104 · South Bank / Waterloo / Lambeth North		Phone	Price in £
Marriott County Hall	Westminster Bridge Rd	020 7928 5200	189
Travel Inn London County Hall	Belverdere Rd	0870 238 3300	104

105 · Southwark / Bankside (West)		Phone	Price in £
The Mad Hatter Hotel	3 Stamford St	020 7401 9222	115

Map 106 · Bankside (East) / Borough / Newington		Phone	Price in £
Novotel London City South	61 Southwark Bridge Rd	020 7089 0400	98

Map 113 · Walworth	Address	Phone	Price in £
Express by Eurotraveller Hotel	18 Amelia St	020 7358 4898	79

Map 120 · Greenwich	Address	Phone	Price in £
Novotel Greenwich	173 Greenwich High Rd	020 8312 6800	145

Map 121 · Camberwell (West)	Address	Phone	Price in £
Park Plaza Hotel	1 Addington Square	020 7021 1800	127

Map 131 · Vauxhall / Albert Embankment		Phone	Price in £
Days Hotel	54 Kennington Rd	020 7922 1331	97
Park Plaza Hotel	18 Albert Embankment	020 7958 8000	119
Plaza on the River	18 Albert Embankment	020 7769 2525	224

Map 134 · South Lambeth	Address	Phone	Price in £
Comfort Inn	87 S Lambeth Rd	020 7735 9494	74
Hotel 87	87 Old South Lambeth Rd	084 5082 2456	134

Map 137 · Wandsworth (West)	Address	Phone	Price in £
Best Western	52 Upper Richmond Rd	020 8874 1598	97

As you might expect from a site constantly inhabited since the Roman invasion of Britain, and probably before, London has managed to assemble a vast array of good, bad and ugly landmarks. The city is, in fact, stuffed with them, and the following is a slightly subjective rumination on a small proportion of some of the most noteworthy.

Historical

London gracefully bears a massive weight of history, and many of its landmarks reflect this. One of the oldest is the remains of the **Temple of Mithras (Map 16)** on Walbrook, built by the Romans when London was Londinium. Parts of the **London Wall (Map 18)**, also originally built by the Romans, still exist, the best fragments are around Tower Hill station. In Medieval times London became a bustling place; celebrate one of its most beautiful churches by visiting the oddly named **St Giles' Cripplegate (Map 7)**, which is ensconced within the brutal **Barbican Centre**, a landmark itself. By the 1600s, London was bustling so hard it got the plague and then some idiot burnt the entire city down in 1666. Celebrate three days of the Great Fire by climbing to the top of the 202 feet high **Monument (Map 18)**, before visiting post-fire architect Christopher Wren's masterpiece, **St Paul's Cathedral (Map 16)**. Into the 18th century, things became a little more sophisticated and some of London's prettiest domestic architecture bloomed. Stroll down Bloomsbury's **Doughty Street (Map 5)**, stopping at Charles Dickens' House, for perfectly proportioned Georgian elegance. The Victorians had a huge impact on London, with whole tracts of the city bearing the stamp of the starched times of chimney sweeps and empire bashing. For the lighter side of Victorian London, poke about the museums quarter from the **Victoria & Albert Museum (Map 37)** up to the **Albert Memorial (Map 36)**. For the darker, dodge the elderly at the **St Pancras Hospital (Map 78)**, an ex-workhouse.

Tourist Bait

London has a host of over-exposed landmarks that are honey to the swarms of tourist worker-bees but over-rated in the eyes of many Londoners. We don't necessarily share this view, but if you want to venture beyond the crowds at **Big Ben (Map 22)**, try some of the following. The aforementioned **St Paul's Cathedral (Map 16)** is an absolute wonder, although try the smaller **Southwark Cathedral (Map 106)** for a more intimate option. **The British Museum (Map 4)** is a beauty made fairer by its recent courtyard renovation; peruse the library to see where Marx pondered upon 'Das Kapital'. **The Burlington Arcade (Map 10)** is how shopping should be, whilst the **Wallace Collection (Map 2)** is probably the perfect townhouse museum to take your mother-in-law. The crypt under **St Mary-le-Bow Church (Map 16)** is 11th century weirdness complete with its own vegetarian restaurant. The Thames is long enough to provide you with your own spot of riverside tranquillity. If you're scared of bridges, burrow under the river at the **Greenwich Foot Tunnel (Map 120)**, or chug across it on the free Woolwich Ferry. For a weekend mooch, try the **Grand Regent's Canal (Map 71)** around **Little Venice (Map 27)**. For a grimier option, avoid local children as they try to push you in the same canal around **Mile End (Map 98)**.

Modern Landmarks

The 20th century blessed the city with some opinion splitting contributions. **The Hayward Gallery (Map 104)** and **National Theatre (Map 104)** are both concrete frighteners which we are learning to love. Despite originally housing a power station, **Tate Modern (Map 105)** has been more graciously received. Meanwhile, further down the river, disused **Battersea Power Station (Map 133)** continues to crumble. The **BT Tower (Map 60)** is like a 1960s lighthouse for central London drunks. **The Lloyds Building (Map 18)** and **Tower 42 (Map 18)** are both absorbing odes to the banker and glare menacingly at their new rival **One Canada Square (or Canary Wharf Tower) (Map 100)**. A more recent contribution to the city is the **Canary Wharf Underground Station (Map 100)**. **The Ark (Map 64)** at Hammersmith is west London's greeting to those driving in from Heathrow. East London is currently revelling in its revamped **V&A Museum of Childhood (Map 92)**.

Lowbrow

In these clean times of starchitects, steel and glass, a few minutes spent gawping at **Elephant and Castle (Map 105)** shopping centre is enough to remind anyone how awry a landmark can go. Even a quick squizz at the nearby **Faraday Memorial (Map 105)** may not lift your gloom, largely as it now forms the body of a clogged roundabout. However, London can do lowbrow with the best of them, starting with the **Westway Flyover (Map 31)**: a noisy, dusty shard of concrete to remind you that the car is still king. The disused **Kingsway Tram Tunnel (Map 4)** is a forgotten piece of prime underground real estate and **Centre Point (Map 4)** and Millbank

Tower (Map 21) are good examples of dodgy skyscrapers that no-one needed. **Battersea Park Gasometers (Map 133)** are imposing monsters, whereas **Lots Road Power Station (Map 50)** is fast becoming London's trendiest disused power station. If you must jump upon band wagons, keep your eyes peeled around east London for art left on walls by Banksy. Mobile lowbrow starts with a trip on a Routemaster, despite the buses being withdrawn in 2005, two heritage routes are still running. Lowbrow (along with logic, aesthetic quality and planning) finishes with **Euston Station (Map 78)**, which is, simply, disgusting.

Map 1 · Marylebone (West)

Marble Arch	Oxford St	Randomly plonked gateway to nowhere.
Speaker's Corner	Cumberland Gate	It's easy—stand on the corner and listen to the 'speeches.'

Map 2 · Marylebone (East)

Hertford House	Manchester Sq	Terribly twee home of the Wallace Collection.
Jimi Hendrix Memorial Blue Plaque	23 Brook St	Jimi lived here. Some bloke called Handel lived next door.

Map 3 · Fitzrovia

BT Tower	60 Cleveland St	A 574 foot tall official government secret until 1993.
Charlotte Street	Charlotte St	Restaurant strip for the advertising in-crowd.
Middlesex Hospital	Mortimer St	Closed-down and spooky-looking.
Pollock's Toy Museum	1 Scala St	Brimming with delightful, traditional toys and Dickensian atmosphere.
Sinner Winner Man	216 Oxford St	Are you a sinner? Or a winner? London's top preacher's patch.
Tottenham Court Road	Tottenham Ct Rd	Buy your electronics 'ere, innit?

Map 4 · Bloomsbury (West)

The British Museum	Great Russell St	Newly-covered Great Court is architectural manna.
Centre Point	101 New Oxford St	Ugly skyscraper looking kinda out of place.
Kingsway Tram Tunnel		Spooky remnant of London's defunct Tram network.
Senate House	University of London, Malet St	Ominous art deco building; Orwell's Ministry of Truth.
Tavistock Square	Tavistock Sq	Has a statue of Gandhi looking as cool as ever.

Map 5 · Bloomsbury (East)

The Dickens House Museum	48 Doughty St	Unassuming from the outside, mecca for Dickens' fans on the inside.
Doughty Street	Doughty St	Exquisite Georgian street in heart of literary land.

Map 7 · Barbican / City Road (South)

Barbican Centre	Silk St	An architechtual eyesore. Bloody good events though.
Bunhill Fields	City Rd	120 thousand dead people, including William Blake. All buried, luckily.
LSO St Luke's	161 Old St	Home to the London Symphony Orchestra. Peaceful gardens for relaxation.
St. Giles' Cripplegate	Fore St	Beautiful church ensconced in brutal Barbican.

Map 8 · Liverpool Street / Broadgate

Fulcrum at Broadgate	Broadgate	Richard Serra's overwhelming steel megalith.

Map 9 · Mayfair / Green Park

50 Berkeley Square	50 Berkeley Sq	The most haunted house in all of London town!
Apsley House	Hyde Park Corner	"Number One, London"—former hip address of Duke of Wellington.
Buckingham Palace	The Mall	Unofficial HQ for Fathers For Justice.
Down Street Station	Down St	Bricked-up Underground station. The Turtles didn't live here.

Map 10 · Piccadilly / Soho (West)

Burlington Arcade	Burlington Arcade	Will anything innovative ever come from here again?
Carnaby Street	Carnaby St	Flash the cash to cut a dash.
Kingly Street Arcade	Kingly St	
Statue of Eros	Piccadilly Circus	God of Love, smothered in pigeon crap: a cautionary tale.

Map 11 · Soho (Central)

Huge Tree In Pub (Waxy O'Connor's)	14 Rupert St	No, you're not drunk, it really is a tree.
Soho Market	Berwick St	Arrive early for traditional Cockney trader songs / off-duty hookers.

Map 12 · Soho (East)

Denmark Street	Denmark St	Guitar land. 'Enter Sandman' forbidden in most stores.
FA Headquarters	25 Soho Sq	Home of English football's top brass.
Old Compton Street	Old Compton St	Dubious gay hub.
The Phoenix Garden	21 Stacey St	A beautiful green mini-oasis in the middle of the city.
Soho Square	Soho Sq	Great atmosphere on hot summer days.

Map 13 · Covent Garden

Oasis Lido	32 Endell St	A lido in central London! In a 50s housing estate!
Seven Dials	Junction of Monmouth St, Mercer St and five others	Slum area in the past. Now great for shopping!

Map 14 · Holborn / Temple

Aldwych tube station	The Strand	Creepy abandoned tube station. With a photo booth... of doom?
BBC Bush House	Aldwych	London calling the world, since 1940.
Inner Temple Garden	Inner Temple	So peaceful even the lawyers look relaxed.
Lincoln's Inn Fields	Lincoln's Inn Fields	Largest public square in London.
The Old Curiosity Shop	13 Portsmouth St	The oldest shop in London is truly Dickensesque.
Royal Courts of Justice	Strand	Witness justice meted out to all, even the McCartneys.
Sir John Soane's Museum	13 Lincoln's Inn Fields	Spooky museum dedicated to the great 18th century architect.
Site of Sweeny Todd's Barber Shop	186 Fleet St	Swing by for a demon haircut and lovely pie.
Somerset House	Strand	18th century palace, beautiful fountains; has various modern functions.

Map 15 · Blackfriars / Farringdon

Daily Express Building	121 Fleet St	Art Deco sleeper.
Millennium Bridge	Millennium Bridge	Footbridge famous for wobbling alarmingly when it was opened.
Postman's Park	King Edward St	Tile memorial for 'average' people who did really cool things.

Map 16 · Square Mile (West)

St Mary le Bow Church	Cheapside	A historic place for City tycoons to save their souls.
St. Paul's Cathedral	St. Paul's Churchyard	Magnificence since 604AD.
Temple of Mithras	Queen Victoria St	3rd century Roman temple foundations. Discovered 1954 and moved here.

Map 17 · Square Mile (East)

Bank of England	Threadneedle St	The 'Old Lady' still churns out the pounds.
London Stone	105 Cannon St	Possibly used by Romans to measure all distances in Britannia.
Threadneedle Street	Threadneedle St	London's original Grope Cunt Lane. Seriously, it's a true story.

Map 18 · Tower Hill / Aldgate

The Gherkin	30 St Mary Axe	Phwoar.
Jack the Ripper Mural	Widegate St	Spooky mural down a gloomy alley. Good for scaring kids.
Jewish Soup Kitchen	Brune St	The kitchen's gone; the stunning ornate façade is still there.
The Lloyds Building	1 Lime St	Dystopia's nicer side.
London Wall	Cooper's Row	Ruins, should be re-built to keep Northerners out.
The Monument	Monument St	Climb 311 coronary-inducing steps for unique, unsung London views.
Pudding Lane	Pudding Ln	Starting point for Great Fire of 1666. No smoking.
Royal Raven Lodgings	Wakefield Tower	Want to upgrade your pokey flat? Become a raven.
Tower 42 (Natwest Tower)	25 Old Broad St	One of London's skyscrapers. Great view (and restaurant) at top.
Tower of London	The Tower of London	Kings and Queens. Surprisingly insightful, annoyingly expensive.

Map 20 · Victoria / Pimlico (West)

Little Ben	Victoria St/Vauxhall Bridge Rd intersection	Big Ben's runty kid brother.
Westminster Cathedral	42 Francis St	Yep, impressive.

Map 21 · Pimlico (East)

Millbank Tower	Millbank	Ugly sore thumb. And Labour Party HQ!

Map 22 · Westminster

Big Ben	House of Commons	The world's most famous clock and pretty damn cool.
Bolan Rock Shrine	Queen's Ride, Putney	Memorial shrine where 70s rock star Marc Bolan died.
Smith Square	Smith Sq	Square with great concert venue—watch out for MPs.
UK Parliament	House of Commons	Parliament buildings where you can watch government debates.
Westminster Tube Station	Bridge St	A daunting, soulless, engineering playground. Good and bad both extinct here...

Map 23 · St. James's

Economist Plaza	25 St James's St	Rotating sculpture installations from bratty young artists.
Giro the Nazi Dog	9 Carlton House Terrace	London's sole Nazi memorial. You'd think there'd be more…
Leicester Square	Leicester Sq	Tragic, tacky, always inexplicably heaving. Avoid.

Map 24 · Trafalgar Square / The Strand

10 Downing Street	10 Downing St	The Prime Minister's house.
The Actors' Church	St. Paul's Church, Bedford St	Somewhat hidden and unique church long-associated with thesps.
The Banqueting House	Whitehall	Unsullied Renaissance cum-shot. Still does private parties.
Cleopatra's Needle	Embankment	Ancient-Egyptian Empire esoterica, with additional Luftwaffe-era 'distressed' styling.
Eleanor Cross	Charing Cross Station, The Strand	A mourning King's tribute to his expired Queen.
Jane Austen Residence	10 Henrietta St	The first Bridget Jones' bachelorette crashed here for a time.
Right-hand Drive Street	Savoy Ct	Britain's only right-hand-drive street. Like being on holiday! (ish)
Sewer Lamp	Carting Ln	Lit by the power of your bowels.
St Martin-in-the-Fields	Trafalgar Sq	Was indeed surrounded by fields once. Just TRY to imagine!
Top Secret Tunnels	6 Craig's Ct (entrance)	Government's WWII tunnels, 100ft below London. But shhh: top secret.
Trafalgar Square	Trafalgar Sq	Hardly an oasis but space to sit, look and think.

Map 25 • Kensal Town

Trellick Tower	5 Golborne Rd	Grade II listed 1960s council estate inspiring love/hate reactions.

Map 29 • Notting Hill Gate

Portobello Road Market	Portobello Rd	Antiques, clothes, food and more. A London institution.

Map 31 • Paddington

Paddington Bear Statue	Paddington Station	The statue's pleasant. But they're milking it with the crap shop.
Westway Flyover		Coolest car route into London

Map 33 • Shepherd's Bush

BBC Television Centre	Wood Lane	Treasure it before the BBC moves out in 2013.

Map 36 • South Kensington / Gloucester Rd

Albert Memorial	Kensington Gardens	The shiniest balding head in town.
Royal Albert Hall	Kensington Gore	One stunner of a music hall, inside and out.

Map 37 • Knightsbridge

Victoria & Albert Museum	Cromwell Rd	Victorian treasure trove, building a beauty itself.

Map 40 • Goldhawk Rd / Ravenscourt Park

Christmas Forest	83 Goldhawk Rd	Just like Norway, but without the bears or hairy women.

Map 43 • West Brompton / Fulham Broadway / Earl's Court

Stamford Bridge	Fulham Rd	That's not sweat you smell but money at Chelsea FC's HQ.

Map 48 • Fulham

Putney Bridge Tube Pill Box	Putney Bridge Station	"We will fight them on the platforms!"

Map 50 • Sand's End

Lots Road Power Station	Lots Rd	Pint-sized power station, now disused.

Map 51 • Highgate

Highgate Cemetery	1 Swain's Ln	Eerily gothic home to Karl Marx and The Highgate Vampire.
Karl Marx's grave	Highgate Cemetry	Exactly what it says on the tin.

Map 52 • Archway (North)

Parkland Walk Nature Reserve	Parkland Walk	Hedgehogs and graffiti to be spotted along this abandoned railway.
Suicide Bridge	Hornsey Ln	Former London entry point, now very much an exit point.

Map 53 • Crouch End

Abandoned Warehouse	Parkland Walk	Dereliction galore along one of the best walks in London.

Map 56 • Hampstead Village

Hampstead Observatory	Lower Terrace	The highest point in London, and open to the public!
Keats' House	Keats Grove	Beautiful buildin' where some bloke wrote some poem. Innit.

Map 57 • Hampstead Heath

Lawn Road Flats	Lawn Rd	c.1934 modern living. Learn to love concrete.

Map 60 • Archway

Banksy's Hitchhiking Charles Manson	Tally Ho Corner (off Highgate Hill)	Early stencil by internationally renowned graff artist.
Dick Whittington's Cat	Highgate Hill	Small stone statue of obscure Mayor's cat.

General Information · **Landmarks**

Map 62 · Finsbury Park

North London Central Mosque (Finsbury Park)	7 St Thomas's Rd ·	New name, ethos for once controversial, now myth-dispelling, mosque.

Map 063 · Manor House

The Castle Climbing Centre	Green Lanes	Fake castle, real climbers.

Map 064 · Stoke Newington

Newington Green Church	39 Newington Green	'ERECTED 1708, ENLARGED 1860'...well, it made us laugh.

Map 67 · Belsize Park

Freud Statue	Fitzjohn's Ave, opposite Maresfield Gardens Junction	Statue by Oscar Nemon near the psychoanalyst's Hampstead home.

Map 68 · Kilburn High Road / Abbey Road

Abbey Road Zebra Crossing	3 Abbey Rd	Go on. Take THAT photo. You know you want to.
State Buidling	195 Kilburn High Rd	Awesome Art Deco building now a scary cult center.

Map 70 · Primrose Hill

3 Chalcot Square	3 Chalcot Sq	Home of poet Sylvia Plath, 1960-61.

Map 71 · Camden Town / Chalk Farm / Kentish Town (West)

Banksy's Maid: Sweeping it Under the Carpet	Chalk Farm Rd	Grafitto symbolising response to African Aids crisis.
Camden Market	Camden Lock Pl	Shop, hang, drink, listen, pose, watch, chill, rock, laugh.
Grand Regents Canal	Grand Regents Canal	London's best bike lane. Or canoe to Birmingham.
The Roundhouse	Chalk Farm Rd	Prominent round building and historic performance venue.

Map 75 · Highbury

St Paul's Shrubbery	St Paul's Rd	All Monty Python jokes welcome, in fact, positively encouraged.

Map 76 · Edgeware Road / Marylebone (North)

Sherlock Holmes' House	221 Baker St	It's elementary my dear Watson!

Map 77 · Mornington Crescent / Regent's Park

Euston Tower	286 Euston Rd	Quite an impressive erection.
Greater London House	Hampstead Rd	Crazy Art Deco building.

Map 78 · Euston

The British Library	96 Euston Rd	Prestigious research library with unmatched collection.
Camden High Street	Camden High St	'Alternative' tourist mecca.
Cheney Road	Cheney Rd	"Chaplin, "Alfie" and many more were filmed on these cobbles.
Euston Station	Euston Rd	So ugly it's oogly.
Platform 9¾	King's Cross Station	This Harry Potter thing has gone way too fucking far.
St Pancras Station	St Pancras Way	Listed Gothic frontage, massive modern Eurostar hangar behind.
St Pancras Hospital	4 St Pancras Way	Ex-Victorian workhouse turned superbug den.

Map 80 · Angel / Upper St

Angel Station Roof	Angel	You can get on the roof here, you epic teens.

Map 82 · De Beauvoir Town / Kingsland

Suleymaniye Mosque	212 Kingsland Rd	Striking minaret silhouetted against Shoreditch Church spire and Broadgate Tower.

Map 84 · Hoxton

Hoxton Square	Hoxton Sq	Great in summer. Buy some cans and join the hipsters.
Village Underground	54 Holywell Ln	How did they get the trains up there?
White Cube	48 Hoxton Sq	Jay Jopling's homage to modern art

General Information · **Landmarks**

Map 85 · Stoke Newington (East)

Abney Park Cemetery	Stoke Newington High St	Egyptian revival-style, spooky nature reserve.

Map 86 · Dalston / Kingsland

Centreprise	136 Kingsland High St	Multi-cultural art centre, cafe, bookshop and venue.
Holy Trinity, The Clowns Church	Beechwood Rd & Kirkland Walk	Every Feb, clowns mourn Grimaldi. In full costume.

Map 87 · Hackney Downs / Lower Clapton

London Orphan Asylum	Linscott Rd	Grandiose remains of historic site now beloved of enviornmental artists.
The Strand Building	29 Urswick Rd	Beautiful Art Deco building, NOT the subject of Roxy Music song.
Sutton House	2 Homerton High St	Music and arts in the oldest house in East London.

Map 88 · Haggerston / Queensbridge Rd

Geffrye Museum	136 Kingsland Rd	English interior design from 1600 to today.

Map 89 · London Fields / Hackney Central

London Fields Lido	London Fields Westside	Open-air swimming for hardy Hackney folk.

Map 91 · Shoreditch / Brick Lane / Spitalfields

Brick Lane Mosque	59 Brick Ln	The area's changes reflect on the building – once a synagogue, now a mosque.
Christ Church Spitalfields	2 Fournier St	Star architect Nicholas Hawksmoor's pretty masterpiece.
Dennis Severs' House	18 Folgate St	Candle-lit cellar, parlour, smoking room - step 300 years back in time.
Spitalfields Market	105 Commercial St	No bargains but certainly one-of-a-kind fashions.
Sweettooth Graffiti Alley	Pedley St	Signature sweeties and skulls – just off Brick Lane.
Ten Bells	84 Commercial St	Where Jack the Ripper got his victims.
Truman's Brewery	Brick Lane	Beautiful old building now a hip weekend market. That's progress...

Map 92 · Bethnal Green

Bethnal Green Tube Station	Bethnal Green Tube Station	Scene of the worst civilian loss of the Second World War.
London Buddhist Centre	51 Roman Rd	Get your freak om.

Map 93 · Globe Town / Mile End (North)

Art Pavilllion	221 Grove Rd	Arts center seemingly designed by the Teletubbies.
Mile End Climbing Wall	Haverfield Rd	Classic climbing centre - one of London's big three.

Map 96 · Whitechapel (East) / Shadwell (West) / Wapping

Battle of Cable Street Mural, St George's Hall	236 Cable St	Celebrating an almighty multi-faith bashing of a 1930s fascist march.
Blind Beggar Pub	337 Whitechapel Rd	A killing here finally led to Ronnie Kray doing porridge.

Map 98 · Mile End (South) / Limehouse

Ragged School Museum	45 Copperfield Rd	Barnado's school 'for the deserving poor' turned East End museum.

Map 100 · Poplar (West) / Canary Wharf (West)

Canary Wharf Tower	1 Canada Sq	You can smell the money yards away. Look, don't touch.
Canary Wharf Tube Station	Canary Wharf	Norman Foster's Jewel in the Jubilee Line Extension.

Map 102 · Millwall

The Docklands Sailing & Watersport Centre	235 Westferry Rd	Award-winning sailing centre.

Map 104 · South Bank / Waterloo / Lambeth North

County Hall	Riverside Walkway	One of London's most historical and vast buildings.
The Hayward Gallery	Southbank Centre	Revered and reviled bruiser.
The London Eye	Westminster Bridge Rd	Two words: Tourist. Trap. Nice view though.
Low Tide at South Bank	South Bank	Go for a walk on the exposed riverbed.

National Theatre	South Bank	South Bank centre-piece, looked like it was from 2050 in 1960.
The Pier at OXO Tower		Screw OXO! Have a picnic on the pier instead.
South Bank Book Market	Southbank (under Waterloo Bridge, opposite BFI)	Little-known outdoor market; heaps of vintage and second-hand reads.
Waterloo Bridge	Waterloo Bridge	When tired with London, come here and watch the sunset.

Map 105 · Southwark / Bankside (West)

Buskers' Archway	Southbank	Excellent acoustics make the decorated tunnel a coveted buskers' spot.
Elephant & Castle	Elephant & Castle	Everything that was wrong with 60s town planning. Concrete hell.
Michael Faraday Memorial	Elephant & Castle	He gave us electromagnetism, we gave him a roundabout.
The Ring	72 Blackfriars Rd	London's first boxing ring was here; now a characterful pub.
Shakespeare's Globe	21 New Globe Walk	The Bard's famous playhouse reconstructed.
Tate Modern	Bankside	Herzog and de Meuron dazzler.

Map 106 · Bankside (East) / Borough / Newington

Cross Bones Graveyard	Red Cross Way	Medieval resting place for London's ladies of the night.
Female Gladiator	Great Dover St	1st centruy AD grave of London's very own Xena.
The Golden Hinde	Clink St	Amazing replica of Francis Drake's Tudor war ship.
The London Tombs	Tooley St	Lesser known Tower experience—beware the plague pits.
Old Operating Theatre Museum	9 St Thomas St	Macabre ancient operating theatre, with gallery for eager spectators.
Southwark Cathedral	London Bridge	Worth the diversion to see Chaucer and Shakespeare's stomping grounds.
Winchester Palace	Clink St	Random 13th century ruins with remarkable rose window.

Map 107 · Shad Thames

City Hall	Queen's Walk, More London	Dubbed 'The Testicle' by Mayor Ken Livingston. Nice.
Fashion and Textile Museum	83 Bermondsey St	DAH-ling, it's just fabulous!
Floating Gardens	31 Mill St	Gardens. Mad tramps. On Boats. What else do you want?
HMS Belfast	Morgan's Lane, Tooley St	Floating WW2 killing machine, much beloved of children.

Map 110 · Rotherhithe (West) / Canada Waters

| Brunel Museum | Railway Ave | Where engineering geeks can seek refuge from being picked on. |

Map 111 · Rotherhithe (East) Surrey Quays

| Surrey Docks Farm | Rotherhithe St | Show the kids what their bacon used to look like. |

Map 113 · Walworth

| East Street Market | East St | Gloriously useless stuff. |

Map 114 · Old Kent Road (West) / Burgess Park

| The Animatronic Fireman | Old Kent Rd | Be afraid. Be very afraid. |
| Peckham Library | 122 Peckham Hill St | Groundbreaking modern architecture or huge, carelessly dropped Tetris block? |

Map 116 · South Bermondsey

| Millwall FC Stadium | The Den, Zampa Road | A football mecca for somebody? |

Map 120 • Greenwich

Greenwich Foot Tunnel	Greenwich Church St	Walk/crawl/skip/limp under the Thames.

Map 126 • New Cross

Ben Pimlott Building	University of London, New Cross	A building of cheerful, dreary, warped, modern fascist fun.

Map 131 • Vauxhall / Albert Embankment

Lambeth Palace	Lambeth Palace Rd	Where the Archbishop of Canterbury lives; no, not in Canterbury, stupid.
Secret Intelligence Service HQ (MI6)	Vauxhall Cross	Real life James Bonds in a not-so-secret location.
Vauxhall City Farm	165 Tyers St	So that's where an egg comes from.

Map 133 • Battersea (East)

Battersea Dogs' Home	4 Battersea Park Rd	Re-house a pooch. Now does cats too.
Battersea Park Gasometers	Queenstown Rd	Rusting monsters.
Battersea Power Station	188 Kirtling St	The world's most beautiful power station, surely.

Map 140 • Clapham Junction / Northcote Rd

Northcote Road	Northcote Rd	Middle-class marketing-types mecca.

Map 143 • Clapham High Street

Clapham Common Air-Raid Shelter	Clapham High St	The depths of government paranoia.

Map 144 • Stockwell / Brixton (West)

Brixton Market	Electric Ave	Caribbean flavours, smells and sounds.
Electric Avenue	Electric Ave	First shopping area in Britain lit by electricity, in 1880.

Map 145 • Stockwell / Brixton (East)

Stockwell Bowls	Stockwell Rd	70's concrete skatepark, take quads and get beaten-up.

Map 152 • Tooting Broadway

Gala Bingo Hall	50 Mitcham Rd	Bingo hall with Grade One listed interior.

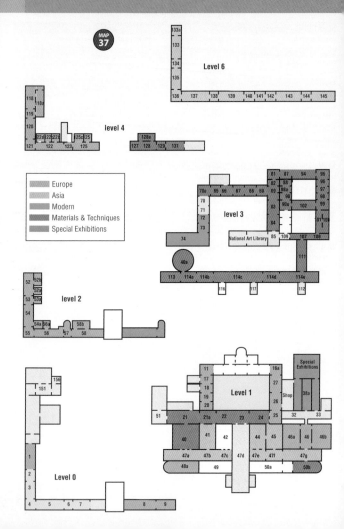

MAP 37

133a
133
134
135
136   137   138   139   140   141   142   143   144   145

Level 6

118
118a
119
120
121   122   123   125
227d 227 227a   225c 25

level 4

128a
127   128   129   131

Europe
Asia
Modern
Materials & Techniques
Special Exhibitions

81   87   94   95
82   88   96
70a   65   66   67   68   69   89   88a   97
70   90   98
71   90a   102   99
72   83   84   101 100
73   85   109   107   108

level 3

National Art Library

74

40a

111

113   114a   114b   114c   114d   114e
116   117   112

52   52b
52a
53   53b
54

level 2

54a 56a   58b
55   56   57   58

156
151

1
2
3
4   5   6   7   8   9

Level 0

11
17   16a
18
19   Level 1   27
20   26
51   21   21a   22   23   24   25   32   33
40   41   42   44   45   46a   46   46b
47a   47b   47c   47d   47e   47f   47g
48a   49   50a   50b

Special Exhibitions
Shop   38a

General Information

NFT Map: 37

Address: Cromwell Road
            London SW7 2RL
Phone: 020 7942 2000
Website: www.vam.ac.uk
Hours: 10 am–6 pm daily,
            Wednesdays until 9 pm.

Admission: Free to the permanent collection. There is a charge for temporary exhibitions. Tickets have an allotted time slot and although they can be purchased on the day, it is recommended you book ahead of time by phone or online, especially with the more popular exhibitions.

Overview

The Victoria and Albert Museum, or the V&A, calls itself the world's greatest museum of art and design and nowhere has there ever been such an eclectic collection of objects inducing so many 'oooooohs', 'aaaaahs' and 'holy shits!'. With a permanent collection of over 4.5 million objects, pretty much all on display in the 145 galleries, you can go everyday for a lifetime and be blown over by something you hadn't noticed before. For the tourist and non-tourist alike, the V&A is a wonderful maze of cultural ramblings. You'll get lost, overwhelmed and flustered, but we promise you won't get bored.

The V&A is a cabinet of curiosities of gargantuan proportions, boasting 5000 years of art and design, in every medium imaginable (from wax dioramas to a little black dress made of bras), spread over seven levels and organised by five themes—Asia, Europe, Materials & Techniques, Modern and Exhibitions. The trouble is where to start. You'll no doubt spend the first 10 minutes mesmerised by the glass Chihuly chandelier over the information booth, but what you do afterwards depends on how much time you have. Got hours? Avoid structure and just wander. Got an hour? Take a look at the map, see what strikes your fancy and head straight there. Just don't forget to hit up the gift shop afterwards—it's killer.

The Greatest Hits

There's no real method to the V&A's madness. Despite their best efforts to categorise everything, Vivienne Westwood gowns are just a stumble away from 1000 year-old Buddhas. But this is a great thing. The best advice is really to ditch the guidebook and go with your instincts. To make sure you take in the best stuff, start in the basement (having arrived through the Tunnel Entrance from the tube station), where you'll find the 17th century **Cabinet of Curiosities**—predecessors to the modern museum—which will get you in the right mind set. Weaving past bits and pieces of **Versailles**, you emerge onto the ground floor (Level 1) which covers fashion, Asia and both Medieval and Renaissance Europe. Highlights of which include the **cast courts**, which boast a life-size replica of **Trajan's Column** in plaster, then onto ancient **samurai swords** and spectacular **kimonos** in Asia, the **Ardabil Carpet**—the largest and most amazing Islamic carpets in existence dating from 1539 (lit up on the hour and half-hour), an extensive costume room covering everything from **18th century crinolines** to **Juicy Couture** worthy of Paris Hilton, and lastly, **Raphael's cartoons** – massive sketches for a 1515 commission of tapestries that now hang in the Vatican. Before heading on, stop for a tea in the **Morris, Gamble & Poynter Rooms** café for teacakes in 1860s arts and crafts surroundings. Level 2 consists of the tucked away **British Galleries**, including the **Great Bed of Ware** as well as the endearing **Lord and Lady Clapham** dolls bedecked in miniature turn-of-the-18th century outfits. Up again on Level 3, you'll find the Materials & Techniques rooms, with its vast collections of **silver, ironwork and musical instruments**, as well as some dynamite paintings. Don't miss **Rossetti's The Daydream** and then **Ron Arad's Chair** in the modern rooms. This floor also houses the **National Art Library**—an art history student's research dream (you have to get a reading pass to study here though). Level 4 has a wonderfully tactile display of **glasswork**, as well as **architecture** and more **British Galleries from 1760-1900**. If you've made it this far, you deserve a knighthood.

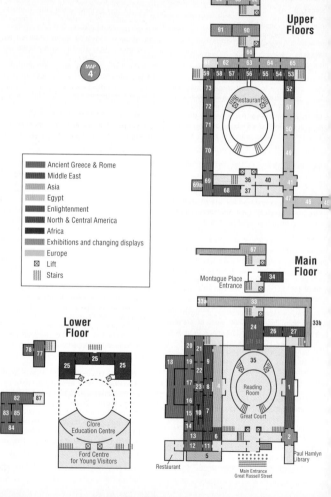

MAP
4

Upper Floors

94 93 92

91 90

66

62 63 64 65
59 58 57 56 55 54 53

73 52

72 Restaurant 51

71 50

70 49

36 40
69a 69 41
68 37 47
46 45

Main Floor

67

34
Montague Place
Entrance

33a 33 33b

24 26 27

20 21
18 19 9 35
22
17 23 8 4 Reading 1
16 Room
15 10 7
14 Great Court
13 6 2
12 11
5 Paul Hamlyn
Restaurant Library
Main Entrance
Great Russell Street

Lower Floor

78 77

25 25 25
25

82 87
83 85
84 Clore
Education Centre
Ford Centre
for Young Visitors

Ancient Greece & Rome
Middle East
Asia
Egypt
Enlightenment
North & Central America
Africa
Exhibitions and changing displays
Europe
⊠ Lift
||| Stairs

General Information

NFT Map: 4

Address: Great Russell Street, WC1B 3DG

Phone: 020 7323 8299 (information) or
020 7323 8181 (exhibition tickets)

Website: www.britishmuseum.org

Hours: The galleries open daily 10 am–
5.30 pm, with selected galleries open
until 8.30 pm Thu & Fri (see website
for details). The Great Court is open
9 am–6 pm. Jan 1, Good Friday,
Dec 24-26: closed.

Admission: Free, with a charge for some
special exhibitions.

Overview

Unless you're Indiana Jones, combining archaeological expertise with the swashbuckling energy to defeat obnoxious school groups, then do not attempt to cover the British Museum in a day. With 13 million items covering two million years of human history in almost 100 permanent and temporary galleries, you are better off treating yourself to different sections when the mood takes you—a perk of having one of the world's largest museums on your doorstep and open for free.

At 250 years, it is also the oldest museum in the world, but forget preconceptions of dusty urns and endless Roman coins—they're there if that's your bag, but this is a very modern organisation. The permanent displays include some of the world's most fascinating treasures, while the temporary exhibitions bring London a chance to see artefacts which would cost a month's salary to see in their original setting, such as the recent display of China's Terracotta Warriors.

However, while preserving artefacts to inspire its visitors, the Museum can also be seen as a testament to the great British pastime of looting. Some of the shining lights of its collection were acquired under the shadiest of circumstances, and the countries which were plundered so that snotty kids could chortle at the genitalia of their sculptures are increasingly vocal about getting the items back. For example the Elgin Marbles, rechristened with their pleasantly playful English name after the earl who helped himself to them, are huge slabs hacked from the 2500 year old Athenian Parthenon (albeit Elgin's entire nose later rotted off due to syphilis: a gratifying example of one-upmanship by nature). The legality of this move is hotly debated, but apart from the damage to the Parthenon, the Marbles undeniably suffered when they were cut into smaller pieces for transport to Britain, and when rowdy schoolboys bopped the leg off a centaur in 1961. The Museum holds firm that returning debated items would empty the museums of the world, but it has extended the occasional olive branch to ease the controversy; compensation was paid for the display of drawings stolen by Nazis, and they returned the Tasmanian Ashes (aboriginal human remains) to Australia after a 20-year battle.

The Greatest Hits

The **Great Court** is not just a Greatest Hit of the Museum, but of London as a whole. Being "the world's largest covered public square" may sound too niche an accolade to be impressive, but it really is stunning. The 150 year old **Reading Room** at its centre is a delight, both for the excellent library and for the wall-mounted list of major historical figures who have sought inspiration within its round walls. Whatever your ethics on plunder, some of the most morally-dubious exhibits are among the absolute must-sees: the **Elgin Marbles** in Room 18 are remarkable, while the **Rosetta Stone** in Room 4 gives you the irresistible buzz of seeing something so legendary up close, or as close at the backpacked hordes will allow, in your own town. A whole **Moai Statue** from Easter Island is in Room 24, the **Lewis Chessmen** set is in Room 42, and the **Mausoleum of Halicarnassus** exhibition displays some of the last remaining fragments of one of the Seven Wonders of the World. However, it is the stories of heartache, adventure, mystery and passion behind the items which bring them to life. Asking the steward of Rooms 62-3 how the **mummies** came to be in the museum, or seeing the pages from **The Book of the Dead**, which recorded lives of the deceased, is a fascinating way to gain insight to people around the world and throughout time. And if that's a bit too deep, just head to one of the four **shops** for a mummy-shaped pencil case or replica Rosetta Stone.

General Information

NFT Map: 36
Address: Cromwell Road, SW7 5BD
Phone: 020 7942 5000
Website: www.nhm.ac.uk
Hours: Daily 10 am–5.50 pm
  (Last admission 17.30)
  "After Hours" events run on the
  last Friday of each month
  during Nov–Apr.
  24–26 Dec: closed.
Admission: Free access to most of the
  Museum. Fee charged for
  some special exhibitions
  (free to Members).

Overview

Visiting the Natural History Museum is like reading National Geographic, if it was edited by JK Rowling. As imagination-tingling to adults as it is to kids, you can mull over serious questions about genetic modification and the environmental cost of modern life, while walking inside a termite mound or knocking on a petrified tree.

With more than 70 million specimens in their collection, you simply won't see it all at once, or for most of us—ever. But with free entry, regularly refreshed exhibits and unforgettable special exhibitions, it's worth

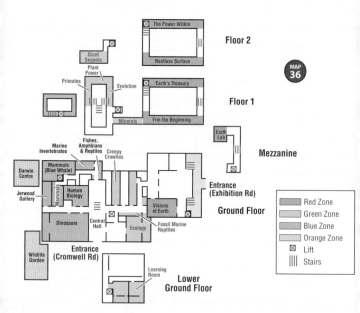

dropping in when you have the opportunity. Grab a free map at the entrance to work out your route, which is colour-coded for a (slightly) easier life: Red Zone for the planet and forces of nature; Green for ecology and the environment; Blue for dinosaurs, mammals and biology; and Orange for the Wildlife Garden and behind-the-scenes peeks.

Weekends are inevitably heaving with hyperactive button-pressing families, spellbound tourists and Londoners trying to rebuild the brain cells they killed off with the night before's drinking; weekdays are amok with school groups. But don't let this put you off. If there's a queue outside the main entrance on Cromwell Road, and you don't fancy killing time by spotting all the different creatures carved around the entrance arch, pop 'round the side to Exhibition Road entrance and you'll fast-track yourself in. You can go early or late for fewer crowds, or stick with the permanent exhibitions, which are superb but not as sexy as the world-class special exhibitions which draw in the masses. Or, if all else fails, just shove the kids out the way: they're smaller than you and the buttons are *so much fun* to press.

The Greatest Hits

Anyone who didn't see the **Dinosaur Exhibition** as a child really missed out: run here and rectify the situation immediately if you haven't been, or revisit and enjoy the modernised exhibits if you have. The **Mammals Exhibition** will get you wondering exactly *how* someone stuffs a giraffe, and gives you a chance to get close to the gaping jaws of a hippo. For a different perspective on this room, go up to the balcony around it: watching people stare agog at the brilliantly-displayed **blue whale** is as entertaining as the exhibits themselves. For proof that even history geeks can make the earth move for you, visit the

Power Within exhibition which recreates an earthquake (though don't expect a Universal Studios experience. The will is there, bless, but the budget just isn't…). Watch blushing parents introduce their kids to the birds and the bees in the **Human Biology** section, where an 8-times-life sized model of a **foetus** will put you off pregnancy forever. The **Wildlife Garden** is an oasis of serenity open from April–October, or you can impress a date (or not, depending on your coordination) by **ice-skating** next to the stunning Victorian building from November–January.

The Museum's Special Exhibitions are superb—check the website for current information. The annual **Shell Wildlife Photographer of the Year**, October–April, is utterly inspirational, while a varying daily programme of events includes **lectures, behind the scenes tours** of the botany department, and **fossil workshops** for kids.

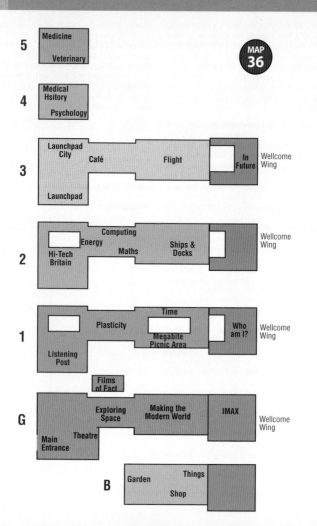

MAP
36

5
Medicine
Veterinary

4
Medical Hsitory
Psychology

3
Launchpad City
Café
Flight
In Future
Launchpad
Wellcome Wing

2
Computing
Energy
Hi-Tech Britain
Maths
Ships & Docks
Wellcome Wing

1
Time
Plasticity
Megabite Picnic Area
Who am I?
Listening Post
Wellcome Wing

G
Films of Fact
Exploring Space
Making the Modern World
IMAX
Theatre
Main Entrance
Wellcome Wing

B
Garden
Things
Shop

General Information

NFT Map: 36
Address: Exhibition Road, South
              Kensington, London
              SW7 2DD.
Phone: 0870 870 4868
Website: www.sciencemuseum.org.uk
Hours: Open 10 am–6 pm every day
              except 24 to 26 December.
Admission: Free, but charges apply to
              IMAX 3D Cinema, simulators &
              a few special exhibitions.

Overview

Museum and Science. Two words known to strike fear into the heart of many a child. And many a grown-up, come to that. But the Science Museum is one of the most visited museums in London. How so? Perhaps it's the heady mix of mildly erotic pistons and shafts; 60s room-sized computers and Bakelite ashtrays; special affects simulators and the mighty IMAX theatre? Or maybe it is the multitude of buttons; red and blue and green actual buttons, as well as Minority Report-style touch screens? We know they're aimed at kids, but we like. Oh and levers, did we mention levers?

The museum has its origins in the popular Great Exhibition of 1851. Prince Albert (no laughing in the back please) suggested the extra cash made by the Exhibition be used to found a number of educational establishments. Following a number of building moves and expansions the Science Museum as we know and love it opened in 1885.

The Greatest Hits

The museum's 300,000 gidgets, gadgets and gizmos attract 2.5 million visitors a minute or something, but venture above the third floor, to the **medical floors**, and you will have the place almost to yourself. The most popular area is the main drag along the ground floor which includes **Exploring Space** hung with real life space probes and other relics that look like they've come from the Doctor Who costume and props department, and **Making of the Modern World** featuring **Stephenson's Rocket**, to titillate your dormant trainspotter.

The third floor's **Launchpad** area has as many interactive displays as an 8-year-old could ever want. Parents hope their little darlings are actually learning something as they race from exhibit to exhibit whirling wheels, spinning liquids in plastic tubes and grimacing through head-sized lenses till tiredness or RSI sets in. For younger kids the tactile **Pattern Pod** on the ground floor makes up for its lack of buttons by its immensely pleasing shape.

Other smaller areas worth a once over include the **Listening Post** that samples and broadcasts words live from blogs and chatrooms – a brain bending experience. Don't even think about going in with a hangover. A huge silver hoop joins the **Energy exhibition** on the second to the ground floor. Answer a question on a nearby monitor, (don't worry they are easy) and watch your initials and age whiz around the inside of the ring. But what's that BUZZ? Like a huge electric fly killer? It's the inspired **'don't touch' display**—irresistible for the naughtiest in the class, one small electric shock later, the rest of the lemmings race over for a turn. Hilarious.

467

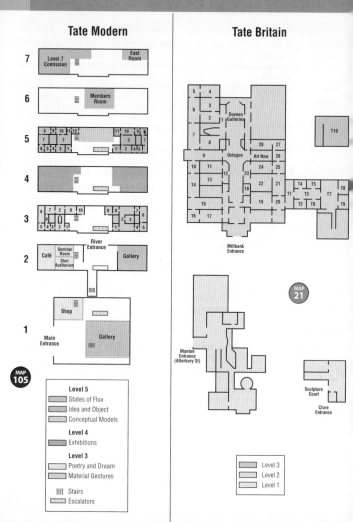

Tate Modern

7
Level 7 Comission
East Room

6
Members Room

5
8 9 10 11 12 | 11 10 9 8
7 2 | 3 7
6 5 4 3 1 | 1 2 4 5 6

4

3
6 7 2 9 10 | 9 8 7
8 | 2 3 6
5 4 3 1 | 1 4 5

2
Café
Seminar Room
Starr Auditorium
River Entrance
Gallery

1
Shop
Main Entrance
Gallery

MAP 105

Level 5
States of Flux
Idea and Object
Conceptual Models

Level 4
Exhibitions

Level 3
Poetry and Dream
Material Gestures

|||| Stairs
Escalators

Tate Britain

5 4
6 3
2
Duveen Galleries
7 1
8
28 27
9 Octagon Art Now 26
10 11 24 25
12 23
14 13 18 22 21
15 19 20
16 17

T10

T4 T5 T8
T1 T3 T7
T2 T6 T9

Millbank Entrance

MAP 21

Manton Entrance (Atterbury St)

Sculpture Court

Clore Entrance

Level 3
Level 2
Level 1

General Information

Tate Britain:

NFT Map:	21
Address:	London SW1P 4RG
Phone:	020 7887 8888
Website:	www.tate.org/uk
Hours:	Daily 10 am–5.50 pm; until 10 pm on the first Friday of each month for Late at Tate Britain.

Tate Modern:

NFT Map:	105
Address:	London SE1 9TG
Phone:	020 7887 8888
Hours:	Sunday–Thursday 10 am–6 pm, Friday and Saturday 10 am–10 pm. Last admission into exhibitions is 5.15 pm (Friday and Saturday 8.15 pm).

Overview

In a city renowned for its galleries and museums, London's Tate galleries shine from the banks of the Thames. The first Tate was founded in 1897 as the National Gallery of British Art, but was renamed soon afterwards after its main patron Henry Tate—he of Tate and Lyle and the sugar cube. Originally on the site of the former Millbank Prison (where Tate Britain remains), the gallery gradually expanded and divided its collection over the four sites, two in London, one in Liverpool and the last in St Ives. In London, Tate Britain houses British art dating from 1500 to the present day, while Tate Modern was created to house—yes you've guessed it—more modern work from 1900 to the present day.

The two Tates carry the same trendy Tate logo and the shops contain much of the same avant-garde merchandise with a great range of children's stuff available in both. But while the more traditional Tate Britain more closely resembles the National Gallery in architectural and artistic flavour, Tate Modern has a very hip feel and draws a slightly broader audience, in part due to its location on the increasingly buzzy South Bank.

Tate Modern

Based in the former Bankside Power Station, Tate Modern has proved to be an extremely popular attraction for tourists and Londoners alike since its opening in 2000. It houses the national collection of modern art (which is art from the 1900s onwards, for those of you lacking an art history degree). The temporary art installations of the five-storey tall Turbine Hall provide much of the draw to the gallery. This huge space displays specially commissioned works from October to May of each year—a programme which was intended to run for only five years, but was extended due to its popularity. Quirky exhibitions fill the vast Turbine Hall, like Olafur Eliasson's 'Weather Project' which encouraged visitors to lie back on the floor in their thousands, gazing at the shadows cast by the synthetic sun. The latest temporary art installation was 'Shibboleth' by Doris Salcedo, a 548-foot-long crack in the floor of the Turbine Hall, representing *'borders, the experience of immigrants, the experience of segregation…'* and a health and safety nightmare for the Tate as visitors came in droves to jump over it/trip/get their feet stuck in it…and of course to ponder the ultimate message of the exhibition.

Tate Britain

The Tate Britain, boasts the most comprehensive collection of British art in the world, and also houses some international modern art. Stone steps lead up to the portico and once inside, the Duveen Galleries' ethereal sculptures lie straight ahead, giving the first taste of a breathtaking collection of artwork. Tate Britain's collection is divided chronologically and dedicates space exclusively to notable artists, such as Turner, Blake and Constable. The gallery also includes significant works by William Hogarth, Stanley Spencer and Francis Bacon. The restaurant and café are popular but to encourage those of us who don't have a subscription to the Tates to sign up, Tate Britain offers a members' room with a café, alluring *'special offers and designated staff'* and probably nicer toilets to those with membership cards. While lacking the hip ambience of its sister gallery across the water, Tate Britain has been attempting to trend-ify itself with 'Late at Tate Britain' between 6pm and 10pm on the first Friday of every month, which aims to lure young'uns from the pub for some after-hours art-appreciation with exhibitions, performances, music, talks and films.

469

General Information

NFT Map: 24
Address: Trafalgar Square
London WC2N 5DN
Phone: 020 7747 2885
Website: www.nationalgallery.co.uk
Hours: 10 am–6 pm daily,
Wednesdays until 9 pm.

Admission: Free to the permanent collection and temporary exhibitions in the Sunley Room, Room 1 and The Space on Level 2. There is a charge for temporary exhibitions held on Level 2 in the Sainsbury Wing. Tickets have an allotted time slot and although they can be purchased on the day, it is recommended you book them ahead of time online, especially with the more popular exhibitions.

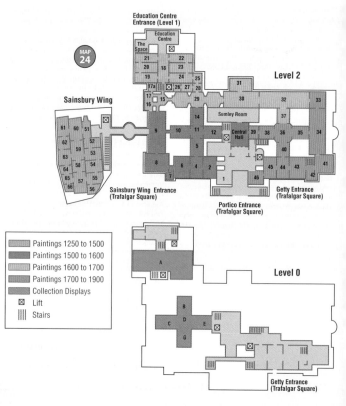

Overview

The National Gallery is home to one of the best and largest collections of Western European painting in the world, coming in at around 2100 paintings on display at any one time. An emphasis on *Western* and *painting* is needed. If you're looking for Roman antiquities or Persian miniatures, head for the British Musuem or the V&A—this is not where you're going to get it. Furthermore, if you're into anything post-Impressionist, make an about face for the Tate Britain. This is a celebration of the arts of Europe in all their old-school occidental glory. Taking the surprisingly manageable tour around the galleries (most of which are on one floor) will leave you wowed by how many works of art you will recognise. This is a collection that has been branded deep into your subconscious – with its oh-yeah-that-one Turners, Hogarths, Rembrandts and Leonardos. Bring a date and even the most culturally-challenged will be able to impress.

The collection came into being in 1824 when the House of Commons paid £57,000 for 38 paintings belonging to a banker, using his Pall Mall home as the exhibition space. Compared to the Louvre, calling a few paintings in some guy's house the National Gallery was a little too embarrassing for the British public. So the great and the good demanded the Government pull their finger out and get to work on a purpose-built gallery worthy of a national art collection. In 1832, architect William Wilkins was given the job, constructing the recognisable porticoed façade in an up-and-coming area known as Trafalgar Square, called by one trustee 'the very gangway of London'. The most recent addition to the gallery is the Sainsbury Wing, designed in 1991 by leading contemporary architects Robert Venturi and Scott Brown after much controversy. Prince Charles, notoriously fussy when it comes to architecture, dismissed one suggested design as "a monstrous carbuncle on the face of a much-loved and elegant friend".

The National Gallery can be tackled in one exhausting afternoon, if you put your mind to it. Take advantage of the fancy benches, as many of the more epic paintings are best viewed from a distance. Be sure to get lost in the many smaller galleries, which house some dynamite, lesser-known, works. If you're feeling hungry, the National Dining Rooms is a critically-acclaimed (read: expensive) restaurant, serving up the best in British fare. If you're feeling like a little culinary nationalism, the more casual National Café serves a very good cream tea.

The Greatest Hits

Starting with the Sainsbury Wing, the collection snakes around, covering European painting in chronological order from 1250 to 1900. There are a lot of paintings and it can get slightly overwhelming, so if you're pressed for time and want to make sure you've 'done' the National Gallery, start in the Sainsbury Wing. Don't miss the **Arnolfini Portrait** (signed with 'Van Eyck was here' above the mirror—hilarious), **Botticelli's Venus and Mars**, **The Wilton Diptych**, and **Uccello's The Battle of San Romano**. Moving onto the 1500-1600 range, you'll recognise **Leonardo's cartoon of The Virgin and Child with St Anne and St John the Baptist**, '**The Ambassadors**' by Hans Holbein the younger (the one where you have to crouch to see the skull), the still-hilarious portrait of **A Grotesque Old Woman** by Quinten Massys (a 1664 example of the classic conundrum—a 64 year-old trying desperately to look 16) and **Titian's Bacchus and Ariadne**. Moving on, the collection houses a rather large collection of Dutch masters, including **Rembrandt, Rubens and van Dyck**. If you're sick of 2-D, a rather cool contraption is **Samuel von Hoogstraten's peepshow**. Peer through the peep hole in this painted box for an eye-popping view of the interior of a Dutch house. Very cool. A trip to the museum is never complete without viewing a **Gainsborough, Turner and Hogarth**, all of which are housed in the 1700-1900 galleries. Do not miss Hogarth's **Marriage a la Mode** a comical rendition of an 18th century arranged marriage—in a series of six paintings. Last but not least, onto the juxtaposition of three epic 19th century history paintings depicting corporal punishment with chilling realism—**Manet's Execution of Maximillian, Delaroche's Lady Jane Gray and Puvis de Chavanne's Beheading of St John the Baptist.** What a way to end it all, quite literally.

471

General Information

Address: Peninsula Square, London, SE10 0DX
Website: www.theO2.co.uk
General Information: 020 8463 2000
Tickets: 0871 984 0002

Overview

Exactly how the Millennium Dome transformed itself from national embarrassment and vortex for millions of taxpayers' money to the slick new home of groovy events is a bit of a mystery. Or maybe it's blindingly obvious—suits are better than politicians at this kind of thing. Anyway, on the outside it looks the same—oversized Bedouin tent graced by James Bond's buttocks in 'The World Is Not Enough.' Inside, gone are the attractions and concepts of 1999, aimed at celebrating all things British, so visionary that visitors stayed away in droves. Instead, the contents of an above-average high street have been stuffed inside—generic bistro food and wine bars, a multi-screen cinema. Whoope-doo you might think. But hold on—people come for the music. No really, they do.

Enter the O2 Arena or its little sis, the IndigO2 (see what they did there?) and be very impressed. The Arena has been engineered to provide sight lines that older venues can only dream of. The air conditioning—usually a rarity at London gigs, actually works. The acoustics have to be heard to be believed. It might not be a destination venue for mosh-loving purists and those who like the sweat and beer to fly, but if you like your music with a bit of comfort and luxury, you know, like toilets that work and don't stink of piss (548 of them!) then the 02 is well worth a look. Wheelchair users are catered for with fully accessible facilities. London seems to have its first venue that feels like some real thought has gone into its creation. If the organisers get their act together and diversify the bands appearing, including more that veer away from mainstream bands then it could become unstoppable.

How to Get There – Driving

Driving to the O2 isn't as daft as it might sound considering its location—previously un-chartered industrial wastelands of south east London. 2,000 parking spaces can be reserved in advance. With decent road links, traveling after rush hour should be bearable. The A102 linking north and south London runs through the Blackwall Tunnel, right next to the venue.

How to Get There – Mass Transit

The O2 has excellent transport links no matter how you travel. The Jubilee Underground line stops at North Greenwich and connects directly with Waterloo and London Bridge overland stations. The Docklands Light Railway is one stop away and several bus routes drop off right outside. But the best way to arrive has to be by boat – the high speed Thames Clipper runs every 15 minutes from several piers including Greenwich, Embankment and Waterloo. It's not only relaxing, but you get to see London at its best on the trip.

How to Get Tickets

Ticketmaster. Naturally. Try Gumtree and Craigslist for swaps, unwanted tickets and scum-of-the-earth touts.

Life in London can sometimes seem like one continuous, eventful film, but if you like your plots to take place on screen then the city has a lot to offer. Going to catch a flick in London can often unravel like some kind of Indiana Jones-esque adventure—the Holy Grail being a reasonably-priced ticket in a clean, comfortable theatre, that can only be sought after battling hundreds of tourists and fellow Londoners all with the same thought. Every year 164 million people visit London's cinemas; now that's a fair few ticket stubs. Thankfully, by leaving The Twilight Zone (a.k.a. the tourist trap of the West End) there are plenty of cinematic treasures to be plundered. Whatever genre of film takes your fancy, whatever time of night and whether you want a velour seat and popcorn or a leather chair and glass of champagne, you are sure to find it in the nation's capital.

For those who are desperate to catch Spielberg's latest offering, and are crazy enough to stick it out in the West End, chain cinemas abound. You'll find **Odeon (Maps 1, 4, 23, 30, 35, 61, 66, 71, 111 & 136)**, **Vue (Maps 12, 33, 43, 66 & 80)** and **Cineworld (Maps 11, 23, 40, 43, 45, 100 & 138)** theatres all over London. If you're brave, or just fancy seeing a star or two at one of the regular premiers, **Odeon Leicester Square (Map 23)** (made up of two separate theatres) could be for you. Another monster on the square is the historic **Empire (Map 11)**, seating an impressive 1,300 patrons is a landmark in itself, although she is a slightly faded leading lady these days. Beware though. While the price of a cinema ticket in the big smoke is normally enough to make you choke on your Butterkist, wandering into any of the theatres in Leicester Square may force you to re-mortgage with prices as high as £17.50 a ticket at peak times. **Apollo West End Multiplex (Map 23)** on Lower Regent Street was formerly the home of Paramount Pictures in the UK but now houses five small, luxurious theatres showing the latest flicks on general release.

It's not hard to find cinemas offering art house and independent films in London. Finding a good one, however, can be more of a challenge. We highly recommend the **Curzon Soho (Map 11)** offering not only a wide range of cinematic gems but also a plush, bar to loosen you up for that three hour Kurasawa number. Remember if the queue is snaking along the pavement, tickets can be bought at the bar downstairs too. Check out the cinema's cousin in **Mayfair (Map 9)** as well as the slightly shabby **Renoir (Map 5)** in Brunswick Square. **Cineworld Chelsea (Map 45)** on the lustrous King's Road is one of London's premier art houses with two-seaters available for the perfect smooching experience. **The Gate (Map 29)** in Notting Hill was created from a restaurant in 1911 and now offers independent releases in a luxurious setting. **BFI Southbank (Map 104)** specializes in film through the ages as well as hosting frequent events. Who would have thought old Charlie would help us save our pennies? **The Prince Charles Cinema (Map 11)** off Leicester Square sits in a perfect location and offers revivals, cult and foreign language films for as low as £1.50. Now that's a bloody bargain. For those with a penchant for 'le cine' courtesy of our French neighbours visit **Cine Lumiere (Map 36)** in South Kensington. Uber-cool Clapham has an equally trendy art house cinema, the **Clapham Picturehouse (Map 143)**, Dalston's Art Deco gem the **Rio Cinema (Map 86)** is worth a look, while Bloomsbury offers up **The Horse Hospital (Map 4)**—the name's almost as avant-garde as the films they show. Just leave Dobbin behind.

There are some wonderful cinematic experiences to be had too. **BFI IMAX (Map 104)** is housed in a curious circular building, south of Waterloo Bridge, with the biggest screen in the UK—the size of five double-decker buses. Then there are those three magic words—**The Electric Cinema (Map 29)** on Portobello Road. Grab a Pinot Grigio, rest your derriere on a soft leather seat and munch away at home-made ice cream all the way from sunny Hampshire while catching the latest Polish release. For those who are lured by bling, bling, bling and the power of exclusivity, get down to Soho's private member's joint, **Rex Cinema and Bar (Map 11)**, where miniature hamburgers and reclining leather seats await you for a mere £250 a year.

Remember Londoners! Those on the Orange phone network get 2 for 1 on Wednesday nights—an ideal opportunity to save some precious pounds.

(**473**)

Cinemas	Address	Phone	Map
Apollo West End	19 Regent St	0871 2233 444	23
Barbican Centre Cinema	Silk St & Whitecross St	020 7382 7000	7
BFI London IMAX	Waterloo Rd & York Rd	0870 787 2525	104
BFI Southbank	Belverdere Rd	020 7928 3232	104
Chealsea Cinema	206 King's Rd	020 7351 3742	45
Cine Lumiere	17 Queensberry Pl	020 7073 1350	36
Cineworld Chelsea	279 King's Rd	0871 200 2000	45
Cineworld Fulham Road	142 Fulham Rd	0871 200 2000	43
Cineworld Hammersmith	207 King St	0871 200 2000	40
Cineworld Haymarket	63 Haymarket	0871 200 2000	23
Cineworld Shaftesbury Avenue	13 Coventry St	0871 200 2000	11
Cineworld Wandsworth	Wandsworth High St & Ram St	0871 220 8000	138
Cineworld West India Quay	11 Hertsmere Rd	0871 200 2000	100
Clapham Picturehouse	76 Venn St	020 7498 2242	143
Curzon Mayfair	38 Curzon St	0870 756 4621	9
Curzon Soho	99 Shaftesbury Ave	020 7292 1686	11
The Electric Cinema	191 Portobello Rd	020 7908 9696	29
Empire Cinemas	5 Leicester Square	0871 471 4714	11
Everyman Cinema Club	5 Hollybush Vale	08700 66 4777	56
Frontline Club	13 Norfolk Pl	020 7479 8950	31
Gate Notting Hill	87 Notting Hill Gate	020 7727 4043	29
Genesis Mile End	93 Mile End Rd	020 7780 2000	97
Greenwich Picturehouse	180 Greenwich High Rd	087 0755 0065	120
Horse Hospital	30 Colonnade	020 7833 3644	4
ICA Cinema	The Mall & Horse Guards Rd	020 7930 3647	23
Lux Salon	18 Shacklewell Ln	020 7503 3980	86
Notting Hill Coronet	103 Notting Hill Gate	020 7727 6705	29
Odeon Camden Town	14 Parkway	0871 22 44 007	71
Odeon Holloway	419 Holloway Rd	0871 22 44 007	61
Odeon Kensington	Kensington High St & Edwards Sq	0871 22 44 007	35
Odeon Leicester Square Cinema	24 Leicester Sq	0871 22 44 007	23
Odeon Marble Arch	10 Edgware Rd	0871 22 44 007	1
Odeon Panton Street	11 Panton St	0871 22 44 007	23
Odeon Putney	26 Putney High St	0871 22 44 007	136
Odeon Surrey Quays	Redriff Rd & Surrey Quays Rd	0871 22 44 007	111
Odeon Swiss Cottage	96 Finchley Rd	0871 22 44 007	66
Odeon Tottenham Court	30 Tottenham Ct Rd	0871 22 44 007	4
Odeon West End Cinema	40 Leicester Sq	0871 22 44 007	23
Odeon Whiteleys	Queensway & Porchester Gardens	0871 22 44 007	30
One Aldwych Cinema	1 Aldwych	020 7300 1000	14
Peckham Multiplex	95 Rye Ln	0870 0420 299	123
Phoenix Cinema	52 High Rd	020 8444 6789	na
Prince Charles Cinema	7 Leicester Pl	020 7494 3654	11
Renoir Cinema	1 Brunswick Sq	0871 7033 991	5
Rex Cinema and Bar	21 Rupert St	020 7287 0102	11
Rich Mix Centre	34 Bethnal Green Rd	020 7613 7490	91
Rio Cinema	107 Kingsland High St	020 7241 9410	86
Ritzy Cinema	Coldharbour Ln & Brixton Oval	020 7733 2229	150
Riverside Studios	Crisp Rd & Queen Caroline St	020 8237 1111	41
Screen on Baker Street	96 Baker St	020 7486 0036	1
Screen on the Green	83 Islington Green	020 7226 3520	80
Screen on the Hill	203 Haverstock Hill	020 7435 3366	67
Short & Sweet	91 Brick Ln	07921 822 749	91
Vue Finchley Road	Finchley Rd & Blackburn Rd	08712 240 240	66
Vue Fulham	Fulham Rd & Cedarne Rd	08712 240 240	43
Vue Islington	36 Parkfield St	08712 240 240	80
Vue Shepherds Bush	Shepherds Bush Green & Rockley Rd	08712 240 240	33
Vue West End Cinema	3 Cranbourn St	08712 240 240	12

It seems that every pub, bench and bridge in London has a tale to tell of past literary greats mulling over their troubles, weeping over lovers lost or launching themselves into the Thames. Ours is a city saturated in literary history and literature-lovers, with an abundance of bookshops and diversity of readers. While so many other retailers are homogenising, our independent bookshops—with their knowledgeable staffs and their often narrow focus—remain as eclectic and enthusiastic as ever. As well as a great selection of specialist independent stores, London is also home to dozens of second-hand bookshops, book markets, a literature festival, a major international book trade fair, and Europe's largest bookshop.

General

The **Foyles** flagship store on Charing Cross Road **(Map 12)** is a London institution, with a history as eccentric as its stock. Along with mainstream books and best-sellers, it offers a good range of second hand and out-of-print books, as well as a specialist Antiquarian department and a chilled jazz café. Venerable **Hatchard's (Map 10)** has been hawking for books for over 200 years, making it London's oldest bookstore. The **London Review Bookshop (Map 4)** offers a huge range of constantly updated books with an intellectual bent and intellectual staff. **Metropolitan Books (Map 6)** is small but perfectly stocked, and Phil the owner makes time for any customer seeking advice or a friendly chat. Kids can find a bookshop wonderland in **Tales on Moon Lane (Map 128)** while parents can find the books they grew up with at **Ripping Yarns (Map 51).** The excellence of the independent stores has meant the chains have had to up their game—and loath though we are to say it, some, such as **Borders (Maps 10, 12, 43 & 80)** and academic specialists **Blackwells (Maps 4, 12 & 74)** have got it very right indeed. In particular, **Waterstone's** in Piccadilly **(Map 23)** attracts all sorts of excitable superlatives, being the largest bookshop in Europe, running a range of literary activities to complement their stock, and even hosting a bar with some of the finest views of London.

Second Hand

Sadly, the world-renowned status Charing Cross Road used to command as the Mecca of second-hand bookstores is fading, and those who go looking for the genteel expertise immortalised in Helene Hanff's bestseller *84 Charing Cross Road* will find a "Med Kitchen" (shudder) at number 84. Many shops still cling to their ideals however, such as **Any Amount of Books (Map 12)** selling titles from as little £1 and offering a leather-binding service so your books can furnish your room as well as your mind. Good places to start if you are scouting for quality second-hand bookshops are: the tardis-like **The Bookshop (Map 129)** staffed by bookworms who have read *everything* (or so it seems) and can always help you find a gem; **John Sandoe (Map 46)** for true bookshop charm (rickety staircases, passionate staff, enchanting atmosphere); and the **Trinity Hospice (Map 136)** and **Oxfam Bookshops (Maps 38, 51, 86)**—not only an astonishingly cheap and broad collection of works, but all for charidee.

Specialist

Finding a bookshop devoted to your passion is like finding a club of old friends, and London caters for all tastes. Bored of cheese toasties? **Books for Cooks (Map 29)** smells as good as the recipes look, as they're tested in their kitchen first, while in-store cooking workshops teach new skills to avid customers. For those who, worryingly, can't decide if they're more in the mood for romance or murder, **Murder One (Map 12)** specialises in just these two genres, while Sci-Fi nerds will be in their element at **Forbidden Planet (Map 179)**. **Gekoski (Map 4)** stocks a good range of modern first editions, or for older and rarer first editions try **Henry Sotheran (Map 10)**, a unique, but pricey, treat for any enthusiast. Head to **Atlantis (Map 4)** for all your occult needs (though no doubt the Spirits had already tipped you off on that one). Arty types are extensively catered for: **Shipley (Map 12)** stocks books on a huge range of arts, and if you register with them they'll help you find a book to meet your needs; **The Photographers'**

Gallery, a treat in itself, has a substantial shop stocking photography titles, artists' monographs and unusual cameras; the **ICA Bookshop (Map 23)** is a great destination for art and film fans, and you can take in an exhibition while you're there; **Travis & Emery (Map 24)** stocks a vast range of music books and scores; comic geeks can get their fix at **Gosh! (Map 4)**. And for those with a passion for passion, pop along to the book section of **Coco de Mer (Map 13)**.

Travel

Feeling lethargic? Head to one of the city's superb travel bookshops to have your energy restored. **Stanford's (Map 13)** has been inspiring London for 150 years, with its enormous collection of travel books and maps. A bookshop for travellers who like to read, **Daunt Books (Maps 2, 28, 57 & 67)** arranges all its books by geographical location, so even its fiction, cookbooks and history are shelved by country. Or to learn any of over 150 languages, head to **Grant & Cutler (Map 10)**, the UK's largest foreign-language specialist.

Politics

Bookmarks (Map 4) stocks left-leaning works on huge range of issues and takes a lively role in political activism, giving it a real and infectious sense of purpose. Also hugely right-on, both representing and driving several lefty social movements, is **Housmans (Map 78)**. Or for a more balanced approach with political works across the parties and even the odd Minister browsing for ideas, try **Westminster Bookshop (Map 22)**.

Talks and events

Publishing is a cut-throat business, and many writers have to sell their soul to get noticed. For them, it means an endless round of book signings and talks; for us, it means a fabulous chance to hobnob with our favourite authors. Most bookshops host occasional signings, but for regular events from the most celebrated authors, the big boys predictably have all the clout. **Foyles (Maps 3, 12, 78 & 104)** and **Waterstone's (Maps 2, 3, 4, 6, 13, 14, 15, 18, 23, 24, 36, 37, 45 & 78)** attract huge names: recent guests have included JK Rowling, Louis de Bernières, Salman Rushdie and AS Byatt. **Stanford's (Map 13)** offers opportunities to hear well-known travel editors, writers and photographers for an inspirational and sometimes career-changing evening. For intellectually stimulating debates and literary discussions, check out the **London Review Bookshop (Map 4)** and **Bookmarks (Map 4)**. Some events are free, some as much as a theatre ticket, but all should be booked in advance to ensure a place.

Bookshops	Address	Phone	Map
Any Amount of Books	56 Charing Cross Rd	020 7836 3697	12
Atlantis	49 Museum St	020 7405 2120	4
Blackwell	119 London Road	020 7928 5378	105
Blackwell Business + Law Bookshop	243 High Holborn	020 7831 9501	14
Blackwell Medical Bookshop	St Thomas Street	020 7403 5259	106
Blackwell University Bookshop	Kings College	020 7240 9723	14
Blackwells	183 Euston Road	020 7611 2160	4
Blackwells	100 Charing Cross Rd	020 7292 5100	12
Blackwells	158 Holloway Road	020 7700 4786	74
Bookmarks	1 Bloomsbury St	020 7637 1848	4
Books etc.	255 Finchley Road	020 7433 3299	66
Books etc.	176 Fleet St	020 7353 5939	14
Books etc.	28 Broadway shopping centre	020 8764 3912	41
Books etc.	263 High Holborn	020 7404 0261	14
Books etc.	115 Buckingham Plalace Road	020 7630 6244	20
Books etc.	66 Victoria St	020 7931 0677	22
Books etc.	Southside Shopping Centre	020 8874 4597	138
Books etc.	Queensway	020 7229 3865	30
Books etc.	30 Broadgate Circle	020 7628 8944	8
Books etc.	Cabot Place East	020 7513 0060	100

Bookshops	Address	Phone	Map
Books etc.	45 Bank Street	020 7719 0688	100
Books etc.	54 London Wall	020 7628 9708	17
Books for Cooks	4 Blenheim Crescent	020 7221 1992	29
The Bookshop	1 Calton Ave	020 8693 2808	129
Borders	122 Charing Cross Rd	020 7379 8877	12
Borders	Parkfield Street	0207 226 3602	80
Borders	Fulham Broadway	020 7386 5451	43
Borders	203 Oxford Street	020 7292 1600	10
Coco de Mer	23 Monmouth St	020 7836 8882	13
Daunt Books	83 Marylebone High St	020 7224 2295	2
Daunt Books	193 Haverstock Hill	020 7794 4006	67
Daunt Books	51 S End Rd	020 7794 8206	57
Daunt Books	112 Holland Park Ave	020 7727 7022	28
Forbidden Planet	179 Shaftesbury Ave	020 7420 3666	12
Foyles	113 Charing Cross Rd	020 7437 5660	12
Foyles	Upper Ground	020 7437 5660	104
Foyles	Pancras Road	020 7437 5660	78
Foyles	400 Oxford Street	0800 123400 ext. 13678	3
Gosh! Comics	39 Great Russell St	020 7636 1011	4
Grant & Cutler	57 Great Marlborough Street	020 7734 2012	10
Hatchard's	187 Piccadilly	020 7439 9921	10
Henry Sotheran	2 Sackville St	020 7439 6151	10
Highgate Bookshop	9 Highgate Highstreet	020 8348 8202	na
Housmans	5 Caledonian Rd	020 7837 4473	78
ICA Bookshop	The Mall	020 7766 1452	23
John Sandoe	10 Blacklands Terrace	020 7589 9473	46
The Lion and Unicorn Bookshop	19 King Street	020 8940 0483	na
London Review Bookshop	14 Bury Pl	020 7269 9030	4
Metropolitan Books	49 Exmouth Market	020 7278 6900	6
Murder One	76 Charing Cross Rd	020 7539 8820	12
Oxfam Bookshop, Highgate	47 Highgate High St	020 8347 6704	51
The Photographers' Gallery	Great Newport St	020 7831 1772	13
R. A. Gekoski	15 Bloomsbury Square	020 7404 6676	4
Ripping Yarns	355 Archway Rd	020 8341 6111	51
Shipley	70 Charing Cross Rd	020 7836 4872	12
Stanford's	Long Acre	020 7836 1321	13
Tales on Moon Lane	25 Half Moon Ln	020 7274 5759	128
Travis & Emery	17 Cecil Ct	020 7240 2129	24
Trinity Hospice Bookshop	206 Upper Richmond Rd	020 8780 0737	136
Waterstone's	Trafalgar Square	020 7839 4411	24
Waterstone's	206 Piccadilly	020 7851 2400	23
Waterstone's	9 Garrick St	020 7836 6757	13
Waterstone's	19 Oxford St	020 7434 9759	3
Waterstone's	Ludgate Circus	020 7236 5858	15
Waterstone's	421 Oxford St	020 7495 8507	2
Waterstone's	82 Gower St	020 7636 1577	4
Waterstone's	87 Brompton Rd	020 7730 1234	37
Waterstone's	151 King's Rd	020 7351 2023	45
Waterstone's	Exhibition Rd	020 7942 4481	36
Waterstone's	1 Whittington Ave	020 7220 7882	18
Waterstone's	Spencer Street	020 7608 0706	6
Waterstone's	128 Camden High Street	020 7284 4948	78
Waterstone's Economists' Bookshop	Clare Market	020 7405 5531	14
Westminster Bookshop	8 Artillery Row	020 7802 0018	22
WHSmith	Surrey Quays Shopping Centre	020 7237 5235	111
WHSmith	Fenchurch Street Station	020 7480 7295	18
WHSmith	Cannon Street Station	020 7626 5643	16
WHSmith	Elephant and Castle Shopping Centre	020 7703 8525	112
WHSmith	124 High Holborn	020 7242 0535	14

Yep you've heard the news. Theatre in the capital is all commercial. Predictable. Repetitive. Uncontroversial. If you believe the whingers, it's all fucking boring stuff. Don't, because it's not. Yes, the West End, that heartland of commercial theatre around Shaftesbury Avenue, is filled with tourist-grabbing, crowd-pleasing musicals. Yes, there are more star-dominated, tried-and-tested plays than ever. Yes, the Mousetrap is still taking up the space at St Martin's after 54 years of we-bloody-well-know-whodunit.

But all that's only half the story. To find the other half, look beyond the glittering billboard signs to find the daring, small West End theatres, such as the **Donmar Warehouse (Map 13)**, bringing the innovative and unusual to Theatreland. There are the Off-West End theatres that proudly fly the flag for new writers, unafraid of being political, controversial and in-yer-face: **The Royal Court (Map 19)**, **The Soho (Map 11)**, **The Bush (Map 33)**. There are the unconventional, anarchic ensemble companies, such as PunchDrunk, shaking up things all the way from the fringe to the West End, while innovative short-play evenings are popping up at pubs across the city (see below).

But lets not forget the cracking double-whammy of the **National Theatre (Map 104)** and **The Old Vic (Map 104)**, two artistic powerhouses currently going from strength to strength. At the National, the unstoppable Nicholas Hytner brings original works to this Southbank concrete colossus (coupled with a £10-tickets offer), while down the road, Hollywood-star-turned-theatre-connoisseur Kevin Spacey is returning the Old Vic into former glory. The refurbished **Young Vic (Map 104)**, meanwhile, is one of the best places to see fresh, new theatre (and get drunk afterwards). And, whatever you do, you're never far from a good Shakespeare production.

The (Real) West End

The Donmar Warehouse (Map 13), the West End's smallest theatre, has gained a reputation for being one of Theatreland's most innovative, yet still crowd-pleasing houses (Jude Law as Hamlet, anyone?). It's quite common for good new plays that have successfully kicked off at a

fringe or Off-West End venue to transfer to the West End, such as Tom Stoppard's guitars-meet-politics cracker Rock'n'Roll The West End is also a great place to catch up on those classics you always wanted to see but never got round to: from Beckett to Shakespeare.

Off-West End & The Fringe – The Best

The underground-led, breakneck guerrilla heyday might be over, but theatre outside the West End is in rude health. Head to rough-around-the-edges Dalston, where the **Arcola Theatre (Map 86)** continues to thrive in its scruffy ex-factory home, thanks to eclectic programming, an early-fringe-days feel and heaps of creative energy. The tiny **Bush Theatre (Map 33)**, in Shepherd's Bush, has long been a fierce champion of new work, and having survived recent funding cuts, will doubtlessly continue to discover exciting new talent. So will **Dean Street's Soho Theatre (Map 11)** and the **Royal Court (Map 19)** on Sloane Square, which remain two of London's finest. For new, innovative work, also keep your eyes on the **Battersea Arts Centre (Map 140)**, which is on fire again (put down your bucket, not literally on fire) after narrowly escaping bankruptcy.

Theatre can't change society? Try telling that to the conviction-led crew of Kilburn's **The Tricycle (Map 65)**—easily London's most radical and most dedicated, political theatre. Islington's **Almeida (Map 80)** is far more conventional, but pretty—and that's got to count for something. If you're up for a laugh, check **The Hackney Empire (Map 87)**, a turn-of-the-century music hall, hosting some of London's best variety shows. **The Old Red Lion (Map 80)**, home inside an Islington pub, stubbornly clings to its unconventional, ale-fuelled fringe attitude, while **Battersea's Theatre 503 (Map 132)** is as provocative as ever. Be surprised.

Tickets

If you know what you're after, check the theatre's website—they will either have their own system, a link to a ticket selling site, or provide a phone number. If not, check www.officiallondontheatre. co.uk, which lists shows by name, theatre and genre. The site also displays shows that are just opening, or just closing, and links straight to the appropriate ticketing website, once you have made your mind up. There's a handy map of all West End venues, too.

Fancy a bargain? The iconic TKTS ticket booth on Leicester Square sells on-the-day tickets for most big shows, half-price. The queue can be mind-boggling, so go early. There's a £2.50 booking fee, but it's included in the price shown. Many theatres also have their own discount schemes. If you don't mind standing, you can get Royal Court tickets for as little as 50p. Yes, that's 50p. Just show up between 6 pm and 6.30 pm on the day of the performance. The National has £5 standing tickets for all shows, but the view ain't always great.

Exciting & New

Enter the ensemble. They are multi-skilled, imaginative and are shaking the cosy, venue-obsessed Theatreland with a vengeance. Ensemble companies like PunchDrunk and Kneehigh are touring their way through London's venues in vigorously anarchic fashion. The result is increasingly physical, increasingly unconventional—and increasingly exciting theatre, which you'd be mad to miss.

PunchDrunk (www.punchdrunk.org.uk) have gained a reputation for site-specific productions, inviting the audience to walk around and follow actors and themes as they please. Their 2006 treatment of Goethe's Faust at the National Theatre was widely hailed as one of the best things to have happened to British theatre in years. Kneehigh (www.kneehigh.co.uk) enjoy setting their nightmarish productions in outside mystical locations, but aren't afraid of West End constraints either. The award-winning Cheek by Jowl (www.cheekbyjowl.com), which have been producing Shakespeare and European classics since 1982, keep discovering hot talent—and ways to innovate.

If that's not grassroots enough, visit one of the themed short-play evenings that are popping up across town. Bringing together writers, actors and directors for twenty-minutes-or-so mini-shows, they have become a popular theatre alternative. Take your pick: Established organisers Nabokov (www.nabokov-online.com) have found a West End home at the **Trafalgar Studios (Map 24)**, SourFeast (www.sourfeast. co.uk) are based at **Brixton's Dogstar Pub (Map 150)**, and relative newcomers DryWrite have made Whitechapel's **The George Tavern (Map 97)** their own. The message is spreading. What you thought was a boozer, really is a stage. The possibilities are endless.

Contemporary Dance

From small company shows to big stage spectacles, contemporary dance is having one hell of a ride. **Sadlers Wells (Map 6)** (www. sadlerswells.com), the grand old lady of dance venues, is still doing a fine job bringing more of the world's best dance to London. Check their Sadler's Wells Sampled programme, showcasing dazzling future talent for as little as £10. **The Barbican (Map 7)** (www.barbican.org.uk) has established itself as a reliable source of powerful dance performances, while the **Royal Festival Hall (Map 104)** attracts increasingly bold and interesting works to its refurbished riverside location. For London's most innovative dance performances, check **The Place (Map 4)**, a stylish venue that combines performance, training and dance education (www.theplace.org.uk).

Theatres	Address	Phone	Type	Map
Adelphi Theatre	The Strand	0870 403 0303	West End	24
Aldwych Theatre	49 Aldwych	0870 4000 805	West End	14
Almeida Theatre	Almeida St	020 7359 4404	Fringe	80
Ambassadors Theatre	West St	020 7369 1761	West End	12
Apollo Theatre	Shaftesbury Ave	020 7494 5070	West End	11
Apollo Victoria Theatre	17 Wilton Rd	0870 4000 751	West End	20
Arcola Theatre	27 Arcola St	020 7503 1646	Fringe	86
Arts Theatre	Great Newport St	0870 060 1742	West End	12
The Astoria	157 Charing Cross Rd	020 7434 9592	Performing Arts	12
Barbican Centre	Silk St	020 7638 4141	Performing Arts	7
Barons Court Theatre	28 Comeragh Rd	020 8932 4747	Fringe	42
Battersea Arts Centre	Lavender Hill & Theatre St	020 7223 2223	Fringe	140
Bloomsbury Theatre	15 Gordon St	020 7388 8822	Fringe	4
Brixton Academy	211 Stockwell Rd	020 7771 3000	Performing Arts	145
Bush Theatre	2 Shepherd's Bush Rd	020 7610 4224	Fringe	33
Cadogan Hall	5 Sloane Terrace	020 7730 4500	Performing Arts	19
Cambridge Theatre	Earlham St	0844 412 4652	West End	13
Chats Palace Arts Centre	42 Brooksbys Walk	020 8533 0227	Performing Arts	90
Cinema on the Haymarket	65 Haymarket	0871 230 1562	West End	23
Comedy Theatre	Panton St	0870 060 6637	West End	23
Criterion Theatre	Piccadilly Circus	020 7413 1437	West End	10
The Dogstar	389 Coldharbour Ln	020 7733 7515	Fringe	150
Dominion Theatre	Tottenham Court Rd	0870 169 0116	West End	4
Donmar Warehouse Theatre	41 Earlham St	0870 060 6624	West End	13
Drill Hall	16 Chenies St	020 7307 5060	Fringe	4
Duchess Theatre	Catherine St	020 7494 5075	West End	14
Duke of York's Theatre	St Martin's Ln	0870 060 6623	West End	24
Etcetera	265 Camden High St	020 7482 4857	Fringe	71
Fortune Theatre	Russell St	0870 060 6626	West End	13
The Forum	Highgate Rd	020 7428 4099	Performing Arts	72
Garrick Theatre	Charing Cross Rd	0870 890 1104	West End	24
Gate Theatre	11 Pembridge Rd	020 7229 0706	Fringe	29
The George Tavern	373 Commercial Rd	020 7790 1763	Fringe	97
Gielgud Theatre	Shaftesbury Ave	020 7494 5065	West End	11
Greenwich Theatre	Crooms Hill & Nevada St	020 8858 7755	Fringe	120
Hackney Empire	291 Mare St	020 8985 2424	Fringe	87
Hampstead Theatre	Eton Ave	020 7722 9301	Fringe	66
Haymarket Theatre	Haymarket	020 7930 8800	West End	23
Her Majesty's Theatre	Haymarket	0844 412 2707	West End	23
Indigo2	Millenium Way	020 8463 2000	Performing Arts	na
Jermyn Street Theatre	16 Jermyn St	020 7287 2875	Fringe	23
King's Head Theatre Pub	115 Upper St	020 7226 1916	Fringe	80
Koko	1 Camden High St	0870 4325 527	Performing Arts	71
Leicester Square Theatre	5 Leicester Pl	0870 899 3335	West End	11
London Apollo Hammersmith Theatre	Queen Caroline St	0870 606 3400	West End	41
London Palladium	Argyll St	020 7494 5020	West End	10
Lyceum Theatre	Wellington St	0870 243 9000	West End	14
Lyric Theatre	29 Shaftesbury Ave	020 7494 5045	West End	11
National Theatre	South Bank	020 7452 3400	West End	104
New London Theatre	Drury Ln	0870 890 0141	West End	13
Noël Coward Theatre	St Martin's Ln	0870 060 6621	West End	24
Novello Theatre	Aldwych	0870 950 0940	West End	14

Theatres	Address	Phone	Type	Map
Old Red Lion	418 St John St	020 7837 7816	Fringe	80
Old Vic Theatre	103 The Cut	0870 060 6628	West End	104
Palace Theatre	Shaftesbury Ave	0870 890 0142	West End	12
Phoenix Theatre	Charing Cross Rd	0870 060 6629	West End	12
Piccadilly Theatre	16 Denman St	0870 060 0123	West End	10
The Place	17 Duke's Rd	020 7121 1000	Performing Arts	4
Playhouse Theatre	Northumberland Ave	0870 060 6631	West End	24
Prince Edward Theatre	28 Old Compton St	020 7447 5400	West End	12
Prince of Wales Theatre	Coventry St	020 7839 5972	West End	11
Queen Elizabeth Hall	South Bank Centre	08703 800 400	Performing Arts	104
Queens Theatre	Shaftesbury Ave	0870 950 0930	West End	11
Riverside Studios	Crisp Rd & Queen Caroline St	020 8237 1111	Fringe	41
Ronnie Scotts	47 Frith St	020 7439 0747	Performing Arts	12
The Roundhouse	Chalk Farm Rd	0844 482 8008	Performing Arts	71
Royal Albert Hall	Kensington Gore	020 7589 8212	Performing Arts	36
Royal Court Theatre	Sloane Sq	020 7565 5000	West End	19
Royal Festival Hall	Belvedere Rd	087 1663 2500	Performing Arts	104
Royal Opera House	Bow St	020 73044000	Performing Arts	13
Sadler's Wells	Rosebery Ave	0844 412 4300	Performing Arts	6
Savoy Theatre	The Strand	0870 164 8787	West End	24
Scala	275 Pentonville Rd	020 7833 2022	Performing Arts	78
Shaftesbury Theatre	210 Shaftesbury Ave	020 7379 5399	West End	12
Shakespeare's Globe	21 New Globe Walk	020 7902 1400	West End	105
Shepherds Bush Empire	56 Shepherd's Bush Green	0870 771 2000	Performing Arts	33
Soho Theatre	21 Dean St	0870 429 6883	Fringe	11
The Space	269 Westferry Rd	020 7515 7799	Fringe, Performing Arts	na
St John's	Smith Square	020 7222 1061	Performing Arts	22
St Martin's Theatre	West St	020 7836 1443	West End	12
Sutton House	2 Homerton High St	020 8986 2264	Performing Arts	87
Theatre 503	503 Battersea Park Rd	020 7978 7040	Fringe	132
Theatre Royal Drury Lane	Catherine St	0870 890 6002	West End	13
Toynebee Studios	28 Commercial St	020 7650 2350	Fringe	91
Trafalgar Studios	14 Whitehall	020 7369 1735	West End	24
Tricycle Theatre	259 Kilburn High Rd	020 7372 6611	Fringe	65
Vaudeville Theatre	404 Strand	0870 890 0511	West End	24
Victoria Palace Theatre	Victoria St	020 7834 1317	West End	22
Wembley Stadium	Wembley Hill Rd	0844 980 8001	Performing Arts	na
Wigmore Hall	36 Wigmore St	020 7258 8240	Performing Arts	2
Wilton's Music Hall	Graces Alley & Ensign St	020 7702 2789	Fringe	95
Wyndham's Theatre	Charing Cross Rd	0870 950 0925	West End	12
Young Vic Theatre	66 The Cut	020 7922 2922	West End	104

There are many great things about London's vibrant art world. The best? It's free. Granted, if you want to see some of the big show-stopping exhibitions that pass through the **Tates (Maps 21 & 105)**, **British Museum (Map 4)**, **National Gallery (Map 23)** and **Royal Academy (Map 2)** you'll have to pay quite a hefty sum, but overall, you can experience visual arts throughout the capital without coughing up much dough. This might be a contributing factor to London's sprawling art scene, as it is so easy to duck in and out of the capital's 300+ museums and galleries on a lunch break.

Of course, there are concentrations of art in locations around Piccadilly and Bond Street (check out Cork Street for its galleries, such as **Messum (Map 10)** and the **Adam Gallery (Map 10)**, running parallel with Savile Row), the East End (funkier affair and an artistic hipster breeding ground—check out Vyner Street in Bethnal Green), South Kensington/Chelsea (a major culture scene as a result of the Great Exhibition of 1851—and not much has changed) and various institutions dotted along the Thames (as seen from the Tate to Tate boat service). But great art is all over the this city, so get out your Oyster Card, and get ready to cover a lot of ground.

Starting with London's modern art, the **Tate Modern (Map 105)**, with its massive smoke stack, has become a major London landmark. This is despite it only existing as a separate entity from the **Tate Britain (Map 21)** since 2000. Check out its spacious turbine hall, with often spectacular installations.

It's not surprising that the Tate Modern is often the London tourist's first stop these days, as the city has become well-known for contemporary art. Due in part to the too-cool-for-school London art scene of the 1990s, which saw the establishment of Turner Prizers Tracy Emin, Rachel Whiteread and Damien Hirst, and made a major mark under Saatchi's guiding light. This light has faded somewhat, as the movement's personalities have slowly sold out a little (Emin designing for Longchamp is a case and point). But certain London galleries remain as monuments to this explosion of counter-culture, and, in addition to the **Saatchi Gallery (Map 19)**,

these include the **Serpentine Gallery (Map 30)**, **Haunch of Venison (Map 2)**, and **Victoria Miro (Map 31)**. Other inspiring alternatives include the **Riflemaker (Map 10)**, **South London Gallery (Map 122)**, **Camden Arts Centre (Map 66)**, the **White Cube** at Mason's Yard **(Map 23)** and **Hoxton Square (Map 84)**.

London is a city with a lot on offer, and if you're looking for something a bit more traditional, start with the **National Gallery (Map 23)** in Trafalgar Square, moving onto the **National Portrait Gallery (Map 24)** next door, which presents you with a who's who of British culture past and present. Stroll up Charing Cross Road to the awesome **British Museum (Map 4)** with its newly covered Great Hall (yet another example of Norman Foster's obsession with glass and geometry). Be sure to take in the Parthenon Marbles, aka Elgian Marbles, before the Greek government makes any attempt to get them back. Then over to the not-nearly-praised-enough **Wallace Collection (Map 2)** behind Selfridge's for some tea and Watteau action. A traditional art-lover's tour of London is not over without a trip to the **Royal Academy (Map 2)** with its epic exhibitions and finally to the **Tate Britain (Map 21)**, where the Pre-Raphaelites reign supreme.

Feeling a little non-conformist? London has a brilliant array of cultural institutions that offer more than just marble and canvas. From ceramics to dolls houses, kimonos to plaster casts of just about every great sculpture in the world—the V&A has it all (not to mention an awesome gift shop). Other alternatives to the mainstream include **The Photographers' Gallery (Map 13)** by Leicester Square, which not only squeezes in the best photographic exhibitions in town, but also boasts the best bookshop on the subject. Odd in its own way is the **Museum of London (Map 7)**, which walks you through the history of the city from prehistoric times to present day. Recent London museum gems also include the newly renovated **London Transport Museum (Map 24)**, **Fashion and Textile Museum (Map 107)**, **Museum of Brands, Packaging and Advertising (Map 29)** and the **Design Museum (Map 107)**, with cars and video games in case you're stuck entertaining your nephew.

A lot of the capital's best museum and gallery treasures are off the beaten path and may even require a trip in a bendy bus (gasp!). **The Geffreye Museum (Map 88)** is a good one to check out when you're in Shoreditch and tired of being hip. Just up Kingsland Road from **Flowers East (Map 91)** (a good British contemporary art gallery), this museum of domestic interiors runs through the history of Britain one living room at a time. Somewhat forgotten are the weird and wonderful **Sir John Soane's Museum (Map 14)**, **Leighton House (Map 35)** and **Dennis Severs'**

House (Map 91)—but we'll let you discover these gems for yourself.

So forget Pret a Manger—feed your soul in one of London's many museums and galleries. They certainly have more to offer than one of those crappy no bread sandwiches, anyway.

Museums	Address	Phone	Map
2 Willow Road	2 Willow Road	020 7435 6166	56
Apsley House	Hyde Park Corner	020 7499 5676	9
Arsenal Museum and Stadium Tour	Drayton Park	020 7704 4504	74
Bank of England Museum	Threadneedle Street	020 7601 5491	17
The Banqueting House	Whitehall	0844 482 7777	24
Benjamin Franklin House	36 Craven St	020 7930 6601	24
Bramah Tea & Coffee Museum	40 Southwark Street	020 7403 5650	106
Britain At War Experience	66 Tooley Street	020 7403 3171	107
The British Library	96 Euston Rd	020 7412 7353	78
The British Museum	Great Russell St	020 7323 8000	4
Brunel Museum	Railway Ave	020 7231 3840	110
Brunswick House	30 Wandsworth Rd	020 7394 2100	134
Cartoon Museum	35 Little Russell St	020 7580 8155	4
Chelsea FC Museum and Stadium Tour	Stamford Bridge	087 1984 1955	43
Chelsea Physic Garden	66 Royal Hospital Rd	020 7352 5646	45
Chiswick House	Burlington Lane	020 8995 0508	38
Churchill Museum and Cabinet War Rooms	King Charles Street	020 7930 6961	24
Clink Prison Museum	1 Clink St	020 7378 1558	106
Clockmakers' Museum	Aldermanbury	020 7332 1868	16
Cuming Museum	151 Walworth Rd	020 7525 2332	113
Dennis Severs' House	18 Folgate St	020 7247 4013	91
Design Museum	28 Butlers Wharf	087 0833 9955	107
The Dickens House Museum	48 Doughty St	020 7405 2127	5
Dr Johnson's House	17 Gough Square	020 7353 3745	15
Fan Museum	12 Croom's Hill	020 8305 1441	120
Fashion and Textile Museum	83 Bermondsey St	020 7407 8664	107
Florence Nightingale Museum	2 Lambeth Palace Rd	020 7620 0374	131
Foundling Museum	40 Brunswick Square	020 7841 3600	5
Freud Museum	20 Maresfield Gardens	020 7435 2002	66
Geffrye Museum	136 Kingsland Rd	020 7739 9893	88
Grant Museum of Zoology	Gower Street	020 7679 2647	4
Guards Museum	Birdcage Walk	020 7414 3271	22
Hampstead Museum	New End Square	020 7431 0144	56
Handel House Museum	23 Brook St	020 7495 1685	2
Horniman Museum & Gardens	100 London Rd	020 8699 1872	na
Hunterian Museum	35 Lincoln's Inn Fields	020 7869 6560	14
Imperial War Museum	Austral St	020 7416 5294	112
Jewish Museum	129 Albert St	020 7284 1997	71

Galleries	Address	Phone	Map
Kinetica	61 Brushfield St	020 7392 9674	18
Kirkaldy Testing Museum	99 Southwark St	01322 332195	105
Leighton House	18 Stafford Terrace	020 7602 3316	35
The Library and Museum of Freemasonry	60 Great Queen St	020 7395 9257	13
London Canal Museum	12 New Wharf Rd	020 7713 0836	79
London Dungeon	29 Tooley St	020 7403 7221	106
London Fire Brigade Museum	94 Southwark Bridge Rd	020 7587 2894	106
London Sewing Machine Museum	293 Balham High Rd	020 8767 4724	151
London Transport Museum	Covent Garden Piazza	020 7379 6344	24
Marylebone Cricket Club Museum	St John's Wood Rd	020 7289 1611	76
Museum in Docklands	Hertsmere Road	087 0444 3857	100
Museum of Brands, Packaging and Advertising	2 Colville Mews	020 7908 0880	29
Museum Of Childhood	Cambridge Heath Road	020 8983 5200	92
Museum of Fulham Palace	Bishops Avenue	020 7736 3233	48
Museum of Garden History	Lambeth Palace Road	020 7401 8865	131
Museum of Immigration and Diversity	19 Princelet St	020 7247 5352	91
Museum of London	150 London Wall	087 0444 3851	7
Museum of Methodism & Wesley's Chapel	49 City Rd	020 7253 2262	7
Museum of the Order of St John	26 St John's Ln	020 7324 4005	15
Museum of the Royal Pharmaceutical Society	1 Lambeth High St	020 7572 2210	131
National Army Museum	Royal Hospital Road,	020 7730 0717	46
National Maritime Museum	Park Row	020 8312 6565	na
Natural History Museum	Cromwell Rd	020 7942 5685	36
The Old Operating Theatre, Museum & Herb Garret Venue	9 St Thomas St	020 7188 2679	106
Petrie Museum of Egyptian Archaeology	Gower St	020 7679 2884	4
Pollock's Toy Museum	1 Scala St	020 7636 3452	3
Ragged School Museum	45 Copperfield Rd	020 8980 6405.	98
Royal Academy of Music Museum	Marylebone Rd	020 7873 7373	2
Science Museum	Exhibition Rd	087 0870 4868	36
Sherlock Holmes Museum	221 Baker St	020 7935 8866	76
Sikorski Museum	20 Princes Gate	020 7589 9249	37
Sir John Soane's Museum	13 Lincoln's Inn Fields	020 7440 4263	14
Smythson Stationery Museum	New Bond St	020 7629 8558	10
Spencer House	27 St James's Pl	020 7499 8620	23
St Bartholomew's Hospital Museum	West Smithfield	020 7601 8033	15
Tate Britain	Millbank	020 7887 8888	21
Tate Modern	Bankside	020 7887 8888	105
Tower Bridge Exhibition	Tower Bridge	020 7940 3985	107
Victoria & Albert Museum	Cromwell Rd	020 7942 2000	37
Wallace Collection	Manchester Square	020 7563 9551	2
Westminster Abbey	Parliament Square	020 7222 5152	22

Overview

It's hard to walk for five minutes in this city without stumbling over a pub, so it shouldn't come as a big surprise that London's nightlife offering can be a bit overwhelming. Soho and Shoho (Hoxditch? Anyway, Shoreditch and Hoxton) have firmly established themselves as the areas with the city's greatest pub/bar/club-density. But the fun doesn't stop there: you will find watering holes, in all colours and shapes, spread across the city. With opening hours relaxed, nightlife is more around the clock than ever—as long as you know (or let us tell you) where to go. And with some of London's most exciting nights now taking place on Sundays and Mondays, the week's come full circle too. But if options are endlessly varied, so are tastes: One Londoner's Camden Town is another Londoner's Brick Lane is another Londoner's Tooting. As far as we're concerned, it's all in the mix. Here are some carefully compiled guidelines.

Real Locals

We know, we know, everyone loves THEIR local. We can't help thinking, though, that there are some local pubs in this city worth checking out even if you're not living in stumbling distance. They include, in no particular order: Highgate's old-school **The Winchester (Map 52)**, real Hackney boozer **Royal Sovereign (Map 85)**, aka The Sov, where crusties try to sell you canto netting, Rotherhithe's dream-of-your-dad **The Mayflower (Map 109)**, and Brixton's **The Effra (Map 150)**, which couldn't care less about what's going on around it. Ah, and so many others.

Traditional Pubs

Chainification. Gastrofication. It's relentless. Although increasingly hard to find, London still has them aplenty: wonderfully time-wrapped, ale-selling drinking establishments. We like getting pissed, or lost, and usually both, in **Ye Olde Cheshire Cheese (Map 15)**, a dark Victorian Dickens was fond of. Borough's **George Inn (Map 106)**, with a dazzling selection of ales, is as ancient as they get, and the clocks stopped

ticking a long, long time ago at the **Nag's Head (Map 19)**, where mobile phones are forbidden. The **Jerusalem Tavern (Map 3)** is a tiny, wood-panelled gem of a pub, tucked away on an otherwise unremarkable Clerkenwell Street. We love philosophising with Bloomsbury's grey literary types at **The Lamb (Map 14)** just as much as drinking up and down the Sam Smith range at Holborn's Grade-II-listed **Princess Louise (Map 4)**. In Hampstead, there's the pretty, and pretty hidden, **Holly Bush (Map 56)**. And we still like **The Carpenter's Arms (Map 39)**, even though it's no longer run by the Kray twins' mum.

Best For Beer

If you're tired of stale-lager-sipping your way through the night—and who isn't?—there are alternatives. Borough's **The Rake (Map 106)** is hard to beat for sheer choice, confusing you with more than a hundred different beer varieties. Round the corner, the fine offer of the **Brew Wharf (Map 106)**, some of which is brewed on-site, makes up for the soulless atmosphere. **The Dove (Map 89)** is best for Belgian, **Quinn's (Map 71)** for German beers. Too fancy? For great ale selections, there's **The Royal Oak (Map 106)** in Borough, where the taps come courtesy of the Harveys brewery, or the **Wenlock Arms (Map 83)**, where the frequently changing line-up is so good we can't bloody decide which ale to go for, usually. Pitfield, Freedom and St Peter's, meanwhile, supply Islington's **Duke of Cambridge (Map 83)** with organic beer, if you like that kind of stuff. We definitely like Guinness and there's no better place for drinking it than Stoke Newington's tiny **Auld Shillelagh (Map 64)**.

Best Cocktails

London got into mixing in recent years—and big time, with new cocktail bars constantly popping up across the city. Hit **Loungelover (Map 91)** for the kitschiest deco, or **Green and Red (Map 10)** for the best tequila. We like rummaging through Fortnum & Mason's wine collection at **1707 (Map 9)**, just as much as settling for a shared bottle at **Gordon's (Map 24)**. Martinis? You'll find us at the **Charlotte Street Hotel (Map 3)**.

At **5th View (Map 9)**, hiding above Waterstone's on Piccadilly, your Kir Royal comes with amazing views towards Big Ben, while the NYC-style **Milk & Honey (Map 10)** comes with eight handy house rules, including "no star fucking". We like Soho's **22 Below (Map 10)** for its down-to-earth attitude, and the plush art deco heaven that is **Claridge's Bar (Map 2)** for the opposite. **Dusk (Map 141)** serves Battersea, **Montgomery Place (Map 29)** Notting Hill, and both do so extremely well. We would also love to praise **The Cinnamon Club (Map 22)**, inside the Old Westminster Library. If only we could find it.

Smoker-Friendly

If the merciless prohibition regime of 2007 hasn't resulted in reluctant surrender, don't despair: from provisionally erected patios to all-year beer gardens to secret backdoors, London's ban-bashing creativity knows no boundaries. Great fag spots include the terrace of **At Proud (Map 71)**, overlooking Camden's roofs, the barbecue-and-beer-can courtyard of **93 Feet East (Map 91)** and the tree-shaded garden of the **Edinboro Castle (Map 77)**. Hang out in front of Highgate favourite **The Flask (Map 51)** or combine a late-night pint with a rollie in the backyard of the **The Dolphin (Map 89)**. For clubbing, consider **Egg (Map 79)**, where you're allowed to smoke in the massive garden. **The Owl & Pussycat (Map 91)** is not just a surprisingly pleasant pub in Shoreditch, it's also got a surprisingly nice garden, where smoking is not just allowed, dear friends, but encouraged.

Clubs

For a classic clubbing night, grandfathers **Fabric (Map 77)** and **The End (Map 13)** still do the trick, but we prefer the slightly more off-beat, mid-sized variety: groovy **Guanabara (Map 13)**, boutique **East Village (Map 84)**, swanky **Images (Map 92)**. The ever-so-eclectic **Notting Hill Arts Club (Map 29)** continues to come up with good nights, as does Brick Lane's **93 Feet East (Map 91)**. For indie moves we trust **Metro (Map 3)**, but much prefer the madness at Shoreditch's **On the Rocks (Map 91)**. **Madame Jojo's (Map 11)** provides exactly the kind of decadence we

demand from Soho clubbing, while Piccadilly's **Pigalle Club (Map 10)** swoops us back to the 40s. For serious rockabilly, find **Ye Olde Axe (Map 91)** gentlemen's club on Hackney Road, where the rock'n'roll starts as soon as the last naked girl has disappeared behind the big-mirrored wall. Last look at your quiff, and move!

Great Bars

Hoxton and Shoreditch might not be as authentic and offbeat and uncommercial as they used to be for us, but more than enough places still do it for us. Try up-beat **Jaguar Shoes (Map 91)**, the hidden **Dragon Bar (Map 8)** and the scruffy, wonderful madhouse that is **The Foundry (Map 84)**, **Freud (Map 13)** or the **French House (Map 11)**—in the West End it all depends on the mood. But there's more out there, so bar-hop your way across the city: from **Barrio North's (Map 80)** caravan to the country-house of **Lost Society (Map 142)**, from **Bloomsbury Bowling Lanes (Map 4)** to the Mojito-fuelled **Mau Mau (Map 29)**. We like standing next to (would-be) artists at the **ICA Bar (Map 23)** and actor types on the terrace of **The Cut Bar (Map 104)**. Or in front of a movie screen, at **Roxy Bar and Screen (Map 106)**. Later on, you'll find us nibbling cheese in Dalston's **Jazz Bar (Map 86)**, dancing to trashy music at **Da Vinci's (Map 104)**, or stumbling down the stairs to the public toilet in front of Christ Church (**Public Life (Map 91)**).

Best Of The Rest

Want to feel exclusive? Members-only clubs are not only becoming ever more popular, but also ever more accessible. So there. Escape Shoreditch's terrifying hordes to the rooftop swimming pool of **Shoreditch House (Map 91)** or the boredom of Shepherd's Bush to the underground ex-toilets that have become **Ginglik (Map 33)**. Get stupidly drunk with the nonsense-talking artists of Soho's **Colony Room (Map 11)** or hopelessly lost in the dusty labyrinth that makes up the excellent **Shunt (Map 106)**, underneath the railway arches of London Bridge Station. Whatever you do, remember: you're in, they're out.

If relying on that notoriously joke-cracking friend of a friend for your evening's amusement sounds a bit risky, consider these alternatives: The standard-setting **Comedy Store (Map 11)** (book in advance), Bethnal Green's **Backyard Comedy (Map 92)** and **Covent Garden Comedy Club (Map 24)**, or, at the pub end of things, the **Monkey Business (Map 72)**, **The Bedford (Map 148)** and the **Camden Head (Map 80)**. If you think that YOU should in fact provide the evening's amusement, well, the **Poetry Café (Map 13)** gives you the stage, if you dare.

Music Overview

From Camden's indie haunts to Soho's jazz clubs to west London's concert halls, London offers a live music spectrum that takes in world-famous names at world-famous venues, and the hottest bands inside the most unassuming looking pub down the road. And everything in between.

Rock, Pop

At first sight, the picture looks depressing. London's time-honoured live classics are dying, one after the other: The Hammersmith Palais is gone. The Electric Ballroom is almost. And the **Astoria's (Map 12)** chances for survival get slimmer by the day. The musical greats of today might be the designer flats and train stations of tomorrow. Meanwhile, annoyingly big stadiums with annoyingly corporate names (the O2, anyone?) get all the attention, throwing frustratingly bland line-ups at us. But all is not lost. For between those two extremes, venues of all sizes, layouts and beliefs are thriving—and keep popping up—bringing a musical variety to stages across the city that is, arguably, still unrivalled.

Camden's **Barfly (Map 71)**, Bethnal Green's **Star of Bethnal Green (Map 92)** (formerly the Pleasure Unit), and Highgate's **Buffalo Bar (Map 80)** are all satisfyingly sweaty, small and loud— and great for bands on the rise. Discover them even earlier at the **Macbeth (Map 84)**, nicely located off the beaten Hoxton track, or **Monto Water Rats (Map 5)**, a low-key legend that continues to bring the best new talent to King's Cross. Shoreditch's **Old Blue Last (Map 84)** has partied its way to the top of the pub gigging scene: always busy, always up for surprises. Mid-sized venues for mid-fame bands? **Scala (Map 78)** and **The Forum (Map 72)** are best. **Barden's Boudoir (Map 86)**, in a dingy Dalston basement, brings live fare of all genres to E8 (there's no sign, just a small door), while the **ICA (Map 23)** has established itself as a fine showcase for fresh bands in its posher-than-thou location on the Mall. For a grungier layout and the matching attitude, try New Cross favourite **Amersham Arms (Map 126)**, one of the city's hottest live stages. Easily.

As for the classics, the **Shepherd's Bush Empire (Map 33)** and the breathtakingly beautiful **Bush Hall (Map 32)** remain west London's finest, while Camden stalwart **Koko (Map 71)** keeps rocking, covering the spectrum from big-name to left-field. The north London show is being stolen by the **Roundhouse (Map 71)**, though, which is quickly rising to top thanks to a £29.7m facelift and a healthy "I am legend"-attitude. **Brixton Academy (Map 145)** might be slightly overrated, but its sky-like ceiling remains awesome. If you have to do stadium-size, do stadium-size in style and get your seat in the **Royal Albert Hall (Map 36)**, which is increasingly luring good non-classical acts. The refurbishment of the **Royal Festival Hall (Map 104)**, meanwhile, has kick-started more pop-oriented programming on the South Bank. Whatever you do, do the **Astoria (Map 12)** before it dies.

Jazz, Blues, World

Camden's intimate **Jazz Café (Map 71)** seems to have no intention of stopping its relentless stream of first-rate jazz performances, getting in more soul, funk and pop at the same time, while **Ronnie Scott's Jazz Club (Map 12)**, London's undisputed jazz original, is equally determined to keep up the good programming. For some of the freshest jazz talent, alongside great contemporary folk and world music, head to Dalston, where the **Vortex (Map 82)** keeps creating a buzz. On the other side of town,

Chelsea's 606 Club (Map 50) is a fine, small jazz venue with crammed, small tables right in front of the stage. Catch excellent blues every night of the week at **Ain't Nothing But The Blues Bar (Map 10)**, or Latin jazz at **Archway's Caipirinha Jazz Bar (Map 52)**. For world music, the **Barbican Centre (Map 7)** leads the pack, but is easily beaten in atmosphere stakes by

the **Union Chapel (Map 80)**, an Islington church doubling as one of London's most beautiful venues. If classical music is your cup of tea, look beyond the obvious venues and settle amid the great acoustics of **Chelsea's Cadogan Hall (Map 19)**, the historical brilliance of **Hackney's Sutton House (Map 87)** or the magnificent **Wigmore Hall (Map 2)**, in Mayfair.

Map 1 • Marylebone (West)

Sequoia@RubyLo	23 Orchard St	020 7486 3671	Dimly-lit, sexy bar with kick ass Mojitos.

Map 2 • Marylebone (East)

Claridge's Bar	55 Brook St	020 7629 8860	Posh and plush and Art Deco. More champagne!
Inn 1888	21 Devonshire St	020 7486 7420	Quiet pint perfection.
The Phoenix	37 Cavendish Sq	020 7493 8003	A quirky gem amidst an ocean of shite chain bars.

Map 3 • Fitzrovia   *Address*

100 Club	100 Oxford St	020 7636 0933	Ancient club that's seen off Nazi bombs and Sex Pistols.
The Albany	240 Great Portland St	020 7387 0221	Swanky, but nice. And the music's good.
Bourne & Hollingsworth	28 Rathbone Pl	020 7636 8228	Fine Fitzrovian basement boutique.
Bradleys Spanish Bar	42 Hanway St	020 7636 0359	60's rock joint with awesome jukebox and disgusting toilets.
Bricklayers Arms	31 Gresse St	020 7636 5593	Advertising types fake no-nonsense boozing.
Charlotte Street Hotel	15 Charlotte St	020 7806 2000	Dirty gossip over dirty martinis.
The Fitzroy Tavern	16 Charlotte St	020 7580 3714	Sam Smith's, anyone?
Ghetto	Falconberg Ct	020 7287 3726	Loud electro at this busy gay club. Thursdays is ladies night.
The Jerusalem Tavern	33 Rathbone Pl	020 7255 1120	A tiny old wooden gem of a pub. And organic ale.
Market Place	11 Market Pl	020 7079 2020	Warm buzz. Hot crowd. Cool prices.
The Metro Club	19 Oxford St	020 7437 0964	Contingency plan for bored indie kids.
Northumberland Arms	43 Goodge St	020 7580 7975	Cosy, old-style bar with a local feel.
Punk	14 Soho St	871 223 1242	Starfucker central. But kinda fun.
The Rising Sun	46 Tottenham Ct Rd	020 7636 6530	Bordering Soundland and Fitzrovia; pretty name, less pretty pub.
The Roxy	3 Rathbone Pl	020 7255 1098	Hip subterranean hangout. More chicks than dicks.
The Social	5 Little Portland St	020 7636 4992	Fab music, nonchalant surroundings and plenty of trendsters.
The Yorkshire Grey	46 Langham St	020 7636 4788	Upstairs is perfect when Oxford Street's pissing you off.

Map 4 • Bloomsbury (West)

All Star Lanes	Victoria House, Bloomsbury Pl	020 7025 2676	You'll be bowled over. Oh yes you will.
Bloomsbury Bowling Lanes	Bedford Way	020 7183 1979	As cool as bowling gets.
The Fly	36 New Oxford	020 7688 8955	For your quick indie fix on New Oxford.
Marquis of Cornwallis	31 Marchmont St	020 7278 8355	Chilled couches.
Old Crown	33 New Oxford St	020 7836 9121	After-work bar that takes itself very seriously.
Point 101	101 New Oxford St	020 7379 3112	Even mass murderers on day release get in here.
The Princess Louise	208 High Holborn	020 7405 8816	Victorian gin palace now serving cheap but good lager.
ULU	1 Malet St	020 7664 2000	Student union, student prices, student bands.

Map 5 • Bloomsbury (East)

06 St Chad's Place	6 St Chad's Pl	020 7278 3355	Stylish wine bar with plastic chairs! SOOO avant-garde, dahhhling!
The Duke of York	156 Clerkenwell Rd	020 7837 8548	You and a hundred cycle couriers.
Monto Water Rats	328 Gray's Inn Rd	020 7837 4412	No rats here, only the best up-and-coming bands.
Smithy's	15 Leeke St	020 7278 5949	Our lunchtime to late-night-wind-down friend.

Map 6 • Clerkenwell

Betsey Trotwood	56 Farringdon Rd	020 7253 4285	Thoroughly likable Shepherd Neame pub renowned for live music.
Café Kick	43 Exmouth Market	020 7837 8077	Creaky, Latin American table football cafe.
Cicada	132 St John St	020 7608 1550	Gorgeous Art Deco interior, original and classic cocktails.
Dollar Grills and Martinis	2 Exmouth Market	020 7278 0077	Forget the grills, go with the martinis.
The Dovetail	9 Jerusalem Passage	020 7490 7321	Small, but perfectly formed Clerkenwell sister to Broadway Market's The Dove.
Filthy McNasty's	68 Amwell St	020 7837 6067	Disappointingly un-filthy or nasty. Sigh.
The Harlequin	27 Arlington Way	020 7837 0090	Livingroom boozer.
Queen Boadicea	292 St John St	020 7354 9993	Full of students paying their lecturers off with pints.

The Slaughtered Lamb	34-35 Great Sutton St	020 7253 1516	Dimly-lit pub that's still packing in the Clerkenwell crowd.
The Three Kings	7 Clerkenwell Close	020 7253 0483	Quirky pub that dies on weekends.

Map 8 · Liverpool Street / Broadgate

The Light	233 Shoreditch High St	020 7247 8989	Light at the end of the tunnel for city revellers.
The Red Lion	1 Eldon St	020 7247 5381	Drinkers near Moorgate can't be choosers. So there.
Sosho	2 Tabernacle St	020 7920 0701	It's so Sosho darling.

Map 9 · Mayfair / Green Park

1707	181 Piccadilly	020 7734 8040	Empty Fortnum & Mason's wine cellar.
5th View	203 Piccadilly	020 7851 2433	Spill Bloody Marys over books in full view of Big Ben.
bbar	43 Buckingham Palace Rd	020 7958 7000	Get drunk behind Elizabeth's back.
Funky Buddah	15 Berkeley St	020 7495 2596	Overpriced, overrated, tacky Z-list haunt. Apart from that, it's great!
Mahiki	1 Dover St	020 7493 9529	Crushingly tropical cocktail bar. Pineapples a-go-go.
Shepherd's Tavern	50 Hertford St	020 7499 3017	For drinking within Shepherd's Market.

Map 10 · Piccadilly / Soho (West)

22 Below	22 Great Marlborough St	020 7437 4106	Table-service cocktail lounge - without being snooty. We love it.
Ain't Nothing But The Blues Bar	20 Kingly St	020 7287 0513	Bracingly raw music in a tiny frontroom.
Bar Red	5 Kingly St	020 7434 3417	Soho cocktail madness. Plush, sexy and red.
Cheers Bar	72 Regent St	020 7494 3322	Sitcom-themed Americana; wags shouting 'Norm!' at regular intervals.
Courthouse Bar	19 Great Marlborough St	020 7297 5555	Drink where Oscar Wilde was in the clink.
Green and Red	51 Bethnal Green Rd	020 7749 9670	Tequila bar worth its post-shot salt - you're spoilt for choice.
John Snow	39 Broadwick St	020 7437 1344	Soho drinkers! Sam Smith's full range and a relaxed upstairs!
Milk & Honey	61 Poland St	0700 655 469	The promised land of after-hours cocktails. Members club, so join.
Pigalle Club	215 Piccadilly	020 7644 1420	Ladies and gentleman, welcome to the 40s.
Strawberry Moons	15 Heddon St	020 7437 7300	Dig the cheese, with your new squeeze.

Map 11 · Soho (Central)

Blue Posts	22 Berwick St	020 7437 5008	Unreformed, scuzzy boozer.
The Blue Posts	28 Rupert St	020 7437 1415	Hey, a decent pub in Soho.
Candy Bar	4 Carlisle St	020 7494 4041	Soho's premier all girl venue.
The Colony Room	41 Dean St	020 7437 9179	Arty pisshead private members' hangout; Shane MacGowan virutally lives here.
The Comedy Store	1 Oxendon St	020 7930 2949	Isn't it world famous for no reason, chuckles.
De Hems	11 Macclesfield St	020 7437 2494	Dutch bar with brain-cell-annihilatingly strong beer. Hic!
The Endurance	90 Berwick St	020 7437 2944	Hang-out for loud media twats.
Freedom	66 Wardour St	020 7734 0071	Neon green cocktail kitsch.
The French House	49 Dean St	020 7437 2799	Boho Soho hang-out for eccentrics.
LUPO	50 Dean St	020 7434 3399	A labyrinth of candlelit corners and sophisticated conversation.
Madame Jojo's	Brewer St	020 7734 3040	Unpretentious club where you won't remain single for too long.
Rex Cinema and Bar	21 Rupert St	020 7287 0102	Rexcellent.
Shadow Lounge	5 Brewer St	020 7439 4089	Gay chi chi lounge.
Soho Revue Bar	11 Walkers Ct, Brewer St	020 7439 4089	For the trashier nighthawk. Cabaret and remorse.
Trash Palace	11 Wardour St	020 7734 0522	Aptly named gay indie bar. Skullz everywhere.
The Village	81 Wardour St	020 7434 2124	Tacky, flirtatious Soho gay bar.

Map 12 · Soho (East)

12 Bar Club	22 Denmark St	020 7240 2622	Ludicrously tiny live club with singer/songwriter focus.
The Astoria	157 Charing Cross Rd	020 7434 9592	Gigging legend. Go before they get serious about tearing it down.
The Borderline	Orange Yard, Manette St	020 7734 5547	Cool basement club, bizarrely got up in Tex-Mex decor.
Comptons	53 Old Compton St	020 7479 7961	Crammed gay pub.
Crobar	17 Manette St	020 7439 0831	Heavy metal and cheap bourbon. Be a man for once.
G-A-Y Bar	30 Old Compton St	020 7494 2756	Poptastic gay bunker.
G-A-Y Late	5 Goslett Yard	020 7734 9858	Cheap drinks and pop videos wipe out brain functions 'til 3 am.
Garlic & Shots	14 Frith St	020 7734 9505	Drunken vampires beware.
Green Carnation	5 Greek St	020 7434 3323	Sexy, Ockar Wilde-inspired lounge that Oscar would have approved of.
Jazz After Dark	9 Greek St	020 7734 0545	Tunes and cheap drinks, until LATE.
Ku Bar	30 Lisle St	020 7437 4303	Newly relocated gay bar for the young and clueless.
Montagu Pyke	105 Charing Cross Rd	020 7287 6039	Cheap beer - in the West End.
Ronnie Scott's Jazz Club	47 Frith St	0207 439 0747	Original, and still the best.
Royal George	133 Charing Cross Rd, Goslett Yard	020 7734 8837	Busy, but the crowd's nice. Board games and food.
The Toucan	19 Carlisle St	020 7437 4123	Small and snug central bolthole for Guinness.

489

Map 13 · Covent Garden

AKA Bar	18 W Central St	020 7836 0110	Proper drinks and proper DJs. And pizza for inbetween.
Bunker	41 Earlham St	020 7240 0606	Beer brewed it in front of your eyes.
Coffee, Cake & Kink	61 Endell St	020 7419 2996	Does what it says on the tin!
The Cross Keys	31 Endell St	020 7836 5185	Tiny old-school boozer.
The End	18 W Central St	020 7419 9199	The beginning is the end is the beginning. This pioneering club's still rockin' it.
Freud	198 Shaftesbury Ave	020 7240 9933	Intimate basement bar that used to be Alex of Blur's living room. Literally.
Guanabara	Parker St	020 7242 8600	Brasil. But in Holborn.
The Lamb and Flag	33 Rose St	020 7497 9504	Cobbled lane leads to a crowded but gloriously timeless inn.
Octave	27 Endell St	020 7836 4616	Dressy but mellow jazz-cum-cocktail bar for Ally McBeal and friends.
Poetry Cafe	22 Betterton St	020 7420 9887	Eat, drink, write, listen or yes, PERFORM!

Map 14 · Holborn / Temple

Cittie of Yorke	22 High Holborn	020 7242 7670	See olde its name has extra e's. A marvellous pube.
Enterprise	38 Red Lion St	020 7269 5901	More Captain Cook than Captain Kirk.
The Lamb	92 Lamb's Conduit St	020 7405 0713	Legendary little place with Victorian touches.
Na Zdrowie The Polish Bar	11 Little Turnstile	020 7831 9679	With 50 types of vodka, even beetroot soup tastes good.
The Seven Stars	53 Carey St	020 7242 8521	Tiny, slightly dusty bar frequented by barristers.
Tutu's	Surrey St	020 7836 7132	King's College students' very own nightclub.
Volupte	9 Norwich St	020 7831 1622	They call it burlesque, we call it strippers with tassles.

Map 15 · Blackfriars / Farringdon

Corney & Barrow	10 Paternoster Sq	020 7618 9520	Champagne breakfast, anyone?
The Deux Beers	3 Hatton Wall	020 7405 9777	Home of the original politically incorrect 100 shooter list.
Fabric	77 Charterhouse St	020 7336 8898	Debauched club mecca for gurners of all persuasions.
Smithfield Bar & Grill	West Smithfield	020 7246 0900	Suits, suits, suits. And chandeliers, jazz and cocktails. And suits.
Ye Olde Cheshire Cheese	154 Fleet St	020 7353 6170	Get tanked up where Dickens used to. Historic.
Ye Olde London		020 7248 1852	It ain't Olde, really, but it sells beer.
Ye Olde Mitre	1 Ely Ct	020 7405 4751	Elizabeth I used to dance here, don't you know?!

Map 16 · Square Mile (West)

Hatchet	28 Garlick Hill	020 7236 0720	Lost in the City? Escape here.
The Mansion House	44 Cannon St	020 7248 1700	Out of the tube, into the House.
The Samuel Pepys	48 Upper Thames St	020 7489 1871	Find it and be rewarded with Thames views.
Ye Olde Watling	29 Watling St	020 7653 9971	Squeeze in.

Map 17 · Square Mile (East)

The Counting House	50 Cornhill	0871 917 0007	A truly magnificent (former) bank. That sells beer now.
Grand Cafe & Bar	The Ctyard, Royal Exchange	020 7618 2480	The courtyard of the Royal Exchange. Fancy, eh?

Map 18 · Tower Hill / Aldgate

Dion Bar	52 Leadenhall St	020 7702 9111	Veuve Clicquot La Grande Dame Rose, anyone?
Kenza	10 Devonshire Sq	020 7929 5533	Belly-dancers, cocktails & couscous.
Pepys Bar at the Novotel Hotel	10 Pepys St	020 7265 6000	Get on the Kir Royales and kiss tomorrow goodbye.
Prism	147 Leadenhall St	020 7256 3873	Cocktails underneath the former Bank of New York.
Revolution in the City	140 Leadenhall St	020 7929 4233	Vodka-drenched, vault-like DJ bar that couldn't care less about the revolution.

Map 19 · Belgravia

The Blue Bar	Wilton Pl	020 7235 6000	It's blue. Mindbogglingly so.
Nag's Head	53 Kinnerton St	020 7235 1135	No mobiles allowed. Says it all.

Map 20 · Victoria / Pimlico (West)

The Albert	52 Victoria St	020 7222 5577	Distinguished, well-preserved period pub. Tourist haunt but rightly so.
The Cardinal	23 Francis St	020 7834 7260	Easier to than to find.
Cask & Glass	39 Palace St	020 7834 7630	Teeny tiny, English country garden-esque drinking hole. Flower-festooned frontage, real ale.
The Plumber's Arms	14 Lower Belgrave St	020 7730 4067	Tradesman's pub from days of yore. Ask about Lord Lucan.

Map 21 • Pimlico (East)

Morpeth Arms	58 Millbank	020 7834 6442	Where Millbank prisoners used to escape to.

Map 22 • Westminster

The Cinnamon Club	Great Smith St	020 7222 2555	Cocktail classiness inside the Old Westminster Library. Try finding it.
The Speaker	46 Great Peter St	020 7222 1749	Good after-worker with guest ales.
St. Stephen's Tavern	10 Bridge St	020 7925 2286	Tiny pub with character, despite being on tourist trail.

Map 23 • St. James's

Aura	48 St James's St	020 7499 9999	If you ain't on the list, you ain't coming in. Seriously.
ICA	The Mall	020 7930 3647	Cutting edge arts complex/bar, weirdly stuck on the upper-crust Mall.
The Sports Cafe	80 Haymarket	020 7839 8300	Umpteen screens of international sport distract from appalling service/grub.

Map 24 • Trafalgar Square / The Strand

Asia de Cuba	45 St Martin's Lane	020 7300 5588	For rum-drinking with the jet set.
The Chandos	29 St Martins Lane	020 7836 1401	All Trafalgar Square pubs tourist traps? Think again.
The Coal Hole	91 Strand	020 7379 9883	Genuine old style.
Covent Garden Comedy Club	The Arches, Off Villiers St	07960 071 340	Good acts play to a friendly crowd drinking awful beer.
Gordon's Wine Bar	47 Villiers St	020 7930 1408	Candle-lit vaults. Romantic perfection.
Heaven	Under the Arches, off Villiers St	020 7930 2020	Epicentre of London's late night gay scene.
Maple Leaf	41 Maiden Ln	020 7240 2843	Just don't ask which State they're from.
Punch & Judy	The Piazza	020 7379 0923	Naff, naff, naff. 'Nuff said?
Retro Bar	2 George Ct	020 7839 8760	Chilled gay bar, hiding from Charing Cross in a small alley.
Roadhouse	The Piazza	020 7240 6001	"You're the one that I want, ooh-ooh-ooh"
The Sherlock Homes	10 Northumberland St	020 7930 2644	Unintentionally sinister, must-see Holmes waxwork upstairs. Expect bad dreams.
The Ship and Shovel	Craven Passage	0872 148 4124	A pub made of two pubs, both obsessed with Sherlock Holmes.

Map 25 • Kensal Town

Book Slam	12 Acklam Rd	n/a	Books for clubbers or DJ-night for literary folks – can't decide.

Map 26 • Maida Hill

The Skiddaw	46 Chippenham Rd	020 7432 1341	West London trendy hang out. Great Sunday roast.

Map 27 • Maida Vale

Bridge House	13 Westbourne Terrace Rd	020 7266 4326	Canal views and comedy. Lovely.
E Bar	2 Warrington Crescent	020 7432 8455	Basement lounge for a quiet drink.
Robert Browning	15 Clifton Rd	020 7286 2732	Cheapo boozer in posh surroundings.
The Warwick Castle	6 Warwick Pl	020 7266 0921	Down-to-earth drinking in Maida Vale. Indeed.
Waterway	54 Formosa St	020 7266 3557	Try not to fall into the canal.

Map 28 • Ladbroke Grove / Notting Hill (West)

Julie's Wine Bar	135 Portland Rd	020 7727 7985	Pleasantly posh wine bar full of pleasantly posh ladies.

Map 29 • Notting Hill Gate

Mau Mau	265 Portobello Rd	020 7229 8528	Ace mojitos and Thursdays open-mic. Wear your dancing shoes.
Montgomery Place	31 Kensington Park Rd	020 7792 3921	The mixers rock. And they know it.
Notting Hill Arts Club	21 Notting Hill Gate	020 7460 4459	Indie cave with bands, visual projections and teenagers.
The Sun in Splendour	7 Portobello Rd	020 7792 0914	Notting Hill denizens' choice.
Uxbridge Arms	13 Uxbridge St	020 7727 7326	Warm fading pub of eccentric old toffs.
Windsor Castle	114 Campden Hill Rd	020 7243 8797	A wood-panelled piece of pub history.

Map 32 • Shepherd's Bush (West)

Bush Hall	310 Uxbridge Rd	020 8222 6955	The red carpet, the ornate walls…the sheer beauty!
The Goldhawk	122 Goldhawk Rd	020 8576 6921	A pub, ladies and gentlemen.
The White Horse	31 Uxbridge Rd	020 8743 0624	Did you call my pint a slag? Outside, now!

Map 33 · Shepherd's Bush

Albertine	1 Wood Lane	020 8743 9593	Drink wine with the Beep set.
Bush Bar & Grill	45 Goldhawk Rd	020 8746 2111	Pre-gig margarita, post-gig wood fired pizza.
Ginglik	1 Shepherd's Bush Green	020 7348 8968	Members-only underground ex-toilets. Join free on the door.
Shepherd's Bush Empire	Shepherd's Bush Green	020 8354 3300	Still among London venueland's finest.

Map 34 · West Kensington / Olympia

Famous 3 Kings	171 North End Rd	020 7603 6071	Brilliant atmosphere for big matches especially rugby. Pool tables too.
Plum Bar	380 Kensington High St	020 7603 3333	Dying for a drink in Kensington? Well there.

Map 35 · Kensington

Builders Arms	1 Kensington Ct Pl	020 7937 6213	Boozy haven from High Street Kensington's shopping madness.

Map 36 · South Kensington / Gloucester Rd

Boujis	43 Thurloe St	020 7584 2000	If you want to see the two princes drunk. And only then.

Map 38 · Chiswick

Carvossos	210 Chiswick High Rd	020 8995 9121	For a glass of wine before dinner.

Map 40 · Goldhawk Rd / Ravenscourt Park

The Dove	19 Upper Mall	020 8748 9474	So perfect for dates that Charles II brought Nell Gwynne here.
Ruby Grand	225 King St	020 8748 3391	Self-proclaimed purveyor of elegance.

Map 41 · Hammersmith

Brook Green Hotel	170 Shepherd's Bush Rd	020 7603 2516	Lost between Hammersmith and Shepherd's Bush? Fear not.
Hammersmith Apollo	45 Queen Caroline St	08448 44 47 48	Still West London's best music venue
Lyric Hammersmith	King St	087 1221 1729	Hammersmith's hottest home of hentertainment..

Map 42 · Baron's Court

Colton Arms	187 Greyhound Road	020 7385 6956	If you're not already a regular, you'll wish you were.
Curtains Up	28 Comeragh Rd	020 8932 4747	Pub which keeps actors in the basement.
The Fulham Mitre	81 Dawes Rd	020 7386 8877	Young, trendy Fulhamites like it. We don't.

Map 43 · West Brompton / Fulham Broadway / Earls Court

The Coleherne	261 Old Brompton Rd	020 7373 8337	Leather, baby!
Nectar	562 Kings Rd	020 7326 7450	Green lights, red lights, and cocktails.

Map 44 · Chelsea   *Address*

Rumi	531 Kings Rd	020 7823 3362	Fulham's secret, chic and cosy jewel.

Map 45 · Chelsea (East)

Apartment 195	195 Kings Rd	020 7351 5195	Hire your personal Kings Road party apartment.
Chelsea Potter	119 Kings Rd	020 7352 9479	Chelsea old school.

Map 47 · Fulham (West)

The Crabtree Tavern	Rainville Rd	020 7385 3929	Great riverside location. So so pub.

Map 49 · Parson's Green

Amuse Bouche	51 Parson's Green Lane	020 7371 8517	Fizzy fun.
Duke on the Green	235 New Kings Road	020 7736 2777	If only all pub food was this good (but half the price).
The White Horse	Parson's Green	020 7736 2115	Victorian pub and a beer drinker's heaven. Book a table.

Map 50 · Sand's End

606 Club	90 Lots Rd	020 7352 5953	Great jazz venue. If you like ten minute sax solos.

Map 51 • Highgate

The Boogaloo	312 Archway Rd	020 8340 2928	Not as cool as it thinks it is.
The Flask	77 Highgate West Hill	020 8348 7346	Great beers, great food, great place. Really, it is.
Highgate Inn	385 Archway Rd	n/a	Chummy, licensed version of your own front room.
Prince Of Wales	53 Highgate High St	020 8340 0445	Friendly local for posh Highgaters and their even posher dogs.
The Woodman	414 Archway Rd	020 8340 3016	Reformed fight club with gastropub intentions.
The Wrestlers	98 North Rd	020 8340 4297	Branded "best pub in Highgate" by residents.

Map 52 • Archway (North)

Caipirinha Jazz Bar	177 Archway Rd	020 7287 1269	Cosiness! Cocktails! Latin jazz! Sherpa required to find it!
The Winchester Pub Hotel	206 Archway Rd	020 8374 1690	Wonky-floored palace of boozy delight.

Map 53 • Crouch End

Harringay Arms	153 Crouch Hill	020 8340 4243	No music, plenty of beer.
Queens Pub & Dining Rooms	26 Broadway Parade	020 8340 2031	God save the Queens.
The Wishing Well	22 Topsfield Parade, Tottenham Lane	020 8340 1096	Goodbye Crouch End gastropub, hello Hornsey cheap boozer.

Map 55 • Harringay Ladder

The Salisbury	1 Grand Parade, Green Lanes	020 8800 9617	A local's secret...no longer! Exceptional.

Map 56 • Hampstead Village

The Flask	14 Flask Walk	020 7435 4580	Hampstead alleyway classic that's been refitted. But nicely so.
The Freemasons Arms	32 Downshire Hill	020 7433 6811	Lovely beer garden.
Holly Bush	22 Holly Mount	020 7435 2892	It's hidden. It's a gem. Really.

Map 57 • Hampstead Heath

The Magdala	2 South Hill Park	020 7435 2503	Ruth Ellis bullet-holed boozer.
Monkey Chews	2 Queen's Crescent	020 7267 6406	Dark and intimate bar and music venue.
Roebuck	15 Pond St	020 7435 7354	Somewhere between cosy pub and stylish bar. And good at it.

Map 58 • Parliament Hill / Dartmouth Park

Bar Lorca	156 Fortress Rd	020 7485 1314	Spanish beer. Spanish tapas.
The Bull and Last	168 Highgate Rd	020 7267 3641	Good place for a post-Heath pint.
The Dartmouth Arms	35 York Rise	020 7485 3267	A fire. Dogs. Old gits. The perfect local.
Duke of St. Albans	Highgate Road	020 7209 0385	Pretty dodgy at times, but also the only pub around

Map 59 • Tufnell Park

Boston Arms	178 Junction Rd	020 7272 8153	Ferociously scruffy but friendly Irish pub, with rock pit attached.
The Lord Palmerston	33 Dartmouth Park Hill	020 7485 1578	Gone a bit plastic, but still worth it.
The Star	47 Chester Rd	020 7263 9067	It's a star.

Map 60 • Archway

Archway Tavern	1 Archway Close	020 7272 2840	Cheap beer, plentiful fisticuffs.
The Mother Red Cap	665 Holloway Rd	020 7263 7082	Begorra! Bejesus! Be better off going to another boozer!

Map 61 • Holloway (North)

Nambucca	596 Holloway Rd	020 7272 7366	Self-proclaimed cult venue.
The Quays	471 Holloway Rd	020 7272 3634	Into bad U2 cover bands? Then you'll love it here.
The Swimmer	13 Eburne Rd	020 7281 4632	No running, diving in the shallow end, or heavy petting.

Map 62 • Finsbury Park

Faultering Fullback	19 Perth Rd	020 7272 5834	Tardis-like local. Avoid match nights unless you're a Gooner.

Map 63 • Manor House

The Blarney Stone	89 Woodberry Grove	n/a	Friendly local.
The Brownswood Park Tavern	271 Green Lanes	020 8809 2846	Enter, before Manor House drives you mad.
Manor Club	277 Seven Sisters Rd	020 8211 0211	Once a historic pub, now a strip club. No brainer.

Map 64 · Stoke Newington

Auld Shillelagh	105 Stoke Newington Church St	020 7249 5951	The best Guinness in London; you won't leave standing up.
The Lion	132 Stoke Newington Church St	020 7249 1318	Nice 'nuff.
Londesborough	36 Barbauld Rd	020 7254 5865	Stokey trendies on leather sofas.
Rose and Crown	199 Stoke Newington Church St	020 7254 7497	Sunday roasts to die for and step-back-in-time décor.
Ryan's Bar	181 Stoke Newington Church St	020 7275 7807	Boho cafe and venue with a noise limiter! Pussies.
The Shakespeare	57 Allen Rd	020 7254 4190	The Bard would be proud.

Map 65 · West Hampstead

The Czech and Slovak Club	74 West End Lane	020 7372 5251	Go Czech.
The Good Ship	289 Kilburn High Rd		Where Kilburn takes music seriously.
The Luminaire	311 High Rd	020 7372 7123	Regular winner of "best live venue" awards, despite the weird decor.

Map 66 · Finchley Road / Swiss Cottage

Ye Olde Swiss Cottage	98 Finchley Rd	020 7722 3487	What can we say.

Map 67 · Belsize Park

The Washington	50 England's Lane	020 7722 8842	Monday night is pub quiz night.

Map 68 · Kilburn High Road / Abbey Road

The Clifton	96 Clifton Hill	020 7372 3427	Not as secret as they want you to believe. But very nice.

Map 69 · St. John's Wood

The Star	38 St. Johns Wood Terrace	020 7722 1051	Drink face-to-face with a huge Highland Terrier.

Map 70 · Primrose Hill

The Albert	11 Princess Rd	020 7722 1886	A local. Cosy and relaxed.
The Engineer	65 Gloucester Ave	020 7722 0950	The classy chandeliers say it all.
The Lansdowne	90 Gloucester Ave	020 7483 0409	Home of the beautiful people.
Princess of Wales	22 Chalcot Rd	020 7722 0354	Traditional pub with occasional jazz performances.
Queens No. 1	1 Edis St	020 7586 3049	Comfy, quaint.
Sir Richard Steele	97 Haverstock Hill	020 7483 1261	Friendly local with quirky decor.

Map 71 · Camden Town / Chalk Farm / Kentish Town (West)

At Proud	Chalk Farm Rd	020 7482 3867	Oh-so-casual, trendy little bar. Fairy lights and arty types.
Bar Vinyl	6 Inverness St	020 7482 5545	DJ Bar. And good coffee.
Bartok	78 Chalk Farm Rd	020 7916 0595	Hip, late-night bar with chilled-out sofa feel.
The Camden Tup	2 Greenland Pl	020 7482 0399	A-spade's-a-spade drinking spot off the beaten track.
Dingwalls	Middle Yard	019 2082 3098	Camden Lock's guitar-smashing heartland.
The Dublin Castle	94 Parkway	020 7485 1773	Famous, small, LOUD.
Electric Ballroom	184 Camden High St	020 7485 9006	Scruffy but essential rock haunt, perennially threatened by developers.
The Enterprise	2 Haverstock Hill	020 7485 2659	Literary Irish pub with tiny indie venue upstairs.
Good Mixer	30 Inverness St	020 7916 6176	Ah, remember those halcyon days of Britpop?
The Hawley Arms	2 Castlehaven Rd	020 7428 5979	The Hawley will rise from the ashes. Camden needs it.
Jazz Cafe	5 Parkway	0207 688 8899	A relentless stream of excellent gigs.
Koko	1 Camden High St	0870 4325 527	From Charlie Chaplin to Lenny Kravitz, playing Koko still kicks ass.
Lock Tavern	35 Chalk Farm Rd	020 7482 7163	Great gigs, Sunday roasts and (unpainfully) hip clientele.
Oxford Arms	265 Camden High St	020 7267 4945	Theatre pub where you may stumble upon Amy Winehouse, stumbling.
Quinn's	65 Kentish Town Rd	020 7267 8240	More German beer than you can pronounce.
The Underworld	174 Camden High St	020 7482 1932	Throbbing pit of angry rock and even angrier metal.
The World's End	31 Jamestown Rd	020 7424 9054	Mammoth rock pub. Bring your eyeliner.

Map 72 · Kentish Town

The Abbey Tavern	124 Kentish Town Rd	020 7485 2131	Fairy-lit, casual beer garden with talented DJs on Saturdays.
Bull & Gate	389 Kentish Town Rd	020 8826 5000	A gigging institution.
The Forum	Highgate Rd	020 7428 4099	Good venue for medium-sized bands.
Monkey Business	289 Kentish Town Rd	07932 338203	Grotty pub, hosting a good comedy club.
The Pineapple	51 Leverton St	020 7284 4631	Backstreet Victorian with good beers and Thai grub.

Map 73 · Holloway

The Lord Stanley	51 Camden Park Rd	020 7428 9488	Dark wood, Edwardian interior, fireplace and secret walled garden.
Shilibeers	1 Carpenter's Mews, North Rd	020 7700 1858	For relaxed drinking on comfy couches.

Map 74 · Holloway Road / Arsenal

The Coronet	338 Holloway Rd	020 7609 5014	The smell of old men's piss is abound, but it's cheap!
El Comandante	10 Annette Rd	020 7607 3961	South American vibe in a Victorian pub.

Map 75 · Highbury

Alwyne Castle	83 St Pauls Road	020 7288 9861	Alright for a pint.
Oak Bar	79 Green Lanes		Eclectic programme of events at this mixed/lesbian venue.
Snooty Fox	75 Grosvenor Avenue	020 7354 0094	Strangely empty - shame for such a great pub.

Map 76 · Edgeware Road / Marylebone (North)

Cellars Bar	222 Marylebone Rd	020 7631 8000	Grand is the word.
The Feathers	43 Linhope St	020 7402 1327	Tiny backstreet den.
Perseverance	11 Shroton St	020 7723 7469	Perseverance in finding it will be rewarded.
Volunteer	245 Baker St	020 7486 4091	Grand old Victorian taphouse great for a lively post-work pint.

Map 77 · Mornington Crescent / Regent's Park

Crown and Anchor	137 Drummond St	020 7383 2681	A pub makeover masterpiece.
Edinboro Castle	57 Mornington Terrace	020 7255 9651	Huge outdoors bit, great BBQ on summer weekends.
Queen's Head and Artichoke	30 Albany St	020 7916 6206	The pinchos are addictive. We have warned, friends.

Map 78 · Euston

The Champagne Bar at St Pancras	Pancras Rd	020 3006 1552	Miss your train!
The Crown & Goose	100 Arlington Rd	020 7485 8008	Delightfully old-fashioned pub with good grub and an open fire.
Purple Turtle	61 Crowndale Rd	020 7383 4976	Rock club that looks like a wacky goth spaceship.
Scala	275 Pentonville Rd	020 7833 2022	Historic venue with plush edges. If these walls could talk...

Map 79 · King's Cross

Big Chill House	257 Pentonville Rd	020 7427 2540	Allow staff 28 working days to process your drinks order.
Canal 125	125 Caledonian Rd	020 7837 1924	Upmarket local bar that draws a swanky crowd.
Central Station	37 Wharfdale Rd	020 7278 3294	Ominous looking cabaret bar-cum-cruise emporium. Check site first.
Cross Kings	126 York Way	020 7278 83 18	Nice little place that tries but usually fails to be 'edgy'.
EGG	200 York Way	020 7609 8364	Big club, big garden, big night out.
Lincoln Lounge	52 York Way	020 7837 9339	Arty, quirky and cool. Does King's Cross proud.
The Tarmon	270 Caledonian Rd	020 7607 3242	Character. Lots of character.

Map 80 · Angel / Upper St

25 Canonbury	25 Canonbury Ln	020 7226 0955	You'll never love it as much as it loves itself.
The Angel	Islington High St	020 7837 2218	Students. The elderly. The unemployed.
Barrio North	45 Essex Rd	020 7688 2882	Groovy little bar with friendly international vibe. And a caravan!
Buffalo Bar	259 Upper St	020 7359 6191	Sweaty, small venue. You'll see them here first.
Camden Head	2 Camden Walk	020 7359 0851	Comedians debut new gags upstairs. Cheap—and mostly cheerful.
Carling Academy	16 Parkfield St	020 7288 4400	Grubby live music. Slap on some skinny jeans first.
The Cedar Room	235 Upper St	020 7704 6417	Happy-hour cocktails.
Compton Arms	4 Compton Ave	020 7359 6883	Islington's only real pub - or so they say.
The Crown	116 Cloudesley Rd	020 7837 7107	Jovial spot for a quiet pint and Sunday roasts.
Cuba Libre	72 Upper St	020 7354 9998	Tank up with mojitos. Salsa with the barman.
Electrowerkz	7 Torrens St	020 7837 6419	Crumbling rave labyrinth.
The Florence	50 Florence St	020 7354 5633	Refurbed, warm Georgian boozer.
The Garage	20 Highbury Corner		Bad sound and a guaranteed black hole in your evening.
Hope And Anchor	207 Upper St	020 7704 2689	Scuzzy pub with even scuzzier bands in the basement.
Keston Lodge	131 Upper St	020 7354 9535	Just the right side of poncy.
King's Head Theatre Pub	115 Upper St	020 7226 1916	Proper, good-time boozer.
Old Red Lion	418 St John St	020 7837 7816	Theatre pub legend.
Salmon & Compass	58 Penton St	020 7837 3891	The old-boozer exterior belies the hip-hop lovin', all night-dancin' crowd within.
Union Chapel	Compton Terrace	020 7226 3750	God's favourite music venue. Hell, everyone's.

Map 82 · De Beauvoir Town / Kingsland

The Northgate	113 Southgate Rd	020 7359 7392	Reliable local despite being—gasp!—a gastro.
The Rosemary Branch	2 Shepperton Rd	020 7704 2730	Theatre pub with great selection of ales and hearty fare.
Vortex	11 Gillett Sq		Dalston's only real jazz bar.
The Wellington	119 Balls Pond Rd	020 7254 4338	Nice little boozer, as they say.

Map 83 · Angel (East) / City Rd (North)

The Duke of Cambridge	30 St Peter's St	020 7359 3066	Feel self-righteous in the world's first organic pub.
Earl of Essex	25 Danbury St	020 7226 3608	For drinking in the day. In the dark.
The Island Queen	87 Noel Rd	020 7354 8741	Where NFT planned the London guide. Sweet.
Narrow Boat	119 St Peters St	020 7288 9821	Cheerful canal-side pub for lazy pints and people watching.
Offside Bar and Gallery	271 City Rd	020 7253 3306	Like a football stadium, but without anyone pissing in the sinks.
Old Queen's Head	44 Essex Rd	020 7354 9993	Trendier than the name suggests.
The Wenlock Arms	26 Wenlock Rd	020 7608 3406	Threadbare, battered old boozer with a magnificent range of real ales.

Map 84 · Hoxton

333	333 Old St	020 7739 5949	The Shoreditch grandfather.
Bar Music Hall	134 Curtain St	0207 613 5951	Nice wallpaper, free music. Who's complaining?
Bedroom Bar	62 Rivington St	0871-223-1252	Saturday's DJ 'n' sax players mean dancing til dawn.
The Bricklayers Arms	63 Charlotte Rd	020 7739 5245	Double bypass heart of 90s Britart scene. Barely still beating.
The Cantaloupe	35 Charlotte Rd	020 7613 4411	Of course YOU'RE not a corporate whore.
Cargo	83 Rivington St	020 7749 7844	Cavernous, sterile hole with bad sound but good gigs. Natch.
Charlie Wright's International Bar	45 Pitfield St	020 7490 8345	Does anyone turn up here sober?
Club Aquarium	256 Old St	020 7251 6136	After-hours swimming pool scuzzfest.
Cocomo	323 Old St	020 7613 0315	Cocktail bar with cakes, comfy sofas and scrumptious staff.
Comedy Cafe	66 Rivington St	020 7739 5706	Fun venue, but invariably a dud in the line-up.
Cordy House	Curtain Rd	N/A	Secret warehouse rave place. Authentically at odds with the authorities.
East Village	89 Great Eastern St	020 7739 5173	Shoreditch clubbing novice where the DJ is king.
The Elbow Room	97 Curtain Rd	020 7613 1316	Pricey, mildly funky pool joint.
Electricity Showroom	39 Hoxton Sq	020 7739 3939	Shark-infested waters.
Favela Chic	91 Great Eastern St	020 7613 4228	Caipirinha-lovin', shabby-chic bar full of clothes-swapping kwaziness.
The Foundry	84 Great Eastern St	020 7739 6900	Like a pretentious art student's dream bar. In a good way.
The Griffin	93 Leonard St	020 7739 6719	NOT the strip bar of the same name...
Hoxton Square Bar & Kitchen	Hoxton Sq	020 7613 0709	Snotty bands and doormen. Wear something uber.
The Legion	348 Old St	020 7729 4441	Free jukebox, quality DJs, cheap beer. Happy times.
The Macbeth	60 70 Hoxton St	020 7739 3844	Hot new bands love it. And so we.
The Old Blue Last	39 Great Eastern St	020 7739 5793	Until the bass drum WILL bring down that pub ceiling.
Plastic People	147 Curtain Rd	020 7739 6471	Tiny, pitch black musical adventure.
Pool Bar	104 Curtain Rd	020 7739 9608	Shiny cocktail shithole sympathetic to noise and club gigs.
The Red Lion	41 Hoxton St	020 7729 7920	Stay forever if you bag the chaise lounge...
Strongroom Bar	120 Curtain Rd	020 7426 5103	Shoreditch's last stronghold of unpretentiousness?
Troy Bar	10 Hoxton St	020 7739 6695	A semi-hidden gem with soul and funk music most nights.

Map 85 · Stoke Newington (East)

The Birdcage	58 Stamford Hill	020 8806 6740	High-ceilinged pub with squishy sofas and lived-in feel.
Blush	8 Cazenove Rd	020 7923 9202	Pink pint-parlour with poker and personable patrons (oh please!).
Royal Sovereign	64 Northwold Rd	020 8806 2449	Pre-gentrified local—like Stoke Newington boozers ten years ago.
White Hart	69 Stoke Newington High St	020 7254 6626	Huge pub, huge beer garden – really it's huge.

Map 86 · Dalston / Kingsland

Bar 23	23 Stoke Newington Rd	020 7241 2060	A slice of weirdness with wacked out DJing and drinking.
Barden's Boudoir	38 Stoke Newington Rd	020 7249 9557	Anything can happen in this basement. The beating heart of Dalston's music shenanigans.
Cafe Oto	18 Ashwin St	020 7923 1231	Mysterious new venue importing music from the hinterlands of psychedelia.
The Haggerston	438 Kingsland Rd	020 7923 3206	Artist-run flea pit. Chaotic crowd surfing most nights.
Jazz Bar	4 Bradbury St	020 7254 9728	Funk and free cheese. Until 5. Need we say more?
Marquis of Lansdowne	48 Stoke Newington Rd	020 7254 1104	Pleases long-standing locals and hip Hackneyites alike.
Passion	251 Amhurst Rd		Tiny basement venue that hosts massive all-nighters.
The Prince George	40 Parkholme Rd	020 7254 6060	Buzzing local favourite. Renowned Monday quiz night, great jukebox.

Arts & Entertainment · **Nightlife**

Map 87 · Hackney Downs / Lower Clapton

Biddle Brothers	88 Lower Clapton Rd	N/A	Almost trendy oasis for the trendy in an eccentric neighbourhood.
Crooked Billet	84 Upper Clapton Rd	020 8806 2747	Proof that Clapton can still be fucking terrifying.
Hugo's Speaker Palace	14 Andre St	020 8968 5704	Clandestine speaker cemetery. Very hush-hush and very cool.

Map 88 · Haggerston / Queensbridge Rd

A10 (aka The Russian Bar)	267 Kingsland Rd	n/a	It's hell and it's heaven and we can't make our fucking minds up.
The Fox	372 Kingsland Rd	020 7254 4012	Half-way stop for Shoreditch-to-Dalston pub crawls.
Melange	281 Kingsland Rd	078 9635 0086	Like your frontroom. With more parties.
Passing Clouds	440 Kingsland Rd	020 7168 7146	Back alley arts collective and live venue.
Plaza	161 Kingsland Rd	020 7613 1319	Sometime gig venue, all-the-time scary East-end boozer.

Map 89 · London Fields / Hackney Central

Baxter's Court	282 Mare St	020 8525 9010	A chain pub, okay, okay. But check the ladies' toilets!
The Dolphin	165 Mare St	020 8985 3727	Pathos sodden karaoke occasionally ruined by post-opening art people.
The Dove	24 Broadway Market	020 7275 7617	Belgian beer paradise.
Pub on the Park	19 Martello St	020 7275 9586	Tap for London Fields.
The Ship	2 Sylvester Path	020 8986 1641	Nicely refurbed ex-dive.

Map 90 · Homerton / Victoria Park North

Chats Palace Arts Centre	42 Brooksbys Walk	020 8533 0227	Fantastic community arts venue—Hackney classic.
The Lauriston	162 Victoria Park Rd	020 8985 5404	As vamped up as its made-be-village surroundings.
Royal Inn on the Park	111 Lauriston Rd	020 8985 3321	Victoria Park's prime boozer.

Map 91 · Shoreditch / Brick Lane / Spitalfields

93 Feet East	150 Brick Ln	020 7247 3293	Enthusiastic, trendy club (to impress out-of-towners).
Anda De Bridge	42 Kingsland Rd	020 7739 3863	Cocktail party, Caribbean-style.
The Archers	42 Osborn St	020 7247 3826	Nice ole pub that's resisted Shoreditchification. Perfect for pre-curry pints.
Bar Kick	127 Shoreditch High St	020 7739 8700	Lemon-yellow table football spot.
Bethnal Green Working Men's Club	44 Pollard Row	020 7739 7170	Saucy amateur burlesque that still confuses the resident Working Men.
The Big Chill Bar	Dray Walk off Brick Lane	020 7392 9180	Still among Brick Lane's better drinking spots.
Café 1001	91 Brick Ln`	020 7247 9679	Like a house party. But one where cans cost £3.
The Carpenter's Arms	73 Cheshire St	020 7739 6342	No longer run by the Kray twins' mother, still felonious fun.
Casa Blue	228 Brick Lane	020 7729 6444	Hookah and bottled beer.
Catch	22 Kingsland Rd	020 7729 6097	Reliably active dance floor, reliably silly hats, reliably good fun.
Club in a Toilet!	82 Commercial St		Yes, a club in a toilet! Tiny. Secret. No longer smelly.
The Commercial Tavern	142 Commercial St	020 7247 1888	Trusty Shoreditch traditional.
Ditch Bar	145 Shoreditch High St	020 7739 4018	Noisy electro bar/scrum.
Exit	174 Brick Lane	020 7377 2088	Sit in a row with fellow Brick Lane trendies.
The George & Dragon	Hackney Rd	020 7012 1100	Witness the E2 gay clique vie for imminent carnage.
The Golden Heart	110 Commercial St	020 7247 2158	Has it all: fires, pints and a lazy resident dog.
The Gramaphone Bar	60 Commercial St	020 7377 5332	Dark basement venue.
Green and Red	51 Bethnal Green Rd	020 7749 9670	Tequila bar worth its post-shot salt—you're spoilt for choice.
Herbal	10 Kingsland Rd	020 7613 4462	It's small enough to shout at the DJ. And groovy.
Jaguar Shoes	32 Kingsland Rd	020 7729 5830	Happy hipsters behind wide windows.
Joiners Arms	116 Hackney Rd	020 7739 9397	Popular gay pub that knows how to have fun.
Loungelover	1 Whitby St	020 7012 1234	Kitsch-colonial glitter-ball of a cocktail bar.
On the Rocks	25 Kingsland Rd	020 7688 0339	Come face to face with oblivion every Friday.
Owl And The Pussycat	34 Redchurch St	020 7613 3628	Crooked little place, tucked in the folds of Shoreditch's blubber.
Prague	6 Kingsland Rd	020 7739 9110	The closest you'll ever get to a romantic bar in Shoreditch.
Pride of Spitalfields	3 Heneage St	020 7247 8933	The only East End boozer left on Brick Lane.
Public Life	82 Commercial St	020 7375 1631	Used to be a toilet. Kinda still is. Moronic fun.
Redchurch	107 Redchurch St	020 7729 8333	Late, loud DJ host.
The Royal Oak	73 Columbia Rd	020 7729 2220	Gentrifying, gentrifying...gentrified.
Shoreditch House	Ebor St	020 7739 5040	Last one in the roof-top pool buys the drinks!
T Bar	56 Shoreditch High St	020 7729 2973	Does cool well.
Vibe Bar	91 Brick Ln	020 7426 0491	Bar in a brewery. Feel the vibe?
The Water Poet	9 Folgate St	020 7426 0495	Mismatched chairs, over-stuffed sofas, philosophy and beer.
Ye Olde Axe	69 Hackney Rd	020 7729 5137	Rockabilly-only weekends. That's right: rockabilly-only. Occasional gentleman's club.

Map 92 · Bethnal Green

The Albion	94 Goldsmiths Row	020 7739 0185	Friendly, footy-mad local. All welcome.
Backyard Comedy	231 Cambridge Heath Rd	020 7739 3122	The comedian's comedy house: this one knows what it's doing.
Bethnal Green Working Men's Club	44 Pollard Row	020 7739 7170	Saucy amateur burlesque that still confuses the resident Working Men.
The Camel	277 Globe Rd	020 8983 9888	Bethnal Green's best kept secret...D'oh!
Florist	255 Globe Rd	020 8981 1100	The Camel's naughty little sister.
Images	483 Hackney Rd	020 7739 5213	When the lapdancing's over, the clubbing madness begins.
The Star Of Bethnal Green (DUP)	359 Bethnal Green Rd	020 7729 0167	Formerly the Pleasure Unit. Still Bethnal Green's live music best.

Map 93 · Globe Town / Mile End (North)

The Approach Tavern	47 Approach Rd	020 8980 2321	Great if you can tolerate the ironic haircuts crew.
Club E3	562 Mile End Rd	020 8980 6427	Purple everywhere. If Prince lived in Bow, he'd come here.
The Fat Cat	221 Grove Rd	020 8983 1412	No fat cats, but a good mix of locals and trendies.
Jongleurs (Bow Wharf)	221 Grove Rd	0844 844 0044	Blandard comedy chain.
The Morgan Arms	43 Morgan St	020 8980 6389	Grab a pint with some gourmet food.
Palm Tree	1 Haverfield Rd	020 8980 2918	Brass walls and retired crooners! Amazingly old-fashioned boozer.

Map 94 · Bow

The Coborn Arms	8 Coborn Rd	020 8980 3793	Nice ales, nice beer garden.
The Lord Morpeth	402 Old Ford Rd	020 8981 9336	Bow boozing's best.
The Young Prince	448 Roman Rd	020 8980 1292	If on Roman Road...

Map 95 · Whitechapel (West) / St Katharine's Dock

The Castle	44 Commercial Rd	020 7481 2361	East End fortress holding it against the City.
Prohibition	1 St. Katherine's Way	0844 800 4153	Gormless bar.
Rhythm Factory	16 Whitechapel Rd	020 7375 3774	The Libertines' old haunt, with all the grimy 'chic' that implies.

Map 96 · Whitechapel (East) / Shadwell (West) / Wapping

The Captain Kidd	108 Wapping High St	0207 480 5759	Pub with nice Thames-side beer garden.
Caxtons	50 The Highway	020 7481 2961	Opens weekdays at 4am. Depressing, but come here to kick-on.
Indo	133 Whitechapel Rd	020 7247 4926	Very narrow and everything but narrow-minded.
Town of Ramsgate	62 Wapping High St	020 7481 8000	Get nautical.

Map 97 · Stepney / Shadwell (East)

The Black Horse	168 Mile End Rd	020 7790 1684	Recently renovated gay local. Drag acts and gogo boys.
The George Tavern	373 Commercial Rd	020 7790 1763	Old men, hipsters and blue-collar poets in imperfect harmony.
The Prospect of Whitby	57 Wapping Wall	020 7481 1095	Ye olde pub(e) on ye Thames(e).

Map 98 · Mile End (South) / Limehouse

The Grapes	76 Narrow St	020 7987 4396	True to its roots East End boozer - natural survivor.

Map 100 · Poplar (West) / Canary Wharf (West)

.Bar 38	West India Quay	0872 148 2408	Great inside and out.
Davy's at Canary Wharf	31 Fisherman's Walk	020 7363 6633	Traditional-style with fine ales, wine and food.
Dion Canary Wharf	Port East Building, West India Quay	020 7987 0001	Docklands warehouse-turned-champagne heaven
Via Fossa	18 Hertsmere Rd	0871 971 5240	Three floors of bankers...

Map 101 · Poplar (East) / Canary Wharf (East)

The Greenwich Pensioner	28 Bazely St	020 7987 4414	No pensioners and not in Greenwich.
The Resolute	210 Poplar High St	020 79871429	In Poplar? Desperate for a drink?

Map 102 · Millwall

Hubbub	269 Westferry Rd	020 7515 5577	Oasis in Docklands desert.

Map 103 · Cubitt Town / Mudchute

Ferry House	26 Ferry St	020 7537 9587	Beer-drenched docks time capsule.
Lord Nelson	1 Manchester Rd	020 7987 1970	Can I have a half, Nelson?
Waterman's Arms	1 Glenaffric Ave	020 7093 0837	Proper boozer on the Island.

Map 104 · South Bank / Waterloo / Lambeth North

Anchor & Hope	32 The Cut	020 7928 9898	For that intellectual pre-theatre/dinner chat.
Cubana	48 Lower Marsh	020 7928 8778	Still riding the mojito trend. But good at them.
The Cut Bar	66 The Cut	020 7928 4400	Enjoy the outdoor terrace with trendy media types and thesps.
Da Vinci's	6 Baylis Rd	020 7928 8099	Cheesy and bizarre late-night fun.
The Fire Station	150 Waterloo Rd	020 7620 2226	Only fun when you're desperate.
The Pit Bar at the Old Vic	The Cut	020 7928 2975	Guzzle champagne with Kevin Spacey and friends.
Royal Festival Hall	Belvedere Rd	087 1663 2500	Increasingly exciting programming amid nicely refurbished surroundings.
Skylon	Belvedere Rd	020 7654 7800	Impress someone with the view, then split the bill.

Map 105 · Southwark / Bankside (West)

Albert Arms	1 Gladstone St	020 7928 6517	Where yuppies meet students meet blow-ins meet locals.
Imbibe	173 Blackfriars Rd	020 7928 3693	Studenty feel, mid-week. Shouty after-workers, otherwise.
Ministry of Sound	103 Gaunt St	020 7740 8600	The sound really IS amazing.
Prince of Wales	51 St George's Rd	020 7582 9696	Cheap local with downright scary karaoke.

Map 106 · Bankside (East) / Borough / Newington

Belushi's	161 Borough High St	020 7939 9700	Drunk Antipodeans. Karaoke. General carnage.
The Blue-Eyed Maid	173 Borough High St	020 7378 8259	It's never too late for a last drink in Borough.
Brew Wharf	Brew Wharf Yard, Stoney St	020 7940 8333	Beer lovers' heaven.
The George Inn	77 Borough High St	020 7407 2056	Grab a home brew in the dazzlingly ancient George Inn.
The Globe	8 Bedale St	020 7407 0043	Bridget Jones' home? Do we care?
La Cave	6 Borough High St	020 7378 0788	So delightful you'll even start liking the French. Briefly.
The Market Porter	9 Stoney St	020 7437 5008	Market traders suck neck real ale. Smell the testosterone.
The Rake	14 Winchester Walk	020 7407 0557	Tiny place with a hundred different beers. Honestly, a hundred.
The Roebuck	50 Great Dover St	020 7357 7324	Cool but calm drinkerie for a pre-night-out drink.
The Rose	123 Snowfields	020 7378 6660	Superb backstreet boozer full of human oddities.
Roxy Bar and Screen	128 Borough High St	020 7407 4057	Mingle with baby yuppies at the Roxy Bar & Screen.
The Royal Oak	44 Tabard St	020 7357 7173	Possibly the friendliest landlords in London.
Shunt Lounge and Vaults	20 Stainer St	020 7378 7776	Dusty dancing under the railway arches. Membership required.
Southwark Tavern	22 Southwark St	020 7403 0257	Traditional ambience and ordinary fare in ye olde Southwark Tavern.
Wine Wharf	Stoney St	020 7940 8335	If you're as crazy about wine as they are.

Map 107 · Shad Thames

The Hide	39 Bermondsey St	020 7403 6655	Slightly odd vibe, but cracking drinks.

Map 109 · Southwark Park

Ancient Foresters	282 Southwark Park Rd	020 7394 1633	Surprise charmer in an otherwise grimy area.

Map 110 · Rotherhithe (West) / Canada Waters

Old Salt Quay	163 Rotherhithe St	020 7394 7108	Pub-by-numbers, but the riverside patio of dreams.

Map 111 · Rotherhithe (East) Surrey Quays

Moby Dick	6 Russell Pl, off Greenland Dock	020 7231 6719	Once here, it's hard to leave. Because it's really far from the tube.
Wibbley Wobbley	South Dock Marina, Rope St	020 7232 2320	Great dinky boat-bar, for short people.

Map 112 · Kennington / Elephant and Castle

Corsica Studios	5 Elephant Rd	0207 703 4760	Sweaty music venue with 'home-made' vibe.
Dog House	293 Kennington Rd	020 7820 9310	Like your scruffy, unpretentious younger brother. Made for chill-axing.
Prince of Wales	43 Cleaver Sq	20 77359916?	Stuart's favourite pub in Kennington.

Map 118 · Deptford (Central)

The Lord Palmerston	81 Childers St	020 8692 1575	Fewer brawls than your average Deptford pub.

Map 119 · Deptford (East)

Bird's Nest	32 Deptford Church St	020 8692 1928	Hilarious 'locals vs. trendies' vibe. Go for monthly Flesh Dunce!
Dog & Bell	116 Prince St	020 8692 5664	Now why can't ALL pubs in Deptford be like this?

(499)

Map 120 · Greenwich

Bar du Musee	17 Nelson Rd	020 8858 4710	"You have beautiful eyes, you know that?"
Greenwich Union	56 Royal Hill	020 8692 6258	Beers galore.

Map 122 · Camberwell (East)

The Castle	65 Camberwell Church St	020 7277 2601	Locals, board games and disco.
Dark Horse	16 Grove Lane	020 7703 9990	A wine pub itching to test its cocktail skills.
Funky Munky	25 Camberwell Church St	020 7277 1806	A local, of sorts, for middle class Camberwellites.

Map 125 · New Cross Gate

The Montague Arms	289 Queen's Rd	020 7639 4923	Semi-legendary, bizarrely decorated local, staffed by the world's oldest barmen and women.

Map 126 · New Cross   *Address*

Amersham Arms	388 New Cross Rd	020 8692 2047	Art school hipdom in grimy New Cross's coolest venue.
Hobgoblin	272 New Cross Rd	020 8692 3193	Get drunk with the Goldsmiths crowd.
New Cross Inn	323 New Cross Rd	020 8692 1866	Someone's gotta keep "the scene" going.

Map 127 · Coldharbour Lane / Herne Hill (West)

The Commercial	210 Railton Rd	020 7733 8783	Roaring fire and mulled wine in winter. Fits like a glove.
Escape Bar and Art	214 Railton Rd	020 7737 0333	The bar's alright, the art's excellent.

Map 129 · East Dulwich

Inside 72	72 Lordship Lane	020 8693 7131	The only bit of cool in Dulwichgastropubland.

Map 131 · Vauxhall / Albert Embankment

Area	67 Albert Embankment		Another massive Vauxhall rave hole. Serious gay clientele.
The Lavender	112 Vauxhall Walk	020 7735 4440	Just popping to the Lav
The Royal Vauxhall Tavern	372 Kennington Ln	020 7820 1222	Fun gay pub with trashy cabaret.
South Central	349 Kennington Ln	020 7793 0903	Fur on tap throughout the week. Sundays recommended.

Map 132 · Battersea (West)

The Woodman	60 Battersea High St	020 7228 2968	A nice Fire. Pint of Badger. Luverleee.

Map 133 · Battersea (East)

The Chelsea Reach	181 Battersea Park Rd	020 7627 8434	Rough around the edges local pub for local people.

Map 134 · South Lambeth

Bar Estrella	115 Old South Lambeth Rd	020 7793 1051	Football on telly, tapas in tummy. The heart of Little Portugal.
Fire	38 Parry St	020 7820 0550	Legendary gay terrordrome with LED ceiling.

Map 136 · Putney

The Boathouse	Brewhouse Ln	020 8789 0476	Riverside pub with loadsa outdoor space.
Duke's Head	8 Lower Richmond Rd	020 8788 2552	Typical gastro pub upstairs. Dark DJ bar downstairs.
Jolly Gardeners	61 Lacey Rd	020 8780 8921	Like all good pubs. And sock monkey classes on Wednesdays.

Map 137 · Wandsworth (West)

The Queen Adelaide	35 Putney Bridge Rd	020 8874 1695	Good beer selection. Mixed crowd. Decent Sunday Roast.

Map 138 · Wandsworth (Central)

The Cat's Back	88 Point Pleasant	020 8877 0818	Atmospheric and busy with loadsa obscure decoration.
GJ's	89 Garratt Ln	020 8874 2271	Party with snow bunnies.

Map 139 · Wandsworth (East)

Adventure Bar and Lounge	91 Battersea Rise	020 7223 1700	Laid back lounging. Friendly crowd. Poncey cocktails.

Map 140 · Clapham Junction / Northcote Rd

b@1	85 Battersea Rise	020 7978 6595	Be at one with a cocktail menu the size of a book.
Jongleurs (Battersea)	49 Lavender Gardens	020 7228 3744	Lots and lots of laughs. Turns into a scary club.

Map 141 · Battersea (South)

Dusk	339 Battersea Park Rd	020 7622 2112	Peppered Vanilla Mules in the shadow of the power station

Map 142 • Clapham Old Town

Frog and Forget-Me-Not	32 The Pavement	020 7622 5230	A first floor terrace that's just made for summer.
Lost Society	697 Wandsworth Rd	020 7652 6526	Country-house drinking, in Clapham.
Prince of Wales	38 Old Town	020 7622 3530	Eccentric, friendly. Run by a magpie.
Rose and Crown	2 The Polygon	020 7720 8265	For the CAMRA purists.
The Sun	47 Clapham Old Town	020 7622 4980	Nice pub. Ruined by surfeit of twats.

Map 143 • Clapham High Street

The Alexandra	14 Clapham Common South Side	020 7627 5102	Join an up-for-it crowd as multinational as the sport here.
Bread and Roses	68 Clapham Manor St	020 7498 1779	Surprisingly pleasant socialist boozer. Without Clapham tossers.
The Clapham North	409 Clapham Rd	020 7274 2472	A bit 'Clapham', but pretty likable really.
The Falcon	33 Bedford Rd	020 7274 2428	"I told Daddy, I've nowhere to even PARK a GTi!"
Green & Blue	20 Bedford Rd	020 7498 9648	For the finest wine. Because you're worth it.
Infernos	146 Clapham High St	020 7720 7633	Oh God no.
The Railway	18 Clapham High St	020 7622 4077	Half-trendy, half-local, three-quarters cool.
The Two Brewers	114 Clapham High St	020 7819 9539	Club nights, gay cabaret, lots of fu-un!
The White House	65 Clapham Park Rd	020 7498 3388	Manhattan in Clapham? Erm, O.K.

Map 144 • Stockwell / Brixton (West)

Duke of Edinburgh	204 Ferndale Rd	020 7924 0509	Warm, traditional pub with massive beer garden.
Plan B	418 Brixton Rd	08701 165 421	Has made a name for itself, but pretty lame really.
The Prince	469 Brixton Rd	020 7326 4455	Behind dealers chanting skunk lies a nothin' special pub.
The Swan	215 Clapham Rd	020 7978 9778	Don't worry about getting on the floor.

Map 145 • Stockwell / Brixton (East)

Brixton Academy	211 Stockwell Rd	020 7771 3000	Overrated, but still a tad awesome.
Jamm	261 Brixton Rd	020 7274 5537	The real deal a little way out.

Map 146 • Earlsfield

Bar 366	366 Garratt Ln	020 8944 9591	Chilled, lounge-type bar.
Box Bar	537 Garratt Ln	020 8879 3599	Always buzzing, but slightly soulless. Dressy crowd.

Map 147 • Balham (West)

The Nightingale	97 Nightingale Ln	020 8673 1637	Untrendified local. Long may it stay so.

Map 148 • Balham (East)

Balham Bowls Club	79 Ramsden Rd	020 8673 4700	A pub. In a bowling club circa 1950. Genius.
The Bedford	77 Bedford Hill	020 8682 8940	Music and comedy pub with great bands but shitty beer.

Map 150 • Brixton

The Dogstar	389 Coldharbour Ln	020 7733 7515	The burritos are great, but leave before the tunes get cheesy.
The Effra	38 Kellet Rd	020 7274 4180	A slice of the real Brixton.
The Fridge	1 Town Hall Parade	020 7326 5100	Techno, trance, hardcore venue avec occasional stabbing.
Mango Landin'	40 St Matthews Rd	020 7737 3044	Reggae-tinged alternative bar.
Mass	Brixton Hill	020 7738 7875	Drum and Bass + Hard House + Fetish Nights = Hedonist Heaven
Prince Albert	418 Coldharbour Ln	020 7274 3771	It's charming, trust us. In a not too obvious kindaway.
Ritzy Café	Brixton Oval, Coldharbour Lane (above Ritzy cinema)	020 7733 2229	Where Brixton sparkles. Cinema, bar, café and free live music.
The Windmill	22 Blenheim Gardens	020 8671 0700	Rough-edged weirdo magnet. Unique and brilliant.

Map 151 • Tooting Bec

The Bec Bar	26 Tooting Bec Rd	020 8672 7722	Pleasant enough. Go for sport.
Smoke Bar	14 Trinity Rd	020 8767 3902	Standard, compact DJ bar.

Map 152 • Tooting Broadway

Garden House	196 Tooting High St	020 8767 6582	Revived Victorian local. Live music and log fire.
Jack Beard's	76 Mitcham Rd	020 8767 8425	Drink. Dance. Drink. Feck - what happened?
The Ramble Inn	Amen Corner	020 8672 2777	Irish/locals bullshit-free boozer.
Spirit	94 Tooting High St	020 8767 3311	For a pint and a cheap bite.
Tram and Social	46 Mitcham Rd	020 8767 0278	Cavernous, funky and cool without trying.
The Tramshed	48 Mitcham Rd	020 8682 7181	Spanking-new kitsch conversion.

It's hard to judge Londoners by their favourite restaurants. We all have such a fully-stocked larder of favourite eateries—adapting to every culinary occasion like cosmopolitan chameleons. We'll rough it over a greasy fry-up day by day (**Alpino** (Map 80)), camp it up deluxe style by night **Les** (**Trois Garçons (Map 91)**) and blow most of our wage on a bottle of champagne over Sunday Lunch, just to celebrate pay day in the first place. The truth is—there's so much choice, we can't really help it. We don't pay out extortionate rents just to cook spag bol ourselves, like the rest of the country. No. We choose to live in London, where the disproportionate amount of restaurants per person leaves us no choice but to accept our fate and embrace the restaurant as the pathway to a damn good night out. After all, we have restaurants to suit every imaginable situation. Everyone has their local Italian; die-hard curry house; girly bistro where rosé becomes acceptable; guaranteed-a-shag-later candlelit brasserie; close-that-deal power lunch spot; greasy caff; and of course, that Sunday lunch gastropub where you can think about all of this over a massive Yorkshire pudding. Probably you don't need us, but we know how fickle London can be. We swear by our local one day, but the minute Jamie O. opens a reasonably over-priced gastropub, there goes that old favourite.

Eating British

From pie shops to posh Sunday lunches, great British food has become our little pièce de résistance in the global restaurant scene. And like everything else, we do it with a bit of a nudge nudge wink wink. We rule the gastropub roost—especially when the likes of the **Eagle (Map 6)**, **Anchor & Hope (Map 104)** and **Great Queen Street (Map 13)** opened their doors, taking a new look at British cuisine and putting it on our tables in ways we'd never seen it before, while other old standards refuse to budge from doing what they do best—partly because there's no one else on earth that can do it like them. **M. Manze's (Map 107)**, for instance, has been serving up pies and jellied eels for over 100 years and still won't give out their prized recipe.

If anything, in this obsession with eating healthily, there seems to be a distinct trend of restaurants

sticking a subtle two fingers up to the likes of Gillian McKeith, by putting the most comforting of comfort foods on tempting familiar (yet strangely somehow exotic menus). **Canteen (Map 104)**, with its macaroni cheese and devilled kidneys; **Roast (Map 106)** with its native breed Mondays (promising only to use British meat); **Boisdale (Map 19)** with its 1870 Jacobite menu, including old-school haggis and **Tom Ilic's (Map 142)** sticky toffee pudding to name a few favourite indulgences.

For a serious Sunday lunch try **Butler's Wharf Chop House (Map 107)**, **Boheme Kitchen & Bar (Map 12)** and **The Admiral Codrington (Map 46)**. Last but not least, London has some of the most sophisticated fish & chips around with über-fresh ingredients like **Fish! (Map 106)**, **Chris' Fish & Chips (Map 38)**, **Tom's Place (Map 45)**, **Sea Cow (Map 129)**, and **Rock & Sole Place (Map 13)**.

London has become a great place to eat British.

Caffs and Breakfast Joints

Few of us have time to actually eat it during the week, but nothing beats a breakfast when a hangover has descended. From a posh crumpet brunch at the **Wolseley (Map 9)** to the most traditional of caffs like **E Pellicci (Map 92)** and **The Regency Café (Map 21)**, breakfast really has become the most important meal of any Londoner's Saturday morning, anyway. All these are well and good, but if you can discover one of those rarities like the absolutely knock-you-on the floor-delicious Latin breakfast at **El Vergel (Map 106)**, you know you must have rock-hard London karma. If you like people watching, there's **Bar Italia (Map 12)** or **Jones Dairy Café (Map 91)**. For healthier fare try **The Larder (Map 15)** and **Giraffe (Map 104)**. The best greasy spoons include **Jeff's Café (Map 18)**, **Mario's Café (Map 72)**, and **Marie's Café (Map 104)**.

Cheap Eats

There's this nasty rumour—spread mostly by those out-of-towners who resent their commute yet insist on living two hours away—that London is no place for the impoverished restaurant lover. Such slanderers should be stopped at the M25 and

Arts & Entertainment · **Restaurants**

made to pay double congestion charge. The truth is, if you know London, you know how to eat out for under £20 (and even under a tenner when particularly skint). We have plenty of true gems where you can boldly shout 'I'll get this one!' all smugly moving ahead in the old restaurant rounds game, with your accompanying party none the wiser. Try **Café Emm (Map 12)** or **The Table (Map 105)** for some really convincing knock-off food that won't break the bank. If you have no qualms re: pretence and just want to eat cheap try **Icco Pizza (Map 3)** and **Maoz (Map 11)**. Stuck in Chelsea without a trust fund? Try **Le Columbier (Map 45)**. Now, go cash in on that overdraft and keep reading...

Fashionable Eats

Let's not call these 'expensive' eats, let's call them just plain must-haves, dah-ling. London is a town where Sloanies and the Land Rover mafia (despite the threat of the latter's own personal congestion charge) still hog the wonderfully chic eateries, where you really do become what you eat. Not in a smoothie-and-wheat-grass way—but in the way that wearing the latest handbag might distinguish you as amazingly in-the-know and undeniably wealthy. Your reservation of choice, which you made, like, a decade beforehand for places like **River Café (Map 47)** and **Gordon Ramsay at Claridges (Map 2)**, matters in this town. Celebrities seem to be judged by where they wash down their dosh and so will you if you're moving in the right circles. But luckily, we're also a city that loves a "bargain" alternative—hence Kate Moss at **Topshop (Map 3)**—and for every celebrity chef hot spot, there's a high street version. If you can't afford the £95 per person price at **Gordon Ramsay (Map 46)** (and that's without splashing out on the £10,000 bottles of wine), you'll love **The Devonshire (Map 38)**. And if you lust over Tom Aikens, try **Tom's Kitchen (Map 45)**, an ever-popular brasserie that still has a lot to write home about. If Sir Jamie (oh, come on, he's almost there!) is your thing try upstairs at **Fifteen (Map 83)** and you can save money for more important things, like that pair of Louboutins you've been after. You'll still need a fairly generous credit card limit, but at least it won't have you re-mortgaging your flat.

For classically chic and delicious, try **Foxtrot Oscar (Map 46)**, **Delfina (Map 107)** or **Chez Bruce (Map 147)**. For a view try **Galvin at Windows (Map 9)**, **Skylon (Map 104)**, **Rhodes 24 (Map 17)** or **Oxo Tower Wharf (Map 104)**. If you're a visiting footballer's wife lurching around in 10-inch heels, try **Balans (Map 11)**, **Deep (Map 50)**, **Eight Over Eight (Map 44)** or **Beach Blanket Babylon (Map 29)**. Hipster deluxe joints include **Village East (Map 108)**, **The Market (Map 106)** and **Bistrotheque (Map 23)**. Take mummy dearest to **Aubergine (Map 44)** or **Morgan M (Map 74)** when she's in town and if you like anything with a label, try **J Sheekey (Map 24)**. But, if you want something worth every penny try Ubon by **Nobu (Map 100)**, **Le Cercle (Map 46)**, and **Wild Honey (Map 10)**. Pretty soon you'll be able to enter your fave fashionable joint and exchange noisy bisous with the maitre d' (that's when you know you're in).

Going for a... (fill in the blank ethnic food)

In such an ethnically-diverse capital as this one, we savour our wide-range of foreign grub. For Londoners 'going for a curry' is an adventure which can encompass such a wide range of cuisines from Nepalese at **Kathmandu Valley (Map 138)** to Eritrean at **Asmara (Map 150)** and a kebab at **Tayyabs (Map 96)** or **Beirut Express (Map 1)** is more than just an ill-advised stop on the way to the night bus. We choose our indulgences carefully. We know how to avoid the incessant menu hawkers along Brick Lane on our way to the **Beigel Bakery (Map 91)**. After all, the best curry houses are rarely on this over-hyped thoroughfare—if you have to, try **The Clipper (Map 91)** or **Le Taj (Map 91)**—but tucked away on neighbouring streets are places like **The Empress (Map 95)** or a good tube ride away at **Spice of Life (Map 139)**, **Mirch Masala (Map 151)**, and **The Punjab (Map 13)**.

The best Chinese food can be found around China Town, which we have to hunt. Try **Shanghai (Map 86)**, **Ping Pong (Map 10)**, **Haozhan (Map 12)** or **Royal China (Map 30)**. But why settle for Chinese when there are a million other Asian foods to try?:

503

Thai at **Yum Yum (Maps 79 & 64)**, Busaba Eathai **(Map 3)**, **Thai Pavillion East (Map 131)** and **Su-Thai (Map 121)**; **Malaysian at Kiasu (Map 30)**; Korean at **Abeno Too (Map 12)** and **Corean Chilli (Map 12)**; Singaporese at **Singapore Garden (Map 66)**; Vietnamese at **Hai Ha (Map 89)** and **Viet Hoa Café (Map 88)** and Japanese at **Bento Café (Map 71)**. Tapas is another thing we get just right with **El Pirata of Mayfair (Map 9)**. And of course, because we're London, for every down-and-out corner spot, there's its posh cousin. Try glamorous Indian at **Amaya (Map 19)**, stylish Thai at **Crazy Bear (Map 3)**, and gourmet Malaysian at **Champor-Champor (Map 106)**.

If you're looking for a neighbourhood Italian, try **San Marco (Map 143)**, **Il Bacio (Map 63)** and **La Luna (Map 113)**. Mexican is another newcomer that's been thriving lately with **Wahaca (Map 24)**, **Taqueria (Map 29)** and **Crazy Homies (Map 29)**. In terms of French, if you haven't noticed, this is the cuisine of choice for any Michelin-starred restaurant in this town worth its salt. But for those of us on a smaller budget there's **Le Petit Prince (Map 72)**, **The Kensington Creperie (Map 36)** and **Savoir Faire (Map 4)**. One cuisine boom, which reflects that of the population, is of the Eastern European variety. For Hungarian, try **Gay Hussar (Map 12)**; Polish, try **Baltic (Map 105)**; and Russian try **Trojka (Map 70)**.

Eating Meat

Here's where we implore you, begging you on both knees, not to let yourself EVER stumble into one of those steakhouse chains, mainly around Leicester Square, that shall not be named. If we succeed in anything with this guide, it should be at least to give carnivores a decent alternative. If you're stuck on the Aberdeen Angus variety of beef, try the **Popeseye Steakhouse (Map 33)**. But if you're open to other options, Argentinian steakhouses are really where it's at right now, with **Gaucho (Map 8)** at the forefront and **Buen Ayre (Map 89)** not far behind. If you want steak with a heart of gold (read: ethically sourced) try **Hawksmoor (Map 91)**.

If you like your meat on a bun, go for **Gourmet Burger Kitchen (Map 24)** (the burgers are like six inches high!), **Camden Bar and Kitchen (Map 71)**, and **Haché (Map 71)**. If you'd rather someone else fired up your barbie, go for **Bodean's (Map 43)** or **Rodizo Rico (Map 80)**. If you're into eating things the rest of us see at the zoo, try **Archipelago (Map 3)** and **Chakalaka (Map 136)**.

Eating Veggie

In a town full of yoga bunnies, eco warriors and Madonna, veggie restaurants are pretty prevalent. And lucky for us, they're not just serving up nut roast. There are places that even sworn meat-eaters love. Get your carnivorous best mate to try the sweet potato curry at **Mildred's (Map 10)** or the home-cooked glutun dishes at **Eat and Two Veg (Map 2)**. If you're looking for a place to impress your new vegan girlfriend (you swear she's the one!), try **Rootmaster (Map 91)**. But there are plenty of other goodies like **Beetroot (Map 11)**, **Blah Blah Blah (Map 40)** and **Alara (Map 4)**. Also, remember Indian is always a good bet, like **Rasa N16 (Map 64)**, **Diwana Bhel Poori (Map 77)** or **Indian Veg Bhelpoori House (Map 80)**.

Our favourite restaurant (because we're all so ethical these days!)

While we're all busy saving the planet, so are London restauranteurs. One of the major new trends in this city has to be the eco-friendly restaurant trying its best to leave a smaller carbon footprint. **Acorn House (Map 5)** has to be our fave with its revolutionary approach to the eco-chic. Named 'the most important restaurant to open in London in the past 200 years', this environmentally-friendly culinary institution manages to combine a restaurant with a cooking school, training 10 aspiring chefs from the community, all underneath a recycled organic roof. The food is ethically sourced and local for the most part (they use boats since it comes from abroad). They serve up breakfast, lunch and dinner, adapting portions to fit your appetite in order to minimise waste. Not that there will be any. The food's brilliant too, with a dynamite seasonal menu. Plus they look good with a swish, minimalist interior. They really are the Gwyneth Paltrow/Chris Martin of restaurants: we love them but also kind of hate them because they're just so goddamn perfect.

Key: £: Under £10 / ££: £10–£20 / £££: £20–£30 / ££££: £30–£40 / £££££: £40+
*: Does not accept credit cards / †: Accepts only American Express / ††: Accepts only Visa and Mastercard
Time listed refers to kitchen closing time on weekend nights

Map 1 · Marylebone (West)

Beirut Express	112 Edgware Rd	020 7724 2700	££	2 am	Chaotic, rude and the best Lebanese in town.
Maroush IV	68 Edgware Rd	020 7224 9339	££	12 am	Wax philosophical while smoking a hookah out front.
Nippon Tuk	225 Edgware Rd	020 7616 6496	££££	11.15 pm	One to avoid for vertigo sufferers—astounding, 23rd floor views.

Map 2 · Marylebone (East)

Diwan	31 Thayer St	020 7935 2445	££	11 pm	Lebanese gorge spot.
Eat and Two Veg	50 Marylebone High St	020 7258 8595	££	10.30 pm	Just like mama's cookin'—only more soya. A lot more soya.
The Golden Hind	73 Marylebone Ln	020 7486 3644	££	10 pm	Fish and chips from the top-drawer. Can do BYOB
Gordon Ramsay at Claridge's	Brook St	020 7499 0099	£££££	11 pm	A rich perfectionist's culinary art deco dream.
Hush Brasserie	8 Lancashire Ct	020 7659 1500	££££	11 pm	European food al fresco. Go on a lunch hour holiday.
La Galette	56 Paddington St	020 7833 1380	£		Pretend you're a hot Parisian at a sexy crêpe breakfast.
Patisserie Valerie	105 Marylebone High St	020 7935 6240	£	9 pm	Boho coffee and pastry.
Sakura	9 Hanover St	020 7629 2961	££	10 pm	Authentic Japanese queue. Worth it for the food.

Map 3 · Fitzrovia

Archipelago	110 Whitfield St	020 7383 3346	£££££	10.30 pm	London's best, alright only, chocolate-covered scorpions and crocodile steaks.
Busaba Eathai	110 Wardour St	020 7255 8686	£££	11 pm	Never mind the shared benches, the food's too lovey.
Carluccio's Caffe	8 Market Pl	020 7636 2228	£££	11 pm	Pretty good for a chain. Have the espresso and ice cream.
Crazy Bear	26 Whitfield St	020 7631 0088	££££	10.30 pm	Thai deluxe. Where the media world feeds its clients.
Eagle Bar Diner	3 Rathbone Pl	020 7637 1418	££	11 pm	Trendy modern American diner; two words: Crocodile Burger.
Elena's L'Etoile	30 Charlotte St	020 7636 7189	£££££	11 pm	Old school French sophistication, politicians and journo's.
Govinda's	9 Soho St	020 7437 4928	£*	8 pm	Cheap Krishna food. You know the deal.
Icco Pizza	46 Goodge St	020 7580 9688	£	11 pm	Zen it is not - but who cares at £3.50 a pizza?
Latium	21 Berners St	020 7323 9123	£££	10.30 pm	Romantic (and pricey) first date place.
Market Place	11 Market Pl	020 7079 2020	£	1 am	Warm buzz all day/night. Hot clientele/tepid Prices.
Navarro's	67 Charlotte St	020 7637 7713	££	11 pm	Delicioso! Smells like Seville, tastes like Seville.
Neel Akash	93 Charlotte St	020 7637 0050	£££	11 pm	Eccentric staff, fantastic food.
Ragam	57 Cleveland St	020 7636 9098	££	10.45pm	Can't dis these dosas (potato crepes) at very decent prices.
Rasa Express	5 Rathbone St	020 7637 0222	£	11 pm	Take-away-priced Indian lunch boxes, seating included.
Roka	37 Charlotte St	020 7580 6464	£££	11 pm	Dazzling Izakaya concept Japanese.
Salt Yard	54 Goodge St	020 7637 0657	£££	11 pm	Intimate and sexy. Take a date. Get laid. Possibly.
Sardo	45 Grafton Way	020 7387 2521	££	10 pm	Hit after hit. Try the crab pasta.
Squat & Gobble	69 Charlotte St	020 7580 5338	£	4.30 pm	Scrumptious, cheap, tiny. Just squat and, um, gobble.
Stef's	3 Berners St	020 3073 1041	££	11 pm	You can't knock the gnocchi.
Thai Metro	36 Charlotte St	020 7436 4201	££	11 pm	Thai food, cooked well, served well, job done.

Map 4 · Bloomsbury (West)

Alara	58 Marchmont St	020 7837 1172	£££	7 pm	Hardcore veggie/vegan mecca, surprisingly good.
Bi Won	24 Coptic St	020 7580 2660	£	10 pm	Manhandling staff but great food.
Savoir Faire	42 New Oxford St	020 7436 0707	££	10.30 pm	Sweet little rustic restaurant, a stroll from Soho.

Key: £ : Under £10 / ££ : £10–£20 / £££ : £20–£30 / ££££ : £30–£40 / £££££: £40+
*: Does not accept credit cards./ † : Accepts only American Express / †† : Accepts only Visa and Mastercard
Time listed refers to kitchen closing time on weekend nights

Map 5 · Bloomsbury (East)

Acorn House	69 Swinton St	020 7812 1842	£££	10:30 pm	Eco-chic: the Gwyneth Paltrow of restaurants.
Aki Bistro	182 Gray's Inn Rd	020 7837 9281	££	11 pm	Almost too Japanese Japanese.
Bread and Butter Sandwich Bar	100 Judd St	020 7713 7767	£	9 pm	Notable for its very cheap al fresco fry ups.
Ciao Bella	86 Lamb's Conduit St	020 7242 4119	££	11 pm	Authentic, rustic feel Italian complete with piano.
Cigala	54 Lamb's Conduit St	020 7405 1717	££	10.45 pm	Great service and gorgeous salty Spanish bread.
The Food Bazaar	59 Gray's Inn Rd	020 7242 6578	£*	9 pm	Casual and friendly with great hot food selection.
Fryer's Delight	19 Theobald's Rd	020 7405 4114	£*	10 pm	No frills chippie; big portions of chunky, salty, greasy tastiness.
Konstam	2 Acton St	020 7833 5040	££	10 pm	All food sourced within London. Should be grim – actually delicious.
La Provence	63 Gray's Inn Rd	020 7404 4920	£	10 pm	Super-friendly staff and a generous hot food deal.
Mary Ward Centre	42 Queen Sq	020 7269 6000	£*	5pm	Hippy educational centre with a great organic cafe.
Swintons	61 Swinton St	020 7837 3995	££	9:30 pm	If Heaven made fishfinger sandwiches, they'd use Swintons' recipe.
Thai Candle	38 Lamb's Conduit St	020 7430 2472	£	10 pm	Cosy, cheerful with a nice lunchtime meal deal.

Map 6 · Clerkenwell

Bada Bing!	120 St John St	020 7253 3723	£	4 pm	Excellent lunch joint. The toasted ciabattas are divine.
Clarks Pie and Mash	46 Exmouth Market	020 7837 1974	£	5.30 pm	A last bastion of a lost London.
Dans Le Noir	30 Clerkenwell Green	020 7253 1100	££££	9pm	Blind waiters serve in pitch darkness: don't wear white.
The Eagle	159 Farringdon Rd	020 7837 1353	££	10:30 pm	London's first gastro pub—just look what they started.
Little Bay	171 Farringdon Rd	020 7278 1234	££	12 am	Posh-people food at cheapy-people prices.
Moro	34 Exmouth Market	020 7833 8336	£££££		DO believe the hype.
The Quality Chop House	94 Farringdon Rd	020 7837 5093	££	10.45pm	OMG it's so BRITISH. Meat and potatoes like nowhere else.
Sandwichman	23 Easton St	020 7833 9001	£	2.30 pm	Office delivery returns. Gourmet—and just 65p. Best lunch in London.
Sofra	21 Exmouth Market	020 7833 1111	££	11 pm	Eccentric little eatery: cheerful staff and a lovely ambience.
Vic Naylor's	38 St John St	020 7608 2181	£££	10.30 pm	Sting's gaff in Lock, Stock And Two Smoking Barrels. Nice.

Map 7 · Barbican / City Road (South)

Carnevale	135 Whitecross St	020 7250 3452	££	11 pm	Veggie on the cheap.
De Santis	Old St	020 7689 5577	££	9.30 pm	Like being in Milan; owner Enzo takes care of you
NUSA Kitchen	9 Old St	020 7253 3135	£	5 pm	People queuing? For ages? For soup? Now I've seen everything.
Warrin Thai Kitchen Stall	77 Whitecross St	n/a	£		Pad thai wokked while you wait.

Map 8 · Liverpool Street / Broadgate

Damascu Bite Kebab	21 Shoreditch High St	020 72470207	£*	1 am	It's the way they grill them from the outside.
Eyre Brothers	70 Leonard St	020 7613 5346	££	10:45 pm	Great place run by the Eyre brothers - Jane no relation.
Gaucho Grill	5 Finsbury Ave	020 7256 6877	££££	11 pm	Divine, ohmigod, melt-in-your-mouth steak. Oops, drooling!
Ponti's Caffe	176 Bishopsgate	020 7283 4889	£	24 hrs	24 hour cafe for the inebriated insomniac.

Map 9 · Mayfair / Green Park

El Pirata of Mayfair	5 Down St	020 7491 3810	£££	11:30 pm	Don't be put off by stuffy location – this is fucking good tapas.
Galvin at Windows	28th Floor, Hilton Park Lane	020 7208 4021	£££££	11 pm	Art Deco French overlooking Buckingham Palace. We're made for it.
L'Autre	5 Shepherd St	020 7499 4680	££££	11 pm	Polish meets Mexican. Surprisingly well.

Nobu	15 Berkeley St	020 7290 9222	£££££	12 am	Rob a bank on the way as it's bloody expensive!
The Ritz	150 Piccadilly	020 7493 8181	£££££	10 pm	High tea amidst ornaments and swank—resist temptation to swipe towels.
Theo Randall at the InterContinental	1 Hamilton Pl	020 7318 8747	£££££	11 pm	Sincere and stylish cuisine unfortunately hidden behind a hotel façade.
The Wolseley	161 Piccadilly	020 7499 6996	££££	12 am	Over-hyped. There. We said it.

Map 10 · Piccadilly / Soho (West)

Cecconi's	5 Burlington Gardens	020 7434 1500	££££	11.15pm	All day menu for the spoilt. Delicious breakfasts.
Dehesa	25 Ganton St	020 7494 4170	£££	11 pm	Faux-rustic protein-rich tapas, sweetie.
Mildred's	45 Lexington St	020 7494 1634	££	10.30 pm	Great food, sometimes crap service. Get the sweet potato curry to takeaway!
Mosaico	13 Albermale St	0207 409 1011	£££	11 pm	Stylish Italian. Prices more for the Mayfair Mamas.
Nordic Bakery	14 Golden Sq	020 3230 1077	£	7 pm	Authentic sticky cinnamon buns, Karelian pies and smoked Moomin.
Ping Pong	45 Great Marlborough St	020 7851 6969	££	11 pm	Don't leave without trying a char sui bun!
Sartoria	20 Saville Row	020 7534 7000	£££££	11 pm	The pick of the Conran restaurants.
Sketch	9 Conduit St	087 0777 4488	£££	1 am	Colossally trendy kitsch palace.
Taro	61 Brewer St	020 7734 5826	£££	10.30 pm	Where London's Japanese locals eat sushi.
Ten Ten Tei	56 Brewer St	020 7287 1738	£££££	10 pm	The Japanese restaurant Japanese people love.
Thanks for Franks	26 Fouberts Pl	020 7494 2434	£*	6 pm	Good sandwiches.
Toku @ The Japan Centre	212 Piccadilly	020 7255 8255	££	10 pm	The best gyoza outside of Tokyo.
Wagamama	10 Lexington St	020 7292 0990	£	11 pm	Reliable, speedy noodle chain.
Wild Honey	12 St George St	020 7758 9160	£££	10.30 pm	This Michelin star's got skillz (and a damn good tête-de-veau).
Yauatcha	15 Broadwick St	020 7494 8888	£££££	11.45 pm	Traditional Chinese tea-house meets star-spangled media haunt.

Map 11 · Soho (Central)

Balans	60 Old Compton St	020 7439 2183	££	3 am	Share a 4am breakfast with the likes of Amy Winehouse.
Bar Bruno	101 Wardour St	020 7734 3750	£*	10 pm	Hidden Italian cafe hidden gem. Authentically loud and friendly.
Beetroot	92 Berwick St	020 7437 8591	£	10 pm	Awesome veggie/vegan place.
Cafe Espana	63 Old Compton St	020 7494 1271	££		Highly recommended. 10% off for eating with castanets (possibly).
Hummus Bros	88 Wardour St	020 7734 1311	££	11 pm	Where hummus is the main dish.
Imli	167 Wardour St	020 7287 4243	£	11 pm	Tapas + curry. Fusion gone insane but somehow works.
Italian Graffiti	163 Wardour St	020 7439 4668	£££	11 pm	Less 'street' than the name suggest. Nice though.
Jerk City	189 Wardour St	020 7287 2878	£	10 pm	Jamaican fast food. In doubt? Go for ackee and saltfish.
Malletti	26 Noel St	020 7439 4096	£	3 pm	Amazing! Use your mobile and you won't get served.
Maoz	43 Old Compton St	020 7851 1586	£*	1 am	Falafeltastic!
Paul	49 Old Compton St	020 7287 6261	£	10 pm	French cafe/bakery chain. Amazing baguettes!
Pizza Express Jazz Club	10 Dean St	020 7439 8722	£	11 pm	Surprisingly, jazz takes the mediocre chain up a notch.
Randall & Aubin	16 Brewer St	020 7287 4447	£££	11 pm	Over-indulgently carnal seafood delights which only call for champagne.
Red Veg	95 Dean St	020 7437 3109	£*	10 pm	Veggie fast food joint.
Soho Thai	27 St. Annes Ct	020 7287 2000	££	11 pm	Thai with a good range. In set meals - go for starter NOT dessert.
St Moritz	161 Wardour St	020 7734 3324	££££	11.30 pm	Swiss cheese heaven.
Sugar Reef	42 Great Windmill St	020 7851 0800	££££	10.30 pm	Wannabe a WAG? Get in 'ere!
VitaOrganic	74 Wardour St	020 7734 8986	£*	10 pm	100% vegan. Superfood stews, warming coconut curries, raw choccy cake to-die-for.
Won Kei	41 Wardour St	020 7437 8408	££	10 pm	AKA Wonky's: institutionally rude service, cheap fast Chinese.

507

Arts & Entertainment · **Restaurants**

Key: £: Under £10 / ££: £10–£20 / £££: £20–£30 / ££££: £30–£40 / £££££: £40+
*: Does not accept credit cards / †: Accepts only American Express / ††: Accepts only Visa and Mastercard
Time listed refers to kitchen closing time on weekend nights

Map 12 · Soho (East)

Abeno Too	17 Great Newport St	020 7379 1160	££	11 pm	Addictive Okonomiyaki (pancakes) flipped and fried on the table.
Arbutus	63 Frith St	020 7734 4545	£££	11 pm	Chocolate soup! Worth it for that alone.
Bar Italia	22 Frith St	020 7437 4520	££	4.30 am	Soho institution; perfect for people-watching at any hour.
Barrafina	54 Frith St	020 7813 8016	£££	11 pm	Seriously, the best (and hippest) place for tapas.
Boheme Kitchen and Bar	19 Old Compton St	020 7734 5656	£££	11.45 pm	You want frites with that? Deliciously snobby comfort food.
Café Emm	17 Frith St	020 7437 0723	££	10.30 pm	Double-take cheap prices and wholesome fare. Wins popular vote.
Chinese Experience	118 Shaftesbury Ave	020 7437 0377	££	11 pm	Popular for a reason. Overwhelmed? Go for the always-great set menu.
Corean Chilli	51 Charing Cross Rd	020 7734 6737	££	12 am	Karaoke and stir-fries with the Korean cool kids.
Ed's Easy Diner	12 Moor St	020 7434 4439	££	12 am	It's like, you know? Soooo, like, American? You know?
Friendly Inn	47 Gerrard St	020 7437 4170	£	1 am	Where Londoners go for Chinese in Soho.
Garlic & Shots	14 Frith St	020 7734 9505	££££	1 am	Garlic, garlic and more garlic. No-go zone for vampires.
Gay Hussar	2 Greek St	020 7437 0973	££	10.45 pm	Everything from strudel to cherry soup at this old-school Hungarian.
Haozhan	8 Gerrard St	020 7434 3838	£££	11 pm	Can't pick? This is the one.
Kettners	29 Romilly St	020 7734 6112	£££££	12 am	Sit and sup with the champagne set.
La Porchetta Pollo Bar	20 Old Compton St	020 7494 9368	££	12 am	Cheap and cheerful Italian. In the West End? Well, exactly.
Le Beaujolais	25 Litchfield St	020 7836 2955	££	10 pm	Get insulted by a Frenchman here in London —Mais oui!
New World	1 Gerrard Pl	020 7734 0396	£	11.45 pm	Crispy duck, Dim Sum, custard dumplings... bring it on!
Stockpot	18 Old Compton St	020 7287 1066	££*	12 am	Fantastically cheap stodge.
Taro	10 Old Compton St	020 7439 2275	££	10.30 pm	Like Taro Brewer Street. But gayer, obviously.

Map 13 · Covent Garden

Belgo Centraal	29 Shelton St	020 7813 2233	£££	11 pm	Thoroughly enjoyable moules et frites. And beer... mmm... beer.
Café Mode	57 Endell St	020 7240 8085	££	11.30 pm	Pizza, pasta, salad. No fuss.
Candy Cakes	36 Monmouth St	020 7497 8979		8 pm	Cupcakes almost too beautiful to eat. But eat them anyway.
Food for Thought	31 Neal St	020 7836 9072	£	8.30 pm	Queues this long mean they've got cheap veg food right.
Great Queen Street	32 Great Queen St	020 7242 0622	£££	11 pm	Affordable and might be London's best gastropub.
Kulu kulu	51 Shelton St	0871 971 3476	£££	10 pm	Tiny conveyor belt sushi joint. Bang on the money.
Mon Plaisir	21 Monmouth St	020 7836 7243	£££	11.15pm	Not up to typical Paris standards, but still très bon!
The Photographers' Gallery	Great Newport St	020 7831 1772	£*	6 pm	Artsy coffee spot with photos on view.
The Punjab	80 Neal St	020 7836 9787	££	11.30 pm	Relive the days of the Raj in this old-school curry house.
Rock & Sole Place	47 Endell St	020 7836 3785	££	11 pm	London's oldest chippie. Est. 1871. On-site, fairy-lit picnic benches. Huge portions.
Sarastro	126 Drury Ln	020 7836 0101	££	11.30 pm	Hilarious over-the-top decor; includes fornicating cherubs.

Map 14 · Holborn / Temple

Asadal	227 High Holborn	020 7430 9005	££	10.30 pm	Go on—venture down those stairs—it's worth it.
Indigo @ OneAldwych	1 Aldwych	020 7300 0400	££	11 pm	Sunday brunch and a movie—all in the same place!

Map 15 · Blackfriars / Farringdon

Beppe's	23 West Smithfield	020 7236 7822	££	3 pm	As classically Italian as oversized sunglasses. Only much, much better.
The Bleeding Heart	Bleeding Heart Yard, off Greville St	020 7242 2056	£££	10:30 pm	Historic, hard to find, eccentric beauty.

Cafe du Marche	22 Charterhouse Sq	020 7608 1609		11 pm	Wonderful French cuisine in delightful venue. Tucked away in Charterhouse Square.
Kurz + Lang	1 St John St	020 7993 2923	£	11:30 pm	Ze German Bratwurst sausage at its zizzling best.
The Larder	91 St John St	020 7608 1558	£££	10:30 pm	Fresh, seasonal food, good breakfast menu and takeaway sarnies.
Pho	86 St John St	020 7253 7624	£	10:30 pm	Steaming bowlfuls for hungry Clerkenwell workers. Specialises in street food.
Portal	88 St John St	020 7253 6950	££££	10:15pm	Astoundingly good Portuguese. Swanky but not stuffy.
Smiths of Smithfield	67 Charterhouse St	020 7251 7950	££	10:45pm	Overflowing with yuppies and trendy types; pricey but tasty.
St Germain	89 Turnmill St	020 7336 0949.	£££	11 pm	Sleek, chic. Bon Appetit.
St John's Smithfield	26 St John St	020 7251 0848	£££	11 pm	This place is ALL about the offal.
Tinseltown	44 St. John St	020 7689 2424	£	24 hrs	Funky diner serving great late-night milkshakes.
Vivat Bacchus	47 Farringdon St	020 7353 2648	£££	9:30 pm	Three wine cellars and a cheeseroom. A ROOM of cheese.
Yo! Sushi	14 St Paul's	020 7248 8726	££	11 pm	Sushi in Paul's shadow.

Map 16 · Square Mile (West)

| Bar Bourse | 67 Queen St | 020 7248 2200 | | 12 am | Known as the Rolls Royce of City bars. And rightly so. |
| Sweetings | 39 Queen Victoria St | 020 7248 3062 | £££ | 4 pm | Old fashioned institution for nostalgia trips. Lunch only. |

Map 17 · Square Mile (East)

Gaucho City	1 Bell Inn Yard	020 7626 5180		11 pm	City clientele but this is the best steakhouse in the city. Located off side-street in former gold vaults.
The Mercer	34 Threadneedle St	020 7628 0001	££	9.30 pm	Proper British grub in a light contemporary atmosphere.
Rhodes 24	25 Old Broad St	020 7877 7703	£££££	8.30pm	Anyone for Gherkin (building) with your Michelin star?
Wasabi	52 Old Broad St	020 7374 8337	£*	10 pm	Delicious sushi and bento for those in a rush.

Map 18 · Tower Hill / Aldgate

Jeff's Cafe	14 Brune St	020 7375 2230	£	10 pm	Cheap as chips (which they serve here, incidentally).
Leon	3 Crispin St	020 7247 4369	£	10.30 pm	Fast food with a conscience. Gets old after a few visits.
S & M Cafe	48 Brushfield St	020 7247 2252	££	10 pm	Not what you think it is, perverts. Sausages and mash!

Map 19 · Belgravia

Amaya	Halkin Arcade, Motcomb St	020 7823 1166	££££	11.30 pm	Where the trendies go for their curry fix.
Boisdale, Victoria	15 Eccleston St	020 7730 6922	£££££	11 pm	Posh Scottish nosh. No deep-fried Mars Bars, sadly.
La Noisette	164 Sloane St	087 1426 9442	£££££	11 pm	Almost perfect. Good job, Gordon Ramsay.
One-O-One	101 Knightsbridge	020 7290 7101	££££	10 pm	One man's fish is another man's pleasure.
Yo! Sushi	102 Knightsbridge	020 7201 8641	££	10 pm	A London institution—we dream in sashimi on conveyor belts.

Map 20 · Victoria / Pimlico (West)

| Grumbles | 35 Churton St | 020 7834 0149 | ££ | 11 pm | Unfashionably unfussy Brit/French home-cooking. Gorgeous pies, no grumbles. |

Map 21 · Pimlico (East)

| The Regency Cafe | 17 Regency St | 020 7821 6596 | £* | 7 pm | Proper British fry-ups and atmosphere in this 1940's cafe. |
| Vincent Rooms | 1 The Victoria Centre, Vincent Sq | 020 7802 8391 | £££ | 7 pm | Brilliant food served by awkward catering students. |

Map 23 · St. James's

Inn The Park	St James' Park	020 7451 9999	££££	7.30pm	Watch the ducks watching you as you eat.
Laduree	71 Burlington Arcade	0207 491 9155	£££	10 pm	Grande Dame of Parisian tearooms and purveyor of cult macaroons.
Stockpot	38 Panton St	020 7839 5142	£*	10.45pm	Treacle pud & custard. Bish bash bosh.

Key: £: Under £10 / ££: £10–£20 / £££: £20–£30 / ££££: £30–£40 / £££££: £40+
*: Does not accept credit cards./ †: Accepts only American Express / ††: Accepts only Visa and Mastercard
Time listed refers to kitchen closing time on weekend nights

Map 24 · Trafalgar Square / The Strand

Bistro 1	33 Southampton St	020 7379 7585	££	11.30 pm	Posh kebabs etc at bargain prices.
Cafe in the Crypt	Trafalgar Sq	020 7766 1100	££	10 pm	Spooky sandwiches and fruit crumble.
Covent Garden Market Cafe	Covent Garden	020 7240 4844	£	10 pm	Cheap egg 'n' chips in heart of tourist London.
Farmer Brown	4 New Row	020 7240 0230	££*	8 pm	Cheap and very cheerful. Great lunches.
Gourmet Burger Kitchen	15 Maiden Ln	020 7240 9617	££	11 pm	Go for the Kiwiburger. Don't question the ingredients. Trust us.
India Club	143 Strand (Second floor, Strand Continental Hotel)	020 7836 0650	£	11 pm	Quirky run-down BYOB eaterie; more character than Brick Lane equivalents.
J Sheekey	28 St Martin's Ct	020 7240 2565	££££	11 pm	Old-fashioned seafood haven that the celebs still love.
RS Hispaniola	Victoria Embankment	020 7839 3011	£££	10 pm	Feel the bloat, on a boat.
Rules	35 Maiden Ln	020 7836 5314	£££££	10.30 pm	London's oldest restaurant with old-fashioned comfort food to match.
Wahaca	66 Chandos Pl	020 7240 1883	£££	11 pm	Tasty Mexican market food/tapas. Always busy.

Map 25 · Kensal Town

Thai Rice	303 Portobello Rd	020 8968 2001	££	10.30 pm	Jaw-dropping food in sterile, bland enviornment.

Map 29 · Notting Hill Gate

Beach Blanket Babylon	45 Ledbury Rd	020 7229 2907	££££	12 am	Maze of baroque nooks and crannies where celebs nibble discreetly.
Cafe Diana	5 Wellington Terrace	020 7792 9606	£	10.30 pm	Creepy, kitsch shrine to Princess Diana with so-so food.
Costas Fish Restaurant	18 Hillgate St	020 7727 4310	££	10.30 pm	Heavenly, Cypriot-run fish and chips. Hellish Notting Hill prices.
Crazy Homies	125 Westbourne Park Rd	020 7727 6771	££	10.15 pm	Avoid first date awkwardness over quality Mexican at this lively get-up.
The Electric Brasserie	191 Portobello Rd	020 7908 9696	££	10 pm	Uber-trendy, worth a visit for the eggs benedict alone.
Geales	2 Farmer St	020 7727 7528	£££	10.30 pm	Feels ever-so-slightly like a front to appease visiting Americans.
Lucky 7	127 Westbourne Park Rd	020 7727 6771	£££	10.30 pm	Atmospheric diner for wistful yuppies.
Taqueria	139 Westbourne Grove	020 7229 4734	££	11 pm	Wash down these fresh mini-tacos with a good tequila.

Map 30 · Bayswater

Berdees Coffee Shop	84 Bishop's Bridge Rd	0207 727 0033	£	9 pm	Hubbly Bubbly Jubbly. Chubbly?
Kiasu	48 Queensway	020 7727 8810	£	11 pm	The best budget Indonesian/Malaysian cuisine. Mmmm....Char Kway Teow...
Royal China	13 Queensway	020 7221 2535	£££	11.15 pm	Keep the Cantonese dim sum comin'!
Tiroler Hut	27 Westbourne Grove	020 7727 3981	££££	12 am	Dementedly kitsch Austrian madhouse with lederhosen-clad waiters.

Map 32 · Shepherd's Bush (West)

Abu Zaad	29 Uxbridge Rd	020 8749 5107	£	11 pm	A colourful Syrian welcome. Posh Kebabs.
Esarn Kheaw	314 Uxbridge Road	020 8743 8930	£	11.30 pm	Outstanding Thai. Transport your taste buds to Bangkok.
Vine Leaves Taverna	71 Uxbridge Rd	020 8749 0325	£	1 am	Friendly staff, traditional grub, huge portions.

Map 33 · Shepherd's Bush

Jasmine	16 Goldhawk Rd	020 8743 7886	££	11 pm	Awesome Thai.
Popeseye	108 Blythe Rd	020 7610 4578	££££	10.30 pm	London's ONLY member of the Aberdeen Angus Society.

Map 34 · West Kensington / Olympia

The Belvedere Restaurant	Abbotsbury Road	027 6021 2380	£££	11 pm	Sublime setting—the same cannot always be said for the service.

Arts & Entertainment • **Restaurants**

Map 35 • Kensington

Byron	222 Kensington High St	020 7361 1717	££	10 pm	London's best burger? Locals in the know say so.
Clarke's	124 Kensington Church St	020 7221 9225	££	10 pm	Elegant, English fine dining. Perfect brunch spot if feeling refined.
Maggie Jones's	6 Old Court Pl	020 7937 6462	£££	10.30 pm	A British culinary time warp, but we like it anyway.

Map 36 • South Kensington / Gloucester Rd

The Kensington Creperie	2 Exhibition Rd	020 7589 8947	£*	11 pm	The best sweet and savoury crepes in London.
Little Japan	32 Thurloe St	020 7591 0207	£*	11.30 pm	Wowzers: bento for a fiver? Suspicious and delicious.
Odonno's	14 Bute St	020 7052 0732	£	11 pm	Gelato fix for homesick Italians and ice-cream freaks alike.

Map 37 • Knightsbridge

Zuma	5 Raphael St	020 7584 1010	£££	12am	If your gal likes sushi, ideal for a romantic night out.

Map 38 • Chiswick

Boys Authentic Thai	95 Chiswick High Rd	020 8995 7991	££	10.30 pm	The staff are as funky and fresh as the food.
Chez Gerard	163 Chiswick High Rd	020 8742 1942	£££	11 pm	"The best steak-frites this side of Paris." Ya wallet'll cry!
Chris' Fish and Chips	19 Turnham Green Terrace	020 8995 2367	£*	12 am	It's all British-ness wrapped in warm, greasy paper.
The Devonshire	126 Devonshire Rd	020 7592 7962	£££	11 pm	A more affordable version of Ramsay.
High Road Brasserie	162 Chiswick High Rd	020 8742 7474	££	11 pm	As good as it looks. The continent comes to the High Road.
Kalamari	4 Chiswick High Rd	020 8994 4727	££	12 am	For those with a feta fetish.
Zizzi	231 Chiswick High Rd	020 8747 9400	££	11.30 pm	Skip the mains - cut straight to the heavenly Apple Crumble.

Map 39 • Stamford Brook

Carpenter's Arms	91 Black Lion Ln	020 8741 8386	£££	11 pm	As gastropub as it gets.

Map 40 • Goldhawk Rd / Ravenscourt Park

Blah Blah Blah	78 Goldhawk Rd	020 8746 1337	££*	10.30 pm	Eccentric, worldly vegetarian. Kinda like your ex, only cooler.
Lowiczanka Polish Cultural Centre	238 King St	020 8741 3225	££	10 pm	Stodgy grub, hard drink, concrete block. So Polish you'll need a passport.
Sagar	157 King St	020 8741 8563	££	11 pm	Yummy South Indian veggie food at a great price.

Map 41 • Hammersmith

The Gate	51 Queen Caroline St	020 8748 6932	££££	10 pm	Light and airy by day, cosy at night. Lovely food.

Map 42 • Baron's Court

Bombay Bicycle Club	352 North End Rd	020 7610 3311	£££	11 pm	Lighter, brighter, more expensive, less authentic Indian restaurant. Still yum.
Ta Khai	100 North End Rd	020 7386 5375	££	10 pm	Decent, cheap food. Interior as tacky as its name suggests.

Map 43 • West Brompton / Fulham Broadway / Earls Court

The Blue Elephant	3 Fulham Broadway	020 7385 6595	££££	11.30 pm	Disney's version of Bangkok--grandiose, expensive, but oh, so good.
Bodean's	4 Broadway Chambers	020 7610 0440	£££	11 pm	Stuff yourself on BBQ pulled-pork sandwiches. Yee haw!
Chutney Mary	535 King's Rd	020 7351 3113	££££	11.30 pm	Get coddled over a curry (at a price).
Vingt Quatre	325 Fulham Rd	020 7376 7224	££	24 hrs	24 hour booze! Incidentally, the food is very good.
Yo! Sushi	Fulham Road	020 7385 6077	££	11 pm	Japanese conveyor belt sushi for beginners.

(511)

Arts & Entertainment · **Restaurants**

Key: £ : Under £10 / ££ : £10–£20 / £££ : £20–£30 / ££££ : £30–£40 / £££££ : £40+
*: Does not accept credit cards./ † : Accepts only American Express / †† : Accepts only Visa and Mastercard
Time listed refers to kitchen closing time on weekend nights

Map 44 · Chelsea

Aubergine	11 Park Walk	020 7352 3449	££££	11 pm	Foie gras, lobster and truffles. Need we say more?
Eight Over Eight	392 King's Rd	020 7349 9934	££££	11 pm	Exotic and dripping with celebs.

Map 45 · Chelsea (East)

Four o nine	409 Clapham Rd	020 7737 0722	££££	10.30 pm	Inviting and intimate, it's nice.
Le Columbier	145 Dovehouse St	020 7351 1155	£££	11 pm	Vive le Bistro!
My Old Dutch Pancake House	221 King's Rd,	020 7376 5650	£	11.30 pm	Sweet or savory pancakey goodness in the heart of Chelsea.
Tom's Kitchen	27 Cale St	020 7349 0202	££££	11 pm	Crush-worthy (maybe just us?) Tom Aiken's British brasserie masterpiece.
Tom's Place	1 Cale St	020 7351 1806	£££	11 pm	Posh chippie.

Map 46 · Sloane Square

The Admiral Codrington	17 Mossop St	020 7581 0005	£££	10.30 pm	Go for simplicity here. Even the chips they get exactly right.
Bibendum Restaurant & Oyster Bar	81 Fulham Rd	020 7581 5817	£££££	11 pm	French institution with a cool (literally) oyster bar.
Foxtrot Oscar	79 Royal Hospital Rd	020 7352 4448	££	10 pm	Tango Alpha Sierra Tango Yankee.
Gordon Ramsay	68 Royal Hospital Rd	020 7352 4441	£££££	11 pm	Mmmmmm...debt...
Le Cercle	1 Wilbraham Pl	020 7901 9999	££££	12 am	Tapas-sized French yumminess. Pears with caramel popcorn, anyone?
Tom Aikens	43 Elystan St	020 7584 2003	£££££	11 pm	Artistic approach to just about everything.

Map 47 · Fulham (West)

The River Café	Thames Wharf, Rainville Rd	020 7386 4200	£££	11 pm	Fine dining by the Thames for champagne socialists.

Map 49 · Parson's Green

Kebab Kid	90 New Kings Road	020 7731 0427	£*	10 pm	Kebabs so impressive you could bring your gran here.

Map 50 · Sand's End

Deep	The Boulevard, Imperial Wharf	020 7736 3337	££££	11 pm	Set for Gordon Ramsay's F-word. F-ing good itself.

Map 51 · Highgate

The Bull	13 North Hill Ave	0845 456 5033	£££	11 pm	Chic eatery with perfectly positioned front terrace.
Cafe Rouge	6 South Grove	020 8342 9797	££	11 pm	Decent French restaurant and cafe chain
Kiplings	100 North Rd	020 8340 1719	££	11.30 pm	Swanky curry joint boasts Raffles Hotel stylings including resident pianist.
Papa Del's	347 Archway Rd	020 8347 9797	££	11 pm	Nice place. Good cookies. £3 pizzas after 9pm!
Red Lion And Sun	25 N Rd	020 8340 1780	££££	10 pm	Excellent Sunday roasts.

Map 52 · Archway (North)

Bengal Berties	172 Archway Rd	020 8348 1648	££	11 pm	Spit and sawdust venue with excellent nosh.
Fahrenheit	230 Archway Rd	020 8347 0333	££	11 pm	Corking Caribbean food with a broad smile.
The Lighthouse	179 Archway Rd	020 8348 3121	££	11 pm	Outstanding fresh fish joint flies beneath radar.

Map 53 · Crouch End

Banners	21 Park Rd	020 8348 2930	££££	11.30 pm	Notoriously child-friendly but the breakfasts make up for that.
Hot Pepper Jelly	11 Broadway Parade	020 8340 4318	££*	5 pm	Pepperphobes probably shouldn't come to this culinary wonder.
Thaitanic	66 Crouch End Hill	020 8341 6100	£	11 pm	Groanworthy name, moanworthy food!

Arts & Entertainment • Restaurants

Map 55 • Harringay Ladder

Sofra	421 Green Lanes	N/A	£*	12 am	A gem amidst gems - cheap and friendly. Get the stew!

Map 56 • Hampstead Village

La Creperie De Hampstead	77 Hampstead High St	N/A	£	11 pm	No crap crepes at this sublime French street stall.
The Louis Patisserie	32 Heath St	020 7435 9908	£	6 pm	Tea and gorgeous cakes beloved of elderly Eastern European gentlemen.

Map 58 • Parliament Hill / Dartmouth Park

Al Parco	2 Highgate West Hill	020 8340 5900	£	10 pm	Probably the best pizza in London.
Cafe Mozart	17 Swain's Ln	020 8348 1384	££	10 pm	Great place for lunch on a sunny day
Kalendar	15 Swains Lane	020 8348 8300	££	11 pm	Pre-Heath brekkie, mid-Heath lunch or post-Heath dinner. All good!

Map 60 • Archway

Archgate Café	5 Junction Rd	020 7272 2575	£	10 pm	Lovely English breakfasts face-off against equally ace Turkish food.
Junction Café	61 Junction Rd	020 7263 2036	£*	10 pm	Greasy. Spoon.
Kingfisher	657 Holloway Rd	020 7263 2163	£	10 pm	Holloway's top fish and chip outlet.
Mosaic Café	24 Junction Rd	020 7272 3509	££	10.30 pm	Head for the back garden sun-trap in Summer.
Nid Ting	533 Holloway Rd	020 7263 0506	£££	11.15pm	Bigger, meatier portions than most Thai Restaurants.
RRC Thai Café	36 Highgate Hill	020 7561 0421	£	10.30 pm	Cheap, tasty and beautifully presented Thai food.
St Johns	91 Junction Rd	0207 272 1587	££££	11 pm	Gastro pub oasis stranded among the pound-shops of Archway.
The Toll Gate	6 Archway Close	020 7687 2066	££	11 pm	On with the pince-nez for slightly self-satisfied veggie venue.

Map 61 • Holloway (North)

The Landseer	37 Landseer Rd	020 7263 4658	££	9.30 pm	Gastropub extraordinaire.
Pasteleiro	22 Seven Sisters Rd	078 7159 9938	£*	6 pm	Brazilian street grub.

Map 62 • Finsbury Park

Fassika	152 Seven Sisters Rd	020 7272 7572	££	12 am	Intimate with lovely food. Distinctly flirty waitresses though...
Le Rif	172 Seven Sisters Rd	020 7263 1891	£*	10 pm	Essential for all your banter and microwaved Tagine needs.
Petek	96 Stroud Green Rd	020 7619 3933	£	10.45 pm	Classy but cheap Turkish.

Map 63 • Manor House

Il Bacio	178 Blackstock Rd	020 7226 3339	££	11 pm	Friendly, reliable and huge portions.
New River Cafe	271 Stoke Newington Church St	020 7923 9842	£	11 pm	Steamy windows and top hangover cure fry-ups.

Map 64 • Stoke Newington

56	56 Newington Green	020 7359 6377	££	11.30 pm	Bring a date.
Anglo Asian	60 Stoke Newington Church St	020 7254 9298	££	11.30 pm	Classic curry house right down to the free sherry.
Blue Legume	101 Stoke Newington Church St	020 7923 1303	£	11 pm	Dreamy eggs benedict, served under a giant aubergine.
Rasa N16	55 Stoke Newington Church St	020 7249 0344	££	11.30pm	Vegetarian-style Indian cooking at its mouth-watering best.
Three Crowns	175 Stoke Newington Church St	0207 241 5511	££	9.30 pm	Impressive Victorian pub that's undergone gastropubification—sofas, sausage n mash, ales n candles.
Yum Yum	187 Stoke Newington High St	020 7254 6751	£££	11 pm	Tasty tasty, Thai Thai. Go for the Kang Mussaman.

Map 65 • West Hampstead

The Green Room	182 Broadhurst Gardens	020 7372 8188	££	11 pm	West Hampstead's newest joint brimming with charm. Nice risotto.

Arts & Entertainment · **Restaurants**

Key: £ : Under £10 / ££ : £10–£20 / £££ : £20–£30 / ££££ : £30–£40 / £££££: £40+
* : Does not accept credit cards./ † : Accepts only American Express / †† : Accepts only Visa and Mastercard
Time listed refers to kitchen closing time on weekend nights

Map 66 · Finchley Road / Swiss Cottage

Bradleys	25 Winchester Rd	020 7722 3457	£££	11 pm	Your friendly face in the neighbourhood that loves wine.
Camden Arts Centre	Arkwright Rd	020 7472 5500	£	6 pm	Excellent food in buzzing artistic setting.
Singapore Garden	83 Fairfax Rd	020 7328 5314	££	11 pm	Surprising flavours make a welcome alternative on a night out.

Map 68 · Kilburn High Road / Abbey Road

Little Bay	228 Belsize Rd	020 7372 4699	££*	11 pm	Crazy cheap. Crazy cute!

Map 69 · St. John's Wood

Tupelo Honey	27 Parkway, Camden	020 7284 2989	££	11pm	A coffee-shop, wine bar and restaurant combined.

Map 70 · Primrose Hill

Cafe Seventy Nine	79 Regents Park Rd	020 7586 8012	£	6 pm	Excellent veggie fare, though you might have to wait.
Fishworks	57 Regents Park Rd	020 7586 9760	£££	10.30 pm	It's a chain, it's expensive but it's really rather good.
The Honest Sausage	Inner Circle, Regent's Park	020 7935 5729	£	7 pm	Great greasy spoon.
J restaurant	148 Regents Park Rd	020 7586 9100	££	11 pm	Excellent food, especially brunch. Tempestous service.
Legal Cafe	81 Haverstock Hill	020 7586 7412	£	10 pm	Great coffee, good food and wifi: a pleasant working environment.
Lemonia	89 Regents Park Rd	020 7586 7454	££	11.30 pm	Fancy a real Greek meal?
Manna	4 Erskine Rd	020 7722 8028	££	11.30 pm	Aesthetically gorgeous veggie restaurant, serving scrumptious food.
Melrose and Morgan	42 Gloucester Ave	020 7722 0011	£	8 pm	Tasty food and coffee. Good for solo snacks.
Odette's	130 Regents Park Rd	02075868569	£££	1 am	Delectably dainty restaurant, high-class service.
Primrose Bakery	69 Gloucester Ave	020 7483 4222	£	6 pm	A deliciously dinky bakery. These cakes can't be missed.
Trojka	101 Regents Park Rd	020 7483 3765	££	10 pm	Authentically spartan but colourful decor. Nice 'n' quirky
Two Brothers	297 Regents Park Rd	020 8346 0469	££	10 pm	Middle class fish & chips.

Map 71 · Camden Town / Chalk Farm / Kentish Town (West)

Bar Gansa	2 Inverness St	020 7267 8909	££	12 am	More buzzing and pleasurable than a rampant rabbit.
Bar Solo	20 Inverness St	020 7482 4611	££	1 am	Where'd they find the waitresses? On the set of Clueless?
Bento Cafe	9 Parkway	020 7482 3990	££	11pm	Exquisite Japanese food at very reasonable prices.
Camden Bar And Kitchen	102 Camden High St	020 7485 2744	££	11 pm	Great burgers at this bohemian gem; sorry, McDonalds!
Camden Kitchen	102 Camden High St	020 7284 2744	££	11pm	Funky eatery, great for a relaxed date.
Cotton's	55 Chalk Farm Rd	020 7485 8388	££	10 pm	No hustle and bustle, just chill Jamaican style.
Gilgamesh	The Stables Market, Chalk Farm Rd	020 7428 4922	*	12 am	Awesome surroundings will confuse the hell out of future archaeologists.
Haché	24 Inverness St	020 7485 9100	££	10.30 pm	Burger heaven for both vegetarians and carnivores.
Kim's Vietnamese Food Hut	Unit D, Camden Lock Palace		£*		Once you pass the Spanish Inquisition, some excellent slop.
Limani	154 Regents Park Rd	020 7483 4492	£££	11 pm	Greek-Cypriot fare in a sophisticated environment. Friendly service.
Marathon Cafe	87 Chalk Farm Rd	020 7485 3814	£*	4 am	Legendary late-night venue serving kebabs, chips and beer.
Marine Ices	8 Haverstock Hill	020 7482 9003	£	11 pm	Fantastic ice cream restaurant with '70s decor and autographed photos.
Market	438 Parkway	020 7267 9700	£££	11 pm	The only restaurant in Camden deserving of the name.
Muang Thai	71 Chalk Farm Rd	020 7916 0653	£	11 pm	Quiet vibe, tinkly music, reliably decent food.
My Village	37 Chalk Farm Rd	020 7485 4996	£	9 pm	Cute ethnic organic shop serving food, tea and coffee.

Than Binh	14 Chalk Farm Rd	020 7267 9820	£	10 pm	Excellent Vietnamese with very friendly and chatty staff.
Viet-anh Cafe	41 Parkway	020 7284 4082	£	11 pm	Surly service, cheap plentiful food. Would it hurt to smile?
Woody Grill	1 Camden Rd	020 7485 7774	£	12 am	Late night post-alcohol food without salmonella poisoning.
Yumchaa Tea Space	91 Upper Walkway, West Yard, Camden Lock Market	020 7209 9641	£	6 pm	Mon-Fri: 8am to 6pm The carrot cake… oh, mama!
Zorya Imperial Vodka Room	48 Chalk Farm Rd	020 7485 8484	££	12 am	Vodka, vodka and more vodka. Oh…and gorgeous food too.

Map 72 · Kentish Town

Bintang Cafe	93 Kentish Town Rd	020 7813 3393	££	11 pm	Good for eating copiously in a gaudy shack.
Café Euro Med	225 Kentish Town Rd	020 7267 7761	£	9 pm	Fry ups with feta. Possibly not OK.
Eat Zone	18 Fortess Rd	020 7485 0152	£*	11 pm	Quick and delicious, with roughly 1 gazillion choices. Addictive.
Le Petit Prince	5 Holmes Rd	020 7267 3789	££	11 pm	Adorable homage to French cartoon character with excellent merguez.
Mario's Cafe	6 Kelly St	020 7284 2066	£	10 pm	Saint Etienne's local greasy spoon.
The Oxford	256 Kentish Town Rd	020 7485 3521	££	9.45 pm	Smug comfort eating.
Pane Vino	323 Kentish Town Rd	020 7267 3879	££	10.30 pm	Staff can be Italian. Food can be fantastic.
Phoenicia	186 Kentish Town Rd	020 7267 1267	£	10 pm	Coffee n baclava, falafel, meze. A real steal.

Map 74 · Holloway Road / Arsenal

Morgan M	489 Liverpool Rd	020 7609 3560	£££££	11 pm	Divine Frenchie. Mais zut alors! £1,200 bottles of wine!
Tbilisi	91 Holloway Rd	020 7607 2536	£££	11 pm	Get your Georgian on.

Map 75 · Highbury

San Daniele Del Friuli	72 Highbury Park	020 7226 1609	£££	12 am	Like mama used to make—well someone had to say it.
Sariyer Balik	56 Green Lanes	020 7275 7681	£££	12 am	Turkish Seafood.

Map 76 · Edgeware Road / Marylebone (North)

Mandalay	444 Edgware Rd	020 7258 3696	£	10.30 pm	Cheap treats await, despite the God awful situation.
Sea Shell Of Lisson Grove	49 Lisson Grove	020 7224 9000	££	10.30 pm	Pescatarians will love this place - sorry, carnivores!
Zen Spice Market	Melcombe Place	020 7723 8890	££*	11 pm	Station sushi.

Map 77 · Mornington Crescent / Regent's Park

Chutneys	124 Drummond St	020 7388 0604	££	11.30 pm	Flavoursome, no-frills, fill-yer-boots affair. Bargainous buffet colossal.
Diwana Bhel Poori	121 Drummond St	020 7387 5556	££	11 pm	South-Indian veggie with tasty dosai and puris.
The Green Note	106 Parkway	020 7485 9899	££	11 pm	Excellent veggie tapas with a side of bongo drums.
Mestizo	103 Hampstead Rd	020 7387 4064	£££	11 pm	Great. The margarita is made by the devil himself.

Map 78 · Euston

Asakusa	265 Eversholt St	020 7388 8399	£££	11.30pm	Authentic Japanese.
Camino	3 Varnisher's Yard	020 7841 7331	£££	12 am	Sophisticated Spanish restaurant in King's Cross. Seems wrong, somehow.
Chop Chop Noodle Bar	1 Euston Rd	020 7833 1773	£	11 pm	Great for a quick and cheap meal. Massive portions.
El Parador	245 Eversholt St	020 7387 2789	££	11 pm	Great tapas. A little ray of sunshine in your mouth.
Great Nepalese	48 Eversholt St	020 73588 6737	££	11 pm	Really the only option in the area.
Kitchin	Caledonia St			11 pm	Round-the-world all-you-can-eat. Vile and great.
Last Word Cafe	96 Euston Rd, St. Pancras	020 7380 1933	£	5 pm	Coffee, croissants with the bonhomous boffins at the British Library.
The Somerstown Coffee House	60 Chalton St	020 7691 9136	££	10 pm	Bistro food in grade II listed pub. Excellent set menu.

515

Arts & Entertainment · **Restaurants**

Key: £ : Under £10 / ££ : £10–£20 / £££ : £20–£30 / ££££ : £30–£40 / £££££ : £40+
* : Does not accept credit cards / † : Accepts only American Express / †† : Accepts only Visa and Mastercard
Time listed refers to kitchen closing time on weekend nights

Map 79 · King's Cross

Addis	42 Caledonian Rd	020 7278 0679			Lovely food with convivial sloth-like service.
Dallas Burger Bar	257 Caledonian Rd	020 7278 4955	£*	9 pm	JR smiles down as you destroy your arteries. Hilarious.
Euro Café	299 Caledonian Rd	020 7607 5362	£	10 pm	Loveable caff with some unusual specials.
Marathon	196 Caledonian Rd	020 7837 4499	££	12 am	Raw meat, ritualistic coffee and crazed dancing.
Menelik	277 Caledonian Rd	020 7278 0679	££	12 am	If only more places let you eat with your hands.
The New Didar	347 Caledonian Rd	020 7700 3496	£	12 am	Friendly staff willing to strike deals. Haggling gets you everywhere.
Oz	53 Caledonian Rd	020 7278 9650	£	10 pm	Unusually well-kempt greasy spoon.
Tony's Natural Foods	10 Caledonian Rd	020 7837 5223	£	11 pm	Vegan salad bar with peaceout garden, man.
Yum Yum	48 Caledonian Rd	020 7278 4737	£	11 pm	Super-cheap Chinese that may even remain in your stomach.

Map 80 · Angel / Upper St

Afghan Kitchen	35 Islington Green	020 7359 8019	£££*	10.45pm	Only a few tables; Islington's smallest - and biggest - Afghan place.
The Albion	10 Thornhill Rd	020 7607 7450	££	10 pm	How many places offer whole suckling pigs? Not enough.
Alpino	97 Chapel Market	020 7837 8330	£	4 pm	This, guv'nor, is a proper tea'n'two slices caff. Alright?
The Breakfast Club	31 Camden Passage	020 7226 5454	££	9.30 pm	Not just breakfast, not a club. But just so gooood.
Candid Café	3 Torrens St	020 7837 4237	£	10 pm	Laid-back, arty cafe for dreamy types. Candle-lit. Perfect for lingering.
Desperados	127 Upper St	020 7226 3222	££	11.30 pm	Garish. More like the Mexico of MTV than the real world.
Elk in the Woods	39 Camden Passage	020 7226 3535	££	10.30 pm	Laid-back, hunting-themed eatery.
Fig and Olive	151 Upper St	020 7354 2605	££	11 pm	Incredibly busy at weekends which can affect service and quality.
Gem	265 Upper St	020 7359 0405	££	11 pm	A good vibe is precious.
House	63 Canonbury Rd	020 7704 7410	£££	10.30 pm	Gastro bar-restaurant where seasonal food's served with flair. For those feeling flush.
Indian Veg Bhelpoori House	93 Chapel Market	020 7833 1167	£	10 pm	Honest all-you-can-eat Indian. Veggie propaganda on walls.
Isarn	119 Upper St	020 7424 5153	££	11 pm	Pretty, flower-adorned food, green curry cooked to perfection. Candle-lit courtyard.
Itsuka	54 Islington Park St	020 7354 5717	£	12 am	Cheap set menus and heartfelt J-Pop.
La Forchetta	73 Upper St	020 7226 6879	££	11.30 pm	Unpretentious, cheap pizza. Eat fast, then leg it.
La Porchetta	141 Upper St	020 7288 2488	££	11 pm	This little pig says yes to good cheap pizza.
Le Mercury	140 Upper St	020 7354 4088	££	1 am	This place will seduce you AND your mother.
Masala Zone	80 Upper St	020 7359 3399	££	11 pm	Cheap, good thalis served on metal trays.
Mem & Laz	8 Theberton St	020 7704 9089	££	11 pm	Mediterranean chaos by candlelight.
Olive Grill	61 Upper St	020 7226 9002	£		The falafels are so good you may quit kebabs. Forever.
Ottolenghi	287 Upper St	020 7288 1454	££	10 pm	Staff you'll want to take home to meet your mum.
Pizzeria Oregano	19 St Alban's Pl	020 7288 1123	££	11 pm	Great pizza and lentil soup. Delicious odd couple.
Rodizo Rico	77 Upper St	020 7354 1076	£££	11 pm	Meat. And lots of it.
Tortilla	13 Islington High St	020 7833 3103	££	10 pm	Damn good burritos!
The Trawlerman Fish Shop	205 Upper St	020 7354 0276	£*	11 pm	Top-notch British stodge.
Zaffrani	47 Cross St	020 7226 5522	££	11 pm	Thinking man's curry.

Map 81 · Canonbury

Sabor	108 Essex Rd	020 7226 5551	££££	11 pm	Latin American; even the tables are tropical.
Zigni House	330 Essex Rd	020 7226 7418	£	12 am	Hearty East African eatery with boho, raffish charm.

Map 82 · De Beauvoir Town / Kingsland

Casaba	162 Essex Rd	020 7288 1223	££	7 pm	Fresh spin on Turkish meze and shisha bar.
Huong Viet	Englefield Rd	020 7249 0877	££	11 pm	A crumbling old bath house? Look again.

Map 83 · Angel (East) / City Rd (North)

Fifteen	15 Westland Pl	0871 330 1515	£££££	10 pm	Lots of Jamie Oliver. Lots of great, expensive food.

Map 84 · Hoxton

The Bean	126 Curtain Rd	020 7739 7829	£*	8 pm	Decent coffee! It's hard to find, you know.
The Diner	128 Curtain Rd	020 7729 4452	£££	10.30 pm	Door-stopper burgers that should come with health warnings.
Macondo	Hoxton Sq	020 7729 1119	£	10 pm	Pleasant blend of cocktail bar and European cafe society.
Rivington Bar and Grill	28 Rivington St	020 7729 7053	££	11 pm	Emin on the walls, meat in the buns.
Yelo	Hoxton Sq	020 7729 4626	£	11 pm	Suspiciously quick service, but cheap and tasty so who cares?

Map 85 · Stoke Newington (East)

Bagel House	2 Stoke Newington High St	020 7249 3908	£*	10 pm	Bagels to rival Brick Lane and without the queues.
Cafe Z Bar	58 Stoke Newington High St	020 7275 7523	£*	11 pm	Popular grease-shop/hangover center for Stokey Lefties.
Testi	38 Stoke Newington High St	020 7249 7151	£££	12 am	Yes, it's named after bollocks. No, it's really not bollocks.

Map 86 · Dalston / Kingsland

19 Numara Bos Cirrik	34 Stoke Newington Rd	020 7249 0400	££	10 pm	Meat, meat, meat – oh and onion, pomegranate and turnip salad.
The Best Turkish Kebab	125 Stoke Newington Rd	020 7254 7642	£*	12 am	Feed your soul. Always buzzing.
Evin Bar and Cafe	115 Kingsland High St	020 7254 5634	££	11pm	Fantastic Turkish place without the grease factor. Speciality is gozleme.
Mangal 1	10 Arcola St	020 7275 8981	£*	12 am	May the grill's smoke guide you, meat-loving friends.
Mangal 2	4 Stoke Newington Rd	020 7254 7888	££	12 am	Gilbert & George aren't the only ones loving this one.
Mr Bagel's	15 Ridley Rd	020 7923 4331	£*	24 hrs	Where gangstas like to get jerk chicken bagels at 4am
Peppers and Spice	20 Kingsland High St	020 7275 9818	£*	10.30 pm	The real deal: jerk, oxtail, festival, plantain, ackee. Everyting irie.
Shanghai	41 Kingsland High St	020 7254 2878	££	10.30 pm	Tasty, good-value Chinese hiding behind the facade of a dingy old Kaff.
Somine	131 Kingsland High St	020 7254 7384	£*	24 hrs	Reanimating red lentil soup, Turkish style. Around the clock.
Stone Cave	111 Kingsland High St	020 7241 4911	££	12 am	Cave look and cave feel. Up-scale(ish) Turkish. And great.

Map 87 · Hackney Downs / Lower Clapton

India Gate	75 Lower Clapton Rd	020 8986 0505	£*	11 pm	Very, very cheap, pretty cheerful and a little rank.
Parioli	90 Lower Clapton Rd	020 75023288	£	9 pm	Best food of any kind in Clapton.
Pogo Cafe	76 Clarence Rd	020 8533 1214	£*	9 pm	Vegan co-op community caff. Real food for thought.

Arts & Entertainment · **Restaurants**

Key: £: Under £10 / ££: £10–£20 / £££: £20–£30 / ££££: £30–£40 / £££££: £40+
*: Does not accept credit cards./ †: Accepts only American Express/ ††: Accepts only Visa and Mastercard
Time listed refers to kitchen closing time on weekend nights

Map 88 · Haggerston / Queensbridge Rd

Faulkner's	424 Kingsland Rd	020 7254 6152	£££	10 pm	Famous fish and fries (oh OK – chips).
LMNT	316 Queensbridge Rd	020 7249 6727	£££	10.45 pm	Eat inside an urn or by a sphinx's paws.
Usha	428 Kingsland Rd	020 7241 0836	£	11 pm	One of few curry houses in the area. Consistently good.
Viet Hoa Cafe	70 Kingsland Rd	020 7729 8293	£	11:30 pm	Bland looking cafe hides gorgeous delicacies.

Map 89 · London Fields / Hackney Central

Buen Ayre	50 Broadway Market	020 7275 9900	££££	10.30 pm	Vegetarians take note - run for the hills.
Cafe Bohemia	2 Bohemia Pl	020 8986 4352	£	11 pm	Feeling Bohemian? Quirky cafe with live blues/jazz/world Saturday nights.
Cat and Mutton	76 Broadway Market	020 7254 5599	££	10 pm	Gastropub without the gastropub nastiness.
Corner Deli	121 Mare St	0208 986 0031	£	9 pm	Nice spot for brunch away from the bustle of Broadway Market.
Hai Ha	206 Mare St	020 8985 5388	££*	11 pm	Brilliant BYO Vietnamese cafe.
R Cooke and Sons	9 Broadway Market	020 7254 6458	£*	8 pm	Lor' love a duck! Pie n' mash shop - liquor an' all!
The Spurstowe Arms	68 Greenwood Rd	020 7254 4316	££	11 pm	Suntrap beer garden, good wine selection and gamey menu. Marvellous.

Map 90 · Homerton / Victoria Park North

The Empress of India	130 Lauriston Rd	020 8533 5123	£££	10 pm	Spiffy menu from brekkie through to dinner in Hackney Village
The Fish House	126 Lauriston Rd	020 8533 3327	££	9.45pm	Not as cheap as chips but still very good.

Map 91 · Shoreditch / Brick Lane / Spitalfields

Beigel Bakery	159 Brick Lane	087 1332 8040	£*	24 hrs	For 3am cravings; salted beef bagel from the Beigel Bakery.
Brick Lane Clipper Restaurant	104 Brick Ln	020 7377 0022	££	12 am	For less spice-oriented connoisseurs, Bengali Clipper's exceptional lamb korma.
Cafe Bangla	128 Brick Lane	020 7247 7885	££	12 am	Popular Bangladeshi adorned with psychedelic and surreal fantasy art.
Drunken Monkey	222 Shoreditch High St	020 7392 9606	££	12 am	Debauched, dimly-lit dim-sum drinking hole. Chinese lanterns and lethal mojitos.
Ethiopian Food Stall	Sunday Upmarket, Truman's Brewery, Brick Lane	N/A	£*		One of many great food stalls, get Brazilian desert after!
Green and Red	51 Bethnal Green Rd	020 7749 9670	££	11 pm	Foot-tappin' Mexican cantina for fab tacos and proper guacamole. Ole!
Hackney City Farm	1 Goldsmiths Row	020 7729 6381	££	4.30 pm	Animals! In Hackney! And some overpriced fry-up.
Hanoi Café	98 Kingsland Rd	020 7729 5610	££	11 pm	Cosy Viet joint, where the whole family's around.
Hawksmoor	157 Commercial St	020 7247 7392	£££	10.30 pm	France and America forget their differences for some serious steakage.
Jones Dairy Cafe	23 Ezra St	020 7739 5372	£	3 pm	Sit back and watch the world go by at Columbia Road
Le Taj	96 Brick Ln	020 7247 0733	££	11 pm	Bengali AND Indian menus, BYO, curry house.
Les Trois Garcons	1 Club Row	020 7613 1924	££££	11 pm	Kitch décor/slick service/fantastic grub.
Noodle King	185 Bethnal Green Rd	020 7613 1032	£*	11.30 pm	Half the normal price; double the normal portions. Come hungry.
The Premises	201 Hackney Rd	020 7729 7593	££	11 pm	Bistro swarming with musicians thanks to next door's recording studio.
Rootmaster	Elys Yard	07912 389314	££	10 pm	Eat on a bus without looking homeless.
Song Que	134 Kingsland Rd	020 7613 3222	££	11 pm	Still Little Vietnam's queen. An authentic, no-nonsense affair.
St John Bread and Wine	94 Commercial St	020 7251 0848	£££	11 pm	Minimalist and meaty. Anyone for deep-fried pig's head?
Story Deli	91 Brick Ln	020 7247 3137	£	9 pm	Lo-tech pizza joint. Think hipster Pizza Express.
Viet Grill	58 Kingsland Rd	020 7739 6686	££	11 pm	Eccentric but tasty. Non edible tropical fish as decor...

Map 92 · Bethnal Green

Bistrotheque	23 Wadeson St	020 8983 7900	££	11 pm	Brunch, burlesque and pianist playing Smells Like Teen Spirit. Fabulous.
E Pellicci	332 Bethnal Green Rd	020 7739 4873	£	4:30 pm	Challenge your hangover to survive their fry-ups.
Little Georgia	87 Goldsmiths Row	020 7739 8154	££	10 pm	Hearty fayre from the former Soviet State. No drinks licence.
Wild Cherry	241 Globe Rd	020 8980 6678	££	4 pm	Buddhist staff serve yummy breakfasts to hungover partiers. Instant karma.

Map 93 · Globe Town / Mile End (North)

L'Oasis	237 Mile End Rd	020 7702 7051	££	11 pm	Well-loved local eaterie.
Matsu	558 Mile End Rd	020 8983 3528	££	11 pm	Japanese food? In Mile End? You're 'avin a giraffe aintcha?
The Morgan Arms	43 Morgan St	020 8980 6389	£££	12 am	Which joker invented the term "gastropub"? This is one of them.
Winkles	238 Roman Rd	020 8880 7450	££	10.30 pm	Outstanding seafood. Fishmonger's and delivery service available too.

Map 94 · Bow

Chicchi	516 Roman Rd	020 8141 4190	£*	7 pm	The Italians reclaim Roman Road.
G.Kelly Pie & Mash shop	526 Roman Rd	020 8980 3165	£	7 pm	Servin' 'ot 'ome-made pies, jellied eels 'n mash since 1937.
The Roman Tandoori	432 Roman Road	020 8980 1390	££	10 pm	If you can't stand eels, 'ave a curry instead.

Map 95 · Whitechapel (West) / St Katharine's Dock

The Empress	141 Leman St	020 7265 0745	££	11:45 pm	Forget Brick Lane. This is where it's at.

Map 96 · Whitechapel (East) / Shadwell (West) / Wapping

Il Bordello	81 Wapping High St	020 7481 9950	£££	11 pm	Upscale neighbourhood Italian.
Tayyabs	83 Fieldgate St	020 7247 6400	£	12 am	Lipsmacking seekh kebabs alone are worth the queues.

Map 97 · Stepney / Shadwell (East)

Wapping Food	Wapping Wall	020 7680 2080	£££	11 pm	Stunning dining in 100 year old powerstation/ art gallery. Go!

Map 98 · Mile End (South) / Limehouse

La Figa	45 Narrow St	020 7790 0077	££	11 pm	Tasty Italian in courtyard setting.
The Narrow	44 Narrow St	020 7592 7950	£££	11 pm	Gordon Ramsay's nod to gastropubs - cracking views.
Orange Room Cafe	63 Burdett Rd	020 8980 7336		11:30 pm	Tasty, fresh Lebanese food in a wasteland of stodgy takeaways.

Map 100 · Poplar (West) / Canary Wharf (West)

1802 Bar	Hertsmere Rd	0870 444 3886		11 pm	Dine inside the warehouse built by Napoleonic prisoners.
Beluga Café	West India Quay	0871 971 5473		11 pm	Overlook the dock and enjoy the seafood.
Browns	Hertsmere Rd	020 7987 9777		11 pm	Always reliable.
la tasca	Hertsmere Rd	020 7531 9990		11 pm	Tapas anyone?
Nicolas	480 One Canada Sq	020 7512 9092	££	10.30 pm	Micro French restaurant and vintners in one.
Plateau	Canada Pl	020 7715 7100	££££	10.30 pm	Striking views and truffle gnocchi.
Tiffin Bites	22 Jubilee Place	020 7719 0333	££	10 pm	Eat curry, watch Bollywood films.
Ubon by Nobu	34 Westferry Circus	020 7719 7800	££££	11 pm	Our favourite Nobu. (We just like saying that).

Map 101 · Poplar (East) / Canary Wharf (East)

Gun	27 Coldharbour	020 7515 5222	£££	11 pm	Enjoyed by 18th century dockers and city workers alike.

Map 103 · Cubitt Town / Mudchute

Mudchute Kitchen	Pier St	020 7515 5901	£	5 pm	City farm's award winning kitchen.

Key: £: Under £10 / ££: £10–£20 / £££: £20–£30 / ££££: £30–£40 / £££££: £40+
*: Does not accept credit cards / ††: Accepts only American Express / ††: Accepts only Visa and Mastercard
Time listed refers to kitchen closing time on weekend nights

Map 104 · South Bank / Waterloo / Lambeth North

Anchor & Hope	32 The Cut	020 7928 9898	££££	10.30 pm	A British gastro-pub obsession, long waits though.
Canteen	Belvedere Rd	084 5686 1122	££	10.30 pm	A menu that sums up the best of British food with aplomb.
The Cut Bar	66 The Cut	020 7928 4400	££	11 pm	Brilliant chips. A cut above the rest.
Giraffe	Southbank	020 7928 2004	££	10.45pm	Good crowd pleaser. Though too much world music and balloons.
Livebait	45 The Cut	020 7928 7211	£££	11 pm	Very fishy, in a very good way.
Marie's Cafe	90 Lower Marsh	020 7928 1050	£	10.30 pm	Greasy spoon by day, a no-frills, super-yum BYO thai by night.
Oxo Tower Wharf	Barge House St	020 7803 3888	££££	11pm	You might have to rob a bank, but the view's amazing.
RSJ	33 Coin St	0207 928 4554	£££	11 pm	Forget about those shitty South Bank chains. Go here.
Skylon	Belvedere Rd	020 7654 7800	££££	10.45 pm	Expensive but staffs' uniforms and view make up for it.
Studio 6	Gabriels Wharf	020 7928 6243	££	11 pm	Service with a reluctant grunt doesn't stop the crowds.

Map 105 · Southwark / Bankside (West)

Amano	20 Sumner St	020 7234 9530	£	10 pm	For post-Tate pizza.
Baltic	74 Blackfriars Rd	020 7928 1111	££££	10.30 pm	Try Polish Hunters stew: made with real Polish Hunters. Probably.
Blackfriars Cafe	169 Blackfriars Rd	020 7928 4034	£	10 pm	Old-school, family-run greasy spoon; amazing fry-ups.
The Table	85 Southwark St	020 7401 2760	£*	10.30 pm	Go and find out why we're all obsessed.
Tapas Brindisa	18 Southwark St	020 7357 8880		11 pm	If you can bear the crowds; lovely market-bordering eaterie.
Tate Modern Restaurant	Sumner St	020 7887 8888	££	6 pm	Stunning views, shit food, clueless staff.

Map 106 · Bankside (East) / Borough / Newington

Amano	Clink St	020 7234 0000	££	10 pm	Trust Amano for stone-baked pizza and freshly-made flatbreads. We do.
Boot and Flogger	10 Redcross Way	020 74071184	££	8 pm	Splendidly gentleman's club-esque—all Savile Row suits and chesterfield sofas.
Brew Wharf	Brew Wharf Yard, Stoney St	020 7940 8333	££	11 pm	Unusual comfort food and tasty home brews.
Cantina Vinopolis	1 Bank End	020 7940 8333	££££	10.30 pm	Gourmet food and wine at a bad museum? Believe it.
Champor-Champor	62 Weston St	020 7403 4600	£££	10.15pm	Jaw-droppingly inspired high-end Malaysian cuisine. Totally inspired.
El Vergel	8 Lant St	020 7357 0057	£		Its Latin breakfast: Oh. My. God. Sooooo good.
Feng Sushi	13 Stoney St	020 7407 8744	££	10 pm	The best sushi in London and available to takeaway. Dangerous!
Fish!	Cathedral St	020 7407 3803	£££	10.30 pm	Great fish. Simple. Let it have its exclamation mark.
Fusebox	12 Stoney St	020 7407 9888	£	5 pm	Quick fusion fare that's well worth the queue.
Hing Loon	159 Borough High St	020 7378 8100	£	11 pm	Stupidly cheap. Very cheerful. The duck rocks.
Roast	The Floral Hall, Stoney St	020 7940 1300	££	9.30 pm	Meat, glorious meat. High-end food. Fab location.
Silka	Southwark St	020 7378 7777	££	11.30 pm	Curry house that won't damage your arse in the morning.
Tas	72 Borough High St	020 7403 7200	£££	11 pm	Meze madness.
Wright Bros Oyster Bar	11 Stoney St	020 7403 9554	£££	10.30 pm	Tastebuds say no, but libido says YES.

Map 107 · Shad Thames

Butlers Wharf Chop House	36 Shad Thames	020 7403 3403	£££	11 pm	What better place for British best than under Tower Bridge?
Delfina	50 Bermondsey St	020 7357 0244	£££	11 pm	Gallery/restaurant offering works of art on your plate.
Le Pont de la Tour	36 Shad Thames	020 7403 8403	£££££	11 pm	Blair & Clinton's rendezvous. Posh but gosh!
M Manze Pie and Mash	87 Tower Bridge Rd	020 7407 2985	£	2.30 pm	As English as it gets. Try it once.
Magdalen	152 Tooley St	020 7403 1342	££££	10.30 pm	Forever fascinating Franco-Spanish cuisine.
Village East	171-173 Bermondsey St	020 7357 6082	£££	11 pm	Superior food. Slick surroundings.

Map 108 · Bermondsey

Arancia	52 Southwark Park Rd	020 7394 1751	££	11 pm	A very decent neighbourhood Italian. Try the pumpkin gnocchi.

Map 109 · Southwark Park

Mayflower	117 Rotherhithe St	020 7237 4088	£££	9.30 pm	The pub Sunday Lunch was invented for.
Simplicity	1 Tunnel Rd	020 7232 5174	££	10.30 pm	Boldly goes where no restaurant has gone before: Rotherhithe.

Map 111 · Rotherhithe (East) Surrey Quays

Café Nabo	Surrey Docks Farm, Rotherhithe St	020 7231 1010	££		Rid the toxins with a healthy farmyard lunch.

Map 112 · Kennington / Elephant and Castle

Dragon Castle	100 Walworth Rd	020 7277 3388	££	11 pm	Odd locale for such a curious pocket of culinary authenticity.
Lobster Pot	3 Kennington Ln	020 7582 5556	£££	10.30 pm	Dine to a soundtrack of seagull caws. We don't kid.

Map 113 · Walworth

La Luna	380 Walworth Rd	020 7277 1991	££	11 pm	Ignore exterior. It's the garlic bread inside that counts.

Map 115 · Old Kent Road (East)

Roma Café	21 Peckham Park Rd	020 7639 7730	£		Escape Peckham and enjoy a good fry-up here.

Map 117 · Deptford (West)

Yellow House	37 Plough Way	020 7231 8777	£££	10.30 pm	The food stands out as much as the yellow building.

Map 119 · Deptford (East)

Kaya House	37 Deptford Broadway	020 8692 1749	££	10.45 pm	Tiny but excellent. Toilet is in the kitchen!
Manzes	204 Deptford High St	020 8692 2375	£		Who ate all the pies? You'll certainly want to.

Map 120 · Greenwich

Inside	19 Greenwich South St	020 8265 5060	£££	11 pm	Surprisingly sophisticated worldly foods for a modest local.

Map 121 · Camberwell (West)

New Dewaniam	225 Camberwell New Rd	087 1426 2594	£	12 am	Mouth-watering Indian takeaway for a tenner.
Su-Thai	16 Coldharbour Lane	020 7738 5585	££	10 pm	Reassuringly delicious Massaman curry & corn fritters.

Map 122 · Camberwell (East)

Caravaggio	47 Camberwell Church St		£		Cheap Italian with impressive fare. Stands out from the rest.

Map 124 · Peckham East (Queen's Road)

805 Bar Restaurant	805 Old Kent Rd	020 7639 0808	£££		West African oasis. In Peckham..

Map 127 · Coldharbour Lane / Herne Hill (West)

Café Prov	2 Half Moon Ln	020 7978 9228	£££	10 pm	Local art (for sale) decorates this relaxed restaurant/bar/ cafe.
Ichiban Sushi	58 Atlantic Rd	020 77387 006		11 pm	The bee's knees.
The Lounge	56 Atlantic Rd	020 7733 5229	£	10 pm	A local favourite for breakfast, recovery and hanging on weekends.
New Fujiyama	5 Vining St	020 7737 6583	£	10.30 pm	This place blows Wagamama's out of the water.

Arts & Entertainment · **Restaurants**

Map 128 · Denmark Hill / Herne Hill (East)

Lombok	17 Half Moon Ln	020 7733 7131	£££	10:30 pm	From stir-fries to curries, a no-fuss pan-Asian standby.
Number 22	22 Half Moon Ln	020 7095 9922	££££	10:30 pm	Gorge yourself on Spanish wine, sherry and loads of brilliant tapas.

Map 129 · East Dulwich

The Palmerston	91 Lordship Ln	020 8693 1629	££££	10 pm	Gastropub that's a lot more gastro than pub.
Sea Cow	37 Lordship Ln	020 8693 3111	££		Fishmonger meets chip shop with Billingsgate beauties.

Map 130 · Peckham Rye

Thai Corner Cafe	44 Northcross Rd	020 8299 4041	££*	11 pm	Tiny, laidback neighbourhood cafe.

Map 131 · Vauxhall / Albert Embankment

Thai Pavillion East	82 Kennington Rd	020 7582 6333	££££	12am	Thai food you will crave in retro round room.

Map 132 · Battersea (West)

Ransom's Dock	35 Parkgate Rd	020 7223 1611	£££	11 pm	Friendly, stylish, likes wine and children.
La Tosca	31 Battersea Sq	020 7978 5395	££		Get some Italian style al fresco action.

Map 134 · South Lambeth

Bar Estrella	115 Old South Lambeth Rd	020 7793 1051	£	12 am	Football on telly, tapas in tummy. The heart of Little Portugal.
Hot Stuff	19 Wilcox Rd	020 7720 1480	£	10 pm	Hard to find. Slightly dinghy. Mental Staff. Amazing food.

Map 135 · Oval

Adulis	44 Brixton Rd	020 7587 0055	£	11 pm	C'mon, it's yummy and cheap. And we can't cook Eritrean.
The Bonnington Café	11 Vauxhall Grove	check website for Chef's mobile	£*	10:30 pm	Wonderful vegetarian meals in a communified (ex-squat) environment.

Map 136 · Putney

Chakalaka	136 Upper Richmond Rd	020 8789 5696	££	10:30 pm	A truly zebra-fied exterior but fantastically authentic South African food.
Talad Thai	320 Upper Richmond Rd	020 8789 8084	££	10:30 pm	Thai-ny, family-run restaurant with Thai market, cooking classes and Thai regulars.

Map 137 · Wandsworth (West)

Miraj	123 Putney Bridge Rd	020 8875 0799	£	10 pm	Curry in a hurry? Cheap, tasty take away joint.
Yia Mas	40 Upper Richmond Rd	020 8871 4671	££		Cosy, welcoming Greek/Cypriot place. No plate smashing.

Map 138 · Wandsworth (Central)

Brady's	513 Old York Rd	020 8877 9599	££	11 pm	Up-market fish and chip cafe and take-away.
Kathmandu Valley	5 West Hill	020 8871 0240	££	11:45 pm	Nepalese is the new black (read: curry).

Map 139 · Wandsworth (East)

Spice of Life	147 St John's Hill	020 7924 2112	££	11:30 pm	Peerless curry restaurant on the hill.

Map 140 · Clapham Junction / Northcote Rd

I Sapori di Stefano Cavallini	146 Northcote Rd	020 7228 2017	££		Totally authentic. Pasta made on site daily.

Map 142 · Clapham Old Town

Benny's	30 North St	020 7622 5868	£	11.30 pm	Marvel at Benny's chest hair, chat and fish and chips.
Mooli	36 Old Town	020 7627 1166	££	11 pm	Good twist on the Italian local.
Tom Ilic	123 Queenstown Rd	020 7622 0555	£££	10.30 pm	British fare that's the business - a result of hard-earned talent.
Trinity	4 The Polygon	020 7622 1199	£££	10.30 pm	How to do local dining really quite fantastically well.

Map 143 · Clapham High Street

Café Wanda	153 Clapham High St	020 7738 8760	££	10.30 pm	Back away from the fantastic dessert counter, real slow.
The Fish Club	57 Clapham High St	020 7720 5853	££	10 pm	Posh fish and chips, worth the extra clams.
The Pepper Tree	19 Clapham Common South Side	020 7622 1758	£*	11 pm	Speedy Thai with soul.
The Rapscallion	75 Venn St	020 7787 6555	££££	10 pm	Good fall-back. Wee bit dear.
San Marco Pizzeria	126 Clapham High St	020 7622 0452	££	11.30 pm	Arguably the best pizza outside Italy – take that New York!
Tsunami	5 Voltaire Rd	020 7978 1610	££££	10:30 pm	The new Nobu. Unbelievable. Unfortunate name.

Map 144 · Stockwell / Brixton (West)

Speedy Noodle	506 Brixton Rd	020 7326 4888	£*	1 am	Prime location and the cheapest, worst food in Brixton.
SW9 Bar Cafe	11 Dorrell Pl	0207 738 3116	£	9 pm	Great hangover curing breakfasts (and hangover causing booze).

Map 146 · Earlsfield

Thai Cafe and Noodle Bar	346 Garratt Ln	020 8874 9036	£	10.30 pm	Reliable, cheap and tasty.

Map 147 · Balham (West)

The Bombay Bicycle Club	95 Nightingale Ln	020 8673 6217	££	10 pm	Award winning curries.
Chez Bruce	2 Bellevue Rd	020 8672 0114	££££	10.30 pm	Worth its fancy-pants (read Michelin) star.

Map 148 · Balham (East)

Dish Dash	Bedford Hill	020 8673 5555	££	11 pm	Tasty food. Tiny portions. Laid back vibe.
Harrison's	15 Bedford Hill	020 8675 6900	££	10.30 pm	Great food if you can tolerate the 'look at me!' crowd.

Map 149 · Clapham Park

Dexter's	36 Abbeville Rd	020 8772 6646	££	3 pm	Perfect brunch spot for hungry hangovers.
Grissini	31 Abbeville Rd	020 8675 6260	££		Cosy neighbourhood joint. Good midweek deals.

Map 150 · Brixton

Asmara	386 Coldharbour Ln	020 7737 4144	££	11.15pm	Disconcerting but delicious curry with pancakes to mop it up.
Khan's	24 Brixton Water Ln	020 7326 4460	££	11 pm	Great curry, and BYO to boot. Have it!
Negril	132 Brixton Hill	020 8674 8798	£	10 pm	Tasty Carribean with veg options (which are joy).
Opus Café	89 Acre Ln	0207 737 3777	£	6 pm	Mon-Fri 8:00-18:00 Cakes and coffee. Niceness.
Upstairs Bar & Restaurant	89 Acre Ln	020 7733 8855	££££	10.30 pm	A real find. Getting discovered. Sshhh.

Map 151 · Tooting Bec

Mirch Masala	213 Upper Tooting Rd	020 8672 7500	£	12 am	Cheap, no frills, award-winning curries. Sublime.

Map 152 · Tooting Broadway

Jaffna House	90 Tooting High St	020 8672 7786	££	12 am	Mediocre curry fare beneath flourescent bulbs.
Radha Krishna Bhavan	86 Tooting High St	020 8682 0969	££	11.30 pm	Busy, buzzing, bhavan of South Indian curry.
Rick's Cafe	122 Mitcham Rd	020 8767 5219	£££	11 pm	Tooting's best kept culinary secret.
Sette Bello	8 Amen Corner	020 8767 5225	££	11 pm	A kiss on each cheek for every diner. Homey Italian.
Urban Coffee	74 Tooting High St	020 8682 9479	£	10 pm	Nifty WiFi caff in the bowels of Tooting.

523

There is a high street chain of estate agents which delights in revamping previously less than appealing neighbourhoods by adding "village" to the end of every name. Lauriston Village sounds infinitely more attractive than South Hackney, no? It's an irritating knock-on effect of the age of spin and marketeering that we live in (and rocketing house prices), but nowhere is it more true than when shopping in the capital—we have a multitude of villages at our fingertips. There are parts of London which are trying desperately to hold on to their traditional roots, holding fast to old-fashioned shopkeeping where everyone knows everyone and every customer counts (such as Lamb's Conduit Street), and there are streets which have been "gentrified" but again, are doing their best to preserve (or in some cases, rejuvenate) a sense of community (such as Broadway Market). These places give a sense of locality even in the depths of London, but even when in the West End, amongst the multinational big boys, it's best to keep this idea of the city as a conurbation and plan which areas will best serve your needs—if only to save your feet. You really can find anything you want in London if you know where to go, and it's this feeling that you can unearth hidden treasure at any given moment that delights residents and keeps visitors coming back.

Department Stores

When it comes to department stores, **Selfridges (Map 2)** is without a doubt the daddy—arguably, you can just get everything you need from here. **Harvey Nics (Map 37)** and **Harrods (Map 37)** are very much for ladies who lunch, and the Knightsbridge set use them like corner shops—that's not to say they don't have their uses. For a more personal touch, **Fenwick (Map 2)** and **Liberty (Map 10)** are wonderful British institutions which take you far from the madding crowd.

Haute

For flexing that plastic, Bond Street has always been the place to spend but Bruton Street, which branches off the main drag, is setting quite a precedent with **Matthew Williamson (Map 9)**,

Stella McCartney (Map 10) and **Diane Von Furstenburg (Map 9)** all in residence. Always one to mix things up and throw us off track, **Marc Jacobs' (Map 9)** London store is to be found on Mount Street—check out the Marc for Marc Jacobs range for affordable designer garb. If you want to feel like Alice down the rabbit hole, make a trip to **Dover Street Market (Map 9)**, owned by Rei Kawakubo of Comme Des Garçons—a real experience even if you're not buying. For those of us on a budget, **Topshop (Map 3)** is the grand kahuna of high street shopping—seventh heaven on three floors for fashionistas. For super-slick, sharp ready to wear you can't beat Spanish stores, **Zara (Map 2)** and **Mango (Map 3)**—rumour has it that some savvy style sharks keep Zara Oxford Street's delivery days in their diary to nab the latest boxfresh fashions. New contenders for higher end highstreet include **Cos (Map 10)** and **Hoss Intropia (Map 10)**, and let's not forget our stateside cousins who have sent ripples of excitement through the fash pack by opening flagship stores of **Banana Republic (Map 10)** and **Abercrombie and Fitch (Map 10)** in our fair city. There are also little shopping oases to be found in the capital. St Christopher's Place is hidden behind the hustle and bustle of Oxford Street and houses cool European brands like **Marimekko (Map 2)** and **Noa Noa (Map 2)** alongside more familiar fare. Kingly Court (behind Carnaby Street—itself a great shopping spot for trend-led labels) has some nice boutiques in **The Black Pearl (Map 10)** and **Twinkled (Map 10)**. The area around Seven Dials in Covent Garden which includes Neal's Yard is eclectic with high-end boutiques like **Orla Kiely (Map 13)** and **Koh Samui (Map 13)** on Monmouth and skatewear at **Slam City Skates (Map 13)** and **Superdry (Map 13)** on Earlham.

Vintage

London is an Aladdin's cave for vintage finds and there are some well-kept secrets in the far reaches of the city's boroughs if you're prepared to make the trip. Some of the best-known, best-loved shops include **Rellik (Map 25)** in Portobello (surely the number one destination for vintage now that Steinberg and Tolkien is sadly no more?), **Annie's (Map 80)** in Islington (a favourite of La Moss), and **Beyond Retro (Map 91)** and **Absolute Vintage (Map 91)** in Shoreditch (famous hunting ground for stylists). For genuine thrift, the turnover of goods in our charity shops is mind-boggling. **Oxfam Dalston (Map 86)** is renowned for being a good rummage: it's hit and miss but then that's the nature of thrifting. The **Salvation Army (Map 80)** in Islington is an extremely busy shop which can turn out some real gems from well-heeled N1 residents. However, if you want some certainty of finding designer threads you can't beat the **British Red Cross** in both **Victoria (Map 19)** and **Chelsea (Map 45)** where you will discover the likes of Ralph Lauren, Armani and pairs of Manolos amongst the knick-knacks. The **Notting Hill Housing Trust (Map 35)** is also a reliable source of local celebrities' cast-offs from like... yesterday. For all you true vintage fashion fiends who want to mingle with like-minded souls and find genuine vintage togs (i.e. pre-1980s) the **Frock Me! Vintage Fashion Fair (Map 45)** and **Anita's Vintage Fashion Fair (Map 140)** are unequalled for choice and variety.

Sportswear

Lillywhite's (Map 10) is the obvious place to go for cheap sportswear—it has earned a bit of a bargain basement tag where once it was prestigious (the Lillywhites were instrumental in the game of cricket during the 19th century) but it doesn't stop the shoppers pouring in, and tourists buying their favourite London team football shirts. **Sweatshop (Map 17)** is a chain of stores but the original Teddington shop is frequented by world-class athletes as well as Sunday joggers. Most of the members of staff have sporting backgrounds and are highly trained so as to find the right shoe for you. In stock is a range of high-tech clothing from the likes of Adidas and Ronhill. More and more Londoners are turning to the speed, efficiency and sheer fun of having a bike, and **Bobbin Bicycles (Map 5)** in Clerkenwell embraces that fun with a range of beautiful vintage and special edition bikes. Their website proclaims "We're more like a boutique than a bikeshop,"—to keep overheads down there is no store but an appointment only service at Bobbin's workshop,

giving a real personal touch. If you don't see getting from A to B is a style event, **Recycling (Map 112)** does a fab job at selling second-hand wheels. **Slam City Skates (Map 13)** is the only place for Southbank skaters to get their duds.

Housewares And Home Design

John Lewis (Map 2) is a British standard and has been the store of choice for middle-class couples' wedding lists over the decades. Their maxim is "never knowingly undersold", with fantastic staff (who all get a share of the profits) they provide a wide range of quality wares with which to set up home. **Twentytwentyone (Map 80)** is a designer's wet dream selling originals as well as new items. So impressive is their collection that they often lend out furniture to film companies who want the authentic look of an era on set. The wonderfully named **Timorous Beasties (Map 6)** make wickedly amusing wallpapers—their most famous being a toile de jouy design for modern days (spot the alcopop-drinking chavs and the Gherkin in the background). For a no-nonsense approach to home furnishing visit the old geezers on Mare Street at **Lazy Days (Map 89)** where they can often be found on the sofas outside. Furniture is bought and sold—some electrical appliances included—and they also do light removals. If you want personable, "Where can I find one of these?" type of service try **Russell's Hardware and DIY (Map 151)** in Tooting.

Electronics

Tottenham Court Road has long been the bastion of bargainous electronic equipment and a stroll down said street will throw up numerous options. In all cases it's best to shop around, play prices against each other and barter until you get the lowest price—often cash payment will get you well below the RRP. **Computer Exchange (Map 3)** is the one-stop shop for gaming, DVDs, computing and phones, which—as the name suggests—will part-exchange and knock money off for cash transactions. For audiovisual, **Richer Sounds (Map 106)** is a trusted chain, and if we're talking electronics in the purist sense,

Arts & Entertainment • Shopping

Maplin (Map 4) is geek central. If you're not interested in getting the lowest price and just want good service and guarantees, **John Lewis (Map 2)**, as ever is your best bet. Photography enthusiasts should check out the **London Camera Exchange (Map 24)** for old-school SLRs and digital cameras. They specialise in Pentax, Nikon and of course, Leica.

Food

London is the place for truffle hunters and sybarites to seek out a smorgasbord of culinary delights. We have New York (and in particular, the Magnolia Bakery) to thank for the invasion of cupcake stores but the original and best is the **Hummingbird Bakery (Map 29)** which makes Red Velvet cupcakes that taste like little pieces of baked heaven. Just try and restrain yourself from licking the last morsels of cake and frosting from the paper. Nostalgia for old style sweetie shops can be satisfied at **Mrs Kibble's Olde Sweet Shop (Map 10)** whether your fetish is for cola cubes, sherbet flying saucers or Wham bars. Shopping in the West End and need a sugar boost? For a bonne-bouche delicieuse, stop in at **Laduree's (Map 23)** Burlington Arcade shop and nab a caramel and salted butter macaroon—the salty-sweet flavour is exquisite. Numerous Italian delis can be found around the city selling cured meats, buffalo mozzarella, biscotti and everything else that Mama used to make—**I Camisa & Son (Map 11)** is small but crammed full of delicacies. Demand for organic groceries is on the up and alternatives to Whole Foods' takeover of Fresh and Wild are cropping up in the unlikeliest places. **The Grocery (Map 91)** in Shoreditch serves the needs of local artists and hipsters. For the cheapest and best coffee to go in Soho try the Algerian Coffee Stores. Looking for Unicum? Look no further than **Gerry's Spirits Shop (Map 11)** where you can find the most obscure liquors as well as favourites like Zubrowka Bison Grass Vodka and good quality Cachaça.

Art And Craft Supplies

Crafty types and closet Van Goghs can pick up supplies at **Cass Art (Map 80)** three-storey flagship store in Islington. There's everything here for aspiring Manga cartoonists and weekend watercolourists alike, and lots of fun bits and pieces for school holiday/rainy day projects in the basement. Much of the high quality stock can be found at cut-price throughout the year—stock up on Moleskine note and sketchbooks which are frequently marked down. The **London Graphic Centre (Map 13)** has more design-led stock as well as fine art material attracting architects and graphic designers. Known for its greeting cards and stationary, **Paperchase (Map 4)** on Tottenham Court Road also has—true to its name—an astonishing array of handmade papers on its top floor—from flocked designs to fibrous papers made with dried flowers. You've got to love **Blade Rubber (Map 4)** just for its name, and for keeping sketches, photos, and memories intact. **Wyvern Bindery (Map 6)** is one of few of its kind to offer book-making services.

Musical Instruments And Equipment

Traditionally, Tin Pan Alley (real name: Denmark Street) has always been the hub of musical creativity in the city. Back in the day when rents were affordable, a community grew up around this little side street which went on to see Jimi Hendrix and The Beatles record in the basements, and a young Elton John sitting on the rooftops penning "Your Song". On any given day you may spot Jack White trying out a Digitech Whammy or Jonny Greenwood looking for some new toy to replace his Marshall Shred Master. There are plenty of independent music stores to be found in London's boroughs, and often they are specialists, happy to have a natter about what exactly it is that you're looking for and what the weather's like. Try **Top Wind (Map 104)** for all your flute needs, the brilliantly named **Duke of Uke (Map 91)** for banjo and ukulele-lovers (and frankly, who doesn't love a uke?), and **Phil Parker (Map 1)** for all you jazz cats needing a hand with your brass. For the medieval troubadour in your life, **Hobgoblin (Map 3)** has its own luthier who makes lutes. Still can't find that elusive, weird and wonderful percussive instrument you need to complete the sound on your latest opus?

Try **Ray Man (Map 71)** in Camden for unusual instruments. For the largest collection of sheet music in Europe, **Chappel of Bond Street (Map 11)** (now on Wardour Street but they've kept the name) is your destination.

Music For Listening

There's a veritable plethora of indie music stores out there and if you thought that vinyl was dead, well you'd be wrong. It seems that even with (or perhaps because of?) the onward march of technology and the ubiquitous white headphones on every other commuter, some of us still want to spend our Saturdays rifling through well-thumbed LPs and other rarities. **Sister Ray (Map 11)** in Berwick Street has long been in music-lovers' little black books, and you can find a member of every possible musical tribe scouring the racks. If you find yourself on the Essex Road, have a gander at **Flashback (Map 83)** and **Haggle Vinyl (Map 83)**: you're sure to find something to please and appealing prices. The **Music and Video Exchange (Map 29)** in Notting Hill was way ahead of its time and has been the swapshop of choice for years. When south of the river, do as Camberwellians do and drop in at **Rat Records (Map 121)**. For chin-stroking, debating Scott Walker's song structure, and arguing over whether if Girls Aloud were a punk band would they be credible (or are they already credible? Is punk an attitude or a genre? Or both? Discuss)? And more obscure chat, try any of these: **Phonica (Map 10)** in Soho, **Pure Groove (Map 60)** in Holloway, and many a muso's all-round fave, **Sounds of the Universe (Map 11)**.

Antiques And Bric-A-Brac, Flea Markets And Stalls

There's nothing more pleasurable on a sunny afternoon (or as is more likely the case, a grey, rainy afternoon) than browsing London's many antique and bric-a-brac markets and stalls, many of which pop up in our neighbourhoods' streets of a Sunday and Saturday. First stop on many shoppers' lists—both serious collectors and weekend browsers—are **Alfie's Antique Market (Map 76)** and **Gray's Antique Market**

(Map 2). Here you'll find art, antiques, jewellery, vintage clothing and rare books all housed under one roof. On a recent trip to Gray's a stallholder was selling a bracelet similar to one seen on the Antique's Roadshow (which had been valued at around £2,000) for £800. He had seen the programme too so was well aware of its potential market value—just one example of the relative bargains to be found.

Once the centre of the Britpop phenomenon in the '90s and a thriving mini-metropolis for vintage and antique stalls, Camden is going through something of an identity crisis with parts of the old Stables market and the Arches being shut down and redevelopment looming: what used to be a hotchpotch high street full of character is fast becoming an identikit of any other shopping street in England. It has a bit of a theme park feel to it with monster Pan-Asian restaurant Gilgamesh **(Map 71)** opening, **Proud Gallery (Map 4)** taking over the listed Horse Hospital building and packs of German and French kids on school trips rifling through the emo and goth gear that overfloweth. There is some gold to be found though in shops like **Episode (Map 71)** and **Rokit (Map 71)**, and certainly the place still has atmosphere.

Well-known to scavengers, **Camden Passage (Map 80)** is a welcome retreat from the mallrat-filled N1 centre across the road in Islington. The Mall and also Pierrepoint Arcade (tucked away behind the passage) offer a cornucopia of clothing, jewellery, military paraphernalia, homewares, prints, and a host of other bits and bobs. On Saturdays, market stalls set up in the street and surprises like vintage Givenchy earrings from 1978 (4 quid!) can be salvaged from amongst the knick-knacks. Again, this is an area threatened by developers as the ever encroaching chain shops like Tesco, Metro and Reiss testify—if you've always been meaning to go then go, the more people who shop in this fantastical locale the better. Use it or lose it!

Brick Lane (Map 91) also opens up on Sunday and in the summer there is a real carnival feel with fruit and veg, plumbing and DIY bits and pieces, electricals, toiletries, furniture (dentist's chair anyone?), clothes, DVDs lining the lane and overflowing into Sclater Street. All manner of weirdness can be observed from performance art (a group dressed in bin bags, making intimidating penguin noises and hobbling on their knees after random punters en masse—really quite normal for Shoreditch) to people seemingly emptying out the contents of their bedrooms onto tarpaulins and sheets looking for enthusiastic buyers. Who wants to buy Teen Wolf on video? Somebody does. Brick Lane also has the added advantage of having many a watering hole and curry house where you can stop and people-watch if it all gets a bit much (which it invariably does). If that's not your thing, (Up)Market is held in the **Truman Brewery (Map 91)** every Sunday and showcases new designers as well as housing some vinyl, vintage

and gourmet street food. Petticoat Lane's name was changed to Middlesex Street to spare our Victorian ancestors from blushing, however the name stuck and although you may be able to find knickers and maybe the odd petticoat, the market is more famous for its knock-down branded clothing in between the kitchen utensils and stereos.

Roman Road Market (Map 94) is proper gor-blimey, lor' love a duck cockney territory and there's lots to be had from fruit and veg, bed linen, and cute polka-dot sundresses for a tenner. In the summer, Saturdays are more of an occasion with stilt-walkers, jugglers and face painters keeping the shoppers entertained.

Map 1 · Marylebone (West)

Maroush Deli	45 Edgware Rd	020 7723 0773	Lebanese food emporium—fresh coffee, ice-creams and best houmous in town.
Phil Parker	106 Crawford St	020 7486 8206	Brass-o-rama.
Spymaster	3 Portman Sq	020 7486 3885	Stab-proof vests, in house P.I., you know, the usual.
Totally Swedish	32 Crawford St	020 7224 9300	Salt liquorice and Plopp bars for scandiphiles.

Map 2 · Marylebone (East)

Browns South Molton Street	24 S Molton St	020 7514 0016	Sleep with someone rich, then bring them here.
The Button Queen	19 Marylebone Ln	020 7935 1505	Antique buttons galore for budding fashionistas.
Daunt Books	83 Marylebone High St	020 7224 2295	Almost intimidatingly beautiful book shop.
Divertimenti	33 Marylebone High St	020 7935 0689	Go and pretend you need a £500 coffee machine.
Fenwick	63 New Bond St	020 7629 9161	A welcome escape from Oxford Street for those in the know.
Gray's Antique Market	58 Davies St	020 7629 7034	A world of bygone beauty a skip away from Bond Street.
John Lewis	278 Oxford St	020 7629 7711	Where John Betjeman would have gone if the world exploded.
Marimekko	16 St Christopher's Pl	020 7486 6454	Retro prints from Jackie Kennedy's favourite Finnish.
Niketown	236 Oxford St	020 7612 0800	Like a real town! Owned by Nike! But without sweatshops.
Noa Noa	14 Gees Ct	020 7495 8777	Desirable Boho Danish label.
Paul Smith Sale Shop	23 Avery Row	020 7493 1287	Cheap designer suits. Sweet.
Selfridges & Co	400 Oxford St	0800 123 400	A Mecca for the shopping elite who want everything.
Zara	242 Oxford St	020 7318 2700	Spiffy suits and cute casualwear from the Balearic brand.

Map 3 · Fitzrovia

Computer Exchange	32 Rathbone Pl	0845 345 1664	Good selection of secondhand DVDs, games and gadgets.
Harmony	103 Oxford St	020 7734 5969	Also known as Butt Plugs R Us.
Hobgoblin Shop	24 Rathbone Pl	020 7323 9901	Folky paradise: impressive/amusing collection of alternative instruments.
Mango	225 Oxford St	020 7434 3694	Let's go Mango!
Maplin	218 Tottenham Ct Rd	020 7323 4411	A whole world of technical geeketry to immerse yourself in.
Paperchase	213 Tottenham Ct Rd	020 7467 6200	More than meets the eye to this high street card shop.
Scandinavian Kitchen	61 Great Titchfield St	020 7580 7161	Smorgasbord!
Stargreen Box Office	20 Argyll St	020 7734 8932	Try here for tickets to sold-out gigs.
Topshop	216 Oxford St	020 7636 7700	Kate Moss still loves it. We do too.

Map 4 · Bloomsbury (West)

Blade Rubber	12 Bury Pl	084 5873 7005	Scrapbooking materials plus traditional and made-to-order rubber stamps.
British Museum shop	Great Russell St	0800 218 2222	Have you lost your Elgin Marbles?
Gosh! Comics	39 Great Russell St	020 7636 1011	A Japanese school boy's wet dream. Comics galore!
London Review Bookshop	14 Bury Pl	020 7269 9030	Big books, big name personal appearances—and cake!
Maplin	218 Tottenham Ct Rd	020 7323 4411	A whole world of technical geeketry to immerse yourself in.
Paperchase	213 Tottenham Ct Rd	020 7467 6200	More than meets the eye to this high street card shop.

Map 5 · Bloomsbury (East)

Bobbin Bicycles	31 Eyre St Hill	020 7253 1058	Making commuting fun - London's nicest cycling enthusiast.
International Magic	89 Clerkenwell Rd	020 7405 7324	When you need some tricks up your sleeve.

Joy	The Brunswick	020 7833 3307	Funky Urban Outfitters type stuff, but cheaper.
Magma Concept Store	117 Clarkenwell Rd	020 7242 9503	
Romanian Charity Shop	Lamb's Conduit St	020 7272 8970	Good quality clothes, good cause, warm feeling inside.

Map 6 • Clerkenwell

The Black Tulip	28 Exmouth Market	020 7689 0068	Think all florists are the same?
Brindisa Retail	32 Exmouth Market	020 7713 1666	Chorizo, salchichon, Serrano ham—famed importers Brindisa have it all. The Family Business
Tattoo Shop	58 Exmouth Market	020 7278 9526	Tatts for all the family.
M and R Meats	399 St John St	020 7837 1781	So meat-savvy they'll even know the best cut on you.
Timorous Beasties	46 Amwell St	020 7833 5010	Outlandish prints for the daringly tasteless home.
Wyvern Bindery	56 Clerkenwell Rd	020 7490 1391	Book binding for theses, portfolios and presentations. Repairs and restoration.

Map 9 • Mayfair / Green Park

Diane Von Furstenberg	25 Bruton St	020 7499 0886	Forget the LBD, every girl needs a DVF.
Dover Street Market	17 Dover St	020 7518 0680	Serious designer wear for people with serious money.
Marc Jacobs	24 Mount St	020 7399 1690	Never out of fashion.
Matthew Williamson	28 Bruton St	020 7629 6200	The boy who knows how to dress real girls.

Map 10 • Piccadilly / Soho (West)

Abercrombie & Fitch	7 Burlington Gardens	084 4412 5750	"Chinese food makes me sick..." Remember that song?
Me neither...Arigato	48 Brewer St	020 7287 1722	Japanese food store and sushi bar. Lychee jelly sweets, anyone?
b store	24 Savile Row	020 7734 6846	Tell the bank you'll look REALLY cool in this shit.
Banana Republic	224 Regent St	020 7758 3550	Your Stateside buddies don't need to ship over your clothes anymore
Behave	48 Lexington Sreet	020 7734 6876	Hipster clothes.
The Black Pearl	10 Kingly Ct	020 7439 0702	Because your earrings should rock as hard as you do.
Burlington Arcade	Burlington Arcade		
Cos	222 Regent St	020 7478 0400	COS you can. See what I did there?
Deal Real	3 Great Marlborough St	020 7287 7245	Hip-Hop mecca. Check out the open mic sessions.
The European Bookshop	5 Warwick St	020 7734 5259	For when you get sick of English.
Fortnum And Mason	181 Piccadilly	020 7734 8040	The world's poshest marmalades.
Georgina Goodman	44 Old Bond St	020 7499 8599	The only shoe worth having since that Mellon woman bought Jimmy Choo.
Hamley's	188 Regent St	0800 2802 444	World's biggest toy store. Terrifying just before Christmas.
Hatchard's	187 Piccadilly	020 7439 9921	Still musty, floors still creak, despite being owned by The Man.
Hoss Intropia	211 Regent St	020 7287 3569	High-end high street.
Liberty	214 Regent St	020 7734 1234	Splendid wood-panelled department store. Beautiful and obscure scents and perfumes.
Lillywhites	24-36 Lower Regent St	087 0333 9600	Good if you know exactly what you're looking for.
Mrs Kibble's Olde Sweet Shoppe	57 Brewer St	020 7734 6633	Tooth-rottingly good sweet shop. Who needs incisors, anyway?
Muji	41 Carnaby St	020 7287 7323	Japanese chain hits London - simple, minimalist goods but great quality.
Phonica	51 Poland St	020 7025 6070	Cutting edge vinyl/CD shop; alas, no Michael Bolton in stock.
Playlounge	19 Beak St	020 7287 7073	Toys for adults, no not those types of toys.
Richard James	29 Savile Row	020 7434 0605	Bespoke contemporary Savile Row tailoring.
Rigby & Peller	22 Conduit St	0845 076 5545	Furnishers of the Queen's basement.
SKK (Lighting)	34 Lexington St	020 7434 4095	Change your bedroom ambiance, light up your love life.
Stella McCartney	30 Bruton St	020 7518 3100	Stella's star keeps rising despite initial doubts in Fahionland.
Twinkled	1 Kingly Ct	020 7734 1978	Awesome selection of vintage clothes and accessories.
The Vintage Magazine Shop	39 Brewer St	020 7439 8525	Yellowing magazines and a million student classic posters.

Map 11 • Soho (Central)

Algerian Coffee Stores	52 Old Compton St	020 7437 2480	Pick up some Blue Mountain beans and a 95p cappu-to-go.
Bang Bang	9 Berwick St	020 7494 2042	Intimate secondhand clothes shop.
Chappel of Bond Street	152 Wardour St	020 7432 4410	...Which is actually on Wardour Street.
Cheapo Cheapo Records	53 Rupert St	020 7437 8272	The name's no lie - Cheapo records and DVDs.
Cowling & Wilcox	26 Broadwick St	020 7734 9556	Good arts supplies shop to spend your Monet in (groan!).
Gerry's	74 Old Compton St	020 7734 4215	A veritable alcoholic's Utopia.
I Camisa & Son	61 Old Compton St	020 7437 7610	The best Italian deli out of Italy.
Paradiso	41 Old Compton St	020 7287 2487	Sexier than most sex shops.
Sister Ray	34 Berwick St	020 7734 3297	Alternative vinyl, CDs and DVDs.
Sounds of the Universe	7 Broadwick St	020 7734 3430	Blow your friends' minds with obscure African vinyl.
Vinyl Junkies	94 Berwick St	020 7439 2923	Get your fix, you grubby vinyl fiend.

Map 12 • Soho (East)

Angels	119 Shaftesbury Ave	020 7836 5678	Chock full of fancy dress outfits.
Fopp	1 Earlham St	020 7845 9770	May Fopp never, ever die again. Long live the music bargain!

Forbidden Planet	179 Shaftesbury Ave	020 7420 3666	Cult/film/TV memorabilia shop that will leave Star Wars fans salivating.
Kokon to Zai	57 Greek St	020 7434 1316	Mad fashion laboratory providing competition for The Pineal Eye.
Macaris	92 Charing Cross Rd	020 7836 2856	Family run instrument shop with historic roots.
Porselli	9 West St	020 7836 2862	Before American Apparel...when only dancers wore dancewear...
Ray's Jazz	113 Charing Cross Rd	020 7437 5660	Convivial Shop/Cafe. Essential for Americana and, uh, jazz!
Turnkey	114 Charing Cross Rd	020 7419 9999	Every musical gadget you need for your next glitchtronica symphony.
Wunjo Guitars	20 Denmark St	020 7379 0737	Mind-bendingly friendly Scot selling lovely vintage gear...

Map 13 · Covent Garden

Cath Kidston	28 Shelton St	020 7836 4803	Kitsch at its most chic, and vice-versa.
Cybercandy	3 Garrick St	020 8801 8815	For when a plain old Mars bar just won't cut it.
David and Goliath	4 The Market Pl	020 7240 3640	Droll, funky t-shirts and other fun stuff.
Duffer of St George	34 Shorts Gardens	020 7836 3722	Rude tees.
Koh Samui	65 Monmouth St	020 7240 4280	Eclectic selection of labels like Chloe and Balenciaga amongst newer finds
Libidex	49 Shelton St	020 7836 5894	Caters for all your kinks. Yes, even that one.
The Loft	35 Monmouth St	020 7240 3807	Designer jumble sale.
London Graphic Centre	16 Shelton St	020 7759 4500	One stop shop for graphics geeks.
Neal's Yard Dairy	17 Shorts Gardens	020 7240 5700	Follow your nose to very fine cheeses.
Nigel Hall	18 Floral St	020 7379 3600	Where to get business casualed well.
Octopus	54 Neal St	020 7836 2911	Makes the everyday so much more fun.
Orla Kiely	31 Monmouth St	020 7240 4022	Trademark cutesy prints from the Irish designer.
Pop Boutique	6 Monmouth St	020 7497 5262	Retrotastic!
Scoop	40 Shorts Gardens	020 7240 7086	Queues out the door for freshly made gelato. Fragola rocks.
Screenface	48 Monmouth St	020 7836 3955	Professional theatre make-up which can withstand the sweat of clubbing.
Slam City Skates	16 Neal's Yard	020 7240 0928	Rambunctious skate shop.
Stanford's	Long Acre	020 7836 1321	Treasure trove of maps, travel books and accessories.
Superdry	35 Earlham St (Thomas Neal Centre)		Super funky pseudo-Japanese urban wear. Friendly staff.
Twosee	17 Monmouth St	020 7494 3813	Many exclusives at this quirky boutique, for those that care.
Urban Outfitters	42 Earlham St	02077596390	Heaps of streetwear and crazy things for your house.

Map 15 · Blackfriars / Farringdon

Flaneur	41 Farringdon Rd	020 7404 4422	Artisanal food hall for those who have time "pour flaner"

Map 16 · Square Mile (West)

Church's Shoes	90 Cheapside	020 7606 1587	An English shoe institution.
Manucci	5 Cheapside	020 7248 1459	Feeling out of place? Get a suit here.
Space NK Apothecary	145 Cheapside	020 7726 2060	Skin care heaven.

Map 17 · Square Mile (East)

Sweatshop (City branch - at Cannon's Gym)	Cousin Lane	020 7626 4324	Ickle version of the athletes' favourite frequented by suits.

Map 18 · Tower Hill / Aldgate

A. Gold	42 Brushfield St	020 7247 2487	Perfect for impressive picnic supplies. But smells like a sock.
Montezuma's	51 Brushfield St	0207 539 9208	Chocolate you'd leave your boyfriend for.
Petticoat Lane	Middlesex St	na	No petticoats here love, but look for the FCUK stall

Map 19 · Belgravia

British Red Cross Victoria	85 Ebury St	020 7730 2235	Green welly-brigade territory. Good range of mens' suits.
Moyses Flowers	Sloane Sq	020 7901 8030	Tastefully delicate posies to enchant your beloved.
Mungo & Maud	79 Elizabeth St	020 7952 4570	Real dogs don't wear clothes! Chihuahuas do though...and pugs...

Map 20 · Victoria / Pimlico (West)

La Bella Sicilia	33 Warwick Way	020 7630 5914	Old-skool deli with cheery old owners and pasta aplenty.
Rippon Cheese Stores	26 Upper Tachbrook St	020 7931 0628	A world of cheese.

Map 22 · Westminster

Haelen Centre	41 Broadway	020 8340 4258	All your hippy, wholemeal, organic needs under one roof.

Map 24 · Trafalgar Square / The Strand

Austin Kaye	425 The Strand	020 7240 1888	Vintage watches. Don't expect e-bay prices.
Australia Shop	27 Maiden Ln	020 7836 2292	Relive the holiday (minus the sun. Or Brad the dive-instructor).

Arts & Entertainment · **Shopping**

The Italian Bookshop	5 Cecil Ct	020 7240 1634	"Of course, there is only one way to read Dante..."
London Camera Exchange	98 Strand	020 7379 0200	My lens is longer than yours.
Rohan	10 Henrietta St	020 7831 1059	Super-friendly fleece-clad staff wielding waterproofs.
Stanley Gibbons	399 Strand	020 7836 8444	World's leading stamp dealer attracts collectors, investors and the curious.

Map 25 · Kensal Town

Honest Jon's	278 Portobello Rd	020 8969 9822	Obscure and rare Jazz, Funk, Reggae and Hip-Hop.
Rellik	8 Golborne Rd	020 8962 0089	Oppsite the Trellik Tower - geddit? Specialises in Queen Viv (Westwood).
What Katie Did	281 Portobello Rd	0845 430 8743	Fabulous 1940s-inspired boudoir boutique for rib-crushing corsets, stockings and pointy bras.

Map 28 · Ladbroke Grove / Notting Hill (West)

Cowshed	119 Portland Rd	020 7078 1944	Express mani-pedis for women who have places to go etc.
The Cross	141 Portland Rd	020 7727 6760	The original London boutique...still going...
Virginia	98 Portland Road	020 7727 9908	If money is no object, what you want is here.

Map 29 · Notting Hill Gate

& Clarke's Bread	124 Kensington Church St	020 7221 7196	All-butter brioche and honey loaves for Harvey Nics, Selfridges - and you.
Bodas	38 Ledbury Rd	020 7229 4464	Everyday underwear that gives M&S a run for its money.
The Grocer on Elgin	6 Elgin Crescent	020 7221 3844	Restaurant standard ready meals for lazy people.
The Hummingbird Bakery	133 Portobello Rd	020 7229 6446	Takeaway cupcakes reminiscent of New York's Magnolia Bakery.
Melt	59 Ledbury Rd	020 7727 5030	Posh chocs made before your bulging eyes.
Music & Video Exchange	38 Notting Hill Gate	020 7243 8573	Invented second hand record shops. Best in London.
Negozio Classica	283 Westbourne Grove	020 7034 0005	Half bar, half store selling high-end Italian kitchen goods.
Portobello Road Market	Portobello Rd		
R Garcia and Sons	248 Portobello Rd	020 7221 6119	Overwhelming selection of Spanish groceries.
Retro Man	34 Pembridge Rd	020 7792 1715	Vintage fixes for modern men. And men only.
Retro Woman	32 Pembridge Rd	020 7460 6525	Exclusive vintage ware that's worth it.
Rough Trade Talbot Road	130 Talbot Rd	020 7229 8541	More character and better records than the soulless East Branch.

Map 30 · Bayswater

Planet Organic	42 Westbourne Grove	n/a	Organic heaven.

Map 32 · Shepherd's Bush (West)

Nut Case	352 Uxbridge Rd	020 8743 0336	About time nuts got some respect.

Map 33 · Shepherd's Bush

Whole Foods Market	63 Kensington High St	020 7368 4500	Overwhelming selection of organic exotica.

Map 35 · Kensington

Buttercup	16 St Albans Grove	0207 937 1473	No other pleasure on earth comes close to these cupcakes.
Notting Hill Housing Trust	57 Kensington Church St	020 7937 5274	There's gold in that 'Hill.

Map 37 · Knightsbridge

Burberry	12 Brompton Road	020 7581 2151	Flagship store of the classic British brand.
Harrods	87 Brompton Rd	020 7730 1234	Arch conspiracy theorist Mr Al-Fayed's still classy department store.
Harvey Nichols	109 Knightsbridge	020 7235 5000	More 1999 than 2009, but still a great department store.
Skandium	247 Brompton Rd	020 7584 2066	For lottery winners who can't shake their love of Ikea.

Map 38 · Chiswick

Oxfam Books	90 Turnham Green Terrace	020 8995 6059	Fantastic fiction selection - the rich read too!
Theobroma Cacao	43 Turnham Green Terrace	020 8996 0431	Which translates as "Chocolate Thrombosis". Choccy penises? Leave it out!

Map 42 · Baron's Court

Curious Science	319 Lillie Road	020 7610 1175	Stock up on stuffed mutant cow heads and cases of eyeballs.

Map 43 • West Brompton / Fulham Broadway / Earls Court

Fulham Broadway Centre	Fulham Road	020 7385 6965	Shopping, cinema, reaturants and tube station all in one place.

Map 44 • Chelsea

Furniture Cave	533 Kings Rd		Swanky. Huge. Quintessentially Kings Road.
The Shop At Bluebird	350 King's Rd	0207 351 3873	Spend a fortune here and become an "edgy" individual.

Map 45 • Chelsea (East)

British Red Cross Chelsea	67 Old Church St	845054 7101	Known locally as La Croix Rouge Boutique.
Frock Me! Vintage Fashion Fair	Chelsea Town Hall, Kings Rd	020 7254 4054	Held every couple of months, "pre-war" tearoom refreshes shopping casualties.
Kate Kuba	24 Duke of York Sq	020 7259 0011	What more could a woman want?! Shoes, shoes, shoes...

Map 46 • Sloane Square

Fresh Line	55 King's Rd	020 7348 7995	Home made cosmetics—fresh!
Space NK Apothecary	307 King's Rd	0207 351 7209	The Superdrug for the Sloane Square ladies who lunch.

Map 51 • Highgate

The Corner Shop	88 Highgate High St	020 8340 1118	Locals' favourite fending off the advance of Tesco's.
Dragonfly Wholefoods	24 Highgate High St	020 8347 6087	Great little organic food shop and juice bar
Highgate Butchers	76 Highgate High St	020 8340 9817	Reassuringly expensive meat. Them cows m.ust have lived like kings.
Le Chocolatier	78 Highgate High St	020 8348 1110	Essential at Easter - not just eggs but whole chocolate chickens.
Oxfam Bookshop, Highgate	47 Highgate High St	020 8347 6704	Musty bookstore with some cracking titles.
Second Layer Records	323 Archway Rd	078 7805 1726	I was into Avant Rock before you were etc. etc.
Sound 323	323 Archway Rd	020 8348 9595	Blisteringly avant record shack.
Wild Guitar	393 Archway Rd	020 8340 7766	Get your retro gear in this brilliant guitar shop.

Map 52 • Archway (North)

Archway Video	220 Archway Rd	020 8340 2986	Local favourite with videos/DVDs for sale and rent.
Magic Carpet	248 Archway Rd	020 8342 9771	You want rugs? They got rugs. Rugs, everywhere.

Map 53 • Crouch End

Walter Purkis And Sons	17 The Broadway	020 8340 6281	Proof fish don't need their tasty batter skins.

Map 57 • Hampstead Heath

Daunt Books	51 S End Rd	020 7794 8206	A right daunty little shop.

Map 58 • Parliament Hill / Dartmouth Park

Corks	9 Swain's Ln	020 8340 4781	Superb selection of interesting wines and beers.

Map 60 • Archway

Pure Groove Records	679 Holloway Rd	020 7281 4877	Cool instore gigs/events and great selection of new indie releases.

Map 61 • Holloway (North)

Michael's Fruiterers	56 7 Sisters Rd	020 7700 1334	Fruit n veg fest. Nowhere's fresher.

Map 62 • Finsbury Park

The Happening Bagel Bakery	284 Seven Sisters Rd	020 8809 1519	Another Haringey gem, with some delicious pastries too!

Map 64 • Stoke Newington

Ark	161 Stoke Newington High St	020 7275 9311	Cute little interiors and gift shop.
The Beaucatcher Salon	44 Stoke Newington Church St	020 7923 2522	Hairdressers and community hub.
Belle Epoque Boulangerie	37 Newington Green	020 7249 2222	Fancy schmancy, delicious pastries.
Bridgewood & Neitzert	146 Stoke Newington Church St	020 7249 9398	Renowned string section repair, exchange and sales.
Metal Crumble	13 Stoke Newington Church St	020 7249 0487	Affordable, flippin' gorgeous, jewellery made on site.
Ribbons and Taylor	157 Stoke Newington Church St	020 7254 4735	Long-standing vintage clothes shop - Stokey original.
Route 73 Kids	92 Stoke Newington Church St	020 7923 7873	Bus inspired toy shop.

S'graffiti	172 Stoke Newington Church St	020 7254 7961	You've been framed.
Sacred Art	148 Albion Rd	020 7254 2223	(Needles + Ink + Skin) x Pain = Art.
The Spence	161 Stoke Newington Church St	020 7249 4927	Bread elevated to an art form.

Map 66 · Finchley Road / Swiss Cottage

Yeomans Grocers	152 Regent's Park Rd	020 7722 4281	Greengrocer that sells flowers and has a great juicebar.

Map 70 · Primrose Hill

Miss Lala's Boudoir	148 Gloucester Ave	020 7483 1888	Dangerously hot underwear. Visit only if your purse is full.
Nicolas (off licence)	67 Regents Park Rd	020 7722 8576	A wide range of wines, including some cheap ones.
Press	3 Erskine Rd	020 7449 0082	Impressive array of brands for a boutique. Good sales.
Primrose Newsagent	91 Regents Park Rd	020 7722 0402	Newsagent, stationers, post office, drycleaners and internet cafe.
Shepherd Foods	59 Regents Park Rd	020 7586 4592	Highly priced but quaint local deli.
Shikasuki	67 Gloucester Ave	020 7722 4442	Affordable vintage and modern design.
Tann Rokka	123 Regent's Park Rd	020 7722 3999	Wildly expensive "lifestyle store" in old Primrose hill train station.

Map 71 · Camden Town / Chalk Farm / Kentish Town (West)

Acumedic	101 Camden High St	020 7388 6704	Chinese medicine offering acupuncture AKA polite masochism.
Black Rose	The Stables Market, Chalk Farm Rd	020 7482 6111	Gothic. Very, very gothic.
Cyberdog	The Stables Market, Chalk Farm Rd	020 7474 3737	Enormous sci-fi set displaying PVC, neon, and leather clubbing gear.
Episode	26 Chalk Farm Rd	020 7485 9927	Unusual vintage store with comparatively low ringworm risk.
Escapade	150 Camden High St	020 7485 7384	Dress up as Wonder Woman! Also caters for females.
Eye Contacts	10 Chalk Farm Rd	020 7482 1701	Opticians that sells uber-trendy spectacles.
Graham and Green	164 Regents Park Rd	020 7586 2960	Wonderfully dinky yet scarily pricey shop.
Know How Records	3 Buck St	020 7267 1526	Pounding dance music and continuous party. Grates after a while.
Music & Video Exchange	208 Camden High St	020 7267 1898	Great secondhand music shop, seemingly staffed by grouches on Mogadon.
Ray Man Music	54 Chalk Farm Rd	020 7692 6261	Wonderful shop full of exotic instruments. Bavarian noseflute, anyone?
Rokit	225 Camden High St	020 7267 3046	Second hand, sorry, vintage clothing store for the stars.
Rough Sleepers	43 Chalk Farm Rd	020 7485 4848	Highly priced designer wear; the proceeds go to charity.
Sounds That Swing	88 Inverness St	020 7267 4682	"It ain't worth a thing..." rockabilly, psych and doo-wop.
Up The Video Junction	Middle Yard, Camden Lock Pl	078 9040 8025	Rare, out-of-print, cult DVD's.
Village Games	65 The West Yard	020 7485 0653	Huge selection of boardgames.

Map 72 · Kentish Town

Dots	132 St Pancras Way	020 7482 5424	Friendly music shop with free hash cakes...OK, just cookies.
Fish	161 Kentish Town Rd	020 7267 0139	Gift shop run by actress Sophie Thompson.
Phoenicia	186 Kentish Town Rd	020 7267 1267	Olives, just-roasted nuts, baclava, ice-cream bar. Meze heaven. Ditch Sainsburys.

Map 73 · Holloway

Bumblebee Natural Foods	33 Brecknock Rd	020 7284 1314	Hot veggie lunches, lush cakes. Organic fruitopia over the road.
DOC Records	5 Cardwell Terrace, Cardwell Rd	020 7700 0081	Probably full of contagious diseases. Worth a rummage.

Map 74 · Holloway Road / Arsenal

21st Century Retro	162 Holloway Rd	020 7700 2354	Mothballs and tweed in this retro paradise.
Fettered Pleasures	90 Holloway Rd	020 7619 9333	Treat your nan to something nice.
House of Harlot	90 Holloway Rd	020 7700 1441	Funky fetish fashion.

Map 75 · Highbury

Cabbies Delight Auto Parts	9 Green Lanes	020 7226 1692	21,000 car parts and 21 years experience.

Map 76 · Edgeware Road / Marylebone (North)

Alfie's Antiques Market	25 Church St	020 7723 6066	Kitsch oddball sanctuary for vintage treats.
Archive Secondhand Books & Music	83 Bell St	020 7402 8212	Old and unusual books.
Beatles London Store	231 Baker St	020 7935 4464	All you need is love, and no taste.
Elvisly Yours	233 Baker St	020 7486 2005	With stalkers like these, it's no wonder Elvis is hiding.

533

J Michael & Daughter	78 Park Rd	020 7722 9000	Georgous vintage to help lighten your purse.
Lord's Cricket Shop	Lord's Cricket Ground, Lisson Grove	020 7616 8570	They won't even ask why you want a cricket bat.

Map 77 · Mornington Crescent / Regent's Park

Chess & Bridge	369 Euston Rd	020 7388 2404	Chess fetishists won't be able to control themselves here.
Greens and Beans	131 Drummond St	020 7380 0857	Wheat grass, supplements and tofu.

Map 78 · Euston

All Ages Records	27 Pratt St	020 7267 0303	Truly independent punk & hardcore record shop. Fuck the system!
Housmans	5 Caledonian Rd	020 7837 4473	Bookshop for progressive peaceniks and radical revolutionaries.
Rock'n'roll Jumble Sale	15 Phoenix Rd	020 7419 6891	Monthly indie-themed bric-a-brac. Cool moustaches everywhere.
Transformation	52 Eversholt St	020 7388 0627	The world's largest shop for transvestites and transexuals. Seriously.

Map 79 · King's Cross

Continental Stores	26 Caledonian Rd	020 7837 0201	1960s Italian deli still run by original Italian owners. Fab.
Cosmo Cornelio	182 Caledonian Rd	020 7278 3947	Old-skool, moustache trimming Italian barbers.

Map 80 · Angel / Upper St

After Noah	121 Upper St	020 7359 4281	Stuff your Nintendo Wiis—these are proper toys, retro-style.
Annie's	12 Camden Passage	020 7359 0796	Proper vintage—1900s to 1940s.
Camden Passage	Camden Passage	020 7359 0190	Thingamebobs, whatsits and doodahs aplenty.
Cass Art	66 Colebrooke Row	020 7354 2999	Large, neat-as-a-pin, extremely pleasing art supply shop.
Gill Wing Kitchen Shop	194 Upper St	020 7503 7963	Splendid array of kitchen gadgetry to keep foodies amused.
Monte's Deli	23 Canonbury Ln	020 7354 4335	Tasty, but look elsewhere if you need a hearty meal.
Palette London	21 Canonbury Ln	020 7288 7428	Islington's eclectic vintage shop—clothes, books, homeware.
Paul A Young chocolate shop	33 Camden Passage	020 7424 5750	"Everytime you go away..." you take a piece of chocolate.
Raymond Roe Fishmonger	Chapel Market	020 7833 8656	Market stall with a sea's worth of fish.
Salvation Army Islington	284 Upper St	020 7359 9865	Ramshackle charity shop. In a well-off area, meaning quality clobber.
Twentytwentyone	274 Upper St	020 7288 1996	Bauhaus to Boontje and beyond.

Map 81 · Canonbury

Get Stuffed	105 Essex Rd	020 7226 1364	Polar bear for the living room, anyone? Taxidermy emporium.
Handmade and Found	109 Essex Rd	020 7359 3898	For something totally unique.
James Elliot Master Butcher	96 Essex Rd	020 7226 3658	So much choice they'd probably stock human if they could.
Raab's The Baker's	136 Essex Rd	020 7226 2830	Crusty white bloomers, chelsea buns. No paninis.

Map 82 · De Beauvoir Town / Kingsland

North One Garden Centre	25 Englefield Rd	020 7923 3553	Dinky little garden centre catering for dinky little London gardens.

Map 83 · Angel (East) / City Rd (North)

Flashback	50 Essex Rd	020 7354 9356	Don't come in whistling Barbie Girl.
Haggle Vinyl	114 Essex Rd	020 7704 3101	Record shop that reminds you how little you know about music.
Past Caring	76 Essex Rd		Oddball collection of furniture, pictures and, if you're lucky, mannequins.

Map 84 · Hoxton

Sh!	57 Hoxton Sq	020 7613 5458	Dildo-tastic! Guys must come (ahem) accompanied by a galpal.

Map 85 · Stoke Newington (East)

Hamdys	167 Stoke Newington High St	020 7254 0681	Porn-free newsagents run by stubborn maverick.

Map 86 · Dalston / Kingsland

Dalston Mill Fabrics	69 Ridley Rd	020 7249 4129	Veritable treasure trove for budding Vivienne Westwoods and John Gallianos.
Oxfam Dalston	570 Kingsland Rd	020 7923 1532	Flagship charity shop. Go find treasures!
Party Party	9 Ridley Rd	020 7254 5168	Fancy dress and party supplies plus an outstanding cake decorating department.

Ridley Road Market	Ridley Rd		Giant (live!) snails, Nigerian DVDs, fresh fish, 'taters, "Pound a bowl!"
Turkish Food Centre	89 Ridley Rd	020 7254 6754	Olives and feta galore, bakery onsite, plus other fresh groceries.

Map 87 · Hackney Downs / Lower Clapton

Umit & Son	35 Lower Clapton Rd	na	Crazed film buff selling vintage porn, super 8 and crisps?!?

Map 89 · London Fields / Hackney Central

Artvinyl	20 Broadway Market	020 7241 4129	The best vinyl and CD covers, printed on canvas.
Broadway Market	Broadway Market		Yummy mummies and Guardian-reading couples peruse.
Burberry Factory Shop	29 Chatham Pl	020 8985 3344	Ever wondered how Burberry became associated with chavs?
Candle Factory	184 Mare St	020 8986 6356	Well-made, well-priced candles.
L'eau a la Bouche	49 Broadway Market	020 7923 0600	Cute French delicatessen shop.
Lazy Days	21 Mare St	078 1632 3848	Not far from Hackney Rd where you'll find more furniture.

Map 90 · Homerton / Victoria Park North

Cheech Miller	227 Victoria Park Rd	020 8985 9900	Everything you need for the park: kites, frisbees, skateboards, unicyclies.
Sublime	225 Victoria Park Rd	020 8986 7243	Boudoir-like boutique selling select and independent labels.
Work Shop	77 Lauriston Rd	020 8986 9585	Beautiful handmade pottery for home and kitchen by Caroline Bousfield Gregory.

Map 91 · Shoreditch / Brick Lane / Spitalfields

A Butcher of Distinction	91 Brick Ln	020 7770 6111	Distinct indeed, impeccable collection of preppy, fresh n' clean stylings.
Absolute Vintage	15 Hanbury St	020 7247 3883	If Imelda Marcos ran a misanthropic clothes shop.
Arckiv	37 Heneage St	07790 102204	Those film kids get their vintage eyewear here.
Bangla City	86 Brick Ln	020 7456 1000	Breaks the rule saying you should avoid smelly supermarkets.
Beats Workin'	93 Sclater St	020 7729 8249	Ideal Record Shop: Interesting stock, friendly and a spouse couch!
Bernstock Speirs	234 Brick Ln	020 7739 7385	Look no further if you're searching for a signature titfer.
Beyond Retro	112 Cheshire St	020 7613 3636	The Daddy of all jumble sales.
Blackman's Shoes	42 Cheshire St	07850 883505	Chaotic hole-in-the-wall selling £5 plimsolls.
Brick Lane	Brick Ln		Nathan Barleys still fucked off their face from the night before.
Caravan	11 Lamb St	020 7739 9009	Quirky interiors shop with items new and old on offer.
Columbia Road Market	Columbia Rd		Get there early, nab outside tables for brekkie then shop.
Duke of Uke	22 Hanbury St	020 7247 7924	For all your many ukelele and banjo needs.
FairyGothMother	15 Lamb St	020 7377 0370	Not entirely "Goth"- a Dita Von Teese of a shop...
The Grocery	54 Kingsland Rd	020 7729 6855	Selling the good life to lower Kingsland Road.
The Laden Showrooms	103 Brick Ln	020 7247 2431	Eclectic bazaar of small labels scavenged by stylists and starlets.
Luna and Curious	198 Brick Ln	079 7744 0212	Curiouser and curiouser...lovely local artists' and designers' co-operative.
No One	1 Kingsland Rd	020 7613 5314	Sporty designer wear. Killer shades.
Nudge Records	20 Hanbury St		Notorious little shack owned by the Brothers Collishaw. Reggae/dub.
Rough Trade East	91 Brick Ln	020 7392 7788	East London outpost of the absurdly cool Rough Trade Records.
Scooter Emporium	10 Dray Walk, Brick Ln	020 7375 2277	Because it's much more fun to be a scooter commuter.
Second Tread	261 Hackney Rd	020 7033 9862	In every fashionista's little black book: seconds and ex-model shoes.
Taj Stores	112 Brick Ln	020 7377 0061	Weird and wonderful Eastern food.
Tatty Devine	236 Brick Ln	020 7739 9009	Bonkers jewellery loved by celebs, fashionistas and hipsters.
Taylor Taylor	137 Commercial St	020 7033 0330	French boudoir-style hairdressers with free cocktail bar. Feel like a princess.
Treacle	110 Columbia Rd	020 7729 5657	Dreamy cupcakes. Don't ask for coffee - this is a TEAshop!

Map 92 · Bethnal Green

AP Fitzpatrick	142 Cambridge Heath Rd	020 7790 0884	Art supplies and expert advice.

Map 93 · Globe Town / Mile End (North)

Massage Table Store	Bow Wharf, Grove Rd	020 8983 9800	For, you know, when you need a massage table.
Paul Mark Hatton	65 Roman Rd		Pocket ashtray anyone? Fans include Jack Nicholson and Liv Tyler.

Map 94 · Bow

Pure	430 Roman Rd	020 8983 2004	The place to spend your wedge in E3.
Roman Road Market	Roman Rd		Big, colourful, cheap as chips—bargain tat hawked by lively east-end traders.

Sew Amazing	80 St Stephens Rd	020 8980 8898	Long established sewing machine shop. Repairs and recycling service provided.
South Molton Drugstore	583 Roman Rd		Branded cosmetics and toiletries at knock-down prices.

Map 97 · Stepney / Shadwell (East)

John Lester Wigmakers	32 Globe Rd	020 7790 2278	Need a syrup?

Map 104 · South Bank / Waterloo / Lambeth North

The Bookshop Theatre	51 The Cut	020 7593 1520	Thesp-oriented but charming, including a tiny stage for performances.
Calder Bookshop	51 The Cut	020 7620 2900	Enduringly fashionable hub for the unfashionably literate.
I Knit London	106 Lower Marsh	020 7261 1338	The UK's only knitting shop with a licensed bar. Wool is cool.
Konditor & Cook	22 Cornwall Rd	020 7261 0456	Yummy scrummy choccies and cake.
Oasis	84 Lower Marsh	020 7401 7074	Friendly independent salon for massages, waxing, facials and fab pedicures.
Radio Days	87 Lower Marsh	020 7928 0800	Cave of vintage wonders.
Scooterworks	132 Lower Marsh	020 7620 1421	Scooter shop has superb coffee. Word spreads. Becomes café too.
Top Wind	2 Lower Marsh	020 7401 8787	Serious flute worship.
Waterloo Camping	37 The Cut	020 7284110	Eccentric army surplus/camping store, run by two friendly brothers.
What The Butler Wore	131 Lower Marsh	020 7261 1353	'60s, '70s vintage boutique—retro-glam party garments plus resident moggy, Binky.

Map 105 · Southwark / Bankside (West)

Elephant & Castle Market	Elephant & Castle		An anti-Portobello Road Market...slightly dodgy but dirt-cheap.

Map 106 · Bankside (East) / Borough / Newington

German Deli	8 Southwark St	020 7250 1322	Sauerkraut and sausages if you like that kinda stuff.
Paul Smith	13 Park St	020 7403 1678	Kitsch and dolls from the fashion designer. Don't ask why.
Richer Sounds	2 London Bridge Walk	020 7403 1201	The original store of this small chain offering low prices.
Vinopolis	1 Bank End	0207 940 8300	Wine tasting and buying megastore. Spitting optional.

Map 107 · Shad Thames

The Design Museum Shop	Shad Thames	020 7940 8753	Stuff you wish you'd thought of.

Map 111 · Rotherhithe (East) Surrey Quays

Decathlon	Surrey Quays Rd	020 7394 2000	The Daddy of sports & outdoors shops.

Map 112 · Kennington / Elephant and Castle

Pricebusters Hardware	311 Elephant & Castle Shopping Centre	020 7703 8244	Impressively cheap, friendly staff and an amusing collection of bric-a-brac.
Recycling	110 Elephant Rd	020 7703 7001	They sell 'em bikes, they fix 'em bikes. Second hand.

Map 119 · Deptford (East)

Deptford Market	Deptford High St		Cheap, busy, eclectic: Proof that there IS life in Deptford.
El-Khadijat International Grocer	147 Deptford High St	020 8692 7333	Run out of Giant African Land Snails? Problem solved.

Map 120 · Greenwich

Mr Humbug	Greenwich Market	020 7871 4944	Infinitissimal old-fashioned sweets to relive your childhood sugar buzzes.

Map 121 · Camberwell (West)

Rat Records	348 New Camberwell Rd	020 7274 3222	Ramshackle and friendly. There's bargains if you've got superhuman patience.

Map 123 · Peckham

Primark	51 Rye Ln	020 7639 9655	More of a chance of scoring that 'it' item at this branch.

Map 127 · Coldharbour Lane / Herne Hill (West)

Blackbird Bakery	208 Railton Rd	020 7095 8800	London needs more lovely independent bakeries (like this).

Map 129 · East Dulwich

The Cheeseblock	69 Lordship Ln	020 8299 3636	Best cheese south of the river.

Map 130 · Peckham Rye

Hope And Greenwood	20 North Cross Rd	020 8613 1777	Twee but tasty old-style sweets.

Map 134 · South Lambeth

New Covent Garden Market	Nine Elms Ln	020 7720 2211	Known as London's Larder. Nowhere near Covent Garden

Map 140 · Clapham Junction / Northcote Rd

Anita's Vintage Fashion Fair	Battersea Arts Centre, Lavender Hill	020 8325 5789	Hardcore collectors, designers, and students find inspiration amongst the rails.
Huttons	29 Northcote Rd	020 7223 5523	Eclectic mix of unusual clothes, furniture and gifts.
Lighthouse Bakery		020 7228 4537	The weekend queue says it all.
QT Toys and Games	90 Northcote Rd	020 7223 8637	Toys for big and small kids. Cool gifts.
Russ	101 Battersea Rise	020 7228 6319	Model specialist—trains, boats, planes and more.
Sweaty Betty	136 Northcote Rd	020 7978 5444	Look like a total Betty, like, even when you're sweaty.

Map 141 · Battersea (South)

Battersea Car Boot Sale	401 Battersea Technical College, Battersea Park Rd	07941 383 588	Yeah! A huge, tumultous boot sale that starts mid afternoon!

Map 142 · Clapham Old Town

M. Moen & Sons	24 The Pavement	020 7622 1624	Butcher for the bourgeoisie, incredibly good, massively expensive.

Map 143 · Clapham High Street

Apex Cycles	40 Clapham High St	020 7622 1334	Bikes fixed, bikes sold.
Paws	62 Clapham High St	020 7720 9962	Attendant, napping canines remind shoppers where the takings will go.
Today's Living	92 Clapham High St	020 7622 1772	Health foods, herbal remedies and other jiggery pokery.

Map 144 · Stockwell / Brixton (West)

Continental Delicatessen	3 Atlantic Rd	020 7733 3766	Portuguese-owned institution, famous for pestos, chorizo and mamma's tortilla.
Lisa Stickley London	74 Landor Rd	0800 876 6339	Dotty 1940s-inspired handbags to tea-towels. Cath Kidston but better.
The Old Post Office Bakery	76 Landor Rd	0207 326 4408	Disused P.O turned artisan baker's. Local loaf? The Brixton Rye.

Map 147 · Balham (West)

Bon Vivant	59 Nightingale Ln	020 8675 6314	Great local deli.

Map 148 · Balham (East)

Moxon's	Westbury Parade	020 8675 2468	Fresh fish for foodies with deep pockets. Knowledgeable staff.

Map 149 · Clapham Park

MacFarlanes	48 Abbeville Rd	020 8673 5373	Gourmet goodness galore.

Map 150 · Brixton

Traid	2 Acre Ln	020 7326 4330	Characterful recycled clothes. Touch of wank, but still we like.

Map 151 · Tooting Bec

Russell's Hardware & DIY	46 Upper Tooting Rd	020 8672 1576	DIY treasure chest. Friendly, helpful owners.
Wandsworth Oasis HIV/AIDs Charity Shop	40 Trinity Rd	020 8767 7555	Thrift store treasure trove.

Map 152 · Tooting Broadway

Tooting Market	21 Tooting High St	n/a	Quaint indoor labyrinth worth nosing about.

does your city need redesigning too?

all-on-one

we redesigned London!

from complexity to simplicity without loss of detail

all-on-one city pocket maps and internet mapmovies of places where people want to go
and how to get there using public transport and walking

let's work together

Street Index

Street Index

Street Index

Street Index

Street	Page	Grid
Bethnal Green Road	91	A1/A2
	92	B1/B2
Bethwin Road	112	B2
	121	A1/A2
Betterton Street	13	B1
Bettridge Road	49	B1
Betts Street	96	B1
Bev Callender Close	142	A1
Bevan Street	83	A2
Bevenden Street	84	B1
Beverley Close	139	A2
Beverley Road	38	A2
	39	B1
Beversbrook Road	60	B1
Beverston Mews	1	A2
Beverstone Road	150	A2
Bevill Allen Close	152	A2
Bevin Close	110	A2
Bevin Way	6	A1
Bevington Road	25	B1
Bevington Street	108	A2
Bevis Marks	18	A1
Bewdley Street	80	A1
Bewick Street	142	A1
Bewley Street	96	B2
Bianca Road	115	B1
Bickenhall Street	1	B1
Bickersteth Road	152	A2/B2
Bickerton Road	59	A1/A2
Bickley Street	152	A1
Bicknell Road	128	A1
Bidborough Street	4	A2
	5	A1
Bidbury Close	114	B1
Biddestone Road	74	A1
Biddulph Road	27	A2
Bidwell Street	124	A1
Biggerstaff Street	62	B1
Biggs Row	136	A1
Bigland Street	96	A1/A2
Billing Place	43	B2
Billing Road	43	B2
Billing Street	43	B2
Billington Road	125	B1/B2
Billiter Square	18	B1
Billiter Street	18	B1
Billson Street	103	B2
Bina Gardens	44	A1
Binfield Road	134	B2
Bingfield Street	79	A1/A2
Bingham Place	2	A1
Bingham Street	82	A1
Binney Street	2	B1
Binns Road	38	A1
Birch Close	59	A2
Birchfield Street	100	A1
Birchin Lane	17	A2
Birchington Road	53	A1
	65	B1
Birchlands Avenue	147	B2
Birchmore Walk	63	B1/B2
Birchwood Drive	56	A1
Bird in Bush Road	114	B2
	115	B1/B2
Bird Street	2	B1
Birdcage Walk	9	B2
	22	A1
Birdhurst Road	139	A1
	152	B1
Birdsfield Lane	94	A2
Birkbeck Mews	86	B1
Birkbeck Road	86	B1
Birkbeck Street	92	B2
Birkdale Close	115	A2
Birkenhead Street	5	A1
Birkwood Close	149	B2
Birley Street	141	A2
Birnam Road	61	A2
Biscay Road	41	B1
Bisham Gardens	51	B1
Bishop Kings Road	34	B1
Bishop Street	81	B1
Bishop Wilfred	123	B2
Wood Close		
Bishop's Avenue	48	B1
Bishop's Court	14	B1
	15	B2
Bishop's Road	48	B1
Bishop's Road	132	A1
Bishops Bridge	31	A1
Bishops Bridge Road	30	B1/B2
	31	A1
Bishops Road	42	B2
	48	A1/A2
	51	A2
Bishops Terrace	112	A1
Bishops Way	92	A1
	93	B1
Bishopsgate	8	B2
	17	B2
Bishopsgate Churchyard	8	B2
Bishopswood Road	51	A1
Bittern Street	106	A1/B1
Black Friars Lane	15	B2
Black Horse Court	106	B2
Black Lion Lane	39	B2
Black Prince Road	112	A1
	131	B1/B2
Black Swan Yard	107	A1
Blackall Street	8	A1
Blackbird Yard	91	A2
Blackburn Road	65	A2
Blackburne's Mews	1	B2
Blackfriars Bridge	15	B1/B2
	105	A1
Blackfriars Court	15	B2
Blackfriars Passage	15	B2
Blackfriars Road	105	A1/B1
Blackheath Hill	120	B2
Blackheath Road	119	B2
	120	B1
Blackhorse Road	118	B1
Blacklands Terrace	46	A1/A2
Blackpool Road	123	B2
Blacks Road	40	B2
Blackshaw Road	152	B1
Blackstock Mews	62	B1
Blackstock Road	62	B1
	63	B1
Blackthorn Street	99	A1
Blacktree Mews	145	B2
Blackwall Lane	103	A2/B2
Blackwall Tunnel	101	A2/B2
Blackwater Street	129	B2
Blackwood Street	113	B2
Blade Mews	137	A1
Blades Court	137	A1
Blagrove Road	25	B1
Blair Close	75	B2
Blake Gardens	49	A2
Blake Street	119	A1
Blakemore Gardens	40	B2
Blakeney Close	78	A2
Blakenham Road	151	B1
	152	A1
Blakes Road	114	B1
	122	A2
Blanch Close	124	A1
Blanchard Way	89	A1
Blanchedowne	128	A2
Blandfield Road	147	A2
Blandford Square	76	B2
Blandford Street	1	A2
	2	A1/B1
Blantyre Street	44	B2
Blasker Walk	102	B2
Blechynden Street	28	A1
Bledlow Close	76	A1
Bleeding Heart Yard	15	A1
Blenheim Court	60	B2
Blenheim Crescent	28	A1
	29	A1
Blenheim Gardens	150	B1/B2
Blenheim Grove	123	B1/B2
Blenheim Road	68	B2
Blenheim Street	2	B2
Blenheim Terrace	68	B2
Blenkarne Road	147	A1
Bletchley Street	83	B2
Bletsoe Walk	83	A1
Blissett Street	120	B2
Blithfield Street	35	B2
Bloemfontein Avenue	32	A1
Bloemfontein Road	32	A1/B1
Bloemfontein Way	32	A1
Blomfield Mews	31	A1
Blomfield Road	27	B1/B2
Blomfield Street	8	B2
Blomfield Villas	30	A1
Blondel Street	141	A1
Bloom Park Road	48	A1
Bloomburg Street	21	A1
Bloomfield Place	9	A2
Bloomfield Road	51	A2
Bloomfield Terrace	19	B2
Bloomsbury Place	4	B2
	139	B1
Bloomsbury Square	4	B1
Bloomsbury Street	4	B1
	13	A1
Bloomsbury Way	4	B1/B2
	5	A1
Blore Close	134	B1
Blossom Street	91	B1
Blount Street	98	B1
Blucher Road	121	A2
Blue Anchor Lane	108	B2
Blue Anchor Yard	95	B1
Blue Ball Yard	23	A1
Bluebell Close	89	B2
Bluelion Place	107	A1
Blundell Close	86	A2
Blundell Street	79	A1/A2
Blyth Close	103	A2
Blythe Mews	33	B2

Street Index

Street Index

Street Index

Street	Page	Grid
Canonbury Lane	80	A2
Canonbury Park North	75	B2
	81	A1
Canonbury Park South	75	B2
	81	A1
Canonbury Place	81	A1
Canonbury Road	80	A2
	81	B1
Canonbury Square	80	A2
Canonbury Street	81	/A1
Canonbury Villas	81	B1
Canonbury Yard	81	
Canonbury Yard West	81	A1
Canrobert Street	92	A1/A2/B1
Cantelowes Road	72	B2
Canterbury Crescent	145	B2
Canton Street	99	B1
Cantrell Road	99	A1
Canute Gardens	109	B2
	111	B1
Capel Court	17	A2
Capener's Close	19	A1
Capern Road	146	B1
Capland Street	76	A1
Capper Street	4	A1
Capstan Road	118	A1
Capstan Square	103	A2
Capstan Way	111	A2
Caradoc Close	29	A2
Caravel Mews	119	A1
Carbis Road	98	B2
Carburton Street	3	A1
Cardale Street	103	A1
Carden Road	130	A2
Cardigan Road	94	A2/B2
Cardigan Street	131	B2
Cardinal Bourne Street	106	B2
Cardinal Place	136	A1
Cardinals Way	52	B2
Cardine Mews	115	B2
Cardington Street	77	B2
Cardozo Road	73	B2
Cardross Street	40	A2
Cardwell Road	73	A2
Carew Close	62	B1
Carew Street	121	B1
Carey Gardens	133	B2
	134	B1
Carey Lane	16	A1
Carey Street	14	B2
Carfax Place	143	B1
Carfree Close	80	A1
Cargill Road	146	B1
Carisbrooke Gardens	114	B2
Carker's Lane	72	A1
Carleton Road	60	B1
	73	A1
Carlile Close	94	B2
Carlingford Road	56	B2
Carlisle Avenue	18	B2
Carlisle Lane	104	B1
	131	A2
Carlisle Mews	76	B1
Carlisle Place	20	A2
Carlisle Road	62	A2
Carlisle Street	11	A2
Carlisle Way	152	A2
Carlos Place	9	A1
Carlow Street	78	A1
Carlton Drive	136	B1/B2
Carlton Gardens	23	A2
Carlton Grove	124	A1
Carlton Hill	68	A1/A2/B2
Carlton House Terrace	23	A2
Carlton Road	62	A1
Carlton Square	93	B1
Carlton Street	23	A2
Carlton Vale	27	A2
Carlwell Street	152	B1
Carlyle Mews	93	B1
Carlyle Place	136	A1
Carlyle Square	45	B1
Carmarthen Place	107	A1
Carmel Court	35	A2
Carmelite Street	15	B1
Carmen Street	99	B2
Carmichael Close	139	A2
Carmichael Mews	146	A2
Carminia Road	148	B2
Carnegie Street	79	B2
Carnie Lodge	151	A2
Carnoustie Drive	79	A2
Carnwath Road	49	B2
Carol Street	71	B2
Caroline Close	30	B1
Caroline Place	30	B1
	141	A2
Caroline Place Mews	30	B1
Caroline Street	97	B2
Caroline Terrace	19	B2
Carpenter Street	9	A2
Carpenters Mews	73	B2
Carpenters Place	143	B1
Carr Street	98	A2/B1
Carrara Close	127	A1
Carrara Mews	86	B2
Carriage Drive East	133	A1
Carriage Drive North	132	A1
	133	A1
Carriage Drive South	132	A1
	133	A1
Carriage Drive West	132	A1
Carriage Place	64	B1
Carrick Mews	119	A1
Carrington Street	9	B2
Carrol Close	58	B1
Carron Close	99	B2
Carroun Road	135	A1
Carter Lane	15	B2
Carter Place	113	B1
Carter Street	112	B2
Carteret Street	22	A2
Carteret Way	118	A1
Carters Yard	138	B1
Carthew Road	40	A2
Carthew Villas	40	A2
Carthusian Street	7	B1
	15	A2
Cartier Circle	101	B1
Carting Lane	24	A2
Carton Street	1	A2
Cartwright Gardens	4	A2
Cartwright Street	95	B1
Cartwright Way	47	A1
Carver Road	128	B1
Carysfort Road	63	B2
	64	B1
Casella Road	125	B1
Casey Close	76	A2
Casimir Road	87	A2
Casino Avenue	128	B1/B2
Caspian Street	122	A1
Cassidy Road	48	A2
Cassilis Road	102	A2
Cassland Road	90	B1/B2
Casson Street	91	B2
Castellain Road	27	A1/B1
Castelnau	40	B2
	41	B1
Castelnau Row	40	B2
Casterton Street	89	A2
Castle Baynard Street	15	B2
	16	B1/B2
Castle Lane	20	A2
Castle Mews	71	A2
Castle Place	38	A1
Castle Road	71	A2/B2
Castle Yard	51	B2
	105	A1
Castlebrook Close	112	A1/A2
Castlehaven Road	71	A2/B1/B2
Castlemain Street	91	B2
Castlereagh Street	1	A1
Castletown Road	42	A1
Castleview Close	63	A1
Castor Lane	100	A2
Catesby Street	113	A2
Cathay Street	109	A1
Cathcart Hill	59	B1
Cathcart Road	43	B2
	44	B2
Cathcart Street	71	A2
Cathedral Street	106	A1
Catherall Road	63	B2
Catherine Griffiths Court	6	B1
Catherine Grove	120	B1
Catherine Place	9	B2
Catherine Street	13	B2
	14	B1
Catherine Wheel Alley	18	A1
Catherine Wheel Yard	23	A1
Cathles Road	148	A2
Cathnor Road	32	B1
Catlin Street	115	A2
Cato Road	143	B2
Cato Street	1	A1
Cator Street	114	B2
	123	A1
Catton Street	14	A1
Caulfield Road	124	B1
The Causeway	138	B1
Causton Road	52	B1
Causton Street	21	A2/B2
Cautley Avenue	148	A2
Cavalry Gardens	137	B1
Cavaye Place	44	B1
Cavell Street	96	A2
Cavendish Avenue	68	B2
Cavendish Close	76	A2
Cavendish Mews North	3	A1
Cavendish Mews South	3	B1
Cavendish Place	2	B2
Cavendish Road	55	B2
	65	A1
	148	A2/B2
	149	A1/B1
Cavendish Square	2	B2

Street Index

Street Index

Street Index

Street Index

Street Index

Street Index

Street Index

Street Index

Street Index

Street Index

Street Index

Street Index

Street Index

Street Index

Street Index

Street Index

Street Index

Street Index

Street Index

Street Index

Street Index

Street Index

Street Index

Street Index

Street Index

Street Index

Street Index

Street Index

Street Index

Street Index

Street Index

Street Index

Street Index